SPYING

ON THE

SOUTH

SPYING

ON THE

SOUTH

AN ODYSSEY ACROSS
THE AMERICAN DIVIDE

TONY HORWITZ

PENGUIN PRESS | NEW YORK | 2019

PENGUIN PRESS

An imprint of Penguin Random House LLC
penguinrandomhouse.com

Map illustrations by Jeffrey L. Ward

Pages iv and 16: Photograph courtesy of the National Park Service,
Frederick Law Olmsted National Historic Site

LIBRARY OF CONGRESS CATALOGING-IN-PUBLICATION DATA
Names: Horwitz, Tony, 1958– author.
Title: Spying on the South : an odyssey across the American divide / Tony Horwitz.
Description: New York : Penguin Press, [2019] | Includes bibliographical references and index.
Identifiers: LCCN 2018056912 | ISBN 9781101980286 (hardcover) |
ISBN 9781101980293 (ebook)
Subjects: LCSH: Olmsted, Frederick Law, 1822–1903—Travel—Southern States. |
Horwitz, Tony, 1958——Travel—Southern States. | Southern States--Description and travel.
Classification: LCC F213 .H768 2019 | DDC 917.504—dc23
LC record available at https://lccn.loc.gov/201805691

Printed in the United States of America
1 3 5 7 9 10 8 6 4 2

BOOK DESIGN BY LUCIA BERNARD

To Geraldine,
the architect of my landscape, in love, life, and work

I WAS BORN FOR A TRAVELER.

Frederick Law Olmsted

CONTENTS

SPYING

ON THE

SOUTH

PROLOGUE: AMERICAN NOMAD

The only lodging in Grafton was a low-slung motel with a smashed door at the entrance. Stepping past shards of glass, I asked the clerk if there were any rooms available.

"You a coal miner?" he answered.

"No. Why do you ask?"

"We sort of cater to them. Special deals."

If so, there were no takers in sight. On a raw Friday evening, my rental car was the only vehicle in the parking lot. The clerk nonetheless rummaged in a drawer for some time before handing me a key. "Fifty bucks," he said.

Miner or not, this seemed like a deal. Until I reached my room: broken heater, broken window, beeping smoke alarm. Either the battery was dead or the last guest had tried to disable it. Cigarette butts swam in the toilet.

I went downstairs to a door by the shattered entrance marked "Pub." Inside, two women stared at video slot machines. After a while one of them served me a beer. It was my second day on the road, and my first in West Virginia. It was also the last night of October, so I asked why I hadn't seen any trick-or-treaters on my way into Grafton.

"Halloween was *last* night," the barmaid said. "It was moved up to Thursday."

"Why's that?"

The other woman snickered. "They say it's because there's a high school football game tonight. Real reason? Parents didn't want their kids out on a Friday with all the drunks and meth-heads partying it up."

This was a haunting image: children staying home on Halloween because there were *real* zombies about. The women returned to staring at their screens, so I drained my beer and followed a road that wound between mountains and railroad tracks: Grafton's main street. Midway along it, a neon sign winked from the window of a creosote-colored pool hall with yellow police tape strung across the door.

The crime scene décor was a Halloween joke. Inside, a dozen people sat at a bar served by a woman dressed as Dorothy from *The Wizard of Oz*. As soon as I sat down, the man at the next stool bought me a beer. "Don't see many new faces around here," he said, clinking bottles of Budweiser.

Ron Childers was a bullet-headed man in his fifties who repaired aircraft in the next county. "Used to be a lot of coal and railroad jobs here, but by the time I left school you had to get out of Grafton if you wanted to work," he said. "Burns my ass, people drawing welfare and doing drugs while I'm busting my butt and paying taxes."

He then told me about a recent spate of drug arrests. Methamphetamines were so rife in West Virginia that cooks had adopted a crude method called shake and bake: tossing pills and volatile chemicals in soda bottles and driving around to mix the ingredients. Vans sometimes burst into flames in midday traffic, passengers fleeing the scene with their clothes on fire.

"Those drugs make folks dumber than the retards in *Wrong Turn*," Ron said. When I looked at him blankly, he explained: "That's a horror flick set in West Virginia, about inbred mutants who trap and hack up people like possum." He smiled. "Gotta have a sense of humor to take all the jokes about how backward we are."

"Amen," interjected the man next to him. He turned to me. "You know the toothbrush was invented in West Virginia?"

"No, I didn't."

"Otherwise it would be the *teeth*brush."

Ron ordered us another round, and introduced me to a young woman named Jess, who wore a tank top, hot pants, fishnet stockings, thigh-high boots, and fake blood smeared across her neck and bare midriff. Jess worked on a road crew but was clad for Halloween as a member of a heavy metal band, the Butcher Babies.

"I'm that one, Carla, except for the knife in the vagina," she said, displaying a picture on her phone of a singer thrusting a bloody dagger at her crotch.

Jess looked up from her phone and studied *my* costume. Jeans, work boots, plaid shirt, horn-rimmed glasses, dun Carhartt jacket with a notebook and pen stuck in one pocket. "Let me guess," she said in an exaggerated drawl. "Yankee boy, spyin' on us hillbillies?"

This was uncomfortably close to the mark. I couldn't muster a witty comeback, so I told her a version of the truth: I was doing research on a famous American who came through here in the 1800s.

Jess pondered this for a moment. "Okay, history guy, here's a question," she said. "Did you know Mother's Day was invented in Grafton?"

I shook my head, awaiting the punch line. Some joke about incest?

Instead, Jess led me to the door and pointed down Main Street. "Few blocks that way, big-time shrine to all our great moms." Then she turned to greet a friend and share her Butcher Babies picture again.

Walking through the drizzle, I reached a statue of a mother and child beside an old church. A historic plaque identified this sanctuary as the site of the first Mother's Day observance, in 1908.

A much larger building loomed directly across the street: an ornate brick-and-granite pile with massive columns, evidently a relic of the town's better days. The hulking edifice was vacant and in poor repair. But at its crown, above elegantly hewn laurels, I could make out the letters "B&O"— the bygone rail line I was following through the hills, on the trail of a long-ago traveler.

IN 1854, A ROVING CORRESPONDENT FOR THE *New-York Daily Times* noted a slang term common in the South: "Gone to Texas." This phrase—or its abbreviation, G.T.T.—was painted on the doors and fence posts of abandoned homesteads as a sign that the inhabitants had fled debt, the law, or other trouble for a fresh start on the frontier.

"G.T.T.," the correspondent wrote, "was almost equivalent, when added to a man's name, to branding him a swindler, defaulter, lawless ruffian or 'scape gallows."

The author of this anecdote was identified in the *Times* as "Yeoman." Such pseudonyms were common in the 1850s, and traveling incognito was a prudent measure in the slave states, where Northern visitors were often cast as abolitionist snoops and stirrers. The pen name Yeoman also spoke to the writer's agrarian identity. He was a proudly independent tiller of the land, on sabbatical from his farmstead, touring the plantation South and following the trail of those "Gone to Texas."

Frederick Law Olmsted is celebrated today as a visionary architect of New York's Central Park, among many other spaces: the US Capitol grounds, college campuses, residential neighborhoods, the Biltmore Estate in North Carolina. During the latter half of the nineteenth century, Olmsted helped create much of the urban and suburban landscape that Americans still inhabit.

But this farsighted designer was molded by an eccentric apprenticeship: as a merchant seaman to China, an experimental farmer, a European wanderer, and—most significantly—the undercover correspondent known as Yeoman, a Connecticut Yankee exploring the Cotton Kingdom on the eve of secession and civil war.

Before embarking on his Southern tour, Olmsted wrote a friend that he sought "reliable understanding of the sentiments and hopes & fears" of Americans on the other side of the nation's widening divide. He wanted to gather "matter of fact matter," which he believed would give ballast to the angry debate over slavery that was tilting the country toward violent breakup.

At age thirty, Olmsted was also restless on his farm and romantically adrift. He hoped that a winter's sojourn in the South would renew him, and further the latest of his many ambitions, to make it as a writer. "Should calculate to leave middle of December & return early in March," he wrote, in time for spring planting.

Instead, the South would consume Olmsted for much of the next decade. As Yeoman, he first traveled the seaboard South, from Maryland to Louisiana, before returning for a much longer trek: across the mountains and Mississippi River to the Texas frontier and back.

He expanded on his newspaper dispatches by publishing three books about the South under his own name. In the preface to the first, Olmsted wrote that he was determined "to see things for himself," with an eye that was tough but fair. "Let the reader understand that he is invited to travel in company with an honest growler."

His writing reached a wide and influential audience, at home and abroad, winning praise from Harriet Beecher Stowe, Charles Dickens, and many other luminaries. But this acclaim didn't translate into strong book sales or a secure perch in what Olmsted called the North's "literary republic."

Nor did his work achieve his stated mission, "to promote the mutual acquaintance of the North and South" with fact and observation rather than invective. By 1860, when the last of his Southern trilogy appeared, few Americans were in a mood for literary statesmanship.

Olmsted's initial faith in reasoned discourse had also waned. In the course of his travels, the South's "leading men" had struck him as implacable: convinced of the superiority of their caste-bound society, intent on expanding it, and utterly contemptuous of the North. "They are a mischievous class—the dangerous class at the present of the United States," Olmsted wrote, seven years before the Civil War.

But this hard-eyed appraisal gave him a new mission. To fortify the nation against the South's slaveholding elite and feudal ideology, the North must uplift its own citizens, to demonstrate the true promise of a free and democratic society.

Olmsted saw many ways to pursue this reformist cause. His own path would lead to a swampy, rock-strewn tract in the middle of Manhattan. In shaping this unpromising landscape, he sought to create a public park that brought together and elevated "the poor and the rich, the young and the old, the vicious and the virtuous."

IN 1953, A CENTURY AFTER THE FIRST OF OLMSTED'S DISPATCHES appeared in the *Times*, Alfred A. Knopf issued a single-volume abridgement of his books about the South, titled *The Cotton Kingdom*. It had first been published in Britain, at the start of the Civil War, but had fallen off the radar of all but a small circle of scholars. Knopf's edition also came with a glowing introduction by a leading historian, Arthur Schlesinger, who extolled Olmsted's work as "indispensable" and a "uniquely candid and realistic picture of the pre–Civil War South."

Thereafter, *The Cotton Kingdom* became a staple of research on the South and slavery, and a fixture in college curricula, including a class I took in 1980. At the time, I knew little about Olmsted the landscape architect, and skimmed the book's six hundred pages for passages I could cite in a term paper. Then I packed the book away, with scores of other college texts I toted around in boxes for decades, imagining that I would one day revisit them.

Of course I didn't, until a few autumns ago when my wife and I fixed up a barn behind our home in New England, fitting it with shelves for our overflowing books. Under spousal orders to "ruthlessly cull" my college library, I unpacked, glanced at, and discarded four years of liberal arts education.

Then I came to *The Cotton Kingdom*, perusing a few passages before consigning it to the give-away pile. I read about riverboat gamblers and gunslingers; the "free, rustic, shooting jacket life" of plantation masters who ruled over "little independent negro kingdoms"; bloodhounds trained to track a runaway slave and "tear him a spell"; and poor whites sharing their scarce space and food when Olmsted sought lodging.

"The woman suddenly dropped off her outer garment and stepped from the midst of its folds, in her petticoat," he wrote of a farm wife, as she lay down on the floor of a one-room cabin with her husband and child. Olmsted, given their bed, battled insects and listened to "the man and the woman, and the girl and the dog scratching, and the horse out in the shed stamping and gnawing himself."

Hooked, I searched out Olmsted's original dispatches for the *Times*, his personal letters, and other writing on the South. Though his principal beat was the region's slave-based agriculture, Yeoman strayed into every byway of antebellum life. He recorded the dialect and songs he heard at black churches, and closely observed the natural and built landscape, however humble, including makeshift, leaning structures that looked as though "too much whiskey" had been drunk in them, and new-sprung "mushroom" towns he dreamed of improving.

Olmsted also described in detail what it was like to be a traveler in the South, and not always with delight. "At this dinner I made the first practical acquaintance with what shortly was to be the bane of my life," he wrote, after choking down corn pone, fatback pork, and "vile coffee" at a rural inn, not realizing "that for the next six months I should actually see *nothing else*."

This scene occurred near the start of Olmsted's journey from Maryland to Texas and on to the Rio Grande. He traveled by train, stagecoach, riverboat, and horseback, accompanied by his brother John, who hoped a long ride in the dry air of Texas would bring relief to his tubercular lungs.

Olmsted rode back north alone, completing a nine-month odyssey that covered thousands of miles at a time of deepening national crisis. In 1854, free and slave settlers took up arms against each other in Kansas. Mob violence erupted over fugitive slave laws, and the two-party system and fragile political compromise that had held together the North and South began to collapse.

"These principles cannot stand together," Abraham Lincoln declared of slavery and freedom in 1854. "They are as opposite as God and Mammon; and whoever holds to the one must despise the other."

Yet Olmsted traversed what would soon be enemy territory, talking and eating and bedding with Southerners against whom he and other Northerners would zealously wage war in the coming years. He wrote unsparingly about the cruelties and inequities he witnessed, but endeavored to communicate with all those he encountered, including a band of Apache that overtook him as he rode in Texas.

"Traveling about, without definite aim, in an original but on the whole, very pleasant fashion," Olmsted wrote a friend during a break in this ride. "It gives me an entirely new appreciation of the attachment of nomad tribes to their mode of life."

These words stirred the nomad in myself. I'd traveled widely, as a foreign correspondent in the Middle East and elsewhere, and as a roaming scribe in my own country. But the vast territory Olmsted crossed on his second Southern journey was mostly unfamiliar to me, including nearly the entirety of Texas.

This journey had also taken Olmsted across the nation's enduring fault line—between free and slave states in his time, and red and blue states in mine. No current issue carried the moral and explosive force of slavery. But there were inescapable echoes of the 1850s: extreme polarization, racial strife, demonization of the other side, embrace of enflamed opinion over reasoned dialogue and debate.

Was the nation unraveling into hostile confederacies? Had that happened already?

The view from my barn-office in New England didn't offer any answers. Autumn leaves floated in the millstream; alpacas munched grass in our paddock; a windmill turned on a neighboring hill. Before the first snow fell, I'd be gone to Texas, too.

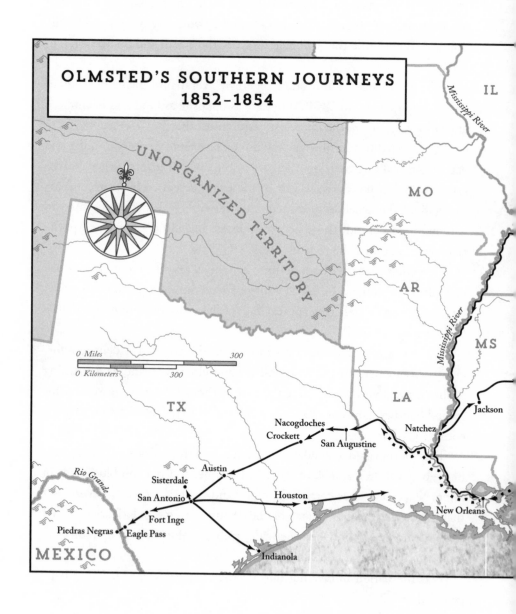

OLMSTED'S SOUTHERN JOURNEYS
1852–1854

UNORGANIZED TERRITORY

IL

MO

AR

MS

LA

Mississippi River

Mississippi River

0 Miles   300

0 Kilometers   300

TX

Jackson

Natchez

Nacogdoches

Crockett

San Augustine

Rio Grande

Austin

Sisterdale

San Antonio

Houston

New Orleans

Fort Inge

Piedras Negras   Eagle Pass

MEXICO

Indianola

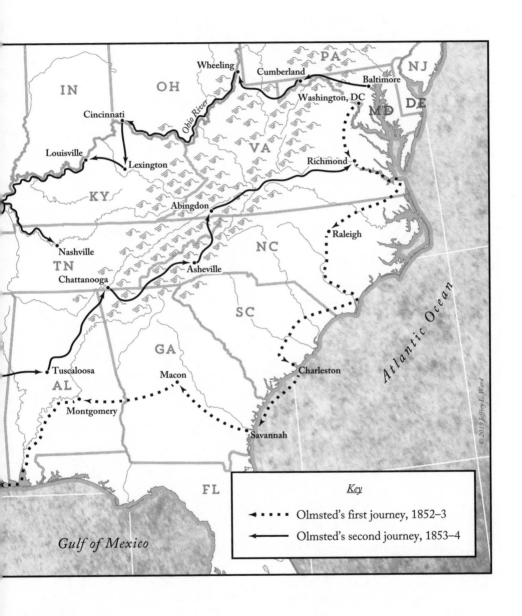

Key

◄····· Olmsted's first journey, 1852–3

◄——— Olmsted's second journey, 1853–4

CHAPTER 1

YEOMAN OLMSTED

"An Enthusiast by Nature"

O lmsted's letter from Texas about the romance of nomadism was tailored to its recipient: Anne Charlotte Lynch, a New York poet, globe-trotting traveler, and eminent convener of literary salons.

"I like her much and shall try to be intimate with her," Olmsted confided in an earlier letter to his father. "She is acquainted with all the distinguished people and her taste is highly cultivated."

Olmsted enclosed samples of prairie flowers in his letter to Lynch and observed of his Texas wanderings that he'd always been "much of a vagabond."

This Bohemian self-styling bore fruit; upon his return north, Olmsted became a regular at Lynch's salons. But the letter also held an element of truth: from an early age, Olmsted *had* been nomadic, drifting between homes, continents, and a bewildering array of courtships, callings, and beliefs.

This vagrancy ran counter to Olmsted's deeply rooted lineage in Connecticut. His forebears were among its first colonists and spawned generations of model Yankees: farmers, deacons, seafarers, Revolutionary War soldiers. Olmsted's father, John, prospered as a dry-goods merchant on Main Street in Hartford, the city his ancestors had helped found almost two centuries before.

Frederick's mother, Charlotte, also came from old Connecticut stock and was raised in a household with a love of Latin poetry. Little else is known about her. She gave birth to Frederick in 1822 and a second son in 1825. Five months later, she died from an overdose of laudanum. The family said she'd been ill and mistaken the potent opiate for a milder painkiller.

"I was so young that I have but a tradition of memory rather than the faintest recollection of her," Olmsted wrote many decades later, in an auto-biographical fragment. As a boy, when asked about his mother, he would say, "I remember playing on the grass and looking up at her while she sat sewing under a tree."

Such pastoral imagery infused almost all his childhood memories. Olmsted grew up at the cusp of New England's Industrial Revolution, when Hartford had only seven thousand residents and a few dozen streets within walking distance of the surrounding countryside. As "a half grown lad," he was free to wander, visiting family friends and relations whose farm-houses "had near them interesting rivers, brooks, meadows, rocks, woods or mountains." Sometimes he got lost and stayed the night with strangers, "encouraged by my father rather than checked in the adventurousness that led me to do so."

The elder Olmsted gave his son latitude that he himself had lacked. Schooled in the puritan virtues of humility, hard work, and self-sacrifice, John Olmsted kept a dry, detailed log of his doings and contributed gener-ously to Hartford's civic institutions. Frederick described his father as an unassuming figure who sought to heed "the authority of Society, Religion and Commerce."

But this convention-bound merchant also possessed a deep "sensitive-ness to the beauty of nature" that strongly influenced his son. "The happi-est recollections of my early life are the walks and rides I had with my father," while perched with him in the saddle or cradled in his parent's arms as they gazed up at the stars.

Soon after Frederick's fifth birthday, John Olmsted married a close friend of his deceased wife. Mary Ann Bull was a pious and orderly woman who shared her husband's "silent habits" and love of nature. The family expanded and so did their rural outings, which included stagecoach and boat trips across New England.

These journeys were "really tours in search of the picturesque," Frederick wrote, though his taciturn parents "did not analyze, compare and criticize" the elements of scenery that gave them so much pleasure. Their "unconscious" absorption of nature would later guide Frederick as he designed landscapes for city dwellers.

His parents' expansiveness, however, did not extend to formal education. John Olmsted had been raised with "a superstitious faith in the value of preaching and didactic instruction," Frederick wrote, and John's second wife reinforced this. Soon after their marriage, Frederick was sent to board with a rural pastor, the first of six clergymen who would oversee his peripatetic education.

In Frederick's telling, these tutors valued child labor and puritan dogma more than academic instruction. He recalled farm chores, a teacher who lifted him by his ears until he bled, and a parson who eavesdropped as Frederick spun tales to fellow boarders—before bursting in, shouting, "Oh! the depravity of human nature!" and beating the youths with a broom handle.

At the age of fourteen, Frederick temporarily lost his vision, an affliction his family later blamed on a poison sumac rash. His father took him to a doctor who prescribed saltwater rinses and a cessation of hard study. So Frederick became "nominally the pupil of a topographical engineer but really for the most part given over to a decently restrained vagabond life," he wrote, spending his teenaged years hiking in the mountains, copying maps, and sketching "ideal towns."

This Huck Finn–ish remembrance wasn't the sum of his schooling. Though never a diligent pupil, Olmsted read widely, borrowing books from libraries and relations who nurtured his omnivorous intellect. His early letters include references to "French Periodicals," Dickens novels, and works of natural history.

Frederick nonetheless entered young adulthood as an outlier among his privileged male peers, many of them bound for college and careers in law, medicine, or the ministry. His merchant father arranged for him to work as a clerk in a Manhattan importing house, but this didn't suit him, either. He found commerce stultifying, "writing at a desk all day & half the night, or practicing assumed politeness or eulogizing a piece of silk or barrel of lamp oil."

This work also took him aboard ships in New York Harbor, stirring what he called his "truant disposition." Just before turning twenty-one, he found a berth as a poorly paid ship's "boy" on a merchant vessel to China. This proved such a nightmarish passage that the crew almost mutinied and the captain was later prosecuted for excessive flogging—brutality that became the yardstick by which the adult Olmsted measured human degradation, including slave labor.

After his year at sea, Olmsted embraced the land and a new passion: agriculture. Moving to a small property his father purchased for him in Connecticut, Frederick became "so full of farming," his brother John wrote, that he talked of nothing except cattle prices, pig litters, and crop rotation. "I hope the present object of his affections, i.e. his farm, will not be as ephemeral as most of them have been."

The brothers were extremely close despite having been separated during most of their childhood. John was sickly from an early age, educated close to home while Frederick boarded, and then enrolled at Yale, en route to training as a doctor. By the time he entered college, John had grown into a handsome and popular young man with a gentle spirit and social ease his older brother lacked.

Their father hoped Fred (as he was called by friends and family) would belatedly follow his brother's example. In his early twenties, Fred frequently visited John at Yale and, though unenrolled, began studying chemistry, mineralogy, and architecture. This informal education ended after just three months due to ill health, a pattern that would afflict Olmsted throughout his life. Hard study and writing brought on headaches, eyestrain, and, at Yale, fainting spells, prompting his father to speculate, "Is it from Mental Causes that he is subject to this tendency of blood to the head?"

Fred's visits and stay at Yale were nonetheless formative, drawing him into an extraordinary circle of bright scholars and young women from New Haven's parlor society. One lasting influence on him was Charles Loring Brace, a polymath with a passion for boxing and debate who would go on to a prominent career as a social reformer. He became a close friend and intellectual sparring partner of Fred's, and the two continued their disputations by letter after Olmsted returned to farming.

"Every time you run your pen against me, you scrape me a little brighter,"

Fred wrote. When Brace visited Fred's farm, the "torrent of fierce argument" lasted all night and through the next day. Impressed by Fred's growing "keenness" and analytic power, Brace wrote a classmate, "I shouldn't be surprised if he turned out something rather remarkable among men."

Fred's brother wasn't so sure. He feared his sibling's "fine capabilities" would never develop due to his irregular education, lack of "stability," and obsession with "harrowing & planting & getting out manure." But the Yalie to whom he confided these doubts saw strength and promise in Fred's unconventional character.

"He is an enthusiast by nature," Frederick Kingsbury wrote John, "and all the Greek and Latin in the world wouldn't have driven that out of him. Well, the world needs such men—and one thing is curious—disappointments never seem to trouble them." He then presciently forecast: "Many of his favorite schemes will go to naught—but he'll throw it aside and try another and spoil that and forget them both while you or I might have been blubbering over the ruins of the first."

READING THIS CORRESPONDENCE, PREPARATORY TO MY TRAVELS with Fred, I felt as though I was listening in on long-ago college bull sessions. The young Olmsted also seemed a rather modern and familiar figure: black sheep in his privileged flock, a drifter and dreamer, a gifted underachiever whose youth was extended with the support of an anxious but loving and indulgent family.

During one of Fred's visits to New Haven, in 1846 or 1847, he posed with his Yale friends for a studio portrait. A daguerreotype shows them clad in formal attire, jauntily leaning into one another, a thick book open on the table before them. John Olmsted, dark haired and fine featured, smiles puckishly while resting his elbow on the shoulder of Kingsbury, a lighthearted future lawyer. Also pictured are the long-faced Charles Brace and Charles Trask, a well-groomed sea captain's son.

The four Yalies face the camera while Fred sits in profile, turned toward the others as if an onlooker in this group of polished young scholars. A solo portrait of him taken a few years later shows a sensitive countenance with wide-set eyes, a broad nose, a small soft mouth, and an untamed wave of brown hair. He was slight in stature, about five feet six inches and

120 pounds. One female admirer thought his face had "the expressive delicacy of a woman's."

Fred's intense personality made a stronger and not always favorable impression. Mary Perkins, who met him when she was nineteen, and would become intimately tied to both Fred and his brother, described Olmsted in his mid-twenties as "full of life and fun," with a keen talent for caricature. But Fred was less inclined to humor than to earnest and heated debate. "He was perhaps over fond of arguments to be pleasing to women," Mary recalled. "Whimsies had no charm for him."

Fred's dislike of chitchat and what he called "flippery" weren't the only impediment to his youthful courting. In romance, as in all his endeavors, he was fervid yet fickle.

"He is dead in love, but with *all* of his acquaintances," his brother wrote Kingsbury, listing a comically long menu of traits Fred sought in a mate. These included "infinite capabilities and longings," "comprehension of what is incomprehensible to others," and "fondness for landscapes, clams, pork and old dressing gowns." John concluded, "He won't be content with less than infinity—while he himself is only finite & a farmer."

Fred, by then, had moved to a different farm, on Staten Island in New York—purchased like the previous one by his father. For the first time Fred showed signs of constancy and achievement. He won prizes at agricultural fairs for his turnips and pears, installed an innovative drainage system, and impressed his neighbors with a tasteful redesign of his property, which he landscaped to create an attractive gentleman's farm.

Fred also found a guiding philosophy in the works of Thomas Carlyle, whom he considered "the greatest genius in the world." Two of the Scottish thinker's precepts had particular influence on him. Carlyle wrote that conviction "is worthless till it convert itself into Conduct," and in choosing a life of service to others, "do the Duty which lies nearest thee."

Olmsted began to cast himself as a secular missionary and apostle of rural reform. "There's a *great* work wants doing in this our generation, Charley, let us off our jackets and go about it," he wrote Brace. While his friend ministered to the urban poor, Fred imagined becoming a model farmer and "Country Squire," paternalistically educating "the *ignobile vulgus*" to appreciate "charity, taste &c.—independence of thought, of voting and of acting."

This aspiring squire, however, still lacked a bride and dreaded becoming an "old bach" on the farm. During a winter visit to Hartford, he seemed to finally find a match in Emily Perkins, "the most lovely and loveable girl," he wrote, with "the most incomparably fine face I ever saw." She went with him on sleigh rides, listened as he read Macaulay's *History of England* aloud, and tolerated his quarrelsome views.

The two kept up a "very vigorous and noble correspondence," Fred's brother wrote, and after an on-and-off courtship over more than two years, they became engaged in 1851.

Then, just weeks later, Fred received a letter from Emily's mother, declaring that her daughter was breaking the engagement due to a

"revulsion of feeling." His brother judged the affair "very strange" and described Fred as stunned. But their father was perplexed by something else.

"Pray tell me what it is makes Fred so happy since his *disappointment*, as it is call'd," he wrote. "He seems like a man who has thrown off a tremendous weight." The elder Olmsted wondered if his son had brought about the break "purposely."

Fred, in his search for "infinity," may have judged Emily limited and said or done something to arouse her unexplained "revulsion." But he also exhibited signs of being unprepared to settle down, domestically or otherwise.

A year prior to his engagement, Fred abruptly abandoned farming and courting to join his brother and Charles Brace on a six-month tramp in Europe. He took careful notes on the trip and was particularly struck by Birkenhead Park in Liverpool. He called it a "People's Garden," enjoyed "about equally by all classes," a new and rare phenomenon in Europe and absent in American cities.

Upon returning to his farm, Fred was glum and restless. "Everybody at home seems to be superficial, frivolous, absorbed in a tide of foam, gas and bubbles," he wrote Brace, who was still abroad. He advised Brace to look for a wife in Europe. "I don't believe there are any left here to suit us."

His brother disagreed. Later that year John wed the Staten Island neighbor of Fred's who had found him argumentative. Meanwhile, Fred's former fiancée, Emily Perkins, quickly fell for a tall, magnetic minister. On the day of their marriage in Hartford, Fred wrote a letter to his good friend Kingsbury, disclosing a new enthusiasm.

Olmsted had just published a "splurgy, thick book" about his overseas ambles. Titled *Walks and Talks of an American Farmer in England*, it was a mix of travel adventure, detailed analysis of rural life, and musings on the mother country. Now he was contemplating a follow-up journey, in another territory foreign to him.

"I have thoughts of going South this winter," he wrote, "mainly with the idea that I could make a valuable book of observations on Southern Agriculture & general economy as affected by Slavery."

Olmsted's views on slavery weren't fully formed. He opposed the institution, telling Kingsbury he "would take in a fugitive slave & shoot a man that was likely to get him." But Fred wasn't prepared to damn all slaveholders or to seek the overthrow of their constitutional right to own human property.

"I am not a red-hot Abolitionist like Charley," he wrote of their friend Brace, "but am a moderate Free Soiler." This aligned him with Abraham Lincoln and others who sought to limit slavery's extension rather than seek its immediate end. "On the whole, I guess I represent pretty fairly the average sentiment of good thinking men on our side."

OLMSTED'S MAINSTREAM STANCE MADE HIM AN EXCELLENT match for the *New-York Daily Times*. Its editor, Henry Raymond, had co-founded the publication in 1851 as a counterpoint to the partisan and over-heated papers of that day. In the first issue of the *Times*, Raymond wrote that the paper would "seek to be temperate and measured" and rely on "fair argument" rather than invective. "We do not believe that *everything* in society is either exactly right, or exactly wrong."

In pursuit of this mission, Raymond sought a coolheaded correspondent to survey the slave South. When Brace learned this, he recommended Olmsted—in part, Fred later wrote, because of the "urgency" Brace felt about abolishing slavery and his desire to win over his skeptical friend.

Raymond was sufficiently impressed by *Walks and Talks* and a brief meeting with Olmsted to offer $300 for a series of "letters" from the South. Raymond didn't interrogate Olmsted about his views on slavery, asking only that Fred write from firsthand reporting, with "honesty of observation and faithfulness of communication."

This edict may sound banal to readers of today's "Gray Lady" (the *Times* dropped the "Daily" from its name in 1857). But at the time, dispassionate reporting on the South was rare. As Olmsted set off in 1852, *Uncle Tom's Cabin* had just become a runaway bestseller. White Southerners answered this heartrending indictment of slavery with a salvo of sentimental paeans to genteel masters and happy "servants."

Hence Olmsted's remark to Kingsbury about wanting to gather "matter of fact matter" to publish "after the deluge of spoony fancy pictures now at its height shall be spent."

Delivering such matter, however, proved much harder than Olmsted anticipated. He embarked in December, the wrong season to observe agriculture or to roam the countryside as he'd done in England. "The roads never were so bad & lots of people here mud bound," he wrote his father from North Carolina.

Another obstacle was the reticence of "planters & gentlemen" he'd hoped to engage on the topic of slavery. "You can't imagine how hard it is to get hold of a conversable man—and when you find, he will talk about anything else but slavery &c.," he wrote Brace. "*Music* I am surfeited with, that is, *talk* on music."

Olmsted also worried that the material he gathered was too small-bore for the *Times*, which introduced his series as a sweeping overview of the South. Much of what he'd written, Fred told Brace, was "merely describing roads and taverns" and other scenes of everyday Southern life.

In reality, Olmsted's ground-level reporting on the region and its people was his strength. It also revealed a current that ran counter to Northerners' image of the South as a stagnant pool in a "go-ahead" nation that was industrializing and pushing west in the 1850s as never before.

"Notwithstanding the youth of the State, there is a constant and extensive emigration from it," Olmsted wrote of Alabama. "The small farmers are constantly going ahead," as well as planters "carrying with them large bodies of slaves."

Most were bound for Texas, "their promised land," hoping to do better than in the crowded districts and "worn-out" fields they left behind. This migration also steered Olmsted in a new direction. He would make a return trip south, he wrote Brace from New Orleans, "to survey upper and interior" parts of the region he hadn't yet visited, before proceeding the next year to "the frontier & Southwest slave states."

Fred made no mention of his farm, or his bachelorhood, or other matters that had previously consumed him. His friends and family may reasonably have supposed that Fred's latest scheme was yet another of his many short-lived passions.

But Olmsted not only stuck to his plan, he advanced the timetable. Returning north in spring, he didn't even finish writing up the material from his first trip before embarking on his second, across the interior South and Texas—a journey that would lead, with characteristic setbacks and indirection, to his greatest and most lasting enthusiasm.

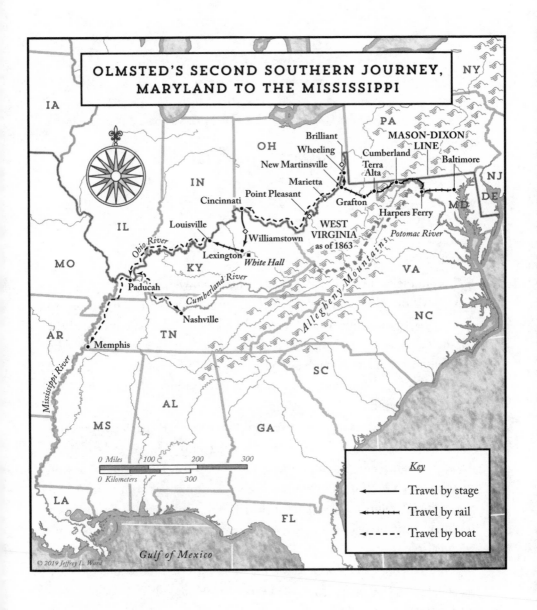

OLMSTED'S SECOND SOUTHERN JOURNEY,
MARYLAND TO THE MISSISSIPPI

NY

IA

PA

OH

MASON-DIXON
LINE

Brilliant
Wheeling
New Martinsville
Cumberland
Terra
Alta
Baltimore

IN

Marietta
NJ
Point Pleasant
DE
Cincinnati
Grafton
MD
Louisville
WEST
VIRGINIA
as of 1863
Harpers Ferry
IL
Williamstown
Potomac River
Lexington
White Hall
VA
MO
KY
Ohio River
Paducah
Cumberland River
Allegheny Mountains
NC
AR
Nashville
Memphis
TN
SC
Mississippi River
AL
MS
GA

0 Miles   100   200   300
0 Kilometers   300

LA
FL

Key

Travel by stage
Travel by rail
Travel by boat

Gulf of Mexico

© 2019 Jeffrey L. Ward

CHAPTER 2

OVER THE ALLEGHENIES

Gateway to the Rust Belt

S cene, the South; bound West. It could be nowhere else."
     With this theatrical flourish, Olmsted raised the curtain on his journey to Texas, while aboard a train in Maryland. He also recorded the "dramatis personae" of his rail trip, including a "Virginia gentleman" who expertly spat tobacco through a hinged window, a "black mamma" nursing a white child, and "buxom, saucy, slipshod girls" at rail-side inns, "bursting with fat and fun from their dresses."

I looked up from my dog-eared travelogue at the coach car on Amtrak's Capitol Limited. Men in suits staring into laptops. A lean spandexed woman reading a yoga magazine. Two boys murdering aliens on their phones. Out the grimy train window, no sign as yet of the "fine farming country" Olmsted described in Maryland. Just endless suburbs: tract housing, graffiti-covered overpasses, a mattress outlet. It could be anywhere else.

Olmsted rode the B&O Railroad, short for "Baltimore and Ohio," a passenger line that no longer existed except on Monopoly boards. The closest I could come to retracing his rail path was aboard the Capitol Limited, Amtrak's daily service between Washington, D.C., and Chicago. The train followed part of the old B&O route and stopped at Cumberland, the western Maryland town where Olmsted spent his first night.

I planned to do the same. Beyond that I had no plan, other than to follow Olmsted's path by whatever transport I could. Parallel journeys, 160
years apart: what he saw then and what I'd see now. No bookings. No
itinerary. Just a ramble across America with long-dead Fred as my guide.

This had all seemed thrilling and plausible earlier in the day as I'd perused
Olmsted's microfilmed letters in a hushed room at the Library of Congress.
"When we were travelling," Olmsted wrote Charles Brace, reflecting on their
tramp around Europe, "we were living a great deal more, getting a great deal
more out of the world, loving oftener, hating oftener, reaching a great many
more mile stones."

Now, two hours after leaving the library, I sat next to a snoring com-
muter as the train crawled through the autumn dusk past malls and subdivisions. Rereading the start of Olmsted's book, I identified with the nervous
"restlessness" and "vague anticipations" he felt at the start of an open-ended
journey.

In his day, rail passengers carried their own provisions or dined at
rail-side inns. I went to the café car, bought a microwaved Italian club sand-
wich, and settled at a table, trying to conjure the "new and wilder beauties"
Olmsted saw along the upper Potomac. In the early dark, all I could see in
the window was my own reflection.

But our rail journeys aligned in one respect. The Capitol Limited kept
slowing, due to curves along the Potomac and track the train shared with
freight traffic. As a result, a conductor told me, our average speed was about
forty miles an hour—not much swifter than Olmsted's pace in 1853, aboard
a steam-engine train.

Arriving in Cumberland on a rainy November evening, Olmsted described it as "a most comfortless place" with "a certain dinginess" that
reminded him of mill towns he'd seen in England. Like the nineteenth-
century British Midlands, Cumberland and its hilly surrounds were rich in
industrial resources: coal, timber, iron ore, water power. The town was also
a major transport hub, at the junction of the B&O, the Chesapeake and
Ohio Canal, and a pioneering turnpike called the National Road.

"Cumberland is destined to become one of the largest inland towns of
America," Horace Greeley assured readers of the *New-York Tribune* four
years before Olmsted arrived. Local boosters later billed their boomtown
the "Gateway to the West."

In the chill autumn air, I stepped from the Capitol Limited onto a small walkway beside the tracks that led past an American Legion and Veterans of Foreign Wars post, a memorial to a native son killed in Iraq, and a homeless shelter with a sign reading, "Doorway to Hope at the Gateway to the West."

At the end of the block rose an imposing but run-down Victorian edifice that housed 2nd Chance Bail Bonds and a corner bar. At 8:00 p.m., the only person in the tavern was the owner, Jim McKenzie. I was his second customer of the night.

"We're a neighborhood bar in a neighborhood that's about gone," he said, serving me a bottle of Miller.

The bar was part of the formerly grand Brunswick Hotel, which had served travelers arriving on the twenty passenger trains that once came through Cumberland daily. Factory laborers also packed the bar, which used to stay open from 8:00 a.m. to 2:00 a.m. to accommodate shift workers.

But since its peak during World War II, Cumberland had lost half its population and almost all its industry, including a textile plant where McKenzie had been one of ten thousand employees. The massive plant was torn down in the 1990s to make way for a state penitentiary.

"Locking people up, that's our industry now," he said, listing eight correctional facilities that had sprung up in and around Cumberland.

On St. Patrick's Day, McKenzie cooked pots of cabbage and corned beef and served it free to the homeless at the nearby shelter. "That used to be a place for people down on their luck for a few days," he said. "Now a lot are long term."

McKenzie apologized that he couldn't offer me a bed, since the three-story, fifty-seven-room Brunswick was no longer a functioning hotel. A sixty-eight-year-old widower, he was the only lodger. "Grew up by the railroad and just don't feel right if I can't hear trains passing in the night," he said.

Only freight traffic did so now. Apart from the Capitol Limited, and a short scenic ride on a restored locomotive, Cumberland no longer had passenger service. But one major artery from the town's transport heyday survived: the National Road, which had linked Cumberland to Wheeling, the end point of Olmsted's ride on the B&O.

So after bedding down at a Ramada by the tracks, I rented a car in the morning at Cumberland's small airport. The rental agent told me that most of his customers came here to see incarcerated family or residents of Cumberland's many rehab and methadone clinics. "Prisons, drugs, and gangs," he said. "It's beautiful."

I steered onto Alt US 40, the inelegant modern designation for the National Road as it runs west from Cumberland. The two-lane highway climbed through a mountain cleft that Olmsted described as "a wooded gorge, into which a road enters as into monstrous jaws."

Sandwiched between tractor trailers, my view of the Narrows wasn't as dramatic. But my spirits lifted with the altitude. Freed from Cumberland and its prisons, I was headed over the mountains on a historic route trod by thousands of wagons and westward pioneers.

I also spotted a picturesque survival from that era on a busy commercial strip in LaVale, a small town just beyond the Narrows. It was a seven-sided brick structure with a wooden cupola: the National Road's first tollhouse, dating to the 1830s. A sign listed "Rates of Toll" for an array of old-world vehicles, including sleighs, chariots, and "Phaeton or Chaise With two Horses or 4 Wheels."

Another marker said the word "Pikers" derived from travelers who tried to avoid paying turnpike tolls by skirting gatehouses like these. Hence the building's nearly octagonal shape; from its many upstairs windows, toll keepers could keep an eye out for some distance in every direction.

"First toll gatehouse!" a voice exclaimed behind me. Startled, I turned and faced a bald black man wheeling a very large bag along the curb of the National Road. He was patriotically clad in a red windbreaker, white shirt, and blue tie, studying the roadside historical marker as I had a moment before.

Then he examined the tollhouse's gatepost. "I can clean that," he said. Pulling a squirt bottle and rag from his suitcase, he sprayed and wiped the post, holding up the cloth to show me all the grime.

He then squirted the side of the tollhouse and took out a heavy bristled brush. "See the mold and mildew go away?"

I nodded, unsure where this was leading—and what to make of the quarters lodged in each of his ears. Following my gaze, he explained, "I want to be successful so I listen to money." He sprayed and buffed a windowsill. "Look at that, a century of dirt. You could use a lot of product here."

David Handy was a salesman, and his product was 20X Citrus Multi-Purpose Cleaner. "If you don't like citrus, I got lavender, green apple, and clear," he said. "Biodegradable, too. As friendly to the planet as I am to you."

"Sorry, I don't work here." I held up my pad and pen. "Just stopped to take some notes. I write books."

"Sell many of those?"

"Try to."

Handy smiled. "Hustling, like me. Traveling around and trying to move product."

I hadn't thought of it that way, but here we both were, by a phantom tollbooth on the National Road, wielding the tools of our respective trades. Handy had been peddling his product for twenty-four years, and he mentored the young people from inner cities that his employer recruited.

"I tell them, 'You got to sell *yourself*, got to have personality. If people like it, they buy it.'" He zipped up his bag. "Want to see how it's done?"

I followed him as he wheeled his bag to a nearby strip of small commerce. He stopped first at a chiropractor's office where the receptionist glanced at Handy a little uneasily. In the nearly all-white hill towns of western Maryland, I guessed that a gaudily dressed black man toting an enormous wheelie bag was an unfamiliar sight. Not to mention the quarters in his ears.

Handy was clearly used to this. He held up his product and said, "I got a spray gun, not a real one. Push soap, not dope."

The receptionist smiled and said the office didn't need any. Handy sprayed a chair leg and held up his rag to show her the dirt. "That's what I used on Michael Jackson, cleaned the black right out of him!"

Now the woman laughed. Handy sprayed a spot on the carpet. "No stain this product won't tame." He rhymed and scrubbed his way around the office until the woman relented and bought a quart of citrus.

At the next stop he gave a similar pitch to a reluctant store clerk, then spread his arms and said, "I tell kids, 'Hugs not drugs!'" The clerk went to his desk to write a check for a quart of lavender, probably to avoid the hug. At a tattoo parlor, where the vibe was distinctly unwelcoming,

Handy declared, "Okay, guys, we got a go-away special today. You buy, I go away."

By the end of the strip, he'd sold all but one bottle in his bag and earned forty dollars in commission from his labor. A company van was parked down the road, waiting to carry Handy to the next town. He declined my offer of a ride but walked me to my car. "I can clean that," he said.

"It's a rental. I don't care if it's clean."

He sprayed and buffed the bumper. "That shine is fine."

I gave him twenty dollars. He gave me a quart of green apple for which I had no conceivable use. "Keep pushing that pen," he said, before wheeling his empty bag down the road.

OF HIS TRAIN JOURNEY THROUGH THE MOUNTAINS BEYOND CUM-berland, Olmsted wrote, "The rails plunge into the wild" and "only by dint of the most admirable persistence in tunneling, jumping, squeezing, and winding, do they succeed in forming a path for the locomotive."

He had entered the Alleghenies, a rugged part of the Appalachian Mountains. Leaving the National Road to retrace the bygone B&O route, I drove hilly roads trafficked by farm vehicles and logging trucks until a sign welcomed me to "Wild and Wonderful" West Virginia.

The wooded scenery didn't change, apart from a sudden proliferation of roadside signs declaring, "Stop the War on Coal!" Meanwhile, on the car radio, a Christian program warned of "America's coming implosion" due to abortion, the removal of prayer from public schools, and an influx of "pagan Muslims" and others "who don't share our culture."

The End Times seemed already to have arrived at the first settlement I reached. Old maps identified Terra Alta as a B&O stop in Olmsted's day, but all I found was a row of abandoned storefronts by the railroad tracks. The only open business was Cheap-O Depot, a variety shop with lawn and car ornaments decorated with the words "I'm a Proud Coal Miner."

I asked the proprietor, a middle-aged woman, if there was much coal mining here.

"Used to be," she said.

"Do trains stop at Terra Alta?"

"Used to." She remembered her father boarding a train when he was drafted during the Vietnam War. "Then they tore the station down."

"What do people here do now?" I asked.

"Nothing." Seeing me to the door, she shut off the lights.

From Terra Alta, the B&O line led to cheerless Grafton—the town where I spent Halloween night at the wretched motor lodge with the coal miner's special—and then northwest toward Wheeling. The tracks had been torn out decades ago, so I meandered in the general direction Olmsted traveled, through hills and narrow hollows. This Appalachian scenery cried out for banjo and fiddle accompaniment. Instead, I listened on the car radio to a college football game that was preceded by a telling rite.

Before entering their home stadium in Morgantown, the West Virginia Mountaineers marched past screaming fans and patted a 350-pound lump of coal perched on a pedestal. This procession, called the Mantrip, was named for the shuttle that carried coal miners underground. The hunk of carbon to which players paid homage came from the Upper Big Branch Mine, where twenty-nine workers had died in a horrific explosion in 2010.

The back-and-forth game—interspersed with ads decrying Washington's "war on coal"—carried me across several rural counties where I saw no evidence of mining, although I passed signs offering "Top $$$$" for oil and gas rights and glimpsed flares from distant rigs.

Olmsted, the future landscape architect, was unusually terse in describing his own passage through this terrain. Earlier in his train journey, he'd admired the "new and wilder beauties at every bend." But he much preferred being *in* nature, on foot or horseback, and wearied of the "monotonous" mountain solitude on view from his train window. "Rocks, forests, and streams, alone, for hours, meet the eye," he wrote. "It is a pleasure to get through and see again the old monotony of cultivation."

He finally did so as the train descended the western slope of the Alleghenies, where the valleys and fields gradually broadened. "At length the fields are endless, and you are following upward a big and muddy stream which must be—and is, the OHIO. You have reached the great West."

At the time, the Ohio was the nation's busiest east-west interstate, linking the Atlantic Seaboard to the Mississippi and a network of other rivers. In the 1850s, some three million people a year rode the river on vessels crammed with livestock, furniture, whiskey, and other goods. The Ohio, for much of its course, also formed a watery divide between North and South, free states and slave states.

None of this was easy to conjure upon my own arrival at the river, beside a bygone B&O junction. I saw no traffic on the water, and the far bank in Ohio, about a quarter mile distant, was a mirror image of West Virginia's: broad fields with gentle wooded hills behind.

Following the river north toward Wheeling, I came to a stone marker denoting another historic North/South divide: the Mason-Dixon Line. It was drawn in the 1700s to clarify the border between Pennsylvania and Maryland, but I hadn't known that surveyors extended the line due west in the 1830s, severing the body of what was then Virginia from a narrow neck of the state that poked north for seventy-five miles, between Ohio and Pennsylvania.

This struck me as a quaint geographic anomaly: a sliver of Dixie that had been stranded *above* the Mason-Dixon Line. But a short drive past the old stone surveyors' post, I entered what *did* feel like a different region from the Southern-inflected backcountry I'd traversed since Cumberland. Chemical plants, bulbous tanks, and a tangle of pipes and electrical grids began to crowd the riverbank. I'd breakfasted an hour earlier on biscuits and gravy, served by a waitress who called me "hon." Now, as I stopped for gas, the men pumping fuel beside me were factory workers clad in Pittsburgh Steelers jackets.

Then Wheeling hove into view. From the elevated highway it looked like a considerable burg, with house-covered hills sloping down to a riverfront of tall buildings and bridges. The city had impressed Olmsted at first sight, too—albeit unfavorably, as a coal-smudged bedlam of transport and industry. "The brightest day would not, I believe, relieve the bituminous dinginess, the noisiness, and straggling dirtiness of Wheeling."

A different pall hung over the streets I navigated after exiting the highway at Wheeling's southern edge. I came first to a rust-colored warehouse with faded letters: "LA BELLE, Cut Nail Plant: The *LARGEST* in the World!" This had been true circa 1885, when Wheeling became known as Nail City. After a long decline, La Belle had closed, as had virtually every other factory in South Wheeling, a formerly vibrant manufacturing district.

Continuing north on wide, almost empty streets, I reached Wheeling's compact downtown and found the McLure, almost certainly the "first class hotel" where Olmsted stayed before boarding a steamboat down the Ohio River. The hotel had opened shortly before his arrival, when the B&O first reached Wheeling, an occasion that dignitaries celebrated at the McLure with a "R.R. Supper" of roast beef, oysters, and champagne. "The pride of Wheeling" later served as host to ten presidents, Marilyn Monroe, and Joseph McCarthy, who famously claimed in a speech at the hotel that he had a list of more than two hundred Communists inside the State Department.

The McLure, like Wheeling, had lost its luster since. It was now a stucco and concrete hulk, the gloomy interior gutted of historical character, a R.R. Supper—or any dining—no longer on offer. But the decayed hotel seemed an appropriate (and affordable) perch as I plotted how to follow the next leg of Olmsted's journey.

A short walk from the McLure brought me to Wheeling's once-busy wharf. "Here are the panting, top-heavy steamboats, surging up against wind and current," Olmsted wrote of the Ohio River traffic. "Here are the flat-boats, coal laden from Pittsburgh, helpless as logs, drifting patiently down the tide."

Wheeling's wharf was now designated a "heritage port," a pleasant little park with no vessels in sight. The only visible remains of the city's river-travel zenith in the nineteenth century were heavy iron rings in a retaining wall, formerly hitching posts for steamboats.

Walking along the river I came to what Olmsted called Wheeling's "only ornament," a single-span suspension bridge "as graceful in its sweep as it is vast in its design and its utility." In his day, it was the longest such bridge in the world and a vital corridor for overland commerce and settlers.

The bridge's cables and towers still gave a grace note to the riverfront. But the span now carried little but local traffic to and from a casino and dog track on an island in the river. Most motorists roared across the Ohio on an interstate highway bridge, or tunneled under Wheeling, or skirted the one-time transport hub on elevated freeways.

Even less remained of Wheeling's manufacturing heyday, in the late nineteenth and early twentieth centuries, when the city's many products included cheap cigars, called stogies, a name believed to derive from tobacco-puffing drivers of Conestoga wagons on the National Road. All this production appeared gone, and the riverbank north of the city was littered with the husks of massive steel plants that sat literally rusting.

So I was startled, while driving through this industrial ghost-scape, to see flames suddenly flaring in a large open shed. Pulling over, I found the small office of the Centre Foundry and Machine Company and several brawny men in hard hats.

"Real old-fashioned industry, I know, a rare sight these days," one of the men said when I asked about the plant. He ushered me to a back room where I met Frank VanSickle, the plant's safety and human resources director, and Patrick Baker, a visiting contractor. Both were in their late fifties, old enough to recall a blue-collar world that had all but vanished.

"It used to be milk and honey in this valley," Baker said. "Dads worked in mines or mills, moms stayed home, families ate dinner together. Now, if people *have* work, they're likely to be on different shifts or one of them has to commute thirty miles."

VanSickle had grown up just a few blocks from here and followed his father into the foundry straight out of high school. "As a kid I could hear the pounding from the foundry and see the soot and flames coming out of the stack. I couldn't wait to get in here."

His father had moved up from shoveler to union president and then "across the street to this office, just like I've done," he said. "My dad did forty-six years here, in the one place. I'm up to thirty-seven. That doesn't happen much anymore."

Centre Foundry, which began in the 1840s, was one of only two companies in the country still producing gray iron castings used in steel plants. It had survived by switching to specialty molds, but its sixty-four-man workforce was a quarter the size of a generation ago, "and the market could dry up any time," VanSickle said.

Baker said the same sense of "impending doom" hung over coal and other industries in West Virginia. "It's got so down that people are really scared and angry." At the EPA, at trade deals, at cheap foreign competition.

VanSickle, a lifelong Democrat, was having second thoughts about his party allegiance. "There's a lot of rhetoric in Washington, years of talk about making things better. Nothing changes here."

He glanced at the clock. "Break's about to end. Want to see some metal cooking?"

VanSickle handed me a hard hat and plastic safety goggles and led me across the road to a corrugated metal shed the length of a football field. The interior was an industrial Hades: bubbling caldrons of molten metal, mountains of black sand, heaps of slag, enormous chains rattling along rails overhead. Workers, clad in what looked like silver-hooded space suits, moved through this underworld wielding blowtorches, shoveling ash, and dangling huge cones over craters.

VanSickle, shouting over the noise, ticked off job titles that sounded almost Neolithic: pitman, melter, molder, rammer, chipper. Their work also put the "heavy" in heavy industry. We watched men "charging the furnace," which meant feeding it enormous chunks of pig iron that arrived in the shape of dinosaur eggs, weighing up to seven tons. Broken into pieces with an enormous spherical crusher called a "headache ball," the iron was then picked up by a giant magnet and dropped into the blast furnace, creating the column of fire I'd seen from the road.

"It's like putting french fries in the fryer," VanSickle said. "We've had people drive by and rush to call the fire department."

Other workers "tapped" the furnace, raising it so the molten metal flowed into an enormous lipped bucket. From a platform above the furnace, I looked down into what looked like the mouth of a bubbling volcano. The temperature of the metal was actually higher than lava, about 2,600 degrees. As protection, workers wore "silvers," a mix of aluminum and flame retardant Kevlar that made the work all the hotter.

At a nearby station, "skimmers" used long wooden paddles to remove surface impurities by raking them into slag pots. Each time they poked at the metal's orange crust, sparks and flames erupted, and after a few minutes their gloves began to smoke.

"We're not pushing buttons; we're a different animal," said Kenny Violet, who served as local representative of the plant's steelworkers' union. "This is hot, dirty, physical work; not everyone can hack it." Over the years he'd seen new hires quit within days, even hours.

The pay wasn't great, either, between $15 and $16.50 an hour, roughly half of what some of the workers had earned at now-shuttered steel mills. The men on this shift worked from 6:00 a.m. to 2:00 p.m., taking two short breaks in a windowless room with vending machines and benches covered in a film of black dust.

I retreated there with VanSickle, who recited the dangers he monitored as safety manager. "Burns, obviously. Crushing injuries, falling into pits, backs giving out." Another issue was air quality, particularly when workers used grinders to remove grit from hardened sand castings. "Sand is one hundred percent silicon; you don't want to be breathing that."

Workers wore dust masks and respirators and watered the floor to keep the sand and dust down. But these and other precautions had come too late for longtime employees like VanSickle, who began shoveling sand at the plant in the 1970s, when no one wore respirators and asbestos pads were used to retard flames. He'd had multiple surgeries on his back and shoulders, and in his fifties, started feeling light-headed and short of breath.

"I went in for a chest X-ray and the doctor said, 'How long have you smoked?' I told him never." VanSickle was diagnosed with asbestosis, a scarring of the lungs for which there is no cure.

He nonetheless felt fortunate to have had steady employment and now, at the age of fifty-seven, a desk job and management salary. "But I don't think I'd want anyone to go through what I've been through." The nature of the work and the uncertainty of the market also made him doubtful that many sons would follow their fathers into this forge, as he'd done.

"I feel like we're the end of an era," he said.

INDUSTRIAL WHEELING HAD BEEN DOWN SO LONG THAT CITY boosters no longer waxed nostalgic for bygone factories. Instead, they touted the city's inexpensive real estate, proximity to Pittsburgh and the "I-70 corridor," and industrial spaces being repurposed as apartments, small offices, and artisanal studios.

"At one time every trash can in the country came from Wheeling. You name it, we made it," said Steve Novotney, a local radio host who took me to a blues and jazz club in a renovated warehouse. "When all the industry was dying, we wallowed in that Rust Belt identity, the coal and steel and nails. Now we're finally evolving."

Politically, however, a counter-evolution was underway in West Virginia. I'd arrived in the state during election season, but learned little about the candidates or issues, apart from the endless ads assailing Washington's "war on coal." Until, returning to the McLure, I noticed campaign posters plastered on a shop front by the hotel. Knocking on the door I was greeted by my first mine worker, or at least ex–mine worker.

Orphy Klempa was a Wheeling native of Slovak descent and the son of a tavern keeper. He'd bolted roofs in coal mines, worked at factories, and risen to become a carpenters' union leader, three-term state legislator, and chairman of the local Democratic Party.

Which was why he now sat alone in the party headquarters, at a desk with three phones, none of them ringing. "If the polls are right, we're going to get our asses kicked on Tuesday," he said, propping his cowboy boots on his desk.

West Virginia wasn't known for cowboys, but Klempa wore the boots, he said, "because they're about the only clothing I can buy that's still made in America." He expressed other views that were conservative by national Democratic standards. Klempa was pro-life, a gun owner and NRA member, and proud of having worked across the aisle with Republicans in the state legislature.

But that middle ground had caved in, and blue-collar West Virginia—staunchly Democratic in the twentieth century—had turned strongly Republican in recent elections. Klempa blamed some of this rightward turn on race. The state was 95 percent white, and even the waning Democratic base was so unenthusiastic about Obama that it had given 41 percent of the vote in the 2012 presidential primary to a jailed felon, Keith Judd.

Klempa added, however, that cultural issues, including "guns and gays," weren't the hot issues now. "It's jobs, or phony promises of jobs. The other side is kicking coal dust in people's eyes so they can't see reality."

Klempa had served on an energy commission in the legislature and knew his fossil fuels. The reality: West Virginia's high-sulfur coal had been under siege for decades, due to reduced demand, competition from natural gas and Western strip mines, and pollution controls dating to the 1960s. Thousands of jobs had also been mechanized, for more than half a century. The industry now accounted for about 3 percent of the state's employment and revenue—much smaller than in sectors like tourism and hospitality.

"Washington's waging a 'war on coal'?" Klempa scoffed. "It's a joke, like having a war on midgets."

But coal remained such a potent symbol and powerful lobby that politicians paid ritualistic homage to it, like the football players patting carbon on their "Mantrip" to the Mountaineers' stadium. In ads, the state's governor took "dead aim" at climate change legislation with a scoped rifle, blasting a hole in it. A Senate candidate dramatized her defense of coal and "our way of life" (a phrase that echoed antebellum defenders of slavery) by pulling a switch to cut off the White House lights.

"It's sad, the world's moving on," Klempa said, "but we're stuck in this mine shaft."

One of the phones on his desk rang for the first time in an hour. He grabbed it: a wrong number. Klempa had a long call list, mostly union members, but found it increasingly hard to compete with the internet, cable TV, and talk radio. "When I was coming up, folks watched network news and talked politics at the beer joint or barbershop or union hall," he said. "Now everyone's in the car or at home, tuning in their favorite rants. We're just shouting past each other."

I left Klempa there, mining for votes, and returned on the morning after the election. The result was a landslide even greater than the polls had predicted. Republicans took control of both chambers of the state legislature for the first time since 1932 and defeated a nineteen-term incumbent who was the sole remaining Democrat from West Virginia in the US House of Representatives.

Klempa appeared shell-shocked. "We've joined the Solid South," he said. "I always thought West Virginia was different and that Democrats were the workingman's party." He paused, blankly stuffing leaflets in boxes. "Now I feel, I don't know, *extinct.*"

WEST VIRGINIA'S POLITICAL REALIGNMENT WAS ALL THE MORE striking because of the history on display down the street from Klempa's office, at a building known as Independence Hall. Before the Civil War, many inhabitants of Virginia's hilly western counties had bristled at taxes and laws favoring plantation masters in the state's east. Olmsted also noted what he called an unusual spirit of "improvement" in western Virginia.

Elsewhere in the state, white elites displayed "not a spark of faith in the capacity of their poor whites" and claimed they could only rely on those "made to work," i.e., slaves. By contrast, he then quoted the *Wheeling Intel-ligencer*, which welcomed "industrious" artisans and mechanics from the North and Europe. "Men will always work better for the cash than for the lash," the paper stated.

In 1861, when Virginia dissolved its ties to the US and joined the Con-federacy, delegates from the state's west gathered at Independence Hall in Wheeling to discuss separating from Virginia. Two years later, West Virginia formally joined the Union as the thirty-fifth state, its seal pro-claiming in Latin, "Mountaineers Are Always Free." This withdrawal from Virginia proved to be the only lasting secession to occur in the Civil War era.

Yet now, 150 years after Appomattox, West Virginia was detaching it-self from the former Union states to join a new, South-based confederacy, in rebellion against the federal government. Coal explained some of this secession, but the museum director at Independence Hall exposed seams I hadn't yet tapped.

"Perversity is part of our character," Travis Henline said. "We've got a split personality."

A curly-haired forty-year-old with an encyclopedic knowledge of state history, Henline had grown up along what he called the state's true Mason-Dixon Line, two hours' drive south of Wheeling. Counties below this di-vide were first settled by farmers from the Virginia piedmont and had always been "more Southern" than Wheeling, with its transport and indus-trial links to the rest of the country.

Many in the state's south resisted Wheeling's lead and fought for the Confederacy, including some of Henline's ancestors. The split persisted after the war as mining took hold in the state's southern coalfields and political power also shifted south, to Charleston.

"We were divided, and then we were conquered," Henline contended. Out-of-state barons bought up the land, timber, and mineral rights, taking advantage of people who lacked written claim to their property or under-standing of its value.

"That's the great irony of West Virginia history," he said. "We declared independence only to become an internal colony, ruled by King Coal."

To this point, Henline had delivered a calm history lesson. Now he became agitated. "The whole Hatfield and McCoy image of West Virginia was perpetrated by outsiders. It's easier to exploit people you've stereotyped as ignorant hillbillies."

What irked him even more was that West Virginians took "perverse pride" in this painful legacy. The riches from extracting natural resources had mostly flowed out of state, leaving behind poisoned streams, blackened lungs, crippled limbs, and communities mired in poverty and isolation.

"So you'd think we'd turn the page and try to develop our human resources," Henline said. Instead, West Virginians displayed a "twisted allegiance" he likened to Stockholm syndrome. "The attitude is, 'We're blue-collar, we dig stuff up, we suffer, but we suffer with dignity.'" He shook his head. "To me, there's nothing dignified about suffering to make other people rich."

BEFORE I LEFT INDEPENDENCE HALL, HENLINE SHOWED ME AN Ohio River steamboat—or, rather, a scale model of one. He also gave me the name of its builder, John Bowman, who painstakingly constructed his museum-quality models in the basement of his Wheeling home, even hammering coal to place bits of it by the boats' miniature furnaces.

Bowman had also authored three books on steamboats. When I named the vessel Olmsted rode on the Ohio, the *David L. White*, he instantly replied, "Registered in 1853, the Wheeling and Louisville line, fleet of seven, finest boats of their time."

These top-line steamboats were known as "floating white palaces," up to three hundred feet long, with plush furnishings and formal dining. However, they were notoriously unsafe due to primitive boilers that frequently exploded, scalding passengers and setting fire to the vessels.

"The boats were made of white oak, hickory, and walnut—all good firewood," Bowman noted. Two years after Olmsted rode the *David L. White*, the boat caught fire. It was relaunched, only to end its brief career in a boiler explosion that blew boat parts one hundred feet into the air and killed sixty-five of those aboard.

Bowman, who was seventy-four, recalled as a child seeing old steamboats tied up near Wheeling. But he said the only stern wheel vessels remaining on the upper Ohio were small hobby craft, operated by enthusiasts who docked at Wheeling and other ports for summer festivals. "Nothing like the *David L. White*," he said wistfully.

Leaving Bowman to his balsa and glue, I walked down to the riverfront to mull what to do next. It was foggy and chill, and the water was as quiet as it had been on my previous visits. Cars sped beside and over the Ohio, but I'd yet to see any traffic on it.

Then, gazing upriver, I glimpsed what looked like a long black snake poking along the surface of the water. As it inched toward me in the fog, I made out a string of low-lying barges, piled with dark hillocks.

"Here are the flat-boats, coal laden from Pittsburgh, helpless as logs, drifting patiently down the tide," Olmsted had written of the Ohio. And here they still were, toting coal at worm speed, a toylike tugboat hitched to the rear.

If I couldn't book passage on a floating white palace, what about a toiling black barge?

CHAPTER 3

OHIO RIVER

Mutants Making Tow

O lmsted set off for the South without training or experience as a roving correspondent, apart from his literary amble around England. His early dispatches for the *Times* were uneven and overfertilized with data about manure use, turnip culture, and other agricultural minutiae.

But he quickly found his feet and displayed a talent for drawing out Southerners from all walks of life. Occasionally, he made appointments to see "well-informed and leading men," he wrote, aided by letters of introduction from "distinguished" Northerners with Southern connections. More often, he relied upon "such chance acquaintance as one may hit upon," he later informed a writer planning his own Southern tour.

"My best finds were coarse men with whom I could take a glass of Toddy in the bar room," Olmsted wrote. "The very best, country practitioners of medicine, third rate tavern keepers, sheriffs & tax collectors & peddlers. Innkeepers wives are not to be neglected."

Olmsted also put high value on "personal acquaintance with the people in their homes," as he'd often done while seeking food or lodging along rural roads. "For this a man must go on horseback and take his chances."

Except for the horse part, I'd adhered to this freestyle approach during my own years as a roving reporter. But Olmsted had several skills I lacked, including a talent for mimicking Southerners' speech and manner.

"There was nothing in his countenance, his dress, his language, or his bearing," Olmsted wrote of his Yeoman persona, "by which he could be readily distinguished from a gentleman of southern birth," at least on "first inquiry."

Olmsted was also a farmer, able to engage Southerners with talk of the land, as well as an experienced rider and a mariner who had not only sailed to China but also piloted small boats off the coasts of Connecticut and Staten Island.

My own facility in these areas didn't extend much beyond mowing the lawn and ferrying to and from my island home on Martha's Vineyard. As for playing the chameleon, my accent, "bearing," and surname tended to mark me as an interloper, or what the Halloween drinker in Grafton had called a "Yankee boy spyin' on us hillbillies."

These deficits came home to me, once again, when I decided to take my chances on Ohio River travel by visiting a coal-loading dock south of Wheeling.

"You want to *what*?" asked the security guard at the entrance.

"Talk to someone about riding a barge," I repeated.

He picked up a phone and called the site supervisor. "Wayne, guy here at the gate wants to talk to you about . . . I'll let him explain."

I found Wayne Dolaman in a shed by a labyrinth of silos, chutes, and conveyor belts. From my encounter at the gate, I gathered that my mission sounded crackpot. So I told him I was a writer seeking insight into coal's journey from underground to river dock to wherever it went from here.

"If you're thinking miners with picks and shovels, those days are long gone," he said. The coal he oversaw was extracted by machinery he likened to the carriage of a typewriter. "It goes across the coal seam with teeth that chew at the coal, and then ratchets back to cross the seam again." With only twelve workers per shift at the coalface, the mine produced six million tons a year.

The coal then traveled here on conveyor belts to be washed, crushed, and sorted for transport to power plants. Dolaman walked me to the desk of a colleague who handled these shipments. He was on the phone, on hold, so I asked him straight out: How might a writer hitch a ride on a river barge?

"Helps if you're coal," he replied. Barges toted coal and other bulk cargo. It was only the boats lashed to the barges that carried people. Oops.

"How far you want to go?" he asked. Olmsted rode the *David L. White* to the largest port on the Ohio before heading overland into Kentucky. So I told him Cincinnati.

"You realize you could probably walk there quicker?"

I didn't, but nodded and stood there until he scribbled down a name and number. "Try this guy, in river ops. Wouldn't get your hopes up."

GREG WALBURN WORKED IN RIVER OPERATIONS FOR AMERICAN Electric Power, one of the nation's largest utilities. When I reached him by phone he seemed to be carrying on three other conversations at the same time, on crackly radio lines.

"It's like air traffic control," he said. Walburn coordinated barge arrivals and departures that were subject to constant change, due to weather and other factors.

Fortunately, he was open to having me document the unsung business of coal transport and said he'd get back to me. When he did, I was killing time at Wheeling's dog track, watching greyhounds hurtle after a mechanical rabbit.

"I can put you on a boat this week, just not sure exactly when or where," he said. The crew would provide everything except footwear. "You'll need some serious steel-toed boots."

I found them the next morning at a century-old "shoe hospital" in Wheeling. The salesman lugged out a pair of his heaviest-duty, industrial-grade boots. "Drop a big chunk of coal on these and you won't feel a thing," he said.

The boots weighed almost ten pounds, sheathing my toes in steel and my shins in leather thick as rhino hide. The high, stiff uppers forced my normally hunched posture upright; huge Vibram soles added another three inches to my height. I walked out of the store feeling like Paul Bunyan.

Two blocks later I felt crippled, as if my feet were encased in concrete. Walburn called again. "I gotta boat leaving out of Brilliant, Ohio, in an hour or two," he said. "You can hop on there."

Hopping anywhere seemed impossible at the moment. But I limped to my car, drove across the river, and followed the Ohio bank to Brilliant, named for a bygone glass factory. The small town was now dwarfed by a massive power station, its squat cooling tower and thousand-foot-high stacks smudging the sky with steam and fumes. This was the Cardinal Plant, my "hop-on" location.

Walburn had told me I'd be boarding a boat called the *Roger W. Keeney* during a crew change. He'd alerted the captain but not the crewmen, who arrived at the plant gate in a crowded van and seemed less than thrilled when I announced I was joining them.

"Too much coffee this morning?" a man grumbled as I nervously stumbled into the packed van, jarring him awake.

No one else said a word as we drove to the plant's dock and boarded a small vessel, standing in a huddle waiting to be shuttled out into the river. After some tentative probing I learned that the men had risen before dawn to meet the van at a pickup point four hours south. They were about to begin a three-week shift, on a cramped boat without alcohol or other diversion—and now, the last-minute addition of a stranger in spanking-new boots, asking questions such as, "How many barges does each tugboat handle?"

"*This* is a tug we're in now," the man beside me muttered. "*Keeney's* a tow."

Tugs referred to small boats that worked at docks and harbors. Tow-boats were much bigger and more powerful and, despite their name, pushed rather than towed barges down the river.

I changed tack, asking what there was to do at ports we'd visit along the Ohio.

"Huntington's got titty clubs," my neighbor replied. "If you're into fat naked ladies with C-section scars, that's your town."

I shut up until the tug motored us out to a blunt-nosed vessel with three decks shoved forward to form a wall-like bow. Five hundred gross tons of diesel-powered muscle, purpose-built to push: the offensive lineman of the river world.

As soon as I boarded the *Keeney*, someone shoved an orange flotation vest at my chest and told me to follow Buck, the first mate, a lanky young man with a shaved head, bushy beard, and a T-shirt stating, "Southern Bred, Venison Fed."

Buck was responsible for my "fire and safety briefing," emphasis on "brief." He strode briskly around the boat, pointing at fire extinguishers and opening hatches to chambers filled with mechanical horrors.

"You pretty much want to stay the fuck out of this one," he said of the tiller room, its hydraulic-powered shafts able to crush a man in "pinch points" along the walls.

Then he ran through a checklist of alarms. The fire warning "is loud as shit," he said, the man-overboard alarm "sounds like a school bell," and if I heard a long continuous ring, "something serious is going down and you head for the galley." Worst was a stuttering alarm. "That basically means we're going to shove her into the riverbank, bail out, and let the fire department deal with it."

The *Keeney* had a lifeboat, but Buck said there wasn't much space aboard, "so if the shit really goes down, I'd swim for it." He hooked an electronic device to my safety vest. "That sets off a signal so someone can fish you out. Hopefully."

Briefing complete, Buck handed me the boat's roster, listing the other nine people aboard, beside their job titles. There was a blank space at the bottom, next to "Spare." Filling in my name, I felt like one of the red-jersey "expendables" in *Star Trek* who are invariably vaporized in the first scene.

The next form wasn't comforting, either. "I, the undersigned voyager," it began, "assume all risk of accident or injury to myself, or loss of life," due to the condition of the boat or docks, or negligence of the crew, or mishaps during "ingress and egress" to wharves or other property.

I, voyager, signed.

"You're good to go," Buck said. Though where I should go was unclear. The crew was busy at various tasks, and wherever I planted myself seemed to be in their way.

When I finally found a quiet spot, Buck paused while rushing past to inform me I was leaning against the cabin of the captain, who was sleeping until his next shift. "If you wake him up, we're all fucked."

He also told me that I'd be "bunking with the pilot," who normally had the only other private quarters, in a cabin next to the captain's. The two men alternated at the helm, and Buck said I should stay out of the pilot's room when he was off duty so he could rest. "Unless you want to have a zombie steering us into a dam."

I'd never met a river pilot outside the pages of Mark Twain, and as I trailed Buck to the top deck to meet my bunkmate, I conjured a grizzled mariner in a stiff cap, standing before a huge wooden steering wheel. Instead, the pilothouse was occupied by a tall, handsome twenty-nine-year-old clad in jeans, flannel shirt, and cowboy boots, seated in a soft swivel chair flanked by computer screens.

Like Buck, Ryan Dawson came from the West Virginia hills and spoke with a mountain drawl, in his case thickened by the Skoal he dipped from a can by the controls. "I was always told you wear out your boots at your first big job," he told me. "All I'm wearing out is my butt."

Ryan didn't seem to mind my presence, and the comparatively roomy pilothouse was the first space I'd found where I wasn't in anyone's path. It had windows on every side, a counter with a coffee machine, and a cushioned bench that doubled as the lid for a toilet, so the helmsman could keep eyes on the river at all times.

I settled atop the "pooper," as Ryan called it, and waited for my trip down the Ohio to begin. It was an hour before Ryan reached for the "sticks," chrome tillers and throttles connected to the boat's rudders and engines. But he motored only one hundred yards before parking again, to collect our tow of fifteen rust-red barges.

It took the crew two more hours to secure the tow with heavy cables and check the mountains of coal in the barges' open beds. Then Ryan swung the *Keeney*'s stern into the Ohio and eased the boat around until the tow pointed downriver.

We were finally underway—at a speed of just over 1 mile per hour. Ryan slowly added throttle until reaching 4.6 miles per hour. "If I dropped the hammer we could go six right now, but we're moving pretty good as it is."

Given our cargo, it was a marvel we moved at all. The *Keeney* pushed over fifteen thousand tons of coal, plus the weight of the steel barges—in all, a load roughly equivalent to 150 loaded railcars. The barges also formed an unwieldy expanse of over two acres, stretching a thousand feet from the *Keeney*'s bow.

Ryan used binoculars to peer at the front of the tow, and his view of the water beyond was blocked by the raised bows of the foremost barges. "In summer, there can be jet skiers and idiots in speedboats that dart right in front of you," he said. "Even if we spot them we can't exactly stop on a dime."

At our current speed, he estimated it would take us a quarter mile to come to a halt. He also had to watch for logs and other detritus that could catch in the boat's propellers and disable the engines. Losing control, with this much tonnage, was unsafe at any speed.

"You hit a wooden pier at half a mile an hour and it's toothpicks," he said. "Hit a bridge pylon and those barges would fold up like an accordion."

Such calamities were rare, and the boat was loaded with radar, satellite, and other systems that buffered the risks. The gear included an alarm that went off if the tiller stick didn't move for ninety seconds—a sign the helmsman might have drifted off.

This was a real hazard, due to the tedium and fatigue of the job. Ryan worked the "back watch," from 11:00 a.m. to 5:00 p.m., and 11:00 p.m. to 5:00 a.m., for twenty-one straight days. While deckhands and mates moved around the boat and barges, the pilot and captain were confined to this room, usually sitting, and most of the time alone. "You have to stay hyperalert up here," Ryan said, reaching for more coffee, "which makes it hard to go straight to sleep when your watch ends."

He managed about three hours of rest after breakfast, and two after dinner. Apart from meals, sleep, and showers, his only off-hours activity was visiting a treadmill wedged into the boat's small laundry room. "Burns calories and kills time," he said.

The coordinates of river travel had a treadmill quality, too. Each location was designated by how many miles it lay from Pittsburgh. Our start point at the Cardinal Plant was Mile 76, and the *Keeney* was scheduled to travel just past Cincinnati, to Mile 474, with multiple drops-offs and pick-ups before turning around.

"I get tickled when I see orders with this many stops," Ryan said, studying the itinerary. "Breaks the monotony."

OLMSTED DESCRIBED HIS STEAMBOAT, THE *DAVID L. WHITE*, AS "A noble vessel, having on board every arrangement for comfortable travel, including a table of which the best hotel would not be ashamed."

He didn't give details of the fare, but in a Wheeling museum I'd found a menu from another opulent boat of that era. It listed entrees in French and English, including "Calves Feet *a la Puceline*," "Filets of Chicken with Truffles," and "White Raisin *a la* Windsor."

Dining on the *Keeney* was a far simpler affair, in a narrow galley with a table at one end and the rest crowded with kitchen equipment. It was overseen by Pam Stewart, who opened a cavernous oven to show me that night's inaugural hunk of ham.

"Country, Southern, that's what these guys want," she said, dishing up sides of hominy and corn bread. "They'll eat a little Mexican, and spaghetti and meatballs, but that's about as foreign as it gets."

Vegetables were also viewed with suspicion, unless heavily fried or well disguised. "Salad—forget it, the closest I can go is coleslaw." But she'd prepared a somewhat exotic dessert recipe, "Better Than Sex Cake," a layered confection covered in pineapple slices, pudding, coconut, and Cool Whip.

"It's easy to get in a rut on a towboat, so I try everything I can to liven things up," she said. Meals were the main entertainment on board, and not only because of the food. The brightly lit galley, overseen by a gregarious cook, the only woman aboard, offered brief respite from the boat's work environment.

"I'm their mother, their sister, their counselor, and sometimes their barber." Married to a truck driver and having raised two sons, Pam said, "I'm used to being around men and their stomachs and bellyaching. I've got guns and farm animals at home, so I can talk about that, too."

As 5:00 p.m. approached, crewmen began to filter in, peeking under dish tops and bantering with "Cookie," as they called Pam. The leading jester was a scruffy engineer in a black bandanna, nicknamed Rat, who had "Kentucky Eye Candy" written on his flotation vest. Spying green collards, he announced, "Cookie's looking after my figure because she's in love with it."

Cookie rolled her eyes. "Rat, your figure is the least of your many problems."

"What's this mess?" another man asked, studying the cake.

"You mean the slob about to drool on my dessert?" Cookie shot back.

The galley table seated only five, and meals coincided with the changeover of shifts. Those about to start work ate quickly, some while standing. Since the two watches worked opposite hours, the men saw very little of those on the other shift.

"I'm the only who sees everyone and hears everything," Cookie said. Among other concerns, the men often came to her for counsel about family issues or for advice on preparing a dish to surprise their wives upon returning home. "Guys gotta be guys with each other. Not with me."

In other respects, her life on board was as limited as it was for everyone else. She rose at 3:00 a.m. to start cooking, while also cleaning, maintaining a constant supply of coffee and snacks, and arranging for grocery pickups downriver. She rarely escaped the galley except for naps in her cabin a few feet away.

"I feel sorry for my husband, because when I get home all I want to do is avoid the kitchen and go out," she said. "I make him eat at the same places he's been going for the three weeks while I've been away."

AFTER AN UNNEEDED SECOND HELPING OF COOKIE'S EXCELLENT ham and hominy, I waddled to the *Keeney*'s other gathering place: "the doghouse," a cramped locker room opening onto the boat's square bow. From here, crewmen went out to the deck and barges as needed and then retreated inside, crowding onto a small bench and milk crates. A heater and the nonstop smoking added to the claustrophobia.

So did the chatter. "We've heard each other's jokes and stories a thousand times," said a deckhand named Dave Lucas, his nose buried in his cell phone.

"Dave's got eight thousand friends online and none at home," another man quipped.

"Except for your horny-ass wife," Dave replied.

"Don't talk about his sister that way!" interjected Rat, the "Eye Candy" engineer. As a "flatlander" from Kentucky, Rat delighted in teasing the West Virginians aboard.

"What does a hillbilly girl say during sex?" he asked me. The other men groaned. "'Get off me, Uncle Bill, you're crushing my Marlboro!'"

Rat's jokes aside, the men said doghouse life was tolerable. Deckhands started at about $40,000 a year, mates and engineers made over $50,000, and all reckoned they were doing better out here than they would onshore.

"It's a good living for country boys," said Buck, the first mate, "a place you can still work from the neck down."

But the schedule was very hard on their domestic lives. Almost all those aboard were in their late twenties or thirties, with young kids at home and wives juggling jobs and single parenthood during their husbands' long absences.

"Seems like everything always goes wrong at home when I'm out here," said the second mate, Travis Roberts. "Pipes burst, car breaks down, kids get sick." In eight years on the water he'd also missed five Christmases and many children's birthdays.

Returning home wasn't easy for Travis, either. "My wife will hand over the kids and say, 'Your turn,' but I'm not up to speed on things and mess up their schedule." By his third week home, he added, "I'm on my wife's nerves and she'll say, 'Don't you have a boat to catch?'"

Rat's wife worked at Wendy's and his three kids were school-age, so during days at home he was mostly alone. "I see more of the guys on my watch than I do of my family." He smiled, adding, "These guys, at least, are all family to each other. You know what they say about West Virginia—no lifeguards in the gene pool."

ASPHYXIATED AFTER TWO HOURS IN THE SMOKY DOGHOUSE, I returned to the top deck, where the captain, Frank Hobbs, was now at the helm, the pilothouse dark except for screens on either side of him. A sixty-two-year-old Kentuckian with a short, graying beard, he was an ancient mariner compared to his crew, having started work on the water at the age of eighteen "and run pretty much all the rivers since."

The Cumberland and Tennessee were "really crooked," he said, the Illinois and Indiana shallow and crowded with small craft, and the Mississippi beset by strong currents and heavy traffic, including ocean freighters and forty-two-barge tows, almost three times the size of ours.

On the Ohio, by contrast, fifteen-barge tows like the *Keeney*'s were "the road hogs" and they had plenty of highway. An hour passed before another tow appeared on one of the captain's screens. Easing us around a bend, Hobbs picked up a radio phone and said, "This is the *Roger Keeney*, I just did the turn."

"I'll see you on the two," the approaching captain replied.

This was old steamboat lingo for passing each other on the starboard side. Before radios and phones, captains blew whistles on bends and still did so occasionally. But the tows moved so slowly, with screens showing their position, that pilothouses rarely had an urgent need to communicate. "We're like a herd of turtles out on the river," Hobbs said.

The Ohio itself had also changed dramatically since Olmsted's day, when vessels often caught on snags or sandbars and couldn't run at all for several months each year due to shallow water. The river now had twenty dams, and the stretches between were called "pools," the water generally placid and at least nine feet deep.

When the water was high and the current strong, "there's a lot of slipping and sliding, like driving on ice," Hobbs said, but in calm conditions "it's pretty laid-back."

This hadn't been so during his early years in pilothouses, when "there was a lot of Jack Daniel's and testosterone on the river." Boats raced each other and ran through fog, despite equipment far less sophisticated than now. Hobbs had felt "invincible" at first, but a few close calls and the counsel of older men settled him down.

"I learned to stop trying to muscle against Mother Nature," he said as the river narrowed and took a sharp turn. We seemed perilously close to the Ohio bank, but Hobbs pivoted expertly and let the current carry us around the bend. He then turned on a spotlight as we approached a dam, and a lock hugging the West Virginia shore. The Ohio dropped almost seven hundred feet between Pittsburgh and Cairo, and locks at each dam lowered or raised boats to the next pool.

The lock chambers were only a few feet wider and longer than the *Keeney* and its tow, so maneuvering into them required considerable finesse. Once safely inside, a lockkeeper turned valves, letting water out of the chamber. "It's like pulling the plug in a giant bathtub," Hobbs said as we slowly sank.

He made it all look and sound easy, but negotiating locks was the greatest danger on the Ohio. A few years earlier, at a lock upriver, barges had hit a wall and broken loose in a heavy current. While trying to corral them, the towboat was swept backward over the dam, killing four crewmen.

"Old-timers warned me long ago that this job is hour after hour of boredom interrupted by moments of sheer terror," Hobbs said.

As I was coming to realize, the job also required excruciating patience.

After exiting the lock, we crawled toward the lights of Wheeling. It had taken me forty minutes that morning to drive from the city to the Cardinal Plant—and five hours to make the return trip by towboat.

I asked the captain what our ETA was for reaching the next city along the Ohio, Marietta, about seventy miles downriver.

"ETA?" he laughed. "Out here it's WAG—a wild-ass guess. There are so many variables." Fog, lock delays, changes in the boat's orders. His WAG for Marietta was tomorrow night.

At 11:00 p.m. there were footsteps on the pilothouse stairs. "Music to my ears," the captain said, turning over the controls to Ryan. The pilot tossed back coffee, reached for his Skoal, and slumped into the chair he would occupy until 5:00 a.m.

I listened to him yawn for a few minutes before heading below to the cabin he'd just vacated. The room was about ten feet square, Ryan's duffel occupying the lower shelf of a bunk bed. Climbing into the top bunk, I lay with my face a few inches from the ceiling.

Ryan had told me that older boats "rattle your teeth," but the *Keeney* had springs that cushioned the ride. Closing my eyes, I had little sense of being on the water, apart from a slight vibration and the low hum of the engines, a drone that matched my first impressions of towboat life.

Front watch, back watch, meals at five and eleven and five. The same few faces and tight spaces, day after day. Sequestered, for a set term, apart from society. A confinement one of the doghouse crew had likened to doing time in a minimum-security prison.

Except with less sleep. I drifted off about 1:00 a.m. and woke to a thud on the door and Buck's booming voice: "It's four fifty, clear the fuck out!"

OLMSTED RECOUNTED HIS OHIO TRIP IN A BRIEF PASSAGE NEAR the start of his second book about the South: *A Journey through Texas*, cumbersomely subtitled *Or a Saddle-Trip on the Southwestern Frontier*.

This was misleading, since Olmsted journeyed for six weeks and more than two thousand circuitous miles getting *to* Texas, by means other than horseback. Another source of confusion: the role of John Olmsted, who accompanied his older brother.

John had been diagnosed with tuberculosis, abandoned his medical studies, and joined Fred with "the hope of invigorating weakened lungs by the elastic power of a winter's saddle and tent-life" in Texas. John wrote this in an editor's note at the start of *A Journey through Texas*. Fred was named as author of the book, but "owing to the pressure of other occupations" after he returned north, John pulled the narrative together. John described his role as "simply that of connecting, by a slender thread of reminiscence, the copious notes" Fred had taken.

He appears to have had a light editorial hand, and much of the book is a stitching together of Fred's dispatches for the *Times*. John is also inconspicuous as a character in the travelogue, until the brothers commence their ride in Texas. This makes him an oddly spectral presence on the Ohio, and elsewhere on their outbound journey: one half of a "we" in a narrative driven by his older brother's eye and interests.

"From some conversational impressions, our anticipations as to enjoyment of scenery on the Ohio were small," reads the account of their river voyage, "and we were most agreeably disappointed to find the book that nature offered occupying us during all our daylight."

Particularly pleasing was the interplay of landscape elements, which would become a hallmark of Fred's park designs. "Primeval forests form the main feature, but so alternating with farms and villages as not to tire." Dramatic bluffs and bends in the river also gave pleasant contrast to the "stately vistas of the longer reaches."

I reread this passage in the *Keeney*'s doghouse, at five thirty in the morning, having spent almost all my ride thus far in the dark, seeing nothing of the riverscape Olmsted described. Someone from the last watch had scrawled on a board in the doghouse: "20 degrees, watch out 4 frost."

Then the deckhands donned headlamps and heavy work gloves to inspect the barges and help guide the captain through another lock. As I followed them outside, our breath clouded in the predawn chill. "Be careful, it's slicker than a wet pussy out here," Dave said, leading us onto the barges.

For the first time I was grateful for my supergrip, steel-toed boots. We navigated a spiderweb of narrow walkways and obstacles that were hard to see in the dark: cables strung at ankle height, heavy metal bitts to secure the lines, winches and hatch lids, gaps between the barges just wide enough to fall into.

It was a quarter mile of careful walking, past mounds of coal that were frosted white, before we reached the front of the tow, where swells had splashed over the bow and formed an ice sheet.

Dave said that on busy days, "deckies" traversed the tow a dozen or more times, logging eight difficult miles on top of other labors. "Summer's the worst. The metal gets hot as hell and the coal captures heat, so you're out here in all this heavy gear boiling up."

"And surrounded by water you can't cool off in," Travis added. Even if they could break from work and find a safe way to dive off the tow, the Ohio ranked as one of the most toxic rivers in the nation, due to mine run-off and other pollutants.

Summer had one plus. There was more to look at, including the occasional bikini-clad woman on a houseboat, or people gazing at the tow from shore. "We watch them watching us," Travis said.

As for the "charming scenery" that Olmsted described, the view was so familiar to the men that they saw it through jaded eyes, like truckers on the interstate. "There's a guy downriver who's building a big house," said a deckhand name Chad. "When we pass that, we note the progress. 'Cool, he's got the garage done.' That's about as thrilling as it gets."

After leaving the lock, we glimpsed the lights of a West Virginia town the crew identified as New Martinsville, founded shortly before Olmsted's steamboat ride. His admiration of the scenery along the Ohio did not extend to the man-made environment. "The towns, almost without exception, are repulsively ugly and out of keeping with the tone of mind inspired by the river."

Olmsted's emerging aesthetic, which he'd later bring to his design of residential settings, abjured ninety-degree angles, dull regularity, and architecture that clashed with its natural surrounds. He particularly disliked "make shift" development plotted solely for commercial ends—a conspicuous feature of towns along the Ohio.

"Each has its hopes," he wrote, "of becoming the great mart of the valley, and has built in accordant style its one or two brick city blocks, standing shabby-sided alone on the mud-slope of the bank." He termed these settlements "mushroom cities" that marked "only a night's camping place of civilization."

In the 1850s, many of these river towns had only just spawned. Those that still clung to the Ohio's bank, like New Martinsville, were old fungi now. The *Keeney* crawled past a cluster of nineteenth-century buildings, strung along a main street running right beside the river. The sun had just begun to rise above the enclosing hills, bathing the town in a gentle reddish glow.

New Martinsville resembled the four-square brick encampments Olmsted judged a blight on the river's grandeur. But I much preferred its picturesque antiquity to the franchise sprawl and other "mushroom" development of my own era.

For the *Keeney*'s deckhands, three hours into their shift, New Martinsville made a different impression. "The regular world, on a regular schedule," Travis said, watching the town stirring to life. "Out here, Cookie's menu is about the only way I even know what day of the week it is. Fish? Must be Friday."

LATER THAT MORNING WE TIED UP TO CIRCULAR BLOCKS TO DROP four empty barges and pick up four filled with limestone. This sounded straightforward, but barges came in different sizes and some rode higher in the water, so they had to be rearranged for balance and visibility.

"It's like taking apart a jigsaw puzzle and putting it back together," Ryan said when I rejoined him in the pilothouse. "Except the pieces aren't alike and they're going to different places. You don't want to bust the whole tow at every drop-off."

The mechanics of this laborious process, called "making tow," engrossed me for about ten minutes—and went on for another four hours. It took Olmsted a day and a half to steam from Wheeling to Cincinnati. I'd been aboard the *Keeney* for almost that long and traveled a tenth the distance.

When the *Keeney* finally got underway again, we entered a long, straight stretch of placid water with wooded hills rising gently on both banks. It was my first sustained glimpse of "the book that nature offered," a peaceful and bucolic passage.

Not so for Ryan, who had traveled the channel hundreds of times. "I *hate* this stretch," he said, fidgeting in his chair. "Not even a single god-damn bend to make the watch go quicker."

This patience-trying leg also encapsulated his career path. He'd spent eleven years working his way up from the doghouse to the pilothouse, and the captain had told me Ryan was a "natural" helmsman. But he couldn't rise to the pay grade and benefits of a captain until one of the limited slots opened up.

"It's a waiting game," Ryan said. "Clock twenty-five more years out here and then maybe I can retire, too."

BY MY THIRD DAY ABOARD, EVEN AS A MERE "VOYAGER," I WAS beginning to feel like Bill Murray in *Groundhog Day*. Buck banging on the cabin door and shouting, "Four fifty, clear the fuck out!" Watching the watches change, watching the crew make tow, watching Cookie prepare another sclerotic meal in the galley.

Then, around Mile 220, the scenery and routine took a dramatic turn. We'd passed a few power plants upriver, in the dark, but for the most part I'd seen little except a misty panorama of river and sky and hills: a Rothko canvas of slate. Now, massive cooling towers and exhaust-spewing stacks loomed at regular intervals.

We stopped at several of these plants to deliver coal or fill empties, the coal pouring out of chutes and into the barge "hoppers" like glasses lined up at a bartender's station. More coal streamed down belts from inland mines, filling silos and forming mountains of coal by the river, a miniature of the dark wooded hills behind.

Coal dust also blew over the tow, mixing with the drizzling rain to form carbon slurries on the deck. The crewmen moved through this gloom like aboveground miners, their headlamps flickering and clothes and faces streaked with grime.

Buck paused while dragging a cable, nodding down at the brownish green scum between the tow and dock. "In summer that'd be filled with stinking dead fish to go with all the other random shit."

Then he went up to the pilothouse to report on our progress. Ryan shared a bag of venison jerky he'd made himself, and the chat turned to hunting and fishing and trapping. Ryan caught muskrat, coyote, and fox, and sold their furs. Buck gave tips on getting meat out of a turtle. "Cut the head off, stick a hose in, and shoot it out."

In the galley and doghouse, I'd half listened to hours of similar talk: the Muzak of the Mountain State. But now, with the boat docked at a plant that ate ten barges of coal a day, belching fumes that blotted out the sky, I was struck by the dissonance in the crewmen's lives.

Country bred, these proud backwoodsmen set traps and stalked wild game—then went back to humping coal along a river corridor so industrial it had once been dubbed America's Ruhr Valley.

At dinner, as the talk turned again to baiting and bow hunting, I asked if anyone found it jarring to inhabit such different worlds.

"All the dirty stuff we do out here pays for the guns and a patch of land to garden and hunt on," Buck replied.

"Someone's got to provide all that power, so why not us?" the captain said. "If money's there, you might as well take it. Don't leave it on the table."

The men didn't pay much heed to coal's impact on the environment either, except to the degree it affected their livelihoods. Many coal-fired plants on the Ohio were closing or switching to natural gas, and tow companies were turning to other cargo, including hazardous chemicals transported on "red flag" barges with double hulls.

"I'd rather push coal," Buck said, "than some scary shit that could blow us to kingdom come if a deckie throws his cigarette the wrong way."

The men also doubted climate change was due to burning fossil fuels, citing "solar cycles" or other factors. "Acid rain, ozone holes, global warming—there's always some scare," Rat said. "It's a power grab by the EPA. They find a puddle in your yard and call it a wetland."

The only dissenting view came from the second mate, Travis, who'd resided for all of his thirty-two years near a power plant downriver, one of the biggest and most polluting in the nation.

"When I was in school, everyone had coughs and headaches, and the sulfuric acid was so bad it'd eat the paint off cars." At times, a pinkish-blue fog hung over the small community. In the early 2000s, as complaints mounted, the plant's owner bought out 450 residents and bulldozed most of their homes.

Scrubbers and other pollution controls had improved the air since. But Travis, who lived just outside the buyout zone, said there was still blow-off from the plant's huge fly-ash dump—"on windy days, it looks like it's snowing"—and chemical-laced waste ponds that gave off what he called "a sewage-like smell."

He worried that his trailer's proximity to the plant was affecting his family's health, including one child with serious asthma and allergies. "Something bad is happening with the air and climate, and burning all that coal isn't helping," he said.

This wasn't easy for him to acknowledge. His grandfather and uncle had worked at the plant, his mother still did, and almost everyone he knew had jobs at riverside plants or, like him, on coal-laden tows. "Man or woman gets a good job, you don't want to take it away from them."

As a teenager, Travis had hoped to train as an anesthesiologist. But he'd married at nineteen, needed a job, and "once you start in life you forget a lot of what you were going to do." He now planned to spend his career on the river.

"I hope the coal goes away in my kids' lifetime," he said as another pair of stacks loomed into view. "I want them to do better than me, in a cleaner world."

THE NEXT DAY, I WAS DOING MY UPSTAIRS-DOWNSTAIRS ROTA-tion between doghouse and pilothouse when Ryan got a call from river ops. "New orders," he announced.

The weather was turning foul, with very high water forecast down-river. Instead of proceeding to Cincinnati, the *Keeney* would halt at Huntington, West Virginia, swap tows with a larger boat that could better handle the weather, and turn around to deliver its new cargo up the Ohio.

"It'll be real slow going, pushing upriver in high water," Ryan said. "Three miles per hour max."

This news scrambled my itinerary, too. Rather than tracking Olmsted's progress, I faced the prospect of revisiting the stretch of river we'd just traveled, in even slower motion. I knew nothing of Huntington, apart from its sad distinction as the most obese city in the nation, and among the worst for opioid deaths. That, and the "titty clubs" a crewman had told me about aboard the tug at the Cardinal Plant.

Ryan mentioned another sight in Huntington. "Saw a dead man there last winter. We were going slow under a bridge and he was lying on a girder." Ryan called the police, who later reported that the man had parked at a Shoney's, climbed down onto the bridge, and shot himself.

I asked Ryan if there was anyplace I might disembark before Huntington.

"Point Pleasant's got a dock," he said. "Okay town, if you're into the Mothman."

"The *what*?"

My ignorance stunned the crewmen, who happily filled me in at dinner. In the 1960s, there had been multiple sightings in Point Pleasant of a winged, red-eyed "thing" that appeared part human. This hit the national media and led to a paranormal book and movie, *The Mothman Prophecies*. Many people believed the creature still haunted the woods and skies around Point Pleasant.

Buck wasn't one of them. "You have to smoke a lot of PCP to see the Mothman."

But Dave, a Point Pleasant native, declared himself a "firm believer." He also offered his mother as a tour guide. "She can show you the Mothman's lair and drop you at the old hotel in town. It's haunted, but so is every place in the Point."

The captain agreed to dock at the town following a stop at a company wharf ten miles north of the Point, to dispose of trash and take on supplies. The crew sprang to these tasks with more avidity than I'd seen thus far, despite drenching rain.

"Feels good to get off this boat and plant your feet onshore," Travis explained, "even if it's only to visit a dumpster."

We were about to depart when the captain informed me that the fog was now too dense to dock at Point Pleasant. If I wanted to jump ship, this was it.

Dave called his mother, who he claimed was happy to head out in rain and fog at 11:00 p.m. to collect a total stranger. Then he walked me to the road by the dock's entry gate, with Buck and Rat: my disembarkation party.

"That book you've been taking notes for," Buck said. "Got a title yet?"

I didn't, and asked for suggestions.

Buck grinned. "How about *Rednecks on the River?*"

"*White Trash on the Water,*" Dave offered.

Rat, as usual, got the last word. "*Mutants Making Tow,*" he said.

We shook hands in the rain and they turned back to the boat, Dave shouting a final salutation: "Tell the Mothman I sent you!"

IN THE DARK AND RAIN, DAVE'S MOTHER COULDN'T SHOW ME THE Mothman's lair, but she kindly dropped me at the lodging her son had described as haunted. The Lowe Hotel stood at the center of Point Pleasant, which resembled another of Olmsted's mushroom towns, a few brick blocks strung along the river.

The hotel had a grandfather clock and antique radio in the lobby and a creaking elevator that carried me to a small room with an iron bedstead. I face-planted for ten hours, blessedly uninterrupted by a four-fifty wake-up shout from Buck, and went downstairs to find the hotel's elderly owner reading a newspaper in an overstuffed chair. Rush Finley said that his guests at the 110-year-old hotel used to include towboatmen on shore leave.

"Rough bunch; all they wanted to do was drink at the bars." Some would tell him, "Lock me in my room so I can sober up for a day before I get back on the boat."

These days, the Lowe mostly catered to Mothman tourists, many of whom claimed to see ghosts at the hotel and posted shadowy photos online. Finley welcomed their business. "But I refuse to modernize myself, or this hotel. If you want spooky, there's plenty of that in the Point without all this birdman stuff."

As evidence, he directed me down Main Street to the site of a colonial fort and fierce battle in 1774 that broke Indian resistance to settlement of the Ohio Valley. The defeated Shawnee leader, known to Anglos as Cornstalk, later sought peace and came to warn settlers of an impending attack—only to be seized and brutally slain. His remains lay at the site, now a small park with plaques describing Cornstalk as noble, well respected, and "atrociously murdered." After his killing, when the river settlement failed to prosper, a legend arose that the chief had cursed Point Pleasant.

This belief resurfaced in 1967, when a bridge linking the town to Ohio collapsed amid Christmas-shopping traffic, dumping cars and passengers and gifts into the icy river. Forty-six people died, one of the worst bridge disasters in US history.

I found the names of the dead etched in bricks at Sixth and Main Streets, by the site of the fallen bridge. Across the street stood a courthouse and memorial to another tragedy. In 1977, the enraged husband of a woman imprisoned at the courthouse jail for killing their two-month-old baby forced his way inside and ignited a satchel of dynamite, blowing up himself and four others.

All this carnage, in such a small town, seemed hard to fathom. "Bridge collapses next to this joint, jail blows up, Indians massacred down the street," said the owner of a bar and grill at Sixth and Main. "Whole world's fallen in on me, too. Cornstalk cursed us, that's what I truly believe."

He also believed it all "tied in with the Mothman," which was first sighted at yet another haunted locale: an abandoned World War II munitions plant outside town. Known as the "TNT area," it was a popular teen-age hangout—until, in 1966, two young couples returned from cruising one night and told police they'd been chased by a winged, fiery-eyed figure.

At first, this report was met with bemused skepticism. "Couples See Man-Sized Bird . . . Creature . . . Something!" the local paper stated. One man told a reporter that the description of the fiendish creature fit his "mother-in-law exactly, especially the red eyes, six inches apart." The county sheriff said the couples had probably seen a giant heron, or what he called a "freak shitepoke."

But other sightings quickly followed, and as the national media converged, the winged thing morphed into a "monster" and then a "moth man." Claims also emerged that the creature had been seen on or near the bridge just before its collapse. This prompted the belief that the Mothman was some sort of angel or demon, a harbinger of catastrophic events.

Paranormal pilgrims now visited all the relevant sites, guided by maps from the Mothman Museum, at the center of town. Following this trail, I glimpsed eerie, abandoned buildings behind razor wire and a gate painted with the words "Mothman Lives!" The only birds I saw were a murder of crows.

More intriguing to me was a historic marker to Samuel and Pamela Clemens, the paternal grandparents of Mark Twain. They had settled this area in the early 1800s and evidently were cursed, too. Samuel, while helping to raise a house, was freakishly crushed to death between a log and tree stump, at the age of thirty-two.

None of this made me any the wiser about what, exactly, so many people had seen in the skies around Point Pleasant. I canvassed a dozen or so locals—at shops peddling Mothman Burgers, Mothman T-shirts, even Mothman Droppings—and heard almost as many theories.

The TNT area had been a party spot; maybe those teenagers in the 1960s had been "liquored up" or smoked enough pot to hallucinate a monster. The area was also a lovers' lane, an older man said, "and a lot of things can be seen through a steamed-up window."

Others noted that multiple toxins had turned up in the TNT area, making it a Superfund site. Perhaps a type of crane with a large wingspan and red patches on its crown had eaten frogs from poisoned ponds and spawned a mutant man-bird.

"Whatever it was, the government covered it up," one merchant assured me. "The TNT area was built by the same people who built Area 51."

Late in the day, as rain began bucketing down, I retreated to a bar that Dave, the *Keeney* deckhand, had recommended. It was a cinder-block tavern by the riverbank, and the rare local business that didn't trade on the Mothman. There was no alien-themed décor—or any décor. Or any person other than the bartender, a man of about forty clad in black and wearing strangely tinted glasses. He looked a little otherworldly, so I tried my luck a last time.

"Have you ever seen the Mothman?" I asked.

"He just left," the bartender replied. "That's why it's empty in here."

"So I take it you're not a believer?"

"If you're making money off the Mothman, you're a believer," he said. "My dad was a miner; he believed in coal, until he died at sixty from silicosis."

He didn't offer more, and I resisted my usual impulse to badger more out of him. His words seemed an apt epitaph to my sojourn in coal country, the river valley, and this Cornstalk-cursed town. When the rain stopped, I'd light out for new territory, in what Olmsted called "magnificent Kentucky."

CHAPTER 4

KENTUCKY

"A Balance Sheet of Good Against Evil"

Olmsted, in matters of belief, was torn between transcendent longings and a hatred of dogma. "I crave and value worshipfulness," he wrote, "but I detest and dread theology & formalized ethics."

One source of this hatred was Olmsted's unhappy tutelage by pastors in his youth. Another was his deeply empirical nature, which made him doubt the authority of the Bible. He ultimately judged belief in scripture to be irrational and regarded the clergy as a hotbed of cant and sectarianism.

Writing in later life to his Yale friend Charles Brace, a man of deep Christian faith, Olmsted recalled his own dalliance with belief in the 1840s, when many of their peers attended revivals and were spiritually reborn. "I repent of nothing more thoroughly than my own sin in superstitious meandering."

Olmsted also came of age at a time when scientists—a term that wasn't in common usage until the 1830s—challenged scriptural authority as never before. He studied and later met Charles Lyell, the British geologist whose work on fossils suggested the earth formed over eons rather than in the six days of Genesis. Lyell, in turn, mentored Charles Darwin, who completed *On the Origin of Species* as Olmsted traveled and wrote about the South.

Darwin closely studied Olmsted's work while finishing his own, praised it in letters to colleagues, and shared many traits with the American. Both were well-born wanderers who went off to sea, and late bloomers who struggled to settle on a career (prompting Darwin's father to warn that Charles would become "a disgrace to yourself and all your family"). Darwin was a religious skeptic, an avid gardener, and a close observer of nature; in later years he lent support to Olmsted's campaign to preserve wild spaces.

Darwin also came from a family of abolitionists and hated slavery. According to his son, the naturalist talked "with horror of his sleepless nights when he could not keep out of his mind certain incidents" in Olmsted's writing.

Another kinship: Olmsted challenged the dogma common to antebellum whites, both north and south, that blacks belonged to a separate and inferior breed, a sort of subspecies out of Africa. This pseudoscience, known as polygenesis—and, to some Southerners, as "niggerology"—buttressed the belief that blacks were innately suited to subservience and hard labor in hot climates.

Olmsted wasn't immune to the racial stereotypes of his day. At times, he described Southern blacks as coarse, slothful, and ignorant. But he cast their degradation as a product of enslavement rather than inborn deficiencies or aptitude. Darwin, of course, also saw humans (and other species) as branches of a common tree, molded by their environment. Abolitionists quickly recognized the racial message inherent in his work, and Brace and others in Olmsted's orbit were among the first Americans to embrace *On the Origin of Species* upon its publication in 1859.

I'd noodled around this intriguing link between Olmsted and Darwin in the archives, judging it the sort of footnote matter that might impress my bookish editor. Until, that is, I resumed my travels with Fred, from West Virginia to Kentucky, where debate over Darwin and the origin of species was very much alive.

Upon disembarking from his steamboat at Cincinnati, Olmsted briefly noted the city's mud, "hubbub," and the "rivers of blood" flowing from its slaughterhouses. The city was then the nation's leading hog butchery, dubbed Porkopolis.

After a day in Cincinnati, the brothers boarded a southbound stagecoach and crossed the Ohio River with evident relief. "We roll swiftly out upon one of the few well-kept macadamized roads in America," Olmsted wrote, "and enter with exhilaration the gates of magnificent Kentucky."

The Porkopolis of his day was now a metro area that extended for miles into northern Kentucky. While attempting to skirt this sprawl, I saw a brown road sign, usually a color denoting a historic site, always catnip for me. This one read, "Creation Museum," with an arrow pointing west.

A few signs later, I reached the museum's entrance, marked by a metal cutout of a Stegosaurus and the words "Prepare to Believe." Another sign, on the door of the museum, labeled it a "Christian environment" where visitors could be searched and anyone with clothing or other items that might be offensive could be removed. Armed security men watched from an SUV near the door.

This rather forbidding portal stood in contrast to the museum's interior, which was airy and bright and filled with kid-friendly displays of animatronic dinosaurs. An opening exhibit showed two paleontologists digging at dinosaur bones, one of them explaining in a video: "I start with the Bible; my colleague does not. We all have the same facts; we merely interpret the facts differently."

Another exhibit, on the Grand Canyon, purported to show how the chasm could have been formed by the biblical Flood rather than carved over millions of years, as "secular scientists" believed. A movie at the Six Days Theater dated God's creation to 4004 BC. Then came the museum's most startling display: a re-creation of the Garden of Eden, with lush plants, trickling water, and bronze-skinned mannequins.

Adam was depicted as a bearded, longhaired hunk; Eve, pretty and lithe, dark locks draped over her breasts. Shown from the waist up, in a pool of water filled with flowers, they looked rather like hippies in a rustic hot tub. Except that the surrounding landscape included dinosaurs.

The Bible makes no mention of dinosaurs, and according to "secular" scientists they died out millions of years before humans appeared. The museum cheerfully disagreed, showing a pair of dinosaurs boarding a model of Noah's ark, behind giraffes. An animatronic Noah explained that dinosaurs were land animals, like others created by God on the sixth day, so "of course they came onto the ark!"

The tone turned darker as the story of our "sin-cursed, post-fall world" entered the modern era. The museum vigorously contested Darwin's evolutionary theories and displayed a copy of his work in a "Hall of Shame," along with *Mein Kampf* and other totems of the descent of twentieth-century man into scientific racism and genocide.

According to the museum, the post-Darwin ridicule and abandonment of scripture also led to "Relative Morality, Hopelessness, and Meaningless-ness." This condition was dramatized in a mock-urban chamber of horrors: alley walls covered in graffiti, shrieking police sirens, videos of teenagers rolling joints while watching porn or talking about getting an abortion.

I pushed on: to the planetarium (which offered alternatives to the big bang), to a movie about global warming (possibly due to "sunspots" or "cosmic rays"), and to Noah's Café, where I ate an Eden Wrap while perusing the museum's arresting literature.

Most of it featured the museum's founder, Ken Ham, an expatriate Australian science teacher and author of tracts such as *The Lie: Evolution*. The museum's exhibits had seemed to suggest that reasonable people could disagree, and that creationism was its own science, alongside the "secular" brand. Ham was much more Manichean.

He fulminated against "the false idea of tolerance" and Christians "deceived into believing they have no right to impose their views on society." True Christianity "cannot co-exist" with "relative morality" and a rejection of "God's absolutes." The result was "a great spiritual war," in which "one or the other will yield."

Ham waged this apocalyptic struggle with strategic and commercial acumen. He'd located the museum (adult admission thirty dollars) in northern Kentucky because it lay within a day's drive of two-thirds of the US population. And this was just one piece of his ministry, Answers in Genesis, which organized conferences and "Creation Vacations," and sold DVD sets of Ham's talks and school curricula.

"Dangerous ideas threaten our families," read a flyer for a teachers' kit on sale at the museum store. "Protect them with biblical answers."

The museum also hosted lectures, one of which I attended: "The Origin of the Supposed Races," by a member of Ham's ministry. His PowerPoint presentation traced racial difference to the Tower of Babel and subsequent dispersal of gene pools. It ended with a Benetton-style video showing beautiful children of varied hues and features declaring, "I did not evolve, I was created."

Afterward, I chatted with the speaker, Joe Owen, a genial man who had emphasized his multicultural message by flashing pictures of his Mexican wife and their six children. He'd contrasted such images with Darwin's *On the Origin of Species* (subtitled *The Preservation of Favoured Races in the Struggle for Life*) and the notions it spawned about the inferiority of "savage" peoples.

"We're not the bigots and bad guys," Owen told me. "The Bible doesn't teach kids to be racist; that comes from what they hear in school, about biology and genetics."

He also explained why the museum seemed so intent on dispelling *any* science—geological, astronomical, biological—that measured the creation of man and the universe in millions or billions of years. Many Christians accepted this timeline, and so-called "Old Earth" creationists had recast the six days of Genesis as eras rather than twenty-four-hour passages.

"We're *Young* Earth," Owen said of the creationist museum and ministry, meaning that God's word in Genesis was "literal and authoritative." But he didn't see it as his job to "slug it out" with secularists, or even to try to sway fence-sitters. "I'm strengthening committed Christians in their faith."

This accorded with the vibe I'd sensed while touring the museum. The crowd included women in long dresses and bonnets and bearded men in suspenders who wouldn't have looked out of place at a tent revival a century ago. Most visitors studied the exhibits with little comment, and I was the only one of seventy-five listeners to Owen's talk who queried him.

For others, it seemed the museum presented a worldview that was altogether familiar and beyond question. Which made me wonder: As a Jew (I didn't mention "secular"), where did I fit into this creationist picture?

"You're part of the Chosen People, with a very rich heritage," Owen replied. "We should be praying for your acceptance of Jesus as a Jewish messiah."

"And what if I don't?" I asked.

"In Romans, Paul says even the remnant of Jewish people are saved through the Gospel." Owen also cited Isaiah, telling me, "Our sin was imputed onto Jesus Christ and His righteousness is imputed, or credited, to your account for those born again into the Last Adam."

The credit part sounded good, if a bit redolent of Jewish moneylending.

About the rest I wasn't so sure. I shared Olmsted's allergy to theology, and all I could recall of Romans was the line about the wages of sin being death.

But Owen saved me, conversationally, by walking over to a poster for the ministry's newest venture, called Ark Encounter. This was a "full-scale" ark, being built to precise biblical dimensions (300 cubits, calculated as 517.5 feet long), "a sign of salvation for this generation" as the original was for Noah's.

"If you're headed south from here, you'll drive right by it," Owen said. He shook my hand warmly. "God will be shown true, always. I pray you keep that in mind."

LEAVING THE MUSEUM, I FELT TEMPTED—NOT BY EVE OR APPLES, but by an urge to dismiss what I'd seen and heard as an appendix of the American mind: a vestigial organ that had lingered a century after the Scopes trial. But that night, sleepless at a roadside motel, I read a Gallup poll in which 44 percent of Americans agreed with the statement that "God created humans in present form within the last 10,000 years," putting them broadly in accord with Young Earth creationists.

I also learned that the museum drew a quarter million visitors annually—and strong protests from scientists and civil libertarians in Kentucky. Foremost among these critics was Dan Phelps, a geologist for the state and head of the Kentucky Paleontological Society.

Phelps's home, a ninety-minute drive from the museum, was easy to spot because of the truck in his driveway plastered with bumper stickers that read, "I Brake for Brachiopods" and "Kentucky Fossils: I Dig 'Em!" Meeting me at the door, Phelps apologized for "the literal man cave" I was about to enter.

"My feng shui guy committed suicide," he said, leading me through dark rooms cluttered with fossils, dinosaur models, and Darwin figurines. Rummaging through this mess, he picked up a spinosaurus tooth.

"This is about a hundred and ten million years old. The Creation Museum would tell you it's from a creature that died in the Flood, in 2348 BC." This date put the Flood *after* the Pyramids were built. "So they have to create an alternative chronology for Egyptian archaeology, along with everything else."

Phelps was fifty-two, tall and geeky, but didn't fit the stereotype of "secular scientists" depicted at the museum. He'd been raised in a very religious Kentucky household and said his church upbringing and contact with clergy had been pleasant, unlike Olmsted's. "My problem with the museum isn't religion. It's bad science, or nonscience."

Kentucky had some of the nation's richest fossil beds, including one near the Creation Museum that was 454 million years old. Phelps walked me through radiometric dating and other techniques used to date fossils. I struggled to follow, but that was the point. "You need a semester of geology to begin to understand all this. The museum is exploiting the fact that Americans don't know much about science."

He recognized that no amount of "secular" evidence would persuade committed creationists. But he worried about the broader impact on attitudes toward science.

"In a weird way, the thinking behind the Creation Museum is postmodern—they're true believers who want to sow doubt," he said. "About Darwin and evolution most of all. But they're also breaking down public trust in scientific reasoning, climate science, vaccines—you name it, all suspect."

Phelps also felt the museum violated the separation of church and state. It received generous tax breaks while requiring employees to sign a "statement of faith" that demanded church attendance and branded homosexuality "sinful and offensive to God," on a par with incest and bestiality.

But Phelps conceded it was hard to make this case in Bible Belt Kentucky, where "it's not polite to bring up religion. When we do, the other side claims they're being persecuted by wild-eyed atheists."

He'd nonetheless kept campaigning against Answers in Genesis, for over a decade, applying his paleontological skills to layers of literature and tax filings. He'd publicized, among other embarrassments, that the man who had served as the model for Adam at the Creation Museum had a sexually graphic website called Bedroom Acrobat.

But Phelps lost many more battles than he won, and he sensed the tide within Kentucky and the nation at large was running against his cause.

"The know-nothingness in this country just seems to be getting stronger," he said. "People are proud of their ignorance, and when you challenge it, they fall back on conspiracy theories and fake facts." He gestured at his man cave filled with fossils he'd painstakingly collected. "It's like centuries of science never happened."

WHILE OLMSTED PUT HIS FAITH IN REASON, AND DISDAINED religious "superstition," he approached nature with a reverence that verged on mystical rapture. "Gradually and silently the charm comes over us; the beauty has entered our souls," he wrote of his youthful tramp in rural Britain. "We know not exactly when or how."

Infused with the writings of transcendentalists and European Romantics, he believed scenery touched our "unconscious" selves, stirring a sense of "mystery and infinity." Olmsted likened this to the action of music on our minds and souls, a sensation that "cannot be fully given the form of words."

This experience might be ineffable, but Olmsted was rarely at a loss for words when describing landscapes he admired, particularly the "magnificent Kentucky" he traveled by stagecoach from the Ohio River to Lexington. "There is hardly, I think, such another coach ride as this in the world," he wrote. "Certainly none that has left a more delightful and ineffaceable impression on my mind."

Antebellum stagecoach travel wasn't always so pleasant. The coaches had leather flaps rather than windows as shields against dust, rain, and cold. Their wooden wheels often broke or mired in mud. And there was little or no cushioning against the violent jolting that occurred in rough terrain and on bad roads.

"We were for some miles tossed about like a few potatoes in a wheelbarrow," Englishwoman Frances Trollope wrote of a very bumpy ride in Virginia. She also termed American stagecoaches "torturing machines" built "to dislocate the joints."

Olmsted rode a later and more comfortable model, on a well-paved turnpike, in November weather so mild that he spent most of his ride on "the box," beside the driver. From this pleasant, open-air perch, moving at animal speed, he lamented the advent of the iron horse, which was rapidly supplanting coach travel.

"This route is now done by railway, with great gain, no doubt, but also with what a loss!" he wrote, contrasting the coach's "free canter" over the Kentucky hills with the train's "sultry drag" along the flattest grade. "Where will our children find their enjoyment when everything gets itself done by steam?"

Olmsted's approach to natural landscapes also reflected his youthful reading of British theorists, who split scenery into an aesthetic triptych. The most dramatic and awesome sights, such as alpine peaks, belonged to "the sublime." Wild but less monumental vistas were classed "picturesque." Gentle landscapes of fields, woods, and water represented the "beautiful," or pastoral.

Olmsted appreciated all three categories and would become an early advocate of preserving the "sublime" at Yosemite and Niagara Falls. But his deepest affinity lay with the pastoral landscapes of his New England childhood and British rambles.

The woodland and meadows of Kentucky moved him in a similar fashion. He relished the "soft, smooth sod, shaded with oaks and beeches, noble in age and form, arranged in vistas and masses, stocked with herds, deer, and game." The terrain was also "charmingly varied," at times a rolling green sward, at others "high and rougher in tone."

Olmsted would later bring these and other elements to his park designs, and he paid the Kentucky countryside a telling compliment: "It is landscape gardening on the largest scale."

As elsewhere in the South, however, he contrasted "this luxuriant beauty of nature" with the "shabby improvements" of man. He described the small farms he passed as having "a slovenly appearance that ill accorded with the scenery." The houses and barns were "thriftless and wretched in aspect," and the village where the travelers stopped for lunch was "small and unattractive."

Stagecoaches, as the name suggests, traveled in segments, with regular stops to change horse teams while passengers ate and rested. The drivers blew horns or trumpets on approach so roadside innkeepers could set out food.

"The meal was smoking on the table," Olmsted reported of his lunch stop, "but five minutes had hardly elapsed, when 'Stage's ready' was shouted," forcing passengers to bolt their food and rush back to their seats on the coach.

This fast-food dining was matched by the quality of the fare: principally, corn bread and bacon, staples that would reappear at almost every table thereafter as the Olmsteds crossed the South. Occasionally, the ubiquitous corn bread and bacon were "relieved" by other dishes. But "taken alone, with vile coffee," they were an affront to the palate and stomach. Corn pone was "a very good thing of its kind for ostriches," Olmsted later concluded, but it did not qualify as "bread."

In the stagecoach, he also observed that his fellow passengers talked a great deal about remedies for indigestion. "It appeared from the conversation that dyspepsia was a common complaint in Kentucky, as God knows it ought to be."

A TWO-LANE HIGHWAY NOW TRACED THE PATH OF OLMSTED'S coach ride. The road ribboned between an interstate and railroad tracks and was fringed with self-storage units, mobile home parks, and other low-rise development. Instead of stagecoach stops, there were regularly spaced cloverleafs by the interstate with gaudy signs rising like selfie sticks: McDonald's, Burger King, Waffle House.

About thirty miles south of the Ohio, gaps opened between the clots of commerce, allowing glimpses of the landscape Olmsted extolled: rolling pasture dotted with black cows and tobacco barns gaily decorated with geometric quilt designs. The hills were softer and less wooded than in West Virginia, the valleys broader, the landscape gently tamed rather than wild or coal gouged.

I pulled over at a sign for Sherman Tavern, a rare surviving stagecoach stop. The clapboard structure had a wide porch, painted plank floors, and giant hearths—little changed from Olmsted's day, except for the absence of travelers or smoking piles of corn bread and bacon.

Fifteen minutes later, I made my own acquaintance with Kentucky's roadside fare at a diner in Williamstown, where I stopped to see the Noah's ark I'd heard about at the Creation Museum. The eatery looked as though it hadn't changed in a half century: Formica, fake flowers, a cigarette vending machine with pull knobs and brands like Viceroy, and a menu that evidently predated the American Heart Association.

The breakfast special: two eggs with biscuits and gravy, hash browns, and a medley of meats that included country ham, bacon, pork tenderloin, and "goetta." The waitress pronounced it "gatta" and said it was a German breakfast sausage "that's big around here, but you kind of have to develop a taste for it."

"What's in it?" I asked.

"Hon, you don't really want to know," she replied, bringing me a sample with the rest of my gargantuan breakfast. The goetta was brown, rectangular, and very flat, like a run-over sausage patty. The texture was gravelly, the taste mostly grease.

"Dessert?" she asked, offering peach cobbler or fudge cake.

Antebellum travelers described Kentuckians as tall, lean, and vigorous—every man "half a horse and half an alligator," in the words of a popular song. Olmsted seconded this, describing male Kentuckians "as stalwart in form and manly in expression as any young men on whom my eyes have fallen."

It seemed doubtful he'd say this of modern Kentuckians. The patrons at the diner oozed out of booths and stubbed cigarettes in their plates of grease and gravy. A tobacco state, Kentucky was also among the heftiest and least healthy in the nation, belonging to what the Centers for Disease Control called the Diabetes and Stroke Belts. In low-income rural counties, life expectancy was actually dropping.

The rest of Williamstown looked distressed in a different way, its traffic and commerce having migrated to the nearby interstate. At one of the few open shops on the main street, I stopped to ask directions to the ark.

The proprietor, a white-haired woman with brilliant blue eyes, told me to turn right at a conical salt dome "we call the Dolly Parton, because it looks like a giant boob." But I'd be wasting my time, she added, because the ark was unfinished and sealed off from view. "They don't want the gay atheists getting in there and causing trouble."

Marlene McComas's store was a one-stop shop for special occasions: flowers, balloons, gifts, tux and dress rentals, and cakes that she made in a kitchen at the rear. "Cradle-to-grave deliveries, too," she said, hoisting a bag of icing and deftly squeezing "Happy Retirement" onto a cake. "You can call 1-800-whatever but they won't know pee-diddly about you. Here, people know me and I know *everything* about them."

Williamstown was the seat of an unprosperous county midway between

Lexington and Cincinnati, a little too far from either to attract much business. "We're the redheaded stepchild of everyone else," Marlene said. This lack of distinction was evident in the slogan painted on the town's water tower: "Gateway to the Bluegrass," a signal to travelers "that there's nothing here and they should keep going," she said. "That's why I'm for that ark. We need all the visitors we can get."

Most locals agreed and objected to "outsiders" who opposed the project, she said. Marlene wasn't much of a churchgoer and didn't share some of the tenets propagated by Answers in Genesis. "But my view? If you don't like that ark, don't go." She reached for a cake mold. "Same as anything. If you don't like seeing boobs hanging out on cable TV, change the channel."

Marlene had many views, which I listened to for several hours as customers passed through, joining the conversation. I learned that Grant County was dry, had eighty-two churches and a very high rate of military service, and like much of rural and small-town Kentucky, had swung in recent years from Democratic to strongly Republican.

Marlene's own political transit had been even more dramatic. "I started as a save-the-world liberal idealist and now I'm a very conservative person."

Raised on a farm, she'd gone to the University of Kentucky on a scholarship and wanted to join the Peace Corps. But her father, scarred by his World War II service, forbade her from going overseas. So Marlene went to work for VISTA in the impoverished mountains of southeastern Kentucky, placing young people in jobs.

"I worked my tail off and had one success," she said, "a gal who got a job as a Cracker Barrel waitress and stuck with it. The rest? Didn't want to work, quit, and went on welfare."

Marlene had also taught at Head Start and remained active in a statewide women's association that helped struggling homemakers. "You know what I've learned from all that?" she said. "You can't help people who don't have a burning desire to help themselves. Handouts only make folks lazier and more dependent."

This was a familiar right-wing refrain, echoing Ronald Reagan's evocation of idle "welfare queens." But Marlene's ire wasn't aimed at urban blacks she'd never met; it was directed at fellow white Kentuckians who didn't share her work ethic.

"Just burns my gizzard when I see people doing everything on God's green earth to get on disability," she said, loading her van with cakes to deliver. "Lord! They're forty-five, what are they going to do and who will pay to take care of them?"

I hustled to help her, not wanting to seem a freeloader, and climbed in the passenger seat. As we drove past Williamstown's water tower, she told me about another one in northern Kentucky that had originally been painted "Florence Mall," to promote its shopping center. This violated a state advertising law. But rather than erase it or pay a fine, locals changed the lettering to "Florence Y'all."

To Marlene, this illustrated "Kentuckians' hatred of being told what to do." In part, this truculence reflected the state's rural character; until 1970, most Kentuckians lived on farms or in towns of fewer than 2,500, a half century longer than in the nation at large.

"Small farmers are self-reliant, rooted in the land, distrustful of distant government," she said. "But in Kentucky you have to double that, because our ancestors came here when this was frontier, to get away from the East. We still want to be left alone."

Marlene nonetheless allowed for exceptions. Pulling into a supermarket to buy catering supplies, she surprised me by saying that she admired Michelle Obama's campaign for healthier school food. "Kentucky has too many fatsos, and our tax dollars pay for junk food and Styrofoam that goes into some landfill until the end of time." She laughed. "Mind you, that's the *only* thing I like about the Obamas."

But as we drove on, she deviated from right-wing orthodoxy on several other issues. Marlene regarded abortion as a "woman's right" and had recently made an elaborate, cowboy-themed cake for the wedding reception of two gay men.

"I was happy to take their money," she said. "What they do behind closed doors is their own business." She wasn't fussed, either, about the legal status of Mexicans she'd hired to work on her family farm. "They're here and they work hard."

Nor was Marlene "a big-business enthusiast." A sign behind the counter of her shop stated: "When You Buy from a Mom and Pop Business, You Are Not Helping a CEO Buy a Third Vacation Home."

Back at her store, as she busily arranged tulips, I tallied the many views she'd shared and observed that they didn't really match her self-characterization as "very conservative." What kind of Republican was she exactly?

She smiled and said, "A Sarah Palin fangirl."

This fandom had more to do with style than substance. She liked Palin's strength and attack-dog persona. At the time of my visit, Palin was publicly flaying Obama for failing to staunchly back the Israeli leader Benjamin "Bibi" Netanyahu. Marlene wasn't a careful follower of Middle East news, but she'd gone on Palin's website that morning to buy a thirty-five-dollar T-shirt that read, "I Stand with Bibi."

"If Obama's against something and Sarah's for it, that's all I need to know," she said. "I stand with Sarah."

We talked until closing time, and she encouraged me to stay in touch by Facebook and phone. At the time of my visit, the 2016 presidential primaries hadn't yet gotten underway, and when Palin didn't enter the race, Marlene became an ardent supporter of Donald Trump.

She didn't always like his tone, particularly when speaking about women. But that and other differences were eclipsed by her hatred of "handout Democrats" and their candidate. When a neighbor put a Clinton sign in his yard, she countered by planting a "Hillary for Prison 2016" in hers.

She and Grant County went on to give Trump a startling 76 percent of the vote, on top of Marlene's other wish: the defeat of those opposing Ark Encounter. The attraction opened in the summer of 2016, drawing hundreds of thousands of visitors in its first few months.

In the view of Ken Ham, head of Answers in Genesis, these events showed, yet again, the falseness of polls and other secular prophecies. As he put it on Facebook the morning after the election: "God, not the media, is in control."

WILLIAMSTOWN'S MOTTO, GATEWAY TO THE BLUEGRASS, MIGHT irk Marlene, but it accurately described the lay of the land in Kentucky. Just south of the town, the hills eased into undulating swells of grassland. Though it wasn't blue, and only appeared so for a brief time in spring, this region was Kentucky's most fecund, its soil nourished by minerals from the underlying limestone.

Central Kentucky's natural splendor, and the wealth it created, put Olmsted in mind of aristocratic estates he'd seen in Europe. "The richest beauty is only reached at the close of the day," he wrote of his coach ride, "when you bowl down in to the very garden of the state—the private grounds, as it were, of the demesne."

Earlier, he'd passed small farms, apple orchards, a husking bee, and only a few slave quarters. In the rich-soiled Bluegrass, by contrast, "accumulation has been easy," he wrote, and the wealth of its "lords" was on full display: in the fine herds of cattle, the "black feudal peasantry," and mansions of "cost and taste" perched on every knoll.

This landscape, he added, gave the environs of Lexington "a rare charm." Olmsted also judged the small city an "agreeable residence" with "firm and quiet" buildings, pleasantly shaded streets, well-supplied shops, and a fine university.

Twenty-first-century Lexington retained much of the ambience he described. The city's compact downtown was girdled by shaded, antebellum neighborhoods and the campus of the University of Kentucky, and the pace was so unhurried that motorists frequently waved me in front of them in the light, center-city traffic. I also caught glimpses of the "rare charm" of Lexington's surrounds at horse farms with rolling swards enclosed by plank fences, drystone walls, and luxuriant hedges.

More often, though, the environs of Lexington—now part of a burgeoning metro area of over half a million—were a man-made mess. A ring road choked with traffic and strip commerce formed a moat between the city center and the remnants of pastoral beauty surrounding it. The Bluegrass was sown for miles with tract housing and malls that were neither rare nor charming.

Paradoxically, Olmsted had a hand in the despoiling of this landscape. Though best known for designing city parks, he was an early architect and advocate of suburbs. Olmsted envisioned these outlying neighborhoods as refuges from urban centers, combining the "ruralistic beauty of a loosely built New England village" with easy access to city jobs and amenities.

In a sense, this vision fell victim to its own success, as trains and trolleys gave way to automobiles and rapid development on the periphery of cities. While Olmsted abjured the "commonplace" and "prosaic" in his designs, the explosion of suburbs ultimately produced the opposite: cookie-cutter subdivisions and commercial sprawl. This was particularly so in the South, which remained largely rural and depressed well into the twentieth century. The region's rapid growth after World War II coincided with the advent of interstates, white flight, and other factors that fueled an exodus to suburbs and exurbs.

Lexington's run-amok sprawl wasn't different from that in countless other locales across the nation. Olmsted would doubtless be appalled by this development, and the corruption of his suburban vision. But perhaps nowhere more so than in the Bluegrass of "magnificent Kentucky."

WHILE OLMSTED EXTOLLED THE PHYSICAL CHARMS OF LEXINGTON and its surrounds, he was searing about the society he found there. Given the region's wealth, learning, and beauty, central Kentucky possessed every "advantage," he observed. "Were it only free."

Olmsted wasn't referring in this instance to slaves, though he described their whip-driven toil at a Lexington hemp factory. Rather, his indictment was aimed at the bound minds and mouths of whites. "Discussion may be learned, witty, delightful, only—not free. Should you come to Lexington, leave your best thoughts behind."

This condemnation spoke to a long-standing grievance of slavery's foes: the stifling of discourse about the South's "peculiar institution." The silencing included a gag on anti-slavery petitions in Congress and the seizure of abolitionist publications mailed to the South. To critics, this censorship showed that the "Slave Power" not only subjugated Africans. It suppressed the fundamental American freedoms of speech and belief.

In Kentucky, however, Olmsted also noted a very colorful and conspicuous exception to the closed minds and careful tongues of whites. On his coach ride, when hogs blocked the road, a fellow passenger observed that the swine bore the brand of Cassius Clay. This prompted a conversation that Olmsted recorded in dialect.

"Well, I ain't sorry to have Cash Clay make money."

"I like a man that, when he's an abolitionist, frees his own niggers fust, and then ain't afraid to talk to other folks."

"He's a whole man, if there ever was one. I don't like an abolitionist, but by God I do like a man that ain't afraid to say what he believes."

One of these speakers owned twenty slaves. Olmsted later recorded similar comments about Clay from other Kentuckians. They thought him "deluded" on the subject of slavery but admired "his courage and great force of character"—highly prized traits in a state known for its frontier independence and fighting prowess. "Even his enemies like him," one man said.

Olmsted recounted all this without context, knowing that his readers would be familiar with Cassius Clay (a name little known today, except in relation to the boxer Muhammad Ali). In the 1840s and '50s, Clay was a nationally renowned firebrand who had a very strong influence on Northerners like Olmsted. Clay went on to help found the Republican Party, appeared on its presidential ballot, and placed second in the voting to choose Lincoln's running mate.

Clay's stature derived from his pedigree, and unlikely betrayal of it. At an early age, he inherited a vast estate from his father, Kentucky's largest slaveholder, and married the daughter of Lexington's leading horse breeder. He was also tall and handsome, a gifted orator, and cousin of the congressional titan and perennial presidential candidate Henry Clay.

Seemingly destined for the gilded life of a Southern gentleman-statesman, Clay instead became a scourge to his caste. He sought "the overthrow of slavery by home-action," aired such views in his fiery newspaper, the *True American*, and wielded fists, guns, and knives in defense of them. "I wanted to show those who lived by force, that it would be met, at all times, and in all places, with force," he wrote.

At one political rally, beset by a mob and then shot in the chest, Clay drew his bowie knife and carved the gunman nearly to death. At another public brawl, he killed his attacker with a knife after being stabbed in the side.

Clay also bristled at abolitionists, calling them "cranks." He clearly rejected their pacifism, and instead advocated for gradual emancipation, building his case against slavery on material rather than moral grounds. "These are better arguments than invective," he wrote a Northern ally, requesting statistics showing that slave states lagged free states in wealth, education, and other areas.

Olmsted, on first reading the *True American*, wrote, "I like Cassius M. Clay and would vote to make him Vice President at least." He shared Clay's wariness of abolitionists, whose Christian zeal and moral absolutism ran counter to his deep skepticism and dislike of "one-idea-ism."

Olmsted followed Clay, too, in seeking "matter of fact matter" to demonstrate that slavery retarded the South's economic and social development, to the detriment of whites as well as blacks. Olmsted also appears to have met the fiery Kentuckian, though he chose not to mention this, except in a letter to his friend Charles Brace, disclosing that he'd carried "a letter from C.M. Clay" (middle name Marcellus) to a Northern-born editor he visited at his next stop, in Louisville.

If Olmsted did meet Clay in Kentucky, it was probably at Cassius's estate outside Lexington (by then, a mob that included Clay's kinsmen had forced his paper's printing press to move to Ohio). The estate was now a small state historic site, but a little hard to find, because the signs I followed to reach it made no mention of the famous emancipationist, only his property, called White Hall.

"If we put 'Home of Cassius Clay' on a sign by the highway we'd get a million more visitors," the park manager, Kathleen White, told me. "But they'd be here to learn about Muhammad Ali, and we get enough of that already."

Before Ali died, motorists often stopped at White Hall and asked, "Is he home?" Other visitors expressed shock when they began the house tour and saw Cassius Clay's portrait in the drawing room. "You mean he's white?"

The staff had to patiently explain that the black boxer from Louisville was named after his father, Cassius Clay Sr., who in turn had been named for the once-famous white Kentuckian. This may have been done out of respect for Clay's antislavery views or because the family's forebears had worked at White Hall.

In the 1960s, Ali rejected what he considered a "slave name" and briefly called himself Cassius X before adopting his Nation of Islam moniker. Nonetheless, there remained a kinship between the boxer and his white namesake. Both were fearsome and charismatic pugilists who loved the limelight.

"Imagine the 'wow factor,'" Kathleen said, leading me inside White Hall's forty-four-room Italianate manor house. "You're in the middle of nowhere and you step into *this*."

The entry room had a sixteen-foot-high ceiling, rose-colored walls, and a grand winding staircase—part of the elaborate facelift Clay and his wife gave to the Georgian manse he'd inherited, on two thousand acres of land.

Kathleen introduced me to the site's curator, Lashé Mullins, a slim-waisted, dark-haired woman who resembled a nineteenth-century Southern belle. Lashé had appeared in drama productions at White Hall while in college, worked here after graduation, and married a fellow employee while dressed in period attire on the estate's front porch.

"We bonded over Cassius," she said. The couple had since coauthored a book on Clay and White Hall and given his middle name, Marcellus, to their own son. "I'll probably fall out with my husband before I do with Cassius."

This obsession became all the more curious as she guided me through the house and the life of its scandal-ridden lord. We entered a palatial drawing room with a chandelier, gilded mirrors, and a portrait of Clay as a young man: wavy dark hair, playful gray eyes, aquiline nose, slight smile curling his full lips.

"Right up my alley," Lashé said. "He was nice looking all the way through his life. He *loved* women and they were really drawn to him."

One of those attracted to him was his wife, Mary Jane Warfield, pictured in the drawing room as a smiling blue-eyed belle with auburn curls. "Her mother hated Cassius's guts," Lashé said, and tried to break their engagement by sharing a letter from an earlier suitor that disparaged Clay's character.

Cassius beat the man in public, challenged him to a duel, and almost missed his wedding to Mary Jane while awaiting "satisfaction." He never received it; the other suitor slit his wrists in apparent shame over failing to fulfill the *code duello*.

Lashé moved on to a portrait of Czar Alexander II and another romantic scandal. In the 1860s, Cassius became US ambassador to Russia, and during part of his term Mary Jane stayed in Kentucky with their children. Rumors appeared in the press of Cassius's entanglement with several women in Russia, and upon his return home, Mary Jane exiled him to an unheated bedroom in the mansion's attic.

Then, in 1872, after ten children and almost forty years of marriage, she left him. Cassius promptly sent for a boy in Russia, presumed to be his illegitimate offspring, and brought him to White Hall as his adopted son. Unapologetic, as always, Cassius later stated that his marriage had soured long before his divorce and "therefore I considered myself free to love anybody."

In his sixties, Cassius also broke with the Republican Party, becoming a Southern Democrat and defender of states' rights. He shot and killed a black man he claimed was poisoning his adopted son and caused yet another scandal by marrying the young sister of a tenant farmer on his property. He was eighty-four, she thirteen or fourteen.

"Cassius said he fulfilled all his husbandly duties—a braggart to the end," Lashé said. The couple soon divorced, and Cassius spent his last years confined to a first-floor library, one leg resting on a gout stool. Even so, he fought off three men who broke into his home, shooting one and stabbing another.

At ninety-two, the "Lion of White Hall" died on the property where he'd been born, from what was termed "general exhaustion"—an apt if medically imprecise close to his long, turbulent life.

By the end of my tour, I didn't know what to make of this violent, mercurial man who hated slavery while enjoying the wealth it bestowed on his family and relishing the trappings of landed aristocracy. Lashé observed that he was also "a real chauvinist," once stating that women "make better bedfellows than voters." Such views, and his strained first marriage, helped inspire his daughters to become prominent suffragettes. "He was for the emancipation of slaves," Lashé said. "Women, not so much."

All of which left me wondering about her comments at the start of our tour, which suggested that she had a crush on this magnetic yet often monstrous figure.

"Call it a fascination with his jaw-dropping life," she replied. "He wasn't a saint, not even close. But all those contradictions he's struggling with, it's the human story, on a big scale and a big stage."

She then cited a letter Cassius wrote to an abolitionist minister in 1855. Clay emancipated his own slaves, but not those he felt legally unable to free, because his father had put them in trust for his grandchildren. He did, however, grant these slaves "privileges and wages" and guarded them from sale or separation.

"I do not set myself up as perfect; far from it," he wrote the minister. "A balance sheet of good against evil is all I aspire to."

CHAPTER 5

TO TENNESSEE AND BACK

A Thorough Aristocrat

O lmsted had embarked on his long journey to Texas aboard a train that chugged thirty or so miles per hour. The boat he boarded in Wheeling steamed at half that speed. Stagecoaches moved slower still, about seven miles per hour. By antebellum standards, Olmsted nonetheless did well, traveling from Baltimore to the Bluegrass without accident or frequent delays.

This luck ran out when he left Lexington, on a train that took five hours to crawl the ninety miles to Louisville. From there, he'd planned to catch another stagecoach, into Tennessee. But this overland route, in late November, required too much travel in the dark and cold, so he "very reluctantly" journeyed by boat instead, via a circuitous route along the Ohio and Cumberland Rivers.

"Were laid up *every* night by fogs and were aground two days, so were a week getting to Nashville," he wrote Charles Brace. "Very tedious & disappointing."

On the Cumberland, he shared a cramped vessel with twenty other passengers, the men "fraternizing loudly" over "their poker and brag," the women "sewing and rocking," while Olmsted "grimly applied" himself to a book of Spanish grammar in anticipation of reaching Mexico.

The fogbound scenery offered little relief, either. "For miles, almost for hours, there is not a break in the line of dripping branches," he wrote. "You turn again and again from listlessly gazing at the perspective of bushes, to the listless conversation of the passengers, and turn back again."

Finally reaching Nashville, Olmsted disembarked for only forty-eight hours before returning to the river, where he "sat five hours in that dismalest of all delays, the waiting to be off." Then he steamed back into Kentucky to catch yet another vessel, headed for New Orleans.

This extended confinement and monotony proved a boon to Olmsted's writing. An afflicted scribe, he complained of what he called "pen-sickness," telling a friend that composing a single page "entirely interrupts my digestion, sets my brain throbbing, my ears singing and half suffocates me—also my eyes twitch." These symptoms, akin to those he suffered as a student, vanished when he left off writing and went for a walk or ride.

There was no such escape on the river. "In a steamboat cabin—dark, shaking, and gamesters and others talking about the table," Olmsted wrote Brace. "I can't collect my ideas." But he did, penning an extraordinary letter that amounted to a manifesto for reforming "this great country & this cursedly little people."

The spur for Olmsted's cri de coeur was his revelatory contact with the Kentucky and Tennessee elite. A year earlier, he'd set off on his first Southern trip seeking "reliable understanding of the sentiments and hopes & fears of sensible planters & gentlemen." In his first piece, he told *Times* readers he would approach the subject of slavery with fair-minded candor.

"I trust in so doing I may be able to encourage the conviction that it is only in the justice, good sense, and Christian sentiment of the people of the South, that the evils of Slavery will find their end." Later, he reminded Northern readers that "the condition of *some* of our laborers" was as bad as those endured by slaves. "There is wrong in both systems."

This studied neutrality showed signs of ebbing soon after his return from his first Southern trip, in 1853. Before embarking on his second journey, he spent seven months in New York, reading and writing about the South as tension over slavery mounted. The new president, Franklin Pierce, was a Northern "doughface," easily plied by Southern interests, as conflict loomed over slavery's status in the Kansas and Nebraska Territories.

A hardening of Olmsted's tone became evident in his writing about Kentucky. He acknowledged that cultured Lexington had fewer of the faults "so offensive to a Northern man" than other Southern cities. But he skewered its white elite, and not only for shutting down speech about slavery.

"These fine fellows, these otherwise true gentlemen," he wrote, displayed "a devilish, undisguised, and recognised contempt for all humbler classes," a trait he found "very repugnant."

Olmsted's indignation curdled into a full-blown crisis of conscience when he landed in Tennessee. Nashville, like Lexington, was a locus of wealth and culture, and home to a man who offered Olmsted exceptional entrée and insight into the Southern gentry. Samuel Perkins Allison was a prominent lawyer and politician, belonged to one of Tennessee's largest slaveholding families, and had attended Yale at the same time as Olmsted's brother John.

"A good specimen of the first class gentleman of the South," Olmsted wrote to Brace. Allison was also much more frank with Northerners than others of his ilk. He had a personal library of six hundred volumes and confided that he was "reading secretly" the works of abolitionist Theodore Parker and a heterodox German theologian. In short, he was exactly the sort of worldly, learned, and "sensible" Southerner that Olmsted had imagined engaging in reasoned discourse.

Allison hosted a dinner for the Olmsteds and was a lively raconteur, telling of his recent run for Congress against a "fighting man" who'd shot a foe in the street the year before. Allison carried two loaded pistols during the campaign, a raucous affair with large crowds "all excited and betting." He lost, as did his body servant, who had wagered his watch on the outcome.

Allison viewed these and other vices with bemused tolerance, Olmsted wrote, believing there was a "happy gentlemanly medium" between religious adherence and "sensual and social pleasures." The Tennessean summed up his personal creed with a wry motto: "Spree moderately."

But this genial equanimity did not extend to Allison's views on slavery. He and his circle saw William Seward, the most prominent critic of slavery in Congress, as "a devil incarnate" who should "be hung as a traitor" for declaring that slavery was subject to a "higher law than the Constitution." The Tennessean also disparaged Northern censure of the South as Yankee cant, devoid of genuine moral outrage.

"Allison & his friends evidently had no power of comprehending a hatred of Slavery in itself," Olmsted told Brace, and "couldn't imagine that the North would be governed by any purpose beyond a regard for self interest."

Also alarming was the Tennesseans' militancy regarding the most volatile issue of the day—whether or not slavery would expand beyond the states where it already existed. "Allison said they *must* have more slave territory," Olmsted wrote. "He thought California would be a Slave State" and coveted Cuba and Mexico, too, if the US could find "some honorable excuse" to "get possession."

This wasn't idle fancy; throughout the 1850s, proslavery adventurers, known as "filibusters," mounted military expeditions to seize land and topple governments in Latin America.

"Allison and other gentlemen I have seen in Nashville & Kentucky have changed the views I had," Olmsted concluded. Not only were these leading men intransigent regarding expansion; "they could not see how the North could be so *foolish* as to determinedly prevent the extension of Slavery." Doing so would harm industry and commerce—which was all they thought truly mattered in the North. "This was the end of their track."

In a sense, writing by candlelight on the Cumberland, Olmsted encapsulated the impasse that would lead to secession and civil war. He realized that he'd underestimated the extremist resolve of the South's leading men, and that they in turn misjudged the motives and determination of Northerners like himself.

Nashville effectively extinguished Olmsted's faith that middle ground could be found, or that Southerners had the "justice" and "good sense" to recognize the evils of slavery and gradually work toward ending them. "They do not seem to have a fundamental sense of right," he wrote.

Nashville also forced Olmsted to reconsider his own beliefs and how best to act on them. What he found most confronting in Nashville wasn't the views he heard about slavery, per se. It was Allison's frank disregard for the common man and his unshakable belief that the South's stratified society was superior to the North's.

"He is, in fact, a thorough Aristocrat," Olmsted wrote Brace, believing "in two distinct and widely separated classes." Allison subscribed to what became known as the South's "mud-sill" theory, which posited that humans were meant to occupy different stations, worker bees at the bottom (or mudsill) supporting a few at the top who advanced civilization and held all the wealth, "wisdom & power," Olmsted wrote.

The flip side of this hierarchical worldview was Allison's disdain for the more democratic and egalitarian North, which he saw as disordered and vulgar. He told his visitors there were virtually "no gentlemen at the North," even among those he'd known at Yale. The only praise he could muster was for "the old Dutch aristocracy" in New York, whom he found "thoroughly well bred."

Olmsted took strong exception, vigorously debating as he'd so often done during his extended bull sessions with Brace. "I tried to show him that there were compensations in the *general* elevation of all classes at the North." But Allison dismissed this, and more painfully still, Olmsted felt there was "a great deal of truth" in the Southerner's critique.

"He silenced us and showed us that our own position was by no means consistent and satisfactory," Olmsted confessed. "Altogether, the conversation [made] me acknowledge the rowdyism, ruffianism, want of high honorable sentiment & chivalry of the common farming & laboring people of the North."

This recognition made Olmsted "very melancholy," exposing not only the flaws of his society but also the deep contradictions in his own character. He often professed a hatred of aristocracy, and had been gratified while touring Britain to find that his family's grand-sounding ancestral home, Olmsted Hall, was a modest farmhouse rather than the manor of "a big murdering Baron." In writing about the Southern gentry, he also expressed his "general loathing of humbugging dignity" and blue-blooded "deference to time honored rules and conventionalisms."

At the same time, Olmsted's own aesthetics and standards were decidedly genteel. Like many of his reform-minded class, he valued cultural refinement, learned discourse, and well-bred speech and behavior, viewing these and other traits as essential marks of a civilized society. He wasn't a Victorian prude or preachy moralist, but he disliked the coarse and tasteless, in society as in corn bread.

So it stung him deeply to hear—and find truth in—the opinion of "a first class gentleman of the South" that Northern society was lowbrow, loutish, and philistine. "What does the success of our Democratic nationality amount to—and what is to become of us?" he despaired in his letter to Brace.

More to the point, what was to become of *him*—at thirty-one, still a muddle of beliefs and enthusiasms: lapsed farmer, writer with pen-sickness, self-styled yeoman and democrat with an effete sensibility. Adrift on the Cumberland, he was "blundering" toward an answer.

"I must be either an Aristocrat or more of a Democrat than I have been—a Socialist Democrat," he told Brace. By this, he meant "a Democrat of the European School," advocating for broad, state-supported uplift of the masses, rather than the laissez-faire individualism of Democrats in the US. "We need institutions that shall more directly *assist* the poor and degraded to elevate themselves."

But Olmsted wasn't the sort to minister directly to the Northern underclass, as Brace had begun doing with his Children's Aid Society in New York. Nor was Fred's principal concern the material well-being of the masses.

"The poor need an education to refinement and taste and the mental & moral capital of gentlemen," he wrote. And it was imperative that he, Brace, and "all our earnest fellows" take the lead, as social engineers, designing institutions and public venues that would draw together and improve Americans.

"Well, the moral of this damnedly drawn out letter is, I believe, go ahead with the Children's Aid," he wrote, "and get up parks, gardens, music, dancing schools, reunions which will be so attractive as to force into contact the good & bad, the gentlemanly and the rowdy."

DURING HIS TWO DAYS IN NASHVILLE, OLMSTED WAS SO IM-mersed in debate with Allison that he devoted little time or ink to the city itself. Arriving at the river wharf, he wrote, "The streets are, as usual, regular," the brick buildings "of a somber hue," and the overall aspect as "dull" and "uninviting" as other young centers of trade and commerce he'd visited. "It is our misfortune that the towns of the Republic are alike, or differ in scarcely anything else than in natural position or wealth."

In the 160 years since Olmsted's visit, Nashville had exploded, like

Lexington, from a compact antebellum town of eighteen thousand to a metropolitan area of well over a million. From the old river wharf, I walked up the main drag, Broadway, past saloons and breweries, cowboy and Opry-themed shops, and tourists drinking aboard bicycles built for many, called "pedal taverns." Guitarists busked on the sidewalk; Japanese teenagers posed for pictures next to a statue of Elvis.

Nashville's historic downtown wasn't "regular" or "dull" in the way Olmsted described. But for all the surface honky-tonk, Music City felt like a themed, blocks-long mall anchored by familiar brands: Hard Rock, Coyote Ugly, Margaritaville.

Fleeing this hubbub, I headed for what Olmsted called Nashville's "one rare national ornament," the Tennessee statehouse. Perched upon "a noble prominence," the capitol was built "of smooth-cut blue limestone, both within and without, and no stucco, sham paint, not even wood-work." He also praised the interior "columns of a very beautiful native porphyry, fine white grains in a chocolate ground."

Olmsted took keen interest in civic architecture, deeming it a gauge of progress and governance. He'd been unimpressed by other Southern capitols but wrote of Nashville's, "Better laws must surely come from so firm and fit a senate house."

These views sound quaint today, when few citizens take notice of government buildings, except to complain of the perfidy of those who labor in them. But I decided to follow Olmsted's example and approach Tennessee's capitol as I might a foreign parliament house, to see what it indicated about the character of the place in which I'd just arrived.

The building's architect, William Strickland, was a leading apostle of Greek Revival who modeled the statehouse on a temple atop the Acropolis. It was Ionic columned, on very high ground, the interior likewise august, with richly marbled columns and ceiling frescoes of "Justice" and "Liberty." In all, a design that projected neoclassical grandeur and loft, suiting Nashville's nineteenth-century image as "the Athens of the South."

The statehouse grounds were another matter: an open-air shrine to bloody defiance. Towering above the main approach to the capitol was a ten-foot-tall statue of a mustachioed man in a frock coat. On the granite pedestal appeared his name and "Carmack's Pledge," a Gothic vow to devote "every drop of my blood" to a Southland "billowed with the graves of her dead."

Edward Carmack was a turn-of-the-century legislator and editor renowned for his violent pen. He crusaded against "demon rum," called for reprisal against "the black wench" Ida Wells for her anti-lynching campaign (inciting the destruction of her newspaper office), and feuded with a rival who shot the cantankerous editor dead in a street duel two blocks from the capitol.

Near the bronze of this dubious idol stood a statue of another martyr-hero little known outside Tennessee: Sam Davis, a Confederate scout captured while carrying plans of "federal fortifications and forces." He refused to disclose their origin—"I would die a thousand deaths before I would betray a friend"—and was hanged as a spy.

The next corner of the capitol grounds was guarded by a helmeted doughboy aiming his rifle: Alvin York, who in World War I single-handedly "silenced a German Battalion of 35 machine guns killing 25 enemy soldiers," the inscription noted.

Then I came to an equestrian statue of Andrew Jackson—in military uniform, victoriously waving his plumed hat—and the tomb of his hawkish political acolyte, President James Polk, who waged war against Mexico.

Tennessee's martial pride spilled across the street, to a plaza studded with more monuments to warriors and an immense, Doric-columned structure with a statue of "Youth," holding a sword, honoring Tennesseans who died in World War I.

Not every monument struck so warlike a chord. One depicted President Andrew Johnson, famed mainly for having been impeached. But the overall message was decidedly bellicose. For all the architectural echoes of Athens, the capitol's surrounds bespoke a different city-state: Sparta. Aliens landing here would conclude these earthlings were fearsome folk and climb right back in their spaceship.

As to whether so "firm and fit" a capitol promoted sound governance, as Olmsted supposed, I couldn't judge—except from bullet marks on the interior marble he so admired. These scars dated to 1866, when gunfire erupted during debate over the Fourteenth Amendment, granting citizenship rights to African Americans.

The legislature wasn't in session on the day I visited, so I continued my tour of Tennessee identity at the state museum adjoining the capitol. It, too, bristled with warriors from the Volunteer State—so-called because of the legions that stepped up to fight in the Mexican War.

But the most popular display related to personal combat: a re-creation, with life-sized cutouts, of one of the many duels fought by Andrew Jackson. I was drawn to the exhibit by its title, *Affairs of Honor*, a subject of keen interest to Olmsted.

Like many other Northern travelers, he was struck by the "intensity of personal pride" in the South and the willingness of a gentleman to violently defend it. "He never values life or aught else more than he does his honor."

This pridefulness, and the brandishing of weapons, was especially pronounced in the formerly frontier states of Tennessee and Kentucky. Riding a train from Lexington, Olmsted saw a pistol poking from a man's pocket and learned from fellow passengers that Kentuckians "very generally" went armed this way, also strapping bowie knives to their backs so they could draw over the shoulder at quick notice.

On reaching Louisville, he found the town abuzz over a recent killing. A school principal had whipped a student for eating chestnuts in class and lying about the infraction. The pupil's adult brother, enraged at this insult to his sibling's honesty, went to the school the next day and shot the principal in front of his students.

The killer came from one of the state's wealthiest slaveholding families, a class renowned for its prickly sense of honor and frequent duels. Refusing to provide "satisfaction" on the dueling ground brought the ultimate disgrace. Your challenger could "post" you as a "poltroon," or coward, in public notices.

Olmsted found the ethos among Tennessee's gentry similar to Kentucky's. The "chivalric" Samuel Allison "believes in pistols and bowie knives," he wrote, and an aristocratic "hodge podge of honor & morality."

The Yankee in Olmsted disapproved of this fixation on self-esteem, inherited status, and hoary codes of conduct. "What a man shows that he thinks of himself is certainly of considerable consequence in estimating his value to others," he wrote. "But it is not everything, or most essential. What he wishes to be, labors to be, is, perhaps, of more consequence."

Olmsted also sensed a dangerous insecurity underlying the South's violent code of honor. Slavery accustomed whites to deference, "uncontrolled authority," and vigilance against any hint of insubordination. They were "always in readiness to chastise, to strike down, to slay, upon what they shall individually judge to be sufficient provocation."

This cavalier wrath, aimed at slaves and each other, menaced the nation, too. In politics, as in personal affairs, slaveholders lashed out at *any* challenge to their power and property. The South's truculent ruling class also relished displays of martial spirit and prowess. "They are brave, in the sense that they are reckless of life," Olmsted wrote in the *Times*, after leaving Nashville, and so "ambitious of military renown" that they "would keep the country constantly at war" if not for fear of hurting cotton prices.

Within a few years, this "dangerous class," as Olmsted called it, would bring on the Civil War and be largely destroyed by it. But defeat didn't extinguish Tennesseans' attachment to "affairs of honor," at least judging from the rapt crowd around the exhibit on Jackson and dueling at the state museum.

While eavesdropping on the chatter, I noticed one man narrating Jackson's duel with Charles Dickinson with particular relish and expertise. He explained that the men took just twelve paces before turning to face each other with .70-caliber flintlock pistols. Dickinson fired first, hitting his foe in the chest; Jackson coolly replied with a fatal shot to the abdomen. "Dickinson almost killed him," the man told his children, "but Jackson was tough and had a lot of guts."

The speaker, David Lewis, was a former museum guide, a history teacher at a local college, and had written his master's thesis on dueling. When I told him I was struck by all the violence enshrined at the state capitol and museum, he laughed and said, "Well, Obama was right—we *do* cling to our guns and our religion."

He walked me over to a reconstructed log cabin. "The first settlers here had to carve a life out of the wilderness. They had to fight, and we're still prepared to." Lewis then mentioned an acquaintance, new to Nashville, who was surprised he didn't need to register his guns. "I told him there's no need for that in Tennessee; we're free men still. It's part of our culture."

Returning to the display on Jackson's duel with Dickinson, he said accounts of their feud differed. But it's known they fell out over a horseracing bet and exchanged the customary flowery insults: "base poltroon," "worthless scoundrel," "cowardly tale-bearer." Dickinson may also have impugned Jackson's wife.

"Right or wrong, you've got to respect what Jackson did," Lewis said. "Defending his honor, his family." This ethos had been diluted by the many newcomers to Tennessee, he added, "but there's still that pride and that belief in defending your clan and your country, right or wrong."

When I asked him to name a modern exemplar of this code, he thought for a moment before citing an unlikely figure: G. Gordon Liddy, who refused to testify against Nixon and went to prison for his role in the Watergate break-in.

"He took his punishment and kept his mouth shut to protect the president," Lewis said. "That's a true act of honor. Liddy's from up north but to me he's an honorary Tennessean."

LIKE THE OLMSTEDS, I HAD AN OLD-SCHOOL TIE IN NASHVILLE to a "first class gentleman of the South." Or so Bruce Dobie had seemed to me when I met him in the 1980s at journalism school in New York. Tall, courtly, and head-turningly handsome, Bruce quoted Faulkner and the Fugitive poets while grilling ribs with red beans and rice—an exotic presence in the squalid student digs we shared on 121st Street.

Bruce went on to work at a newspaper in Nashville, where he had since become a media entrepreneur. We'd stayed good friends, often bantering from afar about the differences between the North and South. But I'd never thought to ask his views on honor until stopping at his Nashville office after my visit to the state museum.

I half expected Bruce to laugh off the subject as Yankee stereotype or Old South balderdash. Instead, he took the question very seriously, both as a personal matter and as a distinguishing feature of the world he inhabited in Tennessee.

"It's not called honor anymore; it's integrity," he said. "Much more than in most places, you don't want to be thought ill of here. If you are, you're on the outs."

Bruce had been introduced to this ethos when he left his native Louisiana for college at Sewanee, in the Tennessee hills. Originally known as the University of the South, Sewanee was founded in the 1850s by clergymen who sought to "resist and repel" Northern influence. The school had evolved a great deal since, but clung to its very traditional code of honor.

"Day one at Sewanee you sign your name in a book, stating that you won't lie, cheat, or steal," Bruce said. "You sign again, at the end of every paper and exam, pledging your honor, and if you break that code you're thrown out." Doors were unlocked, probity esteemed—a contrast to his native south Louisiana, which took rakish pride in its dissolute and crooked reputation.

"When you exit the planet it's ashes to ashes," Bruce said. "You can't take anything with you. What matters is, will people say you were a person of integrity?"

This creed strongly influenced Nashville's business community. Most deals were based on trust and handshakes, he said, and a person's word was presumed to be their bond. "You don't need a lawyer for everything." He had to adjust his expectations on business trips. "I went to raise money in New York and bankers kept telling me, 'Be careful, don't trust anyone, the water here is filled with sharks.'"

In Nashville, he added, the pool was much smaller, and people knew one another and shunned those deemed untrustworthy. "On boards, or at the country club, you're not getting in unless you're good," he said. "It's not the number of zeroes you have, it's the measure of your character."

An insular, old-boy network sustained this system, too. There was no longer a landed gentry of the sort Olmsted encountered, and the music scene had created a cosmopolitan new locus of wealth and status. But a certain pedigree persisted among affluent white natives.

As Bruce explained it, "you grow up in Belle Meade," a wealthy westside neighborhood, "go to Montgomery Bell Academy, then Vanderbilt, then work in law or business and join the Belle Meade Country Club. Your whole life is inside a bubble along West End Avenue."

Bruce had a friend who ticked all these boxes "and then some," including descent from a founding family of Tennessee. If I wanted to talk honor with an old-school Nashville gentleman, this was someone I had to meet.

"Man's been dueling his whole life," Bruce said, reaching for the phone. "He's eighty-four and dying, but that's just an excuse for another fight."

———

JOHN JAY HOOKER MET US THE NEXT MORNING AT A RESTAURANT on West End Avenue. I'd expected to meet a frail octogenarian and instead had my hand crushed by a hearty figure who stood six feet four inches with a full head of silver hair, penetrating blue eyes, and a stentorian voice.

We'd no sooner settled in a booth than he began chatting up our waitress. "You're such a fine-lookin' young lady," he said, which wasn't strictly true but made her smile and blush. "Would you be so kind as to bring us some coffee?"

Courtesy toward the help came with the territory in Hooker's family. His father had been a prominent lawyer, his mother active in charity, both of them often absent. "Black servants raised me," he said. "Mammy, cook, maid, chauffeur, yard man—you never sassed them. Part of being a gentleman was being civil." Affecting a patrician drawl, he quoted a favorite line of his father's: "I respect those most who do what I want to do least."

His mother imbued him with another gentlemanly requisite: pride in one's lineage. She descended from William Blount, whose powder-wigged portrait I'd seen at the state museum. He was a signer of the US Constitution, helped create the state of Tennessee, and served as one of its first senators. "Also a speculator and scoundrel, though that was never spoken of," Hooker said.

His paternal great-grandfather, who lost an arm at Gettysburg, became a respected judge and helped draft Tennessee's post–Civil War constitution. "I grew up feeling I'd been to the manor born," Hooker said, "and had a duty to live up to my ancestors by doing something important."

He dutifully attended the right schools—"it was all 'yes suh, no suh'"— married a Nashville belle, joined his father's law firm, and became an aide to then–attorney general Robert Kennedy. Well connected and oratorically gifted, Hooker entered politics in the 1960s as an integrationist Democrat and critic of the Vietnam War. "Hubris of youth," he said, "I thought I'd become governor and then president. Most people don't have the guts to run, so the field is only so big."

Hooker's liberalism didn't play well in rural Tennessee, where he was branded a "nigger lover" and unpatriotic war hater. Some voters spat at him rather than shake his hand. In the gubernatorial primary, he got 96 percent of the black vote and lost to a segregationist. "I had rather stood up against the war, and for civil rights, than not talked about them and won," he said.

Pausing to hoe into his biscuits and bacon, Hooker told of his subsequent runs for office and repeated defeats as the state's electorate turned increasingly Republican. "I became the biggest loser in Tennessee politics, but I was always more concerned about losing my honor."

This preoccupation had arisen again when he went into business and founded a restaurant chain, Minnie Pearl's, which he freely acknowledged was "a copycat of Kentucky Fried Chicken." The business prospered and was soon worth $250 million, but then the SEC opened an investigation "claiming we'd jiggered the books."

He denied this, and the SEC dropped the case, but in the interim the company's stock price sank from forty dollars to fifty cents. "To save my business and my honor," Hooker said, he put every penny he had into shoring up Minnie Pearl and clearing his name.

"Losing all those political races was painful, but losing my reputation for being honest was far worse," he said. "There are people to this day who think I cheated."

Hooker had gone on to become a political gadfly, filing frequent lawsuits aimed at what he saw as corrupt campaign finance practices and other trespasses of state law. He took to wearing a Lincoln-like stovepipe hat and carrying a copy of the state constitution his great-grandfather had helped draft. "Lost causes, every one," he said, "but I'm not done."

Hooker had recently been diagnosed with metastatic melanoma and told he had less than a year to live. So he'd taken up a final battle, for "the right to die with dignity and honor." His touchstone, again, was the state constitution, which stated, "No human authority may control or interfere with the rights of conscience." He'd brought suit to enforce this language and succeeded in having a bill introduced for debate in the legislature.

"We all have something to live for; it's special to have something to die for," he said. "The right to come, the right to go, that's very fundamental. The government shouldn't make you a prisoner in your own bed, in terrible pain."

He also felt the state forced him and others to consider undignified measures. Hooker owned a gun and thought of "exercising that liberty at the end." But he didn't want to "irritate the man upstairs, eternity is a long time," and he feared the impact on his grandchildren. "I was raised to regard suicide as self-murder, an act of cowardice, embarrassing to one's kin. I don't want to stigmatize my family."

Time was running out, and the odds, as usual, were stacked against Hooker. Medically assisted suicide was legal in only three states, and Tennessee appeared unlikely to become the fourth. But he was determined to "go down swinging."

Wincing in pain as he eased out of the booth, Hooker crushed my hand again and quoted Atticus Finch in *To Kill a Mockingbird*. "Real courage," he said, isn't a man with a gun in his hand. "It's when you know you're licked before you begin and you see it through no matter what."

BEFORE LEAVING TOWN, I HEARD A DIFFERENT PERSPECTIVE ON dignity from the other end of Nashville's social and economic spectrum. Bruce belonged to a church that welcomed the homeless, giving them counsel and food. Bruce had taken this work further, finding jobs and housing for several men and visiting them each week.

"I can't really explain why, but I feel closer to these guys than I do to a lot of my peers," Bruce said as we drove to a homeless shelter south of downtown. "No money, no success, but their attitude is, 'I'm just thanking God for this day and what I have.'"

We stopped to pick up Leon Nickson, a middle-aged black man on a short break from his janitorial job. Nickson had grown up in the Mississippi cotton fields, where his mother died at twenty from sunstroke. He drifted around the country doing odd jobs, and eventually landed in a tent city under a river bridge in Nashville.

"See that second pylon with all the graffiti?" he said as we drove past the site. "That was my spot. Not too bad, except for the rats."

He'd go to the homeless shelter to bathe and get meals but only when he had to. "Metal detectors, pat downs, tickets for the shower, they're always ordering you around," he said. "There's no dignity in that."

With Bruce's help, he'd started work and moved into subsidized housing. "I'm grateful for the second chance," he told Bruce, before returning to work. "Now I got to do some things myself."

In the parking lot of the shelter we then met Robert Wade, a lean black man who'd also come up hard, in "an old shack" in Georgia without indoor plumbing. As an adult he'd worked as a dishwasher and custodian but "drank too much Budweiser, like my dad," he said.

Wade got sober and met a woman who decided they should start fresh by riding the bus to Nashville, where she had family. "That didn't go so well," he said. "When we got here, she left me for her husband."

Broke, knowing no one, he turned up at Bruce's church. He now had occasional work, mostly cleaning and stocking shelves at a Walmart for $7.25 an hour. After bus fare and lunch, that didn't leave him much. He stayed most nights at the shelter, on a chair or the floor if the beds were full. "Guys are coughing and jabbering all night; I have to close myself off or I get depressed."

Wade was fifty-six, the same age as Bruce and me. When he wasn't working, he walked in the park or went to the library. "Been thinking a lot, about my mistakes and the time left to me on this earth," he said.

"Amen to that, brother," Bruce said. "What is it you want from this life?"

Wade's wish list was modest. A good enough paycheck to live on his own. A quiet place. A couch and television. "I'd like to be my own man, independent," he said. "That's what it's all about."

DIGNITY, PURPOSE, AND THE DIVIDE BETWEEN RICH AND POOR were themes Olmsted probed in depth as he wrote aboard riverboats after visiting Nashville. In addition to his long letter to Charles Brace, he penned three summary dispatches for the *Times* that revealed just how much his thinking had evolved.

Gone was the dispassionate observer of a year earlier, seeking "matter of fact matter" about the South. He now branded slavery "shamefully cruel, selfish and wicked," and an institution that "manacles" not only slaves but also "the noble form" of democracy. "It is our duty, as it is every man's in the world, to oppose Slavery, to weaken it, to destroy it."

The question then became: "by what means can we rightly do this." Southern states had a "clear constitutional right to continue their peculiar institution of Slavery, as it is, and where it is." But a sharp line should be drawn and defended against attempts to expand slavery's boundaries or otherwise bolster the institution.

Olmsted, once again, was voicing "pretty fairly the average sentiment of good thinking men on our side," as he'd put it on the eve of his first trip. His riverboat pieces ran in early 1854, as debate raged over the Kansas-Nebraska Act, which opened the door to slavery beyond the boundaries set in the Missouri Compromise.

This galvanized anti-slavery Northerners and led many toward a more confrontational stance against the institution's spread. Should federal power "again be perverted" to "prolong and invigorate" slavery, Olmsted wrote, the nation must stand ready for "combat in aid of Liberty."

Olmsted then returned to the debate he'd had with the Nashville aristocrat Samuel Perkins Allison, and with himself. Beyond vigilance, what "active duty" could Northerners perform against slavery?

He found the answer in the maxim that had moved him when he'd first read Thomas Carlyle's work a decade before. "It is *the duty which lies nearest to us*," Olmsted told readers. The North must reform its own ways, to show the vigor of democratic society and tear down the "theoretic legs upon which Slavery stands."

Foremost among these tenets was "the supposed inherent inability of the negro to take care of himself." Dependent, and innately suited to servitude, white Southerners claimed, Africans were "plainly better off in Slavery" than living in "the miserable freedom" of the North, where whites "neglect them, and cast them out."

Olmsted noted the "cant" in this benign view of slavery, "but the rebuke to us is appropriate and most deserved." Blacks in the North were often "excluded from public conveyances" and subject to "Black-laws" like those in Indiana, which barred them from entering the state, voting, or holding public office.

"The North must demolish these strictures," Olmsted wrote, and let "the negro have a fair chance to prove his own case, to prove himself a man, entitled to the inalienable rights of a man."

More broadly, the North must challenge slaveholders' conviction "that there is something in manual labor, in itself, demoralizing and enervating to the mind," rendering the masses incapable of "reflection" or self-governance.

Southerners buttressed this argument by holding up the North as a nega-tive example, pointing "with animation" at every example of "crime and suf-fering" or restiveness "among the laboring class of people."

To Olmsted, this was a dangerous attempt to undermine democracy and justify the rule of an aristocratic few at a moment when monarchs in Europe were putting out the flames of republicanism. For the American experiment to survive and thrive, there must be "places and times," he wrote, "that the rich and the poor, the cultivated and *well bred*, and the sturdy and self-made people shall be attracted together and encouraged to assimilate."

Such venues would "exert an elevating influence upon all the people," and demonstrate to "enemies of Democracy" the potential for mass uplift and the virtue of seeking "the highest good, of the whole community."

Olmsted apologized to readers that he was "writing in a steamboat, fast aground," and unable to consult library volumes or other "authorities." But in distilling his observations on the South, and what it revealed of the North, he'd begun to articulate a national mission and his own life's work.

Olmsted's catalog in the *Times* of "elevating" venues included "public parks and gardens." Designing these democratic spaces would also draw together the disparate strands of Olmsted's character.

He could be a reformer *and* an aesthete, democratic socialist and civi-lizer, a leveler of "mental & moral capital." Make everyone a gentleman.

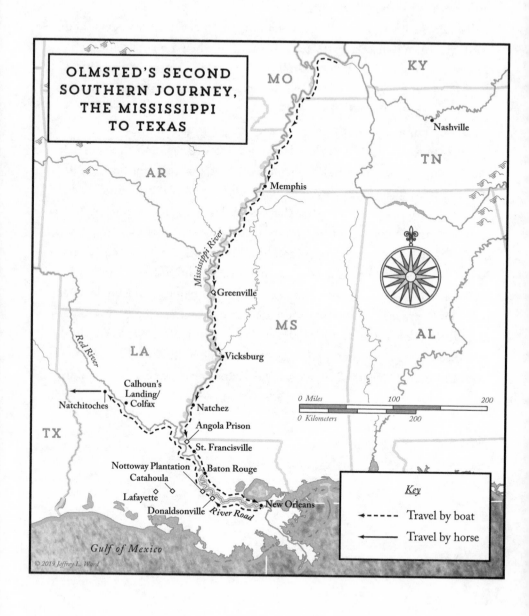

OLMSTED'S SECOND SOUTHERN JOURNEY, THE MISSISSIPPI TO TEXAS

MO

KY

Nashville

AR

TN

Memphis

Mississippi River

Greenville

MS

AL

Vicksburg

Red River

LA

Calhoun's Landing/ Colfax

Natchitoches

Natchez

Angola Prison

St. Francisville

TX

Nottoway Plantation Baton Rouge
Catahoula
Lafayette
Donaldsonville River Road New Orleans

Gulf of Mexico

© 2019 Jeffrey L. Ward

0 Miles 100 200
0 Kilometers 200

Key

- - - - ◄ Travel by boat

◄——— Travel by horse

CHAPTER 6

MISSISSIPPI RIVER

Steamboat Blues

The Olmsteds' slow river trip to Nashville and back concluded on a fortuitous note. As they disembarked at a wharf in Kentucky, "a first-class New Orleans steamer" appeared around a bend and "with hardly a moment's delay we were installed in one of her capacious state-rooms."

For the next six days, they steamed downriver aboard the *Sultana*, "an immense vessel" with "an interminably long saloon," excellent service, and fine cuisine. At no other point in his Southern wanders would Olmsted travel in such style and comfort.

Fortune shone on me, too. There was no need to hitch a ride on a coal barge to retrace Olmsted's river trip to New Orleans. Instead, I could book passage on the *American Queen*, a replica of the palatial steamboats that plied the Mississippi in the 1800s. All I had to do was choose from the offerings in a fat brochure, mostly voyages with pop themes: "Elvis," "Bourbon," "Big Band Swing."

I found a better facsimile of Olmsted's trip in "Southern Memories Last Forever." The write-up touted a journey through "the romance of the antebellum South," including "fertile cotton fields, vast sugar plantations and imposing pillared mansions." The trip to New Orleans lasted a week, as Olmsted's had, with stops along the way at several ports he visited.

And so, on a gray March afternoon, I climbed a gangway in Memphis to board the biggest and possibly the gaudiest steamboat ever built. The *American Queen* stretched more than four hundred feet in length, with a scarlet paddle wheel at the stern and red, white, and blue bunting draped over the balconies at the bow. Its six decks, adorned with gingerbread arches and other "steamboat Gothic" touches, rose like layers of a creamy wedding cake to the cupola-topped pilothouse, a cute little candle at the summit. Even the smokestacks were decoratively filigreed, spraying open like a blossoming flower or the crown of a chess queen.

Bow-tied waiters greeted us at the top of the gangway with platters of seared scallops as a band played Dixieland jazz. The woman just ahead of me turned and flashed a dazed smile. "Sure beats boarding an airplane," she said.

I beamed right back at her. In an era of gridlocked freeways, security frisks, and body-and-soul-crushing flights, it was easy to forget that transport could be a pleasure in itself, and a shared joy, rather than an endurance test and a Darwinian competition for space and other scarce resources.

Nor was anything so grubby as cash required on the *American Queen*. Our fare included board, and we'd been issued laminated IDs with bar codes that doubled as discreet charge cards for spa treatments and other extras aboard what felt like a waterborne resort hotel.

My second impression was of being aboard a floating hospice. I appeared to be the rare passenger not yet eligible for Medicare. Scooting around walkers and wheelchairs, I felt like a moped driver in stalled traffic. Reaching my cabin I met my next-door neighbor, a stripling of about sixty-five who was escorting a tour group from Arizona. "I better go check on the others," she said. "They won't be able to hear the announcements."

On the *Sultana*, Olmsted wrote that nightly poker games in the saloon "frequently broke up only at dawn of day" with loud disputes that kept other passengers awake. This wasn't a risk on the *American Queen*. Dinner seating commenced at 5:15 p.m., followed by a show in the Grand Saloon, which was a theater rather than a bar. The late-night entertainment, at the Night Owls Club, began at nine thirty.

I was the only night owl to appear. By 10:00 p.m. I'd retired to my cabin, a cozy chamber with busy floral wallpaper and carpet, a heavily upholstered chair, and a painting of a sleigh crossing the snow in Maine. Only a faint vibration reminded me that I was berthed on a riverboat rather than at a Victorian bed-and-breakfast.

This was disconcerting, until I recalled my last river trip, pushing coal on the Ohio. If tracking Olmsted now demanded six nights of somnolent comfort on the water, I could handle that. As he wrote of his "long sleeps" and cosseted torpor aboard the *Sultana*: "The monotony is of a kind you are not sorry to experience once in a lifetime."

By day, I also had a more salubrious lookout than the "pooper" I'd perched on in the pilothouse of the Ohio towboat. On the *American Queen*, the best spot to view the river was a well-appointed Chart Room at the bow that featured an antique wooden pilot's wheel, river charts spread on the table, and walls lined with nautical books and Mark Twain quotes from *Life on the Mississippi*.

Best of all, the Chart Room was overseen by the boat's "Riverlorian," a fount of colorful fact and fable about steamboat travel. "Most of what I know is true, and the rest ought'a be," Jerry Hay said.

Case in point: his etymology of "highfalutin." According to some linguistic sleuths, this term for ostentatious display derived from the high fluting of nineteenth-century steamboat stacks, perched atop vessels beside the most luxurious quarters.

Hay had grown up on the Wabash River and worked on many craft, including tows. Unlike the Ohio, the lower Mississippi was undammed, its depth and other conditions in constant flux. "Pushing barges here is like steering a thousand-foot-long wheelbarrow through a muddy ditch," he said.

The Mississippi was also so serpentine that at points in our journey downriver, we'd actually be steaming north. Stranger still, frequent changes in the river's course had created oxbows and cutoffs that left ports high and dry, and even rearranged the shapes of states. Pointing to starboard and what should be the Arkansas shore, Hay said, "That's actually a chunk of Mississippi, stuck on the west bank since the river channel shifted in 1935."

Otherwise, the panorama seemed little changed since Olmsted described his view from the deck of the *Sultana*. "Before and behind are eight or ten miles of seething turbid water; on each side is half a mile of the same, bounded by a sand or mud bank, overhung by the forest."

The Riverlorian said we'd encounter much more traffic down the

Mississippi. "So this is a good chance to kick back and enjoy some quiet river time," he said. I took his advice, settling into a rocking chair on the deck and contentedly watching the wooded shore roll by.

Olmsted, as usual, cast a more discerning eye on the landscape and took pleasure in deflating "spoony" travelogues about the majesty of the Mississippi. "Nothing can be less striking than the river scenery after the first great impression of solemn magnitude is dulled," he wrote. "The eye finds nowhere any salience."

He also punctured the river's reputation as a throbbing artery of commerce. "Human life along the Mississippi is indescribably insignificant," he observed, calling the river valley "a great wilderness of unexplored fertility, into which a few men have crept like ants into a pantry. We give it a vast importance in our thoughts, but it is an entirely prospective one."

At the time he traveled, Memphis and a few other ports were the only stops of even modest size along the 1,200 miles of river between St. Louis and New Orleans. Most settlements consisted of a handful of crude buildings and a woodyard to supply passing vessels.

"Compared with such a *town*," Olmsted wrote of one outpost, "our craft, with its vast population and regal splendor, should rank a great metropolis." Amusingly, he added, these makeshift hamlets announced themselves with large signs facing the river bearing grandiose names like Oratorio Landing.

The *American Queen*'s first stop, in northern Mississippi, bore a similarly inflated sign, at least in size. "Welcome to Greenville," read the immense painted letters by the dock. "Heart and Soul of the Delta."

Greenville represented a new and rather anomalous addition to the steamboat's "romance of the antebellum era" itinerary. The original, tiny settlement of Greenville had been destroyed during the Civil War and rebuilt afterward at its current location. The famed cotton culture of the Mississippi Delta had also bloomed postbellum, in an unromantic era of yellow fever, black peonage, and white supremacy.

American Queen buses, gaily painted like our steamboat, waited at the end of the gangway to take passengers on a short tour. Opting to explore on foot instead, I walked past a pawnshop and entered the old commercial downtown. At 11:30 a.m. on a Sunday, there was little sign of life, apart from the blossoming pear trees. The sidewalk was littered with bricks that had fallen from decaying storefronts.

A few blocks on, I met my first local, Benjy Nelken, who was opening a small museum of local history ahead of the tour buses' arrival. In his late sixties, with a salt-and-pepper beard and swept-back silver hair, Nelken looked and talked like Shelby Foote, the Civil War writer and folksy raconteur. When I mentioned this to Nelken, he laughed and said, "Well, Shelby and I are almost kin."

Foote had been born and raised in Greenville, and his mother was Jewish. So was Nelken and, at one time, a large part of the community.

"This wasn't your typical Mississippi town," he said, leading me to a display on Greenville's Jewish history. In the nineteenth century, immigrant peddlers worked their way up the Mississippi and settled as merchants in the Delta. Greenville's first elected mayor was Leopold Wilczinski, and by the early twentieth century a third of the downtown businesses were Jewish owned. The Jewish community, about seven hundred at its peak, built a grand synagogue on Main Street, the largest such congregation in the state.

"We even had a Jewish president of the local country club in the 1940s, when Jews weren't allowed into clubs elsewhere in the Delta," Nelken said.

This "oasis of tolerance," as he called it, was tested in the 1960s, when civil rights workers from the North, many of them Jewish, descended on Mississippi. Elsewhere in the state, the Klan bombed synagogues, and in Greenville a candidate for town council circulated an anti-Semitic flyer, now on display at the museum.

"Be American and Vote American," it read, noting that the other candidate—Nelken's uncle—was Russian born. "Nationality: A Jew (Does Not Believe in Christ)."

Nelken smiled. "My uncle won in a landslide."

In part, he attributed Greenville's tolerance to the respect for religion that prevailed across the South. "This is the Bible Belt; if you're Jewish and observant, Southerners respect that you adhere to a religious faith, even if it's not theirs."

Greenville also had a history of diversity apart from Jews. In its turn-of-the-century heyday, the town drew Lebanese, Syrians, Italians, and a large Chinese community. I was perusing the museum's display on this immigrant population when I met my second local, Raymond Wong, who helped out at the museum.

"Mississippi, born and bred," he drawled. "I know, not every day you meet an Asian guy with a good ol' boy accent."

His family's assimilation had been harder than that experienced by European Jews. Chinese arrived in the Delta as field laborers, in the late 1800s, and for decades occupied a racial twilight zone in the Jim Crow South. When a yellow fever epidemic hit Greenville, no one knew where to bury the Chinese dead. They ended up in the Jewish cemetery, since neither the black nor the white one seemed appropriate.

In the early twentieth century, when Chinese found a niche as grocery store owners, leaflets circulated in Greenville warning against the "yellow menace" and urging locals to buy "American." Mississippi courts later ruled that Chinese were "colored" and therefore excluded from white institutions.

Born at home in 1952, Wong was raised in the back of his parents' shop, in an otherwise all-black neighborhood. But in his childhood, white schools in the Delta began enrolling Chinese students, almost two decades before integration.

"In a weird way we were lucky," Wong said. "Blacks and whites didn't trust or mix with each other, but they viewed us as neutral. So we Chinese kids had friends from both races, at a time when others in the Delta couldn't."

But this uneasy acceptance had limits. Wong's family attended a white Baptist church but sat separately, and when they tried to build a home in a white part of town, he said, "neighbors started busting bottles at the property and making threats. We never moved there." Later, at Mississippi State, he befriended a fraternity president who urged him to join, but the other members repeatedly denied him entry.

Wong returned to Greenville, married a Chinese American woman from the Delta, ran a Chinese restaurant, and joined the Rotary Club. His three children experienced little prejudice; one married a white classmate.

"The separation these days is more economic than racial or ethnic," Wong said. "You've got black lawyers and doctors living in wealthy areas that used to be all white."

But in other ways, he and Nelken felt Greenville had failed to fulfill the promise of civil rights. In the 1960s, Greenville's newspaper editor and other prominent whites had stood out in Mississippi for their measured support of racial justice. The local police chief protected black protestors, and the town integrated without the tumult and violence that racked so much of the state.

"I thought of all places, we'd get it right and leave segregation behind," Nelken said. Instead, the changes wrought by legal integration had been quickly undercut, mainly by white flight and the opening of private schools dubbed "seg academies." Greenville's public schools were now 99 percent black, "and socially the races don't intermingle much, except in government and business," Nelken said.

A second museum he'd established nearby spoke to another painful chapter of Greenville history: the Great Flood of 1927, which submerged the Delta and displaced almost a million Mississippians. While whites in the Delta evacuated, blacks were confined to tent camps and forced at gunpoint to labor at rebuilding the river levees.

Sated on Greenville's doleful history, I was ambling back to the river wharf when I met my third local, a man with a graying Afro standing in a doorway on the otherwise deserted street. He nodded and said hey, and I said hey back.

This was one of the things I liked best about the South: the obligatory acknowledgment and greeting of others, which had the fringe benefit of making it easier for me to chat up strangers.

"You come off that steamboat?" he asked.

"How'd you guess?"

He smiled, casting his eye down the vacant street. "No other reason to be here."

This begged the question of why *he* was here. I'd find out shortly, but first we talked about the museums I'd visited and his own childhood in 1950s Greenville.

"I didn't know anything about the other side of town," he said. "I knew there were white people, but I didn't know any of them and hardly ever saw 'em."

"What about when you came here to downtown?"

"When I was a boy? Come here and do what—die?" He chuckled. "*Hell* no."

As he remembered it, his parents would simply appear from time to time with new shoes or other necessities. "Maybe they were protecting us, but all we knew as kids was that parents brought shit home, you put it on, no questions asked. That's just the way it was; didn't think nothing about it."

His father had been a minister, the family better off than most in the Delta. "If you lived out on a farm, you didn't have time to be a child, you went to work as soon as you could pick up a hoe and a sack." By adolescence, many of his peers were chopping cotton "sunup to sundown," for three dollars a day. Teenagers also peddled moonshine and did odd jobs at the Delta's many small bars and blues joints.

"First time I heard country and western music, I thought, 'Damn, that's nothing but the white man singing the blues.'" He mimicked a country twang, chanting, "'Someone done me wrong, I'm workin' hard, not making no money, my woman's gone.' Same shit I heard all around here growing up."

He'd left Greenville as a young man and returned in late middle age to find the color line strangely blurred. "I'm living in a neighborhood I wouldn't have had my ass in back in the 1950s, mostly older whites," he said. "They're fine; we wave, make nice, and that's it. We still don't know each other."

He blamed this social distance on himself as well as his neighbors. "There was no big trouble here during civil rights, but when things changed, people my age didn't. We were raised in different worlds. They're not going to invite me over and I don't invite them."

To this point, he'd been vague about his work history—"cars, car parts"—and when I asked what he did now, he nodded at the shop front behind him. It had a generic sign that gave little hint of what transpired inside.

"I book," he finally let on, as in sports bookie, and he agreed—so long as I didn't print his name—to show me his operation. He led me through a front room filled with merchandise that suggested a legal enterprise, and behind it we entered a small barroom with a few men watching college basketball on four TV screens.

"Heavy action on Kentucky," he said, checking the day's betting on a laptop and cell phone. "I'll have to lay some off; don't want too much riding on the one game."

I would have happily taken some of that action and settled on one of his couches to watch, but the *American Queen* was scheduled to depart in fifteen minutes. So before sprinting to the gangway, I asked a final question. Had his glum view of race relations changed at all with the election of Barack Obama?

He shut his laptop and pondered this a moment. "Back in the day, if you'd come in here and bet me there'd be a black president in my lifetime, I'd have given you a thousand-to-one odds," he said. "But I look at it like this. Moneywise, we're still at the bottom. Me, here in Greenville, I'm still on my side of the fence, white folk on the other. What's really changed?"

I RETURNED ABOARD THE *AMERICAN QUEEN* AS WAITRESSES CIR-culated with cocktails in the Mark Twain Gallery, a lounge with Oriental rugs and Tiffany table lamps. In the daintily decorated Ladies' Parlor, a bridge game was underway; in the Gentlemen's Card Room, men snoozed in richly upholstered chairs, with a boar's head, a stuffed bear, and a mounted fish looking on. A champagne reception was about to begin in the Grand Saloon, before waiters clapped cymbals to beckon us into the chandeliered dining room.

"A substantial as well as showy table," Olmsted wrote of dining aboard the *Sultana*, describing "trained and ready servants" and free-flowing wine, "a pleasant relic of French river dominion."

Much the same was true aboard the *American Queen*. The multicourse fare tended toward the filling and fussy: prime rib of beef, braised brisket, shrimp and avocado tower, rich desserts, and ample cabernets, all served by a small army of skilled and obliging waiters.

I was also fortunate in my seating assignment, sharing a table with a convivial group of Brits and Aussies for my six nights aboard. We had two spare seats and were joined one night by deserters from another table. Jamie and Doug were Californians who stood out from the dining-hall crowd, most of it conservatively clad in the "country club casual attire" recommended in the boat's literature.

Jamie, a dark-haired psychotherapist, had blue-painted toenails, rimless glasses, and big dangling earrings. Doug, a car dealer, sported a mustache and loud Hawaiian shirt. They'd originally been seated with octogenarians from the Midwest, one so stroke ridden he could barely speak.

"I listen for a living, but that was hard work," Jamie said. "We managed a little chat about golf and that was about it."

Doug shrugged. "They're going to die on someone else's watch, not ours."

He and Jamie were also avoiding the nightly entertainment at the Grand Saloon, having sampled a program billed as "a musical tour from New Orleans to Memphis." It featured jazz, gospel, and blues—all performed by white entertainers, as the white audience sang along and did the funky chicken. "It just felt weird and wrong," Jamie said.

After my talk about race with the bookie in Greenville, I'd taken an eyeball census of the *American Queen*'s 410 passengers. There were a number of Asian tourists but only four blacks, a family from Canada on board because one was a scholar who'd been invited to give a talk about escaped slaves. He told me it was strange to find his presentation touted in the boat's daily newssheet as a "fun and entertaining lecture about life in the Underground Railroad."

Almost all the boat's officers and senior staff were white as well, while the cleaners and kitchen crew were predominantly black. Apart from the captain and a few others, most of the 162 workers bunked in "the crew hole," a windowless deck in the hull, below the boat's waterline. "I knew we'd be visiting plantations," Jamie said, "but I didn't expect to be floating on one."

I had a chance to query crewmen about this when we docked the next night at Natchez. Employees couldn't drink on the boat but were allowed to do so in port, so long as they were sober in time for their next shift. Natchez offered the perfect opportunity for quick refreshment. We docked at a historic landing, Under-the-Hill, which had catered in the nineteenth century to boatsmen flush with cash after delivering their goods in New Orleans.

"Without a single exception the most licentious spot that I ever saw," one traveler wrote of the landing's saloons, brothels, and gambling dens. A river captain described "dreadful riots" during which "eyes are gouged out, noses and ears bitten and torn off."

Most of Under-the-Hill was gone, along with its rampant vice, but one old tavern remained, a simple brick building with dueling pistols over the bar. Soon after we docked at 11:00 p.m., crewmen flooded down the gangway, which ended almost at the door of the bar.

"It's just good to chill a bit and feel land," said a young black engineer who hadn't been off the boat in three weeks. "Need to free my mind from greasing this or checking that."

When I asked about the racial dynamic aboard, he said "the crew hole" was comfortably integrated, but he rarely saw black passengers. "We stop at a lot of plantations, hoopskirt stuff," he said. "They need to think outside the box and not just market to old white people."

At another table, I joined a young man and woman who had been serving my dinner table the past three nights. I knew them only as pleasant, smiling faces appearing with food and wine. But it turned out they knew quite a bit about me, and the others at my table. Over shots of Kahlúa, they offered observations about our appearance and conversation—nothing unkind, just intimate.

Matt, an openly gay Tennessean, suggested I do something about my chipped fingernails. Cassie, a blond Alabaman, commented on our dinner discussion about the boat feeling like a plantation.

"I'd describe it more as *Downton Abbey*, or *Upstairs Downstairs*," she said, "except that the service isn't downstairs. It's way down in the crew hole, underwater."

Matt agreed that the plantation analogy didn't fit, and most of the crew felt decently paid and treated. But he saw one parallel to the Old South. Like house slaves in the Big House, "We're mostly invisible to the people we're serving," he said, "while we see and hear everything they do."

EARLY THE NEXT DAY, I FOLLOWED A ROAD THAT WOUND STEEPLY uphill, from Under-the-Hill to On-the-Hill Natchez, two very different locales in antebellum times. While bedlam reigned down by the river, "Natchez proper," perched on the bluff above, was renowned as one of the wealthiest and most beautiful towns in the South.

Natchez's prime location—270 miles upriver from New Orleans, and at the terminus of the overland Natchez Trace—made it a major crossroads of the cotton and slave trades. The town also lay close to the richest plantation lands in the South, stretching along both sides of the Mississippi.

This made it an ideal second residence for planters who sought the comforts and culture of town life—and the chance to show off their extraordinary wealth. By the 1850s, Natchez was reputed to have more millionaires than any place in the nation, and it was certainly among the most ostentatious.

"I was amused to recognize specimens of the 'swell-head' fraternity," Olmsted wrote, using a term he'd heard elsewhere in Mississippi for Natchez's nouveau riche. Upon entering town, he passed a carriage carrying a "richly-belaced baby," a French nanny, and two well-dressed ladies sitting "marble-like." Their black coachman perched high up, "on the bed-like cushion of the box," the better to display his showy livery, including a topcoat and velvet cape.

Olmsted also observed white-gloved groomsmen and "a remarkable number of young men, extraordinarily dressed," twirling their walking sticks as they talked of horse racing, a favorite Natchez pastime. In the evening, he leaned against a lamppost for an hour, listening to the excellent violin and piano music being played by an Italian tutor at a home on the main street.

Olmsted didn't enter any of the mansions in and around Natchez, but he noted their "noble grounds," including parklike woods "and the best hedges and screens of evergreen shrubs that I have seen in America."

The landscape feature that impressed him most was Natchez's bluff top, overlooking the river. "I found myself," he wrote, "on the very edge of a stupendous cliff, and before me an indescribably vast expanse of forest, extending on every hand to a hazy horizon."

The Mississippi wound through this vastness in "a perfect arc," and for the first time he appreciated the river's grandeur. From this height, the current and froth were "perceptible only as the most delicate chasing upon the broad, gleaming expanse of polished steel," and the panorama "shamed all my previous conceptions of the appearance of the greatest of rivers."

The bluff top was now a small public park, and the rare spot where I felt certain I was occupying the exact ground Olmsted had. Apart from a bridge to Louisiana, the vista closely matched his description: the mile-wide Mississippi flowing with majestic calm through a boundless wooded plain, the two ends of the river lost "in the vast obscurity," as he put it. From this vantage, even the *American Queen* looked insignificant, like a gaudy toy boat at the edge of an Olympic pool.

The streets near the park also retained some of the antebellum splendor of Olmsted's day. A few blocks from the bluff, I stopped at Magnolia Hall, which was conspicuous for the immensity of its fluted Doric columns and the hoopskirted guide by the door.

She explained that Magnolia Hall was part of Natchez's Spring Pilgrimage, a monthlong extravaganza of house and garden tours, pageants, and other festivities. When a few more tourists appeared, she handed us off to another hoopskirted docent, who led us into the front hallway and parlor.

"This was the last of the great homes built in town before the war," she said, likening antebellum Natchez to Bath in England, where the landed gentry flocked in winter to entertain and display their wealth. Moving on, from room to room, hoopskirt to hoopskirt, we learned a little about the cotton magnate who built the house and a great deal about its expensive furnishings, silver spoons, and marble mantels.

Occasionally, these items prompted mention of shadowy "servants," who emptied the well-disguised chamber pots and answered a parlor bell rung by a needlework pulley. During the Civil War, a Union shell hit the "servants' wing," a guide said, exploding in a tureen and scalding those nearby with hot soup.

Magnolia Hall also served as the headquarters of the garden club that had founded Natchez's Pilgrimage. The top floor was devoted to displays on the festival, including pictures of Pilgrimage "Kings and Queens" in Confederate uniforms and hoopskirted dresses.

I asked the young docent on duty if she found her Scarlett O'Hara attire confining. "Yes, sir," Ariel Gardner replied. The rigid stays inside the tight bodice "force you to stand very straight and squeeze your breath." She sometimes tripped on the skirt when she forgot to lift it on steps or to maneuver the hoop sideways through doors.

Ariel endured this discomfort and "received at homes" because the Pilgrimage was a family affair. Her mother belonged to the garden club, and Ariel had taken classes to learn "cotillion and dining etiquette" so she could participate in Pilgrimage soirées and the season's climactic event: the Historic Natchez Tableaux, from the French phrase *tableau vivant*, or living picture.

This costume pageant told the story of Natchez in ten set pieces, including parties with reels and waltzes, planters drinking before a hunt, and the Confederate Farewell Ball, at which maidens saw off beaux wearing rebel uniforms.

Ariel lowered her voice, adding, "We've made it more politically correct this year." New scenes had been added to include Natchez's slave trade and a black high school student singing about "change-a-coming."

I later learned that the tableaux, begun in the 1930s, had for decades featured blacks as cotton pickers, singing "plantation songs." Women dressed as "old Negro mammies" also greeted visitors on house tours while "pickaninnies" danced on the lawns. Blacks stopped participating during the civil rights era and had only returned to the tableaux following this year's update of the script.

One of the new scenes featured Forks of the Road, Natchez's vast slave market, the subject of a large display at a museum of African American history a few blocks from Magnolia Hall. The Forks at Natchez had been second only to New Orleans in the scale of its slave trade, and a major transit point in the forced migration of slaves from the upper South to burgeoning plantations in the Deep South.

"Labourers are being constantly sent away," Olmsted wrote, describing wretched parties of slaves on trains, boats, and roads. On one thoroughfare in Mississippi, "there were sometimes two hundred negroes brought along together, going South."

Much of this traffic was directed by the nation's largest slave-trading firm, Franklin and Armfield, which dispatched overland caravans from its slave pens in Alexandria, Virginia. Male slaves in these coffles were typically shackled to one another, women and children walking behind, all under the guard of mounted drivers with whips and guns.

After trudging hundreds of miles, the slaves were imprisoned at the firm's Natchez hub and readied for sale. One former slave described this preparation as being fed, washed, and rubbed down like racehorses, then "dressed up" and "put through de paces" to show off their muscles.

Others were transported by sea or via the Ohio and Mississippi, hence the phrase "sold down the river." In all, it's estimated that a million slaves made the second Middle Passage to the Deep South, more than double the number of Africans shipped directly to the US in the first Middle Passage, across the Atlantic.

While studying the displays at the Natchez museum, I met Marcus Chambliss, a tall, mustachioed black man visiting from the nearby town of Port Gibson. We chatted about the Pilgrimage, and I asked if he was surprised that this year's tableaux included the Forks of the Road for the first time.

"I'll be real with you," he replied. "In 2013, the state of Mississippi finally got round to ratifying the Thirteenth Amendment, abolishing slavery. That says something about the state of mind of some white people in Mississippi. So am I surprised that it took these folks eighty years to finally mention slavery in their show? No."

Chambliss worked in economic development for a poor area around Port Gibson. "The Old South is big business, so blacks here learn to live with the hoopskirts and so on because the tourism provides jobs." Like Natchez, Port Gibson had a rich antebellum history and was about to hold its own spring festival.

As part of it, reenactors portrayed soldiers killed in fighting at Port Gibson and buried in a cemetery section called Confederate Row. "They've asked me to come this year so it won't be an all-white thing," he said.

That's why Chambliss was at the museum, to borrow a replica of a uniform worn by black troops in the Civil War. He planned to portray a forebear who escaped slavery and fought with the Union army in Mississippi.

"I'm proud of him and all the Union soldiers that caused Confederate Row to exist," he said. "Never thought I'd be at that place, doing anything. So I guess you can say we're waking up, a little bit."

IN OLMSTED'S DAY, RIVERBOATS STOPPED NOT ONLY AT TOWNS but also at private properties to deliver mail, newspapers, and other goods. Along the Mississippi, these stops included plantations with their own landings, for shipping cotton. Olmsted disembarked at two of these. "On both, the hands were at work picking," he wrote, also describing his visit to "the negro quarters."

The *American Queen* offered a version of this with a bus tour in Natchez called "The Story of Cotton in the Antebellum South." At first, it seemed the sort of group tour I dreaded, our local guide cracking Southern-fried jokes about the "*Wah* of Northern Aggression" and folks doing everything so slowly in the South that it took them an hour and a half to watch *60 Minutes*.

Then we stopped at Longwood, a mansion so ornate and oversized it made Magnolia Hall look like a starter home. The exterior was a massive octagon of brick, with Moorish arches and six floors ascending to a bulbous, bloodred dome. It seemed a mash-up of the Alhambra, Sancta Sophia, and the Taj Mahal—which was more or less what the owner had intended.

Haller Nutt was a cotton mogul with five plantations who became entranced by a sketch in a book of house designs, an "Oriental Villa" blending Byzantine, Persian, and Arabesque themes. He commissioned the architect who'd authored the sketch, and began constructing what was projected to become a thirty-two-room palace with silver-plated fixtures, marble statuary, frescoes, and mosaics.

The docents at Longwood didn't wear period attire, but their presentation was even more sanitized than at Magnolia Hall. "Longwood was intended as a part-time home," our guide explained, "a place for the Nutts to spend the winter social season, between harvesting and planting."

No mention of who performed this agricultural work, or of the slaves who did the heavy labor building Longwood, only of the Nutts and their unfortunate timing. Work on their pleasure dome began in 1860, just before "the nation split." Northern artisans hired for the project "went home," and a Union naval blockade made it impossible for the Nutts to receive the many fine furnishings and other items they'd ordered.

As a result, the family was forced to reside in the partly finished basement rooms and "make do with the furnishing from Mrs. Nutt's family estate," our guide said, walking us past a piano, fainting couch, and ten-foot-tall gilded mirrors.

She also pointed out a ceiling fan with a cord, called a punkah, or "shoofly," which "a servant" pulled to move the air "and keep the bugs away while the family ate." In another room, she noted a portrait of a black man in a red vest, black jacket, and high-collared white shirt: Frederick, "a manservant."

At about the fifth such mention of "servants," Jamie, the Californian I'd met on the *American Queen*, interjected: "Do you mean they were slaves?"

"Of course they were," the guide testily replied.

"How many slaves were here, and where did they live?"

"About thirty house servants; they had quarters out back." She moved briskly on, pointing out where the boudoir and conservatory were to have been.

After a quick stop at the restrooms, located in the former slave quarters, we were herded back onto the bus. "They can't even mouth the S-word," Jamie stewed in the seat beside me. "For them it's like the N-word, too shameful and uncouth to utter."

As we motored out of Natchez, a video played on the bus's TV screen about our next stop, Frogmore, a plantation seventeen miles from town. The narration focused on the stages of cotton cultivation, with passing— and passively phrased—reference to the labor force. Hundreds of slaves "came to call Frogmore home," until "war came" and "many slaves left." I assumed we were in for another Tara-like tour, a suspicion deepened by the appearance of the three people who greeted us on arrival.

"This is Lynette Tanner, the mistress of the plantation," our bus guide said, introducing us to an elegant woman in a long black dress who owned Frogmore with her husband. Beside her stood a young white woman in a hoopskirt and an older black man in a period vest and cravat.

Lynette led us to a clapboard church, where we sat on hard pews for a short program that alternated word and song. The black reenactor sang about toting bales, and Lynette followed this by reading from Solomon Northup, who described the wretchedness of his lash-driven labor in *Twelve Years a Slave*.

At which point it became clear that this "plantation mistress" was very different from our guides in Natchez. She described Frogmore's master, who owned eight hundred slaves across eight plantations, as "the one-eighth of the one percent of his day," and read from a book she'd compiled of interviews with former slaves.

Then she led us outside to a restored slave "street," as the quarters on plantations were called. Olmsted described a typical such street when the *Sultana* docked at a cotton plantation.

"There were a dozen or twenty cheap white-washed board cottages, in a long straight row, without windows." Each cabin had a central chimney and an earthen yard. An overseer's cottage, "larger than the rest," stood at the center of the street.

In one cabin, he found an old woman "cooking the dinner of mush and bacon." Younger women were at work in a nearby field, picking cotton "with a rapid and sullen motion" and carrying it in huge baskets to a ginhouse.

Frogmore's layout followed this pattern: a row of rough-hewn cabins and the overseer's cottage, its two rooms separated by an open breezeway, or dogtrot, a term that came from dogs lying in the shaded central passage to catch the breeze.

We stepped inside a slave cabin made of plank and whitewashed with lime, so crudely constructed that bark still covered the ceiling beams. Each cabin housed two family groups, on either side of the chimney, or about ten people in all. Most slept on mattresses filled with corn shucks.

The front doorway of the cabin framed a view through the back door of the cotton fields stretching immediately behind. A small patch had been left unpicked from last season, and Lynette demonstrated how to pluck the cotton out by hand.

"See the prickly bur at the back side? You want to leave that on the plant and just pull the fiber," she said, expertly holding the boll with one hand and extracting a fluffy ball with the other.

She selected me as the first in the group to stoop down and follow her lead. "Squeeze hard now and pull," she coached.

I yanked, pricking my finger and polluting the white fiber with bits of the woody bur. "Perfect pick," she lied. I tried two more times, with similar results. "Now imagine doing that from sunup to sundown, while dragging an awkward heavy sack," Lynette said.

I couldn't. But I did grasp the literalness of "hands" in the ledger books of cotton planters. A dexterous adult slave, capable of picking a hundred pounds or more in a day, was judged a "full hand" and valued accordingly. Nursing mothers, who left the fields four times a day to suckle babies, were "counted as half-hands," Olmsted wrote. Children new to the job ranked as "quarter-hands." Lynette's volume of interviews with former slaves included one who described picking cotton as a girl until "her sore hands cracked open and bled."

This grueling, labor-intensive cultivation lingered into the 1960s, when newly efficient mechanical pickers arrived. Lynette said two men could now harvest Frogmore's 1,500 acres, while computerized gins processed forty-five bales an hour—enough to make a thousand cotton sheets.

Our tour lasted only an hour, and it wasn't until the bus pulled away that I realized we'd visited a black church, slave cabins, cotton fields, and the ginhouse, without setting foot in or hearing a single word about the handsome, antebellum "Big House" we'd parked beside.

AS WE RETURNED ABOARD THE *AMERICAN QUEEN*, IN TIME FOR that day's signature cocktail, a sloe gin fizz, I felt a more acute discomfort with the faux romance of river travel. Steamboats weren't just bygone passenger vessels plying lazy Southern waters. They had been as critical to the rise of the Cotton Kingdom as Eli Whitney's invention of a gin that separated seed and fiber.

In the first decades of the nineteenth century, goods traveled the Mississippi on simple flatboats that were broken up at the end of downriver trips, their crews returning on foot or horse. It was steamboats that made possible the swift and distant transport of immense amounts of freight, including five-hundred-pound bales of cotton.

The *Sultana* was so heavily loaded that the sides of the lower deck "were on the exact level of the water," Olmsted wrote. In fall, following the cotton harvest, these "floating palaces" became what one historian called "floating warehouses," the bales stacked so high that the only boat parts "visible from the shore were the pilothouse and the smokestacks."

Slaves not only grew this abundant crop, which accounted for 60 percent of the nation's export by the Civil War. They did the hard, gang labor of loading and unloading the cargo central to their enslavement, rolling cotton bales, Olmsted wrote, while singing to ease the labor, "each taking a different part, and carrying it on with great spirit and independence."

He also rode steamboats toting slaves to market or distant plantations. On one, slaves were crowded in the hold, except for a few boys sequestered on deck because their owner "had no handcuffs small enough for them."

In the 1830s, steamboats performed another grim transport, carrying tribes exiled west of the Mississippi as part of Andrew Jackson's Indian Removal policy. During the third day of my cruise on the *American Queen*, we passed the site of a steamboat collision in 1837 that drowned most of the seven hundred Creek packed aboard.

We also steamed by the scene of a tragedy that scarred Mark Twain, the foremost purveyor of riverboat romance. While working as a cub pilot, he found a job on his steamboat for his younger brother, Henry. A few months later, soon after Twain was dispatched from the boat, a boiler exploded, casting hundreds of burned and maimed passengers into the Mississippi.

Twain reached a makeshift hospital in Memphis to find rows of scalded survivors, "every face and head a shapeless wad of loose raw cotton." He stayed six days until Henry—"my darling, my pride, my glory, my *all*"—died from his wounds.

As we steamed out of Natchez, I discussed this with Lewis Hankins, a Twain impersonator on the *American Queen*. Hankins certainly looked the part, a ruddy man with curly white hair and a bushy white mustache, clad in a cream suit and vest. He'd also perfected Twain's walk, which he described as "slow, kind of a shuffle," and his voice, "low and gravelly and folksy."

Hankins had grown up by the river and been hooked on Twain upon first reading *Tom Sawyer*. He went on to become a state trooper but later found work entertaining steamboat passengers with monologues modeled on the author's. "I'll play with a pause the way a cat will play with a mouse," Hankins said, paraphrasing Twain. "I love creating the illusion that it's really him talking."

But Hankins's affinity with the author went much deeper than his mimicry of the man. He'd become a true "Twainiac" as a young father, when he read a biography of the writer while struggling with his own family tragedy. "My oldest son died of leukemia, at age eight, in this arm," he said, tearily raising his right limb. "I never got over it. But when I read about Twain, I saw what he endured and the words he had to express what I couldn't."

Twain's loss of his younger brother left him guilty and haunted for the rest of his life. He also lost his first child and only son at nineteen months and two of his three daughters, at the ages of nineteen and twenty-four. Hankins had been particularly moved by Twain's words about his youngest daughter, who died following a seizure in the bathtub: "Possibly I know now what the soldier feels when a bullet crashes through his heart."

Between his daughters' deaths, Twain also lost his wife. By the time of his own death, at the age of seventy-four, he was described as "outworn by grief." His final spoken words appear to have been addressed to his brother or another deceased family member. "If we meet . . ."

Hankins also identified with the grief-induced anger and bitterness behind Twain's comic mask. "When angry count to four," he drawled, "when very angry, swear." Twain renounced his faith and became a biting critic of religious cant, writing: "Man is a Religious Animal. He is the only animal that has the True Religion—several of them. He is the only animal that loves his neighbor as himself and cuts his throat if his theology isn't straight."

Hankins had drifted, too, despite the urging of devout family members. "My grandmother told me, 'Don't get mixed up with that Twain, he was an atheist and the son of the devil.' Clearly I did not follow her advice."

For Hankins, Twain's writing had become a substitute bible and he read from it every day. He still mourned his son, but found wisdom and solace and the capacity to laugh in the words he'd revisited over many decades.

Twain mocked heaven, complaining that man's version of it lacked both humor and sexual intercourse. "But if there is an afterlife," Hankins concluded, "I like to think he might find it redemptive to know he helped another grieving father."

CHAPTER 7

LOWER MISSISSIPPI

The Absolute South

Moving constantly southward, you find each day pleasant tokens of a milder zone," Olmsted wrote of his steamboat ride, "and you dispense after dinner with your overcoat."

The first signs of this temperate clime were green willows and leafed-out poplars. Next appeared magnolias and Spanish moss "in such masses as to gray the forest green," he wrote. "Then cypress swamps, the live oak and the palmetto along the shore, preluding but little the roses, jessamines, and golden oranges." Olmsted had entered the deep, Deep South, luxuriant even in December, when snow was starting to fall in his native New England.

Retracing his river voyage in March, my transit along the Mississippi unfolded in parallel fashion: cool, wet weather and bare trees gradually giving way to warmth and green, and then the swampy lushness of southern Louisiana. As Mark Twain wrote of his own arrival by steamboat in this subtropical realm, "We were in the absolute South now—no modifications, no compromises, no halfway measures."

The *American Queen* docked in the night at Bayou Sara, named for a slow-moving creek washing in and out of the Mississippi. Like Natchez's Under-the-Hill, this landing was once a riverside Gomorrah, identified on maps as "Bayou Clap." Then fire and flood swept away the brothels, saloons, and gambling dens. All that remained was a dock and drowned shoreline, cypresses rising from the dark water.

As in Natchez, a road climbed from the landing to high ground on which perched a handsome antebellum town. St. Francisville was smaller and less grand than Natchez, the in-town houses mostly cottages with deep porches shaded by long sloping roofs. But on its outskirts Olmsted saw "residences indicative of rapidly accumulating wealth" with "extensive and tasteful grounds."

He particularly admired the roadside hedges, trellises of rose interwoven with trumpet creepers, grapevines, and sugarcane to form an unruly, man-high thicket. "It is not as pretty as a trimmer hedge, yet very agreeable," he wrote, "and the road being sometimes narrow, deep and lane like, delightful memories of England were often brought to mind."

Also splendid were the groves of trees, to which Olmsted brought his eye for landscape design. The magnolia, though beautiful, did not "show well in masses" and looked much finer when set among beech and elm. In these mixed groves, "liquid amber formed the body, and the magnolias stood singly out, magnificent chandeliers of fragrance."

Hoping to glimpse this intoxicating landscape, I headed for a plantation Olmsted passed that still had intact and extensive grounds. The approach to Rosedown, along a long avenue of live oaks, cried out for a horse and carriage rather than my solo amble in scuffed boots. The oaks' ancient limbs, dripping Spanish moss, embowered the lane, creating a perfect frame for the white, columned facade of the mansion at the end of the avenue.

It had been built by Daniel Turnbull, who owned several cotton and sugarcane plantations. "Fat and pockets full of money" was how a neighbor described him. The excess on display on the house tour of Rosedown included rare linen wallpaper imported from France, adorned with courtly panoramas of jousting knights in armor.

Turnbull's wife, Martha, devoted herself to the "pleasure grounds" surrounding the house, inspired by estates she saw on a grand tour of Europe. In Florence the couple bought Carrara marble statues to place on pedestals along Rosedown's oak alley.

These formal touches aside, Martha's eye for plants and design bore a kinship to Olmsted's. Her library included the work of Andrew Jackson

Downing, a leading horticulturalist, tastemaker, and early advocate for a central park in New York. Among the dicta that influenced Fred was Downing's emphasis on mixed plantings and curvilinear lines.

Wandering the sinuous paths through Rosedown's gardens and groves, I tried to channel Olmsted and his admiration of Louisiana's lush flora— badly handicapped, however, by my near inability to identify plants other than dandelions, honeysuckle, poison ivy, and a few other species common to the suburban backyard of my youth.

I cherished trees and flowers as much as the next person but struggled to put a name to them or find descriptors other than "pink" or "pretty" or "rough bark." My impaired sense of smell didn't help.

So I was relieved, while studying a shrub, when a man in a golf cart pulled over. "That's a cherry laurel," he said, breaking off a leaf and holding it under my nose. I could faintly detect an odor I'd describe as . . . cherry- like. He plucked a bud from another bush, which he called banana fiscata. It smelled . . . like a banana.

Dan Rainwater was a lean, pointy-bearded Louisianan who'd tended the grounds for seven years. "Something's always coming into bloom as something else is going out," he said. When the magnolia bloomed, its fragrance mixed with the olive and banana "to make a sweet, spicy scent that's so strong you can barely stand it."

Inviting me onto his golf cart, Rainwater drove to a live oak that was 240 years old. The oaks were called "live" because they were green all year; the feathery "moss" on their limbs was actually a flowering plant related to the pineapple.

Old photographs of Rosedown showed much smaller trees without much growth around them. "The people who planted all this had to have a picture in their head of what it would become," he said. Live oaks took decades to reach their sculptural maturity and had been planted along the alley before the house was built.

This was another aspect of Rosedown that resonated with Olmsted's sensibility. He was "long-headed," as one colleague put it, meaning that he looked far ahead to what Fred called "distant effects" that might take de- cades to realize.

In writing about estates like Rosedown, Olmsted also quoted a phrase common to ordinary Mississippians, who termed owners of grand properties "big bugs." When I mentioned this to Rainwater, he nodded and said, "My people were the little bugs who got squashed."

His striking surname derived from Choctaw ancestors forced from their land in the 1830s. "People such as that," he said, gesturing at Rosedown's Big House, "took land from us so they could grow cotton and get rich."

They also profited from the forced labor of Turnbull's 444 slaves, who serviced a white household of seven. At Rosedown, slaves' duties included the creation and maintenance of Martha's pleasure ground. Skilled gardeners propagated and potted exotic plants, while "invalids" unable to work in the fields did lighter labor such as polishing the statues.

Rainwater knew firsthand how much skill and sweat labor went into the care of these grounds, particularly during the blazing Louisiana summer—a season the Turnbulls usually spent in Europe, at Saratoga Springs, or at other resorts. "We returned home 13th of Sept," Martha wrote of a five-month European tour in 1852, "had a fine garden."

Rainwater headed off to trim hedges. "The lady of the house gets the credit, but who made this place, really?" he said. "Must have been a nice life, so long as you were the ones in charge."

LATER THAT DAY I VISITED A PLANTATION THAT STILL RELIED ON forced labor, much of it performed by the descendants of slaves. In the 1840s, Isaac Franklin, one of the slave-trading magnates at the Forks in Natchez, founded a Louisiana plantation, Angola, named for the homeland of some of those in bondage at his estate. After the Civil War, it became a prison farm, the inmates housed in former slave quarters and leased out to work on levees and in fields.

Louisiana later ended this brutal convict-lease system. But in the twentieth century, the Louisiana State Penitentiary at Angola became notorious for cruel and unusual punishment and violence so rampant it was dubbed "the bloodiest prison in the South." The current warden had instituted faith-based reforms to calm the prison population. Hence the title of our bus tour: "Redemption & Rehabilitation at Angola."

En route to the prison, a guide from the facility told us that Louisiana had the nation's highest incarceration rate and Angola was the country's largest maximum-security prison. Three-quarters of the 6,300 inmates were serving life terms, without possibility of parole; the average sentence of those currently inside was ninety-three years.

"In Louisiana, life means life," he said of the state's strict sentencing laws. The prison also housed the state's death chamber; eighty-three men currently awaited execution.

Entering the prison gate, our first glimpse of the grounds was a disarmingly pastoral expanse of grazing cows and fields stretching to a distant fringe of trees. Walled on three sides by a bend in the Mississippi, and by densely thicketed hills on the other, Angola was in essence an eighteen-thousand-acre Alcatraz. "Not a whole lot of places for prisoners to run," our guide drily noted.

Angola was also an agribusiness, known as "the Farm," with up to a thousand inmates at work each day raising crops and livestock. We passed a hundred or so men in long straight lines, stooping to plant potatoes. They wore jeans and T-shirts rather than convict stripes, but in other respects the scene was an eerie throwback. The current warden once likened the prison to "a big plantation in days gone by."

Almost all the field hands were black, overseen by mounted white guards with rifles. This was the vegetable area; elsewhere, convicts sowed a thousand acres of cotton. They began work at sunup, and lunch was brought to them in the fields. For security, and to save on energy, the inmates used little modern machinery; at one field we saw men load crates onto a horse-drawn wagon.

The plantation legacy loomed again when we passed the prison's canine operation, which specialized in raising patrol dogs and bloodhounds. Most were farmed out to police forces, our guide said. But the dogs sometimes did service chasing and tracking the rare fugitive who got past the guards, double cyclone fences, razor wire, and other security.

Escapes had once been common, and a mass breakout in the 1930s led to the creation of Angola's ghastliest attraction, the Red Hat Cellblock. Named for the red straw hats convicts once wore in the fields, the now-abandoned unit was a reinforced concrete blockhouse built to hold "incorrigible" prisoners. Adjoining it was a smaller building with "Execution" written in red letters above the door.

We climbed off the bus and peered into tiny cells where inmates slept on concrete slabs without heating or cooling. Informational placards chained to the cell doors told of guards' frequent use of the "bat," a thick leather strap attached to a long wooden handle. One man who fell behind in his fieldwork was beaten to death. Another was shot dead in an okra patch.

A passageway connected the cellblock to the execution chamber, where a high-backed wood chair with arm and leg straps sat beside a box extruding a tangle of wires. The prison switched to lethal injection in the 1990s, carried out in a fortified unit where inmates were confined to their cells for twenty-three hours a day.

The same was true at a disciplinary unit we passed, holding four hundred men in "extended lockdown" for serious infractions. Repeat offenders were sentenced to a week of "the loaf," eating nothing but meal scraps cooked into a grayish-brown lump.

Then we parked beside a cellblock and walked through a barred cage and two fences topped with razor wire for the "Redemption & Rehabilitation" part of the program. We entered a small chapel as a crew-cut inmate played an organ donated by the Billy Graham Evangelistic Association.

He spoke briefly to us about his life sentence—"Your world stops; you cling to old memories that get older and older"—before handing the microphone to Hayward Jones, a middle-aged black man with glasses and a shaved head. He, too, carried a life sentence without parole, for second-degree murder, committed during a burglary eighteen years ago.

"A kind of crazy thing at Angola, fifty-two percent of the population is first-time offenders and I'm one of them," he said. "There's the crime and then the prison, no transition. I spent my first few years inside just trying to wrap my mind around this condition I'm in."

He was pulled out of this funk by a prisoner who challenged him "to be better, to do something better. Nobody wants to be judged by the worst thing they did in life."

Jones had gone on to earn a seminary degree at Angola and now mentored "guys who are on shorter sentences and will get back out into the community." He also belonged to a peer-counseling group called Malachi Dads, the name taken from the biblical verse about fathers and children turning their hearts toward each other.

"The reality for most men here is that your family slips away after five or so years," he said, and this had happened to him. But after years without contact, he reconnected with his son and even gained joint custody of him. Father and son, now nineteen and in college, communicated often by phone and letter and saw each other once a month.

Jones's good works earned him small privileges at the prison, "like coming outside the cage to meet your bus," he said. Well-behaved prisoners were also permitted to sell their own arts and crafts and visit with their kids at Angola's famous rodeo, at which thousands of spectators watched inmates in cowboy attire being thrown from broncos and chased by bulls.

But none of this changed the legal status of those sentenced to life without parole. Barring a miracle—a clemency board ruling, signed by the governor—Jones would die at Angola, like roughly 90 percent of the prison's other inmates. The hopelessness this bred was difficult to break.

"It becomes a crutch," Jones said, "a way for guys to say, 'Why rehabilitate?'" His answer was the challenge posed to him long ago, to be better than his worst act in life and believe in the possibility of change. "You have to find something to take that weight off, some hope and reason for living."

Listening to the program, I was moved by the stories while struck once again by the antebellum echoes. For slaves condemned to a life of bondage, Christian belief could be a salve and source of hope, if only for release in the hereafter.

But slaveholders often deployed religion as a tool of social control, tailoring prayers and sermons to stress the duty to obey one's master. Christianizing slaves also served Southern propagandists who claimed that bondage uplifted African "savages" and liberated them from spiritual darkness.

Angola's warden had been candid about using faith, as he put it, to "create a positive group inside [the prison] that I can control." This effort—and harsh measures like solitary confinement—appeared to have borne fruit. During the warden's twenty-year tenure, annual assaults at Angola had fallen by 75 percent. "Moral rehabilitation" also served as a potent PR tool, bringing praise and dollars from Christian groups and talk of the warden as a potential candidate for governor.

The prisoners at Angola weren't born or forced into bondage, but lifers without parole had even less chance than slaves of ever being free. Faith-based programs carried the promise of small leniencies, and for some, a deeper quest that Hayward Jones spoke to in his parting words at the chapel.

"Hope is always there,'" he said. "It's a bird that never perches, but you've got to keep grasping at it."

THE NEXT MORNING, AS THE *AMERICAN QUEEN* RESUMED STEAM-ing south, I rejoined the fraternity of river nerds in the Chart Room, contentedly tracking the boat's progress and calling out the antique names of landmarks we passed: False River, Profit Island, Mulatto Bend. Then, as we neared Baton Rouge, smokestacks poked above the mist, signalling a dramatic shift in the river scenery.

The Riverlorian, Jerry Hay, explained that we'd entered the deep channel and industrial corridor extending from here to New Orleans. Instead of wooded shore and bygone landings, we now passed bulbous storage tanks, mazes of pipes, and other evidence of the oil and petrochemical megalopolis centered on Baton Rouge.

Also startling, after four days of light river traffic, were oceangoing tankers and freighters so immense that the *American Queen* suddenly felt like a little wooden dory. These behemoths couldn't go beyond Baton Rouge due to a bridge built during the reign of Huey Long, Louisiana's famed Depression-era governor.

"The story goes," Hay said, "that Huey had the bridge built low because he didn't want to share the ship traffic with ports in other states upriver."

This tale was typical of Huey Long, a bombastic figure wreathed in lore, much of it his own creation. But our visit to Baton Rouge also revealed Long in a more complex light, as a figure who presaged developments in my own era's politics.

We docked for only a few hours, so I sprinted first to the bizarre governor's mansion that Long erected, using prison labor from Angola. The Georgian, columned facade closely resembled the White House, and the interior included an oval "office," though it actually served as a family room.

"The story goes," a docent said, "that Huey didn't want to be embarrassed when he made it to the real White House. This way, he'd know where the light switches were."

Another of Long's famous edifices, the Louisiana statehouse, towered at the other side of downtown. Here, the story went, Long delayed completion of the structure so he could make sure its height exceeded Nebraska's capitol, under construction at the same time, and thus guarantee that Louisiana's would be the nation's tallest.

The thirty-four-floor Beaux-Arts skyscraper, built in the depth of the Depression, was decorated with two-ton chandeliers and double-life-sized sculptures of Louisiana governors. Even larger was a bronze of Long, towering atop a plinth facing the capitol. "Here Lies Louisiana's Great Son," the inscription read. A bas-relief depicted Huey with outstretched arms, and citizens gazing adoringly at him, as if at Christ.

Pilgrims could also visit the site of his martyrdom beside a chipped marble column in the capitol. Long's dictatorial ways made him many enemies, including a young doctor who confronted Huey one night in 1935 and shot him in the side. Long's bodyguards replied with a fusillade that riddled the doctor with thirty bullets and sent shots ricocheting off walls and columns.

Researchers had since poked holes in this version of events, raising the possibility that it was Long's trigger-happy security men, rather than the aggrieved doctor, who killed him.

The nearby state museum exhibited tommy guns carried by Long's thuggish bodyguards, called brownshirts, one example of why foes often likened Huey to Hitler and Mussolini. Long's political machine so thoroughly rigged elections that a henchman boasted of registering trees as voters.

The cronies he installed at every level also allowed him to maintain his iron-fisted rule of Louisiana, even after he left to become a senator in Washington. Long's brother joked that Huey's handpicked successor as governor, O. K. Allen, was so pliant he once signed a leaf that blew through his office window and onto his desk.

Old newsreels at the museum were also a reminder of Long's fiery populism, radical in his day and strikingly resonant in mine. "None shall be too big, none shall be too poor," he bellowed, waving his fists. He further decried the "financial masters" who "have taken off the barbecue table 90 percent of the food placed thereon by God, even before the feast begins."

As governor, he raised taxes and spent lavishly on roads, bridges, schools, and hospitals. Then, as senator, he launched a national "Share Our Wealth" campaign that called for both a minimum family income and a *maximum*, so that "1 percent of the people" would no longer control so much of the nation's wealth. Heavy levies on fortunes "above the few millions" would be used to fund old-age pensions, health, and other benefits aimed at the masses.

As I listened to Long fulminate against the "favored few" and champion the little man, Bernie Sanders was voicing similar themes on the campaign trail. Trump tapped this populism, too, with a style and tactics that Huey foreshadowed.

A belligerent entertainer, Long mocked Washington "elites" and disparaged the character and appearance of other candidates, calling them "thieves, bugs, and lice," or belittling them with nicknames like "Turkey Head" and "Old Buzzard Back."

He went after judges, told bodyguards to rough up the press, warned supporters to "watch out for the lying newspapers!," and started his own, *American Progress*, so he could speak directly to the public, as he did at huge rallies and on radio.

Long could also be extremely crude. In one of many instances of incivility, he grabbed a dinner plate from a woman at a fancy party, telling her: "I'll eat this for you. You're too fat already."

A dangerous buffoon in the eyes of the political establishment, Long attracted millions of fervent followers and was poised to challenge FDR in the 1936 election. "I can take this Roosevelt," he crowed. "I can out-promise him and he knows it."

Though shot dead a few months later, at the age of forty-two, Long had a very long afterlife in Louisiana, where his family and political machine ruled for half a century. Huey's bridges and roads endured, and so did his legacy of graft, patronage, concentrated power, and flagrant disregard for the law.

"When I took the oath of office, I didn't take any vow of poverty," declared one Long crony who went from the governor's office to federal prison.

A later governor, Edwin Edwards, laughed off the frequent charges against him, boasting that the only way he'd lose an election "is if I'm caught in bed with either a dead girl or a live boy."

He won four times before going to prison for bribery, fraud, and other crimes. But Louisiana was more forgiving of crooked politicians than of the felons I'd met at Angola. Released after eight years, Edwards married a woman fifty-two years his junior, starred with her in a reality show, and won a primary for Congress.

"People say, well, they're all crooks anyhow," Edwards told a reporter, when asked about going to Washington. "You might as well send an experienced one."

It was easy to regard Louisiana's political culture and Huey Long's legacy as lurid exceptions to American norms. But inequality, class resentment, and distrust of "elites" was running strong in the 2000s, as it had in the 1930s, and an emerging candidate bore striking similarities to Long and some of his successors.

A demagogue; a crude and clever bully; a putative champion of the little man who erected towers that exalted him; a divisive figure lashing out at judges, the press, and other brakes on unbridled power; a womanizer and wheeler-dealer of dubious ethics who boasted he could shoot someone in public and get away with it.

Many Americans know Huey Long best from Robert Penn Warren's fictional classic, *All the King's Men*. Warren also wrote nonfiction and had a dark awareness of how the past haunted and weighed on the present.

"History, like nature, knows no jumps," he observed in 1956, writing about white resistance to civil rights. "Except the jump backward."

LEAVING BATON ROUGE, THE *AMERICAN QUEEN* PADDLED IN THE twilight past chandeliers of lights strung along the gas and chemical plants lining the river. The water had been rising for days, due to snowmelt up north, and was so high it had swamped our next scheduled dock site. The captain steered us a few miles past it to an abandoned steamboat landing, then nosed the bow until it touched bottom within gangway distance of the riverbank.

"This is exactly how they did it here 150 years ago," he said, maneuvering carefully to keep the stern out in the river, so the paddle wheel and propeller wouldn't get stuck in the sand and mud.

Securing the bow also required an old-school technique, "choking the stump." Normally, boats tied up to a heavy chain loop onshore. But the one here was now five feet underwater. So crewmen had to tromp through the mud and scrub to find trees large enough to run a line around to hold a 3,700-ton vessel. "When Mother Nature does her thing, you go along," a deckhand said, winching a line in the dark and rain.

The sky cleared overnight, and we woke to another change in the landscape and history of the Mississippi. Baton Rouge wasn't only the gateway to the river's industrial corridor. It also formed a border between the Cotton Kingdom and a smaller but even richer realm in the antebellum South. Call it the Empire of Sugar.

Native to the tropics, sugarcane can't tolerate frost, which occurs even in sultry south Louisiana. The French planters who first brought cane here from the Caribbean mostly failed. But if the risks were great, the rewards were stratospheric. In the 1850s, favorable weather, a tariff on imported sugar, and rising prices helped produce some of the fastest and largest fortunes ever amassed in the United States.

"It is the most complete gambling," Olmsted wrote, after visiting a Louisiana sugar plantation owned by Richard Taylor, a young Yale graduate who had just inherited the property from his father, President Zachary Taylor.

Like other sugar planters, Taylor took on tremendous debt to amass 1,200 acres, 147 slaves, and the expensive equipment needed to crush cane into marketable sugar and molasses. Just two or three bad crops were enough to ruin the venture. But in the flush 1850s, Taylor quickly became one of Louisiana's richest men, allowing him to gamble heavily on cards and horses as well.

Others indulged in the most conspicuous consumption of newfound wealth in the South, building estates so showy that one became known as Le Petit Versailles. The layout of properties on the lower Mississippi amplified this ostentatious display. The lots had narrow river frontage, to maximize access to the Mississippi. Sultans of sugar erected their palaces facing the river and the road beside it, creating a long avenue of impact homes for land and water travelers to gawk at.

Borrowing one of the steamboat's bikes, I rode over the levee by our dock site and came to a sign for Belle Grove, a bygone plantation house that was reputedly the largest ever built in the South, with four floors and seventy-five rooms. The sugar baron who erected it in the 1850s had been fiercely competitive with a neighbor, who was then at work on his own trophy home, called Nottoway.

I reached the latter after cycling past two miles of dead-flat fields, a setting that augmented Nottoway's bulk and made it appear a mirage castle rising from the steamy plain. Some of the houses in Natchez had grace or whimsy in their design; here, size and cost seemed all that mattered.

Standing before the blunt, square-columned facade, a hoopskirted guide ticked off the house's specs: two hundred windows, twelve marble fireplaces, six interior stairways, and an all-white ballroom with Baccarat chandeliers. The main structure had a floor space akin to the White House; the wings brought the total to sixty-four thousand square feet—on a par with Mar-a-Lago and the Hearst Castle.

Almost no evidence remained of Nottoway's forty-two slave cabins and the exceptionally grueling labor that made possible the excessive wealth on display. Slaves on cane plantations cleared swamps, dug drainage ditches, and hoed weeds through the broiling summer—prelude to the backbreaking labor in "grinding season," when planters rushed to harvest and process their crop before the first frost.

"Nearly every man, woman and child," Olmsted wrote of sugar plantations, "were on duty fully eighteen hours a day" in grinding season, including Sundays, for two to three months. Slaves stripped ten-foot-high stalks and toted the cane to mills to be ground and cooked in boiling hot kettles or furnaces. The fires were kept burning around the clock and required cutting huge amounts of wood.

"The severity of the labour," Olmsted wrote, and exhausting schedule was such that planters "liberally" stoked slaves with coffee, tobacco, and hot molasses. Slaves were also "induced, as much as possible, to make a kind of frolic" of the extra rations and intense group effort.

Burns and crushing wounds were common in grinding season, and Olmsted observed that sugar plantations were notable for having "a large number of 'used-up hands'—slaves, sore and crippled, or invalided for some cause." The physical demands of sugar cultivation also skewed the makeup of the slave population. Planters disproportionately sought young men, who were often separated from their families upon sale and shipment to south Louisiana.

Olmsted spoke to one such exile, a slave in his thirties who had been sold away from his family at the age of thirteen. "If I was free, I would go to Virginia, and see my old mudder," he confided. "I would like to do dat fus thing." Then "I'd get me a wife."

Many of those shipped to Louisiana had spouses already, though slave weddings had no legal standing, only the promise of union "until death or distance do you part." The sale of slaves ruptured about a third of first marriages, and demand for young men in the sugar fields made forced separation especially common.

When freedom came, ex-slaves searching for long-lost kin often found that their wives had started new families with other men, out of necessity, on the orders of a master, or because they never expected to see their former partner again.

This legacy made Nottoway all the more grotesque, because the mansion was now a premier wedding venue, touted as the South's largest antebellum mansion. "Every Castle Needs a Queen," one of Nottaway's brochures stated.

On the day I visited, preparations were underway for deluxe nuptials that night and another the next day. While wandering the gardens I met Nottoway's head of maintenance, Randy LaPrairie, who said some couples asked that chandeliers be strung from the live oaks beside the house.

"If you have money and want grandeur, this is the place, always was," he said, noting that Nottoway was erected to outshine nearby Belle Grove. "They were keeping up with the Joneses by building these huge homes, and weddings today are sorta the same."

The front office manager, Jen Donald, said Nottoway was a natural for weddings because of its resort amenities, including forty-one guest rooms and the lavish ballroom, which could accommodate three hundred people. Depending on add-ons, weddings here could cost upwards of a quarter million dollars.

Some brides came through the front gate in horse-drawn carriages, and occasionally they asked to have hoopskirted guides present. But Jen didn't think Old South history and nostalgia was the site's main appeal.

"Really, it's about the house, this *very* big house," she said. "More than anything, a lot of brides want to have it in the background of their wedding pictures."

CYCLING OFF FROM NOTTOWAY, PAST NEWLY PLANTED CANE fields, I came to a much more modest abode where two elderly black men sat out front on chairs. The house stood at the edge of a small community called Dorseyville, established in the 1860s by former slaves who'd worked at the plantations on either side of the settlement, and continued to do so as freedmen.

"Slavery didn't really end with the Civil War," said one of the men, Ulysses Douglas. His grandparents stayed on the plantation, as sharecroppers, using scrip or credit to buy tools and other essentials from the owner's store. "By the end of the year, folks always owed more than they made from their share of the crop. So they worked for no money, just debt."

His parents succeeded in moving off the plantation and into Dorseyville, working for wages rather than a share, "so that was a step up," Ulysses said. He pointed across the street at the weatherboard shack where he'd grown up. "Three rooms, six kids, no plumbing or electricity." As a child in the 1940s, he worked in the cane fields before school, from five to eleven in the morning. "Little boy with a machete, cutting cane that was taller than me, right beside my mother."

The other man, a classmate of Ulysses's, had done the same. "Got up at three a.m. so you could be in the fields by dawn," Herman Hampton said. He stooped to demonstrate the labor. "Bend down, hold the cane, cut the cane. Take a row down, cut a row coming back." He straightened up. "I still do it in my sleep sometimes."

As for the pay, he said, "Shoot, it was like seventy-five cents an acre. You didn't make but a few dollars for working all day."

He'd "left out of here" in the 1950s and became a bus driver in San Francisco. Ulysses departed at the same time and worked in New Orleans as a janitor and mechanic. "We lived in better times than our folks," he said. "There was money for your work and we had options they didn't back then."

Even so, both men had retired to Dorseyville, to small homes they'd inherited. "It's cheap, I can fish, hang out with old friends," Ulysses said, going inside to stir a pot of red beans. "In the city every day is a hurry and hassle."

Herman agreed. "Ulysses and me, we come up together here," he said, before following his friend inside. "Figure we might as well go out the same way."

OVER DINNER ON MY LAST NIGHT ABOARD THE *AMERICAN QUEEN*, we went around the table sharing impressions of our six days on the water. John Young, an Australian lawyer, likened his time aboard the boat to a trans-Pacific flight on a jumbo jet. "It's suspended animation," he said. "The rest of your life doesn't exist."

Brian Coales, a retired Englishman, was also surprised by how easy it had been to forget he was on the water. "I see now why they call it 'seasick' rather than 'riversick.' Barely felt a bloody thing."

Onshore, the experience had been more turbulent. While I was at Nottoway, John and his wife, Anna, had visited a plantation where a cruel master used to roll slaves down the levee in barrels with nails driven into them. "You think you know all the horrible things humans can do to each other," Anna said, "but these slave owners kept shocking me."

We paused as our entrées of red snapper, shrimp Creole, and duck breast arrived. When it was my turn to speak, all I could think was "overstuffed." By the rich food, the plush furnishings, the plantation and prison tours, the swamps and cane and cotton. "Too much of everything to take in."

Our waiter, Matt, had been listening in, as usual. "Just wait until New Orleans," he said, refilling my wineglass. "It's too much of everything, times ten."

CHAPTER 8

NEW ORLEANS

The Gumbo City

I n the course of his travels, Olmsted stopped several times in New Orleans, which was then the South's largest city and second only to New
York as a port of entry for immigrants.

"I doubt there is a city in the world," he wrote, "where the resident
population has been so divided in its origin, or where there is such a variety
in the tastes, habits, manners, and moral codes of the citizens."

Olmsted reveled in this cosmopolitanism, taking in "French noises and
French smells," thick Irish brogues and German gasthauses, architectural
relics of "ancient Spanish builders," and the newer brick edifices of "the
unartistic and dollar pursuing Yankees." New Orleans was also home to
some eleven thousand *gens de couleur libre*, or free people of color, many of
them of French and Afro-Caribbean descent.

"I have rarely, if ever, met more beautiful women," Olmsted wrote, describing daughters of mixed-race unions who had been sent by wealthy
white fathers to France for education and refinement. "They are much better formed, and have a much more graceful and elegant carriage than
Americans in general," he added, "and the way of wearing dresses and ornaments, that is the especial distinction of the women of Paris."

He also noted the pseudo-taxonomy that whites used to distinguish the
many "grades of the colored people" in New Orleans. Those judged to be

the offspring of whites and "mulattoes" were termed "quarteron," or "quadroon." The pairing of white and quadroon produced "octoroon," or *Sangemele*. "Griffe" referred to a "bright" brown-skinned mix of "negro and mulatto." And so on through an arcane spectrum that wasn't exclusive to Louisiana but found its fullest expression there—and that endured, in law, until 1983, when the state repealed a "one drop" standard (technically, one thirty-second black ancestry) used to establish race.

These dubious classifications also served as a marketing tool in antebellum New Orleans, the South's largest slave mart. Darker-skinned men were touted as best able to handle the heat and hard labor of fieldwork. "Bone and muscle," Olmsted wrote, was sold by the lot in New Orleans, including one group of twenty-two young men he saw lined up in front of a "New York clothing store," clad in blue cloth and black hats.

Several Northern firms, including Brooks Brothers, thrived on "plantation clothing," both fine suits for masters and cheaper wares used to dress up slaves for auction. "Dam'd if they ain't just the best gang o' cotton-hands ever I see," a fellow onlooker said to Olmsted.

New Orleans also did a brisk trade in "fancy" girls, light-skinned, curly-haired teenagers whom buyers fancied for their beauty—and the prospect of sexual servitude. White men in New Orleans trafficked in another practice, termed "*plaçage*," cohabiting with women of color until they acquired the means to start a household with a white spouse.

Since interracial marriage was legally barred, the men "make such arrangements 'as can be agreed upon,'" Olmsted wrote, including support for the women and any children they might have by the men. "A tenement in a certain quarter of the town is usually hired, and the couple move into it and go to housekeeping—living as if they were married."

This practice had titillated male visitors to New Orleans for decades and produced a good deal of lore. Travelers often claimed that quadroon mothers trained their daughters to be seductive courtesans and negotiated formal contracts with suitors. Olmsted repeated some of this hearsay, but he also put a practical gloss on a custom that others wreathed in lurid fantasy.

"It is much cheaper than living at hotels and boarding-houses," he wrote of young unmarried men, often newcomers to the city, who moved in with *placées*. "She did the marketing, and performed all the ordinary duties of house-keeping herself; she took care of his clothes and in every way was economical and saving in her habits."

Some of these couples formed "strong attachments," Olmsted reported; other times, women were cruelly abandoned. He didn't approve of *plaçage* but noted the plight of young men in Northern cities who "shrink from marriage" due to the expectation that they be able to afford a degree of "splendor" and "fashion" for their families. In his view, this led to "licentiousness" and other ills "inimical to future domestic contentment and virtue."

It's hard to tell how much this reflected Olmsted's own situation, as a bachelor still trying to make his way in the world. He was clearly attracted to light-skinned black women, referring to their beauty and charms at several points in his travels, and he didn't express the phobia about racial "amalgamation" that infected so many white Americans. But he could only write about this obliquely, treating *plaçage* as a form of starter marriage for young men of modest means and preferable to the "disease" one saw at "the hospitals of New York," an apparent reference to syphilis.

Olmsted was coyer about another exotic feature of New Orleans life: the "quadroon ball." These were masked parties at which white men danced and flirted with women of color—and, according to many travelers' tales, began courtships that led to living together. Earlier in the century, these balls were described as decorous affairs, but by the 1850s they'd become a rowdy industry, the women performing dances and cadging high-priced drinks from sailors and others—an early version of the sex-and-sin tourism on which New Orleans has long traded.

Olmsted didn't say if he witnessed this spectacle during the ten days or so he spent in New Orleans. Instead, he cited an ad for the Globe, an establishment near the docks known for quadroon or "society" balls. The ad listed the door charge as only fifty cents ("Ladies, gratis" and not admitted without masks), weapons were barred, and strict order maintained by "police in attendance."

AT 8:00 A.M. ON A SATURDAY, ROLLING MY BAG FROM MY CABIN on the *American Queen* to much more modest quarters near Bourbon Street, I had to sidestep men and machines hosing and sweeping away butts, beer cups, and other detritus from the previous night's revelry. A drag queen wobbled by in high heels, wig awry, mumbling the doo-de-doo chorus from "Walk on the Wild Side." Two tap dancers no older than twelve were already setting out hats on the sidewalk.

This was the New Orleans that had entranced me in my early twenties, when I worked as a union organizer in rural Mississippi and escaped on paydays to eat rice and beans at Buster Holmes, drink cheap Dixie beer, and dance outside the open doors and windows of blues bars I couldn't afford to enter.

I'd returned to the city several times since but rarely ventured far from the French Quarter and other tourist nodes. This time, with Olmsted as my guide, I'd go farther afield, exploring the beguiling and bewildering mix of races and identities he described.

First, just off Bourbon Street, I found the site of what had once been a venue for quadroon balls. It was now a luxury hotel that made the bygone affairs on its grand second floor sound like debutante balls. "While the air was fragrant with jasmine and sweet olive," claimed the literature given to me at the desk, "quadroon women began seeking liaisons" in a ballroom where "an orchestra filled the richly decorated hall with minuets and waltzes."

One quadroon woman was vocal in her resistance to this ritual. Henriette DeLille rejected *plaçage* and founded a holy order that later bought the ballroom and turned it into a convent and Catholic school. I learned about DeLille at a small museum a mile from the French Quarter, on Esplanade, the wide, tree-lined avenue that borders Tremé, a center of black life in New Orleans since the 1840s.

Le Musée de f.p.c. took its name from the initials used for "free people of color" in censuses and other records. In the early 1800s, free blacks constituted almost a quarter of the city's population and occupied a middle caste between whites and slaves. Most were French speaking and Catholic, literate and highly skilled, and owners of considerable property—in some cases, slave plantations.

White attitudes and laws regarding free blacks hardened in the lead-up to the Civil War, and when hostilities broke out, several thousand f.p.c.s joined pro-Confederate militias, out of allegiance to Louisiana or as a prudent display of support for their white neighbors. Many later switched sides and aided the Union forces that occupied New Orleans early in the war.

"F.p.c.s were caught in the middle, in so many ways," said Beverly McKenna, who founded the museum with her husband. "Yet they left fingerprints all over this city, on the buildings, the culture, the commerce. Black history isn't just about the degradation of slavery."

This distinctive culture endured after emancipation, despite late-nineteenth-century laws that made no distinction between those of free and enslaved heritage. Eight blocks down Esplanade, I came to Li'l Dizzy's Cafe, a green stucco restaurant where the food is "Always Hot & Straight from the Pot." The owner, Wayne Baquet, was overseeing the final preparation of that day's gumbo. A small man with tan skin, Baquet referred to himself and his cooking as Creole, a fluid designation that had been applied over centuries to a shifting cast of Louisianans.

"Creole's a melting pot, just like this," he said, stirring a stew of roux, crab, shrimp, sausage, chicken, green pepper, sassafras, and other herbs. "Gumbo's an African word, for okra, and there's French, Spanish, American Indian, and maybe a little Italian mixed in, too."

He added that, gastronomically, "Creole is the soul food of New Orleans." Elsewhere in the South, soul food was "more country," he said, citing chitlins, oxtail, and greens and peas boiled with pork. Here, the seafood and range of influences made for more varied and strongly flavored dishes.

He was also careful to distinguish Creole from Cajun, the French Louisiana cuisine popularized by Paul Prudhomme. "Creole is a lot better," he said with a smile. "Cajun's peppery, real spicy. Ours is seasoned and subtler."

After I'd sampled his delectable gumbo—along with the other lunch buffet offerings of catfish, gravy-smothered meat, cabbage, and red beans and rice—Baquet came over to my table with a serving of bread pudding. "All good for the soul, maybe not for your waistline."

He then told me about his family, which descended from French-speaking free persons of color and status. Adorning one wall of his restaurant was an 1864 petition from "Free Colored Representatives" in Louisiana, calling upon President Lincoln to grant them voting and other rights. It noted that freeborn blacks in Louisiana had been literate, property-owning, tax-paying citizens for decades and served in the War of 1812. "We are men. Treat us as such."

One of the signers was Wayne's great-great-grandfather. Other luminaries in his family tree included a prominent detective and two pioneering jazz musicians. Baquet's father had been a mailman who went on to open a popular restaurant, as Wayne had since done. One of Wayne's brothers was a senior editor at the New Orleans *Times-Picayune*; another, Dean, had recently become the first person of color to serve as executive editor of the *New York Times*.

"Creoles had education and opportunity that a lot of other people of color didn't," Wayne said. "Pigmentation helped," he added, citing Dutch Morial, the city's first black mayor, who "looked white," which in Baquet's view helped Morial garner a fifth of the white vote upon his election in the 1970s.

But this relative privilege had created tension within the city's diverse community of color. "Back in the day," Baquet said, "Creoles thought they were better than darker-skinned Negroes whose ancestors were slaves and didn't have the same opportunities." Religion was another difference; most Creoles were Catholic, while others of color were mostly Baptist.

Growing up in the 1950s, Baquet came to recognize the hollowness of these distinctions. He played with an Italian boy who lived next door in Tremé, only to be shunned by him as a teenager. "I'd say, 'Hi, Al, how you doing?' and he'd look away. He didn't want his white classmates seeing him associate with me. That's when I saw how things were."

Then came the civil rights movement, and black pride, which he felt had dispelled many Creoles' sense of being separate. "My heritage is Creole; I'm proud of that, but I'm also proud to be black."

Baquet had to get back to work but recommended I visit a frequent patron of his restaurant, Keith Weldon Medley, who'd written several books on black New Orleans. Medley lived nearby in a handsome, double shotgun cottage he'd grown up in, as the son of a plasterer.

Lanky, with a caramel-colored complexion, he was sixty-six and, like Baquet, a graduate of St. Augustine, a prestigious Catholic school in Tremé. He'd gone on to college and a career as a photographer, IT specialist, and author of histories on subjects such as *Plessy* v. *Ferguson*, the famous court case about segregation.

In Medley's view, while nineteenth-century Creoles saw themselves as a people apart, they'd also become leaders in the fight against Jim Crow, on behalf of all blacks. Homer Plessy, for instance, was the son of French-speaking free persons of color and so light skinned he could board whites-only railcars without attracting notice.

In 1892, as part of an organized effort to challenge segregation, Plessy boarded a white car and told the conductor he was one-eighth black, leading to his arrest. The case wound its way to the Supreme Court, which ruled that states could segregate facilities so long as they were "separate and equal." The decision entrenched Jim Crow for the next sixty years, though the lone dissent in the case helped form the basis for its overturning in *Brown* v. *Board of Education.*

Creoles also became integral to the black elite, or what W. E. B. Du Bois called the "talented tenth." Many left for the North and West, and some were so pale they went *passe blanc*, or passed as white, including one of Medley's great-uncles. "He'd nod at us in the street but couldn't hug us because it would show he had colored family. We didn't think that was a sin; it was a way to get ahead in a racist system."

He also recalled a "passing mill" in Houston, where people went to get birth certificates and other documents altered. An aunt and uncle of Medley's had done so for one of their sons, who didn't learn his birth status until decades later.

"In the internet era, a lot of people are just a mouse click away from discovering they're black." Medley laughed, adding a quote attributed to Huey Long: "You could feed all the pure whites and pure blacks in Louisiana with a cup of beans and half a cup of rice."

Another Creole practice was the "brown bag test." Medley hadn't encountered this, but often heard growing up that to enter some parties you had to put your hand next to a paper bag. "If your skin was darker than the bag, you couldn't get in."

Like Baquet, Medley believed "the sixties brought people of color together, rather than let skin tone divide us." But he was less sanguine about relations between blacks and whites in New Orleans. Medley had held well-paying jobs that "wouldn't have been available to me sixty years ago. That's the good side." The bad side: some whites he'd worked with still resented "blacks being on their level."

He'd noticed this most sharply upon Obama's election, when he was the only black working in IT at a bank office. "The whites went crazy, screaming, 'Holy shit, this can't happen!' and they knew I was listening. I couldn't help feeling it wasn't just about Obama. I was making a lot of money and they couldn't handle that."

Katrina had complicated the racial calculus. Some seventy-five thousand blacks driven out by the flooding had never returned, and the rebuilding brought an influx of Hispanic workers and young whites from outside Louisiana. Many of the latter had moved into neighborhoods like Tremé, displacing longtime residents.

Wandering Tremé after my visit with Medley, I stopped at a black-owned barbershop. "Most of my clientele is white," said Invee Burrell, who'd grown up nearby. "Some of them, I can just look at and say, 'What part of Brooklyn are you from?'"

Burrell welcomed the business and said Tremé was safer and had more young families than before. He also felt white newcomers to the city "don't carry all that history and baggage" that locals grew up with. But he understood the fears of many in New Orleans that the city risked losing some of its soul and diversity. "You'll hear black people say, 'If Katrina didn't drive you out, the taxes and house prices will.'"

A dark-skinned man with a goatee, Burrell had tussled as a child in the 1970s and '80s with Creole kids. "We disliked them for thinking they were better than us, and they thought we were wild and dangerous—same prejudices whites had." Some older Creoles might still feel that way, he said, "but they're kidding themselves if they think whites don't see them as black, too."

One difference that lingered was church. Burrell had been raised Catholic and described Creole services as "having a more soulful vibe" than white ones. But he'd since become a Baptist and attended a church in the Ninth Ward that he said was much more akin to traditional black worship in the South.

This caught my attention, because Olmsted wrote at length about his visit to a black Baptist church in New Orleans. On a Sunday walk, attracted "by a loud chorus singing," he entered the open door of a church and was quickly ushered to a seat facing the pulpit. Taking "notes as well as I could," Olmsted struggled with the "grammar and pronunciation," including what he called "vulgarisms and slang phrases." But he judged the preacher "refined and delicately sensitive," his voice "impressive," and his metaphors strange yet "beautiful."

He also overcame his initial discomfort with the fervid piety on display.

During the sermon, congregants shook and convulsed as if stricken with a "violent ague," letting loose groans and shrieks while "stamping, jumping, and clapping." One old woman began a wild dance, "her head thrown back and rolling from one side to the other," before sinking to the floor, "kicking, as if acting a death struggle."

This was very foreign to a descendant of New England Puritans, and not the sort of comportment Olmsted generally admired. So he was surprised "to find my own muscles all stretched, as if ready for a struggle—my face glowing, and my feet stamping—having been infected unconsciously, as men often are, with instinctive bodily sympathy with the excitement of the crowd."

He was also drawn to the musical call-and-response of the preacher, and most of all the hymns. "The collective sound was wonderful," he wrote. "The voices of one or two women rose above the rest, and one of these began to introduce variations, which consisted mainly of shouts of Oh! oh! at a piercing height."

Then suddenly the service ended, the congregants "chatting and saluting one another politely as they went, and bearing not the slightest mark of the previous excitement."

Olmsted was clearly stirred, but he struggled to make sense of his feelings and those of others in the church. Ever the rationalist when it came to religion, he recorded the sermon over several pages, analyzing its message and trying to connect it to the congregation's excitement. He couldn't. Rather, it was the communal setting and the preacher's rousing delivery that produced an unconscious and "wholly unintellectual" response, one that left the congregation inspired and refreshed.

Olmsted didn't make the connection here, but the "unconscious" and "unintellectual" experience he described seemed akin to the spiritual, healing uplift he felt in the presence of nature, and that he would later seek to bring to the masses through his parks.

THE CHURCH THE BARBER IN TREME HAD MENTIONED, FRANKLIN Avenue Baptist, stood at the edge of the Ninth Ward, the distressed, heavily black district that had been severely damaged by Katrina. Almost nine feet of water had flooded the sanctuary, which had since been refurbished.

Some five hundred people crowded the pews, with large video screens by the pulpit so those in back could follow the service.

Collecting a cardboard funeral home fan at the door, I squeezed in beside a retired highway worker named Eddie Gentry. He told me I'd been very fortunate in my choice of churches to visit. The pastor, Fred Luter, was a former street preacher in the Ninth Ward who had gone on to become the first black president of the Southern Baptist Convention. Services here were broadcast on fifty radio stations.

"You'll *hear* some preaching today," Gentry said. He'd joined this church in 1995, and when I asked him where he'd worshipped before, he smiled and said, "Nowhere. I was running with Satan then. Don't get me wrong, I enjoyed running with him, but it was time for a change, and when you hear Pastor Luter you come back again."

Seated to my right was Shirley Parker, a retired cook in her eighties, and her daughter Cora Rayford, a hospital nurse splendidly clad in a white dress, white patent leather shoes, a white jacket with polka dots, and an enormous white hat.

"A woman needs to step out sometimes, be fabulous," she said when I complimented her attire. "Mother was strict about that. Now some young people, it's just come as you are."

I asked if her mother had been strict in other ways.

"Oh yes!" Cora exclaimed. "Today, they'd call it child abuse." Her mother beamed as Cora added, "Scripture says don't spare the child, and Mother never did. We've let children become the parents, telling us what to do; no wonder they go astray."

She paused to smile and nod at a group of white teenagers filing down the aisle. This was a youth church group from rural Tennessee, in New Orleans doing volunteer work in areas affected by Katrina. A few other whites were sprinkled in the pews, and Cora said this was a relatively new phenomenon in Louisiana, and one of which she approved.

"Dr. King used to say that Sunday morning is the most segregated time in America," she observed. "That's changing. With all the divisions we have in this society, this is one place we can come together."

Then the band struck up and the choir, forty strong, began singing "I'm a Soldier in the Army of the Lord." Pastor Luter appeared at the pulpit, a graying, heavyset man, nattily dressed in a dark suit with a white handkerchief poking from his breast pocket. He told us to "worship God with your tithe," by placing money in envelopes for white-gloved ushers to collect. He also urged us, after the service, to buy a book for sale in the lobby, *The Ten Commandments to a Financial Healing.*

The service that followed wasn't far in spirit from the one Olmsted had witnessed in the 1850s. Luter and several other pastors took turns at the pulpit, urging on a congregation that didn't need much encouragement.

"Don't let me dance by myself!" Luter shouted, and instantly congregants rose, swaying and clapping. "Praise the Lord with the horns and drums!" The band went into full roar: two guitars, drums, organ, clarinet, trumpet, and saxophone.

By this point all the congregants were on their feet, and I tried to use Cora as my guide. She thrust her arms over her head, shook her hips, shouted hallelujah. I struggled to keep up, like an exhausted dance partner, but felt buoyed by the shouting and the fast-paced throb of the electric guitars.

"Dance unto the Lord! Make a joyful noise! Hallelujah!"

"I gotta praise! I gotta praise! I gotta get it out!"

The sermon, by a guest minister, was titled "Something Good Will Come From This" and began with Daniel's captivity in Babylon. "Get in my biblical Honda and travel back with me," he said, telling how God "hand-delivered" Daniel to his enemies.

"Daniel is not around church folk no more; he's not at the church picnic. He's thinking, 'I'm your boy, Lord, and you put me in a *bad* situation.'" The minister pivoted to Martin Luther King, who "experienced more down days than up" but told a reporter he continued to fight "because I believe something good is going to come from this."

Then he brought his message into the present. "No matter how cute you look today, you've been in some *bad* situations," he intoned, mimicking both women and men. "I've got this wig on straight, but I've been in some bad situations; I got a nice suit and drive a nice car, but I've been in some bad situations."

He continued for half an hour, toggling between Daniel's captivity and the tribulations of today. Like Olmsted, I didn't catch every reference but was hypnotized by the rhythm and repetition of the preaching, which grew louder and faster as the sermon reached its climax.

"Some folks are super-saved and think, 'I'm too blessed to be stressed!' So I came here this morning to tell you—man, woman, cat, or dog—you've been in a bad situation. God told me, 'Son, I want you to go to Franklin Avenue and say this bad situation isn't to harm them but to teach them.'

"'I told you Crown Royal wasn't the answer to your problems, but you didn't listen!'

"'I blessed you with a job and you thought it was your credentials that made it work!'

"'I blessed you with a spouse and you thought it was your hips and eyeliner that did it!'

"But now God is saying, 'It wasn't you it was me! Nobody but me!' And no matter how bad your situation is, if God is in control some good can come from it."

Then, just as Olmsted described, his preaching turned to song, his voice quivering as the organ played. "Somebody shout Jesus! They hung him on a cross, but something good came from that bad situation!"

"Yeah!" the congregation sang back.

"Jesus, come in, Jesus!"

"All right now!"

"Grab your neighbor," he wailed above the throbbing electric guitars. "Shake 'em and rock 'em, rock 'em and shake 'em!"

By this point the minister had unbuttoned his jacket, loosened his tie, and mopped sweat from his face. I'd done the same, while leaping up whenever Cora did and shaking and shouting. The self-consciousness I'd felt earlier was gone, and I didn't care that I was now a parody of a white guy in a black church, clapping out of unison and jerking like a headless chicken.

I didn't share the religious beliefs expressed, and wasn't in a bad situation, just a tourist in the troubled Ninth Ward. But something good had come from this, a warm and uplifting embrace, and I shouted hallelujah.

As the service wound down and we filed out, every face seemed to glow, and I must have shaken a hundred hands. Cora invited me to hear her preach, as she occasionally did at small churches. I even stood in line to buy *The Ten Commandments to a Financial Healing* ("God personally instructed me to 'let go' of my credit cards").

Outside, on the curb, I was looking for a taxi or bus when an older woman asked where I was going and offered me a ride. This was Lillie

Andrews, who worked with children at the church, and formerly at various government jobs in Louisiana.

She detoured through the Ninth Ward to show me some of the damage still visible a decade after Katrina. There were overgrown vacant lots where houses had stood, and boarded-up homes with orange FEMA Xs still visible. Winding back toward downtown, she also stopped at a plaque by the railroad tracks where Homer Plessy launched his failed challenge to segregation in 1892.

Andrews had grown up under Jim Crow and dropped out of Tulane in the 1960s "because there was so much hostility," she said, including being called "nigger" and denied service in a market. She'd also endured isolation and prejudice as the first black woman to work in her government office.

All of which made me revisit the extraordinary welcome I'd felt at Franklin Avenue Baptist. Given the history here, the racism Andrews had experienced, and the post-Katrina tensions over gentrification, why the warm embrace of a white stranger, and the offer of a ride, which I doubted would happen to a black man wandering the city's white-flight suburbs?

"Yes, there's a lot to forgive, and Jesus is all about forgiveness," Andrews replied. But this went beyond Christian duty. She'd seen a lot change since the 1960s and felt accepted when she returned to Tulane for a degree in the 1980s.

These days, she was most struck by young people—"black, white, Asian, Hispanic"—living and working alongside one another in relative harmony. She felt the rebuilding after Katrina had helped bring the city together, in a common effort, with a civic pride and involvement that hadn't always been evident before.

"The media makes it seem like we're far apart, that it's all negative, but in the real world we're less divided now," she said as we arrived in the French Quarter. "We are not going to allow anyone to tear us apart again."

ONE HARD-FOUGHT VICTORY IN ANDREWS'S LIFETIME WAS THE integration of public spaces, including a park tied to Olmsted.

His career as a landscape architect took off in the decades after the Civil War, when the South was far less urbanized than the North and struggling to emerge from wartime devastation. Ill feelings between the regions also lingered. So it wasn't until late in his career that Olmsted pursued significant landscape work in the South.

"Very soon, our Northern cities will have all been provided with parks," he wrote a partner in his firm, in 1894. Also, "the time has passed in which hatred of Abolitionists is an element of consequence in matter of professional business." He therefore advised that the firm become "favorably known" in the South and establish "good will" there.

Olmsted wrote this from Louisville, where his firm had begun work on an extensive park system that would become a hallmark of his landscape architecture. It included three major parks that respected and enhanced each site's distinct topography, such as riverside bluffs and a "gracefully undulating greensward."

But Louisville also demonstrated the limits of the social vision Olmsted first articulated in his Southern travels, when he wrote of parks as democratic public spaces where all could "assimilate" and be uplifted.

In the early twentieth century, city fathers in Louisville segregated its parks and designated one small piece of Olmsted's design as a separate space "provided for the use of negroes." This policy ended in the 1950s, but housing segregation was by then entrenched, and Louisville's parks, as in many other cities, mirrored their surrounding neighborhoods.

During a brief stop in Louisville, I visited Cherokee Park on the city's mostly white and prosperous east side, where the meadows and glades Olmsted envisioned were well tended and busy with bicyclists, dog walkers, and joggers.

Across town, Shawnee Park, on a bluff top Olmsted thought well suited to "gregarious recreation," adjoined a working-class black neighborhood. The park appeared very neglected, its lagoons muddy and grass growing in cracks on the badly paved footpaths. Nearby Chickasaw Park, once designated for "negroes," abutted a sewage treatment plant.

I saw very few people at either; one reason, a woman told me, was that there had been a number of shootings, including one at Shawnee the previous Thanksgiving that left two people dead.

While working on Louisville's parks, Olmsted was approached about designing one in New Orleans. He retired soon afterward, but his family firm undertook the work, drawing up plans for Audubon Park that hewed closely to Olmsted's precepts, including a serpentine lagoon and moss-draped woods that suited the subtropical setting at what had formerly been a sugar plantation.

Though Audubon's open spaces were never officially segregated, park employees were told to bar blacks from sitting on benches and to keep them "moving all the time." Blacks were also barred from a merry-go-round and other facilities, and the mayor closed the park's pool in the early 1960s rather than allow it to be integrated. A biracial committee finally pressured the city to reopen the pool in 1969.

On the early spring day I visited, Audubon appeared well integrated, though its location in an upscale district by Tulane University made it more accessible to people of means, mostly white, than to residents of poorer black wards across town.

Relatively little remained, however, of "the characteristic flowing, verdant landscape" and "sense of peaceful seclusion" that a historic sign noted were central to Olmsted designs. This was largely due to repeated delays in the park's construction, in an era when attitudes toward public spaces were shifting.

By the early twentieth century, Olmsted's vision of parks as oases for scenic contemplation, and for "civilizing" the masses, was coming to be seen as paternalistic and unmanly. Progressives such as Theodore Roosevelt championed the "strenuous life" and the virtues of athletic facilities that Olmsted had judged inharmonious with the "soothing rural influences" he sought to bring to parks.

At Audubon, this meant the introduction of tennis and swimming, as well as a carousel, pony rides, and other activities. Later came a zoo and aquarium. A lagoon and small wooded area survived, but it was hard to quietly take in this setting in the midst of so much exertion, including the Olmsted Oval Jogging Path, a Paracourse FitCircuit with fifteen stations to do exercises, and herds of people on bikes or skateboards.

"A man moving fast cannot enjoy scenery contemplatively," Olmsted wrote late in life, when he feared the pace of modern travel was dulling appreciation of nature.

Also, a golf course occupied the spine of the narrow park, making it difficult to stray far from perfectly mown fairways and greens—the sort of manicured landscape Olmsted disliked—and the distracting ping of balls and carts zipping past. "Proceed at Your Own Risk," warned a sign as I exited a bridge over the lagoon.

As for Olmsted's dream of bringing people together, the great majority of those I passed (or who ran or cycled or grunted past me) had buds in their ears. It was a public park filled with individuals in private silos, sharing space but little else.

I had a pleasant enough amble, and the fitness on display was a healthy contrast to the excess of the French Quarter. But I couldn't shake Olmsted's voice, and could imagine his dismay that a park linked to his family name now bore so little trace of his aesthetic or social vision.

CHAPTER 9

INTO THE BAYOU

"Dat's How We Roll"

S ince Olmsted took his brother along on his journey to Texas, I went through the motions of asking my own to accompany me. A bro-trip, I suggested, before setting off for the South, a sibling escapade in service of historical verisimilitude.

Josh barely dignified this with a response, except to say, "I have a life." In our twenties, I'd lured him to rural Mississippi to film a documentary, and he hated almost everything about it: the fried food, the furnace heat, the Bubba who threatened to shove a gas nozzle up his Yankee rectum.

In any event, Josh was older and bigger than me, the alpha to my boyhood beta, nothing like Olmsted's younger brother John. But midway through my trip, a more appropriate sidekick turned up, somewhat against my better judgment, and his.

Andrew Denton hailed from Sydney, my wife's hometown, where he'd become an Australian Jon Stewart, a leading comic and TV host renowned for skewering the high and mighty. He often mocked Rupert Murdoch and once raised $200,000 on air to dispatch a bounty hunter after a fugitive robber baron. Slight of build, with large glasses and a cerebral wit, Andrew was also a refreshing contrast to the sunstruck, beer-swilling Aussie bloke of American stereotype.

All of which gave me pause, on a family visit to Sydney, when he proposed tagging along for a portion of my Southern trek. He'd seen little of the US apart from trips to California and New York to interview celebrities, and was eager to glimpse "your outback."

In a follow-up email, he called himself an "anal" traveler, careful to plot in advance, and asked what arrangements he should make. "Accommodation, open-carry weaponry, Confederate casual wear?"

By then I was aboard the coal tow in the Ohio River. I warned Andrew that my travels were the opposite of carefully plotted, and sometimes led to misadventure (or what the Franklin Avenue preacher would call "bad situations"). I also reminded him that Olmsted's travel companion had tuberculosis and didn't come to a happy end.

This spurred rather than deterred Andrew, who declared himself perfect for the role. "I feel constantly in the presence of death," he wrote. In fact, he'd just quit his on-air job to research euthanasia and campaign for death-with-dignity laws in Australia. "I can bring plastic bags and helium if required."

So I suggested we rendezvous in New Orleans soon after I'd disembarked from the *American Queen*. He could then ride shotgun with me across Louisiana to Texas, a second pair of nearsighted eyes in territory that would be new to me and very foreign to him.

Andrew appeared as scheduled, with a return ticket via Oregon so he could research its euthanasia laws. He'd also been intrigued to learn that Louisiana had very high death rates, due to diet, smoking, poverty, and other factors, and was home to a literary publication called *Exquisite Corpse*.

"I'm half-dead from jet lag, so I feel right at home already," he said, gamely agreeing, soon after landing, to dive right in with a nighttime visit to the French Quarter.

We paused first beside the Museum of Death, "Where the Big Easy Meets the Big Sleep," its window touting displays on serial killers, morticians, and cannibals. Then we were sucked into the jet stream of humanity surging down Bourbon Street to the cacophonous strains of blues and jazz and carnival-like barkers.

"Hand grenade!" a man bellowed, shoving in our faces what looked like a bong filled with green liquid. "New Orleans' most powerful drink!"

"Huge-ass beers!" another man shrieked, hawking seventy-ounce cups.

"Tooters, who wants tooters!" yelled a woman carrying a tray of laboratory test tubes filled with shots of brightly colored spirits.

Then we reached the entrance to a strip club. "Titties!" the doorman roared. "Come see the titties!"

Andrew slipped on a gob of something that didn't bear investigating. "New Orleans, just how I pictured it," he said. "The Big Sleazy."

We pressed on through the heaving, sweaty crowd until finding a corner that was relatively subdued, apart from two young women in pink hot pants and bikini tops. One of them approached Andrew and asked if he'd come with her to a nearby club, "to have a good time."

Andrew politely demurred, telling her, "Sorry, I'm jet-lagged." But as we turned back to the hotel, he praised the engaging manner of his first female acquaintance in Louisiana.

"Good eye contact, great smile," he said. "She really liked me. I felt a connection."

Not so the local cuisine. The next day I took him to L'il Dizzy's for fried catfish, butterbeans, mac and cheese, and rice pudding. We also joined a raucous, bead-tossing parade through the Quarter that ended at a park with stalls selling monster cocktails, fried shrimp po' boys, and other fare I urged him to sample.

A light eater and drinker with a delicate constitution—how delicate I didn't yet realize—Andrew claimed after just twenty-four hours that he felt anxious about his health.

"You're trying to kill me," he said, choking down our third or fourth plate of heart-stopping grub. "I'm genuinely concerned that my aorta is going to blow out the side of my chest cavity."

Fortunately for him (or so I thought), we were about to leave for rural Louisiana, where I reckoned that ruinous food and drink wouldn't be so readily available. In a rented sedan, we followed the west bank of the Mississippi, searching for a sugar plantation named Fashion that Olmsted visited.

All that remained of it was a roadside plaque and a gated subdivision, Fashion Plantation Estates. But farther on, we reached a number of sugar estates that had survived, with mansions and grounds open to the public.

After my ride on the *American Queen*, I was plantationed out, so we made short work of the "Big House" tours and lingered at only one site:

Whitney Plantation, which had been purchased by a liberal business-man from New Orleans and turned into a slave holocaust museum and memorial.

At the entrance, sculptured heads bobbed atop steel rods, recalling slaves executed after a mass uprising in 1811, their decapitated heads stuck on pikes along the River Road. There were also black granite walls, akin to the Vietnam veterans' memorial in Washington, etched with the names of 107,000 Louisiana slaves and quotes from WPA interviews in the 1930s. One former slave described seeing his grandmother viciously whipped. "My other grandma got branded with hot irons."

Whitney had been open for only a few months, and our tour guide said she'd been struck by "how little most people know about this history." For instance, visitors sometimes asked, "Why did Africans get on the boat to America in the first place?' They don't grasp that it was a violent transaction and slaves had no say."

Our tour group included a black teacher who said his middle-school students in New Orleans were likewise clueless. "They've got this pseudo-militant view that they can do and say what they want. When I tell them they'd have been whipped or killed for behaving that way on slave plantations, they go, 'Are you serious?'"

We ended our tour at a pavilion bearing the names of 2,200 enslaved children who died in this small Louisiana parish in the space of a few decades. On some sugar plantations, roughly a quarter of children perished by age ten; the death rate for adult slaves was almost as staggering.

The causes included yellow fever, also called the "saffron scourge" and the "black vomit" because victims became jaundiced and threw up dark blood. A yellow fever epidemic shortly before Olmsted's visit in 1853 killed almost a tenth of the population in New Orleans alone.

This harsh environment, however, forced Olmsted to reconsider his sweeping judgment of the South's economy. Elsewhere, he'd found ample fodder for his thesis that slavery was as backward as it was immoral: wasteful of land, labor, and capital, technologically crude, a feudal and stagnant system.

Along the River Road, by contrast, he described large-scale enterprises that bore the hallmarks of the nation's emerging industrial capitalism. Planters invested in the newest steam engines, innovative techniques to process sugar, and other "apparatus constructed in accordance with the best scientific knowledge," he wrote.

Their operations were vertically integrated, turning the raw commodity into syrup and granulated sugar, and factory-like in time management and labor specialization. Olmsted wrote that slaves worked in "divisions," according to their strength and skill, bells regulated their workday, and they "seemed to be better disciplined than any others I had seen." They were also housed in quarters "as neat and well-made externally as the cottages usually provided by large manufacturing companies in New England."

None of this blinded Olmsted to the appalling human toll of "converting the swamps of Louisiana into sugar plantations" amid "the annual assaults of the river, and the fever and the cholera." But he judged the "better class" of sugar planters "among the most intelligent, enterprising and wealthy men of business in the United States," and their profits were "immense."

By this point in my own travels, I was becoming numb to the extravagant wealth on show at plantations like those lining the River Road. Andrew wasn't overawed, either. The oak alleys and white-columned mansions conformed to his film image of the Old South—as did the whips and chains we saw at Whitney. But he confessed to being stunned by the brute scale and systemization of the slave regime.

"I somehow hadn't grasped that these were gulags," he said as we passed the estate of a planter who had amassed one hundred thousand acres of cane, four sugar mills, and more than 750 slaves. "Stalin would have felt right at home here."

THIS STRETCH OF THE MISSISSIPPI HAD ANOTHER EERIE ASPECT. At many points, the sugar plantations intermingled with chemical factories. I'd glimpsed some of this industry from the *American Queen*, mostly in the dark. Driving through it by day, we saw live oak alleys and fields of green cane abutting acres of gray pipes, cylinders, and tanks; old graveyards dwarfed by towers and smokestacks; cows grazing near a pool that looked yellow-orange and radioactive. This corridor of the Mississippi was so toxic that environmentalists had dubbed it "Cancer Alley."

Late in the day, we pulled into a Best Western Plantation Inn on a franchise strip bordered by a prison and two massive factories. One made ammonia, the desk clerk informed me; the other was America's largest nitrogen fertilizer plant. "We've got three Superfund sites in Donaldsonville, too," she added.

When I relayed this to Andrew, he looked at me as though I'd suggested we bed down in Treblinka, where some of his forebears had perished. "I get it, lethal chemicals have to be made somewhere, but right where we're sleeping? How am I going to get in the shower?"

After checking in, we navigated through the industrial maze to the handsome antebellum main street of Donaldsonville. The only establishment that showed much sign of life on a Friday evening was the First & Last Chance Cafe, a low-slung brick joint by the railroad tracks. Inside, a dozen men sat in a semicircle around the bar, most wearing duckbill caps and chatting in a lingo I struggled to understand, punctuated by exclamations like "ha!" and "dat!"

The man seated on one side of us chomped on an unlit cigar, making him even harder to comprehend. "I can see his mouth moving," Andrew murmured, "but I can't tell if he's actually saying anything."

On our other side sat a man named Ronnie, and when I told him I was new to this part of Louisiana, he slapped my back. "You've found the right place, boy," he drawled. "Buncha coon-asses."

This startled me, since "coon" was an old Southern slur aimed at blacks. The bar's patrons appeared to be white. Ronnie explained that "coon-ass" was slang for Cajun, though only between friends. "Means you're country, work with your hands. If you're a coon-ass you take pride in that."

I wasn't yet well versed on Cajuns and hadn't expected to meet them until reaching the bayou, another term I was a little fuzzy on. It turned out there was bayou just back of Donaldsonville, and the swampy territory beyond, Ronnie said, "is coon-ass central."

Ronnie farmed cane but many other Cajuns had found work in the chemical plants around Donaldsonville, including most of the other men at the bar. A very friendly bunch, they bought us beers and shared stories about the industry we'd driven past.

"CF, next to where you're staying," said the barmaid, referring to the nitrogen fertilizer plant, "my husband works there; he's been blown up and flash steamed. My daddy, only burns."

"Our mayor, he's *all* burned up," a man chimed in. "Third degree."

"I got blasted into some pipes and burned some once," another man said. "Hurt my back but wasn't too much scarring."

Still, they considered themselves fortunate. Four people had died in explosions at the CF plant alone since 2000. "Two others got kilt over at the propylene plant," a man added. Another factory had leaked sulfuric acid.

These reports prompted an esoteric debate about the comparative deadliness of chemicals produced in the area. The men ran through a long roster, including chlorine, glycol, urea, jet fuel, and compounds I'd never heard of. The consensus winner was ammonia. "That shit will blow right up and you don't want to breathe it, neither," a man said to general assent.

Even so, the men reckoned they might as well be inside the plants, making good money, since living on the outside wasn't especially safe, either. Emissions, toxic waste dumps, strange odors, unexplained rashes and illnesses. Not to mention the railcars filled with volatile chemicals that ran on the tracks beside the bar.

"If one of those blows, we all go, too," a man said. "Poof!" Everyone laughed and took another swig of beer.

Then a wiry man appeared, identified by Ronnie as the bar and restaurant's owner, Billy Guillot, pronounced "GEE-yat." "Hey, Billy," Ronnie called out, "someone wants to talk to you."

"Who the fuck's asking?" Guillot barked.

I meekly raised my hand.

"So long as you're not a fucking tourist or Yankee," he grumbled.

"Actually, I'm both."

"Why didn't you say so?" he replied, handing me a fresh beer before disappearing into the kitchen. He returned with heaping plates of garlic shrimp, garlic chicken, french fries, fried pickles, hog's head cheese ("that's jellied pig parts"), and boudin sausage.

"Lot of Cajun food's a rip-off—cooks throwing pepper on everything," he said, pushing the entire buffet in front of Andrew and me. "This is the real thing because I'm half-French and half-coon-ass."

"And full asshole!" someone interjected.

Earlier in the day, I'd forced a debilitating lunch on Andrew, and after a few bites at the bar, he insisted he couldn't eat any more.

"I don't give a flying fuck," Guillot said. "Eat your fuckin' boudin."

So we did, along with the rest of the food, until Andrew declared he was about to explode, "and there's been enough of that in Donaldsonville already." The men laughed and urged us to come back, which didn't seem likely after the horrors they'd just told us.

By the time we reached our car, Andrew was wheezing and coughing from all the spice. "I feel like I just ate a garlic enema," he said.

To hose out the fire, we stopped at a drive-through daiquiri shop, where a window server handed us supersized peach coladas in Styrofoam cups. Technically, she said, we weren't supposed to put the straw through the lid while driving. So we joined other motorists who had parked nearby to sip at their frozen cocktails.

"I kept thinking about that barmaid whose husband was flash steamed, whatever that means," Andrew said. "'Katie, do you take this horribly disfigured man to be your lawful wedded husband?'"

It was dark as we drove back to the Plantation Inn, apart from the lights and flares from chemical plants. "Oh, look, there's the nitrogen fertilizer, and there's the ammonia that will blow you right up!" Andrew exclaimed, like a demented tour guide. "If Timothy McVeigh built a town, it would be Donaldsonville, Louisiana."

TO PREPARE FOR THE NEXT DAY'S DRIVE, INTO "COON-ASS CEN-tral," I stayed up late reading Olmsted and others who wrote about the French-speaking parishes of rural Louisiana. "Cajun" was a corruption of "Acadian," the term for restive French colonists on the east coast of Canada who were driven out during the British conquest of the eighteenth century. *Le Grand Dérangement*, as this upheaval was known, scattered Acadians all over the map, and some four thousand eventually found refuge in Louisiana.

Most settled swamp bottoms and slightly more elevated "prairie," raising stock and small crops. Acadians also mixed with other peoples in the crazy quilt of Louisiana, creating a hybrid language and culture that was very hard for outsiders to disentangle.

As Olmsted traveled the region, he met people who called themselves "Italian-French," or "Dutch-French," or who had Anglo-sounding names, like Jack Bacon, a man whose birth name was Jacques Beguin. Farmers switched between French and what they called "American" in the same sentence and couldn't tell Olmsted which one was their mother tongue.

"This mixture of nationalities" and languages, he concluded, "must be breeding for future antiquaries a good deal of amusing labor."

One settlement he passed, pointed out to him as an Acadian hamlet, consisted of "a dozen small houses or huts, built of wood and clay, in the old French peasant style." Wealthy planters held these subsistence farmers in low esteem. One described them to Olmsted as "lazy vagabonds, doing but little work, and spending much time in shooting, fishing, and play." Another informant told him they were "habitually gay and careless, as well as kind-hearted, hospitable, and dissolute."

Olmsted overnighted with several French-speaking farm families, describing one home as a timber and mud cottage with deer hide chairs and floors of "trodden clay." But he found their fields "well-cultivated," their children "gentle and winning in manner," and instead of corn pone and bacon he was served venison ragout and "*café au lait* in immense bowls in the style of the *cremeries* of Paris."

Olmsted traversed this rural, French-speaking territory several times in his Southern travels, by boat and on horseback. "The good-nature of the people was an incessant astonishment," he wrote. On the other hand, he judged the terrain "very wet and unattractive" and beset by swarming mosquitoes and "a black gnat called the 'eye-breaker.'"

This landscape also made for toilsome travel, due to "frequent and embarrassing forks" in the road and "notions of distance we found incredibly vague." The distance to one town, he was variously informed, was ninety-six miles, 120 miles, "a good long way," or "thirty or forty miles, and damn'd long ones, too."

I better appreciated this passage the next day, as we wound our way from Donaldsonville to Lafayette, the center of a twenty-two-parish area now designated Acadiana. The direct distance between the two was only sixty miles, but we had to loop far south and then northwest to skirt a morass of bayous, lakes, rivers, and canals, or coulees.

There seemed to be as much water as land, and to make matters wetter, rain cascaded in torrents so heavy we often had to pull over. This wasn't always easy, since the small roads felt like precarious causeways, at risk of being swamped by the dark water sloshing on either side.

We glimpsed a few raised cottages but little else, and only met people during stops for gas or coffee. None of them seemed perturbed by the apparent monsoon. All had Doppler radar on their phones and checked it the way others did text traffic. "Looks like it's passing through," they'd forecast, or "there's nothing behind this squall so should be fine in an hour. Just rain."

But it kept bucketing down, with an occasional break of unbearable humidity before the thunder and rain resumed. So Andrew and I holed up for seventy-two hours in Lafayette, staying with friends of a long-ago newspaper colleague of mine. Our hosts passed the indoor time force-feeding us étouffée and jambalaya.

We ventured out only once, for literal buckets of boiled shrimp, crawfish, and beer. As our waitress approached with a fresh pail, Andrew ventriloquized, "Would you boys like another ton of something?"

Mercifully, on our third morning in Lafayette, the rain eased from deluge to cloudburst. Our hosts, no doubt eager to be rid of us, studied their phones and judged the radar picture "passable" for part of the day. They recommended we take an airboat ride in the "true bayou," in a nearby parish where more than a quarter of the residents spoke French, the highest ratio in Louisiana.

Andrew and I drove for an hour, seeing little beyond the car's windshield wipers, before taking refuge at a roadside joint that was odd even by the high standard for weirdness in south Louisiana. From the outside, Red's Levee Bar looked drunk, its wooden facade tilted forward at a seventy-five-degree angle. A sign by the road read, "No Credit. Credit Died—Poor Pay Killed Him!"

Inside the bar, we found a dozen drinkers who had been there for some time. Or so it seemed from their animated gestures and slurry patois. In Donaldsonville, I'd struggled with the accents but caught most of the vocabulary. Here, apart from a few nouns, I heard nothing I recognized as English or French or any other tongue. Just voices talking over one another, in most cases rasped by what sounded like decades of chain-smoking.

We eavesdropped on this seeming garble for ten minutes before ordering beers. At which point the others gaily welcomed us and began speaking more slowly, in a dialect we could mostly follow.

"Dey caught dem catfish with some nets," one man said, resuming what had evidently been a discussion of fishing.

"Alligators out dere, too. Oh Lawd, at night all you see is dem red eyes."

This interested me, because Olmsted wrote of "alligator-holes" in Louisiana, describing them as "a disagreeable mixture of mire and angry jaws." I asked if gators here ever attacked people.

"Not regular, but we got some aggressive ones," one man replied. "Kinda like you-all, if you hungry you gonna eat and eat and eat."

The speaker was named Marty, and he'd already caught my eye because he was the most voluble person at the bar, bouncing on his seat and waving his hands as he spoke in rapid-fire bursts. He looked to be about forty-five, lean and deeply tanned, with a pencil mustache and chipped yellow teeth.

"I've lost a few fights but won a lot," he told us, "busted ass and had mine busted." He'd also worked at "some crazy shit," such as underwater oil drilling and "blowing up reefs" in the Caribbean so ships could pass through. "Made a fortune I don't got now," he said. "Easy come, easy go, dat's how we roll."

This echoed Olmsted's description of Acadians as carefree and devoted more to play than to work. When I mentioned this to Marty, he said, "Your man sure got dat right. Where else can you fish in de morning, hunt in de afternoon, and drink and dance all night?" He drained his beer. "Some people save and save; I live for the day. Do what I want, where I want, when I want."

An oil-field worker named Randy put a different spin on Cajuns' independent spirit. "We help ourselves, and each other," he said. "Don't look to no government." A few "swamp people" still lived in houses on stilts and "folks take 'em groceries on boats." Neighbors shared what they caught, he added, and as if on cue, a man appeared with a box full of fresh-killed rabbits that he passed around the bar.

Red's Levee also served as a charity venue in Catahoula, a community of about six hundred. The bar's owner, a woman named Liz Maria, said she hosted fund-raisers whenever someone had high medical bills or other tribulations. "To help a lady with colon cancer, we had the men dress up as women and tell jokes all night," she said.

Liz Maria lived next door, and though the bar was open most days from 10:00 a.m. to 2:00 a.m., "I'll come out in my pajamas at any hour if someone needs help. Like some guys on all-terrain vehicles t'other night, they turned up real late and were desperate for beers."

Red's Levee also drew the occasional traveler from France or Quebec. Regulars at the bar found these Francophone visitors very hard to understand, and vice versa. Formerly isolated, Cajuns had become more assimilated in the twentieth century by service in the two world wars, radio and television, and work in the oil industry.

"Our parents spoke French and most here know some," Liz Maria said, but visitors from Canada and France found Cajun lingo "all mixed up" with English words and grammar. Locals, for their part, thought the foreigners spoke too fast. One commonality survived: "We talk with our hands," Liz Maria said.

We'd been at Red's Levee for ninety minutes when a miracle occurred. The sun emerged. When I mentioned our plan for an airboat ride, Marty shook his head. "Those are pussy boats, for tourists. Lemme show you de real thing."

Just down the road a "drag boat" race was about to start at a small park jammed with pickup trucks, boat trailers, and people hauling coolers to the muddy bank of a brown, still channel. Marty called it a lake, though it looked indistinguishable from the countless swampy waterways we'd crossed, identified on road signs as bayous.

Marty deftly borrowed a few unoccupied lawn chairs and perched them by the water. An emcee's voice crackled on a loudspeaker, announcing the first heat. "They're paired up and off!" he shouted, and two speedboats roared past in a blur of engine noise and exhaust. The race, only an eighth of a mile, was over in seconds.

"One hundred fifteen miles per hour!" the emcee boomed to whoops and cheers. After a long wait, another pair of boats zipped by, and then another, turning the calm lake into a deafening, fume-choked channel.

"I love the sound of dem motherfuckers, and de smell," Marty said, whiffing hard at the exhaust. He said some boats used nitrous oxide and other additives to boost the burn rate of the fuel. "To me it's like a good puff of cocaine."

All I smelled was gas, but Andrew claimed he could detect a subtler cocktail of noxious chemicals. "In Donaldsonville, that would be a mere aperitif," he said.

Between races, Marty studied the water for drifting logs and other obstacles that could cause high-speed disaster. "Seeing dem boats wreck, dat's the biggest thrill," he said. "Dey flip and flop all over."

Then he grabbed my arm and pointed at the water. "See dat gar fish jump!" I didn't, and was amazed a fish of any kind could survive in this polluted mire. "Hit one of dem and bad shit happens."

As Marty described it, gar was "an ugly fucker," half gator, half fish, with a snout "like a torpedo" and jaws filled with nasty needles for teeth. "Some are bigger den you and me."

It was hard to catch these thrashing behemoths, which sportsmen stalked with heavy rods, traps, nets, and even pistols. Marty had another method. He went into the bayou at night in a small boat, armed with a spotlight and crossbow. "Just you and dem gar and de alligators and de snakes," he said. "I'm not scared of nothing, and don't turn nothing down."

Many people considered gar a "trash fish," barely suitable for dog food, but Marty disagreed. "I like it barbecued, with tomato gravy. Coon-ass and a little Italian thrown in." He planned to go after gar the next night and urged us to join him. "Biggest thrill you'll ever have," he assured us.

By then, the skies had opened again, so I gave him my number and told him to check in the next evening. Andrew was not on board with this plan. He spent the rest of our drive replaying all the crazy things Marty had told us: busting ass, blowing up reefs, squirting Cheez Whiz underwater to attract and spear tropical fish.

"He's going to lure us out in the bayou so he can hunt *us*," Andrew said. "Then he'll throw me on the barbie with that garfish."

I had other concerns. Spotlighting and firing crossbows at man-sized prey sounded illegal, not to mention unsafe. Also, at one point while listening to Marty, I'd flashed back to West Virginia. Gaunt and jumpy, smoking and drinking and talking in a manic rush, Marty read like a pamphlet titled *Warning Signs of Crystal Meth Use*. With lots of beer thrown in, to soften the buzz.

When I mentioned this to Andrew, he buried his face in his hands. "Hunting swamp creatures at night," he moaned. "In a little boat. With a crossbow. And a meth-head at the helm. What could possibly go wrong?"

Still, after days of rain and seeing little but the inside of bars and buckets of crawfish, I was restless for outdoor adventure. So we holed up for another day, waiting for Marty's call and the rain to stop. Between bouts of lobbying against the outing, Andrew took solace in studying the Doppler radar forecast.

"Saved by the gods," he announced at 6:00 p.m., turning his laptop so I could see what looked like an angry red fog enveloping the bayou for miles around. "I think the technical word for that is tempest. Or typhoon. Or End Times rain."

An hour later Marty called. The connection was bad and I only caught stray words—"gar," "fucker," "storm"—but surmised that even he wouldn't brave the bayou on a night like this.

Andrew did a celebratory jig around the room. Though disappointed at the washout of our bayou caper, I'd formed a backup plan. The barmaid at Red's Levee had told us about an upcoming event a few hours' drive away, in a town where Olmsted spent considerable time.

"Bunch of crazy drunks in the mud," she'd said, "and people getting nekked."

Spared the gar hunt, Andrew had no objections to this escapade. "Sounds like Australia," he said.

CHAPTER 10

CENTRAL LOUISIANA

The Unreconstructed South

I n the 1850s, there was no easy path across the southern half of Louisiana. The roads were "so wet and bad," Olmsted wrote, and the river
and bayou crossings so "ill-tended" that the overland routes were "scarcely
used."

The only other option was the Red River, a winding course beset with
logjams and rocks that engineers blasted with explosives to keep the waterway navigable. Vessels plying the river were irregular, too. Olmsted described the amenities on one steamboat as "barbarous," and aboard another,
he paid for a cabin only to find it already occupied by a man who "was a
good deal bigger fellow than I, and also carried a bigger knife."

This forced him to join two hundred other passengers without berths,
occupying close-packed canvas cots on the deck, where Olmsted couldn't
sleep due to the "exceedingly offensive smell." By day, he and other unfor-
tunates were "driven to herd" into a saloon where a placard of rules forbade
"smoking, gambling, and swearing." It was crammed, around the clock,
with "drinkers, smokers, card-players, and constant swearers."

Men also amused themselves by firing pistols at birds and river flotsam.
"So large a number of equally uncomfortable and disagreeable people I
think I never saw elsewhere together," Olmsted wrote of the deck
passengers.

Among them were free black travelers, as well as enslaved boat hands, bedded down amid the chaotic freight. "A few white people—men, women, and children—were lying here and there, among the negroes."

Another sight that surprised him: cheap editions of *Uncle Tom's Cabin* being hawked by book peddlers on the docks. A few copies circulated on Olmsted's boat, which also happened to be retracing a passage described in the novel. The villainous Simon Legree, having bought Tom and other slaves at auction in New Orleans, transports his chattel in chains on a steamboat to his Red River plantation, terrorizing them along the way.

Olmsted conversed about the novel with a fellow passenger, a slaveholding merchant and planter who disputed Stowe's depiction. "Cases in which niggers are badly used" were rare, he told Olmsted, and abusive masters were shunned. He also disbelieved the character of Emmeline, a beautiful teenager who recoils in disgust from Legree's gropes and leers.

"No coloured woman would be likely to offer any resistance, if a white man should want to seduce her," he said, before telling Olmsted of a planter in his parish who had recently been prosecuted for mutilating a slave in a jealous rage. Everybody believed him guilty. But blacks couldn't testify against whites. "There was not sufficient testimony to convict him," the planter said.

Olmsted recorded many such instances of racial violence and injustice, either told to him or published in Southern newspapers. Only rarely did he observe physical brutality firsthand. The most vivid instance occurred soon after he disembarked from the Red River steamboat, at a plantation where he described "the severest corporeal punishment of a negro that I witnessed at the South."

As he often did, Olmsted obscured his location and didn't name those he met. But the property was so exceptional, and described by Olmsted in such detail, that it's easily identifiable as the estate of Meredith Calhoun, then the fourth largest slaveholder in the South and owner of four adjoining plantations on the Red River.

Calhoun owned almost a thousand slaves and sold more cotton—by far—than any planter in Louisiana, as well as large quantities of sugar, loaded from his warehouses onto steamboats that made regularly scheduled stops at Calhoun's Landing. Olmsted judged the property "the most profitable estate that I visited."

At the time of Olmsted's tour, Calhoun and his family were visiting the property for only the second time in five years. Like many others among the Southern gentry, the Calhouns preferred to reside at a more cosmopolitan and "healthful estate." Their main home was a grand residence in Huntsville, Alabama, the hometown of Calhoun's wife. The family also took extended sojourns in Europe and named one of their plantations Firenze, after the city of Florence.

"The main advantage claimed for slavery," Olmsted wrote, was "the benefit arising to the inferior race, from its forced relation to and intercourse with the superior." But this supposed, paternalistic uplift "amounts to nothing" on large plantations like Calhoun's, where the absentee owner relied on a manager and overseers who supervised 150 to 250 slaves apiece. "Each laborer is such an inconsiderable unit in the mass of laborers, that he may even not be known by name."

Moreover, control of so many slaves required measures that "would be resisted as barbarously cruel" in other settings. Olmsted spent two days touring the estate, describing slaves at work before sunrise and after sunset, "a hundred or two engaged together, moving across the field in two parallel lines."

Behind them marched a tall and powerful driver, "cracking his whip and calling out in the surliest manner" at anyone who lagged. "They are obliged to keep constantly and steadily moving, and the stupid, plodding, machine-like manner in which they move is painful to witness."

Olmsted was also discomfited by the field hands' reaction—or lack of it—as he cantered between their lines. None lifted their eyes from the ground. "Considering that I was a stranger, and that strangers could but very rarely visit the plantation, it amazed me very much," he wrote. "I think it told a more painful story than any I had ever heard, of the cruelty of slavery."

Then he accompanied an overseer and a "young gentleman" as they rode to another part of the estate. The overseer stopped abruptly at a deep gully covered in brush. He saw or heard something and flushed out a teenaged slave hiding at the bottom. She identified herself as "Sam's Sall" and told a convoluted story about why she wasn't at work and was lying in the gully.

"That won't do," the overseer replied. "You must take some—kneel down." When she did so, he "struck her thirty or forty blows across the shoulders with his *rawhide* riding whip," Olmsted wrote. "They were well laid on, as a man would flog a vicious horse or a thievish dog, or a boatswain would lay it on to a skulking sailor."

When Sall repeated her story, the overseer ordered the girl to "pull up your clothes." She drew her garments above her waist and lay on her side, "her face towards the overseer, who continued to flog her with the rawhide, across her naked loins and thigh."

The girl begged him to stop, "writhing, groveling, and screaming," until Olmsted "could not wait to see the end" and rode out of the gully. He listened from the top of the bank until the whip strokes and screams finally ceased. "Choking, sobbing, spasmodic groans only were heard."

Olmsted had seen sailors and other men "cudgeled and beaten," but never with "a hundredth part of the severity used in this case." After describing the scene in the *Times*, he returned to it in his books. "It was a red-hot experience to me, and has ever since been a fearful thing in my memory."

One source of his horror was the demeanor of the overseer, who remained "perfectly passionless," flogging the girl with a "grim business-like face." He acted, not out of sadistic fury toward Sall as an individual, but in accordance with the brutal logic that prevailed on large estates.

As the overseer explained to Olmsted, if he hadn't punished Sall so severely for shirking work, "she would have done the same thing tomorrow, and half the negroes on the plantations would have followed her example."

Violence against slaves was also seen as a "justifiable and expedient" measure, Olmsted wrote, to ensure the safety of overseers and their families, who lived a mile apart on a vast estate where slaves outnumbered whites by almost a hundred to one.

"I wouldn't mind killing a nigger more than I would a dog," one overseer told Olmsted, and he'd almost done so several times. Once, having been "insulted and threatened" by a slave he was whipping, the overseer "put six buck shot into his hips."

But flogging—and the constant threat of it—was usually sufficient to maintain order. Olmsted likened this regime to the harsh disciplining of seamen. "The lash is constantly held over them as the remedy for all wrong-doing." Overseers also spoke like "ship-masters and officers," telling

Olmsted how it was necessary to "break the negroes in" and teach "them their place." The difference, of course, was that seamen signed up and received pay, rather than being involuntarily "enlisted for their lives in the service of their masters."

Olmsted also toured the slave quarters with the plantation manager, "a gentleman of university education, energetic and thorough in his business." His daily rounds included the sick house, where a woman lay groaning in what appeared to be "very great pain." The manager said she'd had "a chill" when he visited the previous day. But after carefully inspecting her this time, he declared that she was pretending to still be sick. "So you'll just get up now and go to the field," he ordered her, "and if you don't work smart, you'll get a dressing."

Another woman, named Caroline, was unable to get out of bed. "There's nothing the matter with her," the manager concluded, "except she's sore from the whipping she got." She, too, was promptly forced to go hoe in the field.

The manager told Olmsted that Caroline had "been delivered of a dead child about six weeks before," and avoided work ever since. "We have to be sharp with them," he said. "If we were not, every negro in the estate would be abed."

The only patient spared this treatment was a woman "bleeding at the lungs." Others unable to do field labor were put to work at lighter jobs. Olmsted's tour included a workshop where a dozen slaves made shoes and coarse cotton clothing. "One of the hands so employed was insane, and most of the others were cripples, or invalids with chronic complaints."

Materially, conditions were similar to what Olmsted saw at other large plantations. Slaves lived in "well built" cabins and received reasonably ample rations of pork, meal, molasses, salt, and tobacco. They supplemented this with their vegetable gardens and chicken coops, as well as game they trapped.

But these small dispensations also served the disciplinary regime. Runaways relied on fellow slaves for food and rarely strayed far, or for long. If they did, overseers "would make the rest of the force work Sundays," Olmsted learned, "or restrict them in some of their privileges." This collective punishment rarely failed to bring the fugitive in.

OVER FORTY YEARS LATER, A CURIOUS ITEM APPEARED IN THE *Washington Post*, soon after Harriet Beecher Stowe's death in 1896. A general who'd met the author revealed a story he'd been sworn to keep secret during her lifetime. Stowe had told him that she'd modeled Simon Legree on a planter she had heard about from a pilot who worked on the Red River. When she described the location and scale of the plantation, the general, who'd been posted in Louisiana, told her this could only be the estate of Meredith Calhoun. "Well he was my Legree," she said.

The general also sketched Calhoun's life and told of his personal brutality. But many of the biographical details were wrong and his account drew a swift rebuttal in the *Post* from a writer in Louisiana. Unlike the coarse, bullet-headed Legree, Calhoun was "rather effeminate," the correspondent wrote, "educated, refined, humane and polished." He identified a different planter, "a rude, uneducated man, exactly of the Legree type," as the likely model for Stowe's character.

Olmsted's account of his own meeting with Calhoun appears to corroborate this. Instead of Simon Legree, the planter seemed a consummate, arrogant aristocrat of the sort Olmsted had met in Nashville. Calhoun had traveled widely overseas and mingled with "the *higher classes* of the Continent," he told Olmsted, as well as having global contact with servants and laborers. This experience had convinced him that the lot of Southern slaves was "superior to that of any white laboring class in the world."

In the North and abroad, "the laborer was degraded, stupid, unable to take care of himself," at the mercy of men who cared nothing for his welfare. The slave, by contrast, had a master with "a direct pecuniary interest in taking care of him." The only other system of which Calhoun spoke approvingly was feudal: "the good old times in England," when the relation between lord and peasant was "more kindly and happy" and akin to that of "master and slave."

Unlike many planters, however, Calhoun made no claims for Christian uplift of his chattel. He and the plantation manager discouraged religious "exercises" because they excited the slaves and interfered with their labor. "They would be singing and dancing every night in their cabins, and so utterly unfit themselves for work." For the same reason, Calhoun also dealt harshly with a white widow who peddled whiskey to slaves from a "shanty of the meanest description." He pursued her in court, and a few years after Olmsted's visit, some of his employees forcibly evicted the woman, setting her adrift in the Red River before burning down her shanty.

More broadly, in his talk with Olmsted, Calhoun argued that slavery posed less peril to character and morals than other labor systems. In New York or Europe, he noted, impoverished workers were driven to crime and prostitution, and if caught, "their whole future was irretrievably blighted."

Slaves were spared this fate. "Expressly designed by Providence for servitude," their station and status was set forever. When a slave "did wrong," Calhoun said, "his punishment did not degrade him or lead to a worse life than before."

OLMSTED WROTE MORE ABOUT CALHOUN'S ESTATE THAN ANY other he visited and clearly saw it as a leading exhibit in the case he was building against the "conceit, avarice, and folly" of the South's master class. But even as he did so, revisiting Calhoun's practices and attitudes in the pages of his Southern books, Olmsted resisted the "red hot" abolitionism of his friend Charles Brace.

One reason: Olmsted's belief that the ills of slavery were too profound and entrenched to be cured by the "mere setting free of blacks." Or, as he put it: "An extraction of the bullet does not at once remedy the injury of a gun shot wound; it sometimes aggravates it."

He advocated instead for gradual emancipation, followed by a sort of civic and economic apprenticeship for freed slaves, so they would be prepared for full and equal citizenship. Olmsted hoped to play a leading role in this paternalistic project, even after he returned from the South and began work at Central Park in the late 1850s.

At the start of the Civil War, as slaves began flocking to Union lines, he sought a position as a "superintendent" of "negroes in a state of limbo between slavery & freedom." As the war raged on, he told a government inquiry that "cities of Refuge" should be established for protecting and "assimilating" freedmen.

He also warned that military victory for the Union would not vanquish "leaders and desperate men" in the South, who would fight on by other means: paramilitary bands, assassination, electoral intrigue, "and all manner of underhanded annoyance and obstruction." The nation must be prepared for a protracted and uncompromising campaign, "for years," to wear down and eliminate revanchist elements and their support from the mass of "nominally submissive" whites.

Olmsted, in essence, foresaw postwar Reconstruction and the undermining of it by white terror, resistance, and the faltering will and effort of a war-weary North. What he couldn't anticipate was that Calhoun's estate, where he saw the evils of slavery most vividly, would become a pivotal battleground in the long, violent, and unfinished struggle to overturn the legacy of slavery.

FOR ALL HIS WEALTH AND CONNECTIONS TO THE "HIGHER classes," at home and abroad, Meredith Calhoun left little mark on the map of Louisiana. The name Calhoun's Landing had long vanished, as had Firenze and the family's other grand plantations, which once lined seven miles of the Red River. I knew their approximate location but wasn't sure, as Andrew and I headed in search of them, if we'd find any trace of the antebellum world Olmsted described.

The driving, at least, was much easier than before. As we left Lafayette, the rain let up and we sped out of the bayou and into a landscape of reddish chocolate-colored fields, scrubby pinewoods, Baptist churches, and settlements with Anglo rather than tongue-twisting Acadian names.

The cuisine also shifted from Creole and Cajun to country Southern. Andrew, having had his fill of crawfish and spice, rejoiced at this—until the waitress at a roadside diner delivered that day's lunch special: a grayish-brown burial mound of meat and soggy bread, drowned in gravy.

"I've never eaten a meal," he said, excavating with his fork, "that looks like it's been put on my plate by a dredge."

After lunch, we turned onto a rural byway, passing a sign that read, "Experience Greatness in Grant Parish," followed by a dead armadillo, its feet in the air. The route led past fields of cotton and corn to the parish seat, Colfax, a crossroads with the ubiquitous Dollar General, a fish and tackle shop, a chicken and burger joint, and little other commerce. Grant Parish was so lightly trafficked that it didn't have a single stoplight.

But it did have a newspaper office, on Colfax's main street, and the news editor was a well-read history buff. When I asked Glynn Maxwell where I might find traces of the Calhoun estate, he said, "You're sitting in it, or on it."

Maxwell unfurled a map of Calhoun's holdings, which had covered twenty-three square miles, including all of present-day Colfax. During the Civil War, the Red River became the scene of heavy fighting, ravaging the cotton economy and Calhoun's estate. Meredith spent most of the Civil War in Paris, where he died in 1869.

"Almost no one here remembers him," Maxwell said. "It's his son Willie that put us on the map, and a lot of people aren't happy about that."

William Calhoun's age, and other details about him, corresponded to the "young gentleman" Olmsted met while riding on the estate. During the Civil War, in his father's absence, Willie assumed control of the massive property and "turned this place upside down," Maxwell said. "Bunch of bodies in a ditch across the street, some say because of Willie. Still a sore subject around here."

He gave me the name of a Calhoun descendant and drew a map of local sites related to "all the killing." He also recommended I look at a trove of documents at the local library, where I'd dropped Andrew a half hour earlier.

I found Andrew at his laptop and giddily reported on what I'd learned. "My kind of town," I told him, "history haunted, lots of sad sites to visit."

Andrew frowned. "Didn't we see the Dollar General already?" He'd settled in, catching up on his reading about euthanasia. "You do your thing. I'm fine right here, dying with dignity."

He would do so for several days while I burrowed into a tale so Gothic it read like a Flannery O'Connor short story. Olmsted had described Willie Calhoun as "delicate." This was diplomatic. Willie had been badly deformed by a spinal injury in early childhood and spent much of his youth undergoing primitive orthopedic treatments. They didn't work. Contemporaries called him a hunchback.

He was also semi-abandoned by parents who traveled for long stretches, leaving him in the care of a doctor and servants in Paris. A teenaged Alabaman who lived at the Calhouns' Paris quarters, while attending finishing school, wrote about "poor little Willie" in her letters home. She described him as clever and sensitive, pining for his absent parents, and subject to periodic abuse by his carers.

Whether or not this upbringing embittered Willie toward his family, he took a decidedly unfilial turn when he assumed control of the Calhoun estate. In the late stages of the Civil War, and immediately after it, Willie championed the rights of those his father had enslaved: renting them land, giving them livestock, supporting a freedmen's school. He also lived among them, with a mulatto woman by whom he fathered two children.

These acts "endeared [him] to the negroes," a traveling correspondent wrote, and "they flocked thither from all quarters" to settle on his property, which became known as a "Mecca" for freedmen.

Willie also became prominent in the biracial Republican government, backed by the federal military, that replaced the ancien régime in Louisiana. As a state legislator, he engineered the creation of a new parish with a narrow black majority, centered on his family's land, and named it for Ulysses S. Grant: Union war hero, newly elected president, and a figure so reviled in the former Confederacy that he canceled plans to tour the South, out of concern for his safety. The parish seat, at the settlement known as Calhoun's Landing, was renamed after Grant's vice president, Schuyler Colfax, an ardent advocate of Reconstruction.

Willie had effectively erased his father's mark and turned Meredith's former slave domain into what whites derisively called "New Africa," or "Calhoun's Negro Quarter of Colfax." He also oversaw the dissolution of the family's vast estate and battled in court with his sister and only sibling over their dwindling inheritance.

"My family didn't discuss Willie," his great-granddaughter told me, when I visited her home near the Colfax Library. "He was seen as a rascal, the opposite of everyone else, always making enemies."

Mary Bonnette descended from Willie's daughter by his marriage to a second cousin from Alabama, whom he wed after leaving his mulatto partner. A retired teacher, Bonnette had grown up in Colfax, in a house Willie built for his wife, who preferred town life to living on the plantation.

"Piece by piece, they just plain lost everything," she said of the family's holdings.

Few heirlooms had passed down to her, apart from a handful of photographs and letters. Bonnette showed me one that gave a hint of Willie's cool relationship with his family.

Writing from Paris in 1861, his mother told of "soirées," "a delightful Opera," and balls at the Tuileries. "Say to Willie that it seems as if he had forgotten his mother," she wrote, "as I have not had a line from him."

TO WHITES IN GRANT AND NEIGHBORING PARISHES, WILLIE CALHOUN wasn't just a traitor to his family. He represented the worst sort of "scalawag," a white Southerner who collaborated with Yankees and former slaves to impose "carpetbag" rule on Louisiana.

Military defeat and the slaves' emancipation were bitter enough pills. Swallowing the reversal of Louisiana's racial and political order, with blacks holding power over whites—that was unendurable. Or, as a paper named the *Caucasian*, put it: "tame submission to the most desolating war of the negro upon us."

As Olmsted had predicted, defeated whites resisted postwar occupation at every turn, by every means, including voter fraud, Ku Klux Klan terror, and coups against the shaky Republican government in New Orleans. But the bloodiest clash in Louisiana—indeed, in the entire Reconstruction South—occurred in 1873 at the heart of "Calhoun's Negro Quarter of Colfax."

The spark was a disputed state election, which led competing camps to claim control of Grant Parish. When Republican officials occupied the parish courthouse, backed by a black militia, wild rumors spread that ex-slaves were running amok: robbing, raping, and bragging that "they intended killing every white man and boy, keeping only the young women, to raise from them a new breed."

A white posse of about 150 men formed, a third or more of them Confederate veterans, commanded by a former officer under Stonewall Jackson. A black force of similar size, led by a Union veteran, dug a rifle pit in front of the courthouse in Colfax.

The face-off seemed, in miniature, a replay of the war that had technically ended eight years before. Blacks referred to their foes as "the Rebels," and later reports told of whites letting loose a rebel yell as they launched a frontal assault on the courthouse, on the morning of Easter Sunday.

For two hours, the entrenched defenders held the attackers at bay. But the whites had the advantage of horses, a small cannon, and rifles far superior to the shotguns and other arms wielded by their foes. They also found a breach, wheeling the cannon under cover of the river levee until it flanked the defenders' earthworks.

The cannon was small and loaded with buckshot and iron slugs rather than shells. But when fired through a gap in the levee, it raked straight into the exposed trench, with terrifying effect.

"KILLED AND MAIMED SOME, AND SCARED THE HELL OUT OF THE rest," Ben Littlepage told me as we stood in his front yard, studying the little brass cannon that had wreaked so much havoc in 1873. "Today, we'd call that shock and awe."

Littlepage was a retired engineer and pecan grower, a large tanned man in khakis, suspenders, and a John Deere cap. He'd also served in the army, in ordnance, and knew his way around artillery. The twenty-four-inch piece in his front yard was originally a signal cannon, fired by antebellum steamboats to announce their approach. It was then repurposed to rain metal on the surprised courthouse defenders.

Above the cannon in his yard, Littlepage displayed another relic: a heavy bell forged in 1815 in Alabama and brought to Louisiana by the Calhouns to regulate the slaves' workday. The bell had remained in service into the 1960s, when tenant farmers still planted cotton and lived in nearby cabins.

"Rang at noon and at quitting time, for lunch and to call workers in from the fields," Littlepage said. He'd worked beside them in summer, as a teenager, planting cotton with a mule team. The landowner provided the tenants with seeds, tools, and shelter, sold them other goods from a commissary, and took half the proceeds from their crop. After settling debts, each family "might clear a hundred or so bucks a year," Littlepage said. "It wasn't an easy life."

He'd gone on to prosper, developing a high-yielding type of pecan and acquiring 1,500 acres of the former Calhoun estate, including its lone surviving slave quarters. Littlepage walked me to the rough-hewn structure, which he'd moved to the yard behind his brick home. It was made of cypress planks and held together with wooden pins. He used it for storage and as the site of a weekly card game.

"It's history," he said. "The black families I worked with here in the fifties and sixties, some of their ancestors may have lived in this building."

We circled back to the cannon, which whites had hidden at a nearby plantation after the 1873 fight. A century later, Colfax's mayor sent Littlepage to buy it at auction, but the town council refused to pay the bill. "So I kept it," he said. "Another piece of history."

The cannon and slave bell perched prominently beside the main road into Colfax, a mostly black town. In Littlepage's telling, the courthouse fight had "led to a period of white supremacy" in Grant Parish that lasted almost a century.

"There was a lot of consternation when civil rights came," he said. "It's kind of done," he added, though tensions lingered, as did conflicting views over "that little race war we had back in 1873."

Given this history, and the cannon's role in the carnage, I asked if he felt any discomfort displaying the weapon as a lawn ornament. Littlepage shook his head. All were welcome to view the gun, and he'd shared it with what he called "spiritual people," blacks who came to Colfax "to feel the atmosphere and see the cannon that killed so many of them."

Having worked with ordnance, he also viewed the 1873 fight through a military lens. "One thing I learned in the army: you don't fight a battle to lose. If you don't take care of yourself, and take control, someone will take control of you."

In his view, that was what the courthouse fight had been about. "Blacks wanted to take over the community. To maintain order, whites took strong measures," including use of this cannon. "It won the day."

But Littlepage acknowledged that the aftermath of the cannon's deployment had not accorded with military protocol. "Whiskey got into the operation and there were some bad atrocities," he said.

ON THE AFTERNOON OF EASTER SUNDAY 1873, UNDER FIRE FROM the cannon, many of the courthouse's defenders fled their trench for the nearby river and woods. Some escaped, but most were captured or shot down by mounted whites. Sixty or seventy others retreated inside the courthouse, a small brick building with a shingled roof that was formerly a stable on the Calhoun estate.

The attackers quickly surrounded the structure, firing at doors and windows. The defenders' situation appeared hopeless, but so did surrendering to whites, who had murdered unarmed blacks in the tense weeks preceding the fight.

The posse could have laid siege to the courthouse, but this risked a protracted standoff that might bring federal troops to Colfax. Instead, whites forced a black captive to approach the building with kerosene-soaked cotton, stuck to the end of a long pole, setting the shingled roof ablaze.

As the fire and smoke intensified, some of those trapped inside waved white paper and cloth from the windows. Their foes claimed that several whites also hoisted a flag of truce, approaching the courthouse door to negotiate surrender—only to be struck by shots from inside. It was this treachery, they said, that ignited the ensuing slaughter.

When blacks finally fled the burning building, whites "shot them down like dogs," an eyewitness reported, "and those that escaped the first fire were ridden down in the open fields by men on horseback and shot without mercy."

Thirty-five or forty others, many of them wounded, were put under guard at a nearby property. At day's end the white posse began to disperse, but a contingent stayed and celebrated their victory with heavy drinking. That night, they marched their captives into the dark, two by two, and gunned them down. Only a few of the prisoners survived, by playing dead.

"In a war of the races," one of the posse commanders explained to a newspaper two weeks later, "*there can be no quarter* . . . the black flag must prevail."

The morning after the massacre, as black women made their way into Colfax to find out the fate of their kin, a white man on the road laughingly told them, "You'll see plenty of dead beeves." When one woman found her son's body, she later testified, "Dogs were eating him."

A day later, US marshals from New Orleans arrived to find Colfax littered with corpses: charred, shot in the back of the head, mutilated with knives, or with faces "flattened by blows from a gun." The marshals oversaw the burial of fifty-nine bodies, interred in the trench the defenders had dug by the courthouse. Some of the dead were turned over to their families, and an unknown number had been carted away before the marshals arrived. Others died later from their wounds.

It was therefore impossible to make a precise body count. A minimum of seventy blacks died, one of the marshals stated; other investigators put the tally well in excess of a hundred. The white losses were easier to determine. Three men died, including two who whites claimed had been shot under a flag of truce. But after studying their wounds, the marshal concluded that the men had been shot from behind, by wild fire from their own side.

In all, the one-day killing at Colfax constituted the worst single slaughter in the South during the bloody decade following the Civil War, a period in which more than two thousand blacks were murdered in Louisiana alone. President Grant, who had seen his share of carnage, termed Colfax "a butchery" inflicted on "citizens" in an unlawful act to seize power by force of arms. The "miscreants" responsible should not go "unwhipped of justice."

Yet they did. Federal authorities were able to round up and try only nine of the posse, on charges of murder and conspiracy "to injure, oppress, threaten, or intimidate" blacks in the exercise of their rights. Three were found guilty but their convictions were overturned.

Appeal to the Supreme Court resulted in a death blow to the legal basis and dwindling powers of Reconstruction. Justices ruled that enforcement of civil and voting rights, in cases of individual or mob action like Colfax, was a state rather than a federal matter. This effectively stripped blacks of protection against terror.

"No way can be found in this boasted land of civilization and Christianity to punish the perpetrators of this bloody and monstrous Crime," Grant lamented of Colfax. "The spirit of hatred and violence is stronger than law."

FORTY-EIGHT YEARS AFTER THE MASSACRE, CITIZENS GATHERED in Colfax to unveil a monument to the three white men killed in 1873. I'd visited scores of memorials extolling the Confederacy, but very few bore inscriptions as blunt and chilling as the marble obelisk at the Colfax cemetery.

ERECTED TO THE MEMORY OF THE HEROES,

STEPHEN DECATUR PARISH,

JAMES WEST HADNOT,

SIDNEY HARRIS,

WHO FELL IN THE COLFAX RIOT

FIGHTING FOR WHITE SUPREMACY

APRIL 13, 1873

The unveiling was attended by visiting dignitaries, "veterans" of the "riot," and relatives of "the martyrs" who "shed their life's blood in a battle in Colfax in order that white supremacy reign supreme," the local paper reported.

Following speeches and songs, the attendees processed to a pecan tree that had "afforded protection and shelter" to white combatants in 1873. The so-called Riot Tree was also where twenty-five blacks had been over-taken and killed, some of them possibly hanged. Celebrants affixed a plaque to the tree trunk, and a student choir sang "Dixie."

As to the legacy of the "riot," the paper concluded: "the unfortunate event of a half century back has been the means of a more complete and better understanding between the races."

Lightning had since struck down the Riot Tree, but the obelisk honoring white supremacy remained, as did a historical marker erected by the state in 1951, beside the rebuilt courthouse. "On this site occurred the Colfax Riot in which three white men and 150 negroes were slain," it stated. "This event on April 13, 1873 marked the end of carpetbag misrule in the South."

At the time these monuments and markers went up, blacks in rural Grant Parish were powerless to object to the glorification of a massacre as a heroic defeat of "rioting" blacks and their "carpetbag" enablers.

"Back then, you had to get off the sidewalk when white folks passed," Charles Napoleon told me, between lawn mowing jobs in Colfax. He mimed a shuffle, his eyes cast at the ground. "That's how it was. Same with that old-time bullshit on the sign by the courthouse. Just look away."

Another older man, Arthur Milner, recalled crosses burning outside his school in the civil rights era, and the danger of passing over the railroad tracks dividing white and black Colfax. If a black kid ventured to the white side, "they'd call you the N-word and start a fight."

The railroad tracks still formed a rough divide in Colfax, most whites living on one side and blacks on the other, in bungalows and federal housing; the sign on one street read, "HUD Loop." But race relations had gradually improved, and Milner's next-door neighbor had been elected Colfax's first black mayor, in 2006.

The mayor's brother had also begun speaking up about public memory of the "riot." A burly minister in his late forties, Avery Hamilton told me that growing up in Colfax, "I never thought about or questioned that sign, or anything else." Then he'd gone to a historically black college in New Orleans and realized, "Whoa, I wasn't just ignorant about our history. I'd been brainwashed to believe a lie."

After moving back to Colfax in the early 2000s, he researched his family and found ancestors on an inventory of Calhoun slaves. He learned that one of them was later executed by whites, in front of his wife and children while mending a fence a week before the 1873 fight. The killing, well documented in the Colfax investigation, inflamed blacks and convinced courthouse defenders that whites were bent on slaughtering them.

Hamilton walked me to the courthouse, jabbing a finger at the historic sign. "That was no 'riot,'" he said. The phrase "carpetbag misrule" irked him, too, casting Reconstruction and the defense of black rights as crooked and illegitimate.

"This was a battle—a very uneven one, like me going up against Muhammad Ali," Hamilton said, "and then it became a massacre. Let's stop dancing around that and deal with our history."

When Hamilton spoke up about the need to reexamine and reinterpret the 1873 event, some whites agreed. They formed a biracial "heritage association" to research the violence and discuss how to present it. This effort included the use of ground-penetrating radar to discern the 1873 trench-works and mass grave by the courthouse, where bones had turned up during construction work. Hamilton had been optimistic about changing the sign, honoring the black dead, and possibly creating a museum.

"I thought, times have finally changed and blacks and whites can come together over this," he said. "Hear all sides and tell the facts instead of a lie."

But the effort stalled. Funds ran low, and property owners feared their land might be seized if human remains turned up. Others saw the historical work as a scheme by meddlers and "muckrakers" to foment discord.

"Learning for the sake of learning is egg head, intellectual elitism," a local white minister wrote in a letter to the editor, decrying the quest for understanding of this "ancient blight" on Colfax. "We don't want any passer-by to come in and wreck the town's racial and social progress."

To Hamilton's further dismay, many blacks felt the same way. "The view is, 'We get along okay, leave it alone, why rock the boat?'" He shook his head. "When you've been held down so long, you take the view your oppressor wants you to."

So the sign about the "riot" and "carpetbag misrule," and the obelisk celebrating white supremacy, had been left unchanged, even as Confederate memorials were coming down across the South. The only recognition of the black dead in Colfax was a service on the anniversary of the massacre, organized by a woman who had lived in California and become interested in African spirituality. She and a dozen or so others read the names of the dead, burned sage, and said prayers in Swahili. None of the few locals who attended were white.

"The facts still aren't out there," Hamilton said, sweeping his arm in a 360-degree circle, taking in the town center. "Amazing, isn't it? Something so important to American history happened right here, and it's like we've pulled a cloak over it."

MUCH THE SAME WAS TRUE OF THE EXTRAORDINARY, CRIPPLED figure Olmsted met while touring the Red River estate. Willie Calhoun, whatever his tangled motives, had instigated a bold experiment to overturn the world to which he'd been born. And he'd done so in the rural heart of the Confederacy rather than in territory the Union controlled from early in the Civil War. Had Calhoun and Reconstruction succeeded, former slaves and their descendants would have had opportunities and rights that were denied them well into the twentieth century.

Instead, following the 1873 massacre, white vigilantes launched a new reign of terror against blacks along the Red River, as well as against white Republicans. Perpetrators of the carnage also took office, submitting blacks to rule by men who had recently slaughtered their neighbors and kin.

Willie Calhoun narrowly survived the violence. Shortly before the 1873 battle, while trying to deliver a letter beseeching the governor for aid, he'd been dragged off a steamboat and almost lynched. After the massacre, he aided the federal investigation and was again mobbed aboard a steamboat, escaping death by serving champagne to his accosters. "We got tight and he got sober," one of them said.

But Willie couldn't charm or pay his way out of trouble as Reconstruction and his fortunes unraveled. He was ostracized by whites, beset by debt, and stripped of property by seizures and sheriffs' sales. One lot was sold at auction to the commander of the white posse in 1873, a man who'd never been tried and had gone on to serve as a local official.

Upon Willie's death in 1891, the Colfax paper strained to avoid trampling on his grave. He was described as "a remarkably eccentric and noted character" whose management of his family's wealth was "marked by strangeness" and "careless lavishness." He "never refused to secretly bestow liberal charity when he thought it deserved," but "seemed through some inconsistent perverseness to delight in being thought otherwise."

Calhoun was buried by the Red River, the obituary concluded. "May the sod conceal all his faults from human eyes."

CHAPTER 11

THE RED RIVER

Heart of Mudness

De clay must be ya bed
Inspite of all ya toils
De clay must be ya bed.

*Funeral hymn recalled by Catherine Cornelius,
former slave on Calhoun plantation*

Olmsted wrote a lot about mud. He rode horses in it, tramped through it on foot, and boarded stagecoaches that routinely became mired in muck.

"When the wheels sunk in the mud, below the hubs," he wrote of one coach ride, "we were sometimes requested to get out and walk." After traversing just fourteen miles in four hours, the coach toppled on its side. Though uninjured, the passengers had to make their way in the dark to the nearest settlement, where they were literally "mud bound" for days.

On another ride, in Mississippi, a coachman frequently stopped to "make a survey with his lantern" to see if the muddy route was passable. If not, he called on passengers "to assist in road-making," with cut trees or fence rails. The previous night, Olmsted learned, travelers had been recruited to pry "the coach out of sloughs" and they'd endured conditions so sloppy that muddy water "entered the coach body."

Swampy Louisiana was the worst in this regard. The main overland route to Texas "could hardly be called a road," he wrote. "It was only a way where people had passed along before"—a boggy trace filled with "glum, determined," and "mud-bedraggled" travelers.

These westbound pioneers slogged through the morass on foot, or in wagons drawn by mules and oxen. Impossible for them to conceive that their mud march would one day become sport for modern Americans, in vehicles known as "monster trucks."

This was the pastime Andrew and I had heard about from the barmaid at Red's Levee in bayou Catahoula. Called "mudding," the hobby's foremost coliseum was a four-hundred-acre property just south of Colfax, originally part of a Calhoun plantation named Mirabeau. A sugar warehouse, Calhoun residence, and slave quarters had long since vanished, and fields sown with cotton and cane were now plowed with dozers for an annual spring rite: the Louisiana Mudfest.

"White Trash Only," read a sign at the small cabin by the entrance gate, just across the road from Ben Littlepage's lawn display of the cannon and slave bell. Another sign stated, "I'll keep my freedom, my money, and my guns, you can keep the change."

This libertarian ethos extended to the casual fellow manning the gate, Ethan Mudge. Since we weren't planning to stay overnight, he waived the entrance fee—ninety dollars for a week's campout—and explained the rules, such as they were. "No glass bottles, no unattended kids, and the third rule I make up if I feel like it."

This was Mudge's third Mudfest and little surprised him anymore. "One guy arrived with a huge plastic dick on his head. That was different," he said. "Most others, they don't flash their dicks or tits until it's dark and the freak show starts."

Unfortunately for us, he added, that wouldn't happen until later in the week, when the Mudfest really got underway and traffic backed up at the gate for six hours. We'd also come woefully underpowered. The Mudfest's twin mottos were "Run what'chya brung" and "Tear it up." We'd brung a low-slung Kia sedan that struggled on unpaved roads and would be crushed like a bug in any encounter with a monster truck.

"Kia, short for killed in action," Andrew observed as we puttered past a parked truck with tires taller than our car and "Whiskey Bent & Hell Bound" emblazoned on the giant grille.

We barely made it up a low rise to the Mudcat Saloon, where Mudge had told us we could find the Parker family, which owned this land and had turned it into a mud park a decade earlier. Before then, Larry Parker told us, he'd run cattle on the four hundred acres and "mud wasn't something you loved. Just got bogged in it all the time."

But one of his sons had moved to Florida and returned with news of this growing hobby called mudding. The Parker property seemed perfect, its soil a mix of sandy silt and clay that's "really thick and grabs the tires," Larry said. Also, his land was enclosed by a bend in the Red River and an oxbow lake, "so we can pump water onto the fields and make more mud whenever we need it."

The spring Mudfest was now the largest such event in the country, attracting fifteen thousand visitors. "God has blessed me with mud, and boys who know what to do with it," Parker said.

The whole family worked the mud farm, including Larry's adolescent grandson, nicknamed Mud Puddle, and his daughter-in-law Becky, known as Mrs. Mud. She gave us a short tour of the camping area in a Ford F-350 pickup. "If you get to slipping and sliding, you have to gun it," she said, deftly maneuvering along a slick path. "If you stop you're going to sink and bog."

The Parkers had heavy equipment on-site to pull out trucks. But getting stuck in the mud was part of the fun. "Mudders remind me of two-year-olds who see a puddle and have to step in it," Becky said. "Same here, except it's big boys with big toys."

The Parkers also provided showers and porta-potties and sold hundreds of cases of beer, although most visitors brought their own. "These people can *drink*," Becky said, particularly the large contingent of Cajuns. "I try to keep things family friendly, but as long as I don't see it, anything goes."

In any event, the serious partying didn't start until dark. Most of what we'd see today, she said, was early arrivals, "just families camping out and doing family stuff."

Andrew and I met our first such encampment a few hundred yards from the saloon. A family of five sat in a circle on all-terrain, four-wheeled vehicles with heavy tires. The family patriarch, Glen Travis, passed us a mason jar of "apple pie" and shared the recipe. Spiced rum, apple cider, cinnamon sticks, brown sugar, and a fifth of 190-proof grain alcohol.

"Apple pie this time of the morning will open your eyes," he said.

He introduced us to his son-in-law, "Blockhead," a rakishly handsome young man with a red straw cowboy hat and reddish-blond curls halfway down his back. The other members of the troupe were Blockhead's sister and her young sons, who were taking a week off school to attend the Mudfest.

"Family that muds together stays together," Travis said. His own son would be arriving tonight with a monster truck, eighteen more jars of moonshine, and hundreds of alcohol-infused Jell-O shots. "That ain't counting all the beer we got in the cooler."

Travis and his clan were "fixing to roll out" for an exploratory ride through the mud. The others perched on solo vehicles but his was a "side by side" with an extra seat. "Wanna come?" he asked.

I glanced at Andrew, who indicated he was happy to stay with our "monster Kia." So I hopped on beside Travis and we rumbled off, down a trail through scrubby woods. Orange flags flapped from the back of each vehicle "because those trucks are so big they can't even see you," Travis explained. "'Course, when the mud's flying they can't see your flag, neither."

There were no other safety features on his ATV, not even seat belts. "I don't want to get trapped in the vehicle if something happens," he said. There was no windscreen, either, and branches whipped against us as we bounced and swerved along the trail, Travis somehow lighting a cigarette and nipping at the apple pie while steering.

"Being it's your first time, I'll take it easy," he assured me, adding that he drove for a living. Travis trucked hazardous chemicals out of towns like Donaldsonville, the Bhopal that Andrew and I had visited on the River Road. Before each haul he signed a form saying he knew the risks involved.

"One day, I'm doing my paperwork and the safety guy says, 'Son, if you think you're about to wreck, open the door, jump, and run before it blows. That's some *bad* stuff.'" Travis chuckled and took another swig. "I'm sixty, still here, living the life."

We emerged from the woods at what looked like a rain-filled bomb crater. This was one of twenty or so pits the Parkers had dug for mudders to romp in.

"Go find us a mud hole!" Blockhead yelled, and one of the boys raced over a berm and into the crater, splashing water until he bogged in thigh-high mud. Blockhead followed, doing a wheelie before he and the vehicle flopped on one side. Travis got out a winch and used his larger ATV to haul out the others. "You want to get as close as you can to getting bogged," Travis said, "and then see if you can get out."

He was expert at this, churning us through slop so deep it washed into my lap. But the others followed the same routine for an hour: finding a hole, bogging in it, getting pulled out by Travis. Then two shirtless young men approached on their own ATVs, sharing beers and intelligence about other pits.

"Follow those boys!" Travis shouted to his clan, and we hurtled in formation, over berms and across craters, like Humvees I'd ridden during wartime in Iraq. Travis cranked his radio to full volume and wailed along to "Country Boy," a love song to trucks and guns and America "the way it is now," a land where "a couple extra pounds never really hurt," and where "you'll never catch me out of the house without my .9 or .45."

I felt as though I'd been kidnapped by friendly aliens for a joyride in a muddy universe almost the opposite of mine. There was no point in resisting. I got stuck into the apple pie. "It goes down smooth but creeps up on you," Travis said, opening the second jar of the morning.

The 190-proof concoction didn't creep up; it blitzkrieged me. So did the noise and exhaust as we reached the "back flat," a lake-sized morass the liquid brown color of the apple pie in my hand. This was the Mudfest's main arena, and a dozen or so monster trucks, ATVs, and improvised amphibious vehicles were testing the muck while others watched from shore.

Andrew was among the spectators, having sensibly abandoned the Kia and slogged on foot to the back flat. "It's like War World One out here," he shouted as vehicles roared out of deep trenches before plunging into other troughs. "The Somme, on meth."

"On moonshine," I corrected. At which point a man behind us bellowed, "Whiskey up here!" Spectators scurried to a table in front of the man's camper, which had a front-row view of the mud pit. We joined them as our host set out mason jars for tasting, like a backwoods sommelier.

"This one's 150-proof Tennessee corn whiskey," Don Weathers said, hoisting a clear concoction. "You'll feel it all the way down." He opened another jar and sniffed at it, closing his eyes. "Peppermint flavored; it goes down easier. You can mellow out with that."

A third jar, of peach-flavored hooch, was already half-empty. "Medicinal purposes," Weathers explained, holding up his heavily bandaged arm. He'd taken his truck for a test spin the night before and toppled over a berm, breaking a window, smashing the door, and badly gashing his arm.

"Just a Band-Aid thing," said his girlfriend, Sheila, who'd been a passenger at the time. The skin not covered by her very short shorts, tank top, and cowboy boots was purpled with bruises. "With this proof, we don't need to worry about germs," she quipped, handing Don the corn whiskey. "It'd disinfect gangrene."

Of more concern was the status of Don's truck fleet. A bulldozer had righted the truck he'd tipped over, but his other had burned up, due to a bad fuel line. The vehicle's scorched remains perched behind his camper.

"It's toast," Don said. "Just kissed forty thousand bucks goodbye."

Another man raised a jar in memory of the deceased. "We're all broke-ass people," he told me, "because our money is tied up in these trucks."

This prompted a highly technical discussion of the cost and labor that went into the monster vehicles. The basics involved mounting the chassis of a pickup truck on military-surplus axles and massive tires, some of them seven feet tall. The engines were likewise supersized, up to nine hundred horsepower—roughly the power of a Formula One racecar. Exhaust and air pipes rose snorkel-like from the hood and roof, so they wouldn't get clogged with mud.

The other details I scrawled in my muddy notebook made little sense on later inspection. "Front transfer case 2.71 to 1 . . . nitrogen shocks . . . driveshaft upgrade . . . gotta have more torque . . ." The moonshine didn't sharpen my slim grasp of truck mechanics.

What came through clear, however, was the do-it-yourself pride in constructing these Frankenstein vehicles. The actual driving was secondary, and the Mudfest wasn't a sports competition in the conventional sense. It was more like a beauty/beast pageant—an excuse to show off what'chya brung and test its mettle.

"If you get stuck right away, it means your shit's not that good," one man said. "But everyone gets stuck eventually." Returning vehicles to action was part of the show, like NASCAR pit stops. "You tear it up, fix it up, and get right back in the mud."

A contractor named Kenny pulled a crumpled paper from his pocket. His current rig was "just a starter truck," he said, but on the paper he'd sketched the big one he planned to construct. "When you build it yourself, if you have a problem you can find it, because you're the one who did it."

A logger named Will expanded on this, describing the hobby as a throwback to "the good old days" when Americans were artisans and tinkerers. A latter-day Ben Franklin with tattoos and a shaved head, he'd built a vehicle from scratch so massive that others called it a "megatruck." He'd also customized the cab, which teetered ten feet above giant tires and five-ton axles from a military salvage yard. Its features included cushioned seats, a protective roll cage, and a hose for washing off mud.

"It isn't made in China or on an assembly line—it's all my own work," Will said. "People today don't have that experience of building something, of putting that puzzle together." He got a thrill just having it on the back of the trailer he used to haul it here. "Stopped for gas and was there half an hour, because so many people wanted to look at it."

It was harder to command that kind of attention at the Mudfest. Last year, Will had quickly blown out his motor and was idled before the big crowds arrived. Also, a man named Mike explained, "Once you get in the big pit, your truck's muddy so fast that it's hard for people to tell it from any other."

For these reasons, most of the early arrivals were drinking more than driving. But Mike offered to take Andrew and me for a spin in the pit. His truck was named Have a Nice Day, with a smiley face on one side and a rebel flag and "Redneck" on the license plate. Mike pressed a button, lowering a ladder for us to climb into the cab. It was otherwise basic, "a mud bogger," he called it, with tires merely fifty-six inches high.

"Nice hole ahead, ya ready?" he asked as we lurched into the chocolate slurry. For a moment the truck tipped so sharply I thought it was going over. Mike swerved the wheel and spun the tires until the truck righted and pulled out. Then he found another hole and did the same. "Shit yeah, we're slinging some mud!"

My next ride, with Don and Sheila, the wounded moonshiners, was a tad hairier. Don's truck had no ladder, so I had to scale the front right tire and pull myself into the passenger seat. There were no seat belts, and the window on Don's side was still jagged with broken glass from his accident the previous night.

His one concession to safety was a plastic trash bag he'd wrapped over his gashed arm. "If we go in the drink, there's gas and oil and other crap in it," he said. "I don't want that getting in my cut."

Then he shouted, "Hang on!" and plunged into the bog, almost whacking my head into the windshield. "That's some deep shit!" Don whooped, before finding traction and barely making it out.

He headed next for an earthen mogul rising from the center of the pit. We crawled up one side of it, at about a sixty-degree angle, so that all I could see was sky—though I couldn't see much out the mud-spattered windshield. At the top of the rise the truck paused for a moment, like a roller-coaster car, then hurtled down the slope and back into the pit with a titanic, mucky splash.

Don took a victory lap around the pit before climbing the mogul again. This time he paused for a few minutes at the summit, giving me a chance to survey the panorama. Mudders roared all around us: spewing fumes, gunning unmuffled engines, churning huge chunks of mud into the air.

"Just tearing it up," Don said, a phrase I now realized referred to the terrain as much as the machinery. Becky Parker, a.k.a. Mrs. Mud, had told me the back flat was home to beaver, alligator, a swamp rodent called the nutria rat, and other critters. It seemed miraculous that any could survive this assault on their habitat.

Don, in his day job, trucked turbines to new wind farms in Texas. "Puts money in my pocket I can burn out here," he said. Monster trucks, on top of other costs, guzzled monstrous amounts of gas.

"You mean, how many gallons per mile," Don quipped when I asked about fuel efficiency. Then he hurtled down the slope, back into the pool of mud, spilled diesel, leaked battery acid, and empty beer cans.

"This is God's toilet," Andrew said when I rejoined him on the bank of the polluted puddle. While I'd been with Don, he had sampled several other trucks. What had struck him was the contrast between the monster mechanics and macho truck names—Brutus, Bandit, Beast—and the relative tameness of the rides.

"The experience was kind of 'meh,'" he said. "You're riding in a truck, only a lot higher up."

Andrew had also struggled to extract much from the conversation, which he rendered in Mudfest dialect.

"I'm drivin' my big truck into that big hole," he drawled.

"Now I'm stuck."

"Now I'm pullin' out."

"Now I'm goin' in again."

This struck him as a mad liturgy or metaphor for sex. "It's all about drive shafts and mechanical *cojones*," he said, as a truck called Coming in Hott! plunged into the pit. "Funny you don't see any trucks with squishy names. We should call the monster Kia *Remembrance of Things Pissed*."

Caked with mud, we spent the rest of the afternoon trudging between pits and encampments. At each campsite, trucks and ATVs sat circled like wagon trains on a man-made frontier, with generators, other mod cons, and gallons of moonshine.

"You boys look like you done some hard muddin'," said a woman named Angel, offering us lawn chairs and yet another mason jar. "Rest your bones; we'll be mixing some lemonade whiskey shortly."

At day's end, we retired to the Mudcat Saloon, to wash down the moonshine with cold beer and to suck up secondhand tobacco fumes instead of truck exhaust. Outside of New Orleans, it was still legal to smoke in Louisiana bars.

"You can drink and drive, too, least here at the Mudfest," said the man beside us at the bar. "And get naked."

"Saw a topless midget on a quad bike last year," reported the man next to him. "Good knockers for a little girl." He'd also watched a naked couple on the hood of their truck "just pounding away. That was a good show."

The flesh baring got underway in earnest when "party trucks" and a "party barge" roamed the Mudfest. Andrew and I found one of these vehicles parked near the saloon. It was a yellow school bus, jacked up high on monster tires, the bus driver's station intact but the passenger area shorn of its roof and seats. This open space had been carpeted, with a chrome rod rising like a flagpole at the center.

"I had a brain fart one day, trying to think of something no one had done before," said James Bowlin, a broad-shouldered man with sandy hair and beard who was busy installing a new sound system. "This bus was out of service, so I bought it from the parish and made it a monster party bus."

Bowlin was a mechanic with his own shop and plenty of spare parts. He was also a provocateur, nicknamed the Mouth of the South because "I don't bite my tongue," he said. "I'm a mouthy son of a bitch who likes to stand out in a crowd."

Hence the bus, which he'd equipped with disco lights, speakers, a wooden Indian holding a beer can, and the chrome pole, for strip dancing. Bowlin had also retrofitted the school bus's safety equipment. When he hit a switch, warning lights went on and red signs swung out the side of the bus, as they'd done when collecting pupils. Except now the sign in front read "Stop"; the one in back read "Strip."

"School's out when this bus comes along," he chuckled. Testing the sound system, he set off one of his signature blasts—a shrieking police siren. "Gotta make a fuckload of noise out here to compete with all the engines."

Bowlin had a monster truck, too, which he drove by day at the Mudfest. "That's for slinging mud," he said. "This is for slinging tits and ass." As long as passengers weren't underage, anyone could climb aboard to drink, dance, and strip—up to one hundred at a time, jostling where school kids used to sit. Even the wooden Indian got in on the fun. "Chicks like to dirty dance up against him," he said.

Bowlin took us on a test loop around the grounds to make sure everything was in working order. We passed vendors opening stalls to sell Mudfest essentials: safety "glow whips," earplugs, dust masks, rebel flags, whiskey, Tylenol. Bowlin left the driving to a friend, so he could drink freely and participate in the party rather than deal with the traffic and other hazards.

"You've got sons of bitches with big tractor tires, slinging niggerheads at you from all directions," he said, adding, "I'm not a racist; that's just Louisiana terminology" for huge hunks of flying mud.

Also, gawkers scooted too close on ATVs or stopped in the bus's path to snap pictures. Between the engine's growl, the blaring music, and the height of the sixteen-ton bus, "you can't see or hear those fucking fuckheads right in front of you," Bowlin said.

Another challenge: the bus's suspension, or apparent lack of it. As soon as we left the main campground for a muddy trace toward the back flat, the bus jolted so violently I was catapulted into the wooden Indian. Bowlin recommended standing in a bent-knee crouch. "You can build stuff for a soft ride, or you can build it to last," he said, having chosen the latter.

Which made me wonder: How could anyone dance—much less strip—while being tossed around like dice and thrashed by branches in the bus's open bed?

"You have to have good equilibrium," Bowlin acknowledged. This was rare, given the alcohol consumed. "Girls just hang on to that pole and flop all over. Adds to the show."

Less entertaining was the inevitable consequence of mixing strong motion and strong drink. "You just hope they puke over the side," Bowlin said. Others tumbled off the truck. Fights broke out, too, "usually over someone's old lady with her pussy hanging out. A dumb ass will ask her name, and her old man will get all shitty about it."

Bowlin described himself as a fearless brawler—"not a yellow spot on me"—and his friend at the driver's wheel was a mountain of a man, with forearms thicker than my thighs. They rarely had difficulty breaking up fights and getting troublemakers off the bus. But two sheriffs' departments were on hand to handle more serious altercations at the Mudfest. "When Mr. Po-Po shows up with a Glock nine at his side," Bowlin said, "the fighting tends to stop."

As we passed a cluster of campers, Bowlin set off the police siren and then went on the bus's PA system to give us a taste of his customary rap. "Hey, motherfuckers, come on the bus! Hey, bitches, come sling your ass!" A few women waved and smiled. But an older couple, cooking hot dogs with what looked to be their grandchildren, glowered back at Bowlin.

"There's always some haters out here," he said. "I don't give a fuck. You can't hurt my feelings because I don't have any, except on the head of my peter."

The only thing that irked him was the attitude of his "old lady," whom he'd been with for eight years. "She's got a set of eight-thousand-dollar titties," he said. "I want her to show them on the bus, but she refuses."

He unbuttoned his own shirt to reveal tattooed flames rising from each nipple. "Got this done the same time she got her tits," he said. "I like to show 'em. She doesn't."

Fortunately for their relationship, she'd paid for the breast implants on her own. Bowlin was previously divorced and had learned a thing or two. "Set of titties or a college education—buy either of those for your old lady and she's done," he said. "She doesn't need you anymore."

We ended our circuit at the main pit, where Bowlin described what the scene would look like on Friday and Saturday nights. Stadium lights, party vehicles at full tilt, ear-shattering music and dancing and stripping until well after midnight. "Fuck me running, it's a madhouse."

By week's end, the mud pit would also be a vehicle graveyard. "Busted trucks, burning trucks, axles hanging off, wheels in the air, pickups with mud up to the hood." If it rained during the week, the terrain really took a beating. "Won't be a blade of grass left anywhere in sight."

As to the human wreckage, Bowlin pointed to a spot where helicopters could land for medical evacuations. There were always people needing stitches or broken bones set, due to collisions or fights. "Might be a broken neck but nothing worse than that," he said. "Just the normal shit when you have fifteen thousand people partying and tearing it up."

On our arrival at the Mudfest, ten hours earlier, I'd been disappointed that we wouldn't see it at full throttle. And when the first round of apple pie kicked in, I'd giddily suggested to Andrew that we camp here in our monster Kia for the rest of the week. But by sunset, when the school bus dropped us back at the saloon, I'd lost my appetite for mud, moonshine, and monster mechanics.

Andrew was sated, too. Rather than sit at the bar, we moved to the saloon's back deck, which overlooked the Red River and a rare vista of unmangled nature. "Nice sunset," Andrew said, "and all I can think is, 'Let's tear it up!'"

I was mulling something else: how to document our daylong marathon. The mudders we'd met couldn't have been more open and hospitable. They'd generously shared their beverages, hobby, and attitudes—which together comprised a garish stereotype of the rural white South. Unlike Olmsted, I wasn't undercover. But I still felt like an infiltrator.

When I confessed these qualms to Andrew, he diagnosed "a bad case of liberal guilt." Raised Catholic, with Jewish lineage on his father's side, Andrew judged himself "guilty of everything, all the time." But he didn't feel so as a visitor to America, on a moral holiday from the sins and conflicts of his own homeland.

He also had more historical imagination than me. Colfax, just around the river bend, had conformed to Faulkner's famous observation, "The past is never dead. It's not even past." But here, on a plantation where countless slaves toiled in cotton and cane fields, the past not only seemed dead, it lay buried beneath tons of toxic sludge and vehicular shrapnel.

Andrew disagreed. "You have to look at it through mud-colored glasses," he said, pausing as a mud-caked convoy roared past, honking and waving. "This was an evil place, slave masters with whips and chains. Now you've got whites in blackface here, tearing that plantation up. I'd call that unpoetic justice."

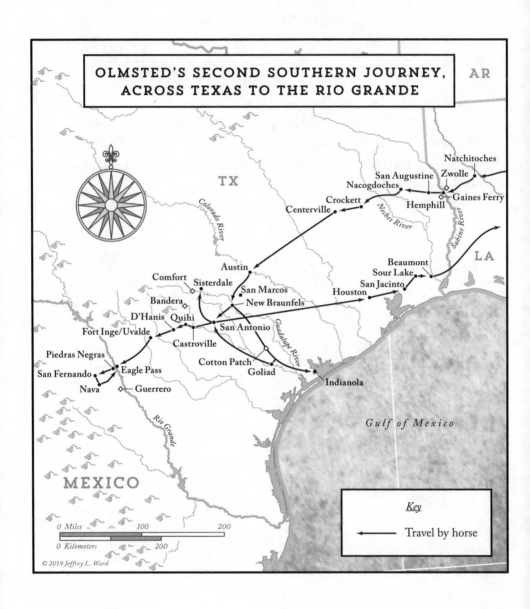

OLMSTED'S SECOND SOUTHERN JOURNEY,
ACROSS TEXAS TO THE RIO GRANDE

AR

TX

LA

Natchitoches
Zwolle
San Augustine
Nacogdoches   Gaines Ferry
Crockett   Hemphill
Centerville

Colorado River

Nueces River

Sabine River

Beaumont
Sour Lake
Comfort   Austin   San Jacinto
Sisterdale   San Marcos   Houston
Bandera   New Braunfels
D'Hanis   Quihi
Fort Inge/Uvalde   San Antonio
Castroville

Guadalupe River

Piedras Negras
San Fernando   Eagle Pass   Cotton Patch
Nava   Guerrero   Goliad   Indianola

Rio Grande

Gulf of Mexico

MEXICO

0 Miles   100   200
0 Kilometers   200

© 2019 Jeffrey L. Ward

Key
⟵ Travel by horse

CHAPTER 12

ACROSS THE SABINE

"Gwine to Texas"

Modern maps can be misleading guides to travel in the hoof and foot era. My trusty *Rand McNally Road Atlas* showed blue-colored interstates slicing straight across Louisiana, and on to Houston and Dallas. Missing altogether was the ancient, winding trace that Olmsted termed "the great thoroughfare of the Texas emigration."

Beginning in the late 1600s, the Spanish blazed El Camino Real, the Royal Highway, linking lands south of the Rio Grande to what was then the northeast frontier of colonial Mexico. The road's terminus, at Natchitoches in present-day Louisiana, became a busy junction of transport and cultures.

"A singularly mixed population lives around here," Olmsted wrote of the town. "The children in the streets speak Spanish, and French, and English (with the negro dialect)."

In the decades before the Civil War, Natchitoches served as the main jumping-off point for emigrants streaming overland to Texas. The riverboat line ended outside the town, railroads lagged far behind, and from here on there was only the "old Spanish trail," Olmsted wrote, which he and his brother "were to follow, with slight deviations" for the rest of their long journey.

For Olmsted, Natchitoches also served as the first dateline for a fresh series of *Times* dispatches, "A Tour in the South-West." These lengthy reports were later incorporated into his second book about the South, *A Journey through Texas: Or a Saddle-Trip on the Southwestern Frontier.*

It was in expectation of this part of the journey, ostensibly a healthful ride, that Olmsted's brother John had accompanied him. In the book's early chapters, recounting their trip *to* Texas, John rarely appears. That changes when they reach Natchitoches and the start of their horseback adventure. Thereafter, the travelogue becomes more dual in voice, and often lighter in tone, beginning with a bemused account of the brothers' "preparations for our vagrant life in Texas."

From a drove passing through town, they purchased Mr. Brown, "a stout, dun-colored, short-legged, cheerful son of a donkey, but himself very much a gentleman." He would serve as a pack mule and interim mount for "the Doctor," meaning John, who had been studying medicine.

For Fred, they bought a "gay little roan creole pony," the property of a local who'd died of yellow fever. "Of excellent temper and endurance," and "full of boyish life and eagerness," the pony was named "little Nack," an abbreviation of the local pronunciation of Natchitoches, which Olmsted recorded as "Nack-i-tosh."

While the brothers were good—or lucky—at securing mounts, they proved less adept at packing them. They'd brought along a cumbersome packsaddle, with iron hooks and wicker hampers, and proceeded to overload it and their other bags.

"Owing to the numerous holds upon civilization we were reluctant to let go," the pony and mule were "so encumbered that we could scarcely find room for the most important articles, viz., ourselves."

Also, "once astride in all this lumber," it was very difficult to dismount. Trotting or cantering posed another challenge, since the heavy, loosely secured gear kept hammering against the riders' legs and the flanks of their mounts. "We set out with some difficulty, amusing rather to by-standers than to ourselves."

After days of trial and error, the brothers learned to adjust their loads to make the travel tolerable for man and beast. But it quickly became apparent that their trip would not resemble the brisk rides they'd taken in New England. "Consideration for your horse as well as yourself soon reduces it to a jogging caravan life," Olmsted wrote, describing a slow trek that was often "laborious and dull."

The brothers' high spirits on setting off were further dimmed by the gloomy woods they entered beyond Natchitoches. They rode all day in "pine shadow," on a rutted quagmire of a road that was royal in name only. The Camino Real's main track was so beset with sand and mud that the Olmsteds generally rode some distance from it, preferring the "pavement of pine leaves."

They also had to maneuver around cotton wagons stuck in mud, and plodding convoys of Texas-bound emigrants. The Olmsteds traveled at the high-water mark of the nation's continental drift; in the 1850s, the geographic center of the US population moved farther west than in any other decade.

This exodus was cast in art and literature as noble and romantic: hardy pioneers, in buckskins and bonnets, cresting mountain passes, cleaving the prairie in Conestoga wagons, crossing the plains and Rockies on the Oregon Trail. But it was Texas that inspired the lofty and enduring phrase for the nation's westward progress. In 1845, on the cusp of war with Mexico, a jingoistic editor, John O'Sullivan, wrote in praise of annexing Texas and declared it America's "manifest destiny to overspread the continent allotted by Providence."

This sanctified tide would wash over Texas to the shore of the Pacific, O'Sullivan wrote, where "already the advance guard of the irresistible army of Anglo-Saxon emigration has begun to pour down upon it, armed with the plough and the rifle."

Olmsted, ever the skeptic, and intent on puncturing "spoony" lore, drew a far less transcendent portrait of the hegira he witnessed. He began by describing Texas-bound emigrant trains from his vantage as a rider approaching from the rear.

"Before you come upon them you hear, ringing through the woods, the fierce cries and blows with which they urge on their jaded cattle," he wrote. "Then the stragglers appear, lean dogs or fainting negroes, ragged and spiritless. An old granny, hauling on, by the hand, a weak boy."

Ahead of them Olmsted glimpsed "the white covers of the wagons, jerking up and down as they mount over a root or plunge into a rut." Reaching closer, he saw the wagons' passengers: invalids, old people, and young mothers and children "whose turn it is to ride," piled together with furniture and other household goods.

"Prime negroes," in better shape than the stragglers, walked behind or beside the wagons, "wrapped in old blankets or gunny-bags." Their masters, clad in homespun and shouldering rifles, appeared glum and spoke little, except to urge on their ox-drawn wagons. "The women are silent, too, frequently walking, to relieve the teams, and weary, haggard, mud be-draggled, forlorn and disconsolate."

Most of these emigrants had trudged all the way from Alabama, Georgia, or the Carolinas, "pursuing, with scarce a halt, their Western destiny." They made ten or fifteen miles a day, "stopping wherever night overtakes them." Roadside amenities were scarce, and the chief occupation of the region's inhabitants was "fleecing emigrants." Adding to this melancholic scene were the many abandoned cabins and wasted fields of pioneers who had come before.

An "inexorable" force seemed to propel these "toil-worn trains" toward Texas. But to Olmsted, the destiny of these refugees and their slaves appeared manifestly doubtful. "What will they be twenty years hence?" he wondered in the *Times*.

The Olmsteds, for their part, could afford to overpay for roadside food, fodder, and lodging, at prices double those in New Orleans. At one stop, they were served cold fatback pork, lard, and stale corn bread. At another, "recommended as one of the best houses on the road," they passed a nearly sleepless night in a crowded, drafty cabin, while dining on food that "was exceedingly coarse and badly cooked," washed down with "the black decoction of the South called coffee . . . it is often difficult to imagine any beverage more revolting."

Grumpily back in the saddle, they found the December weather turning against them. First a chill rain pelted down, then "sleet and snow were soon driving in our faces." They donned all their wraps, including mackintoshes, which became "like a coat of mail with the stiff ice."

By this point, the Olmsteds had seen enough of the Louisiana road and its wretched amenities. So they kept riding through the raw weather toward the river at the state's western edge. "Our animals were disposed to flinch, but we were disposed to sleep in Texas, and pushed on across the Sabine."

AFTER THE MUDFEST, ANDREW AND I FELT READY FOR NEW territory, too. We'd spent four days and nights in and around Colfax, breakfasting at a Cracker Barrel by our motel on the highway and lunching at Colfax's lone eatery, which offered little except fried chicken, fried gizzards, and curly fries.

"It's a worry when McDonald's is your healthy meal of the day," Andrew said, dining on a Quarter Pounder as we drove to Natchitoches, forty miles from Colfax.

Since leaving New Orleans, he'd also developed a gloomy obsession with the many funeral homes we passed, and it was true: Louisiana appeared to have more undertakers per capita than any place in America. "Dying is clearly the growth industry in this state," he observed.

Natchitoches, still pronounced "Nack-i-tosh," turned out to be a pleasant oasis with a tourist trade built around its historic buildings, nearby plantations, and quainted-up commerce: bed-and-breakfasts, shops peddling pralines and fancy soaps, cutely named restaurants like Merci Beaucoup.

Unlike the Olmsteds, we didn't provision ourselves, apart from gorging on fruit and unfried vegetables, food groups we hadn't seen lately and might not see again for a while. "I want to stab this straight into my chest, like an EpiPen," Andrew said, picking up a spear of asparagus.

We also got a foretaste of Texas from three women staying at our hotel. One, a retired teacher named Anna Lou, gaily observed, "This used to belong to Texas so we haven't really left home."

I'd read enough history to know this was a stretch. From the late 1600s to the early 1800s, this borderland was fluid and frequently disputed. Maps of the territory that became Texas sometimes annexed a strip of western Louisiana, though not Natchitoches. When I mentioned this to Anna Lou, she laughed and said, "Close enough. If this wasn't Texas, it shoulda been."

She and the other women were also very Texan in their expansive view of gun rights. There'd recently been a mass shooting in Waco, and I asked if this gave them pause about their state's gun laws.

"The opposite," Anna Lou replied. "Whenever that happens, most Texans think to themselves, 'If I'd been there I could have taken down that shooter before he killed so many people.'"

Her friend, Billy Rose, told us we should presume any Texan we met was packing heat, including women. "If a lady refers to 'little sister,' she's not talking about a sibling. She means she's got a pistol in her purse."

It wasn't clear if this included the three women, but they were fun and lively, joining us for drinks at the hotel and insisting we breakfast with them the next morning. They also urged us to visit if we made it to the Houston area.

Andrew, having never met Texans, was impressed by their warmth and big personalities. "They'll love you right up until they kill you with little sister," he said.

Refreshed by our brief stay in Natchitoches, we climbed back in the monster Kia and left town along a rural road that retraced Olmsted's path to Texas, some forty miles distant. In the early 1800s, this contested borderland had been designated a "neutral zone" where neither the US nor Mexico had full authority. As a result, it became a haven for people on the run or who wanted to be left alone.

Two centuries later, the former neutral zone was still heavily wooded and rather forbidding, much as the Olmsteds had found it. We stopped first to look at a yard planted with a forest of hand-painted signs bearing apocalyptic proverbs. A woman emerged from the house behind and sermonized for forty-five minutes about "false gods" and the run-amok sin destroying America.

"Drink and sex, that's the cheese on Satan's mousetrap," she said, before bringing her hands together with an alarming smack. Then she stared hard at Andrew, telling him, "I can see the demon spirit in someone's eyes."

Our next stop, the small town of Zwolle, welcomed us with a sign for the Holy Water Car Wash ("Will Wash The Hell Out of Your Car") and a huge billboard with graphic photographs of drug-ravaged faces. "Meth Destroys Your Brain, Your Family, and Your Body," it read.

Entering the town center of mostly vacant storefronts, we parked next to a bait and grocery shop with a display of the Ten Commandments and a

Beware of Dog sign. The couple behind the counter stared at us mutely. A few doors down we attempted another conversation, at the small town hall. A local official agreed to talk to us about Zwolle, disappeared into a back office, and never returned.

Across the street we found the town's rhyming food product, Zwolle tamales, sold straight from the door of the kitchen that manufactured them. Except that the man selling the tamales curtly informed us that we had to buy a dozen, and then barked, "No pictures!" when Andrew took out his camera.

While dutifully overconsuming tamales at a booth by the kitchen, we met our first friendly person, though she wasn't local. Bev worked as a food inspector for the state and assured us that the tamale kitchen was sanitary, before regaling us with stomach-curdling details about the many facilities on her rounds that weren't.

But this frank inspector became rather Zwolle-like when I asked about her background. Bev vaguely indicated that she'd lived all over, choosing a term that suited the fugitive territory we were in. "I'm an Else-wherian," she said, declining to share her surname and slipping away before we'd downed the last of our tamales.

At our final stop in Louisiana, we fueled the Kia at a gas station that doubled as a liquor store, across from a bar with a sign that read "Hop in for a Twisted Bunny Daiquiri"—a fitting farewell to our sodden tour of the state. We didn't drink, but I foolishly let Andrew take the wheel for the first time, so I could better observe our crossing into Texas, a moment I'd anticipated since the start of my journey.

Andrew instinctively pulled into the left lane, Australian-style, and hurtled onto the causeway spanning the state divide, forgetting that the speed limit was posted in miles rather than kilometers.

"Goodbye daiquiris, goodbye crawfish!" he whooped. "Yee-hah, we're gone to Texas!"

THE SABINE RIVER TOOK ITS NAME FROM A SPANISH WORD FOR cypress, and Olmsted described it as a narrow waterway fringed by dense woods. At the Camino Real crossing, flatboats had provided regular ferry service since the 1820s, and not only to pioneer families. "The old negro who ferried us over," Olmsted wrote, said that in earlier decades he'd transported many a man "who had ridden his horse hard to get beyond the jurisdiction of the states."

This was the era in which "gone to Texas" had entered the American lexicon, to describe fugitives from debt, legal writs, or other tribulations. The phrase supplanted an earlier term, "French leave," which meant departing without warning or permission. (The French preferred *filer à l'anglaise*, "to leave English-style.")

I'd searched antebellum newspapers for "gone to Texas" and found the tag applied to a range of miscreants, including a forger, an absconding cashier, and an Arkansas governor who pocketed money meant for soldiers.

"You know, sir, the usual course of ruined men," read a typical item. "They sell off secretly, close their shutters, write G.T.T. (gone to Texas) on the door, and are no more heard of."

G.T.T. took on a different connotation after Texas statehood, as settlers streamed in, tripling the white population between 1846 and 1860. In the same period, the number of slaves rose *tenfold*. One of these forced migrants, Betty Farrow, told a WPA interviewer in the 1930s that she'd been raised on a "right-smart plantation" in Virginia. When she was about ten, her master sold out "fo' to gwine to Texas."

For Farrow and other children, this at first seemed an adventure, a "celebration day fo' us." That changed during the grueling overland trek, "from daylight to dark," until the slaves reached a raw farm in eastern Texas.

"I's can't collects how long we'uns was on the way," Farrow said, "but 'twas a long time and 'twarn't a celeb'ation towards the last."

Farrow probably crossed the Sabine where Olmsted and most other travelers did, at the river's intersection with the Camino Real. On the far bank, the ferry's owner kept a tavern and inn of "high rank for comfort," Olmsted wrote, certainly as compared to those he'd encountered on the road from Natchitoches. The two-story log structure was "the first we had met having glass windows," though most of the panes were broken. The fare also exceeded expectations, including mallard ducks from the river that Olmsted deemed "capital."

The proprietor, who owned two cotton plantations as well, displayed less concern for the comfort of his slaves. Their quarters were "mere pens of small logs," chinked "with whatever has come to hand—a wad of cotton here, and a corn-shuck there." Slave girls at the inn wore undersized garments so ragged and filthy they looked as if "they had been drawn through a long stove-pipe."

The site of this rough-hewn Texas welcome center now lay underwater. A 1960s dam had turned the narrow Sabine—pronounced "say-BEAN"—into a reservoir and recreational lake. Crossing a miles-long bridge, we reached a sign welcoming us to Texas and our first glimpse of the Lone Star State: a lakeside marina with RV hookups, DIRECTV, and a motel sign reading, "American Owned and Operated." In the woods behind lay a golf course and split-level homes with satellite dishes.

Andrew was crushed. "I imagined ranch-y, desert-y, cowboy country—a manly landscape, where John Wayne lives." He wrestled the Texas map from my hands. "How far to the Alamo?"

The answer: about 350 miles. El Paso, at the state's western edge, lay five hundred or so miles beyond that, farther away from us than Atlanta or Peoria. Texans might inflate things, but they had a point when it came to the size of their state, which was larger than the entire Northeast, with Ohio and Virginia tacked on.

At the back of the lakeside subdivision we found an old log house, all that survived of antebellum Gaines Ferry. Weldon McDaniel, from the county historical society, was readying the house for a fund-raiser. He said this homestead had belonged to the property Olmsted visited, but it wasn't the inn where he stayed. When the river was dammed, that structure had been disassembled and badly stored. "It rotted away," McDaniel said.

But Sabine County had other historical sites of note. The old jail in the nearby seat of Hemphill was "one of only two in all of Texas with an indoor gallows," McDaniel told us. "Worth a visit."

The jail was a small brick fortress with a Gothic tower at the edge of Hemphill's courthouse square. Its tiny museum displayed an odd mix of artifacts: a tea service, dolls, and other miscellany from locals' attics, and a length of rope used in a hanging at the jail. The pièce de résistance was in the tower. There, a noose dangled from the ceiling, above what had been a trapdoor, right in front of the jail's few cells.

"They used to do the hangings outside in the square," said Louise Adkison, an elderly docent at the museum. "It was a form of public entertainment back then."

She imagined it was less entertaining when the gallows moved inside, in the early twentieth century, affording front-row seats to fellow inmates of the condemned. "Guess it was a deterrent to committing any more crime once you got out of jail."

The only documented execution inside the jail was of a man named Snell, who cut his stepdaughter's throat because she wasn't working hard enough in his field. But the jail figured in a more infamous, extrajudicial hanging.

"There was five blacks, they took them from here to what was called Nigger Hill, and hung 'em from a tree," Adkison said. "Someone took a picture of it."

The full story was so grisly it made national news. In 1908, six young black men had been imprisoned in Hemphill for the alleged murder of a white man. A mob of two hundred whites dragged them from the jail, lynching five and shooting one who tried to escape. Three other blacks were killed later that night.

The photograph Adkison mentioned was reproduced as a postcard, an image of five dangling corpses above several verses of doggerel.

> This is only the branch of a Dogwood tree;
> An emblem of WHITE SUPREMACY . . . .
> The negro, now, by eternal grace,
> Must learn to stay in the negro's place.
> In the Sunny South, the Land of the Free,
> Let the WHITE SUPREME forever be.

Adkison assured us that race relations had greatly improved since. But she startled me by referring to the black part of town as "the Quarters," an eerie echo of slave days. When I queried her about this, she explained, "It's like saying 'across the tracks.' I guess we should say East Mayfield, because that's where it is."

There wasn't much else to see in Hemphill—an apt name for a hang-'em-high town, Andrew noted—so we continued west along Olmsted's path. He described this stretch of the Camino as similar to Louisiana, walled in by pines. Then came "the Redlands of Eastern Texas," where the heavy clay soil was brick colored due to its iron content. "It makes most disagreeable roads, sticking close, and giving an indelible stain to every article that touches it."

Also, though briefly "free from the gloom of pines," the vista remained cheerless: vacant cabins, "deserted wrecks of plantations," and the "truly pitiful" procession of emigrant trains, in driving rain. "Splashed with a new coating of red mud, dripping and staggering," the emigrants "floundered helplessly on."

As yet, there was nothing to reward their long exodus to Texas. "We had entered our promised land," Olmsted wrote, "but the oil and honey of gladness and peace were nowhere visible."

THE PATH OF THE CAMINO THROUGH TEXAS WAS NOW A NATIONAL historic trail, most of it lying along a two-lane rural highway studded with granite markers. Otherwise, the route hadn't changed much from the wooded and semi-abandoned landscape Olmsted described. We passed vacant houses strangled by vegetation, hamlets with no people in sight, and a crossroads with a service station that looked frozen in aspic, circa 1958. An ancient Ford Falcon sat beside the defunct gas pump and a window sign offering "Notions" and "Good Cold Drinking Water and Soft Drinks."

"It's like the Twilight Zone," Andrew said of the eerily empty roadside. "We haven't even seen a funeral home yet."

There were, however, frequent graveyards, in some cases all that remained of bygone settlements. At one, the steeple of the adjoining church had toppled among the graves, mostly rough-hewn slabs of rock laid flat on the ground. Some were marked "Unknown," others etched with images of log cabins and the names of early settlers. "Came to Texas 1824," read one woman's gravestone, as if her life had commenced at that juncture. She died not long after.

Olmsted didn't mention these roadside burial grounds, but they must have added to the gloom of passing emigrants. The first town he came to along the Camino in Texas wasn't cause for cheer, either.

"San Augustine made no very charming impression as we entered," Olmsted wrote, "nor did we find any striking improvement on longer acquaintance." It had fifty or sixty clapboard homes and a half dozen shops fronting "a central square of neglected mud."

As for the inhabitants, he was informed "there was but one man in the town that was not in the constant habit of getting drunk." This was borne out on Christmas Eve, when the Olmsteds witnessed "a pleasant local custom"—townsmen blowing horns and beating tin pans as they went house to house, "kicking in doors, and pulling down fences" until every male had "joined the merry party."

No such jollity was in evidence when we reached San Augustine late on a weekday afternoon. A corner café had a sign reading, "Happy Hour 2–5," but the drinks were alcohol-free. "This is kind of a Christian town," the waitress explained. Bars and liquor stores were illegal.

Old storefronts still ringed the courthouse square and adjoining streets, but many were shuttered, or about to be. "Going Out of Business Sale," read the sign at a medical supply shop, its window filled with walkers, gowns, and wheelchairs. "All Scrubs 1/2 Off." Used goods seemed the town's principal commerce, with several "resale" shops and a flea market called Junk in the Trunk.

One exception was a pleasant, leather-smelling shop on the square called Double EE Boot and Saddle Repair. Its proprietor, Larry Benefield, was also much more chatty than the other shopkeepers I'd approached, including one who'd told me she couldn't talk about San Augustine because "I've only been here thirty years."

When I mentioned this to Benefield, he laughed and said, "Unless you've got a few grandparents in the graveyard, you're kind of an outsider." He'd felt this himself, even though he spent most of his childhood in San Augustine, graduated from its high school, and returned in middle age to take over his father's shop on the square. "They're real clannish here, and set in their ways," he said. "If anyone comes in and wants to change things, folks don't like that."

He attributed this to the area's relative isolation from Texas's fast-growing coast and interior. "Other Texans call this 'Deep East Texas,' or 'Behind the Pine Curtain,'" he said, terms that weren't generally used in a flattering way. "It's like saying we're behind the times, redneck, all kin to each other." He smiled, adding, "They didn't have nothing but mules in the old days, and by the time they finished plowing at the end of the day, they couldn't ride far to get a date."

This farming economy had long since declined, and during World War

II many in Deep East Texas left for the military or defense factories on the Gulf Coast, never to return. Hence the depopulated countryside we'd driven through since the Sabine.

Social change had also lagged. In San Augustine, as in Hemphill, whites referred to black neighborhoods as "the Quarters," and Benefield's high school hadn't integrated until forced by court order in the 1970s. Upon his graduation, there were two sets of homecoming royalty: one white, one black.

He'd gone on to work as a farm manager at state prisons, including one where his entire squad had life sentences. "Hard-core joint, never had a problem, racial or otherwise," he said. "We all got along fine." Then he'd returned to San Augustine and felt as though he'd gone back in time.

"Everybody's still into everybody's business and wants it to stay the same," he said. "This can be a hard little town."

We drove through the rain around the rest of San Augustine. Apart from a few handsome antebellum homes, we didn't, as Olmsted put it, "find any striking improvement on longer acquaintance" with the town. Andrew, however, was gratified to see the San Augustine Monument Company, fronted by tombstones. He also insisted we get out in the rain to inspect two eerie crucifixes.

The first towered by an intersection at the center of town, a graphic life-sized mannequin hanging from tall boards, with a crown of thorns, eyes bugging and mouth agape in shock and torment, bloody hands and feet straining against the nails. The other, on the road leading out of town, depicted Christ as a pallid, faceless blob, a mummy on a cross.

Andrew, a connoisseur of the bizarre, studied this roadside iconography for some time and said nothing until San Augustine was safely in the rear-view mirror. "America is such a fucking weird country, and that town . . ." He shook his head. "Christ was risen, and then they lynched him."

OUR ENTRANCE TO TEXAS HAD DISCONCERTED ME, TOO, THOUGH not because of its strangeness. Rather, it felt oddly familiar. The accents, racial demographics, Baptist churches, and liquor laws seemed closer to the rural South east of the Mississippi than to neighboring Louisiana, with its freewheeling French-inflected character. Nor did East Texas conform to its state's cowboy image, as a swaggering territory that was more Western than Southern.

I later watched the movie *Bernie,* a quirky docudrama about a murder in a town forty miles north of San Augustine. At the start, a local raconteur sets the stage by colorfully explaining that Texas is really five or six separate states.

"You got your West Texas out there with a bunch of flat ranches," he drawls. "Up north you got them Dallas snobs with their Mercedes." Houston and the Gulf Coast formed another region, as did San Antonio and its environs, "where the Tex meets the Mex." Nearer the middle of the state "you've got the People's Republic of Austin, with a bunch of hairy-legged women and liberal fruitcakes."

Last came East Texas. "This is where the South begins; this is life behind the pine curtain." Later in the film, when the trial moves to San Augustine, the local reappears to disparage the jury pool as "cousin-counting rednecks." The defendant, a "highfalutin" fellow who liked fine wine with his fish, didn't stand a chance. "I mean, those people drink warm beer with fried mud cat."

Though comically overdrawn, these riffs held a grain of truth. Texas *was* bewilderingly large and varied, and the region we were in belonged, in many ways, to a separate time and place.

Much of this traced to the world Olmsted described in the 1850s, when the vast majority of Texas's population clustered in the eastern third of the state. The economic staple was slave-grown cotton, the culture and politics staunchly Southern. Texans would vote overwhelmingly to secede in 1861, with their leaders condemning "the debasing doctrine of the equality of all men, irrespective of race or color" and declaring that the "beneficent and patriarchal system of African slavery" should "exist in all future time."

Texas's deep allegiance to slavery and the Confederacy would be obscured in later decades, when the state underwent explosive change and recast its image. But this memo had been slow to reach rural parts of Deep East Texas, like San Augustine County, which gave 46 percent of its vote in 1968 to George Wallace, champion of segregation and the rebel battle flag.

Of which we saw many in East Texas, flying in yards or displayed on vehicles, often in concert with the state flag. Then, forty miles west of San Augustine, we reached a historic town that boasted of its *nine* flags,

including one with a bizarre backstory that was a capsule of Texas's tumul-
tuous history in the G.T.T. era.

Olmsted described Nacogdoches (pronounced phonetically, and not to
be confused with Natchitoches in Louisiana) as "a considerable town" with
several ancient stone buildings and Mexicans "in blankets and *serapes*,"
leaning against posts, "looking on in grand decay." It was one of the oldest
settlements in Texas, dating to the 1600s, and belonged to or was seized by
a host of regimes.

Hence the nine flags that had flown over Nacogdoches, including those
of France, Spain, Mexico, the Republic of Texas, the US, and later, the
Confederate States of America.

But three of the banners were new to me. They dated to the early 1800s,
when freebooters and military adventurers declared mini-empires in Texas,
one of them a short-lived "republic" that had a weird, comic link to
twentieth-century film.

In the early 1800s, Mexico sought to buffer its sparsely inhabited *frontera* against Indians and the expansionist US by contracting with *empresarios*, or agents, granting them land and other privileges in exchange for
settling and developing Tejas. On paper, the *empresarios*, and those they
imported, pledged fealty to Mexico and the Catholic Church. In practice,
the overwhelmingly Anglo-Protestant immigrants inhabited a legal and
social netherworld, outside the US and a thousand miles from central authority in Mexico City.

Stephen Austin, the first and most famous *empresario* to arrive, was a
skilled diplomat who adopted a Spanish name and successfully settled some
three hundred families. But the fourth, Haden Edwards, was obstreperous,
hiking prices and terms of ownership for land in his grant around Nacogdoches. Settlers objected, and Mexico canceled Edwards's contract. But
rather than forfeit the $50,000 he'd spent on his venture, Edwards and a
band of allies declared his defunct grant the independent Republic of
Fredonia.

In 1827, Fredonians took over an old stone trading post in Nacogdoches
that served as a military and official headquarters. In front of it they hoisted
a flag inscribed "Independence, Liberty, Justice," with white and red bars—
an emblem of unity with aggrieved Indians, whom Edwards believed would
rally to his cause.

Few of them did, and both Mexican troops and militiamen aligned with Austin marched on Nacogdoches. Edwards and his fellow insurgents fled to Louisiana, extinguishing the Republic of Fredonia just three weeks after its birth.

But memory of the rebels endured, and so did their adobe "fort." By the time of Olmsted's visit, the ancient Spanish building had been "put to the uses of the invading race," he wrote, and converted into a saloon.

Then, in the early 1900s, a Jewish vaudeville troupe called the Four Nightingales performed in town. Accounts differed, but it appears that the show was poorly received, and when someone shouted that a mule was running amok outside, audience members emptied out to witness the spectacle.

Upon their return, the miffed performers began to ad-lib. They mimicked a mad mule and joked, "The jackass is the finest flower of Tex-ass," among other forgettable gibes.

But the audience loved it. And according to Marx Brothers lore, this was when two of the young brothers in the troupe, Julius and Adolph—better known today as Groucho and Harpo—realized their future lay with slapstick and mocking humor.

As a childhood fan of the Marx Brothers, my favorite of their films was *Duck Soup*, in which Groucho plays "His Excellency," Rufus T. Firefly, the feckless leader of a bankrupt banana republic called Freedonia. Could this have been inspired by the brothers' memorable visit to Nacogdoches?

The Fredonians' fort had been reconstructed outside downtown, as a small museum that made no mention of the Marx Brothers. Yet Fredonia was everywhere: the name of a street, a hotel, a bank, a church, an elementary school, and several small businesses. It was also mentioned on the historical plaques that seemed to adorn every sidewalk and building—even lampposts—in the old district.

"A dentist would be concerned here with all the plaque," Andrew said, channeling Groucho as I dragged him to every marker I could find. "I'm expecting to see a plaque saying that this was the site of the original plaque in Nacogdoches."

Finally, a few blocks from the original site of the stone fort, at Main and Fredonia Streets, we reached a building with plaques identifying it as the town's former opera house. The text mentioned the Marx Brothers' visit and a mule kicking a cart to pieces and dragging it down Main Street—an event that "launched a new direction in their career." It also quoted one of Groucho's riffs. Searching for a rhyme on the town's unwieldy name, he blurted, "Nacogdoches is full of roaches."

We learned, too, that the troupe had been arrested the next afternoon, for playing euchre on a Sunday, on the porch of a hotel across the street. This building was now a mission and soup kitchen with a plaque of its own. Still, no mention of Fredonia and its possible link to *Duck Soup*.

Sarah O'Brien was the only person we met who'd considered the question. She worked at city hall, marketing Main Street, and was always looking for fresh angles.

"Fredonia's all over town; the Marx Brothers must have seen the name and heard the story," she said. "It would have appealed to their absurd sense of humor." During a convention in town, city officials had dressed as the Marx Brothers and a mule and ran down Main Street. "I'm not sure many people got the joke," she said.

Still, she added, "We've always got the real Fredonia, and our nine flags. Texas has had only six flags. Anytime you can beat Texas, it's something to brag on."

A friend visiting her office, Shane Smelley, offered a different view. The Fredonia rebellion was misbegotten, "and lasted, like, a day," she acknowledged. But it was still worth remembering.

"It's a Southern thing," she said. "We take pride in *whatever* happened, even when it wasn't so good, like the Confederacy. As lost causes go, you could do a lot worse than Fredonia."

I'D HOPED TO SHARE MORE OF TEXAS WITH ANDREW BEFORE HE caught his flight to Oregon. But we'd lingered longer than anticipated at almost every stop and been slowed by near-constant rain.

Andrew nonetheless insisted he'd learned a great deal about America and its history. "I came to this country wide-eyed and full of innocence," he said, "'O say can you see,' Davy Crockett, and all that. You've ripped the scales from my eyes."

I wasn't sure how to take this, or Andrew's habit of tapping notes into his phone as he gazed out the car window, or while watching TV ads at motels and restaurants, an odd fascination of his.

Whenever I asked if I could see what he was writing, he'd demur, claiming it was "just some casual observations about America."

After four days touring East Texas, we headed for the Houston airport, sticking to small roads so Andrew could get a final taste of rural Americana— mostly log trucks, self-storage units, and exclamatory church signs. We also detoured to visit tiny Fred, Texas, in honor of Olmsted.

At Fred Grocery, Andrew studied the eclectic bait and merchandise— night crawlers, wiggle tails, hog's head cheese, and pressed ham—and queried two women at the counter about the town's name.

"Just someone named Fred," one of them said. "Fred something. Or something Fred. Used to be called Fred's Mule Lot."

"And what do people do in Fred?" he asked.

"We fish. We hunt. We go to our Fred Walmart—that's what we call the dollar store," the other woman said. "Then there's downtown Fred, which is us."

The women, in turn, were fascinated by Andrew's accent, exclaiming, "Oh gosh, wow, Australia!" and interrogating him about his homeland. Andrew returned to the car flushed with pride. "It was like I'd announced I was a terrapin," he said. "'Look at him—he's exotic!' I felt really special."

To complete his Texas bucket list, we stopped at a gun shop, which also sold crossbows, knives, and camo lingerie, and then at a Western-wear store so I could camouflage myself for the rest of my Lone Star journey. I tried on tight jeans, boots, a ten-gallon hat, and a pearl-button shirt, and asked Andrew's opinion.

He burst out laughing. "You look like a Hasidic cowboy. Rhinestone Jewboy. Shlomo Crockett. King of the Wild Kosher." Trying on similar attire, he dubbed himself Kid Calorie, and declared, "Okay, pardner, let's cook up some beans."

Instead, we had a last meal at a country diner where the menu included fried lug nuts (battered sausage, deep-fried), fried pickles, fried catfish, and fried alligator. Andrew sampled most of it as a final gesture, with a Coke to go. "I drank the first gallon, rest is yours," he said, handing me the trough-sized cup.

As we neared the airport, I felt dejected at the prospect of seeing him off. We'd traveled for weeks without a cross word, except on the subject of spotlighting garfish in the bayou. I'd miss his company, his jokes, even his constant whining about the food.

"Forget your flight," I told him. "Let's power through the rest of Texas."

Andrew chuckled. "If I had a spare aorta, I would."

He was already relishing his arrival in Portland, where he looked forward to kale smoothies and "coffee organically drained through the beard of a hipster." And sure enough, the next morning, I received an email that read: "My breakfast of egg white omelette and fresh fruit plate is now engaged in cell-by-cell combat with entrenched enemy forces of beans, crawfish, and fried shit."

At my repeated urging, he also sent the notes he'd taken on his phone and billed as "casual observations about America." This was like calling *Saw* a movie about loggers. I wasn't anticipating de Tocqueville, but what I got was a phantasmagoric series of snapshots from our journey.

> *"Funeral homes . . . Cemetery St . . . Man brags he never had a*
>   *customer complain. He sells caskets."*
> *"Over-cooled La Shackleton Inn, corpses stay for free."*
> *"Donaldsonville. Ammonia. Urea. Chlorine. Jet Fuel . . . Second-degree*
>   *burns . . ."*
> *"The Crawdad Corridor . . . The Crappie Shack . . . Dead Armadillos."*
> *"McDonald's. Exxon. Cracker Barrel. Burger King. Subway. Same*
>   *shit everywhere."*
> *"Black Belt. Bible Belt. Fat Belt."*

These observations were interspersed with send-ups of the TV ads he'd studied, mainly for medicines (advertising drugs is illegal in Australia) and carrying the obligatory warnings about side effects:

> *"Spine liquefies. Arms fly off. Bladder flies into mouth. Head turns*
>   *backward."*
> *"Explosion of spleen and bladder. Talking in tongues. Gangrene of the*
>   *eyeball."*

There were also bleak observations about riding with me:

"First class tour guide through the not very good."
"The concierge of crap."
"Low expectations will not be exceeded."
"Sad people correspondent."

Then more pages filled with food and anxiety about his health:

"Bag full of gar balls . . . You want the snout or the anus?"
"Smashing vegetables in my face. Putting bananas on me like leeches."
"I want the lord to move inside me, through the layers of corn chips and beans."
"Phantom chest pains."

And finally, toward the end, the notes became frenzied, barely coherent:

"Foot long. Bloated. Blood. Is this it?"
"Put on the full armor of God!"
"He has risen! He is here!"
"Cheese on top of open heart surgery."
"One dollar drive thru daiquiri pawn shop funeral home."
"Self-storagjjijinbbe funeral home. In bbjnb"
"Stop organ harvesting in China. Ok. I will."

That was the last entry. Even allowing for comic hyperbole, it seemed our trip had driven Andrew to the brink of mania and hypochondriac breakdown. His subsequent emails struck a dark tone as well.

"I can taste the high-cholesterol despair from here," he wrote when I reported on my continuing travels in Texas. "Me, I'm deep down the euthanasia mine. Pretty much my entire working day is taken up with death, pain, and dying. Keep 'Little Sister' close by your side and never order the 6lb crawfish. Kid Calorie."

This was all darkly amusing until, after a long and rather confounding silence, I heard from Andrew's wife. Doctors had discovered critical blockage of the arteries, and Andrew was about to go in for emergency open-heart surgery. But she assured me he'd maintained his sense of humor, blaming his condition on crawfish and "mud in the lungs" from our trip.

Andrew pulled through, following a quintuple bypass, and informed me via his "lawyer," Melvin Finagle, that my notes from the road "are now officially evidence in your pending court case. On our advice, Mr. Denton is suing you on two counts of premeditated murder by food and one count of felony blackguarding."

By then, I was gone from Texas, due to a health issue of my own. Cholesterol wasn't the cause, despite my steady intake of Southern grub, Tex-Mex, and the state's brisket barbecue.

The blame belonged to Olmsted—or rather, "the son of a donkey" he took across Texas. This had given me an idea that didn't end well.

CHAPTER 13

GULF COAST

Oil and Water

The passion for bigness—the confusion of size with greatness—is,
like nearly everything else, carried to extremes in Texas.

John Bainbridge, The Super-Americans

O lmsted reached Houston on his return ride across Texas, after a sylvan passage through miles of pine forest "which extends to the town."
He emerged at a port settlement of a few thousand people, at the head of a
bayou so narrow that steamboats could barely turn around.

Houston was then just eighteen years old, having been founded by speculators who bought up barren land and named it for a hero of the new republic, claiming, "There is no place in Texas more healthy." In the annals
of boosterism, this rivaled Erik the Red's naming of Greenland.

"Houston (pronounced Hewston) has the reputation of being an un-
healthy residence," Olmsted wrote. It was low, swampy, and beset by bugs
and fevers, with thin soil that gave only a "meager subsistence" to nearby
farmers.

Townspeople rarely ventured far from the bayou landing; the inhospi-
table territory beyond was "completely terra incognito." Even so, Olmsted
sensed Houston was a coming town. Its inhabitants, many of them German

immigrants, were very enterprising and had made the settlement a major hub for shipping and trading of cotton, slaves, and other goods.

"The principal thoroughfare, opening from the steamboat landing, is the busiest we saw in Texas," Olmsted wrote, also noting the "signs of the wealth accumulated," including fine residences and "a most remarkable number of showy bar-rooms and gambling saloons." Houston was gaining on the more established and much larger Galveston and would "not be easily overridden" by other competitors.

Olmsted, characteristically, took the long view and was prescient in recognizing that this rough-edged bayou port had promise. But even he could not possibly have envisioned that the Houston of 1854 would swell into a megalopolis of six million people, spread across a metro area of some ten thousand square miles—larger than his native Connecticut.

As the urban planner he became, Olmsted would also be appalled by Houston's near-absence of zoning, its despoliation of nature, and the sprawl and spaghetti of highways that made it the antithesis of a walking city. The downtown's sterile street grid, steel-and-glass towers, and multistory parking garages would also leave him cold. Or, rather, hot and bothered, since it was hard to walk more than a few blocks in the smothering heat before retreating to the nearest air-conditioned space.

That was my first impression, while probing for coherence in a place that lacked it, and frequently locked in traffic on the beltways that orbited Houston like rings of Saturn. There seemed an absence of urban density, and little connection between the core and its surrounds, a galaxy of wards and suburbs and exurbs that went on . . . forever. In the home of NASA, I felt like an astronaut lost in the Andromeda nebula.

Once I surrendered to Houston's diffusion, the city became much more agreeable. It had a sultry, good-times undertone of Cajun and Creole, topped with a soupçon of just about every other culture on the planet. As Houstonians were quick to point out, their city was the most ethnically diverse in the nation.

Downtown, new digital parking meters had instructions in English, Spanish, and Vietnamese. On one boulevard I passed, in quick succession, a halal butcher and Arabic-lettered car wash, the office of Dr. Nguyen, countless Latin American shops, and a church sign that said welcome in five languages, including Swahili.

The city also had a lesbian mayor and a plethora of hipsters, hookah lounges, tattoo and piercing parlors, and craft beer bars. The economic contrasts were dizzying, too. East of downtown, Houston was predominantly poor and black, including a ward known as the "Bloody Fifth" because of its gang violence. A short drive west on the freeway—short by Houston standards—brought me to a swank district of baronial homes where I parked between a Porsche and a Mercedes and strolled past "a curated collection of distinctive boutiques and restaurants," one of which offered "an intimate morning of shopping and personal styling."

Houston was way too big and complicated to get my arms around as a blow-through traveler. It also felt very remote from Olmsted's world and the route I'd been tracking in Deep East Texas. I tried to meditate at the Rothko Chapel, ate my first insect taco, went to an Astros game—and felt like a truant from the Camino Real. Olmsted's journey along the Royal Road would lead me later to Austin and San Antonio, settlements where he stayed much longer, so I'd have other chances to scout urban Texas.

But I took the long way back to the Camino, detouring to visit two historic sites Olmsted stopped at during his ride on from Houston. He reached the first after following a "well-marked road" east, which quickly dwindled into "cattle-paths" before reaching a hamlet "laid out upon the edges of the old battle-field."

This was San Jacinto, site of an 1836 battle that was well known in Olmsted's day, and since forgotten by 99 percent of Americans. Except within Texas, where San Jacinto was taught and celebrated as a sacred site of Lone Star independence.

This reverence wasn't obvious from the approach to San Jacinto's hallowed ground. The battlefield lay twenty miles east of central Houston, amidst a petrochemical Mordor so vast it made Donaldsonville, Louisiana, look like a nineteenth-century mill village. Smokestack plumes had replaced the smoke of battle, along with flaring refineries and storage tanks weirdly adorned with murals of 1830s horsemen waving muskets and sabers.

I turned onto Independence Parkway, honoring the fight for Texas liberty and now a testament to the state and the nation's dependence on fossil fuels. I passed the OxyVinyls Battleground plant, Caustic Battleground

ChlorAlkali, and a dozen other facilities before reaching the swampy point of land where Sam Houston led his ragtag rebel army to victory over a much larger and better-trained Mexican army.

The "battle" at San Jacinto lasted eighteen minutes. Houston and his men surprised the encamped Mexicans during a siesta, and after brief combat massacred hundreds of soldiers. They captured most of the rest, including Antonio López de Santa Anna, the notorious commander who had slaughtered the Alamo's defenders six weeks earlier. The fight at San Jacinto effectively secured the independence of the newly minted Republic of Texas, and Sam Houston became its first president.

A hundred and eighty years after this triumph, there wasn't much left of the battlefield to tour, apart from walking trails hemmed by industry and polluted marsh. "Enter Water at Your Own Risk," read a sign by a swampy lake where the greatest carnage occurred.

But the main attraction at the battlefield was its twentieth-century makeover: a tribute to Texas overstatement. Laid out like the National Mall, the park had a reflecting pool and a shaft modeled on the Washington Monument, except the reinforced concrete phallus was a few feet bigger than the one in the nation's capital.

"This is the tallest masonry monument in the world," an elevator operator assured me as I rode to the top for a 360-degree panorama of shipping channels and petrochemical plants. "It's in *The Guinness Book of World Records.*"

Lest the monument's height fail to impress, the inscription at its base put San Jacinto on a par with Waterloo and other exalted fights. The defeat of Santa Anna, the "self-styled 'Napoleon of the West,'" led to the annexation of Texas, war with Mexico, and the "acquisition" of "one third of the present area of the American nation." As such, "San Jacinto was one of the decisive battles of the world."

This narrative elided a fair bit of history and slighted other great battles. The casualties on the Texas side at San Jacinto totaled twenty-three, compared to fifty thousand Americans at Gettysburg. And while Sam Houston was a fine and brave commander, badly wounded in the fight, his foe was no Napoleon.

At San Jacinto, Santa Anna was caught napping, allegedly with a mulatto woman named Emily West. He fled the attack and dressed as a common soldier, although some accounts say as a woman. Among other bizarre ventures, Santa Anna later lived in New York and tried to market a rubbery tree extract called chicle, which his inventor partner turned into chewing gum. Hence, Chiclets.

I learned this and much more at the large museum and bookstore inside the San Jacinto monument. There were tomes on Texas's brief war for independence, fat biographies of Houston, and a slim item titled *The Official Texan's Guide to the Other 49 States*. Its pages were blank. Texans might be the most boastful people on the planet but their braggadocio came with a smile.

On a rainy weekday morning there were few people to talk to about San Jacinto and its outsized fame in Texas. But I found a fitting spokesman the next day as I circumnavigated one of Houston's interminable loop roads. Charlie Fogarty owned a restaurant that stood out from the franchise sameness beside most cloverleaves. The ornate Steamboat House was named for and fashioned on Sam Houston's last home, and in the parking lot stood a twenty-five-foot statue of the famed general and first president of the Texas republic.

"Sorry I'm not in uniform today," Fogarty said, greeting visitors at the door. He was solidly built with silver hair and bushy muttonchops, like Sam Houston in his later years. He often dressed the part, too, for events at San Jacinto and elsewhere.

"Luckily for us," he said in a deep booming voice, assuming Houston's character, "at the time of our attack, the Dick-tator Santa Anna was being entertained by Emily West and deep in the heart of Texas."

Fogarty's fascination with Houston had been sparked decades ago, when he ran a custom frame shop and was given an enormous oil painting of the general that had been displayed at the centennial of San Jacinto. He later went into the restaurant trade and dreamed of "building a place to hang that portrait." The result was the Steamboat House, as much a shrine as an eatery, its rooms and walls crammed with memorabilia and artifacts, not all of them genuine.

"In the framing business you learn to antique things," Fogarty said, leading me down a hall lined with guns and swords. "These were shiny before; now they look old." He stopped at a display of Republic of Texas banknotes. "Replicas. I put coffee on them to get that brown look."

There were also maps, one showing the outline of the original Republic of Texas, which extended into parts of today's Wyoming, Colorado, New Mexico, Oklahoma, and Kansas. For almost ten years, this vast republic had its own ambassadors and other trappings of a nation-state.

This was one reason Texans felt themselves distinct from the rest of the country. "A lot of states were drawn with a ruler and pencil," Fogarty said. "Louisiana was purchased. We fought to become an independent republic and then joined the United States."

We moved on to the formal main dining room, adorned with the oil portrait of Houston and scenes of battle. Beneath them, diners sawed into eighteen-ounce rib eyes and other Texas-sized dishes with names like the General Houston. "Sam was a man of large appetites," Fogarty observed, "for women and booze most of all."

In his view, this helped explain Houston's appeal to Texans. He was tall, handsome, and bombastic, a dandy who wore a jaguar-skinned waistcoat and ordered a plumed hat and green velvet suit from France for his inauguration.

He married twice, to much younger women ("I fancied that you were in my arms, and we were felicitating ourselves," he wrote to one), not counting a native woman he cohabited with while living among the Cherokee, who called him "Big Drunk." Houston also shot a man in a duel and severely caned a congressman in public.

"Texans hate boring and you could never call Sam that," Fogarty said. Olmsted had noted this, too, writing that "Sam Houston and his eccentricities" often came up in conversation, and "there was much laughter at his expense."

Fogarty also admired Houston's refusal as governor to support secession (a stance that cost him his office) and his prophecy that it would lead to a "sea of blood and smoking ruin." Northerners "are not a fiery, impulsive people as you are," he warned Texans, and would overwhelm the South "with the steady momentum of a mighty avalanche." He died two years later, soon after the decisive Union victories at Vicksburg and Gettysburg.

"Sam understood that politics is about compromise and he couldn't be bought, unlike all the crooks in Washington now." Fogarty borrowed my biography of Houston, puffed out his chest, and inhabited the Hero of San Jacinto once again.

"Suh, you prate about sobriety and morality," he intoned, as Houston had to a foe who impugned his honor. "You are a canting hypocrite, whom the waters of Jordan could never cleanse from your political and moral leprosy."

Fogarty closed the book and said, with theatrical *tristesse*, "They don't make 'em like Sam anymore."

FROM SAN JACINTO, OLMSTED RODE THROUGH TERRITORY MARKED by its "lowness, flatness, and wetness," forcing him to sometimes wade through "miles of marshy pools." Then he reached an "odd natural phenomenon" he termed a "fountain of lemonade." This was Sour Lake, formed by two mineral springs that bubbled up with an "outburst of inflammable gas" and gave off a sulfurous smell.

In the 1850s, this strange site was a popular health resort, where visitors drank and bathed in the astringent water. The proprietor promised that a range of diseases would be "permanently cured" by the spa's water and mud treatments, including rheumatism and "secondary syphilis." Its patrons included Sam Houston, who spent a month there in hopes of relieving the pain from his old war wounds. Instead he contracted the pneumonia that killed him a few weeks later.

Olmsted described "rude bathing-houses" at Sour Lake, perched by dense brown pools that had "the properties of the Persian and Italian naphthas," an ancient term for flammable gases, tars, and peats. Unbeknownst to Americans at the time, Sour Lake sat atop an enormous deposit of the petroleum that would transform Texas a half century later.

Sour Lake bordered a densely wooded area known as the Big Thicket, and the drive there took me across the sort of low, flat, and wet landscape Olmsted traversed. The forsaken settlements he described hadn't changed much, either, including Liberty, which he called "a stunted hamlet." I stopped there for a cold drink and asked the man at the counter what people here did.

"Meth," he replied. "And Oxy."

Next came the crossroads of Nome, so-named during the first oil boom, in the early 1900s, when gold-diggers were pouring into its namesake in Alaska. Then I reached a depleted burg with a sign reading, "Welcome to

Historic Sour Lake Where Oil & Water Met." This past-tense slogan was sadly apt, describing the boom-and-bust cycle that had raised and then sunk Sour Lake and so many oil towns.

Pump jacks were strewn all over, rusting in backyards and even beside the library, which had a room with photographs of Sour Lake's heyday. In 1902, drillers hit a series of gushers, among the first major finds in Texas. In a single year, Sour Lake's population soared from forty to almost ten thousand, and spectators flocked to watch regularly scheduled "spoutings" that shot oil hundreds of feet in the air.

The frenzy also spawned a tent city, fifty-six saloons, duels and race riots, oil spills that flooded the streets, fatal gas emissions, and frequent blazes. The close-packed wooden derricks kept catching fire, and soon the business district went up in flames.

By then, crude prices were falling and the easy money had vanished, so drillers moved on from the scorched town to newer, more promising strikes. Described in 1903 as "the largest producing field in the world," Sour Lake boomed for about eighteen months before entering a long decline.

And parts of it were still sinking, literally, due to the massive, watery crater that had formed in the area of the most intensive drilling. I learned this from Steve Radley, whose family extracted small amounts of oil from pumps in and around the town. He offered to show me the sinkhole and other sites in his Super Duty King Ranch Ford.

"I live in this truck; it's my transport and office," he said, climbing into the huge vehicle, its bumper adorned with a Confederate flag. A strongly built man with sandy hair and pale blue eyes, Radley was a libertarian and had disabled the seat belt beeper so he didn't have to strap in.

This truculence extended to his views on race. He had black employees he got along with well, he said, "but my problem with blacks is, don't make me do something because you want to do it. MLK Day? Fine. You celebrate it, but why should I have to?"

He drove past a small black neighborhood he said "some still call 'Niggertown'" and also pointed out a fishpond that had once been a community swimming pool. After integration, he said, "packs of blacks came," and the pool was shut down.

Just outside town, we reached an area once known as Shoestring: a narrow stretch where derricks had stood "bumper to bumper" in the early 1900s.

Only a few sheds and storage tanks remained. The potholed route through Shoestring dead-ended at the sinkhole, which had drowned the rest of the road—along with wells and rigs, a house, and a few cars. Power lines poked above the surface of what was now a fifty-acre water hole.

Sour Lake sat atop a cavernous salt dome, "and once the oil was pumped out of it, the land had no support and down she sank," Radley said. The sinkhole was gradually expanding, and no one knew its present depth.

He drove down another road and said, "Follow me," before taking off on foot through the swampy woods. Trailing him as best I could, bushwhacking through the dense growth and muddy water up to my knees, I began to appreciate the meaning of Big Thicket. When I caught up with Radley, he was standing at the edge of a pond, beside old boards sunk in the mud.

"This was one of the bathing houses at the old spa," he said. At the library, I'd read about visitors in the 1850s plunging into the sulfurous water here, "like a battalion of puddle ducks." Radley pointed across the water to the site of a bygone gazebo. Other resort amenities included a croquet lawn, bowling alley, guest cottages, carriage houses, and the grand wooden inn.

"The story I always heard," Radley said, "was that they burned it all down so they could get at the oil." The only surviving homage to the once-famous spa was a liquor store in Sour Lake called Dr. Mud's, named for a former slave who became renowned for his healing treatments at the resort.

I felt as though I could use one, having been badly scratched by branches and thorns and chewed by mosquitoes during our hike. I'd also sampled the waters at Sour Lake, since I was drenched. "Wouldn't drink it, though," Radley said. "There's all kinds of shit in there from the old wells and crap people have dumped in it."

He and his family still operated a few wells nearby, pulling only about ten barrels of oil a day from Sour Lake's depleted reserve. This was called "stripping" old fields that large companies had abandoned. Like most strippers, the Radleys were a small family enterprise that survived by doing everything themselves and keeping costs low.

"We're old school—poke a hole and hope for the best," Radley said. But strippers were different from wildcatters, who explored undrilled ground. "They have no earthly idea what they'll find. We have an idea—sometimes."

The Radleys were currently probing a field in nearby Beaumont that had produced the first and most famous gusher in Texas, just before the strikes at Sour Lake. Steve suggested I come see the family operation the next day and meet his father, Rhea, who had grown up in Sour Lake and was a true veteran of the oil patch. "You can find him at lunch at the Rockin' A Cafe in Beaumont; he eats there every day."

OLMSTED DESCRIBED HIS TRANSIT THROUGH BEAUMONT AS THE wettest and most difficult of his long ride across Texas. The Neches River bordering the settlement was so high it had turned the surrounds into a "sucking mire" that was shoulder deep. One of the horses became delirious and fell with a "whining snort, upon her side," kicking furiously. Dragging the horse and their drenched possessions from this muddy "porridge," the Olmsteds spent a day "scraping, rinsing, wringing out" at a "little village hotel" before finding drier ground to the north.

Like Houston, Beaumont had since exploded, with subdivisions and refineries sprawling for miles, and the Neches River had been dredged into an industrial shipping channel. Just off the highway I found the Rockin' A Cafe, but locating Rhea Radley wasn't quite so easy. Inside the large, hangar-like restaurant sat a sea of burly white men in duckbill caps, hoeing into fried okra, pork chops, and other Southern fare. "Fat People Are Harder to Kidnap," read a sign on the wall.

After asking around, I was pointed to a deeply tanned man with a full head of graying hair and a camo cap that read, "Have Guns Will Travel." It was Rhea Radley's eighty-third birthday, and he was holding court at a table of fellow oil-field veterans.

"Remember when we made money at three dollars a barrel?" Rhea said to another man. "Now these young people are crying that it's only sixty dollars." He turned to me, adding, "Mind you, that three dollars went a long way in the 1950s."

Radley had since survived all the wild swings in the oil business, which had bankrupted many others. "Oil's a gambling business, just is," he said.

"If you can't handle the dry holes and ups and downs, you don't belong here."

The work also required a high tolerance for filth. "I call the oil field the mud pit," he said. "I'm in it all the time. Fell in a big greasy muddy pit once and lost my glasses. Never did find them."

After polishing off his corn bread, fried catfish, and pie, Rhea drove me to the field his family was working, beside Spindletop, site of the "Lucas Gusher" in 1901 that spouted for nine days, saturating the landscape and setting off the first oil boom in Texas. We stopped at a viewing platform to gaze at the site of the historic strike. The vista was peaceful, birds tweeting in the marsh grass. But as we drove a little farther on, the landscape began to resemble Belgium or northern France circa 1920.

There were trenches and berms, muddy pits that looked like shell craters, shattered pipes and other shrapnel, and miles of ground torn up and denuded of the trees that gave Spindletop its name ("spindle" referred to the cypress grove that once covered the rise).

Adding to the World War I atmosphere were signs reading, "Caution: Poison Gas May Be Present." One of the gases that seeped from wells and tanks was hydrogen sulfide, so potent that it corroded fences and could be lethal to humans after just a few seconds of exposure.

"Smells like rotten eggs," Rhea said, though at higher concentrations it had no odor. "Got gassed badly once, felt so weak I couldn't hold my head up and had to spend four days in bed." His son Steve had once been gassed, too, passed out and hit his head, waking with blood on his face. They weren't wearing respirators and still didn't. Rhea had also incurred injuries from falling pipes and other hazards.

"Like I told you, it's a gambling business," he said. "I'll pick shit with the chickens if I have to, but I'd rather make a living out here."

We drove on to the shed that served as the company office, joining Steve and a few other workers. Steve showed me a map covered with circles and squares, to distinguish active wells from dry holes. Of the last seven they'd drilled, only one had turned up oil. In all they were lifting about one hundred barrels a day on their leases here "and barely breaking even," he said. "I'm not going to be a millionaire stripping oil, but I'll eat real good and I'm driving a King Ranch Ford."

The Radleys were likewise cavalier about climate change and the threat it posed to their livelihood. "The country's too dependent on oil and everything that comes with it," Steve said. "It's in our clothes, polyester. Flush a toilet, that's using PVC pipe. Oil's a commodity the world can't live without, and we're supplying it."

There were echoes in this of Olmsted's opus, *The Cotton Kingdom*, which took its title from the infamous boast of a South Carolina senator and planter three years before the Civil War. Defending slavery, James Henry Hammond mocked Northerners as "our factors," or brokers, in a cotton trade that was indispensable to the national and global economy.

"No, you dare not make war on cotton," he defiantly proclaimed. "No power on earth dares make war upon it. Cotton *is* king."

At Spindletop, ground zero of the Texas oil industry, and close to the world's largest concentration of refineries, it was easy to regard oil as an unassailable monarch, too. But even in Texas, oil's century-long reign was under challenge from the state's many wind farms and from growing environmental concerns. Rhea acknowledged that the end might be coming.

"We're so little I don't get excited about what our oil does to the planet," he said. "I feel like I've been productive for my family and society. But if the scientists are right, my family will have to find something else to do."

Steve, in fact, had advised his own son to consider another career path. Not because of global warming, but because he'd dug so many dry holes that he wondered if there was enough oil left in these fields to strip.

"I told him he should be a chef or in waste management," Steve said of his son. "People are always gonna eat and always gonna shit. Never a recession in those fields."

CHAPTER 14

CROCKETT, TEXAS

"The Drift of Things" in Ruby-Red America

You may all go to hell and I will go to Texas.

Davy Crockett, 1835, upon losing his congressional seat in Tennessee

On their entry into Texas, after crossing the Sabine, the Olmsteds toiled for two weeks through mud, pine, and meager settlements before reaching more hospitable terrain. "Our journey through Eastern Texas was disagreeable in the extreme," Fred wrote in a letter, "an unpleasant country and a wretched people—bad supplies and bad weather."

En route, the brothers took on a guide, "an old original Texas settler, ranger, and campaigner" identified only as "B." They also bought a horse for John that bore some kinship to its less-than-robust rider. The shapely chestnut mare was "dainty" of build, and "took from the first the position of a high-bred girl who had seen better days."

The brothers purchased weapons, too, "for provision as well as defense," including a shotgun for fowling and a deadly new firearm, the Sharps carbine. "In sure hands (not ours)," Olmsted wryly noted, the carbine could fire eighteen times a minute, with a range over a thousand yards.

They also packed Colt pistols, of which Olmsted observed, "There are probably in Texas about as many revolvers as male adults, and I doubt if there are one hundred in the state of any other make." The ubiquitous Colt was known for its accuracy, ruggedness, and easy handling in the saddle. "A border weapon, so reliable in every sense, would give brute courage to even a dyspeptic tailor."

Lastly, the travelers bought tin kettles, a frying pan, and an ax, completing their preparations for camp life, which they were "determined to begin at once," having had their fill of overpriced lodging in "pens of logs" and a steady fare of moldy corn bread, pork "fry," and bad coffee.

Unfortunately, their first nights outdoors in East Texas "met with some blundering difficulties." While their guide B. slept snugly in a blanket by the fire, the brothers preferred the "canvas curtains" of their tent and "lay quietly awake til morning dawned, numb with cold."

The next day, foraging for food, all they found were "a few small and watery sweet potatoes." So they drew on their store of supplies, sampling a newfangled product called "Borden's meat biscuit." Its creator and namesake had recently introduced this "portable meat glue" to great acclaim. Composed of meat extract and flour, and baked into hard crackers, Borden's biscuits needed only boiling water to produce a nourishing soup, ideal for mariners and pioneers crossing the plains.

Or so claimed the early reviews. "After preparing a substantial dish of it, according to directions," Olmsted wrote, "we all tried it once, then turned unanimously to the watery potatoes." Later in their trip, they gave the Borden's a second chance and concluded that the mush "may answer to support life" but that one would need to be starving "before having recourse to it."

Incidentally, Mr. Borden had much greater success with a later invention, which endures to the present day on supermarket shelves: condensed milk.

The riders made their last camp in piney East Texas on New Year's Eve 1853, outside the town of Crockett, where they'd been unable to find flour, butter, or fresh meat. But their guide, B., succeeded in buying a few items from a settler's cabin, including a chicken, which he dressed and put on a spit over the fire.

This promptly attracted a pack of feral hogs so "frantic and delirious with hunger" that they ran into the fire to carry off the chicken, while also devouring most of the horses' corn. "The fiercest of them would resist even a clubbing, eating and squealing on through the blows."

On the first day of 1854 the travelers rested, writing and reading in camp and "making, sailor-like, repairs to such articles as were already giving way." Others did not enjoy this comparative ease. "Near us, within sound, were two negroes all day splitting rails—Sunday and New Year's day."

Olmsted also noted "the largest emigrant train we have seen," a convoy from Alabama, "including 50 negroes, 70 head of cattle, and a large drove of swine, besides wagons, etc."

Two of the slaves "stopped for a moment to drink at a puddle by the roadside." One, an old woman, exclaimed, "Oh my God! How tired I am." The other, "a man of powerful frame," answered, "I feel as tho' I couldn't lift my legs much longer."

Olmsted took note of the time—about noon—meaning the exhausted slaves were only halfway through that day's march.

RETURNING TO THE CAMINO REAL, I HEADED WEST TO CROCKETT, the town nearest to the Olmsteds' New Year's Eve campsite. Like the riders, I felt the need for a break after days of constant motion, and the historic-sounding town seemed a suitable location for a forty-eight-hour flop.

As it happened, I stayed six days, though not because of the town's heritage or charm. Crockett's claim on its namesake turned out to be very slight. The legendary Tennessean came this way in 1836 and briefly camped at a site now designated the David Crockett Spring, a rock memorial with a water fountain, a mural of the frontiersman, and words attributed to him: "Be sure you are right, then go ahead." From here he went ahead to the Alamo, where he died a month later.

Crockett (the town) nonetheless made the most of its link to Davy, holding an annual Crockett Days festival and selling coonskin caps at the chamber of commerce. It was otherwise an unremarkable hub of about seven thousand people, providing goods and services for a rural county of farms, cattle ranches, and timber.

What made me linger was my search the first morning for a nonfranchise meal, which led to a frontier-style building on the small courthouse square. A board on the sidewalk advertised that day's lunch special: chicken and dressing, green beans, yams, rolls, and Coke for $7.95.

Inside, the Moosehead Café was one of those establishments beloved of campaign reporters: a colorful small-town eatery where *tout le monde* gathered to swap local chatter and jaw about the latest news. About eighty people crowded the tables and booths, and the walls were crammed with moose heads, mounted fish, paintings of Davy—and a striking number of political slogans.

On patriotism: "LOVE *Your Country.* FEAR *Your Government.*"
On Benghazi: "*Four Americans Died and Hillary Lied.*"
On Socialism: "*A Great Idea If You Run Out of Other People's Money.*"
On 9/11: "*Terrorist Hunting License,*" emblazoned on a mock
  license plate.

I asked the café's owner, a jolly woman with tinted blond hair and radiant blue eyes, about this décor. Joni Clonts explained that she was county chair of the Republican Party and the Moosehead served as unofficial GOP headquarters.

"I've had a few liberals eat here and complain that they wouldn't have come in if they'd known it was so Republican," she said. "I tell them, 'Fine, don't come back.'"

This didn't happen often, since Democrats were scarce in Houston County, despite a long history of allegiance to the onetime party of states' rights, economic populism, and the New Deal. "My grandfather wouldn't let a Republican come on his property," Joni said, and when she ran for district clerk on the GOP ticket, "even my own uncle wouldn't vote for me."

She lost, but during her two decades as county chair for the GOP, she'd overseen a tidal shift. Of the twenty-one voting precincts in the county, only one remained Democratic: an African American part of Crockett known to whites as Blacktown. "Texans didn't leave the Democratic Party," Joni said. "The Democratic Party left us."

I'd heard this line before in my travels, but I hadn't probed electoral politics since Kentucky and West Virginia. My arrival in Crockett came just before the 2016 primaries in Texas, so I reckoned this was a good moment and place to gauge what Olmsted called "the drift of things" in America.

When I told Joni what I was up to, she led me to a round table beneath a sign reading, "Moosehead Lodge. Hunting, Fishing, and Storytelling Permitted." Seven men in Stetsons and duckbill caps nodded at me and then returned to their discussion of the upcoming presidential primary.

"Not a dime's worth of difference between 'em," one man said of the Republican candidates. "It's all about the money."

"That's bull corn," another man replied. "Cruz is a slick-talking politician. We need a businessman in the White House." This brought support from the man next to him. "It's like around the house, sometimes you've got to clean things out."

"Trump's so dumb he couldn't pour piss out of his boots," the first man persisted. "He talks at a fifth-grade level."

"That's where most Americans are at," replied a Trump advocate. "They're too smart to go to college; they go out and make a living instead."

During a pause in this debate, one of the men asked me why I was visiting Crockett. I told him I was following a nineteenth-century traveler along the Camino Real.

"So you've seen our famous spring," he said. "Every time Davy Crockett stopped to take a shit, they put up a monument."

He mentioned a few other sites of historical interest but warned against going "west of the tracks," to "Blacktown." This steered the conversation back to politics, and to race.

"My mother and sister voted for Obama twice, can you believe that? My daddy would roll over in his grave if he knew they'd voted for that nigger a second time."

"If those niggers don't want to work, I say give them bus tickets out of the country."

I wasn't accustomed to hearing such views expressed so loudly and unapologetically, in the middle of a crowded restaurant. At one point, a black cook at the Moosehead walked past, and the men hailed him by name, in a friendly manner—before slinging around the N-word again.

I was also surprised by my poll of the Lodge. When I asked whom they intended to vote for in the upcoming primary, three men named Trump, two supported Ted Cruz, and the other two were leaning toward "the black guy," meaning the neurosurgeon from Detroit, Ben Carson.

I tried to make sense of this dissonance—as Olmsted had, in a very different time and context. He frequently noted the casual mingling of blacks and whites, laughing and sharing food on trains and in other settings, an intimacy that cohabited with slavery and the white Southern creed that blacks were an inferior race.

When I gently probed the Carson supporters, one of them drew a distinction between "good blacks" and bad. "It's not about skin color; there's niggers black and white," he said. "Carson's a good one, telling his own kind they need to pull themselves up by their bootstraps and stop looking to the government."

After the breakfast klatch dispersed, I stuck around at the café, studying the décor and its small library of local histories until the early lunch crowd began to filter in. This time, Joni introduced me to a former county judge, Lonnie Hunt, who now worked for a state association of county governments.

"When I was in office I sat at the Lodge table twice a day," he said, "but I don't need to anymore. I've heard it all before."

Hunt, a Republican, said one key to grasping politics in East Texas was religion, including the "hard-shell Baptist" beliefs of many residents. "Might only be seventy percent in church on Sunday but ninety-five percent know they ought'a be." This translated into fierce opposition to abortion and gay rights, and the absence of liquor stores in the county (though alcohol sales had recently been permitted at Walmart and a few restaurants).

Taxes were another bugbear. "We have a history of wanting low taxes and not expecting much in return," he said. "If the property tax rate here was two cents, they'd vote to roll it back to a penny."

Olmsted had noted this, too, writing in Texas of the extreme "reluctance of a southern-born man to be taxed, for a mutual benefit." To him this reflected the Southerner's lack of communal spirit, and devotion to speculative adventure. "He instinctively prefers to gamble with his own risks, and would find a life not worth living which was surrounded with recuperative checks and deprived of exciting possibilities."

Hunt put a different spin on Texans' deep-seated aversion to taxes. He saw it as an extension of the founders' fear of tyranny and their creation of checks and balances. "The attitude is, 'Leave us alone, let us live our lives. And the closer to home decisions are made, the better,'" he said. "Texans hate central authority and Big Brother government, whether here or in Washington."

Even so, he'd become alarmed in recent years by the emergence of an extreme and absolutist right wing. "If you're with them on ninety-nine issues but off the reservation on the one-hundredth, you're dead," he said.

Hunt recommended I speak to current officeholders about this, and also introduced me to a local Democrat, though it took him a while to locate one in the lunch crowd at the Moosehead. "We've tried to run them out, but this guy's stubborn," he said, leading me to an accountant named Dick Murchison.

Murchison suggested we meet after lunch at his office across the street. "I didn't want to talk politics over there and risk getting lynched," he joked. He also avoided discussing politics with his clients and didn't allow guns in his office. "I don't want someone in here armed when I'm telling them how much tax they owe."

Murchison enjoyed teasing Republican neighbors, telling them at election time, "I just killed your vote with mine." Problem was, there were about eight GOP voters in Houston County for every one of him.

"I grew up in this county, I care about my fellow man, it's that simple," he said of his party allegiance. "People on the other side are only thinking about themselves. 'I work hard, it's my money, and forget about everyone else.'"

He showed me the four propositions on the GOP ballot for this primary election. "Anti-tax, anti-union, anti-immigrant, anti–federal government," he said, ticking down the list. The referenda on the Democratic ballot were almost the polar opposite, calling for better protection of immigrants, voting rights, and the environment.

"It's like we're on different islands, only ours is much smaller," he said. "The divide is so wide I don't see anything that will bridge it."

TAKING JUDGE HUNT'S ADVICE, I WENT TO SEE TWO STATE legislators whose districts included Houston County. The legislature wasn't in session, so I visited the representatives at their local offices east of

Crockett. Both described themselves as very conservative Republicans, in line with their constituents.

"On social issues, I think you'd be hard-pressed to find a more conservative place in the country than East Texas," said Trent Ashby, a representative in the state's House. One of the bills he was proudest of championing had enshrined in the state constitution the right to hunt and fish, even though there was no threat to this liberty in Texas.

"In other states, radical organizations are trying to reduce bag limits, curtail hunting season, banning hunting of species like bears and wolves," he explained. "We don't want that to happen here."

Texas had recently expanded gun rights to allow open as well as concealed carry. But fervor for the Second Amendment was so strong in Ashby's district that 70 percent supported "constitutional carry," essentially the right to be armed anywhere, at any time, without even a license.

Robert Nichols, a state senator, expressed views similar to Ashby's and was proud that he consistently ranked as "one of the two or three most conservative" senators in Texas. "We have more churches than gas stations in my district. We believe in taking care of our own and being self-reliant, like the pioneers that came here not that long ago. They succeeded or failed depending on themselves, not government."

Nichols and Ashby were so popular in their districts that Democrats hadn't even put up a candidate against them in their last two runs for re-election. But both men had to fend off frequent attacks from insurgents in their own party.

As Nichols explained it, well-funded far-right groups "scored" every vote a legislator made and introduced test amendments "on crazy stuff just to see what you'll do. I've made Cs and Ds and Fs with these people." He'd once been scored poorly, for instance, because he suggested adding a minor provision to a cockfighting bill.

Nichols's district covered an enormous swathe between Houston and Dallas, and he often spoke to Tea Party clubs. In the suburbs and exurbs, he said, "they've gotten really extreme, conspiracy theories, shouting about Agenda 21."

This was a nonbinding UN resolution that passed in 1992 with the support of President George H. W. Bush to promote public health, environmental conservation, and anti-poverty efforts. Extremists in Texas had cast this toothless declaration as a menacing scheme to create "a Soviet-style über-government."

Nichols felt this fear and anger, abetted by social media, had yet to crest. "People are mad at Washington, at everything," he said. "But I'm an engineer by training. We like to solve problems. You can't run a government by simply throwing grenades."

THE NEXT EVENING, BACK IN CROCKETT, I MET THE TYPE NICHols described, during a Republican candidates' forum at the Moosehead Café. Joni Clonts was running the show, with a short staff, so she recruited me to be timekeeper and ring a motel desk–style bell if any of the candidates spoke for more than their allotted two minutes.

A crowd of about a hundred gathered, all of them white and most middle-aged or older. Before the forum started, several men circulated with flyers, one of which noted the "pathetic" score an incumbent Republican had been given by a group called Heritage Action for America.

"He's a cuck-servative," one man said. "No balls, and a conservative in name only." I later learned that the phrase "cuck-servative" derived from a species of porn that portrayed white husbands humiliated by wives who preferred black men.

Another pamphleteer called himself "a voice of the watchdogs," keeping tabs on serving Republicans who had "sold out conservative values." He noted with approval the "top ten hot-button issues" cited by one of his preferred candidates, a retired colonel, including the elimination of "the weaponized IRS." In fiery red letters, the colonel's flyer declared: "I am mad as hell!"

The forum at the Moosehead turned out to be tame by comparison. A pastor offered a prayer, the audience said the Pledge of Allegiance and sang the national anthem, and then a dozen candidates made opening statements, speaking in a folksy manner about their family, church ties, military service, and local roots.

"Been farming and ranching all my life, live on a dirt road, I work hard, and I'm honest," a candidate for county commissioner stated.

Their political stances seemed secondary, in part because they were so similar. All were fierce defenders of religious liberty and the Second Amendment and heated in their opposition to taxes, the federal government, and funding for Planned Parenthood.

The only real debate occurred when a candidate for sheriff spoke about the "uneasiness all across the nation" and called for "twenty-four-hour patrols" in the county. The incumbent defended, at length, his toughness on crime and noted the impossibility of constantly patrolling a 1,250-square-mile county.

This put me on the spot, because he talked for more than two minutes. I couldn't bring myself to ring the bell on this imposing sheriff in a Stetson and cowboy boots with a .357 Magnum strapped to his belt. When I finally did, at the three-minute mark, the crowd sang "God Bless America" and the forum ended.

"You were just enforcing the law," the sheriff said, coming over to give me a bone-crushing handshake.

Joni, meanwhile, was relieved that "the radicals" in the audience hadn't been disruptive. I assumed she meant the extremists I'd met earlier, but apparently there was an even fringier contingent. "They like to talk about storing food, survivalism, and all that."

It also appeared that I was the only non-Republican present, though I didn't confess to this. "I think they were having their own forum tonight," Ray Wilson said of local Democrats. "In a phone booth."

A retired high school principal, Wilson said he used to be a "yellow-dog Democrat," but the growth of government had turned him into a yellow-dog Republican. "What irks the knickers off a true Texan is Washington poking its nose into everything."

Even so, having moved here six years ago from Galveston, he was struck by the depth of the conservatism and religiosity in this part of Texas. "In the yellow pages I counted 348 churches in the county and only one bar," he said.

I hadn't known there was a single bar, and asked him where it was. If I couldn't find any Democrats to canvass, I might as well talk to drinkers.

"Across from the Whataburger," Wilson replied, and ten minutes later I found Wild Bill's Sport Bar & Grill, a shedlike building tucked behind a small restaurant. Inside, it took me a moment to get my bearings because there were no windows, very dim lights, and so much smoke I could barely make out the pool tables and a few TVs broadcasting a women's cage-fighting match.

Eight people sat at the bar and all turned as I approached, apparently startled by the appearance of an unfamiliar customer. When I joined them, the woman next to me asked if I was an oil pipeliner.

"No, just a visiting writer."

"You should write my story," she replied. "'The Single Life of a Married Woman.' Married three times but acted like I was single." She let out a raspy laugh. "I got two kids and three broken ribs to show for it."

The barmaid, named Bunny, had also been through hard times. A slim, buxom woman of about forty, in skintight jeans and black top, she said she'd been married four times, once to a member of the Aryan Brotherhood. As such, she'd been designated a "featherwood," which she defined as "badass girls" attached to "peckerwoods," a prison name for white supremacists.

"I've stepped away from all that," she added, and had also given up her earlier career as a dancer. "The kind where it's not really about the dancing."

She began pouring brightly colored shots into small plastic cups and passing them around the bar. "Wet Pussy," she said of the first, a mix of butterscotch schnapps and tequila. Next came a Redheaded Slut (peach schnapps, Jägermeister, and cranberry juice) and a Blow Job (vodka, coffee liqueur, lots of whipped cream).

"It's not just what's in the Blow Job, it's how you drink it," Bunny instructed, wrapping her mouth around the cup and tilting her head to take it in one swallow.

By this point I was feeling very far from the churchy town of Crockett as I'd come to know it over recent days. When I mentioned this to the others at the bar, a young woman said, "If you don't go to church in this town, you're a heathen. If you're here drinking, you're truly damned."

She was a newcomer to Crockett, from the Dallas area, and worked as a waitress. "A gay couple came in the other day and everyone was staring at them," she said. "One woman even said aloud, 'That's an abomination.' I wanted to tell her my brother is gay, God says to love everyone. The Bible is a guide, it's not a hammer."

She disliked the racial dynamic, too. "It's all smiles one minute and the

N-word the next. They don't think they're racist because there's a few black people they know and like."

At Wild Bill's, two of the drinkers were black, as was the bar and grill's manager, who emerged at one point to share puppy pictures on his phone with Bunny, the former Aryan "featherwood." I'd seen little such social interaction in Crockett, or elsewhere in East Texas.

"Don't even try making sense of this town," Bunny said, pouring another round of obscenely named drinks. "When people ask me what Crockett's like, I tell them it's somewhere between Mayberry and *Deliverance*."

IN THE MORNING, I TOOK A COLD SHOWER AND RETURNED FOR my fourth visit to the Moosehead Lodge breakfast club and its rotating cast of locals. The topic of the day was immigration and terrorism.

"I like that Trump wants to keep Muslims out; they're exporting their war here."

"We have a pussy in the White House, paying Muslims to kill us."

"And Saudi Arabian Wahhabis paying for a Muslim compound in our own backyard."

This comment came from a man named Don, the loudest and most openly bigoted of the Lodge members. He told me he'd worked for an oilfield services company and spent time in the Persian Gulf. "There's a mosque and a training camp," he said of the "compound" south of Crockett, "guarded by guys with automatic weapons."

Perhaps it was my hangover, but for the first time I took issue with the Lodge, telling the men I'd heard rumors of this sort elsewhere in Texas and very much doubted them. I also mentioned that I'd been a Middle East correspondent and spoke a little Arabic. "Tell you what, I'll go down there and check it out and report back to you," I suggested.

After much hemming and hawing around the table, Don drew me a map of how to find the "compound," just beyond the county's southern border, outside a town called Groveton. "Be real careful," he said.

I drove through pasture and woodland for about thirty miles, turned down a farm road and then an unpaved route that brought me to a heavy metal gate, as Don had described. It had a security keypad and a high fence running to either side, but no phone or call button. I followed the fence line for a few hundred yards, trying to see what lay beyond, but glimpsed only trees and a bit of rolling open land.

I couldn't find neighbors, either, so I circled back to Groveton and visited the small police station. The county sheriff, Woody Wallace, sat behind a desk on which perched his very large Stetson. When I told him I was a writer, curious about the "Muslim compound," he let out an audible sigh.

"You were at the right place," he told me. "It's caused me all kind of bother."

As soon as construction began at the site two years earlier, he said, "the rumors started flying. It's a mosque. A Muslim school. A terrorist training camp." Then a story circulated that people from the compound had tried to buy guns and the storeowner kicked them out.

"People went nuts over that," he said. "We'd get calls about armed men being out there. Folks were seeing all kinds of strange things and telling me, 'Woody, you got to do something.'"

He did—going to the property several times when the security system set off false alarms and no one was there to turn it off. "What's actually there," he said, "is a big-ass house." It belonged to a doctor from Houston, of Indian or Pakistani descent, who'd bought the property as a second home and visited occasionally with his extended family. They were rarely seen except during shopping trips into Groveton.

"The women cover their hair but not their faces, and the men wear skullcaps," he said. "I don't know for sure if they're Muslim or something else. Not my business, unless they do something illegal, which they haven't."

But the rumors persisted, and when a YMCA camp elsewhere in the county announced plans for an educational seminar on Islam, "people went berserk again," he said. Protestors camped outside the facility and cooked pigs, "to offend Muslims," and in the end the seminar was canceled.

Woody tried to ignore the clamor and get on with the business of policing crime, of which there wasn't much in this rural county. "Mostly just dope and the theft to support it," he said. "Can't tell you the last time we had so much as a bar fight."

Why then, I wondered, were people so quick to panic about a far-fetched and nonexistent threat of Muslim intruders?

"People are scared," he said. "We've got open borders; people see what's happening overseas and are scared it will happen here. Everyone's on edge."

This anxiety wasn't confined to immigration. He mentioned that day's news, which included Black Lives Matter protestors scuffling with Trump supporters at one of the candidate's rallies.

"It's like things are breaking down," he said. "Civil unrest. Nobody trusts anyone they don't know, and they certainly don't trust Washington."

He counted himself in this camp and planned to vote for Trump. But he wasn't optimistic about the future. "Something's going to happen, somewhere. Then people will come here to hide, because everyone here has guns and knows how to use them. This will be a safe place, though maybe not for that Muslim doctor and his family."

I RETURNED TO CROCKETT DEPRESSED OVER THE FEAR AND division Woody had described. But I also felt a perverse elation at the prospect of sharing what I'd learned with the Moosehead Lodge. "Busted my bubble" was a phrase one of them used when others set him straight on some point of fact. I couldn't wait to bust the whole table's bubble regarding the "Muslim compound."

So I was there bright and early the next morning, enjoying my breakfast as the others talked about Trump's proposal for a border wall. Then I mentioned that I'd driven to the compound, seen no gunmen or anything else, and spoken to the sheriff.

"We all know Woody," one of the men said. "Good guy."

Then I told them the sheriff had debunked all the rumors about a mosque, or training camp, or gun-toting Muslims.

"Woody has to say that," replied Don, the oil-field veteran. "He's probably getting paid by them."

The others concurred, except for one man, new to the table, who ran a grocery in Groveton and had met the doctor and his family when they came in to buy deer feeders. "They're from Pakistan, I think, and the women wear colorful clothes. They spend a lot of money."

"That's their strategy," another man countered. "Spend a lot of money so everyone's happy and doesn't ask questions."

"Damn right, they send in someone real quiet-like, so no one realizes what's coming."

Don reiterated that he knew "for a fact" there was a "camp" and armed guards, and when I asked his source for this, he replied, "I've got photographs taken while flying over it."

"Can I see them?"

"I don't give anything to the press. You're just a pack of liars."

Another man chimed in, "Come back in a few years and you'll see, it'll be all Muslim around Groveton."

"At least by then," Don added, "we won't have a Muslim in the White House anymore."

I drained my coffee and decided it was time to get out of Crockett. I went over to thank Joni Clonts for the café's fine food and service and her hospitality in letting me use the Moosehead as my office for much of the week. She gave me a hug and offered two bumper stickers for the road, my choice of Cruz or Trump.

She hoped the latter would win. "He may have a mouth on him, but that's okay, a lot of Texans do, too." And though she doubted he was a sincere Christian, "that could change. God will touch him. God is good, he'll give our country another chance."

She also hoped God would touch misguided liberals in Houston County and beyond. "I pray for them. They're wrong in their politics, but they don't know they're wrong."

I pondered this as I drove out of town, past church signs declaring "He Is Risen!" and "Jesus Is Lord—And His Word Is Our Authority." I liked Joni and many others I'd met in and around Crockett. They'd been very welcoming and open about their beliefs, while doubtless suspecting I didn't share them.

But the Moosehead Lodge left a bad taste in my mouth, and not only because of the bigotry at the table. Like Olmsted, I'd embarked on my journey believing—or at least hoping—that Americans on opposite sides of the national divide could listen to each other and air their differences in a rational and coolheaded fashion.

Not so in Crockett. The Lodge members were intent on walling themselves off from any dissenting view or contrary information. No amount of "fact" about the "Muslim compound," not even the word of a familiar sheriff, could penetrate their protective shell. I felt as though I'd been firing a BB gun at an armor-plated vehicle.

A few dozen right-wingers at a small-town café obviously didn't comprise a scientific sample. But I'd heard enough similar commentary at other stops—and incessantly on the car radio—to sense the political "drift of things" in the territory through which I'd traveled.

Leaving Crockett, I felt as Olmsted had after his testy encounter with slave masters in Nashville. "Very melancholy" and pessimistically wondering "what is to become of us . . . this great country & this cursedly little people."

CHAPTER 15

AUSTIN AND BEYOND

The Loon Star Republic

W e came to-day upon the first prairie of any extent," Olmsted wrote of his ride west from Crockett. "After having been shut in during so many days by dreary winter forests, we were quite exhilarated at coming upon an open country and a distant view."

"Prairie," derived from an Old French word for meadow, had taken on a broader meaning in the vastness of America. It connoted grassland that was much more expansive than pasture and more fertile than the barren plains farther west.

Olmsted described Texas's prairie as undulating "like the swell of the ocean after the subsidence of a gale which has blown long from the same direction." At the crest of each wave the brow of the next appeared in the distance, "dark against the sky, following Hogarth's line of beauty and of grace with mathematical exactness."

Trees added vertical adornment to this rolling sea of grass. Olmsted particularly admired the post oak, "a somewhat small broad-leaved oak of symmetrical shape," standing in groves that formed pleasing "islands in the large prairies."

The riders' camp life settled into a tolerable routine, too. They traveled no more than twenty miles a day, leaving ample time and light to choose a sheltered site, feed the animals, gather wood and water, and plan "rather dolefully" for supper, which often consisted of "hot corn-meal." Afterward came lounging by the fire, "toasting your various fronts, and never getting warmed through," and then retirement to the tent, wrapped in blankets, with "a candle and a book or pencil."

At the first settlement west of Crockett, the riders also found protection against their "dirty persecutors, the hogs." They procured a bull terrier named Judy, a compact bundle of muscle "behind a pair of frightful jaws." If commanded to fend off hogs, she "would spring upon them like a hungry lion, and route a whole herd."

The only real drama during the Olmsteds' weeklong prairie ride to Austin was a "norther," the Texas term for sudden chill storms sweeping in from the plains. Balmy skies and sixty-seven-degree weather quickly turned to freezing temperatures and driving sleet, forcing the riders to seek refuge at a drafty inn with the usual drab fare. "Supper was, however, eaten with such rapidity that nothing had time to freeze on the table."

On another night, the riders sheltered from a norther at the home of a large slaveholder where Olmsted noted the behavior of the planter's eight-year-old son. "We heard him whipping his puppy behind the house" and berating the animal, he wrote. "I've got an account to settle with you," the boy shouted. "I've let you go about long enough; I'll teach you who's your master."

When his father told him to stop cursing, the boy tartly replied that the planter cussed in exactly this fashion when he was mad. As Olmsted drily observed, the boy's bullying treatment of the puppy "was an evident imitation of his father's mode of dealing with his slaves."

THIRTY MILES WEST OF CROCKETT, I REACHED CENTERVILLE, where the Olmsteds acquired the terrier, Judy, from the keeper of a log hotel. The hotel was long gone and Centerville seemed the center of very little, just a sleepy courthouse square. I was about to drive on when I noticed a long line of cars pulled up at a curb piled with boxes. This was the Lord's Produce Drop, a monthly distribution of fruit, vegetables, and other goods trucked in from a city food bank.

"God bless you," volunteers said to each motorist, before asking, "How many families?" and then loading the vehicle with groceries.

The event's organizer, a local woman named Roberta Allen, had previously run a small food bank at a Centerville church and found there was a broader need across this poor, rural county. "Anyone can come, no questions asked," she told me. The crowd—both volunteers and the motorists lined up in well-worn cars and trucks—was divided about evenly among whites, blacks, and Hispanics.

I lingered for an hour, warmed by the contrast to the uncharitable attitudes I'd encountered in Crockett. When I queried Roberta about this, she said, "It's true, Texans don't like handouts, giving or getting them. But here, folks are comfortable, they don't have to give any information, and there's no government involved."

A shared Christian spirit helped, too. "God puts what we need in our hands," she said. "There's abundance, and it's our duty to share it. Is that so complicated?"

As I drove on from Centerville, my spirits were further buoyed by the change of scenery. Piney woods and log trucks gave way to open ranchland and red-brown fields sown with cotton, corn, and milo. Meandering down farm roads, I caught glimpses of the vistas Olmsted described: prairie rolling for miles between gentle crests, though the "vastness and simplicity" he observed was somewhat diminished by power lines and ribbons of pavement.

I also searched for the trees he so admired, but found post oaks hard to identify, even with the aid of my laminated guide, *Trees of Central Texas*. Pulling over to inspect grove after grove, I studied green, bushy, and not very tall trees that looked alike. It didn't help that my guide listed eight types of oak, distinguished by tiny variations in their acorns and leaf structure.

Spotting a road sign for Post Oak Loop, I circled it for several miles, vainly scanning the fringe of trees for the striking symmetry and grace Olmsted extolled. No forester, I, the only other option was to plead for help.

"Lost tourist," I burbled to a man in oil-stained overalls, stooped over a Toro in front of a mower repair shop. Waving my laminated guide like a demented tree spotter, I asked if he could point me to a post oak.

He kindly walked me to a nearby clump of four trees, about forty feet tall. "Post oaks, you can tell by the rough bark," he explained. "They do better in dry times than other oaks."

I nodded and stared at the oaks, trying to channel Fred. Their branches swayed pleasingly in the breeze, like . . . every other tree. I asked the man if there was anything else distinct about them.

"Not to me," he replied. "Just post oaks. Common as dirt around here."

THIS ARBOREAL MYSTERY UNSOLVED, I SPED ON TOWARD AUSTIN, which the Olmsteds looked forward to, as a "bourne" of civilization after weeks of hard travel. Even without this expectation, Olmsted wrote, "it would still have struck us as the pleasantest place we had seen in Texas."

Austin occupied a "fine situation" beside the clear, blue-green Colorado River, surrounded by rolling countryside "with many agreeable views of distant hills and a pleasant sprinkling of wood over prairie slopes." Fifteen years earlier, this hilly setting had impressed Texans as a Rome-like "seat of Empire" for their new republic. The remote hamlet at the site, Waterloo, was rechristened Austin and hastily laid out as the capital.

Elsewhere, Olmsted derided the "mushroom" development of insta-towns along the South's frontier. But he approved of Austin's layout and architecture, describing its capitol as "a really imposing building of soft cream limestone," set upon a hill toward which "nearly all the town rises." The broad avenue linking the capitol to the river was lined with a nice variety of wood and stone buildings, including "pretty dwellings" and a church with a "German turret."

Olmsted wasn't so impressed by the "very remarkable number of drinking and gambling shops" and the capital's meager lodging. At a hotel recommended to the Olmsteds, they were shown to "the best room in the house," a filthy chamber they shared with another man. The food was worse: "a succession of burnt flesh of swine and bulls, decaying vegetables, and sour and mouldy farinaceous [starchy] glues, all pervaded with rancid butter."

Informed that Austin's other hotels were even ghastlier, the Olmsteds rented a room in a private home, buying and cooking their own food, "thus really coming back to caravansarism."

In other respects, they spent a refreshing five days in Austin, meeting "many cultivated, agreeable and talented persons." These included the state's Connecticut-born governor, a progressive advocate of railroads and

public schools. Olmsted also visited the state legislature, praising its parlia-
mentary decorum, "honest eloquence," and the "simple manly dignity" displayed by members.

"One gentleman, in a state of intoxication, attempted to address the
house," he added, by way of example, "and he was quietly persuaded to
retire."

LIKE OLMSTED, I APPROACHED THE TEXAS CAPITAL WITH PLEAS-
ant anticipation. Austin routinely placed at or near the top of national
surveys—most livable city, most economically vibrant, most appealing to
millennials, among other metrics. For decades, it had also ranked as one of
the nation's fastest growing. Since 1970, when Austin's peers in population
were Akron and Wichita, it had become the nation's eleventh largest city
and the center of a metro area of over two million.

Growth this explosive was rarely kind to urban planning, and I spent an
hour inching through exurbs and suburbs to reach the city center. However,
in contrast to the flat, formless straggle of Houston, Austin still had a core
anchored to its hills and river and rising, as in Olmsted's day, toward the
lofty capitol grounds.

Before exploring the downtown, I was lured off the gridlocked interstate by a sign for the French Legation, a quaint relic of Austin's brief reign
as capital of an independent republic. Texas established diplomatic relations
with all comers, including Hanseatic city-states, the short-lived Republic
of Yucatán, and a handful of European nations that opened consulates in
Austin.

"This place was meant to impress, and show what *La France* was all
about," said the Legation's irreverent tour guide, Mary Braunager-Brown. In
1840, when Austin was a newborn capital of dirt streets, the French envoy to
the republic constructed an elegant two-story house with a wine cellar,
perched on a hill "so that he could literally look down on the Texans."

Alphonse Dubois de Saligny was also a fraud: a faux nobleman who
paid bills with counterfeit currency, or didn't pay them at all. This sparked
a bizarre international crisis when de Saligny and an innkeeper went to
court over unpaid expenses and an additional matter: the envoy's servant
had killed the hotelier's roaming swine.

De Saligny, in high French dudgeon, claimed diplomatic immunity and called on his superiors in Paris to intervene, with force. The so-called Pig War of 1841 ended peacefully when the consul fled his post after only a year.

"He probably had PTSD, living here instead of in Paris," Mary speculated, "and realized he didn't want to stay." The legation soon passed into private hands, but the survival of a property known as the "French Legation" remained a source of confusion. "A French tourist in Texas contacted us; he'd lost his passport and asked if we could issue a new one," she said.

In her view, the story of the Legation and its roguish envoy was illustrative of Texas's early history. "Ours is not a genteel heritage," she said, recommending I also visit the nearby Texas State Cemetery. "We're kind of proud of our scoundrels."

I followed her advice, walking a few blocks to a rolling meadow established in the 1850s as a burial ground for notable Texans. Those interred or honored with monuments included more than two thousand Confederates, the author James Michener, and Tom Landry, who coached the Dallas Cowboys to five Super Bowls.

Then, on a rise called Republic Hill, also known as the Hill of Heroes, I came to a scoundrel of the sort the Legation guide had mentioned. The name etched in granite was familiar from my research on "gone to Texas" and the "rascality" it implied.

Robert Potter served five years in the US Navy without rising above the rank of midshipman, allegedly because of his dueling and whoring. He then brawled his way to a seat in Congress from North Carolina—until, in 1831, he came to believe that a teenager and a fifty-five-year-old minster were both "violating the sanctity" of Potter's marriage bed. Taking justice into his own hands, he hogtied and castrated the purported adulterers, a well-publicized maiming that gave rise to the phrase "potterized" and landed its namesake in prison.

Upon his release, Potter won election to the state legislature—only to be quickly expelled for cheating at cards and brandishing a knife and pistol. At which point he was G.T.T., arriving just in time to become a belligerent in the Texas Revolution. Sam Houston regarded his military schemes as mad and wrote that Potter's "infamy was wider than the world and deeper than perdition."

He nonetheless rose to become secretary of the Texas Navy and served as a senator in Austin while living bigamously with his second "wife." Then another violent feud cut his career short. Set upon by a mob of hostile neighbors, Potter was given a chance to run for it and jumped in a lake, only to be shot dead when he came up for air.

His lurid demise was widely reported and caught the eye of Charles Dickens, who cited it in *American Notes* as an example of the brutish vigilantism in slaveholding states. But none of Potter's notoriety was noted on the Hill of Heroes. His remains lay beneath a large headstone recording the offices he'd held and his patriotic service to the republic. There was even a Texas county named after him.

Olmsted didn't mention Potter by name but described his ilk when writing of the swashbucklers who flocked to Texas on the eve of its fight against Mexico: "A more reckless and vicious crew was seldom gathered." This legacy—less than two decades past when Olmsted reached Texas—inclined him to soften his view of the rough-and-tumble world he'd traveled en route to Austin.

"Society," he concluded, "has certainly made a great advance there in becoming even what it is."

MODERN AUSTIN SEEMED WELL SCRUBBED AND CIVIL, BEARING little trace of its early days as the haunt of a deadbeat French diplomat, a potterizing senator, and other dubious characters. But the city still clung to a maverick self-image that traced to the 1960s and early '70s, when Austin was much smaller and scruffier, a university town that attracted musicians and other creative types in a state unrenowned for bohemianism.

As corporate headquarters and cookie-cutter suburbs arose, a battle cry emerged: "Keep Austin Weird." This slogan had persisted ever since, more as a brand than a descriptor. On my first day's tour of town, I passed a Museum of the Weird, a billboard for the Austin rodeo ("Where Weird Meets Western"), Live Weird Realty (with pictures of expensive condos in the window), and countless businesses with "Unique" or "Odd" or "Off-the-Wall" in their names.

Along South Congress Avenue, a once-seedy strip recast as SoCo and lined with upscale shops, I watched street performers doing self-consciously weird things. Like composing love poems on demand, on a manual typewriter, or wearing a top hat and shouting megaphoned compliments at pedestrians. "You have a beautiful smile!" "Nice man pecs!" "I like that slo-mo walk, it's working well for you!"

This was all mildly offbeat. But it's hard for a city to stay weird when few of its inhabitants are. Austinites often referred me to a waggish illustration that had recently caused a stir. Titled *Judgmental Austin Map*, it showed the metro area with neighborhoods tagged by their stereotypical residents, such as "Old $$ Hippies," "Boring Gays," "Big 'N' Dull Wealth," "Mall Zombies," "Lance Armstrong Types," and "Blacks Resisting Gentrification."

The last referred to East Austin, where I'd visited the French Legation and state cemetery. Traditionally black and Mexican American (and designed as such, by segregationist city fathers in the twentieth century), East Austin's bungalows and small businesses were now filling with hipsters and house flippers. Near the cemetery, I passed a characteristic strip: espresso joint, craft beer pub, boutique hotel, and a formerly black-owned drugstore repurposed as an oyster and wine bistro called Hillside Farmacy.

This trend wasn't unique to Austin, but it seemed especially conspicuous in the liberal capital of a state that was now majority minority. Compared to polyglot Houston, Austin felt bleached, the rare major city that was getting demographically whiter. As if to emphasize this, a striking number of those I encountered were recent transplants from the Nordic states of the upper Midwest.

Typical was a handsome young couple I met while studying a menu of "provisions" and "libations" at a bar on Sixth Street, Austin's downtown music corridor. Erik and Leah were from Wisconsin and Minnesota and had decided to make a "lifestyle move," selecting Austin over Portland, Seattle, and Denver.

"It was sort of like a college tour," Erik said of their search. In Austin, he'd quickly landed a job at Apple; Leah was still mulling several options. "After Wisconsin, it feels so sunny here, in every way," she said.

They invited me the next night to a party in a fifteenth-floor condo in one of the new apartment towers downtown (a district labeled "Ex-Frat Highrises" on the *Judgmental Map*). The host told me he was "in finance"; others I spoke to worked "in software." Most were from the upper Midwest, with a sprinkling of Californians. They chatted about start-ups, made

Cheesehead jokes, and played beer pong. Easily the oldest person present, I felt like a chaperone at a very tame college party.

The next night I met a more jaded Cheesehead, Paul Wainwright, a bartender who had moved from Milwaukee eight years ago. A philosophy grad in his early thirties, he described Austin as "ground zero for monetizing a certain demographic—young, white, well educated, seeking a counterculture that's not counter anymore, it's a mainstream product." He missed what he called the "edginess and authenticity" of Milwaukee, where "for six months of the year everyone is experiencing seasonal affective disorder, which makes for dark humor that's lacking here."

Paul then turned this humor on himself, noting that he'd become an "Austin cliché." He'd adopted a monthlong cleanse called the Whole30 diet, worked by day as a video editor for a project called Happiness Is a Choice, and lived in East Austin, where "most of my neighbors are buying, renovating, and flipping homes."

He shrugged, mixing me a house special called a Cool but Rude, expertly reciting its contents: mint-infused Milagro *reposado* tequila, mango liqueur, and jalapeño. "When in Rome," he said, filling my glass.

The cocktail went down much more smoothly than the last I'd consumed, a Blow Job at the only bar in Crockett. I also sampled Austin's excellent barbecue, made a pilgrimage to the first Whole Foods Market, and scaled Mount Bonnell to gaze across a lake at pleasure boats and villas dotting the wealthy hills to the west (labeled "1%" on the *Judgmental Map*).

Then I returned to Olmsted's trail, following Congress Avenue from the Colorado River to the hilltop statehouse he'd admired. At the capitol visitors' center, I was chuffed to find an exhibit quoting Olmsted, who described the handsome statehouse and its surrounds as "Washington, *en petit.*"

There was nothing *petit* about the capitol now. The three-story structure Olmsted judged "very imposing" had been replaced in the 1880s by a domed building taller than the US Capitol. Though not quite so lofty as Huey Long's tower in Louisiana, Texas's limestone and red granite statehouse ranked as the largest in the nation when measured by square footage.

This obligatory supersizing seemed incongruous, given that the state legislature only convened every other year, for 140 days—a testament to Texas's long history of hostility to centralized authority. In the space of a few decades, early Texans rebelled against Mexico, joined the Confederate rebellion against the US, and fiercely resisted federal Reconstruction. When freed of this yoke, the drafters of the 1876 state constitution studded the document with restraints on "big government."

The monuments ringing the capitol amplified Texans' truculence. One, to the "Heroes of the Alamo," cited William Travis, the hotheaded commander who proclaimed, "God and Texas, Victory or Death," and "I shall never surrender or retreat." True to his word, he was among the first to die at the Alamo.

Another statue honored Hood's Texas Brigade, a Confederate unit renowned for suicidal charges. "They have shown on many battlefields their willingness to die for Dixie," the inscription read, quoting Jefferson Davis.

For added emphasis, two howitzers from 1836 and three cannons from the Civil War guarded the capitol's main entrance. This air of defiance extended to the traditional separation between church and state. One large monument, displaying the Ten Commandments, had narrowly withstood challenge in the Supreme Court.

The atmosphere inside the statehouse was more peaceful, since it was an off year for the legislature. But a guard told me that a committee hearing and other meetings were underway in a basement annex. Bizarrely, the first gathering I came to was a congress of rattlesnakes, writhing and thrumming on the floor of an atrium.

"Unlike true Texans, they prefer flight to fight," a man said, herding the vipers with a metal poker. "Producing venom takes a lot out of them." This turned out to be a promotional display for an upcoming rattlesnake roundup.

I then waded through a scrum of burly sheriffs, state troopers, and men in FBI jackets, all carrying guns, most of them at the capitol for a meeting of a law enforcement association. Some were also there to testify at the legislative committee hearing—on incarceration rates in the Texas prison system, the nation's largest.

After listening in, I stopped at the open-doored office of a House staffer whose boss represented a strongly pro-gun district. Speaking off the record, he expressed doubts about Texas's new open-carry law, which allowed licensed civilians to openly bear arms in all but a few proscribed spaces.

"If you're a bad guy committing a crime," he said, "who's the first person you're gonna shoot? The idiot with his gun in the open."

The aide, however, had a concealed-weapon permit so he could pack heat when working alone or driving at night. "Never needed it, probably never will, but I like to have the option." For his district's constituents, the attachment to weaponry went much deeper. "The attitude is, 'You can't take it away from me; it's my last defense!'"

Against what? I wondered. In this building alone, I'd just encountered lawmen carrying enough firepower to repel a small army and listened to legislators discuss the hundreds of thousands in Texas locked up for non-violent offenses.

"Exactly," the staffer replied. "All that power in the hands of the state scares people." He then mentioned Jade Helm 15, a military exercise that had recently caused a furor in Texas. This was a routine, role-playing war game held in six states, to prepare Navy SEALs and other special ops for unconventional combat. But when a map of the operation went public, labeling Texas a "hostile" territory, conspiracy-mongers cast Jade Helm as a covert federal plot to occupy the state, disarm civilians, and declare martial law.

Rumors spread that shuttered Walmart stores near military bases were being retrofitted as mass detention camps. A leading talk radio host claimed "Helm" was short for "Homeland Eradication of Local Militants." The panic led to angry meetings across the state, the forming of armed civilian "surveillance" units, and the governor ordering the Texas State Guard to monitor the exercise to ensure that no civil liberties were infringed.

"That nonsense blew over," the staffer said, "but there's always another." His current bugbear: secessionist groups that bombarded legislators with phone calls and petitions, seeking a referendum on Texas independence. Their lobbying had contributed to approval of interim measures such as the repatriation of Texas's share of gold from the Federal Reserve.

"This stuff used to be lunatic fringe," the aide said. "Now we have to take it seriously, or pretend to."

After leaving his office, I checked the website of the largest group he'd mentioned: the Texas Nationalist Movement, which claimed 250,000 adherents and held regular "information" sessions to distribute literature and petitions. One of these events was scheduled for the next day in the town of Goliad, which Olmsted visited during a side trip from the Camino Real.

So I followed him there, speeding away from the hills and into the rolling prairie between Austin and the Gulf Coast. Olmsted rode this way in spring, when the prairie bloomed with flowers. He also expressed rare admiration for a rural town, Seguin, praising its "shaggy live oaks" and streets "not always at right angles," a contrast to the grid layout and raw ugliness of other frontier settlements.

Goliad had a different distinction. Though a mere hamlet when Olmsted visited, it lay close to a gory shrine to Texas independence. The modern-day town announced itself with a gigantic water tower emblazoned with the words "REMEMBER GOLIAD" and an image of a bleeding severed arm—emblem of the Texans slaughtered nearby in 1836. I also passed a monument to the "massacred" and an oak called the "Hanging Tree," where executions "were carried out immediately, by means of a rope and a convenient limb."

Goliad seemed an otherwise tranquil town, its streets shaded by pecan trees and the courthouse square ringed with stalls for a monthly open-air market. Amid the vendors of candles, kettle corn, and crafts, the Texas Nationalists were easy to spot. Their red, white, and blue tent had a banner proclaiming, "Texas Independence Now!" and a table with exclamatory literature: "Stand Up for Texas! Stand Up against D.C.!"

The three people in lawn chairs under the tent appeared mellow by comparison, at least in manner. I was greeted by the head of the district chapter, Regina Cowan, a genial woman of about thirty-five clad in shorts, sandals, and a "Texas Is Rising" T-shirt.

"All we want is legal, peaceful separation from the United States," she said. "Texas can take better care of Texans than the federal government can."

Next to her sat Dave Fitts, a small business owner wearing a "Most Likely to Secede" T-shirt. "One size never fits all," he said. "We don't need all those laws and ABC agencies in Washington." He handed me a flyer that called for repeal of the Fourteenth and Sixteenth Amendments ("birthright citizenship" and income tax) and the elimination of virtually every federal agency, including the National Wild Horse and Burro Program and the Administration on Intellectual and Developmental Disabilities.

"As far as I'm concerned, we could do without *any* of it, except the Second Amendment," Dave said. "You can get all the law you need in the Bible." He also felt Texas possessed every resource necessary to go it alone. "Food, energy, shipping, guns, you name it, we have it."

The Nationalists offered me a chair and cordially fielded my questions about how this separation would work. What about interstates, or Texas's many military bases, or Social Security, which Dave and another man in the tent received?

"I don't like it because it's 'social,' like 'Socialism,'" Dave replied. "But I paid for it, so I should still get it once we're independent."

Regina acknowledged, "A lot of details will have to be worked out, like in any divorce settlement." She was also careful to distinguish the Nationalists from other separatist groups, like the Republic of Texas, which had tangled with authorities—sometimes violently—and begun minting its own currency. "They're kind of out in left field," she said. "We're in center."

As evidence, she noted that the Nationalists had helped amass over 125,000 signatures for a petition to the US president, asking for Texas's peaceful withdrawal. This had legally obliged the Obama White House to respond, with a terse message stating that the Constitution "did not provide a right to walk away" from the Union.

"We don't want another Civil War," Regina said. "If Washington would just let Texas be independent again, we'd avoid all that trouble they had back in that day."

I took a lunch break at the Hanging Tree Restaurant and returned to find that a rather unlikely spokesman had joined the Nationalist tent. Regina's husband, Roger, was a bearded musician with a tattoo of a microphone and a "Willie for President of Texas" T-shirt, meaning Willie Nelson. He was also part Hispanic and had in tow his son by a previous marriage and a light-skinned black nephew.

"My great-grandmother came here illegally from Mexico," he said. "She swam the Rio Grande. But the moment she crossed, in her heart she became American. Not like today, where a lot are just coming to sell drugs or collect food stamps."

An even bigger beef of his: distant federal government telling Texans what to do, as Mexico had before the revolution. "I don't need another mommy and daddy, and I sure don't need Michelle Obama telling me what to feed my boy." He gestured at his overweight son, his face planted in a snow cone. "I know vegetarians who are sick because they're not getting enough protein."

This sparked discussion of what Dave Fitts called "all the freedoms that have been taken away" in his lifetime. "Stuff we used to do, you'd get arrested for now."

"Like what?" I asked.

"Throwing water balloons, old-fashioned horseplay," he said, an activity I wasn't aware had been criminalized.

"Fireworks," added Charles Bibb, a retired chemical plant worker. "We can't buy them except a few weeks a year, around July Fourth and other holidays."

"Speaking our minds," Regina said, speaking hers. "They're taking that away with political correctness."

We went back and forth—about taxes, limits on ammo clips, Jade Helm, and other instances of what they saw as government menace—while I struggled to fathom the wellspring of their discontent. By their own accounts, these amiable Texans led fairly comfortable and freewheeling lives. So why did they feel so burdened by bureaucrats in Washington?

"Bottom line?" Dave finally exclaimed. "The government won't let us do whatever the hell it is we want to do. That's it."

This brought a chorus of amens and echoed the fifty-year-old book I'd been reading at night since finding it at a bookstore in Austin: *The Super-Americans*, by John Bainbridge, a title that perfectly captured its thesis.

Bainbridge argued that Texans, for all their Lone Star pride, weren't a species apart from other Americans. Rather, the qualities associated with their character—braggadocio, cowboy culture, brash enterprise, rugged individualism—were a magnification of the nation's frontier identity.

"Texas is a mirror in which Americans see themselves reflected," Bainbridge wrote, "not life-sized, but, as in a distorting mirror, bigger than life."

The Nationalists, in turn, struck me as Super-Texans, taking the spirit of the state's revolution to its libertarian extreme. *No* authority—save God—should tell them what they could or couldn't do, anywhere, at any time.

Or, as Roger Cowan put it, "If you come after our freedom, you'll have to tear it from our dead cold hands, like happened here at Goliad." He turned to his son and nephew, slurping the last of their snow cones. "Wanna go see where those brave Texans got waxed?"

I piled with them into Roger's pickup truck for the short drive to

Presidio de la Bahía, a stone-walled garrison and church built by the Spanish in the 1700s. At the start of the Texas Revolution, rebels seized the bastion from the Mexicans, renamed it Fort Defiance, and hoisted a flag bearing the image I'd seen on the Goliad water tower: a muscular arm clutching a bloody sword to its shoulder, in apparent self-amputation.

"That meant they'd cut off their own limb rather than submit to tyranny," Roger told the boys as we gazed up at a replica flying from a pole in the presidio's parade ground. "They were just a bunch of hunters, farmers, everyday rednecks willing to die standing up to a dictator."

The full story, as told in the presidio's museum, wasn't quite so uplifting. The fort's commander, Colonel James Fannin—a planter and slave trader trained at West Point—had been ordered by Sam Houston to withdraw from the isolated presidio.

Fannin delayed doing so and was forced to surrender when a Mexican army caught up with his force in open prairie and marched the captives back to the presidio. Then, under orders from Santa Anna to treat "perfidious foreigners" rebelling against Mexico as pirates, soldiers executed more than 340 prisoners and burned their corpses—a toll roughly twice that at the Alamo, which had fallen to Santa Anna three weeks earlier.

Texans took revenge the next month, at San Jacinto, and later by pillaging Presidio de la Bahía. Olmsted, arriving eighteen years after the Goliad massacre, described the presidio as a large, limestone-walled quadrangle, its barracks and other buildings in ruins.

To his surprise, he found a priest living in a corner of the ravaged chapel. The curate had been sent by the Catholic Church to care for the Mexicans who had long dwelled around the presidio, in *jacales*, wood huts made of poles, mud, and stones.

"The Americans destroyed it as much as they could," the priest said of the ransacked church. They'd also mistreated the resident Mexicans, who lived "like chickens," having lost much of their land to the Anglos and been cheated "in every business."

The priest offered his visitor a cigar and showed him around the "dim damp vault-like" chapel. The gloom and poverty at La Bahía, Olmsted wrote, was a stark contrast to the small but well-stocked Anglo settlement at Goliad. He also noted the prevailing view of Mexicans, not as heretics to be converted, "but rather as vermin, to be exterminated." Soon after his visit, Anglos began persecuting Mexicans who carted goods from the coast, lynching a number of them from the hanging tree I'd seen earlier in the day.

The church and other presidio buildings had since been restored, and while Roger took the boys up on the ramparts, I wandered over to the adobe birthplace of Ignacio Seguín Zaragoza, whose father was posted at the garrison in the early 1800s. Zaragoza went on to become a national hero in Mexico, leading a reformist revolt against Santa Anna and defeating an invading French force on May 5, 1862, the date celebrated as Cinco de Mayo.

While exploring the birthplace, I met Alberto Perez, a history and social studies teacher in the Dallas area who was visiting with his family. When I confessed my ignorance of Zaragoza, he smiled and said, "You're not alone. A lot of Texans don't know him, either, or even that Mexico had its own fight for independence."

The son of Mexican immigrants, Perez had taught at a predominantly Hispanic school in Dallas named for Zaragoza. Even there, he'd found it hard to bring nuance to students' understanding of Mexico and Texas in the nineteenth century.

"The word 'revolution' slants it from the start," he said. "It makes kids think of the American Revolution and throwing off oppression."

Perez tried to balance this with a broader, Mexican perspective. Anglos had been invited to settle Texas and were granted rights, citizenship, and considerable latitude in their adherence to distant authority. Mexico's abolition of slavery, for instance, had little force on its northeastern frontier, where Southerners needed only to produce a "contract" that technically labeled their human chattel as indentured servants.

"Then the Anglos basically decided, 'We don't like your rules,'" Perez said. "'This is *our* country now.'"

He wasn't an apologist for Santa Anna, whom he said was reviled by most Mexicans today as a despot and a traitor for allegedly giving up territory to save his own skin after being captured at San Jacinto. "But many Mexicans still see what happened in the 1830s and '40s as outright robbery of their land."

Returning to the presidio, I shared these views with Roger. Predictably, he didn't concur. "Yeah, this used to be part of Mexico, but the US continent used to be controlled by Indians, too," he observed. "Not anymore."

He wasn't happy, either, with the large bronze statue of Zaragoza, donated by Mexicans, which stood just outside the presidio. "We recognize Cinco de Mayo, but July Fourth isn't a holiday in Mexico or France or other countries."

Roger also recommended I get another viewpoint, from the Mexican American proprietors of a music venue he'd be performing at that evening, not far from Goliad. "We play outlaw country, which is country with no rules," he said. "Sort of the way we'd like things to be here in Texas."

THE DIRECTIONS ROGER GAVE ME WERE CONFUSING, AND I wandered for some time before reaching a low wooden building at a rural crossroads, about all that remained of a community known as Cotton Patch. The building, formerly a general store and dance hall, displayed the US and Texas flags and a sign reading, "cold beer."

The interior was likewise plain, with an unpainted wood floor and bar, plank ceiling, and patrons drinking two-dollar beers from cans and bottles. I found Roger setting up on a stage outside, and he introduced me to Esther Puente, who ran the place with her husband. She brought out a file of newspaper clips from the 1940s, when Cotton Patch catered to a large population of farmers and sharecroppers.

"Look how skinny and well dressed they are!" she said, showing me photographs of women in white dresses and men in white shirts crowded on the dance floor.

The only person of color in any of the photographs was a black waiter. Blacks were otherwise barred from the dance hall, as were locals of Mexican descent. In the Texas of that day, laws and customs known as *Juan* Crow subjected Hispanics to discrimination and segregation similar to that inflicted on African Americans.

"My parents couldn't have afforded a night out here anyway," Esther said. They were migrant farmworkers, picking cotton in this area and other crops as far north as Michigan. Esther grew up in a shack without running water and showered under a hose her father hooked up inside a phone booth at a junkyard. She entered school late, speaking only Spanish.

"I learned quickly and looked white, so in second grade they put me with the white class," she said. "But when the teacher found out my Mexican heritage, she persecuted me the rest of the year." Things didn't improve much in later grades, "and there was no way a white boy would date me. There were black families we got along with, but whites treated them even worse than they treated us."

Her own children, raised in the 1980s and '90s, had a very different experience. They spoke little Spanish, "didn't feel much discrimination," and one became, in his twenties, a school board member and city manager in the nearby town of Yorktown.

"I tease my grandkids, telling them they're Mexican, and they say, 'No we're not!' They don't associate with it at all and can't imagine the life we lived."

Esther had mixed feelings about the dramatic change she'd seen over six decades. Despite the segregation of her youth, and to a degree because of it, "we were a big happy family, lots of cousins and elders, looking out for each other and caring for the little ones while their parents worked," she said. "Today, if someone's raising grandkids, it's because their own children are up to no good."

She believed life was healthier then, too, with the vigorous work and a diet of beans, green vegetables, and a little meat. "Soda and other stuff people consume all day now, that was a special treat."

So was a night out at the dance hall, at least for whites. The lean, ruddy, dressed-up dancers in her photographs bore little resemblance to the current crowd at the Cotton Patch: a mix of Anglo, Hispanic, and a few blacks, most of them very well fed, spilling out of jeans or shorts and T-shirts.

"We're all Texans now, for better and worse," Esther said. Roger's band started blaring outlaw country, making further conversation difficult. So I asked her one last question: How did she feel about this movement to make Texas independent?

Esther answered tactfully. "Texas could handle being on its own, if it had to."

But she and her husband had done well by America and enjoyed annual car trips around the country, including to states where her parents had picked crops. Many of the patrons here, and at a second venue she and her husband managed in San Antonio, were oil workers, or military, or other migrants from outside Texas.

"I love my Hispanic heritage, I love America, and I'm a proud Texan," she said. "Why choose just the one identity? Let's not put people in separate boxes, like they did here when I was coming up."

CHAPTER 16

SAN ANTONIO

High Holy Days at the Alamo

One sometimes wonders if Bowie and Travis and the rest would have fought so hard for this land if they had known how many ugly motels and shopping centers would eventually stand on it.

Larry McMurtry, In a Narrow Grave

Olmsted had a special relationship to trees. His mother sewed beneath one in Fred's sole memory of her, when he was not yet four. Seven decades later, during his last great work as a landscape architect, he proposed "a museum of living trees" along the entrance to the Biltmore Estate and urged its owner to preserve the nearby mountain woodlands in their wild state.

"Years ago I rode alone for a full month through the North Carolina forests," he wrote George Vanderbilt, recalling his journey back from Texas. "There is no experience of my life to which I could return with more satisfaction."

It wasn't just the "mystery" and "solemnity" of untamed forest that moved Olmsted. As I'd seen while tracking his prairie ride to Austin, he found virtue and beauty in almost every tree, including the humble post oak.

This esteem for trees was inextricably bound to the broader landscape; in the instance of post oaks, the way they punctuated the open, horizontal prairie. In later writing, Olmsted noted that observers of scenery tend to focus on the most dramatic features, such as waterfalls or peaks. But he believed the true power of landscape lay in the dynamic interplay of trees, sky, water, and topography. All combined, like the human face, to create a whole larger than "a measured account" of its parts.

Upon resuming his ride along the Camino Real, from Austin to San Antonio, Olmsted extolled another variant of oak, one he'd often seen before. Though the live oak appeared stunted in central Texas, and "lacking the rich vigor and full foliage" it possessed in lush districts of the Deep South, it was "thickly hung with the grey Spanish moss, whose weird color, and slow, pendulous motions, harmonize perfectly with the tone of the tree itself."

This was especially so in places where the tree's "distorted roots" clung to rocky ledges. The oaks also stood "alone or in picturesque groups," dotting the prairie, which "rolled in long waves that took, on their various slopes, bright light or half shadows from the afternoon sun." In all, the gnarled trees, "clean sward" of grassland, and other features created an effect that was fresh and striking to Olmsted, "like a happy new melody."

Or so he felt upon first entering this landscape, lingering just beyond Austin to sketch "a superb old tree" and the vista beyond. "Had we known that this was the first one of a thousand similar scenes," he added, "we should have perhaps, spared ourselves the pains."

Thereafter, the scenery changed little, for days, until the live oaks grew scarce and the prairie ever more monotonous. "The groundswells were long, and so equal in height and similar in form, as to bring to mind a tedious sea voyage."

Then, on their fourth day's ride from Austin, the Olmsteds ascended a hill and beheld what seemed a mirage: "The domes and white clustered dwellings of San Antonio below us." Seven miles distant, the city lay "basking on the edge of a vast plain" through which wound a tree-lined river. To the south and west stretched "limitless grass and thorny bushes," to the north a gradual sweep upward to mountain country.

"We stopped and gazed long on the sunny scene," Olmsted wrote, before descending into the enchanted city.

SAN ANTONIO, AT THE TIME, WAS ALREADY 130 YEARS OLD, THE largest and only long-established "city" in Texas, with about six thousand inhabitants. Its size and character were also distinctive, Olmsted wrote, because San Antonio was "outposted" on the frontier, geographically and culturally remote from the rest of the nation.

From my parents' description, San Antonio had still felt that way a century later, when they lived on an air force base at the city's dusty edge during the Korean War. Since then San Antonio had exploded, like Texas at large, becoming a hub of oil, defense, medicine, tourism, and other industries, and the nation's seventh largest city.

It was also linked to burgeoning Austin by an eighty-mile corridor of almost continuous development. Thirty miles south of the capital, I came to San Marcos, a settlement Olmsted described as "three shabby homes." It now had sixty thousand people and had recently topped the rankings for fastest-growing population center in the nation, for a third consecutive year.

Other once-modest communities along I-35 had grown almost as rapidly, and bled into each other, making it hard to judge where the sprawl of greater Austin ended and that of greater San Antonio began. At points, narrow strips of scrub separated one exurb from another, but I searched in vain for live oaks, which had been supplanted by groves of signs for "Prime Corridor Property!" or "New Homes 0$ Down!" or big-box malls under construction.

The meteoric growth of greater Austin and San Antonio, and all points between, was unlike any I could recall seeing in my years of roaming the continent as a reporter and writer. It was also a striking contrast to the distressed and depopulated areas I'd so often passed on my journey. Postindustrial Cumberland and Wheeling, the Mississippi Delta, countless vacant rural crossroads and derelict main streets elsewhere—all that seemed a different country from the throbbing I-35 corridor.

Twenty-first-century America was once again "gone to Texas," or at least to its mushrooming metro areas, joined by throngs of immigrants from overseas. I later checked the census data. Texas was adding almost a half million people a year, more than any other state, and its growth rate was double that of high-tech California, which it was projected to surpass in population within a few decades.

Texas already ranked first in the nation when it came to exports and production of electronics and other goods, and the state accounted for an astounding 30 percent of all new jobs created in the US since 2000. I might dislike some of the industries and policies abetting this explosive growth—oil, defense, deregulation, hostility to unions and taxes—but the "drift of things" was impossible to ignore.

In Olmsted's day, expansionism in Texas, and the conflicts it aroused, drove the nation ever farther apart in the decades before the Civil War. The state had played an outsized role in the polarized politics of my own era, too. A short list of pivotal figures from the past quarter century included the Bushes, Karl Rove, congressional right-wingers Dick Armey and Tom DeLay, maverick Ross Perot, libertarian Ron Paul, and now Ted Cruz, loudly decrying Washington as he sought its highest office.

"Today, just like the brave heroes of the Alamo," Cruz declared in a campaign speech during my Texas drive, "we are besieged by a government that is undermining our basic constitutional rights. And I believe now, just as in 1836, it will be the people of Texas who stand together and say, 'Enough is enough!'"

However events played out in the short term, it seemed inescapable that fast-growing Texas would remain a crucible of the nation's escalating conflicts: over immigration, gun rights, religion, the environment, and other hot-button issues.

Olmsted foresaw the state's influence at a time when Texas was newly born, with about three hundred thousand citizens, compared to twenty-eight million today. The scale of its land and resources, he wrote, gave Texas a natural "preeminence of positions among our States" and sterling prospects. Or, as he put it, in words that applied to the state and nation, then and now, Texas has "an opulent future before her, that only wanton mismanagement can forfeit."

NEARING SAN ANTONIO AND IN NEED OF GAS, I WAS LURED OFF the interstate by a huge sign depicting a cartoonish beaver beside the name

Buc-ee's. This referred to a franchise that was supersized even by Texas standards. I pulled into a pit stop with *120* fueling stations and a hangar-sized store filled with Buc-ee's-themed merchandise.

"If It Harms Beavers, We're Against It" claimed one of the brand's cutesy slogans, though the surrounds of the super-station had been stripped of vegetation that might sustain an actual beaver or other wildlife.

Olmsted cited a different creature on the last leg of his ride from Austin. Almost every road into San Antonio, he wrote, was bordered by dense, prickly undergrowth, "and so the city bristles like the porcupine, with a natural defense."

In contrast to the city's sprawl today, San Antonio was also "closely-built." Soon after reaching the first houses at the city's outskirts, the riders entered "the square of the Alamo." Olmsted described this plaza as "all Mexican," ringed by simple homes made of adobe, or wood stakes "plastered with mud and roofed with river-grass."

The Alamo itself was "a mere wreck of its former grandeur," he added, "a few irregular stuccoed buildings, huddled against the old church, in a large courtyard surrounded by a rude wall." This former mission sanctuary, "all hacked and battered in the battles it has seen," he wrote, survived as a monument to the courage of its defenders—and was now in use "as an arsenal by the U.S. quartermaster." Photographs from the mid-nineteenth century show horses drawing wagons through the front door of the church; its first floor was mainly used for storing animal fodder.

Not until the twentieth century did Texas designate the Alamo "a sacred memorial to the heroes who immolated themselves upon that hallowed ground." The state also appointed, as custodians of the shrine, the Daughters of the Republic of Texas, a group that helped save the Alamo from further desecration.

Before leaving Austin, I'd visited the Daughters' headquarters and museum, which was filled with locks of hair, whittled crosses, and other holy relics of the heroes of the revolution. The group's treasurer told me that the Daughters had recently relinquished their role as caretakers of the Alamo, after more than a century. But they remained active in the rites held on the anniversary of the 1836 sacrifice.

These tributes included battle reenactments, and honored not only the Alamo's dramatic fall but also the twelve-day siege that preceded it. "We call this the High Holy Days," she said, a phrase I associated with rabbis and yarmulkes, not Crockett enthusiasts in coonskin caps.

The observance was approaching, so I timed my arrival in San Antonio for the High Holy Days, and prepared by dipping into the vast scripture of literature and scholarship devoted to the Alamo. What I failed to do was consult a map of modern San Antonio, having blithely supposed that I would quickly arrive, as Olmsted had, at the city's famous shrine.

Instead, upon exiting the interstate, I entered a labyrinth of one-way streets, river crossings, and office towers blocking my sightline. After circling in traffic for half an hour, I lowered the car window and pleaded with a pedestrian, "Where's the Alamo?"

He pointed down the street I was on and told me to "go left at the plaza." Parking my car, I headed there on foot, but couldn't see much that looked like a plaza, or the Alamo, just a street named for it that was lined with tourist traps: souvenir shops, a wax museum, a game arcade, and Ripley's Believe It or Not!

Then I turned and saw, directly across from this gaudy commerce, the iconic facade of worn yellow stones and ancient columns, topped by a humped crown. Exactly as I'd imagined it, since my boyhood reading of *Remember the Alamo!* I could almost conjure Davy Crockett swinging his musket in front of the church, as he did on the cover of my Landmark Books classic.

Except the real thing looked so . . . puny. Like Plymouth Rock, which towered in American imagination and turned out to be a cracked little boulder. I'd read enough to know the Alamo wasn't a grand cathedral. But at first glance, the shrine's size and shape wasn't much different from the Mexican restaurant where I'd lunched.

It didn't help that just behind me, a legless figure called Stumpy the Ghoul kept cackling maniacally from the entrance of Ripley's Haunted Adventure. Seeking a better vantage, I crossed the busy street and joined a group of men sitting on a low wall that formed a front-row pew for worship of the Alamo.

Or so it seemed from the pilgrims I met there, who referred to the wall as their "perch" and to themselves as "Alamaniacs." Almost all were sixty or older and cited common sources for their devotion: the 1950s Disney series and film on Davy Crockett, and the 1960 Hollywood epic *The Alamo.*

"Fess Parker and John Wayne, that's how all of us got the bug," one man explained, before breaking into a verse of "The Ballad of Davy Crockett."

"I see the John Wayne movie as a boy," added an Italian man. "It is a big tragic story, like an opera."

Some of the men took their passion to a deeper level, poring over the fine print of battle. Soon after I arrived, they began debating a favorite subject: whether Davy Crockett actually died swinging "Old Betsy" to the last, as generally depicted in Alamo lore.

"You don't get to be a forty-nine-year-old frontiersman by acting like a kamikaze," said a shaggy-haired man who'd wandered over to the perch. "Davy was a survivalist; he respected danger. I think he kept falling back, until he was seized."

The speaker was Gary Foreman, a filmmaker and writer from Indiana who'd been so infected by "the Alamo and Crockett craze" of his boyhood that he'd attended the High Holy Days for thirty-five years, proposing to his wife on one of these visits. He'd also devoted much of his career to Alamo preservation and memory, recording hundreds of interviews with the perch sitters and other visitors.

The takeaway, for him, was that most people were drawn to the Alamo by the story's existential dimension: taking a stand of life-or-death consequence in the face of impossible odds.

"The guys who fought here, no matter how messed up their lives were to that point, they had that 'Alamo moment,'" Foreman said. "People come here to feel and understand that, and to ask themselves, 'What would I do in that situation?'"

Unfortunately, in his view, it was hard to conjure this experience because so little of the 1836 setting remained, and what did was commonly misunderstood. For instance, many visitors thought the church *was* the Alamo, rather than one corner of a fortified mission compound that had covered four acres.

Foreman then led me on a brisk tour, weaving through a hodgepodge of monuments, street vendors, street preachers, and car traffic. Striding past

Ripley's and Stumpy the Ghoul, he stopped at what had been the Alamo's north wall and the main point of attack on March 6, 1836.

"Mexicans poured across that lot," Foreman said, pointing at what was now Alamo Parking, "straight into cannon and musket fire."

Outnumbered roughly ten to one, the Alamo's defenders fell back to a barracks within the compound, shooting from doorways at Mexicans who had breached the walls. These "separate last stands," as Foreman called them, ended when the Mexicans turned the Alamo's cannon around, raking the barracks and shooting or bayoneting survivors.

"Much blood has been shed, but the battle is over," Santa Anna wrote an aide, "it was but a small affair."

This understated the ferocity of the short fight, which killed or wounded six hundred or so of Santa Anna's men. On the other side, every combatant died, a much-debated toll ranging from 185 to more than 250.

By most accounts, the fight lasted only an hour, and Foreman believed the true combat was even briefer. "We imagine the battle as a John Wayne shoot-out, but these guys were zombies," he said of the Alamo's defenders, who had been under siege and artillery bombardment for days. Citing military studies of fatigue and stress, he speculated, "They probably only had about ten to twelve minutes of adrenaline before they collapsed."

Foreman ended this rather deflating tour at the church, where he punctured another myth. Little fighting took place at the chapel. And if Crockett died in front of it, this likely occurred after the combat, when Santa Anna ordered the execution of Davy and five or six other captives.

Foreman glanced at his watch. For all his dislike of the commerce intruding on the Alamo, he had his own to transact: signing copies of his latest book beside a fudge stand at the gift shop. "Not exactly an 'Alamo moment,'" he acknowledged. "But you could say I'm a survivalist like Crockett, selling books instead of shooting bear."

AS OLMSTED OBSERVED, EIGHTEEN YEARS AFTER THE "HEROIC defense" of the Alamo, the site had become a half-ruined compound, repurposed as a US Army depot. Soldiers also gouged bricks as souvenirs, removed religious statues, and carved their names on the walls. "You couldn't take a selfie back then, so this was how you left your mark," a guide in the chapel said of the graffiti.

After the Civil War came other indignities. The Alamo was leased to merchants who adorned its barracks with mock battlements and used the compound as a grocery and liquor warehouse. The state and Daughters of the Republic of Texas saved what remained from being razed, but they couldn't halt the garish development that grew up around it.

While purists like Foreman bemoaned this, the Alamo's longtime historian and curator noted an ironic twist. The first man to buy up property around the Alamo was Samuel Maverick, who escaped death at the Alamo by riding off as a courier a few days before its fall.

"So it's an Alamo survivor who gets rich from developing this area," Bruce Winders said. He also noted that the Texas revolutionaries were fighting, in part, for economic opportunity. "If the others here had lived, they'd have done the same as Maverick and built the equivalent of a Fuddruckers, too."

I'd encountered Winders by the front door of the church and at first had mistaken him for a visiting Alamaniac. Bearded, and clad in a cravat, top hat, and frock coat, he stood before a clot of visitors, reading from William Travis's letters from the Alamo proclaiming, "God and Texas! Victory or Death!!"

Winders told me after the presentation that dressing in period attire during the High Holy Days "makes me more approachable. People actually listen to my history lessons, even if they don't always like what they hear."

Popular culture, as I'd seen at the "perch," explained much of the appeal of the Alamo, which attracted 2.5 million visitors a year, on a par with Mount Rushmore. But literature and Hollywood also bred fictions that Winders and his staff struggled to dispel.

One of many enduring shibboleths: the Alamo was an abandoned mission in the middle of nowhere, as depicted in the John Wayne film. "Visitors ask me, 'How did the Alamo get here, in downtown?'" Winders had to explain that San Antonio was a long-established city in 1836, and control of it was the reason for Santa Anna's attack.

He'd also spent his twenty years on the job trying to give nuance to the traditional American view of the Alamo, which he characterized as "the heroes of Texas fighting foreign villains and invaders!"

In reality, only eleven of the Alamo defenders were Texas born, and nine of those were men of Mexican or Spanish descent who opposed Santa Anna's regime. One of the garrison's leaders, Jim Bowie, had Mexican citizenship and a Tejano wife. Over twenty of the defenders came from Denmark, Wales, and elsewhere abroad.

In addition, Crockett and other new arrivals to Texas "were effectively illegal immigrants," Winders said, since Mexico had barred further immigration from the US in 1830 and sought the expulsion of squatters.

Meanwhile, Santa Anna's army included European officers and mestizos of mixed Spanish and Indian descent, conscripted for up to ten years. "So who exactly were 'the Mexicans' and who were 'the Texans,' and why were they here?" Winders asked. "It's not a black-and-white story."

Except that in part, it was. Mexico had abolished slavery and attempted to restrict its spread in Texas, inciting many Anglos to take up arms. Santa Anna hoisted a red flag from a church within view of the Alamo, signaling he would show no quarter to its defenders. But after slaying all the combatants, he spared Jim Bowie's slave and another black man, freeing them with about a dozen women and children huddled in the church.

Winders had succeeded in adapting the Alamo's interpretation and museum, but he also had to contend with latter-day Travises among right-wing Texans. The Alamo and four nearby Spanish missions had recently been designated UNESCO World Heritage Sites. This boosted the missions' international profile, aided in their preservation—and enflamed conspiracy theorists who cast UNESCO's move as a dark, globalist plot.

"'The blue berets are coming! To take the Alamo and tell us what to do, like Santa Anna and the Mexicans!'" Winders said, mimicking the new battle cry. "It's the same old story here. Perception trumps reality and becomes the reality."

AFTER ARRIVING AT THE ALAMO UPON HIS ENTRY TO SAN ANTO-nio, Olmsted spent a week touring the city and its surrounds. In many ways, he approached human landscapes as he did scenery and park designs, expressing a dislike for uniformity and a strong preference for admixtures, contrast, and an element of mystery.

"We have no city, except, perhaps, New Orleans," he wrote, that rivaled San Antonio's "odd and antiquated foreignness" and picturesque "jumble of races, costumes, languages and buildings."

This "composite character" was palpable from the moment he rode into town, past German homes made from "fresh square-cut blocks of creamy-white limestone." Later came the flat-roofed adobe homes of Mexicans, "washed blue and yellow." Then multistory brick "American dwellings" set behind picket fences. On the streets, "the triple nationalities break out into the most amusing display," a mingling of "bearded Germans," "sauntering Mexicans," "and "sallow Yankees."

Olmsted would soon become well acquainted with Germans in Texas, who had migrated in large numbers over the previous decade. But he was mesmerized, first, by the exotic-seeming Mexicans, with whom he'd had only glancing contact thus far in his journey.

"There is a permanent company of Mexican mountebanks," he wrote, parading in "spangled tights with drum and trombone" and giving performances "of agility and buffoonery." This spectacle attracted vendors of whiskey, tortillas ("corn slap-jacks," Olmsted called them), and tamales ("hashed meat in corn-shucks"), the torchlight scene "ruddily picturesque."

Strolling by moonlight, Olmsted gazed through the open doors of Mexican homes, generally single rooms with floors of beaten clay and little furniture. "We were invariably received with the most gracious and beaming politeness and dignity," he wrote. "Their manner towards one another is engaging, and that of children and parents most affectionate."

Olmsted paid particular attention to young women, as he had in New Orleans. He admired their "blushing olive" complexion, glossy and luxuriant hair, "animation of tongue and glance," and captivating eyes, "deep, dark, liquid, and well-set." Also, their ample curves, or what he delicately called their "soft embonpoint," meaning fleshy and buxom figures.

"The common dress was loose and slight," he wrote, "frequently but a chemise, as low as possible in the neck, sometimes even lower, with a calico petticoat," an ensemble that "seemed lazily reluctant" to cover the women's charms.

He described the Mexican men as "admirable laborers," working as drovers and shepherds and transporting goods in crude carts and ox-drawn wagons. But they were poorly paid and badly treated by Anglo Texans, who were always careful to "distinguish themselves as 'white folks,'" Olmsted wrote, while disdaining Mexicans as mixed-race, thievish, and threatening.

This "contempt and suspicion" was strongest among slaveholders. In other slave states, runaways typically headed north in search of freedom; in Texas they ran *south* toward Mexico. Also, those of Mexican descent in Texas "consort freely with the negroes, making no distinction from pride of race," Olmsted wrote. "Most of them regard slavery with abhorrence."

In some Texas counties, Mexicans were driven out altogether. San Antonio, with its large immigrant presence, resisted this. Still, "a day or two after our arrival," Olmsted wrote, "there was the hanging of a Mexican" and the "whole population" went to watch, including children hoisted high to witness and be warned by the spectacle. "The Mexicans looked on imperturbable."

WITH THE AID OF OLD MAPS AND THE ALAMO HISTORIAN, BRUCE Winders, it was relatively easy to reconstruct Olmsted's tour of the city. He entered on Commerce Street, which bridged the San Antonio River, a beautiful waterway "of a rich blue and pure as crystal," Olmsted wrote, "flowing rapidly but noiselessly over pebbles and between reedy banks. One could lean for hours over the bridge-rail."

The narrow wood bridge of his day had been replaced by a concrete span, and the water below looked more like a lazy, greenish-brown canal than the rapid, crystal-blue river he described. But Olmsted would likely have approved of San Antonio's River Walk, the landscaped promenade that wound below street level, a sinuous strip of green extending to the missions on the city's southern edge.

On the other hand, he envisioned green spaces as a therapeutic refuge from the hubbub and materialism of city life. The River Walk's core, in downtown San Antonio, was thronged with tourists, stores peddling "Mexican curios," and bars and restaurants: Waxy O'Connor's Irish Pub, Coyote Ugly, Hard Rock Cafe.

Wading through this jostle, I came face-to-face with a stunning woman of exactly the sort Olmsted admired: olive-skinned, liquid dark eyes, luxuriant black hair, and voluptuous curves rising from her low-cut blouse.

She was also animated of "tongue and glance," returning my gaze with a beguiling smile. "Two-dollar margaritas," she said, waving me toward the Cafe Olé behind her. "Happy hour now till six!"

Returning to Commerce Street, I reached San Antonio's main plaza, once busy with what Olmsted called the city's "rattling life" and overlooked by an old stone cathedral with a cracked bell "clunking for vespers." The plaza remained intact, if empty of much life apart from pigeons. The cathedral's Spanish facade had been remodeled a decade after Olmsted's visit and now resembled Paris's Notre-Dame. Its interior had also been colonized by a sarcophagus that allegedly held the burnt remains of the "Texas Heroes," Travis, Bowie, and Crockett.

As Olmsted observed, San Antonio was a "conquered" city, the "intruding race" busily converting Mexican buildings into "drinking-places," or leaving them to decay into relics of a near-forgotten heritage. He saw this most vividly at the eighteenth-century Spanish missions that formed an eight-mile necklace along the river winding south from the Alamo.

These had once been thriving settlements, peopled by natives seeking protection from Apache and Comanche raiders. They lived in the walled mission compounds, herded livestock, worked quarries and iron forges, spun and wove cloth, and tended fields and orchards watered by a sophisticated network of aqueducts and irrigation canals.

By the time of Olmsted's arrival, however, the missions seemed as remote as Mayan temples. "All are real ruins," he wrote, "beyond any connection with the present—weird remains out of the silent past."

The missions had since been restored, but they still felt disconnected in time and place, like medieval abbeys transported to the outskirts of a modern American city. The largest, Mission San José, had a domed church decorated with Moorish arches, cherubs, and an ornate rose window. The walled compound also included a *convento* for the missionaries, and white-plastered "Indian quarters."

The priests required Indians to learn Spanish and Latin and worship three times a day, while being taught carpentry, blacksmithing, and other trades. Even in ruins, Olmsted wrote, the missions impressed upon him "the strangely patient courage and zeal of the old Spanish fathers," who "persuaded and compelled" natives to construct these striking testaments to "the glory of the faith."

They had a similar effect on me. Standing at the center of San José's vast courtyard, as the church bells tolled, only the hum of traffic beyond the walls broke the spell of a carefully ordered colonial world a century older than the rough-hewn Anglo settlements Olmsted encountered along most of the Texas frontier.

Eerier still was Mission Concepción, a less-restored site in a run-down area at San Antonio's southern edge. Only crumbled ruins remained of the walls, and the heavy stone church looked gloomy and grimed, like the "ponderous but rudely splendid edifices" Olmsted described on his tour.

But inside there were colorful frescoes, one depicting an adobe-colored sun with eyes, a mustache, and crown-like yellow rays. A guide explained that this was native art, mixing Spanish, Christian, and indigenous motifs. "It may have been an effort to present God in the image of a Spaniard," he said. Another theory: it depicted God as a mixed-race mestizo.

The Franciscan priests acknowledged the "Imperfect Conversion" of natives at the missions. Many Indians deserted the compounds or alternated between Christian and native ritual, ingesting peyote for spiritual visions and dances. They were also ravaged, as elsewhere across America, by epidemic disease, and by the ongoing raids of hostile tribes. In 1794, the missions were secularized and their lands distributed to the surviving inhabitants.

Despite this failure to bring lasting benefit to converts, the guide at Mission Concepción, an elderly man named David Garrett, felt the Spanish had compared favorably to "other invaders." The Franciscans provided food, clothing, training, and "a path to citizenship," he said, rather than segregating themselves from natives or seeking to expel them.

Late-arriving Anglos nonetheless branded the Spanish legacy in Texas as brutish and uncivilized. "Pot calling the kettle black," Garrett said, turning to show another visitor the church's startling frescoes.

I RETURNED TO THE ALAMO, ORIGINALLY MISSION SAN ANTONIO de Valero, to find troops mustering for battle beside food trucks named Big

Mike's Barbecue and Truck'n Taco. Those representing the Mexicans wore formal military uniforms: white pants, blue coats, and tall red shakos.

Their foe, for today, was a ragtag outfit, mostly clad in buckskin and an assortment of headwear. Many appeared to be sixty or older, at least double the age of most combatants in 1836. Also ahistorical: the Texas ranks were larger than the Mexican, which had massive numerical superiority at the time of battle.

"I switched teams today to keep the numbers up," said one of the "Mexicans," David Martin, a retired aviation worker. "We can't all be Texas heroes." Another "Mexican," Bart Tyler, said he preferred playing a *soldado.* "I like the uniform and the discipline of being a regular soldier," he said. "On the Texas side, it's loose; everyone feels they're in charge and can dress any way they like."

"Damn right!" interjected a Texan with straggly grayish-red hair, a top hat, and a frayed frock coat. The man beside him, playing the part of Davy Crockett, wore a mismatched ensemble of rough trousers, vest, coat, and a fur cap. "When I see a dead raccoon on the road, I think 'hat,'" he said.

This irregular, faux-military scene was reminiscent of the many Civil War reenactments I'd witnessed—and sometimes participated in—when I lived in Virginia. Allegiances to North or South were often stylistic rather than regional or ideological. Blue and regimented on the Union side; gray and brown and ragged in the rebel camp, which tended to be larger and rowdier.

The Alamo defenders, like Confederates, also had underdog appeal. "Our cause is doomed today, but we'll die like men," said the man playing Crockett, before marching with his comrades to take up position in front of the wax museum on the plaza.

Then, over the hum of the food trucks, a man regally clad in a plumed bicorn, sash, saber, and epaulets began barking orders in Spanish. *"Atención! Armas al hombro! Marche!"* As he led his soldiers into the plaza, saber held stiffly to his shoulder, a woman ran up and asked, "Are you-all the Mexicans and Santa Anna?"

"*Sí, señora.*"

"Hon!" she called to her husband. "Bring the camera and get me with the bad guys."

Another tourist, evidently not a history buff, spotted the Mexicans and shouted, *"Viva Zapata!"*

Hundreds of spectators lined Alamo Street, the set for today's battle. The Texans stood behind chest-high Styrofoam "walls" on either end of the street, some of the men having inserted earplugs.

"This reenactment is called 'For God and Texas,'" an emcee announced to the crowd, "and will be a realistic presentation of how the Alamo defenders died. It is now an hour before dawn on March sixth. Let the battle proceed!"

Following a few lines of stilted dialogue between William Travis and his aides, the Mexicans charged the Styrofoam walls, accompanied by fife and drum. *"Levante sus armas!"* Santa Anna shouted. *"Apuntar! Fuego!"* The soldiers fired their muskets, which were loaded with powder blanks and aimed above the heads of their foes.

The Texans bit at paper cartridges, poured powder down their musket barrels, and returned fire. "Give 'em hell, boys!" Travis shouted. "Make every shot count!"

The two sides exchanged repeated volleys from about thirty yards apart, filling the street with smoke and the acrid smell of gunpowder, but not with bodies. It had been agreed beforehand that no one would risk flopping onto the hard pavement.

"Steady, boys, keep it hot on 'em!" Crockett shouted, his fur cap awry. A drone buzzed overhead, prompting one spectator to bellow, "Air support!"

Then the Mexicans rushed forward, shouting *"Viva Santa Anna! Viva la República!"* When they reached the Styrofoam, there was a bit of musket swinging and mock bayoneting before the Texans turned their guns over and bowed, signifying defeat and death.

"Remember the Alamo!" the emcee concluded. "And we'll see you back here at three thirty for another reenactment of the battle."

The spectators cheered lustily, crying, "Long Live Texas!" Many seemed genuinely moved, solemnly approaching the reenactors and telling them, "Thank you for remembering," or "Thank you for your service," as if actual combat had transpired.

"De nada," one of the *soldados* replied. Then to me: "My Spanish is terrible. When Santa Anna said 'about face,' I thought it was 'left face' and marched the wrong way."

I followed the reenactors as they marched from the plaza to rehydrate between battles at the bar of the Menger Hotel, Teddy Roosevelt's favorite haunt while mustering the Rough Riders. One of the "Mexican" reenactors removed a shako to reveal a long braid of dark hair. This was Renae Avery, a preschool director, and today a lancer who had dispatched Davy Crockett.

"If any of the guys give me grief," she said, "I tell them, 'At five foot three and a hundred and twenty pounds, my body's much more historically correct than you six footers with beer bellies.'"

Drinking across from her was Doug Cohen, a former cop in his late sixties with a fringed buckskin jacket and strong Brooklyn accent. "There were three Jews at the Alamo—probably a doctor, lawyer, and accountant," he quipped. "So why not me?"

There were in fact a few Alamo defenders believed to have been Jewish, although little was known about them. Cohen had another tie to the Alamo, having appeared as a teenaged extra in the John Wayne film. "I was a kosher ham, got on camera as much as I could," he said. "How often do you get to be killed on the big screen?"

The reenactors conceded that today's mock battle hadn't been their best, due to the highly improvised set and backdrop of Häagen Dazs, Ripley's, and other modern intrusions. But the Alamo was just one stop in an annual pilgrimage known as the Texas Independence Trail, each historic contest commemorated with reenactments. "I like killing and winning all the way to San Jacinto," said a *soldado*, "then I switch sides so I can give it to the Mexicans."

Returning to the Alamo, I met a man in Mexican uniform who took his role more seriously. Martin Vasquez wasn't participating in this year's reenactment, but he played Santa Anna at San Jacinto and was dressed as the general today for a presentation by the church called "Who Were the Mexican Soldiers?"

Accompanied by two men in *soldado* attire, Vasquez explained that most of Santa Anna's men were mestizo conscripts who marched to San Antonio barefoot or in sandals, in cold and snow. Much better equipped and trained were elite *zapadores*, who served as assault infantry as the Mexicans stormed the Alamo's twelve-foot walls with axes, crowbars, and ladders.

"The foot soldiers were merely doing their duty," Vasquez said, and they suffered grievous losses scaling walls under heavy fire. Yet there was no monument of any kind to them at the Alamo. "Instead, they have been called murderers and cowards when in reality they were sons, brothers, and fathers fighting for their country."

To further humanize these neglected *soldados*, the reenactors sang a Mexican Army tune from the period. The lyrics translated in part: "While there's wine in our glass let's be merry, for tomorrow the trumpets may call us to die."

As for Santa Anna, Vasquez described him as "charismatic, ruthless and brave," more comfortable in the saddle than in his presidential office. Like Napoleon, whom he idolized, Santa Anna came from a modest background and rose quickly due to his military skill and imperial flair.

One example: two years after his defeat at San Jacinto, Santa Anna became a war hero again in a fight with the French called the Pastry War. When cannon fire shattered his left leg, he interred the limb with full military honors in a mausoleum, replacing it with an elaborate prosthetic of wood, leather, and cork.

Vazquez's talk was a new addition to the High Holy Days. In earlier years, he said, there had been strong resistance to any presentation of the Mexican side. "People would write the newspaper saying, 'Why are we remembering these savages and murderers?'"

He'd grown up in San Antonio with a similar perspective, despite being a third-generation Mexican American. "John Wayne was my entry point, the movie hooked me, and it wasn't until I went to college that I realized there was another side and that I should help tell it."

He'd done so as a history teacher and now as a reenactor. Santa Anna was a tall, handsome dandy, and Vasquez fit this role, standing ramrod straight in white pants, embroidered green frock coat, white gloves, and cravat, speaking to visitors in a formal yet engaging manner.

Sometimes he was too convincing. "People think I'm Santa Anna for real, or because I talk like he did, about Texans being land grabbers and pirates, they assume I approve of everything about him."

Vasquez didn't. But he did enjoy expressing Santa Anna's position "that this was Mexico and he had to defend it against illegal invaders pouring into Texas." He also hoped this perspective resonated in the present.

"The problem Mexico had with Americans then," he observed, "is what Americans are having now, with undocumented Hispanics."

AS OLMSTED TOURED SAN ANTONIO, HE KEPT RETURNING TO ITS "chief interest," the city's "jumble" of nationalities and cultures. Anglos, Mexicans, and Germans predominated, but there were also blacks, Irish, Native Americans, and others.

This mix had since changed, but the city's population remained a striking mélange. I witnessed this most vividly at an event where I didn't expect it: a High Holy Days ceremony at the Alamo sponsored by a local chapter of the Daughters of the Republic of Texas.

I arrived to find Daughters in red jackets and Sons of the Republic in blue blazers and white Stetsons, most of them elderly and almost all of them white. They'd gathered to watch performances by students from Thomas Jefferson High School: junior ROTC cadets drilling in the plaza; a dance group called the Lassos in cowboy hats and boots, slinging ropes; a jazz band playing "Texas, Our Texas."

The program was quintessentially Lone Star, including prayers and pledges to the US and state flags—all led by a student body that was about 90 percent Hispanic, Asian, and African American. It was a multiculturalist's dream, deep in the heart of Texas, without a hint of the self-conscious and self-congratulatory atmosphere that might attend a similar display of diversity in blue-state America.

I was also unexpectedly stirred by the climactic ceremony on the holiest of the Holy Days: a predawn observance of the Alamo's fall on March 6, 1836. Five a.m. on a Sunday turned out to be the perfect time to visit the site, the church's facade lit and the rest of the plaza undisturbed by traffic, Stumpy the Ghoul, and other clamor.

Several hundred spectators had gathered by the time the ceremony began at 6:00 a.m., with an emcee briefly narrating the battle that had raged at this hour 180 years ago. Boots clattered on the flagstones as reenactors marched into the plaza and stood silently facing each other, much more solemn and convincing than they'd been in the heat of mock battle the day before.

Descendants of those killed at the Alamo lit candles and laid wreaths, while others read from eyewitness accounts of the battle, on both sides, telling of the confusion, carnage, and "desperate terrible cries" of alarm and agony. After a prayer for peace, in English and Spanish, a bugler performed the *Oracione*, a plaintive Taps-like tune of the Mexican Army, and a bag-piper played "Amazing Grace" as he walked along the wall of the barracks where the Alamo's defenders staged their bloody last stand.

For the first time all week, I felt a twinge of time travel and awe as the sun rose behind the Alamo church, illuminating, at the exact place and hour, what would have been a scene of terrifying slaughter in 1836. Those around me seemed similarly moved, sitting or standing silently long after the ceremony ended.

In 1836, the fight for the Alamo was over by about 7:00 a.m. Not so on the last of the High Holy Days, which like Yom Kippur became a long march through a series of solemn services. In this case, repeated speeches about "hallowed ground" and "supreme sacrifice," with Travis's letters read liturgically and prayers and pledges offered to the Alamo defenders, the nation, and the Texas flag.

Between ceremonies, I met several Crockett descendants, including a Seventh-day Adventist from Idaho who gave a religious cast to his fore-bear's demise. "Davy's fighting beside a church, there are women and chil-dren inside, that's faith and chivalry," he said. "When you die for a purpose, people take notice. In the Middle Ages, the blood of the martyrs was the seed for the spread of the Gospel."

Others invoked the continuing sacrifices made by the military, and men in uniform appeared on almost every podium. As one lieutenant general put it: the Alamo "reminds us to cherish our freedoms, and inspires us to defend them."

I soldiered on because I wanted to see the closing ceremony, conducted by the wise and irreverent Alamo historian, Bruce Winders. He abjured further worship, or praise of the military, talking instead about the fate of the Alamo defenders' bodies.

"There was a long-standing tradition of burning enemy dead," he said, "and of burning heretics," which the mostly Protestant defenders repre-sented to Santa Anna. After the fight, Mexican soldiers dragged wood and bodies onto pyres, alternating layers of corpses and mesquite. Then, at about 5:00 p.m. on March 6, the fires were lit.

"So at this hour, 180 years ago, you would have seen the smoke and fire of the funeral pyres," he concluded. "Always remember the Alamo."

As the crowd dispersed, Winders took historical exception to the words he'd just solemnly uttered. During the High Holy Days, "remember the Alamo" carried a mournful, elegiac message. But its original usage, in 1836, was as a battle cry at San Jacinto, six weeks after the carnage at the Alamo.

"It was a way of saying to the Mexicans, 'We remember what you did and will take revenge.'" The Texans promptly did so, slaughtering hundreds of *soldados* after the battle had already been decided.

Winders also shared some important news about the historic ground we stood on. The state had agreed to purchase the buildings that housed Ripley's and other entertainment, for renovation as an Alamo museum and visitors' center.

"Maybe next year at this time, we'll build a funeral pyre and throw Stumpy the Ghoul on it," Winders joked. "Bring your marshmallows."

CHAPTER 17

GERMAN TEXAS

Olmsted in Arcadia

Americans don't generally regard Texas as a sanctuary for Socialists, utopians, and adherents of heterodox faiths from abroad. Yet this was the case in the 1840s and '50s, when the migrant tide included a rainbow of ethnic, religious, and political refugees.

Near San Antonio, Olmsted encountered pockets of Alsatians and what he called "a sort of religious colony of Silesian Poles." At the city's Institute of Texan Cultures, I also learned about groups entirely unfamiliar to me, such as French Icarians, who believed in "perfect democracy and universal suffrage," and the Wends, a Slavic people so dour in their beliefs that brides wore black wedding gowns, "to symbolize the end of a carefree childhood and the approaching hardships of married life."

Also exotic to modern eyes—and much more consequential for Texas and Olmsted—was the *Adelsverein*, a league of petty German nobles that dreamed of "bringing new crowns to old glory" by planting a second fatherland in Texas. They sponsored mass migration of peasants and artisans but lacked the acumen for their grandiose project and were duped by land speculators.

The group's semifeudal leader, Prince Carl of Solms-Braunfels, founded a town named for one of his ancestral castles and decamped to Europe. The *Adelsverein* soon went bust. Thousands of vassals the nobles landed on the Gulf Coast were ill-equipped for the long trek inland; many died en route or soon after reaching land plots on what was then the frontier of settlement.

But Neu Braunfels and a few other settlements survived and more Germans kept coming, impelled not only by economic distress at home but also by the failed revolution against monarchial rule that erupted across Europe in 1848. By the time Olmsted reached Texas, Germans constituted about a fifth of the state's white population and the vast majority of inhabitants in the hills between Austin and San Antonio.

"The first German settlers we saw, we knew at once," Olmsted wrote. Their log cabins and timber-frame homes were simple but very well kept, as were their tidy and "judiciously cultivated" fields. These plots included rectangles of the South's great staple, sown and picked by German men, women, and children.

"It caused us a sensation to see a number of parallelograms of COTTON—FREE-LABOR COTTON," Olmsted exulted. To underline this point, he reminded *Times* readers that cotton and free labor weren't words he'd ever used together in print. In "the WEST," he added, emigration was diluting rather than expanding the Slave Power. "Cotton comes to market this year from *beyond* Slavery."

Soon after, the riders reached Neu Braunfels, an orderly town of cottages, workshops, gristmills, and *"seven wagon manufactories."* Olmsted judged the town to have a higher proportion of skilled workmen than any he'd visited in the South.

Also astonishing was the inn where he and John lunched. In contrast to the makeshift, "cheerless" establishments they'd become accustomed to on the Camino Real, the Schmitz Hotel had pink walls with stenciled panels and lithographic prints. The dining table was set with a white cloth and there was no sign of bacon or corn pone. Instead, the travelers enjoyed "an excellent soup" followed by "two courses of meat, neither of them pork, and neither of them fried," as well as salad, peach compote, and wheat bread with delicious sweet butter.

"I never in my life, except perhaps, in awakening from a dream, met with such a sudden and complete transfer of associations," Olmsted wrote, likening the hotel to "delightful little inns" along the Rhine. "In short, we were in Germany."

The company pleased him, too: thick-bearded, pipe-smoking men, "all educated, cultivated, well-bred, respectful, kind, and affable." The travelers were so delighted that they lingered, overnighting at the inn. Strolling in the dark, Olmsted paused by a cottage "to listen to some of the best singing I have heard for a long time."

Riding out of town the next day, he was likewise charmed by the school-children he passed, "all with ruddy, cheerful faces, the girls especially so, with their hair braided neatly," he wrote, "smiling and saluting us—'gutten morgen'—as we met. Nothing so pleasant as that in Texas before; hardly in the South."

Olmsted was predisposed to swoon over this Teutonic milieu. Like many of his peers, he'd drunk deeply of German literature and philosophy and felt an Anglo-Saxon kinship with an immigrant group often typecast in the North as clean, thrifty, and hardworking—in contrast to the reviled Irish. His pleasant time in German lands while tramping abroad deepened this admiration.

But Olmsted's enchantment with Neu Braunfels—and later, his rhapsodic writing on other German settlements—reflected more than his delight at finding a cultured European enclave deep in the interior of Texas. Up to this point in his travels, his case against the slavocracy had been built on negatives and invidious contrasts between North and South. The Germans presented a positive, free-labor model *within* the region.

"Patient, industrious and persevering," the Germans "contrast remarkably with the American Southerners," building wealth through steady labor and enterprise rather than seeking quick riches from speculative adventure. Moreover, though new to the frontier, Germans were forging genuine communities with schools and civic groups devoted to horticulture, music, mechanics, and political debate.

"In these associations you see evidence," Olmsted wrote, "of an active, intellectual life, and desire for knowledge and improvement among the masses of the people, like that which distinguishes the New-Englanders, and which is unknown wherever Slavery degrades labor."

THE NEARLY ALL-GERMAN ENCLAVE OF NEU BRAUNFELS NO LONGER existed as such. Anglicized to *New* Braunfels, the compact, country town of Olmsted's day had metastasized into a bedroom community of sixty-five thousand strung along the interstate corridor northeast of San Antonio.

Even so, like Olmsted, who "knew at once" when he'd reached German settlement, the change was obvious as soon as I crossed the franchise moat between I-35 and New Braunfels's historic center. There were handsome *Fachwerk* cottages like those Olmsted described, half-timbered with steep shingled roofs; beer gardens and a bakery selling strudel; and businesses bearing German names or plays on them, such as Blumen-Meisters (a florist) or Opa's Wheelhaus (a car rental).

I passed a huge fairground devoted to the town's annual Wurstfest, with a billboard of a buxom Bavarian in a dirndl beside the words, "*Sprechen sie Fun?*" Then I came to the office of the *New Braunfels Herald-Zeitung*, descended from a German paper Olmsted noted in 1854. It had stopped publishing in German in 1957 but still printed a section called "*Stammtisch,*" or regular meetings, including yodelers, *Kinderchor* singers, and players of an old German card game called *Skat.*

The paper's publisher, David Burck, was a transplant from Minnesota and told me the German-ness in Texas felt different than it did in the Midwest. "I don't think you see people wearing cowboy hats with their *lederhosen* anywhere else," he said. "And here, when people make sauerkraut, they add jalapeños."

This Tex-Mex-German blend was evident when I checked into the Faust Hotel and snacked at the bar on "German Nachos," *Kartoffel* chips topped with wurst, peppers, and cheese. The woman sitting next to me was of mixed German and Mexican heritage and jokingly referred to herself as "a beaner schnitzel."

I moved on to the Friesenhaus restaurant, where the menu catered to local tastes with dishes like schnitzel smothered in Texas gravy. "I meet many people here who insist their family recipes are German, but you would never find them at home," said one of the owners, Cornelia Dirks, a native of Kiel who'd lived in New Braunfels for a decade.

She and other German-born residents I encountered, many of them married to US servicemen, also expressed amusement at the vocabulary and diction of "Texas Deutsch" speakers. Nineteenth-century migrants spoke many dialects, and their descendants used words that had dropped out of common usage in Germany, while also mixing in Spanish, English, and a Texas twang.

"*Die car. Der cowboy. Luftschiff* for jet plane," Cornelia said, citing examples of this creole tongue. "To me, *Luftschiff* means 'air vessel,' like a Zeppelin." The nearby town of Gruene—"GrOOn-eh" in German—was now pronounced "Green."

This linguistic and cultural fusion hadn't been altogether voluntary. For several generations after Olmsted's visit, New Braunfels remained an insular and staunchly German community. At the Sophienburg, the town's excellent museum, I toured displays on the many associations that once thrived here, including nine-pin Kegelen bowling clubs and a society that Olmsted noted: the *Turnverein*, which mixed gymnastics with civic and political engagement.

"Germans had this togetherness thing," said Charles Nowotny, a museum guide and descendant of early settlers. "They loved their clubs and being clubby."

This cliquish world came under siege in the twentieth century, which brought English-only laws to Texas public schools and two world wars that aroused strong anti-German sentiment. "A lot of the heritage was lost or went underground," Nowotny said.

Still, there were older residents who had remained "German from the word go," and he recommended I visit a man named Carroll Hoffmann. I found him at his small office on the main street where at eighty-four he still advised retirees on their finances. In dress and manner, he was more buttoned-down than most Texans, telling me rather stiffly, with a slight German accent, that I should "make appointments to see experts" rather than talk to him.

Instead, I shared some of Olmsted's observations about the town's tight-knit world, at which point Hoffmann nodded and opened up. "When I was young it was still very clannish here. We stayed in our own village, you could say." This extended to religion. The early settlers were a mix of Protestants, Catholics, and a few Jews, and for roughly a century it remained verboten to date across sectarian lines.

Another rule: absolute respect for elders. "If we talked back or didn't help an older person, we had a lesson back home we did not forget," he said.

Authority figures outside the home could deliver corporal punishment, too. "Three people could kill you almost: the teacher, preacher, and sheriff."

Hoffmann had entered school in the 1930s speaking only three words of English: "My name is." But World War II brought rapid change to this inward community. "We felt looked at and watched," he said. "There was a feeling we had to become fully American, and our parents wanted us to speak English."

The war also brought military bases and scores of non-German newcomers—an influx of what Hoffmann called "foreigners" that had accelerated in the decades since. This had been good for the town's economy and its annual Wurstfest, of which he'd been president.

"It is okay now to celebrate our culture, and beer and sausage is what has hung on more than anything." But he lamented the loss of an ethos Olmsted observed—hard work, shared joy, a certain egalitarianism—that had remained strong in his youth.

"My father worked in a laundry and as a foreman, making fifteen dollars a week. The attitude was 'All you need is what you need, not what you want. Don't kill to make a buck,'" he said. "Everyone was pretty much the same; we wore the same shoes and had the same gardens, and if we had too many carrots we took them to neighbors."

He saw little of that spirit in the very *Amerikaner* world that New Braunfels had become. "Today money talks," he said. "People what come here now, they drop big money and have so much stuff they don't know what to do with it."

RETURNING TO THE SOPHIENBURG, I MET HOFFMANN'S DAUGHTER, Keva Boardman, who helped me search the museum's archives for material relating to Olmsted's visit. Among the items she dug out was an 1857 article from the local *Zeitung*, reviewing *A Journey through Texas*. Other German papers in Texas had praised and excerpted the book; not so the editor in Neu Braunfels.

"Our local German population surely deserves credit for industry and cleanliness," the paper stated. But Olmsted's "overly favorable report on Neu Braunfels" was a biased effort to paint a "hateful contrast" between the

Germans and slaveholding Anglos. "In fact there is no mutual mistrust between the two nationalities here, as Olmsted depicts it."

The editor had his own biases, favoring accommodation with the pro-slavery majority in Texas and opposed to what he called "German alumni of 1848"—exiled revolutionaries who agitated for change in their adopted land. But Keva, after translating the review, said the *Zeitung* accurately reflected a large part of the German community, and Olmsted may have misapprehended what he called its "universal repugnance" to slavery.

"Germans liked doing things themselves, and never thought anyone could do it as well as them," she said. "Farming on their own, rather than with slave labor, was a kind of quality control." Most Germans in antebellum Texas also lacked the large landholdings or capital needed to make slave labor practicable.

More broadly, Keva questioned Olmsted's writing that "the manners and ideals of the Texans and of the Germans are hopelessly divergent," and that the latter might become an anti-slavery fifth column behind Southern lines.

"Germans are conservative by nature in that they tend to resist change," she said. "That's part of why the culture endured here as long as it did."

Over time, Germans also found points of strong cultural kinship with other Texans, including a love of music and dancing (many of the dance halls in Texas were founded by Germans), brewing beer (Shiner being one of the state's most popular brands), and the recreational use of guns (there were once sixty shooting clubs in and around New Braunfels).

"They were German first and wanted to keep their heritage," Keva said. "But once they chose Texas they affiliated with that very strongly."

GERMANS' GRADUAL EMBRACE OF LONE STAR WAYS EXTENDED TO politics. At the time of my visit, a Republican primary for state legislator pitted the incumbent—motto: Our Conservative Champion—against a right-wing firebrand and German culture enthusiast who'd weathered controversy for dressing as a "gay Hitler" at a costume charity event. In campaign ads, he appeared in sniper attire, aiming a gun at the camera. He won the primary easily and ran uncontested in the general election.

"I'm blown away every day by how conservative it is here," the *Herald-Zeitung* editor told me. Whenever the state discussed aid programs, such as rich school districts subsidizing poor ones, "people complain, 'That's So-cialist!'" This was somewhat ironic, since early German settlers included avowed Socialists.

While listening to a German choir group, I met the rare local who con-fessed to being a liberal Democrat, though not for attribution. When the Episcopal Church accepted gays and the ordination of women, he said, "Ninety percent of the people here left the church." And when the county's Democratic Party—"all ten of them"—joined oompah bands and other groups in a jolly July Fourth parade, they were lustily booed.

On my third day in New Braunfels I woke to a different crowd on the main street, streaming toward the civic center for the Liberty Gun Show. A sign at the door forbade open carry of firearms, but inside the arsenal on display included AR-15s, silencers, scopes, body armor, and antique Ger-man Lugers. To buy from a private dealer at the show, one needed only to produce a picture ID proving Texas residency or military posting to the state, no background check required.

But there were a few irksome rules. "You can't pick up the long guns unless you're eighteen, and it's twenty-one for handguns," a salesman told a man whose young sons wanted to handle the wares. "Stupid law, but that's the way it is."

The boys went instead to fire BB guns at a "shooting education range" run by a "faith-based outreach" group, devoted to "guiding the next genera-tion to Christ through the outdoors." One vendor at the show had a sign reading, "Bullets & Bibles."

Oddly, in this sea of arms, ammo, and men in camo, I met a woman selling Nuluv soaps and lotions made from "raw Nubian goat milk." She usually sold these wares, along with German baked goods and organic sau-sage, at a nearby farmers' market. But she was doing a brisk trade at the gun show, too.

"People around here are very particular about eating and washing well," she said. "I don't know if that's a German thing. But if these guys want to pack goat soap with their guns, that's good by me."

AFTER VISITING NEU BRAUNFELS AND SAN ANTONIO, THE OLM-steds originally planned to continue their southwesterly ride to the Rio

Grande. This meant crossing an arid, sparsely settled borderland roamed by Comanche and cutpurses. "We should wear out about one horse a week, and would be robbed each day," they were warned.

So the brothers made it their "first business" in San Antonio to find a military convoy or other wagon train to accompany to Mexico. Unfortunately, such forays were "infrequent and precarious" due to the many hazards. Also, the guide who'd accompanied them on parts of their ride announced that he had urgent business elsewhere and abruptly decamped.

"This more completely blocked our wheels," Olmsted wrote. The brothers' resolve to hasten to the Rio Grande also went into apparent remission. Instead of continuing south, they "gladly accepted an invitation" from a German newspaper editor in San Antonio to accompany him on a ride "into the mountains to the northward."

Olmsted cast this change in itinerary as "A Pause," citing the difficulty of finding safe passage south. But he'd overcome many prior obstacles, and in this case protested too much. The "pause" turned into a two-month sojourn as the Olmsteds became ever more infatuated with the land and people of German Texas.

Foremost among them was Adolf Douai, their editor-guide on the mountain trip. He was a kindred soul, having lost his mother as a child, like the Olmsteds, and an intellectual who'd learned seven languages, written a doctoral dissertation on Hegel, and become a freethinker, or what he called an "infidel," believing that religious doctrine should be subject to rational analysis.

"There are certain persons with whom acquaintance ripens rapidly," Olmsted wrote of Douai, who had settled in Texas two years earlier, after being imprisoned for his political agitation during the republican revolution in Germany. As they rode off from San Antonio, the three men quickly fell "into discussions that ran through deep water, and demanded all our skill in navigation."

The riders became so immersed that "our horses took advantage of our absence" and strayed into prairie, "only keeping their heads towards the north." Once back on course, the men entered hills "rugged with projecting strata of limestone," a peculiar topography "that leaves very much the impression of a crumbling, overgrown pyramid." The vegetation was also striking: "large cacti, yuccas, and agaves, scattered over the arid rocky elevations."

On their second day, the riders reached a summit with "a wide and magnificent view of misty hills and wooded streams." This was the valley of the Guadalupe River, and descending into it, the riders encountered two horsemen in slouch hats, searching for stray cattle. One was a doctor of philosophy from Berlin; "the other a Baron," Olmsted wrote, who "took us to his castle, which was nearby."

This "castle" was a log house plastered with mud, and the travelers lunched on bread and broth. Their host was indeed a baron, though a renegade: Edgar von Westphalen, a classmate, follower, and brother in-law of Karl Marx.

The riders had reached Sisterdale, a singular outpost of German intellect and radicalism in the Texas hills. Almost all the settlement's ten or so farmsteads belonged to distinguished former professors and "Forty-Eighters" who, like Douai, had been driven into exile for their activism and beliefs. Also inhabiting the river valley were what Olmsted called "political hermits," single men who lived in "huts or caves" along the Guadalupe, "earning a tough livelihood chiefly by splitting shingles."

After leaving the baron's "castle," the travelers called at "a double log cabin, upon a romantic rocky bluff," the home and courthouse of the local justice of the peace—also an exiled German nobleman and eminent naturalist. "We had interrupted him at work at notes upon a meteorological table."

The travelers stayed for a "Texan" dinner of corn bread, beans, and coffee, and Olmsted, for once, didn't complain about the plain fare or the tin cups it was served in, because "the talk was worthy of golden goblets."

Olmsted was even more enchanted by a log home where the brothers overnighted. Their host, a formerly wealthy banker "of unusually large education," now farmed sixty acres with his teenaged offspring.

"These sons were as fine pictures of youthful yeomen as can be imagined—tall, erect, well knit, with intelligent countenances, spirited, ingenuous, gentle and manly," Olmsted wrote. Schooled in the morning, they farmed and hunted in the afternoon, bagging a fat turkey for the visitors to dine on.

After supper, neighbors gathered at the log house to sing opera tunes and waltz "to the tones of a fine piano" with two women "of distinguished beauty, grace and accomplishments." One guest told Olmsted that "German tyrants" would be chagrined to see this display of gaiety, since almost every man in the room had been condemned to death or life imprisonment.

The brothers lingered four days in tiny Sisterdale, and returned the next month for a weeklong encampment on the Upper Guadalupe. By the end of this Hill Country tour, Olmsted wrote like a man besotted, as he'd been while courting in his twenties.

"It is a strange thing," he effused in the *Times*, "to hear teamsters with their cattle staked around them on the prairie, humming airs from 'Don Giovanni,' or repeating passages from Dante and Schiller." Or, to "engage in discussions of the deepest and most metaphysical subjects of human thought" with men who live in caves and "earn their daily bread by splitting shingles."

Yeoman had found his Arcadia: an agrarian domain of "unsurpassed" beauty, honest labor, and intellectual and artistic refinement. A world where manual toil and material poverty was no bar to possessing the "mental & moral capital of gentlemen" that Olmsted dreamed of bestowing on all Americans.

His brother was likewise smitten, and the siblings considered ending their travels at the Guadalupe. Olmsted disclosed this in a letter to Anne Charlotte Lynch, his poet friend in New York. "We have fallen among a German population very agreeable to meet: free-thinking, cultivated brave men," Fred wrote. "We have, indeed, been so much pleased that we have been considerably inclined to cast our lot among them."

This was more than a passing fantasy, cooked up by siblings around the campfire. "We now await advices" from "folks at home," Fred told Lynch, "upon which we may determine to become a settler."

ON THE LAST OF MY FOUR DAYS IN NEW BRAUNFELS, I STOPPED AT the Schmitz Hotel, where the Olmsteds had dined and stayed with such pleasure on first visiting the town. The building had been converted to other uses, but a Realtor on the ground floor said he rented out rooms upstairs and agreed to let me lodge for a night.

I felt momentarily triumphant. Olmsted slept here and so would I!

Then I revisited his description of the hotel. He likened it to "one of those delightful little inns" on the Rhine, his room a gay, blue-walled chamber with potted plants, porcelain, a book-lined bureau, and roses trailing from the window. Mine was a blandly renovated suite with a kitchenette and humming refrigerator.

The lone historical touch: a wall display picturing a melancholy pioneer who'd delivered the last of her thirteen children on a wagon with a broken wheel after her husband died of smallpox. When she sought aid from a passerby, he replied, "Your troubles ain't my troubles old lady."

Lying awake in the night, listening to the refrigerator, I pondered my own journey and its much more minor travails. In New Braunfels, as in many other places along Olmsted's route, I'd struggled to unearth vestiges of the world he described. This no longer surprised me, but at 3:00 a.m., it filled me with gloom. I felt like a bloodhound dispatched on the trail of a long-dead scent.

Another source of angst: Olmsted's passion for German Texas, which I'd thus far failed to duplicate. Some of this reflected my inbred, Semitic discomfort with Aryanism—an aversion that the Lugers and Nazi regalia at the gun show had done nothing to dispel. Also, while Olmsted relished German fare, I found a steady diet of sausage, sauerkraut, and dumplings as agreeable as he did corn pone and fatback. The massive *Wurstplatte* I'd consumed for dinner wasn't sitting well.

Olmsted had also raised expectations that couldn't possibly be met. I'd hoped that I might, just maybe, meet a few small-spectacled freethinkers paying homage to their forebears. Instead, I'd mostly found a German heritage embalmed in kitschy commercialism. "*Sprechen sie Fun?*"

More troubling still: I'd begun to suspect that Olmsted, my trusty guide, wasn't the reliable narrator I'd supposed. From my visit to the Sophienburg, and other research, it seemed clear that he'd misconstrued or embellished the free-labor, communitarian society he described in New Braunfels—a burg that Adolf Douai and other Forty-Eighters regarded as bourgeois and reactionary.

Nor, I'd come to realize, was Olmsted forthright with readers about the time and attention he lavished on German Texas, a subject to which he ultimately devoted a third of his *Times* series, "A Tour in the Southwest."

It was true that Fred and John were stalled in San Antonio, and scouted the Upper Guadalupe to learn "for our own benefit, what were the prospects for a northern man who should fix on this point as a future home."

But in doing so, they weren't thinking only of themselves, or merely of the land and other advantages on offer to prospective settlers. The Yeoman who'd once claimed to dispassionately seek understanding of the South had become an agitator, conspiring with a covert cell in the hills to overthrow slavery in Texas.

CHAPTER 18

———

THE HILL COUNTRY

True to the Union

T he two-lane road winding west from New Braunfels took me into gently rolling hills and then a rugged landscape of rocky outcrops, cacti,
and gnarly live oaks. This matched the "Sonoran" scenery that Olmsted
described on his ride with Adolf Douai to Sisterdale.

But a short way farther on, the road intersected with a highway running
north from San Antonio, and I entered a landscape gouged with unfinished
malls, new subdivisions, and property signs touting "Big Views, Great Pri-
vacy," which seemed unlikely to be the case for long.

This despoiled scenery was in tune with a program on my car radio.
Two commentators were bantering about Texas's cowboy-themed official
symbols, including sage (state shrub), rodeo (state sport), and chuck wagon
(state vehicle). "We should change that to the Chevrolet Suburban," one of
the speakers observed.

Then I turned north, into territory just far enough from San Antonio
and the I-35 corridor to not yet have been overrun. I crossed and recrossed
the serpentine Guadalupe, still the beautiful river Olmsted described, embowered by cypress and walled with cream-colored rock shelves. The hills
grew steeper and the views more expansive until I reached a summit that
closely matched one the riders scaled on their second trip along the Guadalupe. "The whole upper valley now lay before us," Olmsted wrote, with "a

wild array of tumbled hills to the north." Using "the glass," a handheld telescope, he could make out "three houses in the dale."

I lacked a spyglass, but the natural grandeur was still plain to see. Ranchland and rocky hills extended for miles, a boundless and rugged vista I associated with the West. This wasn't an illusion. The escarpment at the heart of the Hill Country was part of a rough geographic divide extending into Oklahoma and Kansas, between prairie and woodland to the east and the semiarid plains stretching west to the Rockies.

Descending into the valley, I crossed the Guadalupe again and pulled over at a roadside shop. The building was low-slung and weatherboard with a rust-red metal roof and a sign that read, "General Store: Sisterdale, Texas."

This surprised me. I hadn't noticed a road sign welcoming me to Sisterdale, and on a Sunday afternoon the only evidence of life was a man lying in a hammock in front of the shop, beside a goat paddock.

"This is Sisterdale all right," he assured me. "I'd call this the lower downtown of our business district. You're looking at about a fifth of Sisterdale's commerce."

Bret Cali didn't fit my image of a rural Texas storekeeper. A handsome man in his forties, blue-eyed with unruly black hair, he tuned the store's sound system to jazz and popped two bottles of Shiner Bock. The store's walls had *Pulp Fiction* and *Blues Brothers* posters; plastic pink flamingoes perched in the yard.

The store was also general in an untraditional sense. In addition to a small range of groceries (jerky, salsa, moon pies, canned goods), Bret sold leather bags he made himself, rented out kayaks, and had turned two trailers out back into what he called the Moon Pie Motel, bookable on Airbnb.

"I'm an industrious hippie, like the freethinkers who used to live around here," he said. "Actually, I take that back. I'm much more of a capitalist than they were."

Whatever he was, Bret seemed a serendipitous introduction to the heterodox settlement Olmsted described. Settling at a picnic table, I learned of Bret's "varied and stormy life," as Olmsted wrote of listening to Adolf Douai's. He was of Sicilian rather than German descent, attended military school as a teenager ("earned the highest number of demerits in its history"), and went on to become a fisherman in Alaska, a wilderness survival guide, and an entertainer at a beach resort in Australia, among many other unusual pursuits.

Returning to his native Texas a few years ago, Bret heard that Sisterdale's general store was available for lease and moved into a back room with his dog, gradually building a small, thriving enterprise. "But I'm still a newcomer and I'm reminded of that daily," he said. "Around here, you don't really belong unless you have a road or creek named after your family."

Present-day Sisterdale wasn't much larger than in Olmsted's day, an unincorporated community of about forty inhabitants. Several hundred others lived in the rural surrounds, including most of the old German families that remained. "When I opened," Bret said, "some of the old-timers would come in and say, 'Just wanted to let you know I won't be shopping here.'" When he asked why, they'd tell him, "You haven't been here long enough."

He'd also found Sisterdale riven by obscure feuds—a fault that Olmsted acknowledged in his otherwise glowing portrayal of Hill Country Germans, writing of their "insane mutual jealousy, and petty personal bickering, that prevents all prolonged and effective cooperation."

Bret had naively supposed he could remain neutral, "a Switzerland or Sweden." But when he hired a young man from an old German clan, neighbors who held a grudge against the employee or his family shunned the store. Bret had also stirred ire by holding popular music and steak nights, competing with the saloon that anchored the other end of Sisterdale's tiny business district.

"Hustling's what I do," he said, "and that rubs some people the wrong way."

Many locals, including most of the old German families, also didn't share Bret's liberal politics and cultural tastes, despite Sisterdale's revolutionary heritage. When he saw conservative neighbors approaching, Bret switched the store's soundtrack from NPR or jazz to country music. "Being Texan is such a hard-core identity," he speculated, "that the Germans who stayed here gave in to it, or took it on extra-strong to prove they were really Texan."

This hypothesis accorded with the impression I'd formed in New Braunfels. But Sisterdale's settlers had been far more iconoclastic. In fact, some of them, including associates of Olmsted, were later massacred by fellow Texans.

Or so I'd discover. After another round of Shiner Bock with Bret, I ambled along the Guadalupe and felt "greatly pleased," as Olmsted wrote of his visit to the area. So I settled in, as he had, staying at the Moon Pie Motel for what became an extended Hill Country tour: by car, by foot, and ultimately in the saddle.

IN COMING TO AMERICA, GERMAN "FORTY-EIGHTERS" LOOKED TO the New World as an exemplar of the republican ideals they'd fought for in Europe. But many were disillusioned by what they found and began agitating for reform, particularly in Northern and Midwestern cities with large German populations.

Doing so in distant, slaveholding Texas was far more difficult and dangerous, requiring a great deal of discretion. A month before Olmsted's arrival in the state, Adolf Douai and other Forty-Eighters had quietly formed *Der Freie Verein* in Sisterdale, to foment change and mobilize like-minded Germans.

This "free society" was likely the reason for Douai's mountain "excursion," and for his "invitation" to the Northern travelers to join him. Douai later named four of the "welcome acquaintances" the Olmsteds made in Sisterdale—all radical allies of the editor. The gathering of exiles at which Olmsted described waltzing and "student-songs" was likely a political meeting, too.

On Olmsted's return trip to the Upper Guadalupe, he and his brother camped by a creek they didn't name, "visiting and visited by" settlers they didn't identify, for what Olmsted blandly termed a "tour of observation." But the secretary of the *Freie Verein* wrote that Fred and John "put up a tent on the banks of Sister Creek," a stream that joins the Guadalupe at Sisterdale's heart.

Two months later, the *Verein* convened other German groups in Texas and won approval for a platform ahead of the 1854 midterm election. Much of the manifesto drew on European democratic socialism, calling for a progressive income and inheritance tax and the abolition of capital punishment. But it also took aim at a distinctively American ill.

"Slavery is an evil, the abolition of which is a requirement of Democratic principles," the plank stated. Treading carefully, delegates cast slavery as a state matter in which the federal government should not interfere. "But if a state resolves upon the abolition of the evil, such state may claim the assistance of the general government."

By the time of the platform's adoption, the Olmsteds were on their way out of Texas. But before leaving, Yeoman penned the last of his *Times* pieces, a summary dispatch that amounted to a legalistic brief in support of the Sisterdale cell and its allies.

The 1845 congressional act annexing Texas included a provision allowing settlers of the vast territory to subdivide it, creating up to four additional states. On this basis, Olmsted argued for for the separation of what he called "Western Texas," roughly the territory between the Guadalupe and the Rio Grande.

He described the land in this district as well suited to grazing and small farming, rather than plantation cotton. Furthermore, its proximity to Mexico made slave property "insecure," since fugitives could flee south to freedom. Most significantly: "A majority of the citizens of the whole of Western Texas are Mexicans and Germans, who have no attachment to the institution of Slavery."

Should this "new Western State" emerge, and prohibit the further importation of slaves, it would become very "attractive to free emigrants" and grow rapidly into a land of "varied industry" and agriculture—essentially, a scaled-up version of what the enterprising Germans had already built. Also, its inhabitants would be "*voting citizens*" whose interests diverged from those of their Southern neighbors.

"There is, then, I conclude," he wrote, "a most favorable territory and a promising basis of character for a prosperous, wealthy, healthy-minded, and happy community, and a great, free, independent state. And such a State, self-governed by such a people, I hope to live to see here. YEOMAN."

This confessional endnote was far from a full disclosure. Olmsted failed to mention his close contact with Forty-Eighters and knowledge of their free-state ambitions. At the least, he acted as their propagandist in the *Times*. He may well have been the principal architect of the entire Western Texas scheme.

Olmsted was a man of varied enthusiasms and talents, in an era before rigid professions and specialization. But at heart, he was a master planner, seeking to landscape society as he did public spaces.

"The result of what I have done is to be of much more consequence than anyone else but myself supposes," he immodestly confided to an old friend, near the end of his career. His parks, he added, "are having an educative effect perfectly manifest to me—a manifestly civilizing effect."

Olmsted was also exceptionally far-sighted, and dogged in pursuit of visions that others couldn't imagine or dismissed as harebrained. "I have all my life been considering distant effects," he wrote, in another late-career letter, "and always sacrificing immediate success & applause to that of the future."

Western Texas was just such a project: a grandiose scheme, germinated in secret, and unlikely to bear fruit for years. As laid out in private correspondence with Adolf Douai and other co-conspirators in Texas, the plan called for the "immigration of one or two thousand staunch and steadfast northern men, supporters of Freedom." These infiltrators should come quietly and in small groups at first, forming a "nucleus" in alliance with free-state Germans. Thereafter, migrants from the North and Europe would "pour in," aided by new railroad lines.

Olmsted kept refining and expanding on this plan, long after his return from Texas. It became, in effect, a dry run for his career as a landscape architect, including blueprints for a string of planned communities across the frontier of the Cotton Kingdom.

"I have a private grand political hobby which I must display to you," he disclosed to a Northern ally, in a letter filled with geometric shapes, lines, and arrows. The sketch was nothing less than a sweeping design for winning what Olmsted called the "war between the power of Slavery and of Freedom on this continent."

SISTERDALE'S "BUSINESS DISTRICT," AS BRET CALI CALLED IT, WAS a quirky collection of buildings strung along a two-lane road running north from the Guadalupe. The strip included a former cotton gin converted into a small winery, a repair garage with a rusted Sinclair gas pump, a gift shop called the Shabby Shack, and a nineteenth-century dance hall now used as a wedding venue.

In front of the hall, a historic plaque cited Olmsted's admiration of the "free-thinking intellects" he met here. It also noted the origin of Sisterdale's name. "Since nearby landmarks were named Bosom Hill, Sister Hills and Twin Sisters," the settlers continued the feminine theme in christening their town.

Across from the dance hall stood the Sisterdale Saloon, a functional brick building where I found four drinkers in cowboy attire trying to chat up the barmaid. When I inquired about descendants of German settlers I might speak to, the saloon crowd recommended Joe Spendrath, with a caveat. "He's a hard-core, reserved old German," the barmaid said, and was nicknamed "Smiles" because of his dour manner.

Following her directions—"right on the farm road, pass the third cattle grid, lot of junk piled in a yard"—I came to three men in muddy jeans perched on all-terrain vehicles. A fourth figure sat on an ATV about ten yards apart from the others.

I went into my reflexive, traveling-writer routine—big grin, curious about history, heard Joe Spendrath might be a good source—only to be met with silence and downward gazes. Two of the men motored off and the third remained impassive before telling me that he was Joe Spendrath's brother.

Jerome Spendrath appeared to be in his seventies, and I asked general questions about the Sisterdale of his youth. But for half an hour I did almost all the talking. "You really should speak to my brother, Joe," he said.

Throughout our "interview," the fourth man had sat on his ATV within earshot, smoking and staring into the distance. Having got nowhere with Jerome, I asked who this other man was. "My brother, Joe," Jerome replied.

So I walked ten paces to *his* ATV and started all over. A gray-bearded man in a John Deere cap, Joe said nothing as I told him about Olmsted and what he'd seen in Sisterdale. Then he uttered, "Used to be all German through here, but someone sold to an outsider and den de old farms got broke up."

The Spendraths had held on to 280 acres of the property their forebears had settled in the mid-nineteenth century. "We were always working," Joe said of his youth. "Whatever was on our plate we ate." Blood sausage, liver sausage, sauerkraut, and other German dishes, cooked on a woodstove. They bathed in metal tubs.

I asked what he and his siblings had done for fun as children.

"Fun?" He thought about this. "My sisters made me eat mud pies they baked in the sun." That was the only frolic he could recall.

As an adult, Joe had worked in construction before returning to the family farm. Both he and Jerome had married women of non-German descent, and most other old families had also become "Heinz 57," as he put it.

"When we butcher a hog," he said, "we talk to the young people about the old traditions, but those will be gone when we're gone." Joe still bartered eggs and other produce and preferred "the old days" when "nobody owed anybody anything" and all shared what they had. "Now, people stick to themselves, and the first thing they want to know is, 'What are you going to pay me?'"

His attitude seemed resonant of the Forty-Eighters' disdain for capitalism. But Joe was no Socialist. He felt the government should "keep its nose where it belongs" and stop taxing and redistributing wealth. He also threw out census questionnaires and other surveys, telling me, "The government just wants more control."

It had taken me over an hour to elicit this opinion, by which point the sun was setting and it seemed clear I'd worn out my "welcome." I asked the brothers to pose for a picture, which they did reluctantly, standing so far apart that I struggled to get them in the same frame.

"I'll come back again, if you don't mind," I said, though Joe's expression indicated he did. When I returned the next evening, he wasn't exactly chatty, but he showed me his hog pen and chicken coop before ducking inside his one-story stucco house and returning with a jar of triple-distilled cactus pear whiskey.

The concoction was equal parts sweet and searing, and after a few slugs I broached the subject of Sisterdale's freethinkers. Did any of their mindset remain?

"All of us have our own views and some of dem are strong, because we're always right," he replied. "All chiefs, no Indians. When we butcher a hog, someone will say how to cook it and we all start disagreeing. Always the way here."

There was another, much clearer survival of freethinking ways. Sisterdale had never had a church, and Joe said his family had rarely spoken of religion except to dismiss it. "Dad would tell us, 'Dat's for Catholics,' or

'Dat's for Lutherans, not us,' and said that if he wanted to talk to God he could do it in the fields."

This deviation from Texas norms did not extend to private property. Since arriving at Sisterdale's general store, I'd toyed with retracing the Olmsteds' return trip to the area by boat, camping as they did by the water. The Spendraths' property bordered a long stretch of the Guadalupe, so I asked Joe how he felt about kayakers coming ashore on his family's land.

"I'd tell them, get back in your boat and get on," he said.

And if they didn't? I asked. What would he do—shoot at them?

For the first time during our conversation over two days, a hint of a smile appeared. That and a shrug was his only reply.

RETURNING TO SISTERDALE'S GENERAL STORE, I FOUND BRET Cali drinking beer with Josh Cravey, the young local he'd mentioned having hired. Josh fit my stereotype of a German farmer, bearish and heavy-bearded with meaty, callused hands. But he had a ready, chipped-tooth grin and a warm, open manner. When I told him about my labored interrogation of the Spendraths, he laughed and said Joe was his uncle by marriage, "and always boasting that his sausage was better than ours."

Josh had spent much of his youth working with another "hard-ass" uncle: hauling hay, building fences, and doing other farm labor, dawn to dark. "He'd always say to me, 'You work and you die, that's all you get.'" Josh's family didn't attend church and told him, "Sunday's a workday like any other."

To escape constant farm labor, Josh had played every sport in high school, driving a tractor thirteen miles to get there when he missed the school bus. In his twenties, Josh left the area to work as a stagehand and light technician at rock concerts. But he'd returned eight months ago when his father was diagnosed with advanced cancer, and resumed working the farm with his uncle. His father had since shot himself with a hunting rifle, leaving a handwritten note about his life.

"There is nothing great or important for me to write," the letter said in part, "just working every day, that was the way I was taught."

Josh was determined to "ease up" in raising his own child, now a toddler. "She'll work, but not like my father and uncle." His upbringing had also made him appreciate Sisterdale's early settlers. "I love those freethinkers; they believed in working to live, not living to work," he said. "Too bad they were driven out."

IN 1854, WHEN THE SISTERDALE CELL WON APPROVAL OF AN anti-slavery manifesto at a German convention in San Antonio, the backlash was swift and furious. Foes damned the plank as a thinly veiled call for abolition, abetted by the federal government—tantamount to sedition in a Southern state, at a time when the nation was fracturing over slavery. Anti-immigrant fervor was also on the rise, stoked by the Know-Nothings, a national movement also known as the American Party, which cast native-born Protestants as besieged and sought to bar those born abroad from voting or from holding office.

Conservative Germans in Texas feared they would be lumped with Forty-Eighters as abolitionists and foreign troublemakers. They loudly disavowed the platform's "designing men," in print and at mass meetings, declaring that few Germans were agitated over slavery or other issues in the radicals' plank.

The brunt of this attack was aimed at the editor of the large-circulation *Zeitung* in San Antonio, Adolf Douai, who published the anti-slavery platform and advocated for it in his paper. Skittish businesses withdrew ads, readers canceled subscriptions, and "the press and many Americans spoke aloud of lynching," Douai wrote the Olmsteds, who by then had returned to New York.

Douai also cited a letter Fred had sent, asking what more he could do "for freedoms sake in Western Texas" and mentioning "wealthy friends" who might aid the effort. "Help us to save our paper," Douai wrote, requesting supplies and a loan to cover his mounting debts.

The Olmsteds quickly circulated appeals for funds, telling of Douai's plight and the movement "silently at work" to create a state "*secured to free labor* & real republicanism." They raised most of the money Douai needed and sent it as a gift rather than a loan, along with printing paper and types.

"I never before witnessed in friends of so short an acquaintance such a readiness to help," wrote Douai, who began sending copies of the *Zeitung* to his Northern patrons, as well as to Frederick Douglass, in exchange for copies of the black abolitionist's paper.

But fury over Douai's advocacy for a free state in Texas became so intense that he took to sleeping in his office with a gun. Deep in debt, and fearing for the safety of his large family, Douai left San Antonio, ultimately finding work as an educator in Boston and becoming a pioneer of the kindergarten system in the US.

Olmsted carried on his free-state Texas mission with another extraordinary Forty-Eighter, Charles Riotte, a former Prussian judge and railroad director who shared Fred's love of grand plans. "We see one and the same aim, and are spiritually linked together," he wrote, working for "the cause of humanity at the heart of American life."

Riotte fought to keep the *Zeitung* and free-state effort alive, but like Douai he was worn down by foes who "vomit fire and poison against me." Rather than "act the part of Sisiphus," he planned to found a new German colony in northern Mexico to "build up a more solid wall against slavery" than was possible in the US.

In his letters to Olmsted, Riotte also delineated, with keen transatlantic insight, a divide that he felt had doomed their efforts from the start. "We are judged from the standpoint of an American—indeed a very strange people!" he wrote.

Riotte and his ilk viewed society "as a *congregation* of men; whose aim it is to elevate the wellbeing of the aggregate by the combined exertion." Americans, by contrast, "look first upon themselves as private *individuals*, entitled to ask for all the rights and benefits of an organized community even to the detriment of the whole. . . . We idealize the community—you the individual! How is it possible, that we ever should amalgamate?"

Riotte closed by praising Olmsted's writing on the South but expressed doubt that it would diminish the Slave Power. "I don't know of any historical record of an Aristocracy giving up their privileges, except in the case of revolutionary pressure."

FROM SISTERDALE I DROVE THIRTEEN MILES TO COMFORT, A town founded by like-minded Germans the year of Olmsted's visit to Texas.

At its start, Comfort hewed to "a sort of communism," wrote the wife of the town's founder. "One would give to others what could be spared, and take in return what was lacked."

Comfort had since grown into a community of 2,400 and now billed itself as "an antique town," though this was hard to discern from its un-quaint perimeter of fast-food franchises and tangle of highways. Tucked behind this sprawl lay a tidy street grid with *Fachwerk* cottages and old stone buildings, many of them converted into antiques stores and other businesses catering to Hill Country visitors.

On the main street, there was also a striking homage to the town's "Founding Freethinkers (*Deutsche Freidenker*)." The plaque, set in a large stone, said that freethinkers "advocated reason and democracy over religious and political autocracy," believed in "equal rights for all persons," and op-posed slavery and the Confederacy, a stance that "cost many their freedom and lives."

At the other end of the main street, I visited the yellow wooden home of Anne Stewart, a descendant of early German settlers. She wore a pink sweater and polka-dotted pants and, after inviting me inside, kicked off her shoes before flopping on a couch.

"Ooh, Olmsted, what a wonderful man!" she said when I told her of my journey. "He does carry on a bit about Sisterdale being heaven on earth. But that's the romantic way I look at Comfort."

A retired school librarian, Stewart had authored several local histories and saw clear traces in Comfort of the freethinking ways Olmsted de-scribed. "There's still a deep orneriness," she said, citing the town's repeated refusal to incorporate, leaving it without a local government or municipal services. But a communitarian spirit endured. Volunteers mowed parks, collected trash, and raised funds when needed, including support for a cancer-stricken "hippie who no one liked," she said.

Like Sisterdale, Comfort had also been notable for its religious noncon-formity. A Presbyterian missionary, visiting three decades after Comfort's founding, called it "an infidel" town that boasted of having "no church building or religious services."

Later, as railroad workers arrived, churches belatedly sprang up, and Stewart had been raised Episcopalian. But she recalled her grandmother saying of Bible stories, "by age thirteen or fourteen, you should know they're fairy tales."

Religious belief, or its absence, had nonetheless become a ferocious point of contention in the late 1990s, when admirers of Comfort's founders won permission from the county and state to erect a monument in the town's park. They put up a thirty-two-ton hunk of limestone to which they planned to affix a plaque lauding freethinkers.

Then word got out that some among the monument's donors and supporters planned what they called a "Freethought-Atheist Volksmarch" to the cenotaph. This prompted a backlash and a petition, "NO MONUMENT TO ATHEISM IN COMFORT," likening the rock to "a slab of discarded Stonehenge" erected for the hidden purpose of attacking religion.

The controversy played out in the media and at fiery public meetings for several years, until a local opponent hired a crane, lifted the slab onto a truck bed, and dumped it in a pasture outside town. Supporters of the cenotaph had to settle for the much smaller monument to freethinkers I'd seen on Comfort's main street.

To Anne Stewart, this was "history repeating itself." In her view, "the early freethinkers rejected dogma, but were too dogmatic to win over others, and got crushed." She believed Olmsted's allies in the Hill Country "made a huge mistake" by publicizing their anti-slavery platform and putting a target on their backs. Then they picked another fight they couldn't win, against the Confederacy in Texas.

"The Civil War killed Sisterdale and the society of educated freethinkers your man Olmsted so loved," she said.

THE VIBRANT SOCIETY OF FORTY-EIGHTERS OLMSTED ENCOUN-tered in Sisterdale struggled to sustain itself in the years immediately after his visit. Some returned to Germany, or died, or fled the hostility they encountered due to their political activism. Others came to recognize that they lacked the skills and temperament to fulfill their dream of living on the land. "Our honest peasants understood farming better than we did," wrote a law-trained German who left Sisterdale after two years.

But those who remained held to their beliefs, and joined other Hill

Country Germans in strong opposition to Texas's secession from the Union. When war came, they formed secret, armed groups to avoid service in Confederate units and, if possible, give aid to Union forces.

Prominent in this resistance was a family Olmsted had stayed with in Sisterdale: the household of Edward Degener, the Forty-Eighter of "unusually large education" at whose log home Fred had enjoyed a wondrous night of singing and waltzing. It was there, too, that he'd extolled Degener's sons as "fine pictures of youthful yeomen as can be imagined."

The anti-Confederate underground the Degeners joined, behind Southern lines, so alarmed Texas authorities that in 1862 they declared martial law in the Hill Country. Soldiers were dispatched to "remove" all "disloyal persons," register white males above the age of sixteen, and to force "aliens" to swear allegiance to the Confederacy. Those who refused were summarily hanged.

"Civil war is on the eve of breaking out," Edward Degener wrote in a letter to family and friends in Germany. Young Unionists had taken to "the Mountains & ravines" and were being "chased by Confederate troops, like Indians," while their families suffered from the deprivations wrought by war and martial rule.

"This is my last piece of paper; no more coffee in the house," Degener wrote, citing two shortages of particular concern to intellectuals like himself.

Faced with arrest, conscription, or guerrilla war that would further devastate the Hill Country, Degener's sons, Hugo and Hilmar, fled toward Mexico with sixty-six other Unionists, some of whom hoped to link up with Northern forces on the Gulf Coast. The brothers rode off with bread their mother had baked and the letter their father had written to family and friends in Germany, for safe mailing from Mexico.

This fugitive band camped sixty miles from the Rio Grande, at the Nueces River, singing and doing acrobatics before bedding down, unaware that a German informant had betrayed them and led a Confederate unit in hot pursuit. The Unionists awoke before dawn to gunshots, an ambush that the colonel in command of the Confederates stated, in his official after-action report, cost two of his own men while killing thirty-four of the enemy. "They offered the most determined resistance and fought with desperation, asking no quarter whatever," he wrote, "hence I have no prisoners to report."

According to other accounts, the fight at the Nueces was more massacre than battle. At least seven wounded captives were executed after the fight ended. Of those who escaped the slaughter, seventeen were hunted down and slain: shot while swimming the Rio Grande, hanged, maimed, or "used as shooting targets." Many more Unionists were shot or lynched during a reign of terror in the Hill Country that lasted for two years.

Two of those wounded and then executed at the Nueces were the yeoman sons of Edward Degener that Olmsted had so admired. On one of their bodies, Confederates found the letter their father had written, telling of Unionist resistance and stating, "If the south is victorious, it may become necessary for the Germans to emigrate again."

As a result, Edward Degener was imprisoned for trial as "a dangerous and seditious person" and "enemy" of the Confederacy. The trial testimony included mention of Olmsted's writing, which neighbors of Degener said had hardened him against slavery. But witnesses also claimed that Degener's sons had acted independently, and that their father hadn't given active aid to Unionists. Found guilty of lesser charges, he was released on a $5,000 bond, on condition he "conduct himself during the War as a good and loyal citizen to the Confederate States."

Many in the Hill Country had done so from the start of the conflict. At Comfort's small museum and archives, Brenda Seidensticker showed me documents that made the 1860s Hill Country sound like occupied France during World War II. There were resisters, active collaborators, and those caught between, serving as Confederate teamsters, mail carriers, or in militias, if only to avoid persecution and spare their families harm.

"Some Germans were upset at these young and excited guys who made life hard for people who wanted to lay low," Brenda said, and "bad feelings" lingered for generations between Unionist families and those that had served the Confederacy.

Her own feelings were mixed. "I'm more Texan than anything," she said, "and believe a lot of that war was about states' rights, not just slavery. Texas voted to be Confederate, and you can argue that the military had every right to go after Germans who resisted or ran."

But even if the Unionists were traitors to their state, she felt they didn't deserve to be massacred. She led me to a case filled with bullets and other artifacts from the Nueces slaughter. "It's Texas history, a chapter that should be much better known."

The tragedy might have been forgotten altogether, were it not for the efforts of Edward Degener. As soon as the Civil War ended, he engineered a difficult expedition to retrieve the remains of his sons and other slaughtered Unionists. Those killed at the Nueces had been left unburied by the Confederates, at a remote site far from any road. The party that went to collect them wrapped the skulls and bones in quilts and carried them sixteen miles to a wagon for transport to Comfort, where they were interred on a hill at the edge of town. A detachment of Union troops fired a salute in honor of the dead.

Degener and other mourners also marked the grave with a simple obelisk—the first Civil War monument in Texas, and the first in the former Confederacy erected at the burial site of Union remains. Etched on the stone were the names of those *gefallen* (killed) at the Nueces, or *gefangen genommenund ermordet* (captured and murdered) afterward. The roster of dead included Pablo Diaz, a Mexican captured by Indians who had been rescued and adopted by German settlers in Sisterdale.

Even more striking was the terse inscription honoring the fallen: *Treue der Union*, a proud statement of loyalty to the Northern cause, in the heartland of a just-defeated and embittered Confederate state.

"The sacrifice that we, the fathers of the slaughtered, made to our country and to liberty is great and dolorous," Degener declared in an oration at the grave site. "We shall, however, console ourselves: we shall be proud of having offered our sons to the Union, if the glorious victory of its arms bear all the fruits that this nation and the whole of humanity justly expect to reap."

STANDING BEFORE THE MONUMENT, 150 YEARS LATER, I WONdered whether Degener would be consoled by the fruits reaped since his dedication speech. He'd gone on to become a Republican congressman during Reconstruction, before the forces of reaction triumphed in Texas and across the South, as they had in Europe after the initial success of the 1848 revolution.

The radical German legacy in Comfort had been erased, too, apart from the *Deutsche Freidenker* plaque on the town's main street and the True to the Union monument, which now stood across from a church of which the early freethinkers would have disapproved.

The fate of the Sisterdale community so beloved of Degener and Olmsted was even more forlorn. By the end of the Civil War, very few of the Forty-Eighters Olmsted had described, singing and dancing at Degener's home, "in exile, but free," remained in the Hill Country.

"How times have changed since 1854," wrote August Siemering, a schoolteacher in Sisterdale and secretary of its "free society" at the time of Olmsted's visit. In a later life reminiscence, Siemering fondly recalled "Mr. Degener's salon" and quoted at length from Olmsted's description of the community, counting himself as one of the few in Texas who was still alive to recall that golden era.

"There is hardly any trace left of what was once Sisterdale," he lamented. "No more lectures are given, and even the memories of the pleasant days once witnessed by the lovely valley die with those who lived to see them. Only the old hills are still there, the river and its streams murmur their old song."

CHAPTER 19

UPPER GUADALUPE

And Absalom Rode Upon a Mule

The frontispiece of *A Journey through Texas* is a woodcut depicting an idyllic encampment beside a shaded stream. The bivouac appears in miniature, framed by arching boughs and set against a backdrop of undulating prairie. A small tent is strung between trees; two horses are at rest; a man unpacks a mule as another tends the campfire; and a faithful dog looks on.

The illustration is likely based on one of Olmsted's travel sketches, and bears a close resemblance to the landscapes he described during his leisurely travels with John along the Guadalupe River in the early spring of 1854.

"Always in the evening we search out a pleasant spot by some water-side," Fred wrote Anne Charlotte Lynch, "and take plenty of time to pitch our tent securely & make every thing comfortable about us. So we have had from fifty to a hundred pleasant homes of our own selection, construction & furnishings in the most beautiful spots we could find in this great wilderness."

This spring sojourn, "travelling about, without definite aim, in an original but on the whole, very pleasant fashion," became a touchstone for Olmsted in later years as he formulated his philosophy of park design.

"What is the beautiful?" he asked in an 1868 address to the Prospect

Park Scientific Association in Brooklyn. Olmsted cited his Texas trip and the elements that had guided his and John's daily choice of a "pleasant camp." They sought unhindered access to water, wood, and pasturage, a safely secluded and "cosy" location, and "as much beauty as possible in the view from our tent door."

These practical and aesthetic considerations were intertwined. Intrinsic to beauty, Olmsted stated in his address, was the "quality of ease" that flowed from the gratification of basic human needs: shelter, shade, prospect, and economy of effort.

These impulses were universal and largely unconscious, he wrote, and a park was a "work of art" that spoke to them. It should be a "hospitable landscape" that "invites, encourages & facilitates movement," with "occasional shelter and shade" and "opportunities for agreeable rest."

Not every aspect of a park need conform to this "easy flowing topography." Rocks, thick woods, and other features provided contrast and "obscurity" of view, stirring imagination and drawing the visitor deeper into the park. But nothing should demand "severe exertion" or obstruct the park's essential mission: to "invite and stimulate the simplest, purest and most primeval actions of the poetic element of human nature."

Over a century after Olmsted delivered this address, scholars discovered a pencil draft of the speech rolled up with unrelated documents. They published it as part of Olmsted's multivolume papers, hailing the talk as "his most complete discussion" of "the nature and effect of the pastoral scenery he wanted in parks." Accompanying the text was a reproduction of the woodcut of the brothers' Texas encampment.

Olmsted was still citing that experience four decades after his journey, when he wrote one of his sons who'd gone to work as a surveyor in Colorado, preparatory to entering his father's profession as a landscape architect.

"Pick up all the woodcraft that you can," Olmsted advised, by which he meant a range of skills, including plant identification, keeping one's sense of direction when "pursuing a devious course," and "guessing at distances" of approaching objects. "All the knack that I gained by my Texas experience in this way has been professionally useful to me."

Reading this letter was a bit shaming. I had little knack for "woodcraft," and my Texas experience had thus far failed to enhance it. I'd learned to navigate the devious course of highway cloverleafs and could guess the distance to the next Buc-ee's service plaza. If pressed, I could distinguish a post oak from a live oak. That was about it.

Olmsted's beloved Hill Country seemed the appropriate place to do more in the woodcraft line. Stunted as my skills might be, I could at least wander on foot or by water and scout campsites along the Guadalupe that possessed that magical "quality of ease." The more ease the better.

But when I proposed a tramp of this kind to Bret Cali and Josh Cravey at the Sisterdale General Store, they almost choked on their Shiner Bocks. Last July Fourth, they'd rented kayaks to two teenaged girls and dropped them ten miles downriver to paddle back for pickup near the store.

"Next thing we know, they're running across a field in their bikinis shouting and screaming," Bret said. As they'd floated by a nearby farm, an eighty-year-old woman came out and shot at them, claiming they were trespassing on her property.

The riverbed was public but not the shore, "and if you see posts painted purple, watch out, that means the owner will shoot if you trespass," Josh said.

Bret raised another uncomfortable topic. "Happy to rent you a kayak—and a bulletproof vest if I can find one. But didn't you tell me that Olmsted came through here on horseback?"

Indeed, I had, without mentioning that my own experience in the saddle consisted of pony rides at summer camp, circa 1970, and two or three ambles since on fat slow mounts. Also, my wife was a horse lover, and through her I'd met a number of equestrians—on crutches, in casts and neck braces, or with limbs bristling with metal pins.

Bret and Josh were unimpressed. Surely I could find an expert guide, as the Olmsteds had during their ride in Texas. Also, there was an obvious place to hire one, less than an hour's drive away: Bandera, which billed itself as the "Cowboy Capital of the World."

At first glance, the town lived up to this slogan. Bandera's main street had movie-Western buildings with false-fronted facades, shops with names like Gunslinger, and a quaint eatery called Old Spanish Trail, where the morning menu featured steaks with creamy gravy, eggs, refried beans, and thick-cut "Texas Toast."

I opted for the Little Wrangler's Breakfast, from the kids' menu, trying to avoid the macho gaze of John Wayne, pictured across the walls. Every other patron wore cowboy attire, and several men entered in spurs.

Bandera had once been a staging post for cattle drives, before becoming a rodeo center. Guest ranches and trail-riding stables lined a road south of town, and the breakfast diners advised me to go there in search of a guide to hire.

I stopped first at the Hanging Tree Ranch, site of yet another mass lynching of "traitors" during the Civil War. Then I pulled in at five ranches with stables and received the same news at each. The busy spring season had just begun, and the few guides who led overnight trips were typically booked months in advance.

Another complication: one couldn't just ride the range as I'd romantically supposed. "We do have fences and barbed wire in Texas," a dude ranch manager drily informed me. In fact, an astonishing 96 percent of the state's land was in private hands, and the one public domain close to Bandera was small, arid, and scrubby, with little resemblance to the Hill Country Olmsted toured.

I retreated to a cowboy bar in town to cool off and consider my options. The ceiling was draped with the signed bras and boxer shorts of exuberant patrons, including the woman sitting next to me, who could barely speak due to her smoker's hack. When I asked her occupation, she finally coughed out, "I'm a barfly."

I was on my second Lone Star, feeling glum, when I got a call from a trail guide I'd spoken to earlier in the day. She knew a fifth-generation Texan whose family had come to the Hill Country in the 1850s. He led extended rides and "would be perfect for what you're after," so long as I didn't mind one adjustment to my plan.

"He's a mule man extraordinaire," she said.

I knew almost nothing of mules apart from what I'd read about "Mr. Brown," the stout "son of a donkey" the Olmsteds acquired for their Texas ride. He carried John until the brothers bought a second horse, and thereafter served as a stellar pack mule for six months and "two thousand rough miles."

I had in mind a ride of four or five days, in comparatively gentle countryside. Guided by a mule man extraordinaire, how difficult could that be?

———

UPON PUBLICATION OF *A JOURNEY THROUGH TEXAS*, THE SOUTH'S leading editor and critic lambasted Olmsted's writing on the region as "wordy" and "abounding in bitterness and prejudice." J. D. B. DeBow also mocked the Yankee author, for whom "the opportunity is too tempting to be resisted to revile and abuse the men and the society whose open hospitality he undoubtedly enjoyed."

In reply to this charge of "ingratitude and indelicacy," Olmsted wrote that he admired and felt grateful to "numbers of men" he met in his travels. "There are others for whom I have a quite different feeling." But he had not identified the "true name" of such figures, or "facts of private life" that could "be readily localized."

In this spirit, I will refer to my mule man extraordinaire as Buck. When I called him from Bandera, he gave me detailed directions to his property, which lay seven miles from the nearest town. The landscape was stunning and Southwestern, complete with cactus and antelope, and I got completely lost, arriving at Buck's lovely, shaded house forty-five minutes after the time we'd agreed upon.

"What the heck?" he said by way of greeting, clearly peeved by my inability to follow directions—a leitmotif of the time we'd spend together.

Buck was as ruggedly handsome as the natural surrounds. Sinewy and tanned with pale blue eyes and fair hair, he wore jeans, red suspenders over a denim work shirt, and a jaunty, wide-brimmed straw hat. Paul Newman as Butch Cassidy, crossed with the Marlboro Man.

It was almost sundown and he had a lot to do, striding so briskly that I scurried to keep up. He toted saddles and hay and said nothing until a mule wandered over and I instinctively ran my hand from its head to its mane and back.

"Most people, first time, give them a sort of slap," he said. "What they really like is what you just did, a long, gentle pat."

This was pure luck on my part but it seemed to open Buck up. He told me that he currently looked after twenty mules, half of them sent to him for training because they were "green" or giving their owners difficulties.

This was common, he said because mules had "an image problem" and were easily misunderstood. Though they were typecast as dull, plodding, and obstinate, their "mulish" behavior was in fact a reflection of the animals' wary intelligence.

"Mules read humans like a book before we've read their first page, and they need to be convinced of your mastery and ability to keep them safe." He also likened them to thirteen-year-old boys. If asked to do something, "their first response is, 'Why?' Then, 'Make me!' Until you become captain of that ship, it can be frustrating."

Buck was clearly admiral of his fleet. The mules obeyed his verbal commands, even mounting a truck tire in response to a tongue click and remaining until he told them to come down. My own thirteen-year-old son wasn't nearly so compliant.

I was also struck by the mules' bulk, having thought of them as smaller than horses. In reality, due to what geneticists call "hybrid vigor," mules tended to improve on their parents, inheriting the general build of mares and the sturdiness and smarts of their donkey fathers, called jacks.

After finishing his chores, Buck led me to the porch of his house to discuss the trip I'd broached on the phone. At the mention of Olmsted and Sisterdale, he nodded, telling me he was a descendant of a German from there who had been killed at the Nueces during the Civil War.

He suggested I map out a route of about fifteen miles a day, along small roads around Sisterdale if I couldn't get permission to ride on private land. I'd also need to locate a campsite.

The rest sounded straightforward. I'd need a half day of training and then we'd load the mules in a trailer with camping and other supplies he'd provide. Transport, food, shelter, and an expert guide with deep roots in the Hill Country, all for what seemed a very reasonable price. Perfecto!

I was also pleased by Buck's homework assignment: a nineteenth-century treatise by a man who supervised thousands of mules on the frontier and during the Civil War. Reading it that night back at the Moon Pie Motel, I learned all about mules' use and abuse since biblical times. The author, like Buck, felt mules' reputation for being difficult was undeserved, though some of what he wrote contradicted this thesis.

"Mules, with very few exceptions, are born kickers." They were also "what may be called a tricky animal" and "naturally more stubborn" than horses. "Whenever the mule finds that he has the advantage of you, he will keep it in spite of all you can do."

Evidently, mules did not suffer fools. Nor, I'd sensed, did Buck. It also dawned on me that I'd have a hard time documenting my trip while staying aboard a tricky, kicky beast and performing the labor required before and after each ride.

In short, I could use a hand, and the perfect candidate appeared for work in the morning at the Sisterdale General Store. Josh Cravey was an experienced rider and a big, strong, and agreeable guy I could lean on (or hide behind) when necessary. As a local, he could also open doors and run interference with property owners.

"Sounds great—I'm in!" he said. His only concern was whether Buck had a mule that could handle his 260-pound frame. The answer was yes: mules could carry up to 20 percent of their body weight, and Buck said a few of his weighed more than half a ton.

But he added that Josh's familiarity with horses might complicate his handling of mules. So he'd need training as much as if not more than a complete novice like me.

"A horse is like a high-maintenance woman," Buck explained when we began our training day at a café in the town nearest his ranch. "A mule's more like a country girl. She doesn't need fancy feed or shoes or a lot of pampering. I like the economy."

Mules also didn't require frequent visits to the vet, though that's where we headed after lunch—so Buck could get treated for a large, angry boil under his collar.

"Grit your teeth," the vet said, lancing the boil and mopping a bloody sludge that he described to his patient as "Thousand Island dressing gushing out your neck."

Buck didn't so much as wince, and told us the vet had previously stitched the top of his thumb back on after an accident.

"Okay, I get it," Josh muttered as we returned to our car. "He's a hard-as-nails cowboy."

Any doubt about Buck's toughness was dispelled by our afternoon boot camp. He briskly demonstrated how to tack up mules, expertly swinging saddles with one arm from his hip onto the animals' backs. "I'm only doing this for you once," he said, cinching and tying off straps and showing me a "bank robber's knot," among many other maneuvers I struggled to duplicate.

Then he leaned down to put protective boots on a young mule's hooves, which had been trimmed the day before. "He didn't like his first pedicure," Buck said as the mule froze, reared up, and kicked.

Buck waved his arms, made a spitting noise, and whipped the mule's flank, but it kept kicking wildly. So he looped a rope around one of its legs and brought the animal to the ground. "This is a tough life lesson, buddy," he told the mule, which whimpered for five minutes before calming enough to accept the booties.

Then he turned and handed the mule's lead to me, announcing, "Tony, that's your beast." It would henceforth be my job to handle its tender hooves.

Buck demonstrated how to do so one more time, removing the boots and repeating his earlier struggle, bringing the beast to ground. "Mules have a lack of trust in the captain, which is us," he said. "If you're not the leader, they're going to feel insecure."

Which was exactly how I felt as I approached my eight-hundred-pound mount, still breathing hard from the shoe ordeal. Hatcher was a handsome reddish-brown four-year-old, and I put my face right up to his, summoning what I imagined to be a commanding gaze. His dark eyes, staring right back at mine, conveyed all the warmth and trust of a prison inmate meeting the new warden.

"Okay, boys and girls, time to mount up," Buck said, instructing me to put my boot toe in the stirrup and jump with my calf rather than pulling with my arms. Somehow, I succeeded on the first try, swinging out over the saddle before settling onto it. Hatcher didn't budge and Buck nodded approvingly.

We also set off smoothly. I found the reins simpler to understand than all the other tack, and Hatcher's gait was easy and comfortable. My spirits lifted as we followed Buck and his mule through thin woods, Josh bringing up the rear on a very large mount named Doney.

Then we reached a rocky stream. Buck's mule splashed right across it before bounding up a steep ledge on the far bank. Hatcher followed—and froze at the base of the rock shelf. Josh's mule did the same.

We circled round and tried again, and again. I squeezed my legs against

Hatcher, gave a few kicks, rocked forward, shouted, "Cummon, boy!" and other commands.

"Señor Horwitz, he does not *comprende*," Buck said. "He understands mule."

I learned that I was "putting on the gas and brakes at the same time," by kicking while leaning back and tightening the reins. After a few more tries, I managed to get Hatcher up the rock shelf, and Josh's mule followed.

We continued along the rocky stream and scrambled up several more ledges, each time leaving me very impressed by Hatcher's sure-footedness. I began to feel confident in our partnership, a sentiment that wasn't reciprocated.

When I reached for a pocket tape recorder I'd stashed in a saddlebag, Hatcher immediately veered toward a low-lying tree limb. I ducked in time but lost my baseball cap and didn't want to risk dismounting to retrieve it.

After an hour or so we reached a towering rock in the stream, and Buck scaled it on his mule with the ease of a Hollywood cowboy charging up to a lookout. Hatcher and I, once again, experienced failure to launch. Eight times. Josh wasn't having any better luck with Doney.

"You know what those mules are saying?" Buck shouted, looking on from the stream bank with conspicuous disgust. "'I ain't gonna do it, 'cause you don't have a clue how to make me go!'"

With his instruction, I finally achieved liftoff and was rewarded at the top of the rock with a majestic view of hills and valley. I had ample time to admire this vista, because Hatcher refused to descend, standing as rigid as an equestrian statue, impervious to my clicks, kicks, and other coaxes. I had to ignominiously dismount and tug Hatcher off the rock.

"Guys, I know I'm being a bit of a rear end," Buck said, after Josh again failed to mount the rock. "But there will come a point over the next few days when you're gonna have to handle your mule or someone gets hurt. And if I'm choosing between the well-being of you or the mules, I'm looking after the mules."

My own being, by this point, wasn't well. Sunburnt and sweat soaked, I was sure that Hatcher had already read me like a book. Or like a comic strip. Charlie Brown came to mind.

Buck offered a little encouragement on the ride back, telling me that Hatcher would be easier to handle away from this ranch. "Here, he knows there's twenty mules in the pasture, and he'd much rather be hanging with his buds than with some Yankee jerking on his mouth."

He also said I'd done well mounting and staying aboard my first time out, despite Hatcher "being a bit ornery." But this mild, rookie competence was more than offset by my utter ineptitude at handling the cinches, straps, and other tack.

Simply looking at this apparatus brought on a sudden aphasia, or contact dyslexia, the way I felt when forced to assemble IKEA furniture. Except in this case, the equipment came with an animal five times my weight that wouldn't function if a single piece was out of place.

"It's like checking the water and oil in your car," Buck said. "If you don't take care of your vehicle, you're not going anywhere."

Or worse. While I combed Hatcher, the rare task that seemed simple and pleasant, Buck warned that if I missed a single burr or mud clot on the mule's underside, "he'll be taking you on a rodeo ride next time you get in the saddle."

Determined to avoid this fate, and to improve on my opening day performance, I spent an hour that evening poring over another of Buck's recommended treatises: *Knots, Hitches and Their Uses*. Studying the illustrations, I tried to duplicate the most essential knots with a shoelace. This exercise in futility left me so dispirited that I felt like tying a noose. If only I knew how.

But I was buoyed by the last of our evening mule chores. Helping Buck fill and loop feedbags over the animals' tall ears, we watched them contentedly munch on a mix of corn, peas, oats, and alfalfa.

Buck mellowed, too, patting and nuzzling the mules. "There's a time to be a disciplinarian," he said, "and calm times like this, when it's good to bond."

He also told me that Hatcher belonged to a Texas woman who'd rescued him from a "kill pen" in Louisiana, where mules were sent before processing in Mexico and shipment of their meat to restaurants in Europe. "Bleeding hearts sometimes step in and buy them," he said. "If it wasn't for that nice gal near Dallas, Hatcher would be on a plate in France."

This softened me toward my mount. I found further solace at bedtime, in a spare room of Buck's house. Revisiting my well-worn copy of *A Journey through Texas*, I was reminded that the Olmsteds and their mule had gotten off to a rough start.

"He was endowed with the hereditary bigotry of his race," Olmsted wrote of Mr. Brown, who objected when his new owners overloaded the wicker hampers he had to carry. Unburdened at one of the Olmsteds' first campsites, the mule fled and wasn't recovered until he'd escaped for four miles.

On another occasion, Mr. Brown took off "with a snort of fat defiance," tearing through heavy brush and rolling in a creek to try to shed his hampers. Then he struck out in a beeline across open plain. "A short-legged mule, when fully under way on a stampede, is 'some pumpkins' at going," Olmsted wrote, but on horseback the brothers quickly overtook him.

These incidents were exceptions. With time, Mr. Brown proved "amenable to reason," gentle persuasion, and the occasional disciplining. After the "some pumpkins" breakout, he never again displayed "symptom of insurrection."

Perhaps the same would be true of Hatcher, the mutineer in his system cleansed by his tantrum over his hooves and his periodic noncompliance during our ride. Once I learned to handle him, he'd accept me as captain and we'd sail smoothly around Sisterdale. And maybe pigs would fly.

BUCK WOKE ME AT 5:00 A.M. SO WE COULD READY THE MULES FOR transport on the trailer that the veterinarian—a.k.a. Doc—would bring in two hours, Josh meeting us at the other end, near Sisterdale. In addition to our mounts, we'd be taking two pack mules. The loading proceeded without drama, except for Hatcher, who balked and resisted boarding. "Eight thousand pounds of mule flesh and eight hundred pounds of orneriness," Buck said, after finally dragging Hatcher inside the trailer with the others.

We also loaded several hundred pounds of tools and supplies, including feed for animal and man, which Buck had spent hours sorting and weighing the previous night. Upon arrival at the start point for our ride there was another hour's labor, as he fitted out the pack mules with fifty-pound bags on either flank, another twenty pounds strapped on top. Then he tied canvas over the whole to form a tight, carefully balanced load, secured with an Arizona box hitch.

My own contribution to launching the trip had been light lifting by comparison. I'd spent a pleasant few days studying old maps, consulting with a Hill Country historian about the trails and landmarks Olmsted described, and charting a course that roughly retraced part of the brothers' ride. I'd also scouted our start point, at a pull-off on a two-lane highway seven miles from Sisterdale.

"Our road took us over a rugged ridge to the valley of the Guadalupe," Olmsted wrote, and the spot I'd chosen for the start of our own ride closely matched this. We began by following a narrow road along the ridge, Buck at the front leading the pack mules.

He'd told me to stay thirty yards back until the pack mules settled. Josh brought up the rear on Doney, who was a slowpoke and soon fell well behind Hatcher. This made conversation difficult, but left me free to take in the landscape and learn to handle Hatcher and the tape recorder at the same time, while making fumbling moves without Buck's close surveillance.

It was a perfect spring morning, sunny and in the high seventies, with a soft breeze. Ambling along the road's grassy fringe, we had glimpses of the "wide and magnificent" valley Olmsted described, threaded with wooded streams and bordered by misty hills.

Then we turned onto a farm road that wound between pasture and clumps of cactus and longhorn cattle. Olmsted subtitled his Texas book *Or a Saddle-Trip on the Southwestern Frontier*, and here I finally was, in the saddle on a hot dry day with rugged hills in the distance and majestic clouds overhead.

A few cars passed, the drivers waving or pulling over to admire us as we clopped by. I'd borrowed a cowboy hat to go with my jeans, boots, and bandanna, and for the first time didn't feel ridiculous in this attire.

I also pitied the drivers in their metal, gas-fueled, climate-controlled boxes. So much better to travel at mule height and hoof speed, in the open air, along a roadside blanketed with spring flowers!

The night before, Buck had talked of his ambition to trek on muleback to California and make a reality show about it, called *Three Miles an Hour*. This had sounded like a wretched idea at the time, but now it struck me as inspired. Experiencing our great land as Olmsted prescribed, slowly and tranquilly, rather than at the warp speed of "civilized life."

Before long, I lost track of time and distance and felt positively transported, as if on a drug trip. At one with this beautiful world, hyperalert to the slant of shadows and thrumming of insects, and rocking in rhythm with a gently huffing beast that seemed a different species from the obstreperous child of the day before.

How, I began to wonder, had this transcendent experience eluded me until now? I repented for having mocked my wife's equine enthusiasm and her horse-crippled friends. I felt ready to join them on the trail. Maybe even buy a mule, become a dude, a real Rhinestone Jewboy.

"Mr. Hoooorwitz," Buck bellowed, "you're falling behind!"

I trotted to catch up, bouncing uncomfortably in the saddle and struggling to keep hold of my hat and tape recorder and the reins. Then, after resuming our pleasant saunter, we arrived at our first obstacle: a cattle guard in the road, its twelve rounded metal bars impassable for mules. A fence ran to either side.

Josh located a gate in the adjoining brush so we could ride around the cattle guard. But we soon came to several more of them, slowing our pace as we detoured into pastures or took down fence posts or wire to create a temporary passage.

Buck glared at me and asked how many more cattle guards lay ahead. I had no idea, having plotted our course without realizing that these would be impediments. He rolled his eyes and tapped a finger to his head, as if to say, "Use your noodle, if you have one."

The ride went smoothly for a short stretch until we reached a field filled with horses and donkeys that loped over to the fence line by the road. This spooked several of the mules, causing them to pull away amid an equine cacophony of neighs, donkey brays, and the mules' peculiar whinnies.

Buck described the mules' cries as "halfway between a horse's and a donkey's. Sort of begins like a neigh and ends like a hee-hawing bray." He also said that mules, being bred of mares, were generally comfortable around horses, though the opposite wasn't usually true.

This seemed an intriguing family dynamic, but I didn't learn more because a man pulled over in a truck and began quizzing Buck about our mounts.

"That's my uncle Bobby I told you about," Josh said, the one who always told his nephew that you work and you die. "He's a man of few words, unless he's yelling at you."

So I looked on with some surprise as Bobby and Buck, not the loquacious sort either, had an animated conversation about the cost, breeding, and care of mules. Josh's analysis: "They're both more comfortable with animals than with people."

As we rode on, Josh also kept pointing to either side of the road, saying, "That's Uncle Pudgie's land" or "There's my grandpa's house" or "That's my aunt Irene on her ATV." His own home stood nearby, behind a fringe of trees. "In high school I had to watch who I dated because around here we're all related."

A short way on, we reached the homestead of Buck's forebears, a spot I'd noted on an old map and thought might be a place he'd want to stop. But he pressed on, noting that it was already noon, we had many miles still to go, and we needed to reach camp with ample time and light to set up and look after the animals.

To my dismay, we then came to a formidable obstacle I'd failed to recognize as such: a narrow bridge with a cattle guard, bordered by barbed wire and a concrete embankment that plunged about forty feet down to a rocky streambed.

Josh's uncle Bobby had evidently anticipated this, because he reappeared in his truck with plywood to lay over the cattle guard. Buck succeeded in leading his mount and one of the pack mules across, but the second one balked and pulled back violently, breaking the line linking it to the mule ahead.

Buck ran through his toolbox of commands and persuasion, without success. He then began studying the barbed wire and the steep embankment, and sent me to look after his mount, tied up out of sight about twenty-five yards on the far side of the bridge.

I stood in the shade, patting the mule, until I heard shouts and a clatter of hooves and rushed back to see what was happening. I arrived just in time to witness Josh descending the embankment with Hatcher and Doney.

It was not only very steep, but also slick with mud and wet leaves. Near the bottom, Hatcher slid in front of Josh, forcing him to let go of the lead. Then Doney toppled down into the streambed.

I stood there gawking until Buck shouted, "What's wrong with you! Get control of your mule before he runs off!"

Hatcher had wandered a short way down the streambed, and I quickly retrieved him. Doney righted herself, and Buck said of her topple, "That was no biggie; a mule can roll down the side of a mountain and get up and rejoin the pack."

But the bridge snafu had delayed us another forty-five minutes and drained what little remained of Buck's patience, or faith in my route-planning.

Reaching the outskirts of Sisterdale, we encountered a property owner who'd seen us on the road that morning and told us we were welcome to ride on his land by the Guadalupe. He also invited us to tour an old farm-house on his land that had belonged to a German family Olmsted visited.

This was just the sort of excursion after Fred I'd hoped for, and the riverbank was lovely, much cooler than the road, and covered in flowers. I suggested pausing to compare Olmsted's description of the river with the scene before us.

"Really?" Buck replied, before riding on. He showed even less interest in the stone farmhouse, staying outside with the mules while Josh and I toured the cool, thick-walled interior with our host, Coby Knox, gratefully accepting his offer of water, since we'd been riding for four hours without drinking any.

Coby had moved here six years ago with his wife, who was of German descent, and he'd read Olmsted's account of the freethinkers who once lived in the area.

"They were looking for their utopia, and had the right ideas, but their timing was wrong," he said. "We think of California in the 1960s as radical. But *here*, in the 1850s, standing up for their beliefs the way those Germans did? They were way, way ahead in their thinking."

I could happily have lingered, but knew Buck was waiting impatiently outside. We wolfed down a handful of dried fruit before remounting and turning onto a road bordered by the most spectacular flowers I'd yet seen. Josh identified them for me: purple verbena and salvia, yellow coreopsis, and a red-and-yellow bloom called Indian Blanket.

"The whole prairies became radiant and delicious," Olmsted wrote of riding in spring near the Guadalupe. "A quick flush spread over all; the bosom of old Mother Earth seemed to swell with life." At another point he described the prairie "new-clothed in its most agreeable garb," flowers "jeweling the smooth and even verdure." He picked some of them to enclose in his letter to Anne Charlotte Lynch, also telling her of the rich, grape-like "perfume" of a shrub known in Texas as frijolito.

I might have picked flowers, too, to send to my wife. But we'd fallen behind again, and Buck had sped up the pace, forcing me to trot to keep up—and punishing my crotch, which already felt very raw after five or six hours of riding. I tried leaning forward or back, or half standing in the saddle, but none of these adjustments seemed to spare my bruised groin and aching thighs.

Before our trip, I'd secured permission to camp at a ranch four hilly miles from Sisterdale. By the time we reached it, I was riding on empty. There was another mile and a half I hadn't accounted for, from the ranch gate to our campsite by the Guadalupe. "How much longer?" Josh asked, looking as exhausted and glazed as I felt.

We reached the river at five thirty, having ridden sixteen miles, not counting detours. I fell from the saddle and hugged the grassy bank like a shipwrecked sailor.

"Mr. Hooorwitz," boomed Buck, "unsaddle your mule and stake out the grass."

This was a straightforward task that required pacing off distances, planting stakes, and Velcro-ing a long line to the mules' legs so they could graze without straying. But I felt so fried, and anxious about screwing up, that of course I did, putting the line too high on the mules' legs. Ordered to correct this, I made things worse and allowed one of the mules to wander off.

After I made a hash of a few other tasks, Buck handed me a shovel and flashed a rare smile. "Here's a job even you can do. Shovel the mule shit away from our campsite."

This I did. It was almost dark as we gathered wood and set up camp. Our site was magnificent, not unlike the frontispiece of *A Journey through Texas*: a sloping bank fringed with pecan and elm trees, the Guadalupe "quick and perfectly transparent," as Olmsted described. Fireflies flickered in the dusk.

Buck had a chuck wagon at his ranch that he took out for "cowboy camp" dinners of steak, chicken, quail, and other dishes. I knew we wouldn't be dining that way tonight, having helped him pack our food, mostly dehydrated meals that were light. But we'd also packed a cast iron Dutch oven that Buck said was for cooking cowboy bread.

Instead, he produced a large can of Chef Boyardee ravioli he'd picked up during a stop on our drive that morning, the only food that appeared.

I'd brought a bottle of whiskey and passed it around, trying to cheer up the proceedings, and told Buck how much my rear hurt. "You'll be a hard-ass by Friday," he replied. It was now Wednesday.

I also shared Olmsted's writing about choosing campsites and how "the beautiful" was bound to the "quality of ease" that came from satisfying basic needs. For all my other failures, I felt I'd triumphed in finding us exactly such a spot.

Buck seemed to concur with Olmsted. "Being content and getting quality rest has a lot to do with serenity and the animals being taken care of," he said. But he added that "ease" wasn't the word he'd choose to describe our long day, which had started in the dark at 5:00 a.m. and gone downhill by noon.

As we were cleaning up, the ranch's owner, Wayne Wright, appeared with bottles of wine and the property's caretaker, a cowboy named Paulo. Better still, after surveying the remains of our camp dinner, Wayne whispered to Paulo, who returned ten minutes later with a medley of noodles, rice, and vegetables his wife had cooked, and that Josh and I devoured.

I'd first met Wayne at the Sisterdale store, where he often stopped to chat with Bret and other locals. A white-haired man with a white mustache, Wayne was a very successful lawyer in San Antonio, specializing in product liability cases, and the owner of a rum business and several other enterprises.

He was also dedicated to the preservation of Sisterdale and its heritage, having paid to renovate the old dance hall and erect the sign about free-thinkers in front of it. Upon learning of my journey after Olmsted, he'd immediately offered his 380-acre Eagle Dancer Ranch as a campsite.

"I was raised on a working ranch in North Dakota, but this one's a little different," Wayne said of the touches he'd introduced to the property, including a fountain, covered bridge, and a herd of exotic Thai deer.

Given his wealth and business ventures, I was curious why Wayne was such an admirer of the freethinkers, who advocated, among other things, for a progressive income and inheritance tax.

"I don't think their philosophy was rooted in any one system," Wayne said, opening the second bottle of wine he'd brought from his cellar. "They were naturalists and realists, not beholden to supernatural beliefs." In his view a freethinker could be a capitalist or a Socialist, or, like himself, a mix of the two.

"You listen to what they were saying, they could have been Bernie Sanders. Free college, equal rights for women, against oppression of all kinds."

Also, having been raised in the Church of the Nazarene, in a family that included Mennonites, Wayne said he'd "got enough of religion" and admired the freethinkers' secularism. Plus they loved opera, as he did, and had come to this area "looking for their piece of paradise."

Wayne had certainly found his. The sward of grass by our campsite rose to a pasture carpeted in bluebonnets and Indian paint. Wayne told us that the river abounded with bass and trout, and the trees along its bank included the largest stand of American elm on the Guadalupe.

He also said that thousands of arrowheads had turned up along the river. "Natives here had grass, water, timber, game, and a protected spot," he said, giving further substance to Olmsted's view about the universal attraction of ease and beauty. "It was perfect for them, and now it is for us."

OLMSTED, FOR ALL HIS SKILL AT LOCATING IDEAL CAMPSITES, wasn't always adept at the "woodcraft" he later wrote about to his son. Upon finding one fine site near the Guadalupe, he and John "began to burn the grass off a small circle of the ground, that we might have a place to cook our supper upon without danger of setting fire to the prairie at large."

The grass was "perfectly dead and dry," a strong wind blew from the southwest, and "just as the fire was touched to the grass, came an unusually violent gust." This sent the flames "*leaping* along the top of the grass before the wind."

The Olmsteds flailed at the blaze with corn sacks and kept it from setting alight "our tent, ammunition, and camp-stores." But the wind drove the fire up a slope by their camp. "There were now several acres of black, smoking ground, beyond which the flames and white smoke still roared frightfully and entirely obscured the view." But the brothers knew what lay in the inferno's path. "We were very fearful of the damage that might be done," the fire now threatening pasture, fences, cabins, and "fodder stacks and cattle."

Fortunately, Olmsted's keen eye for terrain led him to a military-style maneuver. Half suffocated by heat and smoke, he and John lit grass along the fire's windward flank "to cut off its fuel," soaked their corn sacks in a bog, and beat the edges of the bonfire to channel it into a gully.

"Hotly engaged for more than three hours," they collapsed to watch the flames die down, their hair singed and clothes partly burnt. "We amused ourselves with each other's appearance, our faces, red with heat, being painted in a very bizarre fashion, like Indian warriors', with streaks and spots, and clouds of soot and coal."

Olmsted was likewise self-deprecating about his hunting skills. He'd often crept within rifle range of game and "blazed away without result." Then, along the Guadalupe, he got much closer to a deer and felt "venison was certain," taking aim while thinking of the "tender steak" he'd offer visitors to the brothers' camp.

He fired and advanced to collect his trophy, only to spot "my venison going at a spanking rate, down the mountain, a stiff white tail, derisively hoisted, like the colors of a runaway prize."

On their camping trip, the Olmsteds also spied a snake that seemed "an ugly customer," seven feet in length. "We interrupted his siesta with a pistol-ball." But their triumph was diminished when they discovered the snake was a species "harmless to anything else than eggs, for which they have an irresistible hankering."

I, TOO, HANKERED FOR EGGS WHEN MORNING ARRIVED WITH A bang on a pan and Buck announcing, "Don't know when you lounge lizards want to get up, but it's after six."

He'd retired early while Josh and I had polished off the wine with Wayne and Paulo. I hadn't even bothered to get inside my sleeping sack, instead collapsing on a tarp with my knapsack as a pillow. Stiff, sore, and a bit hungover, I poured a cup of coffee from the pot on the fire before Buck told me to go ask Paulo if there was a shorter route from our campsite back to the road.

I had trouble finding him on the large ranch and returned to find the stove and food had been packed. Josh told me later that Buck had opened a sack of dehydrated scrambled eggs and bacon, spooned a little of the powder into the cup Josh had been drinking coffee from, added boiling water, and eaten his own out of the pouch.

This sounded about as appetizing as the Borden's "portable meat glue" the Olmsteds sampled. Still, it was more than what I got: a few quick forkfuls of leftover rice from the dinner Paulo had brought, before rushing to saddle up.

Hatcher had been fairly tractable on our first day, but he seemed to have awakened on the wrong side of the pasture. He made a fuss over having his boots put on and then kept shifting as I tried to mount.

Buck walked Hatcher in tight circles to calm him and "let him know that for today, a human that looks somewhat like me is going to be in charge." This was said with heavy sarcasm. "We'll do the best we can with what we've got, and pray that Mr. Horwitz comes out the other side in one piece, more or less."

He also lengthened the stirrups so that I wouldn't bounce so much in the saddle. This gave a little relief to my crotch, but the readjustment, or Hatcher's and my respective bad moods, put us in poor sync. As soon as we left camp, he took off across a pasture, and by the time I got him under control I'd lost a saddlebag that I'd failed to tie on properly.

"How many car accidents have you had?" Buck asked as I reassembled my gear and remounted. When I told him I'd had only one of consequence, in the Australian outback thirty years earlier, he shook his head in disbelief. Then he rode at a brisker pace than before, leaving Josh and me far behind and turning every ten minutes or so to shout at us to catch up.

Unbeknownst to me, Josh's mood had curdled, too. "I've tied a million fucking knots in my life, but every time I do a bowline Mr. Hard-Ass comes over and reties it," he said. "Treats me like a slow child. And you like a kid with special needs."

Josh had accepted Buck's drill-sergeant demeanor on training day and at the start of our ride. "He was teaching us a lesson, I get that." But Buck's behavior since had made him wonder.

"Why did he give me the laziest mule and you the craziest?" Josh said, kicking Doney hard to keep up with me. "He's got spurs and is probably up there laughing at us. He enjoys making us feel like idiots."

I tried to cheer Josh up, assuring him that Buck would chill by the time we reached Sisterdale. I'd received permission to ride around several home-steads Olmsted visited, and had also arranged with the Hill Country his-torian I'd consulted to have a photographer take pictures and make a video of part of the day's ride.

The county historical society wanted footage of the homesteads, and I thought it would be fun to have some of us, too—as well as offering Buck a chance to perform for the camera.

Our first stop was certainly photogenic: the junction of the Guadalupe and Sisterdale's smaller waterway. "I have rarely seen any resort of wood-nymphs more perfect than the bower of cypress branches and vines that overhang the mouth of the Sister creek," Olmsted wrote. "You want a silent canoe to penetrate it; yet would be loath to desecrate its deep beauty."

The spot remained very pastoral, though somewhat less tranquil due to the road bridge overhead. Also, after admiring the water for a few minutes, we had to ford it. Almost all the Olmsteds' serious mishaps occurred at river crossings, including one attempt at the Guadalupe that ended with Fred's horse slipping on wet boulders. "Over we rolled, helter-skelter, puff-ing, sneezing, kicking and striking out among one another generally."

No one was hurt during this "hydropathic course," but the brothers re-alized "it was useless to think of getting over dry on the short pegs of Mr. Brown." Elsewhere, while crossing a "crooked, dirty stream," their mule became so mired in the turbid water that "nothing whatever was visible of Mr. Brown, save the horns of the pack-saddle and his own well-known ears, rising piteously above the treacherous waves."

The mule then "gave up with a loud sigh, and laid upon his side to die," at which point the Olmsteds waded in to rescue him. But Mr. Brown regained his footing, and fortitude, emerging "like a drowned rat," the wicker hampers filled with muddy water. "We thought, bitterly, for a moment, of our pistols and sugar, our Epsom salts and gunpowder, our gingerbread, our poets and our shirts," Olmsted wrote, "then broke into an uncontrollable fit of laughter."

Fortunately for us, the Guadalupe's current at our crossing was swift but the water low, wetting little more than our boots. Then we rode up a rise to Sisterdale's first European homestead, established in the 1840s by a German surveyor seeking *den Garten der Welt*, meaning "garden of the world."

He then sold the property to Edward Degener, the Forty-Eighter who hosted the Olmsteds and later lost his sons at the Nueces. The current owners showed us a cabin dating from the late 1840s, made of ax-hewn boards chinked with mud. A larger house, where the Olmsteds stayed and enjoyed the night of singing and dancing, had since vanished.

But the setting was little changed. "His house stands upon a prominence, which commands the beautiful valley in both directions," Olmsted wrote of Degener's home, and this matched the view as we rode to the edge of a bluff by the water.

When I dismounted to take pictures, Buck said, "Keep it snappy," and then rode off the wrong way, ignoring the directions I'd relayed from our hosts.

Correcting course, we reached the onetime property of Baron Ottomar von Behr, the professor and local judge the Olmsteds dined with on their first day in Sisterdale. The site of Behr's "double log-cabin" was now occupied by a handsome limestone house of slightly later vintage, which had passed down to a direct descendant of the baron's, Charlie Kohl.

I'd visited Kohl a few days earlier and found a copy of Olmsted's book on the kitchen table, open to the passage describing his great-great-grandfather recording the temperature and wind. "A man of marked attainments at home," Olmsted wrote, von Behr was "an intimate associate" of the famous geographer Alexander von Humboldt and "Goethe's Bettina." His cabin was cluttered with guns, wool from his sheep, snakeskins, and "Romances and philosophies" he shared with his neighbors, believed to be the first lending library in Texas.

Kohl wasn't home at the time of our ride, but he'd told me it was fine for us to explore what Olmsted called the "romantic rocky bluff of the Guadalupe," beside von Behr's home. There was still an ancient cave with a wood door on the face of the bluff, which Kohl said had served as a hideout in case of Indian attack. In his childhood, adults didn't want kids playing there and dressed as a werewolf-like creature, the "Behr Bluff Monster," to scare them away from the steep, rocky ridge.

Josh and I dismounted to look at the cave and bluff for a few minutes while Buck sat impatiently in the saddle. We were due in an hour to be let in a gate at another historic property, where the photographer would meet us for an extended shoot. "Our Facebook cowboy doesn't want to miss that," Josh grumbled as we trotted behind Buck to the other end of Sisterdale. "A tryout for his reality show."

We arrived at the gate early, and Buck adjusted and retied every piece of gear on Doney and Hatcher, evidently keen to make the mules camera ready. As we waited in the ninety-degree sun, I tried to lighten the mood by casting *Three Miles an Hour*, the show Buck had proposed making about his cross-country mule trek.

For contrast and entertainment, I suggested, his sidekick should be a clod who talked too much, like me, or perhaps a Native American.

"I don't want anybody," he said.

"But then the show won't have any dialogue."

"I don't like words," he replied. "Words to me are highly overrated."

I zippered it until we entered the property, once a hydrotherapy spa founded by Ernst Kapp, a prominent German geographer and philosopher. "The delicious brook water has been turned to account by him for the cure of disease," Olmsted wrote of Kapp's land along Sister Creek, "and his house is thrown open to patients."

The therapies included *sitzbads* (sitting baths) and being rubbed with a wet sheet, as well as gymnastic exercises beneath a shade tree. "To any friend of mine who has faith in pure air and water," Olmsted wrote, "and is obliged to run from a Northern winter, I cannot recommend a pleasanter spot to pass his exile than this."

His tone hinted at skepticism toward water cures, but the property was as beautiful as he described. We rode down a tree-lined lane, rather like an oak allée at Southern plantations, except that here the trees were pecan.

This led to a cluster of well-restored buildings from Kapp's day, one a cabin of hand-hewn cypress logs.

After taking a leisurely ride around the grounds for the camera, we drank cool, fresh spring water that ran from a pipe behind the old buildings. I felt refreshed, and relieved that Hatcher had been relatively easy to handle since he'd taken off as we left camp that morning.

Perhaps this had lulled me. Or maybe Hatcher had simply been waiting for the right moment to get me off his back. For no apparent reason, as we sat in our saddles in the shade, Hatcher bolted like "some pumpkins," as Olmsted would have put it, headed straight at a live oak with a high stone wall behind.

"Whoa! Whoa!" I shouted, unable to rein him in. Then I let go of the reins so I could throw myself back against Hatcher, to avoid being clobbered by the elbow of one of the oak's sturdy limbs. I cleared it by an inch or two and managed to halt Hatcher just before he hurtled me into the wall.

"*Holy fuck*, are you okay?" Josh shouted, rushing over to help. I was shaken, thinking of the Absalom-like fate I'd narrowly avoided. But more than that, I was confused. Buck had readjusted everything a half hour earlier, and I couldn't figure out what I'd done to provoke Hatcher's sudden attempt to decapitate me.

I glanced over at Buck for guidance. He shook his head disdainfully, turned his mule, and wandered off.

Josh glared after him with a look that said, "I'm gonna rip your fucking throat out." I appreciated his being protective of me. But I didn't relish the prospect of my 260-pound guardian assaulting our slimmer but very tough hombre of a guide.

"How's about we ride down to the creek," I said, with as much cheer as I could muster. "From what Olmsted wrote, it's really special."

And it was, the most spectacular spot we'd yet visited and exactly as Olmsted described the two branches of Sister Creek. "The water of both streams has a delicate, cool, blue-green color; the rocky banks are clean and inviting; the cypresses rise superbly from the very edge, like ornamental columns."

It was also easy to see why this property had once been a water-cure spa. There were deep pools by a small waterfall, white stones at the bottom of the perfectly clear water, the whole shaded by cypresses that Josh judged to be twenty feet in diameter. "Just looking at the water makes you feel better," he said.

Buck seemed soothed, too, allowing us to linger and splash around on the mules before we rode off to rejoin the cameraman for our next photo op, at the old dance hall on the main street.

After Buck and his mule performed, effortlessly mounting a wood platform by the dance hall and leaping off it, I suggested we go across the street for a drink at the saloon. To my surprise, he didn't object. Josh, party to the general store's obscure feud with the saloon, stayed outside with the mules while Buck and I sipped beers.

I chatted first with a Mexican-born cowboy at the bar who said the Spanish word for mule was *mula*, which he believed was the origin of the term "moolah," for cash. "Mules are for working and make you the money," he said.

Buck, always animated by talk of mules, chimed in. "They'd be perfectly happy *not* working. All they really want to do is eat, sleep, and excrete. They'd be as fat as butterballs if they could."

I also learned that accidents like the one I'd nearly had at the Kapp property weren't all that rare. Buck said he'd had two concussions, one from a "low tree limb to the forehead," another soon after, when he wasn't fully recovered and was jarred by a bucking mule before falling from the saddle. Also, two people he'd taken on rides had been evacuated by helicopter, due to back and head injuries. "That's why I'm such a stickler for doing everything right."

I nodded, and felt consoled at having avoided a concussion or the need to be airlifted. But Buck's momentary mellow disappeared as soon as we left the saloon. He took Josh to task for the way he'd tied up our mounts, then led his and the pack mules briskly down the street.

As we trailed behind, Josh finally lost it. "He's as stubborn as a mule, an asshole on an ass," he fumed. "All he cares about is the camera. My ass has taken enough of a pounding. I'm done."

I pleaded with Josh, telling him I'd be lost without his assistance and company, which was true. But he couldn't be moved. A friend of his father's had just died, and there was an open-casket viewing in a few hours. "I didn't like the guy and he didn't like me," Josh said of the deceased. "But I'd rather look at his dead face than spend another night in camp with that asshole and his ravioli."

Buck received the news of Josh's departure with a shrug. The forecast called for heavy thundershowers, he said, and without Josh present there'd be more room in the tent for the two of us and any gear we needed to keep dry.

While he hitched Doney behind the pack mules, I popped into the general store. Bret had already received a download on our trip while I'd been drinking with Buck at the saloon. "I gather Josh is abandoning ship, leaving you alone with your cowboy Captain Ahab."

I confided my dread of riding and camping without Josh as a buffer between Buck, Hatcher, and me.

"It won't be that bad," Bret said, airily waving his hand. "He'll probably just tie you to a cactus and sodomize you."

This gave me a much-needed laugh. I'd been through worse, and would just have to suck it up and endure saddle soreness and verbal abuse until Doc returned with his trailer to collect the mules.

It helped that Buck rode off toward Wayne Wright's ranch at an even faster clip than usual. The late-afternoon sky had turned threatening, and he wanted to make camp ahead of the rain. Unmentioned was his apparent desire to put as much distance between us as possible. He didn't even turn in the saddle to badger me to catch up, as he'd so often done.

This was fine by me. I tried to enjoy the quiet and the splendid roadside flowers, while attempting to ignore the raw open wound forming on my butt. Until, about a mile from the general store, Hatcher began acting in a way he hadn't before: shaking his head from side to side, whipping his tail, and snorting. Then he suddenly reared up and backed into the road.

During our training, I'd asked Buck what to do in a truly bad situation. He'd told me to find the middle of the rein, bring the mule's head to the side, and turn him in a circle. If that didn't work, make sure to position my toes in the stirrup so I could bail cleanly. "Otherwise, you won't get your feet out and that never ends well."

I managed to rein Hatcher in a circle and out of the road, but he kept rearing and trying to throw me. Buck was far ahead, the wind was blowing in my face, and he evidently didn't hear my shouts. I watched as he and the other mules disappeared over a ridge.

When I'd encountered other difficulties, Buck had chided me by saying, "If there's a problem there's a source. Analyze and fix it." He'd also said something that struck me as wise at the time. "It's never the animal's fault. Nothing they do in their world is wrong. You just have to learn to understand and speak their language."

So I carefully dismounted and held Hatcher as best I could while searching him for burrs or other problems that might explain his agitation. Nothing seemed awry. All I could see was a bit of strap hanging from one of his boots, so I tightened that. Then I tried to remount.

Hatcher reared and backed into the road again. Terrified that a truck might roar over the nearby ridge, I yanked with all the strength I had left, pulling him onto the grassy fringe.

But I felt bereft of other tactics to control him. So I put my face up to his, and reached to give his forehead a soothing pat. Before my hand got there, Hatcher jerked his head forward.

I'd often heard the expression "seeing stars," and when I came to on the ground I saw an entire constellation. Hatcher had head-butted me into semiconsciousness. The brunt of the blow had landed on the bridge of my nose, and for a moment I thought it might be broken.

But I was as much stunned as physically hurt, a little the way I imagined an abused spouse might feel. "What the fuck, Hatcher?" I yelled. We'd had our issues and I was far from blameless. But what had I done to deserve this?

As Buck might have told me, Hatcher didn't *comprende*. His ears were back and his eyes wild. So I decided to walk him the rest of the way. But he kept rearing, and all I could do was clutch the lead and turn him in circles away from the road.

We'd been engaged in this struggle for a wretched ten minutes or so when Buck appeared, having noticed I'd fallen far out of sight. I anticipated a tongue-lashing, but he couldn't identify a physical source for Hatcher's displeasure, or fault my report on the measures I'd taken.

Buck patiently worked with the mule and waited out his tantrum. Then he hitched Hatcher behind the others. "All right, we'll make it *real* easy for you," he told me. Mounting Doney, who was tied between Hatcher and the others, I didn't have to do anything other than sit in the saddle and be part of the mule train.

This went okay for about a quarter of a mile. Then Hatcher started trotting up alongside Doney, who picked up the pace, bunching the mules together. This annoyed one of the pack mules so much it kicked back at Doney.

At which point all hell broke lose, the mules agitated and circling until the rope Buck was holding them by became wrapped around both of us. I felt like a passenger in a skidding car, without a steering wheel or brake to reach for, clutching Doney's saddle horn while Buck struggled to bring four tons of frantic mule flesh under control before being pulled to the ground.

He somehow maneuvered out from the rope and traffic jam, and succeeded in herding the mules back in line. We still had about three miles to go, and I suggested that I ride ahead on Doney, to lessen the risk of a repeat scrum.

For the first time all week, Buck agreed with my judgment and told me to remove Doney's bridle from the saddle horn. I was so rattled, and still feeling woozy from being head-butted by Hatcher, that I probably couldn't have untied a shoelace.

"Give it to me, stupid!" Buck shouted, grabbing the tangled bridle out of my hands. "I've never seen anyone in my life with so little common sense!"

I feebly replied that I was "really trying." He took off his sunglasses and brought his pale blue eyes close to mine. "Does it look like I believe you?"

I silently remounted Doney and rode ahead toward the ranch. Doney was much wider than Hatcher and very hard to keep moving without constant kicks. Still, after being aboard Hatcher, I welcomed the lack of drama and felt unaccustomedly secure, at least physically.

Buck's words had stuck in me like a barb. Not because of wounded pride in my competence at dealing with straightforward tasks. *Klutz* comes from the Yiddish for "wooden block." If I was a blockheaded stumblebum who couldn't untie a bridle from a saddle horn, so be it.

What stung much more was my failure in a department of which I'd felt I was chair: finding a way to reach and get along with just about anybody, no matter how different our backgrounds or beliefs or temperaments. This was one reason I'd identified with Olmsted. I shared his missionary spirit, believing that there was always room for dialogue, and great value in having it, if only to make it harder for Americans to demonize one another.

With a few exceptions—my contretemps with the bigots in Crockett came to mind—I felt I'd honored Yeoman in that regard. Not so during this ride. It was obvious Buck loathed me, as much as or more than Hatcher did. I'd come to resent him right back, with an animosity I couldn't recall since falling out with a bullying sports coach in high school. In adolescent fashion, I'd even taken to giving the finger to Buck's upright, red-suspendered back during our ride.

In Josh's view, "that man only wants to make us feel little." But Buck had shown flashes of fellowship. Surely, I could analyze and fix this situation. Learn to speak his language, as he'd told me to do with mules.

"Don't be sweet; smack him on the butt," Buck said as he overtook me near the entrance to Wayne's ranch. He then rode ahead as I struggled to get Doney to move at more than turtle pace through the last of the day's fourteen miles.

By the time we reached camp, I was as bedraggled as I'd been the evening before, and in dread of "staking out" the mules and other tasks. Not to mention sharing dinner and a tent with Buck.

Mercifully, due to the forecast of heavy storms, he decided to shift our camp from the riverbank to the porch of one of the ranch buildings Wayne had said we could use. He also told me to stay out of the way while he attended to the mules, and invited the ranch caretaker, Paulo, as well as the photographer who'd trailed us during the day, for dinner on the porch once he was done.

This made me wonder, once again, if I'd misjudged the man. It also stirred hope that he might bring out the Dutch oven, or at least something more than the can of ravioli we'd consumed the night before.

But no, not even the dehydrated meals we'd packed. Or plates. Instead, Buck took out a plastic container with leftovers from Paulo's largesse to us the previous evening, forked some of it into his mouth, and passed the container to the photographer. After going around once, the food was finished.

The only sense I could make of this was that Buck, having given up on

me, and our trip, had decided he wouldn't expend another iota of our provisions. Supplies, he'd told me, that were part of the package I'd paid for.
I wasn't agitated over the money, and felt oddly without appetite. But it
seemed an appalling way to treat guests he'd invited to our so-called
dinner.

I could have spoken up, or opened the bags he'd packed away on the
porch and cooked something myself. But I lacked the energy, and didn't
want to risk Buck reacting in a way that would finally make me explode.
Instead, I passed around the rest of my whiskey, until the cowboy I'd
chatted with at the saloon unexpectedly turned up with a pot of pork
and beans.

This redeemed the culinary portion of the evening. But as soon as our
guests left, I felt depressed at the prospect of another long day in the company of a man and a mule that couldn't bear my company, or I theirs.

"You know what," I said as casually as I could. "I'm thinking, rather
than ride in the rain tomorrow, and you doing all the work, maybe we
should call it quits and hang here until Doc can come with his trailer."

"Sounds good to me," Buck replied, laying out his bedroll at one end of
the porch. I took mine to the other, separated from Buck by a border wall
of gear, and was lulled by the rain into the deepest sleep I could recall in
months.

IN THE MORNING THERE WAS A FAINT AIR OF MUTUAL CONTRI-
tion, or perhaps just relief that the riding portion of our trip was over. I
went through my notes and tapes, asking Buck about details I wasn't sure
I had right. He answered agreeably, even complimenting my "physicality"
in having mounted smoothly (with one or two exceptions) and avoided
tumbling from the saddle during our ride.

I felt we'd lowered the temperature, and I followed him to help move
the mules from the pen where they'd spent the night. He asked me to open
the gate, which I did, pushing it in toward the pen.

"Common sense!" he shouted. "Gates always open out!"

After that, we avoided each other until it came time to ready the mules
for transport home. I hadn't touched Hatcher all day, but he refused to

cooperate with Buck either, rearing up before going to the ground, where he lay whinnying and kicking his hooves in the air.

He was still there when the trailer arrived. Doc walked over to Hatcher and quipped, "Lying down on the job?"

I resisted a cruel urge to quote Buck, "The animal is never wrong," and instead mocked myself. "I think I've set his training back a year."

"That's perceptive," Buck observed.

We said little more until the mules and gear were loaded and we reached the Sisterdale store, where I'd asked to be dropped off. I shook hands with Doc and thrust my hand at Buck, struggling to find words that wouldn't seem ludicrously insincere.

"Well, it's been an experience," I finally mustered.

"That it has," he replied.

I found Bret in the hammock, listening to Josh, who was still venting over our trip. I tossed in a few details about the rest of the ride and the evening Josh had missed. Then Bret half rose in the hammock, like a slacker judge, to issue his opinion.

Buck had told us that his family ranch had suffered, due to wild hogs and other factors beyond his control. Before becoming a muleteer and guide, he'd worked for a telephone company, as a welder, and at other jobs, "anything to scratch out a living in this beautiful Hill Country," he'd said. On a social media profile, next to "studies at," he'd written "collage of hard nocks."

In Bret's view, all this made Buck bristle at those dealt a more fortunate hand in life. "He needed to put your East Coast writer's ass in its place, at the bottom of the pecking order."

"What about me?" Josh whined, citing his own school of literal hard knocks, delivered by his uncle Bobby. "Why'd he have to treat *me* like a sack of shit?"

"Because he knew you were onto him from the start," Bret said.

This all sounded plausible, but I'd stopped caring. I felt drained and ill, which I put down to the heat, weariness, and tension of the last few days. So I retired early to the budget quarters at the Moon Pie, a half trailer six feet across.

In the mirror I glimpsed a figure about as collected as Hatcher mid-tantrum: swollen nose, hat hair, rope burn on my upper arm from a mishap

I couldn't recall, and blank, bloodshot eyes. Not visible was the very painful saddle sore on my butt.

I face-planted on the bed and stayed there for hours as one of Bret's steak and music nights got underway on the patio outside. A very loud R & B band played on a stage about five feet from my trailer. Near midnight, the audience shouted, "Encore!" and a musician broke into an electric guitar solo, Jimi Hendrix's "Purple Haze," each shrieking chord like a nail driven into my cortex.

The next day I still felt very out of sorts but forced down a pot of coffee and drove to San Antonio to start plotting my journey to the Rio Grande, the last leg of my trip in Olmsted's wake. I missed a highway exit sign and had trouble focusing well enough to read the next. Pulling over, I called a friend in San Antonio for the name of a hospital and drove very slowly to the emergency room.

A nurse took my vitals and a doctor examined me. It's hard to get a laugh in an emergency room, but when I told of my ride and tête-à-tête with Hatcher, they both cracked a smile.

The doctor asked me to close my eyes and bring a finger to my nose, and walk with one foot right in front of the other. If this had been a roadside sobriety test, I would have gone to jail. Then he asked if I felt nauseated (yes), if I had a headache (yes, crushing), and if I was experiencing confusion and blurry vision (absolutely).

He sent me for a CAT scan and told the nurse to hook me up to an IV since I appeared extremely dehydrated. I'd been guzzling water for the past twenty-four hours, but he said the condition could linger for days after my parched, hot time in the saddle.

"Good news," the doctor said, returning with the scan results. "No fracture or sign of hemorrhage. Everything is consistent with a concussion."

The bad news: "No stress, no strenuous activity, do as little as possible, mentally and physically, until you're better."

"How long will that be?"

"In severe cases, symptoms can last for months," he said, but if I took care of myself, I'd likely feel better in about three weeks. With a smile he added, "Absolutely no mule riding."

I found the nearest motel, pulled the shades, and blurrily studied my discharge instructions, which said to watch for "warning signs" like swelling, high fever, or "bloody drainage from the nose or ear." After two very dull days and nights, lying in bed listening to the air conditioner, I felt able to putter back to Bret's store to collect my baggage.

Like Olmsted, I'd lingered in and around Sisterdale for weeks and grown fond of the area and its inhabitants. But I rather doubted that the Moon Pie and the music and constantly flowing beer constituted the sort of R & R the doctor had in mind. The Rio Grande could wait; I was flying home for a spell.

"Given how things have gone," Bret said, "you deserve a refund I'm not going to give you." He'd actually collected little. The mini-trailer ran fifty dollars a night, and he'd let me sleep on the store floor when the motel was fully booked.

I'd also been fortunate to arrive when I did. Bret had just learned that his landlord planned to sell the store and its surrounds to out-of-state developers. He sensed this was part of a larger trend, to chase the remaining quirk out of Sisterdale and turn the sleepy community into a boutiquey getaway for wealthy weekenders.

"Next time you're here," he predicted, "the saloon will be an English tea parlor." Kapp's former sanitarium by Sister Creek, he added, would become a new age spa with "high colonics." As for Bret, "I'll be selling overpriced stinky cheeses to the winery crowd. Or I'll have been driven out, like those free spirits Olmsted wrote about."

A month later, he emailed to report that his landlord had canceled his lease and served him with an eviction notice. Bret hired an attorney and turned his music nights into fund-raisers for legal fees. I chipped in from afar, as the Olmsteds had done to help keep Douai and his besieged newspaper afloat. But before long, Bret could no long afford inventory. As a final protest, and what-the-hell stunt, he kept the store open with a single product.

"A container of ketchup always lives up to the promise of its contents," he wrote on the store's Facebook page. "Ketchup does what it says it is going to do. Ketchup is the Atticus Finch of condiments. We hope this serves as a reminder to all that there is a moral standard and we should all strive to live by it."

Soon afterward, Bret was finally forced out. But with his usual resourcefulness, he found a store deeper in the Hill Country to lease and restart his music nights and other enterprises. Last I heard from Josh Cravey, he was back working the family farm with his uncle Bobby.

As for our mule man extraordinaire, we exchanged a few brief emails about the snaps and video the photographer had taken. I mentioned my concussion and said it was taking me weeks to start to feel better.

"Sorry to hear that for sure," he replied, adding of Hatcher, "Took him just about as long to recover as well, ha ha."

CHAPTER 20

TO THE RIO GRANDE

Border Disorder

I n later life, reflecting on his "vagabond" years, Olmsted wondered if his youthful wandering had conditioned him to "lose the thread I wish to follow and go off wool-gathering."

This propensity for drift was on conspicuous display during his ride in Texas. Initially, Olmsted cast the journey as an extension of his Southern reporting, and as a healthful excursion for his ailing brother. Then came the extended "pause" in San Antonio and the brothers' flirtation with settling among the Germans.

While exploring that possibility, Olmsted divulged yet another design. "We expect to go on to California," he wrote between trips along the Guadalupe. A letter of John's also mentioned their "California plan." Though sketchy, it appears the brothers envisioned riding south of the border and then across northern Mexico to the coast.

But upon returning from the Hill Country to San Antonio, they couldn't find "company for any long route in Mexico," Olmsted wrote. "We abandoned the idea, and set out on the first of April for a short ride across the frontier, by ourselves."

The brothers traveled light, taking "Little Nack" and the mule Mr. Brown, leaving behind John's "worn down" mount as well as their tent and pack, toting little apart from their weapons.

"We might lose our scalps, should we chance to be seen by any stray band of Comanches," Olmsted wrote of the dangerous stretch they'd need to cross before reaching the Rio Grande. But mail riders risked this passage once a week, for little pay, so "we might well afford to do the same once in a lifetime, for the pleasure of the thing."

At first, the ride was easy and delightful, the early April weather "Italian" and the prairie "a rolling sheet of the finest grass, sprinkled thick with bright, many-hued flowers." This pleasing landscape west of San Antonio was also newly planted with European immigrants, mostly from Alsace.

Beyond the last of these settlements, the riders entered dry, rugged terrain devoid of foliage other than brushy mesquite. "We saw that we were approaching the great chaparral desert of the Rio Grande valley," Olmsted wrote. At its edge stood Fort Inge, one of a cordon of federal outposts established along the Texas frontier following the war with Mexico.

The military base was little more than a mesquite stockade from which soldiers periodically gave "lumbering" pursuit to Comanche and Apache warriors skilled at lightning attacks on mail trains, cattle droves, and homesteads. "Keeping a bull-dog to chase musquitoes would be no greater nonsense," Olmsted wrote.

The travelers nonetheless enjoyed dining at the officers' mess and were fortunate "to procure at Fort Inge a good guide for the Rio Grande." John Woodland "could assume the Mexican manner and tongue," speak several Indian languages, and "use the signs of various other tribes." The London-born, Ohio-raised scout was also reliable, neat, and "communicative without being garrulous and tiresome—a combination of good qualities we found in no other frontiersman."

Olmsted further approved of Woodland's views regarding "Indian character." The scout complained that writers always misrepresented natives by rendering their speech in a phony, "highfalutin way." He then told of translating for a lieutenant "talking up in the clouds," until he was interrupted by an Apache elder who asked that the officer plainly state his business, rather than spouting nonsense as if to babies.

Woodland also had a healthy respect for native guile, having survived capture by the Comanche, from whom he escaped after a month. On the riders' first day out from Fort Inge, during a break at a rare shaded spot,

Olmsted lay down for a nap—only to learn that three men had been killed there the year before, when set upon while slumbering.

That night, after Woodland expertly dressed and cooked rabbits on mesquite skewers, he advised his companions to retire with their heads on their saddles, Colts hidden beneath. This would keep the guns dry and allow the men to reach for them quickly and without rustling.

"I slept little," Olmsted confessed, but he was rewarded with a magnificent night canopy. "The Germans have a saying that the sky seems *nearer* in Texas," and this seemed true, the stars and nebulae shining more vividly than in any part of the globe he'd traveled. The only disturbance in the night was "a mouse, or something like it," that got under his blanket and nuzzled his throat.

But in the morning, the riders came upon an enormous rattlesnake and then countless more of the species, "*hanging* in bushes" or sunning by the trail. "I share, with many of mankind, a peculiar dread of serpents," Olmsted wrote. The snakes, however, became "so common as hardly to excite an exclamation," and gave clear warning of danger by coiling and clattering. "Its rattle is a piercing noise, like that of an August grasshopper, and cannot be mistaken."

He also deflated fearful tales about "the peculiar venomous insects of Texas," describing the tarantula as "very rare" and the scorpion as "a minute flattened crawling lobster" with a sting no worse than a hornet's. Much more intriguing was the horned frog, which seemed a weird hybrid of lizard and toad.

The Olmsteds captured two of the frogs and later mailed them in a box to John's wife and young children in New York. Miraculously, the reptiles arrived "in good spirits and flesh"—although in advance of "the letter of introduction" the brothers had sent. This caused "some explosive consternation," but once the strange creatures were found to be harmless, "they became household pets."

There was little else to recommend the hostile territory the brothers and Woodland traveled for two days after leaving Fort Inge. "The soil is generally gravelly, arid, and sterile, and everywhere covered with the same dwarf forest of prickly shrubs." As they neared the Rio Grande, the more "desolate, dry, and barren became the scene; the more dwarfed and thorny the vegetation."

At one point the riders spotted an avian that Woodland identified as a bird of paradise. "It must have been so denominated in irony," Olmsted wrote, "for a more dreary country, of equal extent, I never saw."

A MONTH AFTER MY MULE TRIP, HAVING MOSTLY RECOVERED, I decided to extend the "pause" in my own journey to the Rio Grande. It was June, a lovely season in New England and already a frying pan in South Texas. I delayed flying back to San Antonio until early autumn, when the afternoon temperatures cooled to about ninety degrees.

I also took it easier than before, upgrading to two-star lodging when available, and loitering west of San Antonio before plunging into the drear beyond. Just past the city's far edge I came to Castroville, the first and largest of the Alsatian communities Olmsted passed through. "The cottages are scattered prettily," he wrote, "the whole aspect being as far from Texas as possible."

Castroville still had a quaint Old World air: clustered and gaily colored cottages, a cathedral plaza, streets named after European capitals. In other respects, the town's Continental roots felt attenuated. Its "Alsatian" bakery mostly sold glazed donuts; there were businesses with names like Alsace Tan & Salon; and at the town's fringe I reached Ville d'Alsace, an upscale golf community.

Following a farm road, I reached a more far-flung Alsatian settlement, Quihi, which Olmsted described as a "picturesque" village of whitewashed, thatched-roofed cottages, "artistically placed in the shade of large dark live-oaks." The riders overnighted with a "peasant" family that had amassed a considerable farm with a fine garden and other "improvements."

But Quihi was beset from its founding by cholera, Indian raids, and drought, and never really thrived. It now verged on ghost village status: the post office and school long gone, a shuttered shop, and little sign of life apart from a tall-steepled Lutheran church beside a small cemetery. The nineteenth-century gravestones were etched with spired Gothic buildings, reaching heavenward, a celestial vision of the Franco-German world the immigrants left behind.

The only person I encountered was Larry Schott, who was hauling hay on land that had been in his wife's family for five generations. The couple had recently gone on a "roots" trip to Alsace. "The houses looked like the old ones here," he said, "except they're stacked together in town, not spread out, and had nice flower boxes."

He took me inside a restored cottage, one wall bearing photographs of worn, unsmiling pioneers. In Alsace, Schott had been very impressed by the region's fine wine and rich cropland. "Made me wonder," he said. "A lot of the ones who left there long ago? Probably wished they hadn't once they got here."

Driving on, I crossed Verde Creek, which was absent of water or greenery, and then a parched creek called Seco, Spanish for "dry." I crossed a baking plain where trees became "stunted and rare," Olmsted wrote. The riders then came to the westernmost of the Alsatian colonies, which he called "a singular spectacle upon the verge of the great American wilderness."

The twenty or so "cottages and hovels" in D'Hanis were built of vertical mesquite stakes with peaked thatched roofs. The floors were beaten dirt; the windows had no glass. "It is like one of the smallest and meanest of European peasant hamlets."

The riders slept on a floor of one cottage, and learned that the settlers, on their arrival five years earlier, had endured times so lean that they'd eaten weeds. Olmsted described the women as "very coarse and masculine" due to constant and demanding labor.

The D'Hanis he visited was now little more than a collection of graveyards, the settlement having been abandoned when it was bypassed by the railroad in the 1880s. "New" D'Hanis, by the tracks a few miles away, looked as if it might suffer a similar fate. Parts of the tiny downtown business district were in ruins due to a tornado a year before my arrival.

At a market lunch counter I met John Bergmann and his wife, Margaret, both retired teachers of Alsatian descent. They gave me a taste of parisa, a spicy ground meat for spreading on crackers, a rare survival of their forebears' diet and customs. "It's amazing *they* survived," Margaret said.

John took me to see the remains of an 1850s fort on a bluff outside town, walking me past a few crumbled walls and foundations surrounded by cactus and mesquite: a bleak, prickly outpost. "Settlers were lied to about the fertility of the land," he said. "When it's dry around here, it's *really* dry, and if it's raining it floods."

The Alsatians had also served as the civilian vanguard of continental conquest, a buffer of population that helped justify the establishment of garrisons like this one, for subduing Indians. The fort was abandoned just three years after its construction, when the front line of settlement and conflict shifted farther west.

"Immigrants built this country and have always done the hard work and suffering," John said. This made him bristle at the loud campaign talk about building a border wall. "Our families did what they had to, to survive. Same with people now, and you're not going to stop them."

LEAVING THE FORT, I CROSSED THE FRIO RIVER, WHICH WAS parched, and the Dry Frio River, entering territory Olmsted described as treeless and almost uninhabited. At one of the rare homesteads he passed, a slave boy of about ten ran after him, asking how long it was to Christmas. When Olmsted inquired why he wanted to know (it was April), the boy said he'd been hired out until then, to this lonely property, and wanted to "go back whar I belong."

The riders then reached Fort Inge, "adjacent to a singular conical rocky hill," a formation known to geologists as a volcanic plug. Little trace remained of the fort, where the Olmsteds hired their border guide, John Woodland. I was thinking of doing the same, since my Spanish was meager and my familiarity with Mexico even slighter.

So before crossing the near-desert between the fort site and the Rio Grande, I stayed the night at a considerable town that had arisen nearby when the railroad arrived. After my two-day tour of Alsatian settlements, Uvalde felt familiarly Texan. I passed a gym named Shotgun CrossFit, adorned with crossed rifles and a sign with the words "Never Retreat Just Reload." Then I came to a sports bar where brawny riggers and roughnecks were drinking a Texas beer named Guns & Oil.

One of the barmaids appeared to be Latina, so I asked her for advice about finding a guide and translator for my trip along the border. She said she avoided going to Mexico, because family members had been kidnapped and held for ransom while driving to and from their native Guatemala. Also, the border area Olmsted visited in Mexico "is *really* bad news," she said, notorious for its drug cartels and frequent murders.

But her sister often crossed the border to shop, and was also an able translator. "She needs the work and I'm sure she'd go with you," the barmaid said, adding an odd caveat. "You should know, she likes to eat a lot."

I gave the barmaid my number, and she promised her sister would call me that evening. By late morning the next day, having still heard nothing, I gave up and hit the road alone. This was just as well, since there was nothing to eat in the barrens I entered soon after leaving Uvalde.

I drove for miles without seeing another car, or any life, only a run-over rabbit and a hawk soaring overhead. The bird of prey shadowed me for fifteen minutes, as if hoping I'd become roadkill, too.

"In riding sixty miles, we encountered but two men," Olmsted wrote of this expanse. Mounted and armed, the men "met us with the abrupt inquiry: 'Seen any niggers?'" When the answer was no, the slave catchers rode off.

Given the landscape, it seemed incredible that any fugitive crossed it on foot without dying of thirst or exposure or being spotted and chased down by horsemen. I stopped once, to walk some of the terrain, and instantly became mired in what Olmsted called a "dwarf forest of prickly shrubs." I could see for miles and there was no sign of shade or cover, just low spiky brush. The temperature in October was 94; in summer, it sometimes reached 115.

Retreating to my car, I came to a crossroads and the first person I'd seen in an hour: an officer in a white SUV that had a green stripe on the side and the words "Border Patrol." A short way on, I came to a clot of these vehicles and an officer in the road, stopping cars in the oncoming lane. Then tall surveillance towers began sprouting in the otherwise desolate plain. The scene was a mirror image of Olmsted's day, with border rather than slave patrols searching for fugitives who now fled *north*, into the US.

Nearing the Rio Grande, Olmsted described rugged hills and "a sudden flash of light from the tin roofs of a cluster of military store-houses." This was Fort Duncan, perched on a plateau by the river. "On the opposite bank we see the wretched-looking Mexican town of Piedras Negras, and beyond it another dreary, hilly desert."

On the Texas side, the Olmsteds could also make out the roofs of a settlement called Eagle Pass. They rode toward it with pleasant anticipation due to "a rose-colored little book" that had recently been published by a resident whose pen name was Cora Montgomery. She depicted Eagle Pass as a vibrant frontier outpost and model of westward expansion, a "true miniature of Americanism."

The author's real name was Jane Cazneau, and she was the wife of a major speculator who had invested heavily in the area. "Perhaps, if we had known this, we should have been a little less disappointed," Olmsted observed of their arrival at Eagle Pass.

The riders came to "half a dozen tottering shanties, mere confused piles of poles, brush-wood, and rushes," then a few huts and adobe stores, no people in sight. "I asked our guide where was the town. This was it, he said."

Finally, at a mud-walled cabin that served as a pool hall, they found an inhabitant. He said everyone else was at the burial of a local who'd died the night before.

"What killed him?" Woodland asked.

"Whisky."

He then showed them to a gated yard to tie up their horses to a tree that had chains and padlocks affixed to it. "See any niggers?" he asked.

Apart from slave catching, he told them, most people lived by smuggling or "selling liquor and gambling." He himself was a barkeeper, serving from barrels of "rot-gut" in a hut beside the yard, which doubled as lodging. He offered the riders a bed, warning that it was flea ridden.

That night, returning to "our quarters," Olmsted wrote, "we found them occupied by a crowd of drinking and brawling Irish soldiers." The travelers chose to sleep in the yard by their horses.

"The bed, we soon discovered, did not contain all the fleas on the premises," Olmsted wrote. "There were other creeping things also, desirous of paying their respects to the strangers in the establishment."

THIS BLEAKLY COMIC PORTRAYAL OF EAGLE PASS MAY HAVE BEEN overdrawn. Olmsted disliked "spoony fancies" like Jane Cazneau's book and took apparent delight in contradicting it, as he had other romantic depictions of the South and frontier.

The two authors were also in opposed ideological camps. Cazneau and her husband were prominent advocates of American expansionism and downplayed the boost this might give to the slave economy. Olmsted not only opposed slavery's spread, he saw America's ceaseless pioneering as toxic to civic values and institutions.

"Every tub must stand on its own bottom," he wrote of frontier individualism, also decrying the greed, impermanence, and general "barbarism" that reigned in far-flung communities. "Incompleteness, makeshift effort, that is the law where civilization encounters the wilderness."

Eagle Pass was no longer a mud-and-whiskey bedlam at the edge of the American frontier. But it still felt roughshod, and visually, the town made almost as bad a first impression on me as it had on Olmsted.

Instead of sun glinting off tin roofs by the river, my first glimpse of the border town was a miles-long straggle of car lots, heavy equipment yards, and franchise outlets. A welcome sign listed Eagle Pass's population at twenty-six thousand, but it felt much larger, and very congested, with stalled traffic, a spaghetti of overpasses and loop roads, and freight trains that further clogged circulation as they puttered on tracks bisecting the town. There seemed a complete absence of zoning or planning or regard for aesthetics.

One reason for this disarray became apparent when I finally crawled within a few hundred yards of the Rio Grande. The traffic flow, such as it was, funneled onto a two-lane bridge flanked by border and customs booths. The adjoining town center, originally oriented toward the river, had also been scrambled in the service of border security.

The nineteenth-century main street now ended at an imposing, fourteen-foot-high fence, about 150 yards from the river. Oddly, there were openings large enough to drive through, and people were playing soccer and walking dogs on the grassy floodplain leading down to the water.

The Rio Grande was known in Mexico as Rio Bravo, meaning "wild" or "fierce." But at first glance, the river appeared neither grand nor fearsome. It was about fifty yards across and looked waist deep. Men sat in lawn chairs, poles draped in the water, across from boys chattering and skipping stones on the Mexican bank. Golf carts tootled by, traversing the fourth hole of the Eagle Pass Municipal Golf Course.

It all felt placid and recreational—apart from border patrol SUVs parked in the shade and border patrol airboats periodically zipping down the river. Also, the Mexican bank was brushy while the Texas side had been shorn of vegetation to deny cover to illegal crossers.

Returning to the commercial part of Eagle Pass, I toured a crowded flea market where women held umbrellas against the blazing sun, and mariachi music blared on boom boxes. I couldn't communicate beyond pleasantries because no one I approached spoke English. On a nearby shopping street, almost every car had a Mexican license plate.

This sunstruck, noisy, colorful, Spanish-speaking street scene was the sort I'd anticipated finding in Mexico, not on the Texas side of the river. The sudden foreignness was refreshing, but hard for me to make much sense of. After forty-five sweaty minutes of wandering like a lost tourist, asking, "*Habla usted inglés?*" I wondered if I should have waited in Uvalde to hear from the barmaid's sister who ate too much.

Then I stumbled on the small office of the local chamber of commerce. A woman at the desk gave me a map and brochure—*Eagle Pass: Where Yee-hah Meets Olé*—and recommended I speak to a restaurateur who knew a lot about the area. This was helpful, except his premises didn't have a name, she didn't know the address, and it took me some time to locate the "yellow house on a street near Main" she described.

I also struggled to explain myself to the dark-haired woman I found shredding chicken in the restaurant kitchen. She smiled warmly but shook her head when I said I was a writer seeking information on Eagle Pass.

"Carmen is English challenged," explained her husband, Edward Roberts, who joined her in the kitchen a moment later. He was lean, sandy haired, and fair skinned, with blue eyes, but said he was a "half-breed," his father Anglo and mother Hispanic. "How can I help you?"

The couple appeared busy, so I hastily told of my journey and asked if I could come by another time, to chat about Eagle Pass and get advice about finding a guide and translator to accompany me across the border.

"Got your passport?" Edward asked.

"Yeah, in the car."

"Let's go then," he said, speaking in Spanish to Carmen and gathering up his wallet and keys.

LIKE EAGLE PASS, PIEDRAS NEGRAS HAD BEEN FOUNDED JUST after the war between Mexico and the US as a border garrison town. While military tensions remained high in the 1850s, border control was lax. The

Olmsteds and their guide paid a dime to ride a skiff from the Texas bank to a narrow beach where women washed clothes in the river and a man reclined in the shade smoking a *cigarito*. Woodland identified him as a Mexican corporal, "*standing guard* over the landing."

The Olmsteds carried "informal" passports from the Mexican consul in New York, but no one asked to see them. So they searched the town for the *alcalde*, or mayor, who doubled as captain of the local garrison. Finding his home, they were informed that he had "not yet wakened from his siesta."

When, "at length," the mayor appeared, he commended his visitors for taking the "precaution" of presenting their papers. A clerk then questioned the travelers and recorded, in triplicate, "a minute description of our persons." He gave one copy to them, said another would be sent to Mexico City, and filed the third in an "official bureau," a small box "distinctly labeled, COLGATE'S PEARL STARCH."

After paying a "moderate fee" for these formalities, the Americans were free to resume their tour. "The town is regularly laid out, with streets crossing at right angles," Olmsted wrote, and "a considerable square of open ground" that was "destined to be a grand plaza." Most of the town's residences were "made of poles and mud," the inhabitants "lounging outside their doors, chatting cheerfully, laughing, and singing a great deal, nearly all smoking."

Then, turning a corner, the travelers "came suddenly upon two negroes, as they were crossing the street." One seemed startled and briskly walked away. The other tipped his hat before heading off while whistling with apparent insouciance.

"Wishing to have some conversation with him, I followed," Olmsted wrote, and the man "very civilly informed me" that he'd been born in Virginia, transported to the Deep South by a slave trader, and "sold to a gentleman who had brought him to Texas, from whom he had run away four or five years ago."

Olmsted also learned that "runaways were *constantly* arriving here." Many more crossed at other points along the Rio Grande, and in all, an estimated four thousand slaves succeeded in escaping to Mexico before the Civil War.

The fugitive in Piedras Negras told Olmsted that most runaways, before escaping, hoarded a little money from hiring out, or stole small items from their masters. "When they first got here they were so excited with being free," he reported, "and with being made so much of by these Mexican women, that they spent all they brought very soon."

Since his own arrival, the man had become fluent in Spanish, joined the Catholic church, and found steady work, mainly as a mechanic. By and large he felt well treated by the Mexicans. "In fact, a colored man, if he could behave himself decently, had rather an advantage over a white American, he thought. The people generally liked them better. These Texas folks were too rough to suit them."

The status of runaways, however, remained very insecure, since they lacked Mexican citizenship or US documents, and armed parties often crossed the border to kidnap and return them to bondage. This violated Mexican law and sovereignty, but enforcement along the far-flung frontier was erratic at best.

Furthermore, white Texans were so enraged by large numbers of runaways taking refuge in Mexico that they were demanding the seizure of border territory or other aggressive action. They got their wish in 1855, when 130 Texas rangers and volunteers invaded from Eagle Pass, intent on destroying the protection given fugitives by Mexicans and allied native tribes. The Texans were driven back, but not before looting and burning down Piedras Negras.

Olmsted, traveling a year before this attack, passed through the town a second time and had another encounter with the proud black mechanic he'd interviewed. This time, the man was exiting a "dram-shop" filled with "Mexican girls" and asked Olmsted for a "loan," having spent all his earnings.

Olmsted wryly noted that his interlocutor evidently wasn't as provident or self-sufficient as he'd made out during their earlier conversation. But he also observed, "Where is the man who does not sometimes make a bad use of freedom?"

He also reminded readers what fugitives like this man had endured. First bondage, then escape across "the great dry desert country" at great peril from Indian attack, slave hunters, thirst, and "famishing in the wilderness," as well as panthers, poisonous snakes, and stinging reptiles.

"He faces all that is terrible to man for the chance of liberty," Olmsted wrote. "I fear I should myself suffer the last servile indignities before setting foot in such a net of concentrated torture."

At the last, within sight of freedom, came the risk of "drowning miserably" in the Rio Grande, which was much wider and deeper in the 1850s than now. If they made it, the runaways arrived in an alien land where few of them had the language or resources to start a new life. Yet they kept coming, and scratching out what meager existence they could.

"I pity the man whose sympathies would not warm to a dog under these odds," Olmsted concluded. "How can they be held back from the slave who is driven to assert his claim to manhood?"

EDWARD AND CARMEN ROBERTS, THE RESTAURANT OWNERS IN Eagle Pass, went to Piedras Negras two or three times a week to buy propane and other supplies. My drop-in had been well timed, since they'd been considering whether to make a shopping trip that afternoon.

As we inched toward the international bridge, Edward helped interpret some of what I'd seen thus far. "Eagle Pass is really just a suburb or extension of Piedras Negras," he said. The Texas town had one tenth the population of its Mexican neighbor, 95 percent of its residents were Spanish speakers, and it was swollen each day by people streaming across the river to work, shop, and attend school (many students used post office boxes or relatives' addresses in Texas to claim residency).

Close to two million vehicles and pedestrians crossed this bridge into the US each year, while two nearby bridges carried trucks and railcars. All of it carefully monitored, causing traffic to frequently back up for hours.

"Big Brother is everywhere, even when you can't see him," Edward said of the boats, helicopters, drones, seismic sensors, and other surveillance. "It's a DMZ."

Our own crossing was uneventful, just a cursory passport check on the Mexican side. But as soon as we exited the bridge, a jeep and a truck sped past, bristling with machine guns and soldiers wearing bulletproof vests. Edward pointed out a sniper on a catwalk and translated a large banner strung across the road that stated: "Piedras Negras: Home of the Mexican Army."

"They're trying to make a big show of force," he said, "to convince people the state's in control and it's safe to be on the streets."

Piedras Negras means "black rocks," a reference to coal deposits in the area. But *piedra* was also slang for crack cocaine, and the border city was a major transit point for drugs entering the US. Weapons were smuggled in the other direction, since Mexico had much tighter gun laws than its neighbor. Cartels had bribed and shot their way into power over parts of the city, and the state to which it belonged, Coahuila.

This had overshadowed two points of historical interest. Piedras Negras was the birthplace of Marilyn Monroe's mother, Gladys, an American whose father was working on a Mexican railroad at the time. And in the 1940s, a local barkeeper nicknamed Nacho invented the famous snack of the same name.

"It's sad, but Piedras Negras's claim to fame now is bad news," Edward said. He'd seen this firsthand while working as a US Customs courier, ferrying documents and currency across the border by bike as cartels battled the military, police, and each other. "I was like a Pony Express rider; I liked the thrill," he said, telling of street battles, grenade launchers, cars blasting through checkpoints, and narcos hijacking trucks to blockade a military post, forcing closure of the border bridges.

The fighting had eased over the past year, and at 3:00 p.m., driving on a busy commercial thoroughfare, I assumed there was little chance we'd witness any trouble. "Actually," Edward said, pulling over to fill propane tanks, "a lot of the killing happens mid- or late afternoon so it will appear on the evening news. The cartels want to show how badass they are."

We made only a few, short stops, and from the window of the minivan, Piedras Negras looked like an unlovely big cousin to Eagle Pass, its sprawl dotted with chains like McDonald's, Burger King, and Office Depot, and the multinational factories, *maquiladoras*, which had proliferated as a result of NAFTA. Carmen, who came from central Mexico, said this border region was regarded as "dirtier and less beautiful" than other parts of the country, but more prosperous due to its proximity to the US.

The cuisine was also more Americanized and beef-centric than elsewhere. We stopped to eat at a small restaurant where the dishes included a "gringo tortilla," covered in cheese, grilled beef, and cilantro. Our substantial meal and beers for three cost less than four hundred pesos, or about eighteen dollars.

These low prices, by US standards, extended to the fuel and groceries the Robertses purchased, and to the movies they crossed over to watch for four dollars a ticket. But many residents of Eagle Pass no longer came to Piedras Negras at all.

The previous Christmas, the most murderous of the cartels, Los Zetas, had decapitated four people and deposited heads outside a supermarket, city hall, and a restaurant, attaching crude signs warning that this would be the fate of anyone who aided an elite anti-cartel unit—itself known for "disappearing" noncombatants.

Edward advised, should I return on my own, that I stay near the church plaza and street market by the river, close to a military garrison. On a brighter note, he suggested I stop by his restaurant again on the weekend, so he could introduce me to a couple who often visited family in Piedras Negras and the rural area beyond that Olmsted toured.

"The Day of the Dead is coming up," he said as we crossed back into Eagle Pass. "You'll want to be back in Mexico for that."

IN RIDING TO THE RIO GRANDE AND NORTHERN MEXICO, OLM-sted paid particular attention to the borderland as it related to slavery. But he also wrote at length about his encounters with native tribes, informing readers that his prior contact had been limited to "tamed sort of Indians" in upstate New York and Canada, a population he'd found "by no means as degenerate sons of the forest as I used to think."

This casual bigotry, toward natives and others, was an aspect of Olm-sted I'd struggled to reconcile with his humanistic principles. A child of the Enlightenment, he believed in the family of man and the right and capacity of all to pursue life, liberty, and happiness. But his philosophical broad-mindedness cohabited with stereotypes and prejudices common to his day, and more freely expressed than in our own.

Olmsted generally cast Irishmen as drunk and lazy, Jews as scheming money-grubbers, and Mexicans as gracious but indolent peasants. His guide, Jack Woodland, called them "greasers," a phrase Olmsted noted without approbation.

This mix of bias and benevolence extended to Indians. En route to the Rio Grande, Olmsted accompanied a military party at Fort Inge on a visit to a Lipan Apache encampment. He wrote that the teepees, bright blankets, and campfires at first formed "a pleasant sketch of the natural socialism of the uncontaminated man."

But on closer approach, the "noble savages of the plains" presented "nothing but the most miserable squalor." Their horses were half-starved, their teepees filled with filthy blankets, and their children so "eager for a dime" that they "went through any amount of degrading nonsense to secure it."

The Olmsteds later met the band's chief, when overtaken on their return ride from the Rio Grande by "a squad of armed Indians." As the natives slowed to the Olmsteds' pace, the brothers felt like "prisoners under escort" and feared the natives "could not have fallen on a prettier prize than the mule and horse we rode, the guns and Colts we carried, and the comely scalps we wore."

The troop's leader wore buckskin, beadwork, and a wreath of oak leaves, his face streaked with vermillion and his eyelashes and brows plucked clean. "Assuming as much native dignity as I could command," Olmsted nodded at his escort and in reply received "a grunt, which I was unable to translate."

Then, after an extended silence, Olmsted asked his chaperone if he and his comrades were Lipan Apache.

"*Sí*," the man answered. He was a chief known to Anglos as Castro, and in halting English "entered upon a general conversation on the various merits of whisky, corn, horses, and Germans." They rode in amicable if awkward company until parting at the nearest settlement.

The next day, the Olmsteds learned that a ranch they'd planned to visit had been raided in the night and a shepherd killed. Then another homestead was attacked, leaving a man and two children dead. "The trail, when found, had evident marks of Lipan origin," he wrote, and Castro fled with stolen horses after a shoot-out that killed one of his band. "Open war at once broke out," the Lipan Apache "to be shot down at will."

The riders' brush with Castro, and the many Indian attacks they heard about on their trip, gave Olmsted a degree of sympathy for the bellicose stance of borderland inhabitants. "If my wife were in a frontier settlement,

I can conceive how I should hunt an Indian and shoot him down with all the eagerness and ten times the malice with which I should follow the panther."

But he rejected the prevailing Anglo view of nomadic Indians as innately and incurably savage—"blood-thirsty vermin, to be exterminated." Rather, he saw hostile Apache and Comanche as products of their environment and harsh treatment by whites. "Nothing can be more lamentable than the condition of the wandering tribes," forced "step by step" from their lands and hunting grounds. "It is no wonder they are driven to violence and angry depredations."

The only hope, he believed, was the settling of Indians on reservations and "the power of even a little education" to assimilate natives. "Some other future than extermination will then, at least, be open."

BEFORE REACHING THE RIO GRANDE, MY OWN CONTACT WITH Indians in Texas had been limited to historic displays at museums and mission sites. The state's natives hadn't been exterminated, as Olmsted feared, but in the quarter century after his visit, the Apache, Comanche, and others were hunted down and largely driven out.

Modern Texas, in sharp contrast to its much less populous neighbors, New Mexico and Oklahoma, had only three small reservations, two of them for refugee bands from other states. The third, just outside Eagle Pass, was home to one of the most traditional and radically displaced tribes in North America.

I first learned of the Texas Kickapoo at Fort Duncan in Eagle Pass, a garrison Olmsted viewed as dimly as he did other "nominal" forts on the frontier. He thought it "badly placed, in a military view," on an exposed plateau by the Rio Grande, and its four hundred troops "in admirable condition for marching upon Mexico" but incapable of keeping Indians from stealing horses, cattle, and provisions "from under their guns."

Robert E. Lee concurred. Posted at Fort Duncan and other Texas garrisons before the Civil War, Lee wrote that the scattered frontier defenses "afford but a feeble guard against marauders." He also grew despondent, describing the territory as a "desert of dullness" in which even the plants were hostile.

"Every branch and leaf in this country nearly are armed with a point, and some seem to poison the flesh," he wrote his family. "I can think of nothing that would interest you in this paradise of the Texans."

Lee's quarters at Fort Duncan had survived along with a few other old buildings, a rare oasis of history and green space in Eagle Pass—albeit intruded upon by a surveillance tower rising by the old barracks. "Eagle Pass began as a border garrison and essentially it still is," said Jeff Taylor, curator of the fort's small museum. "It's always been a hard town, too."

As illustration, he showed me a nineteenth-century death register that listed causes such as drowning, "Fright," and "Saddness." An early town ordinance declared, "If any person shall cast or throw or use any nigger-shooter"—slang for slingshot—they could be fined one hundred dollars. Another display told of tickets being sold for the hanging of a man who'd murdered an entire family to get their land.

Then I came to an exhibit on the Kickapoo, whose name is believed to mean "he who moves here and there." Once woodland dwellers along the Great Lakes, the Kickapoo had been steadily driven south and west. One of the tribe's bands continued all the way to Texas and northern Mexico, where they were granted land in exchange for defending *la frontera* against cross-border raiders. Olmsted mentioned the Kickapoo as one of the tribes he briefly encountered near the Rio Grande.

In the mid-twentieth century, drought and other hardships forced the Kickapoo to resume their exodus. Many became migrant farm workers in the western US, their base a squatter camp beneath the international bridge in Eagle Pass. Dwelling in huts of pole, thatch, and cardboard, with a single spigot as water supply, they belonged to no nation, traveling with papers granting them safe passage, issued at an Illinois fort in 1832.

These antique passports were replaced in the 1950s by cards bureaucratically labeling the carriers "Parolee-Kickapoo Indians pending clarification of status by Congress." No clarification came until the 1980s, when the tribe won federal recognition and relocated to a small reservation six miles outside Eagle Pass.

"A lot of people here wanted them out of sight and mind," the Fort Duncan curator said of the reservation, initially a ragged settlement on a dirt road in scrubland by the river.

It had since become home to the Kickapoo Lucky Eagle Casino, the area's premier attraction, drawing busloads of gamblers and locals who watered at bars in the casino's cool, dark interior. I quickly discovered there was no better place to meet all manner of sources—including employees of the many agencies related to border security, and known by a sea of acronyms: ICE, INS, DEA, DOD, CBP.

"I'm a greeter at Walmart," one man said with a smile when I asked about his occupation. Like others, he loosened up after a beer or two and told me his real job was with Homeland Security.

"If you meet an Anglo in Eagle Pass, you can be pretty certain they work for one of the agencies," he said, though most border patrols and others who interacted with migrants on the ground were Spanish speakers. "We're a big dysfunctional family."

In low voices, he and others also told me about the cat-and-mouse intricacies of border enforcement. Drug traffickers used both new technology (scanners, GPS, night-vision gear) and old-school tricks, like recruiting morticians to stuff corpses with heroin for transport in hearses for "burial" on the US side of the border.

Narcos also deployed an army of *las focas*, meaning "seals," hiring newspaper vendors and others as street-level lookouts and informants. Those they couldn't bribe, they terrorized. "Drug gangs didn't used to seek attention," one investigator told me. "It was like a mobster movie; people vanished. 'Tony? Haven't seen Tony.'"

Now, he said, cartels "want everyone to know they cut off Tony's head. That scares people and attracts wannabes who are looking to join the baddest team."

The flow of illegal migrants had also changed, the overwhelming majority now "OTMs," or "other than Mexicans," fleeing violence in Central America. People smugglers sent them across the Rio Grande on inner tubes and hid them in "stash houses," often in company with smuggled drugs. Others waded the river and ran the 150 yards to downtown Eagle Pass, where they melted into the Hispanic population.

But crossing the border was only half the game. It was much harder to slip through the gauntlet of checkpoints and surveillance in the harsh, open terrain stretching fifty or so miles beyond Eagle Pass. "A lot of illegals get trapped in this shit hole of a town," said one disgruntled border agent, "just like us."

None of the enforcers I spoke to thought a border wall was feasible, or would do much to deter illegal traffic. "Any barrier is only as good as its weakest point," one agent said, and it was impossible to effectively fortify the 1,200 miles of border in Texas alone, much of it floodplain or remote and rugged terrain. "It'd be like building a house on sand."

He also showed me pictures on his phone of tunnels, ramps, and other stratagems that drug and people smugglers used to get around the barriers that already existed. "If there's a will—and a lot of money at stake—there's always a way," he said.

BY MY THIRD NIGHT OF TROLLING THE CASINO'S BARS, I'D MET A cross-section of Eagle Pass's inhabitants, with the conspicuous exception of the Kickapoo. At other Indian casinos I'd visited around the country, there were tribal members working the floor, and displays of native history and culture on the walls, in brochures, at the gift shop. Here, nothing.

The residential part of the Kickapoo reservation adjoined the casino, but it was fenced off and guarded by tribal police, who turned me away when I asked if I could drive through. I called the tribal office to request an interview. No one called back.

Finally, on my fourth visit to the casino's bars, I met a local who knew a Kickapoo woman and offered to introduce me. Jodie Logan was a tall, handsome middle-aged woman with a wide face, light brown skin, and a long braid of black hair. She worked in the engineering department at the casino hotel, its only Kickapoo employee, and served on the tribe's police commission.

When I asked her about Kickapoo culture and belief, she recommended what she said was the best work on the subject: a sixty-year-old monograph by anthropologists who wrote on the first page that their inquiries were frequently met with "curt refusal and extreme suspicion." After a short visit, they were ordered to leave.

"We're called the Kickapoo Traditional Tribe of Texas because we hold to the old ways and are hush-hush about it," Jodie said. "Other tribes are into powwows and selling crafts. We don't do that."

She'd been raised among a band of Kickapoo in Oklahoma she described as "more open and integrated with the outside world." So it had been an adjustment when she married into this tribe, where most spoke Kickapoo at home and had traditionally resisted Western education to the point of burning down schools.

This opposition had eased, but Kickapoo students struggled, Jodie said, because many parents were barely literate in English, and removed their children from school for long periods to attend tribal ceremonies. The main one occurred in Nacimiento, the Kickapoo's sacred ground 120 miles away in Mexico. "It's hard for kids to even play school sports, because there are times of year when we're not allowed to do that," she said.

Religious observances also made steady employment difficult. Kickapoo might be gone a week, or a month, depending on the lunar ceremonial calendar and other factors. "The world doesn't wait for us to come back," Jodie said, "and companies aren't used to letting people come and go like that." Few Kickapoo worked at other than tribal jobs.

There was also lingering prejudice, which I'd picked up in conversations at the casino. Many locals still spoke of the years when the Kickapoo lived under the international bridge in a shantytown without plumbing. "People always tell me it was an eyesore in their community," Jodie said, "though I don't see how you can be an eyesore in Eagle Pass."

The dismal image of Kickapoo as "drunk and dirty" had been compounded by an epidemic of huffing paint fumes. Some Kickapoo lived in parks and under overpasses, in brush littered with empty spray cans. "Paint abuse is a big issue," Jodie acknowledged, "but so are other drugs in this country. We have a problem as a society, as American society."

Economically, the fifteen-year-old casino had been a boon to the once-destitute tribe, which spent the gambling proceeds on social services and annual disbursements to its nine-hundred-odd members. "But it's also brought more materialism, pushing tradition and culture aside," Jodie said. "Kids expect the excitement they get from computer games and don't want to spend a week doing beadwork or tanning hides in Mexico. I tell them, 'That's exactly why you need to go.'"

She spoke in only general terms about the ceremonies at Nacimiento, which were closed to outsiders. But she said of the beadwork and other crafts, "God gave these tasks to women to deal with daily stress. When you're done you have a beautiful finished product and have forgotten what was heavy on your heart."

I LEARNED A LITTLE MORE THAT NIGHT, READING THE 1950S anthropological study she'd mentioned, written by two scholars from Wisconsin who'd been struck, most of all, by the endurance of Kickapoo custom and belief. Though living in arid settlements, two centuries after being displaced from northern woodlands, the Kickapoo still spoke an Algonquian dialect, played lacrosse, held deer sacred, and lived in "mat-covered Woodland wigwams," substituting rushes for birch bark.

Young people courted by whistling, and men sought mates who "should not be too heavy for a horse." The Kickapoo had adopted some Western dress and food, but otherwise displayed an "almost fanatical will and effort to keep out foreign influences." They believed their deity gave them everything they needed to know, and "when the tribe becomes extinct, God will destroy the whole world by fire."

In the morning, Jodie took me on a short drive through the reservation. The homes were a mix of plywood shacks, brick houses, RVs, and FEMA trailers donated after Katrina. Almost every property was ringed with a high fence. "People break into houses to feed their drug addiction," Jodie explained, and smugglers crossed the nearby river to "hide drugs wherever they can," for others to collect.

Also striking: bundles of stalks leaning against the houses and fences. These were cattails, drying in preparation for being woven into mats for the tribe's traditional structures. One such *wickiup*, a dome of poles and matting used for funerals, stood near the back of the reservation.

There was otherwise little to see, apart from a pecan orchard and a cluster of modern tribal buildings, including a medical clinic and day care center. "The main goal of the tribe is to keep everyone and everything in harmony," Jodie said.

This communitarian instinct went very deep. She showed me a guide to the tribe's language, which stated: "Kickapoo culture does not require one to say thank you for a good deed done," since "it is a pleasure for the giver to provide the good deed." Nor was it necessary "to say please when issuing a command," because it was understood that verbal instructions "are not intended harshly" or meant to be rude.

Circling back to the casino, Jodie told me that she sometimes struggled to balance the very different worlds she inhabited.

"As Kickapoo, we're taught to be humble, to not chase money, to put the group before the individual," she said, as we reentered the clamor of the casino's slot machine floor. "Those aren't the top priorities in here."

CHAPTER 21

LA FRONTERA

Days of the Dead

S etting out from Eagle Pass a second time, the Olmsteds bathed in the Rio Grande, took their mounts on a skiff across the river, and began a seventy-two-hour tour of the countryside beyond Piedras Negras.

Their guide, John Woodland, led them through "trackless, bleak, rugged and barren hills" before descending to the main road south. In contrast to major thoroughfares the Olmsteds had traveled in Texas, the road was wide, well cleared of brush and stones, and "moderately smooth," having been built for a visit by the region's governor.

This fine road was all the more striking because it crossed a "dreary, desolate plain, sometimes as barren and bare as the Sahara." The only variety was "the alternate predominance of one sort of thorny shrub over another." Olmsted called this landscape "the most monotonous and uninteresting that I have ever seen."

After thirty miles, the riders sighted "a dark mass of lofty trees" and entered the agricultural surrounds of San Fernando, its fields and orchards well irrigated by aqueducts. Like other Spanish colonial towns, San Fernando was laid out in square blocks with a grand plaza at the center, the better homes built of stone and ornamented with brightly colored stripes and stenciled rosettes.

"The place had a comfortable look," Olmsted wrote, "and the people

had the characteristics of a slow, kind, light-hearted and contented peasantry." The inhabitants also showed considerable curiosity about "*los Americanos*," coming out of their homes to gaze at the visitors.

Olmsted, in turn, made a "pretty study" of a woman slapping a tortilla
between her hands, at a home where the riders found lodging. "She stopped
a moment to look at me, and, dropping her arms, her chemise—the only
garment she wore—fell loosely off her shoulders, disclosing a beautiful
little bust." Tossing back "thick, dark locks from her face," she smiled
"frankly and cordially" before resuming her labor.

The travelers were served *frijoles* and a kid stew with onions, leeks, and
red chili, Woodland having cautioned their hosts not to make the meal too
hot. The brothers weren't sure, at first, how to handle "the absence of fork
or spoon, but we soon learned from Woodland the secret of twisting a tortilla into a substitute." They deemed the beans "excellent" and the maize
tortillas "decidedly superior" to Southern corn pone.

This pleasant sojourn was marred only by the travelers' unease over Indians "riding helter-skelter" in the streets, shooting arrows for sport and
"carrying themselves everywhere with such an air as indicated they were
masters of the town."

At one point, as Olmsted spoke to a merchant, an Indian rode up and
demanded whiskey and tobacco from the storekeeper, drawing his bow
when refused. Another grabbed Olmsted's arm and tried to wrest away his
gun. "I spurred my horse, and, with my free hand, disengaged myself,"
Olmsted wrote. "He followed me for a few rods, yelling and gesticulating
violently."

Woodland warned that one Comanche had "squeezed his eye" covet-
ously at the Olmsteds' mule. As a precaution, the scout decided they should
sleep in a high-walled courtyard, beside their mounts, "a Colt and knife
under each pillow."

The travelers were undisturbed, but woke to find more Indians on the
streets than before. "They seemed to regard us with a skulking malice, and
we resolved to withdraw from their neighborhood as soon as possible,"
Olmsted wrote.

The riders briefly visited several nearby settlements before returning to
Texas. "After one lonely, dewy, snaky, starlit camp in the desert," the Olmsteds also parted "with our guide as from a friend."

Woodland went on to ply his risky trade for seven more years, as a frontier scout, interpreter, and mail carrier. On a furlough in Ohio, he became engaged, returning to Texas to earn a larger stake before his wedding. Then, while accompanying a small troop tracking Apache, Woodland counseled the officer in command against chasing native horsemen into a high-walled canyon near the Rio Grande.

The lieutenant ignored this advice and the pursuers were ambushed, as Woodland foresaw. One among the military party survived and escaped to a fort, returning to the canyon with a recovery party. They found hats, boots, dead horses, and the body of only one of the fourteen men slain. No trace was found of Woodland, though his distinctive sleeve buttons were sighted months later, at an Apache scalp dance.

WHEN I ASKED PEOPLE IN EAGLE PASS ABOUT THE TERRITORY Olmsted visited beyond Piedras Negras, the response was a shake of the head or a grimace. The settlements he toured were located in or near the municipality of Allende, which had been the scene of the worst cartel violence anywhere in Coahuila.

In 2011, leaders of Los Zetas learned that someone had snitched on them to the DEA, and sent truckloads of young *sicarios* to punish alleged informants and terrorize the populace. During a days-long rampage, from Allende to Piedras Negras, they looted and bulldozed homes; kidnapped and murdered men, women, and children; and incinerated their bodies. The death toll was unknown, with estimates ranging as high as three hundred. Parts of Allende remained in ruins.

But I found another option for touring rural Coahuila upon returning to the restaurant I'd visited my first day in Eagle Pass. Edward Roberts introduced me to the young couple he'd mentioned as possible guides, Frank and Kristel Sanchez. They were in their early thirties, he bespectacled with a well-trimmed beard and mustache, she a brown-eyed beauty with a long braid of dark hair.

"We're tremendous nerds," said Kristel, who worked at a community college. Frank, a high school teacher, added, "We're into history, literature, and NPR."

Their family backgrounds were characteristic of the fluid borderland.

Frank, short for Francisco, was the son of migrant farm workers. Born in rural Oregon, where his family picked beets and other crops for part of the year, he'd worked in the fields as a child until his family settled in Eagle Pass.

Kristel had grown up in Piedras Negras but crossed the bridge to attend school in Eagle Pass and later found work in Texas. Her family also owned property in a rural town thirty miles from Piedras Negras, and she and Frank made regular family visits. I was welcome to join them on an excursion the next day.

So on Sunday morning, I climbed into their sedan next to an eighteen-month-old in a car seat. We'd collect their other son at his grandmother's house in Piedras Negras after a walk around the plaza and marketplace by the river.

"How are your teeth?" Kristel quipped as we entered a street, just off the international bridge, that was lined with dentists' offices and signs in shaky English stating, "Acquire Best Smile at Lowest Price" or "Extraction of Wisdom."

Inexpensive dental care was a big, cross-border business, as were pharmacies and opticians. Eagle Pass residents also brought pets across for treatment—though one couple had told me they no longer did so, because Los Zetas had murdered their veterinarian when he refused to treat a cartel racehorse.

We stepped inside a nineteenth-century pink-stone church with a mannequin of Christ, enclosed in a glass box. The figure was littered with written prayers, inserted through a slot. "A lot of the prayers are for the disappeared," Kristel said. Mourners sometimes added pictures of their lost relatives.

A few blocks on, we reached a lively open-air marketplace and entered what seemed a spice shop. Mixed in with mustard seed and cinnamon sticks were packages with names like Milagro, meaning "miracle," and promises of "sex pronto." Beside these aphrodisiacs were "potions and spells for all occasions," Kristel said, translating their promises. "Will make you smarter. Thinner. Someone will love you. Punish an enemy. Counter witchcraft and envy. Get more business and take it away from your competitor."

This faith in charms and spells was intermingled with Catholic belief.

There were shelves of religious figurines, one depicting a mustachioed man with dark eyes and brows that Kristel identified as Jesús Malverde, a Robin Hood–like folk hero in Mexico. Drug cartels had adopted Malverde as a "narco-saint" and appropriated Day of the Dead symbols such as altars with skulls "to keep the drug lords safe and let them outlive their rivals."

Kristel told me all this while also trying to emphasize positive aspects of her hometown. "People think they're going to come here and see bodies floating in the Rio Grande," she said as we ambled along a willow-shaded river walk busy with joggers and baby strollers. Elsewhere near the river, minstrels played accordions and bongo drums, families promenaded, and children chased pigeons in the plaza.

"Eagle Pass is dead by comparison," Frank observed. "Everyone's inside Xboxing or watching sports on Sundays. Here, it's much more public."

But the specter of the cartels was inescapable. Returning to the car, we drove through a residential district of eucalyptus trees and mission-style villas with two-car garages that looked like an upscale neighborhood in Southern California. Except that some structures were charred and gutted, the surviving walls covered in graffiti.

Kristel said this area had traditionally been home to doctors, lawyers, and businesspeople. Then drug lords moved in, and when fighting broke out between them, cartel leaders recruited poor people to loot and burn their rivals' mansions. "Now people are scared to touch these properties," Kristel said, "so they're just shells, like monuments to the drug violence."

We drove on to her mother's home in an older neighborhood lined with bougainvillea. Behind the family's brick house was a lovely terracotta patio with monarch butterflies fluttering in the banana trees. The only jarring note was the fortress-like security: heavily bolted door, high fence, barred windows.

"My mother watches too many crime shows," Kristel explained. "When I told her we were bringing a guy we'd just met, she wondered if you might be a serial killer."

Indeed, her mother greeted me warily, before handing over the Sanchezes' older son. We then drove to the family's property thirty miles from Piedras Negras, through a dead-flat, arid plain very much like the "Sahara" Olmsted described.

The highway we traveled was known as La Ribereña, a notorious corridor for drug smuggling, and a frequent site of cartel murders. It was empty of traffic until we reached a military checkpoint where heavily armed soldiers in black uniforms looked in the windows and questioned the Sanchezes. A second checkpoint was guarded by soldiers in full combat attire, in Humvees with mounted machine guns.

Kristel visibly tensed at both stops. The cartels had infiltrated and re-cruited from the military, and there was also the danger that "you get con-fused with someone else and are picked up," she said. "We all know someone who disappeared."

Then a clump of trees appeared, which Olmsted noted was a sign of a settlement in the Mexican chaparral. The town we entered, Guerrero, resembled the handsome settlements he visited south of Piedras Negras. There was an aqueduct system (parched by drought), streets lined with pecan and palm trees and adobe houses painted in vivid colors—turquoise, lime, peach, tangerine—with decorative stripes and curlicues.

Founded in the 1700s, Guerrero also had the classic, colonial Spanish layout of streets centered on a shaded plaza with a whitewashed church. It seemed an intact version of the regular and "comfortable" settlements Ol-msted described, with one notable exception: the only other person we saw during our two-hour stroll was the cashier at the one open shop where we stopped for soft drinks.

Kristel said the local population had been draining away for decades, and not only because of drug-related violence. NAFTA had brought com-petition from US farmers, and job opportunities at factories, depleting the once-busy rural district.

Her father came from a family of ranchers and had inherited a mustard-colored stucco home behind a high wall. We found Kristel's mother bus-tling around the garden, assisted by a lean man of about fifty, named Vincente, who had worked in the border factories of companies that had moved to Mexico after NAFTA.

As Kristel translated, Vincente described standing all day while labor-ing at plants that made fan blades, auto fuses, and surgical sutures. "They lure you in with promises of benefits and bonuses," he said. "But after you've been there a few months, those go away," leaving hard labor that paid only about twenty dollars a day.

Like other Mexicans, Vincente was paying close attention to the US presidential campaign. When I asked him about claims that Mexico had been stealing jobs, he scoffed, "If Trump wants those jobs back, he can have them. He's going to find Americans who want to do that work, for such low wages?"

Vincente also shrugged off talk of a border wall. Since the 1980s he'd entered Texas illegally several times to do stone masonry in Dallas. "It wasn't like the TV show, but the money was good." He currently had enough work in Mexico but would go back north if required. "They'll need people like me to build that wall," he said with a smile. "Then we'll just build a bigger ladder to get over it."

ON OUR RETURN DRIVE TO PIEDRAS NEGRAS, KRISTEL EXPRESSED more anxiety than Vincente had about the campaign rhetoric concerning the border. "Mexicans have a strong and dark sense of humor, but we're also very sensitive when people say bad things about us." She'd been particularly stung by Trump's comments about murderers and rapists streaming across the border.

"I feel like our families have been invisible," she said, noting that her uncles, grandparents, and other relations had worked in the US, legally, at farms, restaurants, and other jobs. "We've been in and out of the US for generations, but people talk about us like we just got there."

By the time we reached Piedras Negras it was dark, which I'd been warned multiple times was not the safest time to be in the city. But this night was different from other nights: the opening celebration of *Día de los Muertos*, or Day of the Dead, at a plaza by the city hall.

The holiday traced to pre-Columbian rituals honoring the dead and welcoming their spirits, which were thought to return at this time. This ancient belief had been overlaid with Catholic iconography of saints, virgins, and crosses. "It's a perfect marriage of our native and Spanish heritage," Kristel said.

The holiday also embodied the spirit of her troubled hometown, carrying on after years of violence and terror. "We honor death, but we laugh at it, too," she said as we entered a crowd of people with faces painted to look like skulls and shirts striped with faux ribs. One skeleton woman led a skeleton dog, while others wore nuns' habits over their ghoulish faces. Strobe lights, mambo bands, and men on stilts added to the carnival air.

More solemn were the altars to the dead, one to disappeared students, another to twenty-five miners buried alive. The latter was made of papier-mâché, to resemble a mine entrance, with wooden tracks and a cart, pictures of the miners, crosses, and non-Christian symbols associated with the Day of the Dead. "Souls need a guide, and the dog is there to lead them," Kristel explained. "The owl scares off witches; the mirror keeps away bad spirits."

Other altars were tiered, like wedding cakes, each level bearing special items: the ceremonial bread of the dead, a cane or toy belonging to the deceased, their favorite food and drink. "I want to believe my grandma will come back for a cigarette, so I put one on an altar to her," Kristel said.

This made me wonder. I would soon part ways with Olmsted, for whom I'd developed some affection after our long journey together. What would be appropriate on an altar to Fred? Not corn pone or bacon, certainly. Crosses or supernatural imagery weren't his thing, either. Maybe just a tree, a post oak or . . .

"Look, the dead are coming!" Kristel shouted, grabbing her boys by the hand and running to the curb to watch a raucous parade of marching bands, honking cars, hearses, fire trucks, and motorcycles, most of the revelers dressed or painted like skeletons. At the back came jeeps filled with soldiers in camo clutching guns, the only participants whose costumes were real. (The city's mayor, circulating at the festivities, was later assassinated with a shot to the head while taking a selfie with a supporter.)

By the time the parade ended, the boys were falling apart, so we went to get them ice cream before the slow trip back across the bridge. Beside the food stalls I noticed a man with a curious box and cage mounted on a stand.

"Want your fortune read?" Kristel asked.

Inside the man's cage was a canary, which at his command picked bits of folded paper from the box, forecasting aspects of my future. A "spiritual message" told me, "you are happiest on Sundays" and should do business then. The second said Tuesdays were my "best and luckiest."

The next, *El Oraculo*, stated: "Me, the humble bird, warns you that in your path there are two persons that pretend to be your friends, but they will betray you."

Kristel glanced at Frank and nodded at me. "Should we sell him to a human trafficker, or make him our drug mule?"

The last paper the canary plucked was much more sanguine. "Soon you will have the best luck ever. Play with consistency the lottery. Focus on numbers that have four or five digits and end in zero, and you will see your dreams come true."

The soothsayer wrapped my fortunes in a horoscope to form an amulet for me, charging one hundred pesos. "Gringo price," Kristel murmured, "five times the usual rate."

The bridge traffic was so backed up that we left the car with Kristel's mother and hiked instead. At the US end, half the pedestrians, including the Sanchezes, were ushered into an office for extra questioning and document inspection.

It was 10:30 p.m. by the time we reached Eagle Pass, footsore and sweat soaked, the boys asleep in their parents' arms. I reckoned I'd now seen what I could of the territory Olmsted toured along the Rio Grande. But the Sanchezes urged me to linger one more day, so I could visit Frank's classroom and come out the next night with their sons, on Halloween.

Before collapsing at the casino hotel, I heeded my fortune and played the slots for the first time. I chose a machine that promised "4 corners—4 balls, wins $400," and tapped a series of fours and zeroes, and "Big Win!" flashed on the screen with a clatter and flashing lights. After twenty minutes I was up $158.

"What's your system?" asked the woman at the machine next to me.

I hadn't known there was a system for slots, other than avoiding them. "Listen to the birdie," I said, which I knew sounded loco but seemed as good advice as any.

UPON LEAVING MEXICO, THE OLMSTEDS RODE STRAIGHT TO SAN Antonio and "prepared for more rapid travel," shedding "useless weight" for their journey out of Texas. Having spent more than four months traversing the state, they exited it in three weeks, via Houston and Beaumont.

By the time they neared Louisiana, "the hot, soggy breath of the approaching summer was extremely depressing." This was particularly so for

John, who'd set off for Texas with "the hope of invigorating weakened lungs."

Instead, the "abominable diet, and the fatigue" had "served to null the fresh benefits of pure air and stimulating travel." While slogging through a swampy plan near Beaumont, John fell from the saddle "in faint exhaustion," lying facedown on the ground for half an hour, "hardly breathing, and unable to speak."

Their mounts were also "much jaded," and the Olmsteds exchanged one of the horses and the mule Mr. Brown for a "fresh, lusty, good-natured American stallion." But John's decline worsened as they crossed "the alligator-bayous" of Louisiana. He became "so prostrated by the heat," he wrote in a letter, that he "gave it up as worse than useless expense & suffering" to carry on. He boarded a steamboat for New Orleans and from there caught a ship to New York.

Fred rode on, atop the stallion, accompanied by the terrier Judy the brothers had acquired in East Texas. Her paws had become so ulcerated that the Olmsteds covered them with moccasins, but "the wet country had proved for her a great relief" and "she was able to accomplish the rare canine feat of over two thousand miles of steady travel."

Fred spent the summer crossing upland Mississippi, Alabama, Tennessee, North Carolina, and Virginia, collecting material for another newspaper series and what would become the third of his Southern trilogy, *A Journey in the Back Country*.

"From Richmond I went with my horse and dog direct to New York by the steamer," he wrote. Of Judy he later reported, "Her tired bones have now found a last rest upon Staten Island."

Olmsted was exhausted, too, having traveled for almost nine months and over four thousand miles. "Fred took many notes," John wrote a friend two months later, and was "ostensibly engaged" in writing. "But he is not strong enough to work with energy."

Fred nonetheless took time to write a long letter to his half sister Bertha, then studying in France, sharing what he'd learned about travel. "The great key," he told her, "is to place oneself in situations & circumstances, where one will be most liable to *accidents*. I don't mean disagreeable accidents. To place oneself where (I mean) one does not know *what to expect next*."

OLMSTED'S PHILOSOPHY OF TRAVEL SPOKE TO ME AS I SHED MY own "useless weight," discarding unread brochures, crumpled maps, a torn and chili-stained T-shirt, and my third ruined paperback of *A Journey through Texas*.

It was two years and a day since I'd set off aboard Amtrak's Capitol Limited, with little clue what to expect. Though now "much jaded" by travel, like the Olmsteds' horses, it still felt strange and unforeseen to find myself, at journey's end, at a Kickapoo casino hotel in arid scrub by the Rio Grande—far removed, in every sense, from my barn-office in New England, or from my autumnal train ride along the Potomac.

Cars and airplanes and telecommunications had radically shrunk distance since Olmsted's day. But this hadn't diminished the wonder I'd often felt at the diversity and capaciousness of America. My last day in Eagle Pass proved a prime example.

Driving to the high school where Frank taught, I arrived at a low brick building with sports trophies and pictures of homecoming royalty in the lobby. It looked like a hundred other public schools I'd visited, except that the lunchroom was a sea of brown skin and black hair, the students speaking a mix of Spanish and English, often in the same sentence.

One hall had a "wall of heroes" with pictures of the many graduates who had served in the military. Another was covered in drawings and writing on the theme "my favorite childhood memory." Many pupils told of relatives south of the border, including one girl whose fondest memory was her fourteenth birthday, "the last time I celebrated with my family."

I found Frank in his audiovisual classroom, where he shared podcasts his students had made about family elders. He translated one student's interview with her grandmother, Maria, just two generations removed from a fugitive slave named Romulus who had married a Mexican and moved his family back and forth across the border.

"There was a lot of hunger and poverty, and as soon as the kids were of working age, they went to the fields," Maria told her granddaughter. She'd picked cotton and other crops from the age of ten. "I had one pair of shoes, two dresses, no socks. Sometimes we ate, sometimes we didn't. Life went on."

Her mother died young, leaving Maria to care for her many siblings. She described herself as "so old" by the time she was free to marry, in her thirties. But she'd been blessed with a husband and child, and "we continued our struggle to overcome."

At the age of seventy-seven, Maria looked back at "all I went through" and felt fulfilled. "We were taught that you had to be respectable and honorable, this is what you struggle for, with God's help." She'd done so, and was rewarded with a daughter and grandchildren who had a better life than hers. "I'm here and very happy."

Frank, whose own parents had been migrant workers and left school after second grade, said Maria's generational story was common to the families of many of his students. They spoke Spanish at home, while often Anglicizing their names at school, striving to "become American" and get ahead.

This assimilation was on colorful display that evening when I rejoined the Sanchezes for Halloween at their modest brick home in a neighborhood off one of Eagle Pass's loop roads. Frank and their older son put on matching Superman outfits; Kristel and their younger son both dressed as Batman.

I donned my Rhinestone Jewboy attire for a last time: cowboy boots, fake-pearl button shirt, tight jeans, and red kerchief. I regretted this costume as soon we headed out at 6:00 p.m., the sun still glaring and the temperature over ninety, not weather I associated with the crisp Halloweens I'd spent with my own boys in New England.

Nor was I accustomed to the style of trick-or-treating in South Texas. The kids' costumes looked all-American—superheroes, ghosts, princesses, an unfortunate child sweltering in a bear outfit—but there were as many adults as children, some with faces painted like Day of the Dead skeletons. I heard very little English as we wandered the crowded streets.

"People sit in traffic and come from all over to bring their kids here for a true American experience," said Lina Cruz, handing out candy by her home. Like others, she distributed candy from a chair on her front lawn, rather than from the door. Another difference from my prior Halloween experience: there were very few homes with jack-o'-lanterns. One reason: pumpkins didn't fare well in the South Texas heat, and those I saw looked prematurely rotted.

Also, there wasn't a Spanish equivalent to "trick or treat," so the children just said "tricky-tricky" as they held out buckets. "Halloween's new for most people here; we're still learning," Lina said.

In other yards, families set up barbecues and played music, offering me sausages while children collected candy. The overall air was that of a neighborhood fiesta rather than a kids' spooky night out.

"In this culture, everyone has to be in on the fun," said a burly border patrolman named Harold, the only Anglo I encountered. Perched on a lawn chair, he had a walkie-talkie and was on volunteer duty, "making sure everyone's safe." He laughed. "The only danger tonight is cavities."

At some point, having lost the Sanchezes in the swarm of other Batmen and Supermen, it dawned on me that my last Halloween outing had been at the start of my journey, in Grafton, West Virginia. There, I'd seen no trick-or-treaters, because parents feared their kids being out on a Friday night, amidst drunks and drug addicts.

Grafton had been my welcome to a heartland hollowed out by economic and social decay. Here, at the nation's edge, celebrating a Northern European holiday in a Spanish-speaking semi-desert, the atmosphere seemed much more hopeful and . . . American. Neighborly, immigrant, vibrant, and family-centered, three generations often represented among the trick-or-treaters and those gathered on lawn chairs.

It was also upwardly mobile. When I reconnected with the Sanchezes, Kristel was carrying her little Batman while Frank hauled his weary Superman in a red wagon. Returning to the house, the couple put the boys to bed, opened a bottle of wine, and talked about their plans for the future.

Both parents were studying for graduate degrees after work, Kristel's in business and Frank's in physiotherapy. Once they'd saved enough money from their current jobs, they hoped to marry their skills and open a rehabilitation center. The couple also had high ambitions for their sons.

"I want my boys to go to Ivy League schools," Kristel said. "We've had a black man as president, and it looks like next week we'll elect a woman. Sometime soon it will be one of our sons or daughters in the White House."

CHAPTER 22

CENTRAL PARK RAMBLE

I am one of those men who work best with a strong head of steam on.

Frederick Law Olmsted to Henry Whitney Bellows, 1861

In his late sixties, Olmsted penned a confessional letter to Elizabeth Baldwin Whitney, a literary belle he'd ardently courted in the 1840s, until she told him it was "neither right nor best" for them to correspond.

Writing forty-four years later, he wondered "how such a loitering, self-indulgent, dilettante sort of a man as I was when you knew me and for ten years afterward, could, at middle age, have turned into such a hard worker and *doer* as I then suddenly became and have been ever since?"

He also recalled a transcendentalist sermon from their New Haven days, "Having, Doing, and Being," and reflected on the price paid for his metamorphosis from the questing "vagabond" she'd known to the remorseless pursuer of success and esteem he'd become. "I have been selling being for doing," he wrote.

The timing of Olmsted's transformation was clear. He'd been close to Elizabeth in his mid-twenties and abruptly shed his loitering ways at the Dantean life midpoint of thirty-five, following a period of professional disappointment and personal loss.

Upon returning from Texas in 1854, Olmsted began adapting his dispatches to book form. He also sought to further his ambition of becoming a "recognized litterateur" by partnering in a high-toned publishing firm, with $5,000 borrowed from his father. He moved to a room on Broadway (leaving his brother John to manage the Staten Island farm) and began consorting with the likes of Emerson, Melville, Longfellow, and Karl Marx, whom he dined with during a business trip to Europe.

But Fred chafed from the start at his "cursed" financial responsibilities and "unaptness" for commerce. "I wonder how I could have been swerved from my repeated resolution not to be a business-man," he wrote his father, when forced to seek another parental loan.

He was also preoccupied with his continuing work on behalf of radical Germans in Texas. Olmsted had returned from the South as the nation was convulsed by conflict over Kansas, a new territory whose fate as either a free or slave state would be determined by referendum. Emigration societies arose to aid (and arm) Northern settlers to swing the balance against pro-slavery forces.

Olmsted joined this campaign and characteristically sought to expand its mission. Don't stop at Kansas, he urged leaders; seize the "feasible opportunity to forestall further aggressive movements of the slave powers" by spurring emigration to other parts of the contested frontier.

It was in connection with this scheme that he drew military-style sketches ("the opposing forces face each other on line A.B.") and plans for a string of settlements linking the Midwest to free-state forces he still believed could be mobilized in Texas. "In four years' time a line from Iowa continuously to the Gulf may be occupied with free labor farms," he wrote. This cordon sanitaire would "completely *turn* the flank of the South" and "Slavery will retreat upon itself."

Far-fetched in hindsight, this plan appealed to the New England Emigrant Aid Company, which helped sway Kansas in favor of free labor. As that fight wound down in 1857, the company proposed sending Olmsted as its agent to territory south of Kansas, and to England, where he'd begun lobbying cotton manufacturers to buy their staple from free-labor producers.

Olmsted was very keen to pursue what he called his "grand" scheme to win the "war between the power of Slavery and of Freedom." But in the summer of 1857, a financial panic gripped the North. Olmsted's distressed publishing venture went bust, leaving him "hopelessly in debt" and at risk of legal action by creditors.

"I have not determined not to go on your business, my heart is in it," he wrote the Emigrant Aid Company, "but I am under the necessity now, much more than I have been, of making a permanently lucrative disposition of myself."

The next month, he reported another circumstance that prevented further work on the company's behalf.

"I have to-day received notification of my appointment to the office of Superintendent of the Central Park of New York," he wrote. "My duties at the park will occupy my time & mind very closely for some time to come."

THIS MOMENTOUS TURN FOR OLMSTED, AND THE NATION, RE-sulted from a serendipitous encounter at a Connecticut inn where Fred holed up to finish his Southern writing. Scribbling in a barn behind the inn, he became so pen-sick that his eyesight failed and he couldn't write for weeks.

At tea one day, he ran into an acquaintance who had recently been named to the board of commissioners overseeing Central Park. At the time, there wasn't yet a park, just a tract the city had acquired on rocky, boggy land deemed ill-suited to commercial or residential development. It was home to a mostly black village and scattered other inhabitants, as well as goats, pigs, and "nuisance" industries like boiling bones to make grease and glue.

The commissioner told Olmsted he should hasten to New York and apply for the new job of park superintendent. "I'll take the boat tonight and think it out as I go," Olmsted replied. "If no serious objection occurs to me before morning, I'll do it."

The opportunity appealed to him on multiple levels, apart from his desperate need for a paycheck. One theme of Olmsted's evolving critique of the South was that slavery prolonged and exacerbated the "frontier" state of society, a condition he saw as makeshift, dispersed, and lacking in common purpose and spirit. His encounters with Southern gentry had also stirred his missionary impulse to "elevate" the North, as a rebuke to aristocratic slaveholders and European monarchists who claimed the masses were incapable of uplift and self-governance.

Many Northerners shared this undemocratic view. The *New York Herald* opined that an Astor and "Sam the Five Pointer" (referencing a rough district of Manhattan) could not "enjoy the same place" because the latter was too "coarse" and rowdy to mingle with his social betters. "Central Park," the paper predicted, "will be nothing but a huge bear garden for the lowest denizens of the city."

Olmsted was ardently committed to demonstrating the opposite. "The first real park made in this country," he wrote, would represent "a democratic development of the highest significance," and its success would drive progress in many other areas on which "this country is dependent."

Apart from this passion, Fred wasn't an obvious fit for park superintendent. He had little experience or training for the task of overseeing a large workforce that included policemen, and laborers clearing the site. The post also demanded a great deal of bureaucratic and political finesse.

"The strongest objection to me," Fred wrote his brother, was that commissioners regarded him as a "literary" rather than a "practical" man. One reason he won out over the other candidates: he wasn't tainted by local politics and patronage and was deemed palatable to conservative Democrats on the faction-riven board.

"You will, of course, be cautious not to give offence in your new position and particularly careful in your accounts," advised Fred's merchant father, who had just lost the thousands he'd invested in his son's publishing venture. Olmsted's brother was likewise cautious, writing their father that he was glad Fred "is settled for a while on something," but predicted he would be "turned out next election."

John was in France at the time, having gone abroad seeking relief from his worsening tuberculosis. Two months after his brother's appointment as park superintendent, John sent a letter from Nice.

"Dear dear Fred," he began. "It appears we are not to see one another any more." Though "kept wild with opium," John could see he was in rapid decline. "I never have known a better friendship than ours has been & there can't be greater happiness than to think of that—how dear we have been & how long we have held out such tenderness."

John died two weeks later, at the age of thirty-two, widowing his wife,

Mary, with three young children, one of them a newborn. John went "gently" and "without a struggle," his father wrote, continuing "to the end his quiet ways." John Sr. also lamented to Fred: "In his death I have lost not only a son but a very dear friend. You almost your only friend."

As so often before, the father was perceptive about his oldest son. Fred had many acquaintances but few soul mates. Eight years after John's death, Fred wrote of joining a crowd singing "Glory! Hallelujah!" at news that the Civil War had ended. In the midst of this celebratory embrace, he wrote, "I stood alone—and my heart cried back stronger than ever to my poor, sad, unhopeful brother, who alone of all the world, ever really knew me and trusted me for exactly what I was and felt."

The depth of their bond, and the pain of losing it, was manifest in Fred's career and personal life. He threw himself into his work with remorseless dedication, supervising Central Park by day while working feverishly at night to win a competition to design its grounds in collaboration with Calvert Vaux, an experienced English-born architect and landscape gardener.

Their plan was titled Greensward, which spoke to its open meadows and emphasis on the pastoral rather than statuary, structures, or formal gardens. They also devised an ingenious system of underpasses and bridges to separate pedestrian from carriage, dung cart, and other traffic. When Greensward beat out thirty-two other submissions in the spring of 1858, Olmsted became architect in chief of Central Park and redoubled his labors to bring the design to fruition.

During this same period, he also let go of his search for romantic "infinity," and answered his brother's dying wish. "Don't let Mary suffer while you are alive," John had written at the end of his last letter to Fred.

After John's death, Mary returned with her three children to the Staten Island farmhouse where she'd lived for several years previously. Then they moved to Manhattan, close to Olmsted's office and quarters. Nineteen months after John's death, Mary and Fred were wed at a small ceremony on a hilltop in Central Park.

Fred had first met Mary when he was a farmer newly arrived on Staten Island, and she nineteen, living nearby. Writing at the time to his Yale friend, Kingsbury, Fred described Mary as "comfortably pretty," "a real earnest thinker," and "just the thing for a rainy day. Not to fall in love with, but to talk with."

He also asked Kingsbury to send him two knives, one sharp and one small and blunt, so he could give them to Mary with a poem he'd written. The verse expressed hope that the softer blade would grow in her. "The steel of the larger, as pure as thy mind/Can be—just as cutting—can not be as kind."

Mary, in turn, had found the young Fred argumentative and lacking in whimsy, unlike his wry, gentle brother. By the time of their marriage twelve years later, in June 1859, Fred was also obsessively devoted to his labors at Central Park.

"I am capable of stronger passions than many men and I have never had a more desperate passion than that," he later wrote Calvert Vaux, explaining his overwrought behavior at the start of their work together. "A great deal of disappointed love and unsatisfied romance and down-trodden pride fastened itself to that passion."

Three months after his wedding, Fred wrote his father that he was "used up, fatigued beyond recovery, an older man than you." He blamed overwork, but also cited a home filled with sick children, a wife "half distracted with her multitude of anxieties," and "other squalls." When "blue" pills and a retreat to Saratoga Springs failed to cure him, he took a leave of absence to travel alone in Europe.

This appeared to help, but the next year, "close on the edge of a brain-fever," Fred fainted while driving a carriage and was thrown from it, breaking one leg so severely that he limped for the rest of his life. Soon after, his first child by Mary died from cholera, at the age of two months.

He nonetheless returned to work, toted about on a "litter chair," and by the spring of 1861, the park below Seventy-Ninth Street was effectively complete. It was also an immediate sensation, drawing one hundred thousand people on some days, with little friction (the most common crime: speeding, on horseback, punishable with a ten-dollar fine). "Park" entered an American encyclopedia for the first time, the entry written by Olmsted.

"Both in conception and execution," the *Atlantic Monthly* declared, Central Park represented "the beau-ideal of a people's pleasure-ground" and "the most striking evidence of the sovereignty of the people yet afforded in the history of free institutions,—the best answer yet given to the doubts and fears which have frowned on the theory of self-government."

This was exactly as Olmsted had hoped, but too late to serve as a reproach to the South. A few weeks after the *Atlantic* article appeared, Confederates bombarded Fort Sumter, and Lincoln called for volunteers.

"We are full of fight," Olmsted wrote his father, five days after Fort Sumter. He was mustering employees for military drills at the park, had submitted his resignation, and talked of volunteering for the navy. "The impulse of patriotism sweeps everything before it."

A WEEK AFTER ENDING MY JOURNEY FOLLOWING OLMSTED AT THE Rio Grande, Donald Trump won the presidential election. This wasn't on a historical par with secession or Fort Sumter, but still a political jolt unlike any in the forty years since I'd cast my first vote. Also, marinated as I'd been in Olmsted's writing on the prelude to national breakup, I couldn't help seeing commonalities between his troubled era and mine.

The most glaring parallel was the retreat into tribal and partisan camps, tuned to frequencies so divergent that the reasoned discourse Yeoman had initially sought was a virtual impossibility. Also resonant was the role of what he called "ultraists," who stoked and exploited the nation's divisions and spread conspiracy theories, especially in the South. One of many examples: fire-eaters' success in convincing a large swath of the white South that Abraham Lincoln, a peace-seeking accommodationist, was a "Black Republican" in league with radical abolitionists bent on destroying slavery.

Many Northerners were possessed by an opposing specter: the "Slave Power," viewed rather like the Koch brothers today, as a sinister cabal pulling the strings at every level of government, including the Supreme Court.

"My thoughts are murder to the state," Thoreau wrote, as violence erupted in Boston over enforcement of the Fugitive Slave Act. William Lloyd Garrison branded the Constitution "an agreement with hell" and publicly burned it on July Fourth. "So perish all compromises with tyranny!" Secessionists took the ultimate, uncompromising step, leaving the Union rather than abide by the result of the 1860 election.

Americans, in short, not only despaired of their government and laws.

They abandoned the fundamental compact and creed that citizens of diverse regions, backgrounds, and faiths were united by a common history and allegiance to founding principles.

Lincoln spoke eloquently to this breakdown, appealing on the eve of war to the nation's "bonds of affection" and "mystic chords of memory." He also urged his "dissatisfied fellow-countrymen" to "think calmly and well" about the crisis at hand. "Before entering upon so grave a matter as the destruction of our national fabric," he asked, "would it not be wise to ascertain precisely why we do it? Will you hazard so desperate a step while there is any possibility that any portion of the ills you fly from have no real existence?"

I thought of these cautionary words during the campaign, as Trump kept up a drumbeat of divisive and inflammatory falsehoods: about voter fraud, Mexican rapists pouring over the border, Muslims on rooftops cheering on 9/11. While on the other side, a presidential candidate appeared so contemptuous of Trump's supporters, and seemingly unconnected to their genuine ills, that she barely sought their votes.

"Color me deplorable," said Joni Clonts, the Moosehead Cafe owner in Crockett, Texas, when I called her a few days after the election. "Trump has a mouth but he says what a lot of us are thinking, and no one here believes *anything* Hillary and the media say about him."

Many others I contacted from my travels expressed delight, above all, at the middle finger that Trump brandished at coastal "elites" by whom they felt despised.

"It tickles me to death every time I hear another commentator say the polls were wrong," exulted Marlene McComas, the florist I'd met in small-town Kentucky. "Well you didn't talk to the right people; you didn't reach *us*." She disagreed with Trump on abortion and a few other issues, "but I love that the press thought they could fix the election, and the common man and woman stood up and said, 'You're not pulling the wool over our eyes.'"

More nuanced was the view of Frank VanSickle, who'd shown me around the iron foundry in West Virginia, a working-class state that went more strongly for Trump than any except Wyoming. VanSickle was a lifelong Democrat and had voted for Obama. His daughter taught English to Somali refugees. He didn't think highly of Trump's intellect or statesmanship, but the candidate's talk of trade and job losses had stirred him, as it did most others in his union shop.

VanSickle told me he went into the voting booth intending to vote for Clinton, circled the oval by her name, "but just couldn't fill it in." After hesitating for some time, he got a clean ballot and voted for Trump. When I asked what he thought had tipped him in the end, VanSickle cited claims about Hillary's failing health, her actions in Benghazi, and a much more bizarre story he was surprised I hadn't heard.

"That tape of Tim Kaine cursing out his young daughter," he said. This had made him question the VP candidate's image as a good Catholic and family man.

I looked into this. The recording was actually nine years old, of the actor Alec Baldwin, telling his eleven-year-old daughter in a voice mail that she was a "thoughtless little pig" and threatening to "straighten your ass out." The tape had recirculated on social media a month before the election, with a photo of Kaine as the alleged speaker.

It was hard to gauge the impact of this sort of chicanery. I sensed that VanSickle had been leaning toward Trump and looking for anything that might justify his abandonment of Democrats. But it seemed yet another alarming sign of national estrangement—and derangement—that otherwise reasonable people were primed to believe toxic fictions on the internet, and to dismiss factual reporting as "fake news."

Or, on the other side, to believe that every Trump voter was an irredeemable bigot. When I talked to my New England neighbors about deep-red Texas, it was clear they regarded it as arid, alien, and hostile, like ISIS-controlled parts of Syria. The self-righteous certitude of others on the left reminded me of a different Middle Eastern country: Saudi Arabia, where the religious police surveilled and punished citizens for even the faintest deviation from Wahhabi orthodoxy.

America's divide wasn't 1861-level, not by a long shot. But our "bonds of affection" were badly strained, and I listened in vain for a swelling "chorus of the Union," touched by "the better angels of our nature."

THREE MONTHS AFTER LINCOLN INVOKED THIS IMAGE IN HIS first inaugural address, Olmsted wrote a prominent friend that he was "pining" to find his "mission" in the war. The role he most wanted was as "superintendent" of slaves flocking to Union lines. Instead, Olmsted was chosen to direct the US Sanitary Commission, which inspected soldiers' conditions and supplied them with food, clothing, and medicine.

"Talent and energy most rare," George Templeton Strong, the Sanitary Commission's treasurer, wrote of Olmsted in his diary. "Decidedly the most remarkable specimen of human nature with whom I have ever been brought into close relations."

But Olmsted also vexed his colleagues, as he had at Central Park, by becoming so "fanatical about his duty," and convinced of his vision, that he behaved autocratically and labored to the point of collapse. "Most insanitary habits of life," Strong wrote of Olmsted in another diary entry. "Works with steady, feverish intensity till four in the morning, sleeps on a sofa in his clothes, and breakfasts on *strong coffee and pickles*!!!"

This monomania also displeased Mary Olmsted, who was pregnant and felt abandoned and nearly "impoverished" when her husband decamped for Washington. Upon receipt of a letter full of war news and Fred's ceaseless labors, Mary termed the missive a blustery "rhodomontade" rather than a "letter to a wife," and urged her husband to come home for an extended visit.

"Stay a fortnight at least if you love me," she wrote. "I wanted you to go because I thought you would be happier there, than here with me," but now she worried, "you are, I am afraid, so much given over to the contemplation of the enemy that you will forget all about the temporal wants of your wife and her babies."

The family eventually joined Fred in Washington, but he often slept at the office and traveled for long periods, visiting Gettysburg and other battlegrounds and riding hospital boats and trains filled with dead and wounded. This experience completed his decade-long transit from moderate, dialogue-minded Yeoman to committed warrior against the South.

"I want to exterminate the Slaveholders—or rather slaveholding and the state of society founded on it," he wrote in 1862, later adding: "I would rather die than live with the possibility of an attempted Union with that people again. I know that they are my enemies. . . . Down with them, damn them!"

Olmsted drew up a congressional bill for the protection and aid of freed slaves, and strongly supported the enlistment of black soldiers. "I believe many of them are capable of making military heroes," he testified before a government commission. But this self-described "soldier of the republic," whose "righteous hatred" of the Confederacy grew "stronger than my love of life," burned out after two years of exhausting service and political infighting.

He also needed money. Central Park had brought him great esteem but modest earnings, and he was still in debt from his publishing fiasco. So in 1863 he decamped again, to administer a gold-mining enterprise in California—only to discover that the venture was failing and corrupt. However, he found rewarding work drawing plans for Bay Area landscapes, and as head of the first commission overseeing Yosemite Valley.

With exceptional farsightedness, Olmsted wrote that Yosemite, then a remote and little-visited site, was a treasure of the "deepest sublimity" that would one day attract "millions," and "should be held, guarded and managed for the free use of the whole body of the people forever." His report was shelved at the time, but revived a half century later, by one of his sons, who helped draft legislation creating the National Park Service.

At war's end, Olmsted was still mulling multiple career options. But Calvert Vaux convinced him to return east and resume their partnership as landscape architects—a term coined in connection with their Central Park work. Olmsted disliked the title. "The art is not gardening nor is it architecture," he wrote Vaux, but rather a more comprehensive "sylvan art" and urban planning that included an "artistically arranged system" of roads, public spaces, and other features.

Whatever one called it, Olmsted had finally settled on his life's mission, at the age of forty-three, and would pursue it with astonishing success for the next three decades. As the North's economy and cities rapidly expanded after the Civil War, Olmsted and his partners became the go-to designers of parks, transport systems, residential neighborhoods, campuses, the World's Columbian Exposition, and the grounds of hospitals, libraries, museums, and government buildings, including the US Capitol.

"Of all American artists," declared Charles Eliot Norton, a Harvard art historian and leading thinker of the late nineteenth century, Olmsted "stands first in the production of great works which answer the needs and give expression to the life of our immense and miscellaneous democracy."

As his career blossomed, Olmsted also settled domestically. Fred and Mary raised two children of their own, in addition to the three she'd had by John and that Fred adopted. In 1881, he moved his family from New York to a comfortable suburban home in Brookline, Massachusetts, that also served as the office of a landscape architecture firm two of his sons would join.

But Olmsted remained prone to the "blues" and "the dumps" and periodic collapse from his "faculties and talents" being "severely and steadily bent," as he put it in one letter. "I am liable to break down entirely and suddenly—and I see that it's the worst feature in my life."

In his writing about "park-making" or "scenery-making," terms he preferred to "landscape architecture," Fred often seemed to be outlining a cure for himself. Natural scenery soothed "the severe and excessive exercise of the mind which leads to the greatest fatigue," he wrote, and helped city-dwellers "resist" and "recover" from the stresses of their hectic lives. "It is thus, in medical phrase, a prophylactic and therapeutic agent of vital value."

However, as Calvert Vaux sagely observed, Olmsted was a poor advertisement for the tranquility of mind he attributed to parks. "Upon my word Olmsted I will *not* forgive you if you do not make a better show," Vaux wrote, during one of his partner's absences due to mental strain. "Who will be tempted to a study of nature and the polite arts if the best paid and most popularly appearing professor cuts such a lugubrious sallow bloodless figure as you insist upon doing."

Vaux also noted the dissonance between Olmsted's ideals and his "*un-democratic*" tendencies. Vaux complained of dealing with "two characters"— Olmsted "the artist & republican," and "Olmsted the bureaucrat and imperialist with whom I never for a moment sympathized."

The two men ended their fraught, brilliant partnership in the 1870s. But they corresponded until their careers ended in tragic concordance, months apart. And for all their differences, they shared an immense pride in Central Park.

Vaux, in one letter to Olmsted, called it "the big art work of the

Republic." Fred answered in less grand and more personal terms. "There is no other place in the world," he wrote, "that is as much home to me."

IN THE AUTUMN OF 2018, I ENDED MY TRAVELS WITH FRED BY spending a long weekend in Central Park. I'd lived in New York in the early 1980s and returned many times, but I hadn't visited the park in years, and never with an eye to its underlying philosophy and design.

At its most fundamental level, the park had been intended to provide sanctuary from the crowded and unsanitary conditions in New York, at a time when the city's population was doubling by the decade. But Olmsted saw it as a refuge from a host of other ills, including the excessive materialism and "artificial things" of urban life.

These afflictions were on garish display as I emerged from the subway at Times Square: building-high ads, wall-to-wall paving, and man-made sensory overload. If, as Olmsted imagined, parks were places to nurture humankind's "poetic" side, Times Square was the polar opposite.

Olmsted also wrote that crowded city streets "compel us" to "walk circumspectly," guarding against others, "without any friendly flowing toward them, but rather a drawing from them." Within a block of the subway, I'd instinctively assumed the protective crouch of my student days in the city: head down, shoulders braced against the jostling crowd, eyes averted from hawkers and hustlers. The mien of a busy man on his way to . . . a park, where I just as quickly unlimbered and began ambling in no particular direction.

This was an aspect of parks I'd always taken for granted. But as I strolled along a winding path, channeling Olmsted, I saw the degree to which he and Vaux had engineered my experience. Cities don't just compel us to walk protectively; numbered street grids like New York's also *propel* us in a straight line, toward some goal or destination, an internal Fitbit logging the blocks achieved. Olmsted and Vaux intentionally scrambled this mind-set.

"I love it when people come up to me and say, 'I'm lost,'" said the first person I approached, Jack Intrator, a green-shirted volunteer "greeter" for the Central Park Conservancy. We stood at one end of the Mall, a

European-style promenade that Olmsted and Vaux were required to include in their proposal. It was the only straight path in the park.

Other walkways curved and looped to disrupt pedestrians' hurried urban pace and draw them deeper into what Olmsted called the "mystery and infinity" of the natural surrounds. The conservancy respected this by posting relatively few signs or maps in the park, which has fifty-six miles of trails.

"The whole point is to lose your bearings and leave the city behind," Intrator said, while also noting a historical development that complicated this mission. In 1857, as Olmsted began work at the park, the first Otis passenger elevator was installed in a New York building, a technology that enabled the erection of high-rises that now loomed above the tree line, including the gold-crowned Trump Parc condos on Central Park South.

Even more intrusive were new "super-towers" soaring over a thousand feet, casting shadows on the park and in winter blotting out the sun for extended periods. The cost of living in them was likewise lofty, rising as high as $100 million. "Olmsted wanted this to be a people's park," Intrator said. "But some people always try and grab more of it than others."

Nonetheless, I only had to wander ten minutes deeper into the park before I *did* feel lost, particularly when I reached one of Olmsted's favorite spots, the Ramble. Here, the woods and shrubs were so dense, and the paths so labyrinthine, that it was easy to forget I was at the center of a throbbing megalopolis of seventeen million people.

The Ramble also bore traces of Olmsted's Southern travels. Its lush and aromatic density felt more like Louisiana or the Carolina Low Country than the mid-Atlantic, and the plantings included swamp magnolia, a tree he'd admired on his journey. The rustic benches and bridges were made of Alabama cedar. Elsewhere in the park, the lagoon-like water features felt Southern, too, as did the elms arching over the Mall in the cathedral-like fashion of live oak allées on grand plantations.

Olmsted and Vaux introduced many non-native elements, in part because large stretches of the park site bore little trace of its native state, having been stripped and disfigured by loggers, bone-boilers, and others. The two men, in effect, produced a highly engineered and romantic artifice of nature, including a man-made "loch" and waterfalls fed by piped-in city water. Such picturesque facsimiles, Olmsted wrote, allowed "hundreds of thousands of tired workers" to freely experience what "the White Mountains or the Adirondacks is, at great cost, to those in easier circumstances."

Wherever possible, however, Olmsted believed in discerning and respecting "the genius of the place," meaning its intrinsic and singular nature. He'd exhibited this eye when admiring the rolling swards of Kentucky, or the interplay of trees and plain in Texas. So, too, in his designs, which sought to bring out and enhance a setting's essence.

In central Manhattan that essence was rock, and Olmsted foresaw its fate in the fast-growing city. "The time will come," he wrote park commissioners in 1858, "when the picturesquely-varied, rocky formations of the Island will have been converted into foundations for rows of monotonous straight streets, and piles of erect angular buildings."

So, in addition to preserving and showcasing the park's rocky outcrops, he sought to "judiciously" enhance the rocky bluffs at the park's Harlem end, to bring out "these particularly individual and characteristic sources of landscape effects."

In other instances, Olmsted expressed a preference for the untamed. "More mowing or dug ground I object to," he wrote of landscaping his family's property in Brookline. "Less wildness and disorder I object to." He also inveighed against park maintenance that diminished the element of mystery he sought in his designs. "How will it be," he complained, "when the way of the lawnmower has at all points been made plain, and the face of nature shall everywhere have become as natty as a new silk hat?"

In a similar vein, he lamented the "fashion" among wealthy homeowners in Newport, Rhode Island, of giving "a lawn-like finish" to properties along shore that was "rocky, wild, sea-beaten." When the town's mayor asked him for a plan of "improvement" for a local beach, Olmsted replied that the site's rough strand, "and the waste of the sand back of it, thrown up by the breakers" was what made the beach "moving" and distinct.

"Nothing better can be done than to let it alone," he wrote.

OLMSTED'S RESTRAINT IN RESHAPING LANDSCAPES DID NOT EXtend to his related vocation, as an architect of American society. This was the calling he'd outlined in his 1853 letter to Charles Brace, in which he first mentioned parks as among the venues necessary to "elevate" and assimilate the masses, "and force into contact" the rich and the poor, the highbrow and low.

On my second day in Central Park, I tried to gauge the legacy of this vision by focusing on the visitors. From surface appearances, the democratic coming together that Olmsted imagined was evident at every turn, the park crowd as diverse as the surrounding metropolis, with tourists from all over the world added to the mix.

At the most popular spot, the fifteen-acre Sheep Meadow, women wearing hijabs unfurled an Oriental carpet near a lightly clad couple entwined on the grass; black and Asian and Hispanic families shared the shade of a large tree; young people lofted footballs and Frisbees and kites, and strangers casually joined in or tossed back wayward projectiles.

The scene also spoke to what Olmsted called the "gregarious" aspect of parks: the convergence of "all classes" and backgrounds creating "an attractive and diverting spectacle," with "each individual adding by his mere presence to the pleasure of all others." In park surveys, I later learned, people-watching ranked as visitors' main activity.

Farther on, while resting by a fountain, I also glimpsed evidence for Olmsted's thesis that strangers interacted more easily and amicably in the park than in the wary and "heart-hardening" atmosphere of the city. On the bench next to mine, an older man struck up an animated conversation with a young woman, and after they'd talked for a while, I went over and quizzed them about their encounter.

"I asked what she was reading," said Jeffrey Sado, a retired real estate broker.

"I told him I was sketching," said Silvia Marazzi, an Italian-born dancer, "and it went from there."

Jeffrey said he frequently met people this way at the park. "All *sorts* of people. We're more open and at ease here."

This was seconded by a young black musician wearing a backward baseball cap and a boa constrictor wrapped around his shoulders, which he offered to passersby to pose with for photographs, charging them a few dollars. This wasn't "strictly legal," he said, and therefore declined to tell me his name. But he did share a thought. "Some people are scared of my snake, but not of me. That's not always true in this city."

Nearby, I visited the Chess & Checkers House, beside a large rock worn smooth by kids sliding down it. The woman on duty, Diann DeFebbe, told me that first-time visitors were often surprised to learn they could borrow games and just sit and play in the shelter with whoever else appeared. "This is a rare building in New York where no money changes hands," she said.

That afternoon, I met Adrian Benepe, who had spent almost his entire life attached to the park. He walked and played there as a child, worked as a pushcart vendor as a college student, then was a park ranger, and ultimately served as Commissioner of the New York City Department of Parks & Recreation for eleven years. He also married in the park.

Benepe took me for a bike ride through the northern reaches of the park, less visited than the area below Seventy-Ninth Street and freer of monuments and other additions that were grafted onto Olmsted and Vaux's design. It was also a part of the park that became extremely neglected in the 1960s and '70s, when the city was in dire financial straits and the park beset by vandalism, drug-dealing, and muggings.

Since then, the Central Park Conservancy had raised millions to restore and maintain the park, in partnership with the city. Benepe said park use had risen fivefold since 1980, to about fifty million visits a year, while felonies had fallen from more than a thousand annually to less than a hundred.

The park had become tamer in other ways, too. Benepe, who began working there in the 1970s, recalled a vibrant and eclectic scene: "happenings," disco Rollerbladers, and "gay, black, and Hispanic liberation all on display at the same time." While these sorts of gatherings had waned, Benepe said, Olmsted's "deliberate, democratic experiment is still going on," in ways that went beyond the "benign voyeurism" of many visitors.

"People come together serendipitously; they see others who don't look like them, who are doing and enjoying the same things," he said. "That contributes to a tolerance and harmony you don't see in many other cities."

This cosmopolitan intimacy also occurred on the subway, Benepe noted, "but it's forced and grim," in contrast to the voluntary and open-air mingling at the park. "Plants and grass have a pacifying effect. I've never seen a fistfight in front of a flower bed."

We then stopped at one, the Conservatory Garden near 105th Street. A spectrum of races and ages shared benches, chatting as children played by the garden's fountain. "Exhibit A," he remarked.

We rode on to the heavily wooded Ramble, which in Olmsted's day had quickly become popular as a trysting spot. Or, as an art critic in the 1860s delicately described it, a secluded setting that gave "excuse to a pair of lovers to pause awhile" and rest under a "canopy of vine." A nearby pond was another instant attraction when the park opened, since ice-skating was the rare Victorian setting where single men and women could mingle—and tumble into each other's arms.

In the 1970s, the Ramble had become a trysting spot of a different sort: for gay men. Benepe said that a nearby meadow, where men sunbathed in Speedos, had been dubbed by its habitués "the fruited plain."

Olmsted may not have anticipated these and other comings together. But to Benepe, the park's changing use and character illustrated the endurance and flexibility of Fred's vision. "This city's always evolving and so is its park," he said.

The original design had been overlaid with ball fields and other facilities, walled by high-rises, crowded with tourists, and intruded on by air traffic overhead. But the genius of the place remained.

"This was the first of its kind, an experiment that worked and that's been reproduced all over," Benepe said. "I really believe Central Park changed the world."

AS I'D COME TO SEE IN MY TRAVELS, OLMSTED'S INFLUENCE EXtended far beyond urban parks, in ways that didn't always accord with the aesthetic and social vision he brought to his early landscape work. Suburbs were the most obvious example. Olmsted envisioned them as residential extensions of his parks, describing the ideal suburb as a "picturesque, sylvan and rural" sanctuary from the density and drab regularity of urban street grids. The planned communities he and his partners designed, such as Riverside, Illinois, had shaded parkways (a term Olmsted and Vaux coined), curvilinear streets, house lots with deep setbacks, and other now-familiar features.

But early suburbs weren't as democratic as parks. Few but white Americans of means could afford to live in them, and in the early twentieth century, cities like Atlanta (where Olmsted and his sons planned the suburb of Druid Hills) passed ordinances to codify residential segregation. Other practices, such as redlining, further excluded blacks and confined them to separate, less desirable neighborhoods.

Olmsted's son and namesake played a role in this development. During World War I, he headed an agency that built and oversaw segregated housing for defense workers, and he later served on a federal zoning committee that also enabled segregation.

"Racial divisions," Frederick Jr. wrote in 1918, had "to be taken into account" in any housing plan, and one should not "force the mingling of people who are not yet ready to mingle"—a complete reversal of the barrier-lowering ethos that had driven his father in designing public parks.

Developers in the twentieth century also betrayed Olmsted's vision of suburbs as varied and semi-rural "villages," or what he termed a "series of neighborhoods of a peculiar character." Instead, modern suburbs had filled with cookie-cutter subdivisions and malls, not to mention the hum of lawn mowers Olmsted so disliked. What he imagined as distinctive became banal and a byword, in my 1960s youth, for stifling conformity.

Other aspects of Olmsted's legacy traced more directly to a shift in his own thinking, and a dimming of the democratic fire that had burned in him at the start. In the 1880s, while working on Boston's "emerald necklace" and other public projects, Olmsted took many private commissions, including the grounds of grand homes. The project that consumed him during the last seven years of his career was the Biltmore Estate in North Carolina, owned by George Washington Vanderbilt, the young heir to a vast industrial fortune.

"It is far & away the most distinguished private place, not only of America, but of the world, forming in this *period*," Olmsted wrote his partners, later describing Vanderbilt as "a very rich man who for his own pleasure can be drawn to serve art and Science and popular education in a rarely good way."

He prevailed on Vanderbilt to buy thousands of acres of woodland for the preservation and study of forestry, launching this field in the United States. Olmsted also designed an arboretum for experimenting with plants, and a network of roads and gates that allowed visitors to tour part of the estate.

"The public is more and more making a resort of the place," he wrote his partners in 1894, "and I more & more feel that it is the most permanently important public work and the most critical with reference to the future of our profession."

But there was no escaping the irony of his last great endeavor. The young Olmsted had ridden this part of North Carolina in 1854 as a decrier of aristocracy and proponent of state-aided uplift of the masses. He'd returned to the region to end his career designing the grounds of a 250-room French-style chateau, the largest private home in the nation.

While pursuing other landscape work in the South, Olmsted also strayed from his once-ardent concern for the welfare of freed slaves, and his conviction that whites would do all in their power to resist blacks' advancement. Advising on the grounds of the Alabama capitol, he suggested ways to display the site's Confederate monument to better advantage, and diplomatically answered questions from the governor's secretary about his views of the post–Civil War South.

"The Negroes have been doing a great deal better as freedmen than I had ever imagined possible," he wrote, and "the whites have accepted the situation about as well as it was in human nature that they should."

He stood up strongly for equal rights, and objected to whites not "playing fair" at elections. But he praised the region's "firm, lasting, and progressive" recovery from war, and said Northerners were "only anxious to have the more intelligent people of the South" lead the way in resolving the racial injustices that remained.

Olmsted wrote this in 1889, as Southern states were vigorously stripping blacks of the hard-won rights they'd gained since the Civil War. Two years later, he rebuffed a Massachusetts businessman and former abolitionist who thought Olmsted's work "the best books ever written" on slavery and sought to reissue *The Cotton Kingdom* in condensed form.

"I have seen a tendency in recent literature to re-establish a romantic view of the condition of things in the Slave States before the War," Olmsted replied, a "false and most mischievous view" that he believed *The Cotton Kingdom* contradicted. But he saw no "commercial demand" for the volume's republication, and his landscape work in the South had allowed him "to review the field of my former travels. . . . The revolution has been a tremendous one and I am well satisfied with the present results."

He returned to Biltmore, working as hard as ever, until May 1895, when he wrote from the estate to one of his sons, "My memory as to recent occurrences is no longer to be trusted." He'd had several serious lapses, and looking "at the situation from an outside and impersonal point of view," he realized "I cannot be depended on to properly represent the firm."

He stayed on at Biltmore, with assistance, but his faculties did not improve, and he became "over-strung and nervous." That autumn, while he recuperated in Maine, his partners engineered his retirement from the firm, at the age of seventy-three.

Olmsted expressed bitterness over this. But resentment gradually gave "way to a realization of the truth," he wrote, closing one of his last letters to his partners with an exhortation:

"The firm! No. The Art!"

"*Exit*, bowing, not ungratefully,"

"F.L.O."

THE FALL OF 1895 ALSO MARKED THE EXIT OF THE MAN WHO had convinced Fred of his destiny as a landscape architect. Calvert Vaux, after splitting from Olmsted, had struggled to succeed, and appears to have succumbed to mental demons of his own. Vaux's body was found off a pier in Brooklyn, an apparent suicide. For all his talent, and coaxing of his difficult partner through their work at Central Park and on many other projects, Vaux died a man of modest renown and wealth.

Olmsted's family withheld the news of Vaux's death from Fred, fearing it would agitate his impaired mind. While acknowledging the "gradual decay" of his "faculties," Olmsted expressed terror at the prospect of being sent to an institution. "My father was a director of an Insane Retreat," he wrote, and "having been professionally employed and behind the scenes in several, my dread of such places is intense."

But his dementia, or what one doctor diagnosed as "slight hemorrhages on the brain," steadily worsened. In 1898, his family committed him to an asylum near Boston whose grounds he'd drawn plans for decades earlier. He died there five years later, at the age of eighty-one. After a small private service, appropriate given his dislike of pomp, Olmsted's cremated remains were interred in a family crypt at the Old North Cemetery in his native Hartford.

Mary outlived Fred by eighteen years, and their sons carried on Olmsted's landscape work for more than four decades, contributing to thousands of park and other designs. Olmsted's writing on the South also lived on, and not only as a resource for academic scholars.

In 1949, when Frederick Law Olmsted Jr. retired, a young black inmate was combing the library at a prison twenty miles from Fred's former home and office in Brookline.

"I will never forget how shocked I was when I began reading about slavery's total horror," Malcolm X later recalled, citing Olmsted's work as among those that "opened my eyes" and "made such an impact" that the street hustler turned toward the Nation of Islam and a fiery career challenging the racial injustice that afflicted America a century after emancipation.

MY LAST DAY IN CENTRAL PARK WAS RAINY, AND FEW PEOPLE were out. So I walked from one end to the other, unaccustomedly alone with my thoughts, reflecting on Olmsted's transit from Yeoman to Central Park to the Biltmore Estate.

In a sense, Fred had remained the figure he'd described to his friend Kingsbury on the eve of his first Southern journey: "I represent pretty fairly the average sentiment of good thinking men on our side." Olmsted's evolution over the next decade, from "moderate Free Soiler" to Union crusader who wanted to "exterminate" slavery and the "society founded on it," was broadly in line with the arc of mainstream Northern opinion.

So, too, was his gradual retreat from the idealism and sacrifices of the Civil War era. "I see what ought to be done but I can't get other men to see it," he wrote in the 1860s, when he felt foiled by bureaucrats in both New York and Washington, where his knowledge of the South and slavery was "snubbed & set down and made of no account."

Despairing of government, he also came to believe that money spoke and that he needed to make a sufficient pile of it. "First: I should not be under temptation to work for purposes which my own convictions did not approve, as I am now," he wrote. "Second: people—capitalists & men controlling capital—would have some real confidence in my practical sagacity."

After a final flirtation with heading a freedmen's agency, he abandoned the cause that had animated him for so long. Like much of the nation, which lost its will to reconstruct the South, he turned instead to the challenges posed by fast-growing cities and grasped the considerable opportunities on offer in the Gilded Age.

"Seek the best society," he wrote his youngest son upon the youth's entrance to Harvard. "Seek to make yourself desirable in it. Make yourself a well informed man on matters of conversation of the best and most fortunate sort of people."

This was yet another aspect of Fred's life and era that resonated in my own. I'd witnessed the turn from 1960s idealism to the Reagan-era embrace of free markets, conspicuous consumption, and the measuring of success in dollar terms—an ethos, though periodically challenged, that had prevailed since.

Many of my peers had once talked, like Olmsted, of making a sufficient stake so they could act in accordance with their convictions, only to settle into careers as corporate lawyers. I hadn't been immune to this drift. After college, I'd worked as a union organizer in Mississippi, gone on to a well-paid job at the *Wall Street Journal*, and collected generous book advances to travel the world and write about whatever piqued my curiosity.

As Olmsted had in speaking of his work at Biltmore, I liked to think there was a worthy "public" dimension to my labor—albeit on a much tinier and less consequential canvas than his. But at times, while pursuing some historical obscurity in the archives or on Southern byways, I felt uncomfortably like the "loitering, self-indulgent, dilettante" Fred had described in his letter to his long-ago flame, Elizabeth Baldwin Whitney.

The fallout from our own Gilded Age was evident at Central Park, too, beginning with the super-towers and Trump buildings that loomed over it. On my last day touring the park, I spent several hours perusing the plaques on the hundreds of benches, put there by devoted park visitors.

"Reserved for Lovers Only."
"Toi et Moi, Toujours. Eddy and Hannah always."
"This bench of Barbara's, by the Lake, Her Place of Joy to Contemplate."

Then I came to an area just off Fifth Avenue where many of the plaques bore names of modern-day robber barons, including the Madoffs. It now costs $10,000 to secure a bench plaque.

This money went to the upkeep of the park, for all, and as I'd seen on my bike ride with Adrian Benepe, the most striking revitalization had occurred in the section adjoining Harlem and the far Upper East and West Sides. But the gentrification of these neighborhoods had also changed the park's demography.

As the rain slackened, I spotted and then joined an elderly black woman striding briskly on her "daily route" through the park above 100th Street. A retired financial industry worker, she'd followed this course for decades and "couldn't exist without it." She also said the park was much safer and better maintained than it had been before about 1985.

But something had been lost, too. "It's become sterile," she said. "Used to be all shades, all types, lots of music." She didn't blame this change on park management. Rather, it was due to "so many who used to live here moving away," she said. "Some days I feel like it's just me, tourists, and young white people doing their exercise thing."

Waiting for the light to change at the park's 101st Street exit, she left me with a more positive appraisal. "Park's not perfect, nothing ever is," she said. "But imagine this city without it. We'd be like rats, scratching each other's eyes out."

Olmsted had spoken to this in 1866, in a proposal he submitted with Vaux for the design of what became Prospect Park in Brooklyn. He described parks as pressure valves, providing relief and escape "from the cramped, confined, and controlling circumstances" of urban life. In the next sentence he expanded on this theme in a way that tied his thought and career together.

As Yeoman, Olmsted's essential subject had been freedom, or the absence of it. Slaves yearning to be free; slave owners whose thoughts were not; an entire society chained to a system that inhibited free labor, free expression, and the flourishing of free enterprise and free institutions.

Olmsted may have turned away from the South and its iniquities after the Civil War. But the central quest of his travels and writings endured in his landscape design. As the Brooklyn park essay stated: *"A sense of enlarged freedom* is to all, at all times, the most certain and the most valuable gratification afforded by a park."

This came home to me during my final hour in Central Park, when I rested on a bluff above the Harlem Meer. Below, a lone man fished in the drizzling rain, across from a men's prison just north of the park on West 110th Street. I was wearily debating whether to hike down to the Meer for a final interview when a black kid scooted past me on a Hoverboard, trailed by a youngster on a bicycle.

I watched as they rode over to a tree, where they stood for a full ten minutes, mesmerized by the squirrels scampering up and down the trunk. Then I went over to speak with them.

They seemed wary of me at first, having doubtless been cautioned about talking to adult strangers. Then the older boy told me his name was Justin, he'd just started sixth grade, and he came to the park every weekend with his little brother from the apartment block where they lived in Harlem.

"What do you like best about the park?" I asked.

"Just exploring," he said. "Going where I want. Sometimes I get lost."

I told him the man who created the park would be pleased to hear that.

"What's his name?" he asked.

"Frederick Law Olmsted—Fred, to his friends and family. I can tell you all about him."

At which point Justin got back on his Hoverboard and motioned to his brother. Then he turned back to me.

"Tell Fred he did good," Justin said, before leading his brother down a winding path and into the woods.

ACKNOWLEDGMENTS

My first and loudest shout-out goes to Charles Beveridge and Charles McLaughlin, the Olmsted and Vaux of scholarship on FLO's life and work.

Professor McLaughlin was the founding editor of the Olmsted Papers Project—and, coincidentally, father to my high school girlfriend. I enjoyed many long-ago bull sessions with him about history and architecture and am saddened that he and his wife, Anne, who encouraged me as I undertook this project, are no longer present to thank in person.

Charles Beveridge has carried on his colleague's work, as series editor of the Olmsted Papers, an ongoing, multivolume compilation of FLO's writing and other documents related to his career. My own research would have been infinitely more difficult without the decades-long labor of Beveridge and his associates. Charlie, as I've come to know him, was also generous in sharing his insights and doctoral dissertation on Olmsted's formative years.

I'm very grateful, too, that McLaughlin, Beveridge, and colleagues deposited the documents they compiled at American University in Washington, D.C. Olmsted's copious papers reside across town, at the Library of Congress and, until recently, were accessible only on microfilm. I relished being able to also consult the hard-copy files and transcriptions at American University's Special Collections, with the expert and obliging guidance of Susan McElrath, the library's archivist.

In my travels beyond library reading rooms, I depended as Yeoman did on the hospitality and openness of those I met along the way. My travels after Olmsted, from Maryland to Mexico, were too extended for me to thank everyone who helped me. But here's a short list of people to whom I'm especially indebted.

In West Virginia: Orphy Klempa, Frank VanSickle, Steve Novotney, and Greg Walburn, who inflicted me on the unsuspecting crew of the *Roger Keeney*. Warm regards to all those aboard the coal tow for the kindness you showed a clueless supernumerary on our journey down the Ohio River.

In Kentucky, thanks to Marlene McComas, Dan Phelps, the staff at Cassius Clay's White Hall, Lee Carroll, and Griggs Powell, with regrets that my experience of "Blue Nation" ended up on the editing room floor. Also, Emily Bingham and Stephen Reily, gracious hosts and guides to Louisville, home to several of Olmsted's finest parks.

In Tennessee, I'm indebted (again) to Bruce and Laura Lee Dobie, old friends and the finest advertisement I can imagine for Nashville, where Olmsted was filled with despair and I with excellent food and conversation. The same was true when I boarded the *American Queen* in Memphis. Thanks to the steamboat's gracious crew, the free berth offered a feckless writer, and my delightful co-passengers: Jamie and Doug, John and Anna, Christine and Cherry.

In New Orleans, I leaned on a bevy of friends. Stephanie Stokes and Dan Shea helped orient me with an expert guided tour, and scholars Blake Gilpin and Jonathan Earle provided essential historical perspective. Thanks also to new acquaintances: Wayne Baquet, Keith Medley, and Lillie Andrews and her fellow congregants at the Franklin Avenue Baptist Church.

During my onward travel in Louisiana, as I hope I've communicated in this book, Andrew Denton was a very wise and comic companion, and bravely endured what became a muddy and gastronomically challenging adventure. Mate, should you ever choose to return to Donaldsonville, Catahoula, or the Mudfest in Colfax, I'm sure you'll be shouted a round. Thanks also to our absurdly tolerant and generous hosts in Lafayette, Steve and Cherry May.

Texas, before I traveled there for this book, was a state I barely knew and tended to view in stereotype. For advance guidance, I'm indebted to proud native son Mit Spears, keen analyst of all things Lone Star. Also Mimi Swartz, an exceptional reporter and commentator on Texas and a welcoming guide to a traveler lost in the immensity of Houston.

In Austin, special thanks to the inspired historical novelist and Texas know-it-all Stephen Harrigan. In addition to his insights, and excellent taste in Mexican food, he introduced me to Katy and Ted Flato, the most delightful and informative couple I met in San Antonio.

While visiting the Alamo City, I was further blessed by the lively and provocative company and insights of Dr. Bruce Winders, Martin Vasquez (a.k.a. Santa Anna), and Martha Fleitas from the Daughters of the Texas Republic. Historian Catherine Clinton hosted, educated, and steered me to a hospital when I realized I needed it, as well as introducing me to fellow scholar Pat Kelly, an invaluable guide to Civil War–era Texas.

In New Braunfels and other German settlements I visited, thanks to Keva Boardman and the outstanding work of the Sophienburg; Bryden Moon, a generous researcher on settlement in the Hill Country; and Paul Barwick, the rare student and practitioner of landscape architecture I met in my travels.

As I've indicated in the text, Bret Cali lodged, amused, and advised me throughout my long stay in and around Sisterdale. Huge thanks also to Josh Cravey, for his invaluable aid and protective company during a mule ride neither of us enjoyed. I'm also very grateful to Wayne Wright, who let us camp on his spectacular ranch, its caretaker Paulo Dominguez, and other landowners who shared their properties: Cina Alexander Forgason, Charlie Kohl, Coby Knox, and Susan Taylor.

In Eagle Pass and along the Rio Grande, special thanks to Edward and Carmen Roberts and Frank and Kristel Sanchez for warmly welcoming me into your lives, and taking me along on trips to Mexico.

Off the road, I'm grateful to Petra Lent and Emi Gonzalez for German and Spanish translation; to historians Andrew Cohen, Tera Hunter, Jill Lepore, and Wolfgang Hochbruck, for expert consultation on parts of this manuscript; and to Adrian Benepe, Tim Francis, and Ken Wells for weighing in with local knowledge. Thanks also to friends who perused parts of my manuscript with wit and support: Martha Sherrill, Bill Powers, Joel Achenbach, and Michael Lewis.

For hard-core editing, I'm indebted to Angelina Krahn, copy editor extra-ordinaire, and Thera Webb for her invaluable aid with the endnotes and bibliography. Also Mia Council, at Penguin, for expertly (and very patiently) guiding my overdue manuscript to print.

This book would never have come about without Kris Dahl, my literary agent and friend over several decades. She had the wisdom to hook me up, in this project, with the incomparable Scott Moyers, my editor at Penguin: a deep thinker, probing inquisitor, and host of the funnest poker game I've ever played in, even though I lost.

Finally, I was blessed, as I've been with every book I've written, by the input of my mother, Elinor Horwitz, an indefatigable reader and editor. Deep love and gratitude as well to my wife, Geraldine, and our history-averse sons, Nathaniel and Bizu, who gave me counsel and perspective as I lost myself in Olmsted and his era.

NOTE ON SOURCES

Olmsted wrote sixty-four dispatches for the *New-York Daily Times* and ten pieces for the *New York Daily Tribune*, and adapted and expanded on this reporting in three books, as well as *The Cotton Kingdom*, a one-volume compilation of his Southern trilogy.

The extent, time frame, and changing character of this writing pose several challenges for researchers. As I've indicated in the text, Olmsted took pains to conceal or obscure the identities and locations of many of those he met, and at times he narrated events out of sequence to further disguise his whereabouts.

Olmsted's views about the South and slavery also changed in the course of his 1852–4 travels, and even more so in the years after his return, when he put his reporting and conclusions into book form. As a result, episodes described in his newspaper dispatches often appear in quite different form in his books.

In navigating this, I've leaned heavily on the spadework of Beveridge, McLaughlin, and their associates at the Frederick Law Olmsted Papers Project, who painstakingly reconstructed Olmsted's Southern itineraries and matched his newspaper and book writing. A summation can be found in the *Papers of Frederick Law Olmsted*, vol. 2, pages 459–82.

My own itinerary hewed very closely to the path of Olmsted's second Southern trip, as recounted in his *Times* writing; the book-length version of his tour, *A Journey through Texas*; and in his private correspondence. I've also incorporated material on people and places along his route that he wrote about elsewhere: for instance, book passages and letters about New Orleans, which he visited several times in the course of his Southern travels.

NOTES

EPIGRAPH

ix **"I was born for a traveler"**: Frederick Law Olmsted to John Olmsted, Mar. 27, 1856, box 6, reel 5, Olmsted Papers, Library of Congress.

PROLOGUE

3 **"lawless ruffian or 'scape gallows"**: Olmsted, "A Tour in the Southwest," *New-York Daily Times*, Mar. 21, 1854.

4 **"reliable understanding of the sentiments and hopes & fears"**: Frederick Law Olmsted to Frederick Kingsbury, Oct. 17, 1852, in Olmsted, *Papers of Frederick Law Olmsted*, 2:82.

4 **"Should calculate to leave"**: Frederick Law Olmsted to Frederick Kingsbury, Oct. 17, 1852, in Olmsted, *Papers of Frederick Law Olmsted*, 2:82.

4 **"Let the reader understand that he is invited to travel in company with an honest growler"**: Olmsted, *Journey in the Seaboard*, 1:v.

5 **"literary republic"**: Frederick Law Olmsted to John Olmsted, Dec. 9, 1855, in Olmsted, *Papers of Frederick Law Olmsted*, 2:376.

5 **"to promote the mutual acquaintance of the North and South"**: Olmsted, *Journey through Texas*, xiii.

5 **"leading men"**: Frederick Law Olmsted to Charles Eliot Norton, Sept. 19, 1878, Letter File, box 11, Olmsted Documentary Editing Project.

5 **"They are a mischievous class—the dangerous class at the present of the United States"**: Olmsted, "The South," *New-York Daily Times*, Jan. 12, 1854.

5 **"the poor and the rich, the young and the old, the vicious and the virtuous"**: Olmsted, "To the Board of Commissioners of the Central Park," Sept. 9, 1858, in Olmsted, *Papers of Frederick Law Olmsted*, 3:213.

5 **"uniquely candid and realistic picture of the pre–Civil War South"**: Arthur Schlesinger, introduction to *The Cotton Kingdom*, by Frederick Law Olmsted, ix.
    Since Schlesinger's day, Olmsted's reputation as a reliable chronicler of the South has come under attack from scholars of the slave economy. Critics note that Olmsted visited relatively few large plantations and was so intent on demonstrating that slavery was a drag on the South's development that he miscast the institution as a woefully unproductive use of labor, capital, and other resources.
    An example of this argument can be found in Fogel and Engerman, *Time on the Cross*. More recent studies of the slave economy have highlighted the role of torture and control in maximizing profits and productivity, and the centrality of slave-grown cotton to the world's emerging capitalist economy.

Leading exponents of this school include Edward Baptist, Sven Beckert, and Walter Johnson, whose books are cited in the bibliography. For a critique of their work, see Hilt, "Economic History, Historical Analysis, and the 'New History of Capitalism,'" and Olmstead and Rhode, "Cotton, Slavery, and the New History of Capitalism."

6 **"free, rustic . . . tear him a spell"**: Olmsted, *Cotton Kingdom*, 70, 374, 388.

6 **"stamping and gnawing himself"**: Olmsted, *Cotton Kingdom*, 377–8.

6 **"too much whiskey"**: Olmsted, *Journey in the Seaboard*, 1:69.

6 **"mushroom"**: Olmsted, *Journey through Texas*, 6.

6 **"that for the next six months I should actually see *nothing else"***: Olmsted, *Journey through Texas*, 15–16.

7 **"whoever holds to the one must despise the other"**: Lincoln and Delbanco, *Portable Abraham Lincoln*, 73.

7 **"the attachment of nomad tribes to their mode of life"**: Frederick Law Olmsted to Anne Charlotte Lynch, Mar. 12, 1854, in Olmsted, *Papers of Frederick Law Olmsted*, 2:273–4.

CHAPTER 1

11 **"I like her much . . . highly cultivated."**: Footnote to letter to Anne Charlotte Lynch, above, Olmsted, *Papers of Frederick Law Olmsted*, 2:274. Full letter is Frederick Law Olmsted to John Olmsted, May 19, 1853, box 5, reel 4, Olmsted Papers. Library of Congress.

11 **"much of a vagabond"**: Frederick Law Olmsted to Anne Charlotte Lynch, Mar. 12, 1854, in Olmsted, *Papers of Frederick Law Olmsted*, 2:274.

12 **"I remember playing on the grass and looking up at her while she sat sewing under a tree."**: Olmsted, "Autobiographical Fragment A: Passages in the Life of an Unpractical Man," in *Papers of Frederick Law Olmsted*, 1:99. This reminiscence is believed to have been written by Olmsted when he was in his fifties.

12 **"a half grown lad"**: Olmsted, "Autobiographical Fragment B," in *Papers of Frederick Law Olmsted*, 1:115.

12 **"had near them interesting rivers . . . led me to do so"**: Olmsted, "Autobiographical Fragment B," in *Papers of Frederick Law Olmsted*, 1:116.

12 **"the authority of Society, Religion and Commerce"**: Olmsted, "Autobiographical Fragment A: Passages in the Life of an Unpractical Man," in *Papers of Frederick Law Olmsted*, 1:115, 98.

12 **"The happiest recollections of my early life are the walks and rides I had with my father"**: Olmsted, "Autobiographical Fragment A: Passages in the Life of an Unpractical Man," in *Papers of Frederick Law Olmsted*, 1:99.

12 **"silent habits"**: Olmsted, "Autobiographical Fragment A: Passages in the Life of an Unpractical Man," in *Papers of Frederick Law Olmsted*, 1:100.

13 **"really tours . . . compare and criticize"**: Olmsted, "Autobiographical Fragment A: Passages in the Life of an Unpractical Man," in *Papers of Frederick Law Olmsted*, 1:99–100.

13 **"'unconscious' absorption of nature"**: Beveridge, "Olmsted—His Essential Theory," http://www.olmsted.org/the-olmsted-legacy/olmsted-theory-and-design-principles/olmsted-his-essential-theory.

13 **"a superstitious faith in the value of preaching and didactic instruction"**: Olmsted, "Autobiographical Fragment A: Passages in the Life of an Unpractical Man," in *Papers of Frederick Law Olmsted*, 1:100.

13 **"Oh! the depravity of human nature!"**: Olmsted, "Autobiographical Fragment A: Passages in the Life of an Unpractical Man," in *Papers of Frederick Law Olmsted*, 1:109.

13 **"nominally the pupil . . . vagabond life"**: Olmsted, "Autobiographical Fragment B," in *Papers of Frederick Law Olmsted*, 1:117.

13 **"ideal towns":** Kalfus, *Passion of a Public Artist*, 65.

13 **"French Periodicals":** Olmsted, *Papers of Frederick Law Olmsted*, 1:126.

13 **"writing at a desk . . . lamp oil":** Frederick Law Olmsted to Charles Loring Brace, June 22, 1845, box 4, reel 3, Olmsted Papers, Library of Congress.

14 **"truant disposition":** Olmsted, *Papers of Frederick Law Olmsted*, 5:327–31.

14 **"I hope the present . . . have been.":** John Hull Olmsted to Frederick Kingsbury, Mar. 12, 1847, box 5, reel 4, Olmsted Papers, Library of Congress.

14 **"Is it from Mental Causes . . . blood to the head?":** Kalfus, *Passion of a Public Artist*, 55.

14 **"Every time you . . . little brighter.":** Olmsted, *Papers of Frederick Law Olmsted*, 1:284.

15 **"I shouldn't be surprised if he turned out something rather remarkable among men.":** Charles Loring Brace to Frederick Kingsbury, Oct. 1848, in *The Life of Charles Loring Brace, Chiefly Told in His Own Letters*, edited by Emma Brace (New York: Charles Scribner's Sons, 1894), G 1–2.

15 **"fine capabilities . . . getting out manure":** John Hull Olmsted to Frederick Kingsbury, May 1847, Letter File, box 1, Olmsted Documentary Editing Project.

15 **"enthusiast by nature":** Frederick Kingsbury to John Hull Olmsted, May 8, 1847, Letter File, box 1, Olmsted Documentary Editing Project.

16 **"the expressive delicacy of a woman's":** Katharine Prescott Wormeley, cited in Olmsted, *Papers of Frederick Law Olmsted*, 3:113.

16 **"Whimsies had no charm for him.":** Olmsted and Hubbard, *Landscape Architect*, 80.

16 **"flippery":** Frederick Law Olmsted to Charles Loring Brace, Aug. 4, 1844, Letter File, box 1, Olmsted Documentary Editing Project.

16 **"He is dead in love, but with . . . finite & a farmer":** John Hull Olmsted to Frederick Kingsbury, Dec. 17, 1849, Letter File, box 1, Olmsted Documentary Editing Project.

16 **"the greatest genius in the world":** Frederick Law Olmsted to John Olmsted, Aug. 12, 1846, *Papers of Frederick Law Olmsted*, 1:272.

17 **"is worthless till it convert itself into Conduct":** Olmsted's version of this is in his letter to John Hull Olmsted, Dec. 13, 1846, in Olmsted, *Papers of Frederick Law Olmsted*, 1:279, and original Carlyle in footnote, Ibid., 291.

17 **"do the Duty which lies nearest thee":** This is from Carlyle's *Sartor Resartus*, one of Olmsted's favorite books. A discussion of this can be found in Olmsted, *Papers of Frederick Law Olmsted*, 2:269, 11n. Other strong influences on the young Olmsted included Horace Bushnell, a leading New England theologian, and Johann Georg von Zimmermann, a Swiss physician.

17 **"There's a *great* work . . . go about it":** Frederick Law Olmsted to Charles Loring Brace, July 26, 1847, box 5, reel 4, Olmsted Papers, Library of Congress.

17 **"Country Squire . . . voting and of acting:"** Frederick Law Olmsted to Frederick Kingsbury, June 12, 1846, box 4, reel 3, Olmsted Papers, Library of Congress.

17 **"old bach":** Frederick Law Olmsted to Charles Loring Brace, Aug. 4, 1844, in Olmsted, *Papers of Frederick Law Olmsted*, 1:199.

17 **"the most lovely and loveable girl":** Frederick Law Olmsted to Frederick Kingsbury, June 12, 1846, box 4, reel 3, Olmsted Papers, Library of Congress.

17 **"very vigorous and noble correspondence":** John Hull Olmsted to Frederick Kingsbury, Sept. 12, 1851, Letter File, box 1, Olmsted Documentary Editing Project.

17 **"revulsion of feeling . . . very strange":** John Hull Olmsted to Frederick Kingsbury, Sept. 12, 1851, Letter File, box 1, Olmsted Documentary Editing Project.

17 **"Pray tell me . . . purposely":** John Olmsted to Sophie Stevens Hitchcock, Oct. 28, 1851, Letter File, box 1, Olmsted Documentary Editing Project.

18 **"People's Garden" . . . absent in American cities":** Olmsted, *Walks and Talks*, 2:79.

18 **"Everybody at . . . gas and bubbles"**: Frederick Law Olmsted to Charles Loring Brace, Nov. 12, 1850, box 5, reel 4, Olmsted Papers, Library of Congress.

18 **"I don't believe there are any left here to suit us"**: Frederick Law Olmsted to Charles Loring Brace, Jan. 11, 1851, box 5, reel 4, Olmsted Papers, Library of Congress.

18 **"splurgy, thick book . . . affected by Slavery"**: Frederick Law Olmsted to Frederick Kingsbury, Oct. 17, 1852, in Olmsted, *Papers of Frederick Law Olmsted*, 2:82.

18 **"would take in a fugitive slave & shoot a man that was likely to get him"**: Olmsted, *Papers of Frederick Law Olmsted*, 2:83.

18–19 **"I am not a red-hot Abolitionist . . . men on our side"**: Frederick Law Olmsted to Frederick Kingsbury, Oct. 17, 1852, in Olmsted, *Papers of Frederick Law Olmsted*, 2:83.

19 **"seek to be temperate . . . right, or exactly wrong"**: "A Word about Ourselves," *New-York Daily Times*, Sept. 18, 1851.

19 **"urgency"**: Frederick Law Olmsted to Letitia Brace, Jan. 22, 1892, in Olmsted, *Papers of Frederick Law Olmsted*, 9:468.

19 **"honesty of observation and faithfulness of communication"**: Olmsted, "The South," *New-York Daily Times*, Feb. 13, 1854.

19 **"matter of fact . . . be spent"**: Frederick Law Olmsted to Frederick Kingsbury, Oct. 17, 1852, in Olmsted, *Papers of Frederick Law Olmsted*, 2:82.

19 **"The roads never were so bad & lots of people here mud bound"**: Frederick Law Olmsted to John Olmsted, Jan. 10, 1853, in Olmsted, *Papers of Frederick Law Olmsted*, 2:113.

19 **"planters & gentlemen"**: Frederick Law Olmsted to Frederick Kingsbury, Oct. 17, 1852, in Olmsted, *Papers of Frederick Law Olmsted*, 2:82.

19–20 **"You can't imagine . . . that is, talk on music"**: Frederick Law Olmsted to Charles Loring Brace, Feb. 23, 1853, in Olmsted, *Papers of Frederick Law Olmsted*, 2:210.

20 **"merely describing roads and taverns"**: Olmsted, *Papers of Frederick Law Olmsted*, 2:210. On Feb. 16, 1853, Henry Raymond introduced the series to readers as a "complete and dispassionate statement of *facts* concerning the industrial, social, educational, religious and general interests of the Southern States."

20 **"Notwithstanding . . . bodies of slaves"**: Olmsted, "The South," *New-York Daily Times*, Aug. 26, 1853.

20 **"their promised land . . . worn-out"**: Olmsted, "The South," *New-York Daily Times*, Aug. 26, 1853.

20 **"to survey upper . . . slave states"**: Frederick Law Olmsted to Charles Loring Brace, Feb. 8, 1853, in Olmsted, *Papers of Frederick Law Olmsted*, 2:203.

CHAPTER 2

22 **"Scene . . . their dresses."**: Olmsted, *Journey through Texas*, 1–2.

23 **"When we were travelling . . . many more mile stones."**: Frederick Law Olmsted to Charles Loring Brace, Nov. 12, 1850, box 5, reel 4, Olmsted Papers, Library of Congress.

23 **"new and wilder beauties"**: Olmsted, *Journey through Texas*, 2.

23 **"a most comfortless . . . dinginess"**: Olmsted, *Journey through Texas*, 3.

23 **"Cumberland is . . . towns of America"**: Smith, *Chesapeake and Ohio Canal*, 51.

27 **"The rails plunge . . . the locomotive"**: Olmsted, *Journey through Texas*, 4.

28 **"new and . . . old monotony of cultivation"**: Olmsted, *Journey through Texas*, 2, 4.

28 **"At length . . . the great West"**: Olmsted, *Journey through Texas*, 4.

29 **"The brightest . . . dirtiness of Wheeling"**: Olmsted, *Journey through Texas*, 5.

30 **"first class hotel"**: Olmsted, *Journey through Texas*, 4.

30 **"Here are the panting . . . patiently down the tide"**: Olmsted, *Journey through Texas*, 4.

30 **"only ornament"**: Olmsted, *Journey through Texas*, 5.

35–36 **"not a spark of faith . . . than for the lash"**: Olmsted, *Journey in the Back Country*, 281–2.

38 **"Here are the flat-boats"**: Olmsted, *Journey through Texas*, 4.

CHAPTER 3

39 **"well-informed and leading men . . . take his chances"**: Frederick Law Olmsted to Charles Eliot Norton, Sept. 19, 1878, Letter File, box 11, Olmsted Documentary Editing Project.

40 **"There was nothing in his countenance . . . first inquiry"**: Olmsted, *Journey in the Back Country*, 404.

45 **"a noble vessel, having on board every arrangement for comfortable travel"**: Olmsted, *Journey through Texas*, 5.

51 **"the hope of invigorating . . . tent-life"**: Olmsted, *Journey through Texas*, xii.

51 **"owing to the pressure of other occupations"**: Olmsted, *Journey through Texas*, xiii.

51 **"simply that . . . notes"**: Olmsted, *Journey through Texas*, xii.

51 **"From some conversational . . . our daylight"**: Olmsted, *Journey through Texas*, 5.

51 **"Primeval forests . . . reaches"**: Olmsted, *Journey through Texas*, 5.

52 **"charming scenery"**: Olmsted, *Journey through Texas*, 6.

52 **"The towns . . . by the river"**: Olmsted, *Journey through Texas*, 5.

52 **"make shift"**: Olmsted, *Cotton Kingdom*, 108.

52–53 **"Each has its hopes . . . civilization"**: Olmsted, *Journey through Texas*, 5–6.

53 **"the book that nature offered"**: Olmsted, *Journey through Texas*, 5.

61 **"magnificent Kentucky"**: Olmsted, *Journey through Texas*, 10.

CHAPTER 4

62 **"I crave and value . . . formalized ethics"**: Frederick Law Olmsted to Mary Perkins Olmsted, July 29, 1863, in Olmsted, *Papers of Frederick Law Olmsted*, 4:683.

62 **"I repent . . . meandering"**: Frederick Law Olmsted to Charles Loring Brace, Mar. 15, 1887, in Olmsted, *Papers of Frederick Law Olmsted*, 8:369.

63 **"a disgrace to yourself and all your family"**: Fuller, *Book That Changed America*, 18.

63 **"with horror . . . incidents"**: "Letter no. 3256," 5n, http://www.darwinproject.ac.uk /DCP-LETT-3256.

63 **"niggerology"**: Desmond and Moore, *Darwin's Sacred Cause*, 168. For a discussion of Olmsted and Darwin, see pages 308–9.

63 **"hubbub . . . rivers of blood"**: Olmsted, *Journey through Texas*, 7–9.

63 **"We roll swiftly out . . . Kentucky"**: Olmsted, *Journey through Texas*, 10.

65 **"the false . . . other will yield"**: Ham, *The Lie: Evolution*, 30–34.

69 **"Gradually and silently . . . when or how"**: Olmsted, *Walks and Talks*, 2:155.

69 **"mystery and infinity"**: Olmsted, Lecture to Architecture Students, *Papers of Frederick Law Olmsted*, 9:1006.

69 **"cannot be fully given the form of words"**: Frederick Law Olmsted, *Notes on the Plan of Franklin Park and Related Matters* (Boston: Massachusetts Department of Parks, 1886), 106.

69 **"There is hardly . . . my mind"**: Olmsted, *Journey through Texas*, 11.

69 **"We were . . . dislocate the joints"**: Trollope and Smalley, *Domestic Manners*, 192, 335.

69–70 **"the box . . . done by steam?"**: Olmsted, *Journey through Texas*, 11–12.

70 **"soft, smooth sod . . . the largest scale"**: Olmsted, *Journey through Texas*, 10–11.

70 **"this luxuriant beauty . . . unattractive"**: Olmsted, *Journey through Texas*, 10, 14–15.

70 **"The meal was . . . shouted"**: Olmsted, *Journey through Texas*, 15.

71 **"taken alone, with vile coffee"**: Olmsted, *Journey through Texas*, 15–16.

71 **"a very good . . . bread"**: Olmsted, *Journey in the Back Country*, 394.

71 **"It appeared . . . to be"**: Olmsted, *Journey through Texas*, 14.

72 **"half a horse and half an alligator"**: The song is "Hunters of Kentucky," one version of which can be found online at the Library of Congress: https://www.loc.gov/item/amss.as105650.

72 **"as stalwart . . . have fallen"**: Olmsted, *Journey through Texas*, 20.

76 **"The richest beauty . . . the demesne"**: Olmsted, *Journey through Texas*, 11.

76 **"accumulation" . . . taste**: Olmsted, *Journey through Texas*, 11, 16.

76 **"a rare charm . . . quiet"**: Olmsted, *Journey through Texas*, 16.

76 **"ruralistic beauty of a loosely built New England village"**: Frederick Law Olmsted to Mariana Griswold Van Rensselaer, June 11, 1893, in Olmsted, *Papers of Frederick Law Olmsted*, 9:644.

76 **"commonplace . . . prosaic"**: Olmsted, *Papers of Frederick Law Olmsted*, 9:153.

77 **"Were it only free . . . thoughts behind"**: Olmsted, *Journey through Texas*, 18.

77 **"peculiar institution"**: Olmsted, "The South," *New-York Daily Times*, Feb. 13, 1854.

77–78 **"Well, I ain't . . . enemies like him"**: Olmsted, *Journey through Texas*, 12–13.

78 **"the overthrow of slavery by home-action"**: Clay, *Life of Cassius Marcellus Clay*, 75.

78 **"I wanted . . . force"**: Clay, *Life of Cassius Marcellus Clay*, 81. For more on Clay's extraordinary career, see Smiley, *Lion of White Hall: The Life of Cassius M. Clay*, and Blumenthal, *The Political Life of Abraham Lincoln*, vol. 2.

78 **"cranks"**: Clay, *Life of Cassius Marcellus Clay*, 187.

78 **"These are better arguments than invective"**: Cassius Clay to Salmon Chase, Dec. 21, 1842, cited in Foner, *Free Soil*, 63.

78 **"I like Cassius M. Clay and would vote to make him Vice President at least"**: Frederick Law Olmsted to John Olmsted, July 1, 1846, box 4, reel 3, Olmsted Papers, Library of Congress.

78 **"one-idea-ism"**: Frederick Law Olmsted to Charles Loring Brace, Sept. 20, 1847, in Olmsted, *Papers of Frederick Law Olmsted*, 1:301.

79 **"a letter from C.M. Clay"**: Frederick Law Olmsted to Charles Loring Brace, Dec. 1, 1853, in Olmsted, *Papers of Frederick Law Olmsted*, 2:232.

79 **"slave name"**: Remnick, *King of the World*, 305.

80 **"therefore I considered myself free to love anybody"**: Mullins and Mullins, *History of White Hall*, 70.

81 **"Lion of White Hall . . . general exhaustion"**: "Death Has Gripped Gen. Cassius Clay," *Atlanta Constitution*, July 23, 1903.

81 **"make better bedfellows than voters"**: Mullins and Mullins, *History of White Hall*, 142–3.

81 **"I do not set myself . . . evil is all I aspire to"**: Cassius Clay to John G. Fee, 1855, cited in Mullins and Mullins, *History of White Hall*, 39.

CHAPTER 5

82 **"very reluctantly"**: Olmsted, *Journey through Texas*, 22.

82 **"Were laid . . . disappointing"**: Frederick Law Olmsted to Charles Loring Brace, Dec. 1, 1853, in Olmsted, *Papers of Frederick Law Olmsted*, 2:232.

82 **"fraternizing loudly . . . grimly applied"**: Olmsted, *Journey through Texas*, 28.

82–83 **"For miles . . . turn back again"**: Olmsted, *Journey through Texas*, 30.

83 **"sat five . . . be off"**: Olmsted, *Journey through Texas*, 37.

83 **"pen-sickness"**: Olmsted, *Papers of Frederick Law Olmsted*, 5:54.

83 **"entirely interrupts my digestion . . . eyes twitch"**: Frederick Law Olmsted to Edwin Godkin, Dec. 25, 1863, in Olmsted, *Papers of Frederick Law Olmsted*, 5:160.

83 **"In a steamboat cabin . . . this cursedly little people"**: Frederick Law Olmsted to Charles Loring Brace, Dec. 1, 1853, in Olmsted, *Papers of Frederick Law Olmsted*, 2:235–6.

83 **"reliable understanding . . . gentlemen"**: Frederick Law Olmsted to Frederick Kingsbury, Oct. 17, 1852, in Olmsted, *Papers of Frederick Law Olmsted*, 2:84.

83 **"I trust in . . . find their end"**: Olmsted, "The South," *New-York Daily Times*, Feb. 16, 1853.

83 **"the condition . . . systems"**: Olmsted, "The South," *New-York Daily Times*, Mar. 30, 1853.

84 **"so offensive to a Northern man"**: Olmsted, *Journey through Texas*, 18.

84 **"These fine fellows . . . very repugnant"**: Olmsted, *Journey through Texas*, 18.

84 **"A good specimen of the first class gentleman of the South"**: Frederick Law Olmsted to Charles Loring Brace, Dec. 1, 1853, in Olmsted, *Papers of Frederick Law Olmsted*, 2:232. Allison graduated from Yale in 1847, studied law in Nashville, and was described upon his early death from tuberculosis in 1858 as having been "handsome and manly," "bold and fearless in the avowal of his opinions," and possessed of a "high literary and legal" mind. Obituary, *Nashville Union & Democrat*, Apr. 6, 1858, https://www.newspapers.com/newspage/83322677/.

84 **"reading secretly"**: Frederick Law Olmsted to Charles Loring Brace, Dec. 1, 1853, in Olmsted, *Papers of Frederick Law Olmsted*, 2:234.

84 **"fighting man . . . betting"**: Frederick Law Olmsted to Charles Loring Brace, Dec. 1, 1853, in Olmsted, *Papers of Frederick Law Olmsted*, 2:232.

84 **"happy gentlemanly . . . moderately"**: Frederick Law Olmsted to Charles Loring Brace, Dec. 1, 1853, in Olmsted, *Papers of Frederick Law Olmsted*, 2:234.

84 **"a devil incarnate . . . law than the Constitution"**: Frederick Law Olmsted to Charles Loring Brace, Dec. 1, 1853, in Olmsted, *Papers of Frederick Law Olmsted*, 2:233.

84–85 **"Allison . . . self interest"**: Frederick Law Olmsted to Charles Loring Brace, Dec. 1, 1853, in Olmsted, *Papers of Frederick Law Olmsted*, 2:235.

85 **"Allison said they . . . get possession"**: Frederick Law Olmsted to Charles Loring Brace, Dec. 1, 1853, in Olmsted, *Papers of Frederick Law Olmsted*, 2:233.

85 **"Allison and other gentlemen . . . the end of their track"**: Frederick Law Olmsted to Charles Loring Brace, Dec. 1, 1853, in Olmsted, *Papers of Frederick Law Olmsted*, 2:233–6.

85 **"They do not seem to have a fundamental sense of right"**: Frederick Law Olmsted to Charles Loring Brace, Dec. 1, 1853, in Olmsted, *Papers of Frederick Law Olmsted*, 2:235.

85–86 **"He is, in fact . . . wisdom & power"**: Frederick Law Olmsted to Charles Loring Brace, Dec. 1, 1853, in Olmsted, *Papers of Frederick Law Olmsted*, 2:233–4. For a discussion of mudsill, see Faust, *James Henry Hammond and the Old South: A Design for Mastery*, 346–7.

86 **"no gentlemen . . . well bred"**: Frederick Law Olmsted to Charles Loring Brace, Dec. 1, 1853, in Olmsted, *Papers of Frederick Law Olmsted*, 2:234.

86 **"I tried to show . . . very melancholy"**: Frederick Law Olmsted to Charles Loring Brace, Dec. 1, 1853, in Olmsted, *Papers of Frederick Law Olmsted*, 2:234.

86 **"a big murdering Baron"**: Frederick Law Olmsted to John Olmsted, in Olmsted, *Papers of Frederick Law Olmsted*, 1:352.

86 **"general loathing of . . . rules and conventionalisms"**: Frederick Law Olmsted to Charles Loring Brace, Dec. 1, 1853, in Olmsted, *Papers of Frederick Law Olmsted*, 2:235, 234.

86–87 "What does the success of our Democratic nationality amount to—and what is to be-come of us": Frederick Law Olmsted to Charles Loring Brace, Dec. 1, 1853, in Olmsted, *Papers of Frederick Law Olmsted*, 2:234.

87 "blundering": Frederick Law Olmsted to Charles Loring Brace, Dec. 1, 1853, in Olmsted, *Papers of Frederick Law Olmsted*, 2:235.

87 "I must be either an Aristocrat . . . to elevate themselves": Frederick Law Olmsted to Charles Loring Brace, Dec. 1, 1853, in Olmsted, *Papers of Frederick Law Olmsted*, 2:234–5.

87 "The poor need an education . . . and the rowdy": Frederick Law Olmsted to Charles Loring Brace, Dec. 1, 1853, in Olmsted, *Papers of Frederick Law Olmsted*, 2:235–6.

87 "The streets are . . . or wealth": Olmsted, *Journey through Texas*, 35–6.

88 "one rare national ornament . . . in a chocolate ground": Olmsted, *Journey through Texas*, 36.

88 "Better laws must surely come from so firm and fit a senate house": Olmsted, *Journey through Texas*, 36.

88–89 "Carmack's Pledge . . . the black wench": Will T. Hale and Dixon L. Merritt, *A History of Tennessee and Tennesseans: The Leaders and Representative Men in Commerce, Industry and Modern Activities*, vol. 2 (Chicago: Lewis Publishing, 1913), 506; "demon rum" cited in William Majors, *Editorial Wild Oats* (Macon, GA: Mercer University Press, 1984), 162; and for Carmack and Wells, see Tennessee Encyclopedia entry, s.v. "Memphis Free Speech," by Kenneth W. Goings, "Memphis Free Speech," Tennessee Encyclopedia, last updated Mar. 1, 2018, https://tennesseeencyclopedia.net/entries/memphis-free-speech/.

90 "intensity of personal pride": Olmsted, *Journey in the Back Country*, 414–5.

90 "He never values life or aught else more than he does his honor" Olmsted, "The South," *New-York Daily Times*, Jan. 12, 1854.

90 "very generally": Frederick Law Olmsted to Charles Loring Brace, Dec. 1, 1853, in Olmsted, *Papers of Frederick Law Olmsted*, 2:233.

90 "chivalric . . . honor & morality": Frederick Law Olmsted to Charles Loring Brace, Dec. 1, 1853, in Olmsted, *Papers of Frederick Law Olmsted*, 2:232, 234.

90 "What a man shows . . . more consequence": Olmsted, *Journey in the Back County*, 415.

91 "uncontrolled authority": Olmsted, "The South," *New-York Daily Times*, Jan. 12, 1854.

91 "always in readiness . . . sufficient provocation": Olmsted, introduction to *The Englishman in Kansas*, in Olmsted, *Papers of Frederick Law Olmsted*, 2:407.

91 "They are brave, . . . hurting cotton prices": Olmsted, "The South," *New-York Daily Times*, Jan. 12, 1854.

91 "dangerous class": Olmsted, "The South," *New-York Daily Times*, Jan. 12, 1854.

91–92 "base poltroon . . . tale-bearer": Robert Brammer, "Frontier Racing and Injured Pride: The Duel Between Andrew Jackson and Charles Dickinson," *In Custodia Legis* (blog), Apr. 15, 2015, Library of Congress, https://blogs.loc.gov/law/2015/04/frontier-racing-and-injured-pride-the-duel-between-andrew-jackson-and-charles-dickinson/.

97 "shamefully cruel, selfish . . . destroy it": Olmsted, "The South," *New-York Daily Times*, Feb. 13, 1854.

97–99 "by what means can we rightly do . . . laboring class of people": Olmsted, "The South," *New-York Daily Times*, Feb. 13, 1854.

99 "that the rich . . . of Democracy": Olmsted, "The South," *New-York Daily Times*, Jan. 12, 1854.

99 "the highest good, of the whole community": Olmsted, "The South," *New-York Daily Times*, Feb. 13, 1854.

99 "writing in a steamboat, fast aground": Olmsted, "The South," *New-York Daily Times*, Jan. 26, 1854.

99 **"public parks and gardens"**: Olmsted, "The South," *New-York Daily Times*, Jan. 12, 1854.

99 **"mental & moral capital"**: Frederick Law Olmsted to Charles Loring Brace, Dec. 1, 1853, in Olmsted, *Papers of Frederick Law Olmsted*, 2:235.

CHAPTER 6

101 **"a first-class" . . . fine cuisine**: Olmsted, *Journey through Texas*, 37.

102 **"frequently broke up only at dawn of day"**: Olmsted, *Journey through Texas*, 39.

103 **"long sleeps . . . once in a lifetime"**: Olmsted, *Journey through Texas*, 39.

104 **"Nothing can be . . . entirely prospective one"**: Olmsted, *Journey through Texas*, 39–41.

104 **"Compared with . . . great metropolis"**: Olmsted, *Journey through Texas*, 40.

109 **"A substantial . . . and ready servants"**: Olmsted, *Journey through Texas*, 37–40.

110 **"Without a single exception the most licentious spot that I ever saw"**: William Richardson, 1816, quoted on historical plaque at Natchez.

110 **"dreadful riots . . . torn off"**: Capt. J. E. Alexander, 1833, quoted on historic plaque at Natchez.

112 **"I was amused to recognize . . . shamed all my previous conceptions of the appearance of the greatest of rivers"**: Olmsted, *Journey in the Back Country*, 35–8.

112 **"in the vast obscurity"**: Olmsted, *Journey in the Back Country*, 37.

114 **"Labourers are being . . . along together, going South"**: Olmsted, *Cotton Kingdom*, 87, 356.

114 **"dressed up" . . . their muscles**: Isaac Steer, quoted in James Mellon, *Bullwhip Days*, 171.

115 **"On both, the hands . . . quarters"**: Olmsted, *Journey through Texas*, 42.

117 **"There were a dozen or . . . sullen motion"**: Olmsted, *Journey through Texas*, 42.

118 **"full hand"**: Johnson, *River of Dark Dreams*, 153–4.

118 **"counted as half-hands"**: Olmsted, *Journey in the Back Country*, 47.

118 **"quarter-hands"**: Johnson, *River of Dark Dreams*, 154.

118 **"her sore hands cracked open and bled**: Tanner, *Chained to the Land*, 6.

119 **"were on the exact level of the water"**: Olmsted, *Journey through Texas*, 37.

119 **"floating palaces . . . and the smokestacks"**: Johnson, *River of Dark Dreams*, 93.

119 **"each taking a different part, and carrying it on with great spirit and independence"**: Olmsted, *Journey in the Seaboard*, 2:195–6.

119 **"had no handcuffs small enough for them"**: Olmsted, *Journey in the Seaboard*, 2:207.

120 **"every face and head a shapeless wad of loose raw cotton"**: Twain, *Life on the Mississippi*, 122.

120 **"my darling, my pride, my glory, my *all*"**: Powers, *Mark Twain: A Life*, 88.

120 **"Possibly I know now what the soldier feels when a bullet crashes through his heart"**: Mark Twain, *Mark Twain's Own Autobiography: The Chapters from the North American Review*, edited by Michael J. Kiskis, 2nd ed. (Madison: University of Wisconsin Press, 2010), 246.

120 **"outworn by grief"**: "Obituary," Associated Press, Apr. 22, 1910.

120 **"If we meet . . ."**: Powers, *Mark Twain: A Life*, 627.

CHAPTER 7

122 **"Moving constantly southward, . . . golden oranges"**: Olmsted, *Journey through Texas*, 39–40.

122 **"We were in the absolute South now—no modifications, no compromises, no halfway measures"**: Twain, *Life on the Mississippi*, 221.

122 **"Bayou Clap"**: "Bayou Sara–The Town and Stream," USGenWeb Archives Project, http://files.usgwarchives.net/la/westfeliciana/history/bsarah.txt.

123 **"residences indicative of . . . chandeliers of fragrance"**: Olmsted, *Journey in the Back Country*, 13–15.

123 **"Fat and pockets full of money"**: Davis, "Bennet H. Barrow," 434.

123 **"pleasure grounds"**: "Rosedown Plantation," National Historic Landmark Nomination, United States Department of the Interior, National Park Service, 6.

124 **"long-headed"**: Henry Whitney Bellows, quoted in Olmsted, *Papers of Frederick Law Olmsted*, 4:89.

124 **"distant effects"**: Frederick Law Olmsted to Frederick Law Olmsted Jr., Sept. 5, 1890, in Olmsted, *Papers of Frederick Law Olmsted*, 9:204.

125 **"big bugs"**: Olmsted, *Journey in the Back Country*, 12.

125 **"We returned home . . . fine garden"**: "Rosedown Plantation," National Historic Landmark Nomination, 29–31.

125 **"the bloodiest prison in the South"**: From display in Angola Museum.

126 **"a big plantation in days gone by"**: Quoted in the documentary film *Angola for Life*, Atlantic Documentaries, Jeffrey Goldberg, reporter, https://www.theatlantic.com/video/index/404305/angola-prison-documentary/.

128 **"create a positive group inside [the prison] that I can control"**: Atlantic Documentaries, *Angola for Life*.

130 **"O. K. Allen, was so pliant he once signed a leaf that blew through his office window and onto his desk"**: White, *Kingfish*, 150.

130–1 **"None shall be too big . . . favored few"**: Huey P. Long, "Share Our Wealth," https://www.americanrhetoric.com/speeches/hueyplongshare.htm.

131 **"elites . . . watch out for the lying newspapers!"**: White, *Kingfish*, 4, 194, 32, 213.

131 **"I'll eat this for you. You're too fat already."**: White, *Kingfish*, 185.

131 **"I can take this Roosevelt . . . knows it"**: White, *Kingfish*, 241.

131 **"When I took the oath of office, I didn't take any vow of poverty"**: White, *Kingfish*, 270.

132 **"is if I'm caught in bed with either a dead girl or a live boy"**: Sean Sullivan, "The Greatest Quotes of Edwin Edwards," *Washington Post*, Mar. 17, 2014.

132 **"People say, well, they're all crooks . . . experienced one"**: Gloria Borger, Kevin Bohn, and Brian Rokus, "Fresh Act: 87-Year-Old Felon Wants Back in Congress," CNN Politics, Sept. 19, 2014, https://www.cnn.com/2014/09/18/politics/edwin-edwards-gloria-borger/index.html.

132 **"History, like nature, . . . backward"**: Cited in Jon Meacham, "Southern Discomfort," *New York Times*, Apr. 10, 2010.

133 **"It is the most complete gambling"**: Frederick Law Olmsted to Frederick Kingsbury, Feb. 26, 1853, in Olmsted, *Papers of Frederick Law Olmsted*, 2:213.

134 **"Nearly every man, woman and child . . . hours a day"**: Olmsted, *Cotton Kingdom*, 255.

134 **"The severity of the labour . . . a kind of frolic"**: Olmsted, *Cotton Kingdom*, 255, 329.

134–5 **"a large number of 'used-up hands'—slaves, sore and crippled, or invalided for some cause"**: Olmsted, *Cotton Kingdom*, 329.

135 **"If I was free, I would go to . . . get me a wife"**: Olmsted, *Cotton Kingdom*, 260–2.

135 **"until death or distance do you part"**: Hunter, *Bound in Wedlock*, 6, 26.

CHAPTER 8

138 **"I doubt there is a . . . codes of the citizens"**: Olmsted, *Cotton Kingdom*, 235.

138 **"French noises . . . pursuing Yankees"**: Olmsted, *Journey in the Seaboard*, 2:227–9.

138 "I have rarely, . . . women of Paris": Olmsted, *Journey in the Seaboard*, 2:243.

138–9 "grades of the colored people . . . mulatto": Olmsted, *Journey in the Seaboard*, 2:231; and Johnson, "The Slave Trader," 13–38. See also Johnson, *Soul by Soul*, 256, 10n.

139 "Bone and . . . New York clothing store": Olmsted, *Journey in the Seaboard*, 2:233, 222.

139 "plantation clothing": *Purchased Lives: New Orleans and the Domestic Slave Trade, 1808–1865* (New Orleans: The Historic New Orleans Collection, 2015), 14–15.

139 "Dam'd if they ain't just the best gang o' cotton-hands ever I see": Olmsted, *Journey in the Seaboard*, 2:233.

139 "fancy" girls: For discussion of "fancy" trade, see Johnson, *Soul by Soul*, 113–4, and Clark, *Strange History*, 164.

139 "*plaçage*": The most comprehensive study of *plaçage* is *The Strange History of the American Quadroon: Free Women of Color in the Revolutionary Atlantic World* by Emily Clark. She observes that the practice that became known as *plaçage* was mostly limited to free women of color from Haiti, and their daughters, who greatly outnumbered free men of color in New Orleans in the early 1800s.

139 "make such arrangements . . . were married": Olmsted, *Journey in the Seaboard*, 2:244.

139 "It is much cheaper . . . and saving in her habits": Olmsted, *Journey in the Seaboard*, 2:248.

140 "strong attachments": Olmsted, *Journey in the Seaboard*, 2:246.

140 "shrink from marriage . . . and virtue": Olmsted, *Journey in the Seaboard*, 2:249–51.

140 "disease . . . New York": Olmsted, *Journey in the Seaboard*, 2:253.

140 "quadroon ball": For a discussion of so-called quadroon balls, see Clark, *Strange History*, 172–81.

140 "Ladies, gratis . . . in attendance": Olmsted, *Journey in the Seaboard*, 2:245.

142 "We are men. Treat us as such": For a discussion of the petition and delegates' meeting with Lincoln, see Hirsch and Logsdon, *Creole New Orleans*, 224–6.

144 "You could feed all the pure whites and pure blacks in Louisiana with a cup of beans and half a cup of rice": There are several variations of this quote, though no proof it can be traced to Huey Long. See discussion at "Revisiting Descriptors Again," Louisiana Historic and Cultural Vistas, May 23, 2015, http://www.mylhcv.com/revisiting-descriptors-again/.

145–6 "by a loud chorus . . . wholly unintellectual": Olmsted, *Cotton Kingdom*, 240–7.

151 "Very soon, our Northern . . . good will": Frederick Law Olmsted to John Charles Olmsted, Mar. 13, 1894, in Olmsted, *Papers of Frederick Law Olmsted*, 9:755.

151 "gracefully undulating greensward": Frederick Law Olmsted to Thomas H. Sherley, Aug. 26, 1891, in Olmsted, *Papers of Frederick Law Olmsted*, 9:380.

151 "assimilate": Olmsted, "The South," *New-York Daily Times*, Jan. 12, 1854.

151 "provided for the use of negroes": Burnette, *Parks for the People!*, 103.

151 "gregarious recreation": Beveridge and Rocheleau, *Designing the American Landscape*, 96.

152 "moving all the time": "Segregation in Audubon Park," NOLA Parks History, May 18, 2014, Internet Archive, https://web.archive.org/web/20160810114735/http://www.nolaparkshistory.org/category/segregation-of-new-orleans-parks/.

152 "strenuous life": "Strenuous life" is quoted on page 25 in Nels Abrams's thesis "The Making of Audubon Park: Competing Ideologies for Public Space," which has an excellent discussion of the change in park philosophy.

152 "soothing rural influences": Frederick Law Olmsted to Paul Dana, Dec. 22, 1890, Olmsted, *Papers of Frederick Law Olmsted*, 8:257.

152 **"A man moving fast cannot enjoy scenery contemplatively"**: Frederick Law Olmsted to Mariana Griswold Van Rensselaer, June 18, 1893, in Olmsted, *Papers of Frederick Law Olmsted*, 9:654.

CHAPTER 9

157 **"My other grandma got branded with hot irons"**: Silas Spotfore, quoted in Tanner, *Chained to the Land*, 16.

158 **"apparatus constructed in accordance with the best scientific knowledge"**: Olmsted, *Cotton Kingdom*, 257.

158 **"divisions"**: Olmsted, *Cotton Kingdom*, 254.

158 **"seemed to be better disciplined . . . companies in New England"**: Olmsted, *Cotton Kingdom*, 248–9.

158 **"converting the swamps of . . . the cholera"**: Olmsted, *Cotton Kingdom*, 253.

158 **"better class . . . immense"**: Olmsted, *Cotton Kingdom*, 256–7.

161 **"Cajun . . . Louisiana"**: For more on this history, see Richard, *History of the Acadians of Louisiana*.

161–2 **"Italian-French . . . American"**: Olmsted, *Cotton Kingdom*, 317–8, 325, 323.

162 **"This mixture . . . deal of amusing labor"** Olmsted, *Journey through Texas*, 395. Olmsted added further confusion by referring to Acadians, at times, as "*habitants*" or "poor white French Creoles." Olmsted, *Journey in the Seaboard*, 342.

162 **"a dozen small . . . shooting, fishing, and play"**: Olmsted, *Journey in the Seaboard*, 2:332.

162 **"habitually . . . dissolute"**: Olmsted, *Cotton Kingdom*, 328.

162 **"trodden clay . . . *cremeries* of Paris"**: Olmsted, *Cotton Kingdom*, 322–4.

162 **"The good-nature of the people was an incessant astonishment"**: Olmsted, *Cotton Kingdom*, 317.

162 **"very wet and unattractive . . . 'eye-breaker'"**: Olmsted, *Cotton Kingdom*, 324–5.

162 **"frequent and embarrassing forks . . . long ones, too"**: Olmsted, *Journey through Texas*, 393–4.

164 **"alligator-holes . . . and angry jaws"**: Olmsted, *Cotton Kingdom*, 391–2.

CHAPTER 10

168 **"so wet and bad . . . scarcely used"**: Olmsted, *Journey through Texas*, 43.

168 **"barbarous"**: Olmsted, *Journey through Texas*, 44.

168 **"was a good deal bigger fellow than I, and also carried a bigger knife"**: Olmsted, *Cotton Kingdom*, 271.

168 **"exceedingly offensive smell . . . elsewhere together"**: Olmsted, *Journey in the Seaboard*, 263–8, and *Cotton Kingdom*, 271–5.

169 **"A few white people—men, women, and children—were lying here and there, among the negroes"**: Olmsted, *Cotton Kingdom*, 273.

169 **"Cases . . . badly used"**: Olmsted, *Cotton Kingdom*, 276.

169 **"No coloured woman . . . to convict him"**: Olmsted, *Cotton Kingdom*, 277–8.

169 **"the severest corporeal punishment of a negro that I witnessed at the South"**: Olmsted, *Journey in the Back Country*, 83.

169 **"the most profitable estate that I visited"**: Olmsted, *Cotton Kingdom*, 445. Olmsted gave slightly varying accounts of his visit to the Calhoun estate in two *Times* dispatches and two of his books, *Journey in the Back Country* and *Cotton Kingdom*. For discussion of how the plantations he described correspond to Calhoun's, see Olmsted, *Papers of Frederick*

Law Olmsted, 2:222–3. For Calhoun's ranking among Southern slaveholders, see http://freepages.genealogy.rootsweb.ancestry.com/~ajac/biggest16.htm.

170 **"healthful estate"**: Olmsted, "The South," *New-York Daily Times*, Nov. 21, 1853. For more on the Calhouns and their Alabama connections, see Nancy Rohr, "The O'Shaughnessy Legacy in Huntsville," http://huntsvillehistorycollection.org/hh/hhpics/pdf/hhr/Volume_21_2_Jan-94.pdf.

170 **"The main advantage . . . painful to witness"**: Olmsted, "The South," *New-York Daily Times*, Nov. 21, 1853.

170 **"Considering that I was a . . . of slavery"**: Olmsted, *Cotton Kingdom*, 452.

170 **"young gentleman"**: Olmsted, *Cotton Kingdom*, 455.

170–1 **"Sam's Sall . . . skulking sailor"**: Olmsted, "The South," *New-York Daily Times*, Nov. 21, 1853.

171 **"pull up your clothes . . . groveling, and screaming"**: Olmsted, *Journey in the Back Country*, 85–86.

171 **"could not wait to see the end"**: Olmsted, "The South," *New-York Daily Times*, Nov. 21, 1853.

171 **"Choking, sobbing, spasmodic groans only were heard"**: Olmsted, *Cotton Kingdom*, 455.

171 **"Olmsted had seen . . . on large estates."**: Olmsted, *Cotton Kingdom*, 455.

171–2 **As the overseer explained . . . "lives in the service of their masters"**: Olmsted, "The South," *New-York Daily Times*, Nov. 21, 1853.

172 **Another woman . . . "chronic complaints"**: Olmsted, "The South," *New-York Daily Times*, Nov. 26, 1853.

172 **Slaves lived in "well built . . . fugitive in"**: Olmsted, "The South," *New-York Daily Times*, Nov. 21, 1853.

173 **"Well he was my Legree"**: "Model for Mrs. Stowe," *Washington Post*, July 19, 1896.

173 **"rather effeminate . . . the Legree type"**: "About Uncle Tom's Cabin," *Washington Post*, Aug. 31, 1896.

173–4 **"the *higher classes* of the Continent . . . utterly unfit themselves for work"**: Olmsted, "The South," *New-York Daily Times*, Nov. 26, 1853.

174 **"shanty of the meanest description"**: Olmsted, "The South," *New-York Daily Times*, Nov. 21, 1853. Olmsted referred only to "poor whites within a few miles" who "would always sell liquor to the negroes" and were "spoken of with anger by the overseers." But Calhoun's eviction of the widow was well documented in a case that went to the Louisiana Supreme Court, *Antoinette Boullard v. Meredith Calhoun*, 1858. For more see Kathryn Page, "Defiant Women and the Supreme Court of Louisiana in the Nineteenth Century," in *A Law unto Itself?: Essays in the New Louisiana Legal History*, ed. Warren M. Billings and Mark F. Fernandez (Baton Rouge: Louisiana State University Press, 2001).

174 **"their whole future was irretrievably blighted"**: Olmsted, "The South," *New-York Daily Times*, Nov. 26, 1853.

174 **"Expressly designed by . . . a worse life than before"**: Olmsted, "The South," *New-York Daily Times*, Nov. 26, 1853.

174 **"conceit, avarice, and folly"**: Olmsted, *Journey in the Back Country*, iii.

174 **"red hot" abolitionism:** Frederick Law Olmsted to Frederick Kingsbury, Feb. 26, 1853, in Olmsted, *Papers of Frederick Law Olmsted*, 2:213.

174 **"mere setting free of . . . aggravates it"**: Olmsted, *Journey in the Back Country*, iii.

174 **At the start of . . . "slavery & freedom"**: Frederick Law Olmsted to Henry Whitney Bellows, June 1, 1861, in Olmsted, *Papers of Frederick Law Olmsted*, 4:118.

174 **he told a government . . . "assimilating" freedmen:** Olmsted testimony before the

Special Inquiry Commission, Apr. 22, 1863, in Olmsted, *Papers of Frederick Law Olmsted*, 4:610–1.

174–5   **He also warned ... "nominally submissive" whites:** Frederick Law Olmsted to Charles Eliot Norton, Apr. 30, 1863, in Olmsted, *Papers of Frederick Law Olmsted*, 4:619.

176   **"delicate":** Olmsted, *Cotton Kingdom*, 456.

177   **"poor little Willie":** Nancy M. Rohr, *An Alabama School Girl in Paris* (Huntsville, AL: Silver Threads Publishing, 2006), 164.

177   **These acts "endeared [him] to the negroes" ... for freedmen:** Keith, *Colfax Massacre*, 78. Keith's book is one of several invaluable secondary sources on Colfax. The most thorough book-length study, including keen legal analysis, is Charles Lane, *The Day Freedom Died*. Nicholas Lemann's excellent *Redemption* sets Colfax in the context of Reconstruction's failure. The legal and political fallout from Colfax is also discussed in Eric Foner's magisterial *Reconstruction: America's Unfinished Revolution, 1863–1877*. Another fine scholarly treatment is James Hogue, "The 1873 Battle of Colfax: Paramilitarism and Counterrevolution in Louisiana," http://www.libertychapelcemetery.org/files/hogue-colfax.pdf.

    Among primary sources, extensive testimony and documents related to Colfax can be found in the Congressional Record, including House Miscellaneous Documents, Forty-Second Congress, second session, "Testimony Taken by the Select Committee to Investigate Affairs in the State of Louisiana," and House Reports, Forty-Third Congress, second session, "Conditions of the South."

177   **"New Africa ... Calhoun's Negro Quarter of Colfax":** Keith, *Colfax Massacre*, 78, and Lane, *The Day Freedom Died*, 43.

178   **"soirées ... from him":** Mary Calhoun to "My Dear Husband," Jan. 1861, courtesy of Mary Bonnette, Colfax, LA.

178   **"tame submission to the most desolating war of the negro upon us":** Lemann, *Redemption*, 24. For more on the *Caucasian*, which can be read online, see "About the Caucasian. (Alexandria, La.) 1874–1875," Chronicling America: Historic American Newspapers, Library of Congress, http://chroniclingamerica.loc.gov/lccn/sn86053765/.

178   **"they intended killing ... a new breed":** Keith, *Colfax Massacre*, 90.

179   **"the Rebels":** Lemann, *Redemption*, 14.

181   **"shot them down like dogs ... without mercy":** "A History of the Colfax Riot," *Colfax Chronicle*, May 25, 1912.

181   **"In a war of the races ... must prevail":** George Stafford, *Louisiana Democrat*, May 14, 1873, cited in Lane, *The Day Freedom Died*, 133.

182   **"You'll see plenty of dead beeves":** Lane, *The Day Freedom Died*, 108.

182   **"Dogs were eating him":** Keith, *Colfax Massacre*, 110.

182   **"flattened by blows from a gun":** Keith, *Colfax Massacre*, 112. For a detailed analysis of casualties at Colfax, see Lane, *The Day Freedom Died*, 265–6.

182   **"a butchery ... unwhipped of justice":** Ulysses S. Grant, Special Message to the Senate, Jan. 13, 1875, American Presidency Project, UC Santa Barbara, https://www.presidency.ucsb.edu/node/204094.

182   **"to injure, oppress, threaten, or intimidate":** Charles Lane, "To Keep and Bear Arms," *Washington Post*, Mar. 22, 2008, http://www.washingtonpost.com/wp-dyn/content/article/2008/03/21/AR2008032102540.html.

182   **"No way can be found in ... is stronger than law":** Grant, Special Message. For more on Grant and Louisiana, see Chernow, *Grant*, 758–63.

183   **The unveiling was attended ... "understanding between the races":** "Colfax Riot Monument Unveiled," *Colfax Chronicle*, Apr. 16, 1921, Chronicling America: Historic American Newspapers, Library of Congress, http://chroniclingamerica.loc.gov/lccn/sn88064176/1921-04-16/ed-1/seq-2/.

185 **"Learning for the sake of learning . . . racial and social progress"**: "Your Mail," *Alexandria Daily Town Talk*, Feb. 4, 2007.

186 **"We got tight and he got sober"**: Keith, *Colfax Massacre*, 130.

186 **"a remarkably eccentric and noted character . . . faults from human eyes"**: "Obituary," *Colfax Chronicle*, Jan. 17, 1891.

CHAPTER 11

187 **"De clay must be ya bed."**: Tanner, *Chained to the Land*, 103.

187 **"When the wheels sunk . . . requested to get out and walk"**: Olmsted, *Cotton Kingdom*, 129.

187 **"mud bound"**: Frederick Law Olmsted to John Olmsted, Jan. 10, 1853, in Olmsted, *Papers of Frederick Law Olmsted*, 2:113.

187 **On another ride, in Mississippi . . . "entered the coach body"**: Olmsted, *Cotton Kingdom*, 343–4.

188 **"could hardly be . . . along before"**: Olmsted, *Cotton Kingdom*, 284.

188 **"glum, determined . . . mud-bedraggled"**: Olmsted, "A Tour in the Southwest," *New-York Daily Times*, Mar. 6, 1854.

199 **"The past is never dead. It's not even past."**: William Faulkner, *Requiem for a Nun*, act 1, sc. 3.

CHAPTER 12

201 **"the great thoroughfare of the Texas emigration"**: Olmsted, "A Tour in the Southwest," *New-York Daily Times*, Mar. 6, 1854.

201 **"A singularly mixed population lives . . . dialect)"**: Olmsted, "A Tour in the Southwest," *New-York Daily Times*, Mar. 6, 1854.

201 **"old Spanish trail . . . follow, with slight deviations"**: Olmsted, *Journey through Texas*, 53.

202 **"preparations for our vagrant life in Texas"**: Olmsted, *Journey through Texas*, 45.

202 **"a stout, dun-colored, short-legged, cheerful son . . . the Doctor"**: Olmsted, *Journey through Texas*, 45–46, and Olmsted, "A Tour in the Southwest," *New-York Daily Times*, Mar. 6, 1854.

202 **"gay little roan creole pony . . . little Nack"**: Olmsted, *Journey through Texas*, 46.

202–3 **"Owing to the numerous holds . . . pavement of pine leaves"**: Olmsted, *Journey through Texas*, 53–55.

203 **"manifest destiny to overspread . . . the plough and the rifle"**: *United States Magazine and Democratic Review*, July–Aug. 1845, "Annexation," reprinted in Greenberg, *Manifest Destiny*.

203–4 **"Before you come upon them . . . forlorn and disconsolate"**: Olmsted, *Journey through Texas*, 55–57.

204 **"pursuing, with scarce a halt, their Western destiny"**: Olmsted, "A Tour in the Southwest," *New-York Daily Times*, Mar. 6, 1854.

204 **"stopping wherever night overtakes them . . . fleecing emigrants"**: Olmsted, *Journey through Texas*, 56, 62.

204 **"inexorable"**: Olmsted, *Journey through Texas*, 55.

204 **"toil-worn . . . will they be twenty years hence?"**: Olmsted, "A Tour in the Southwest," *New-York Daily Times*, Mar. 6, 1854.

204 **"recommended as one of the . . . badly cooked"**: Olmsted, "A Tour in the Southwest," *New-York Daily Times*, Mar. 15, 1854.

204 **"the black decoction of the . . . more revolting"**: Olmsted, *Journey through Texas*, 61.

204–5 "sleet and snow were soon driving . . . across the Sabine": Olmsted, *Journey through Texas*, 64.

207–8 "The old negro who . . . jurisdiction of the states": Olmsted, *Journey through Texas*, 64.

208 "You know, sir, the usual . . . more heard of": "Blind Squatter," *Bangor Whig and Courier*, Oct. 26, 1850.

208 "right smart . . . 'twarn't a celeb'ation towards the last": Betty Farrow, in Waters, *I Was Born in Slavery*, 123–5.

208 "high rank for comfort . . . capital": Olmsted, *Journey through Texas*, 65.

208 "mere pens of small logs": Olmsted, "A Tour in the Southwest," *New-York Daily Times*, Mar. 15, 1854.

208–9 "with whatever has come to hand—a wad of cotton here, and a corn-shuck there": Olmsted, *Journey through Texas*, 66.

209 "they had been drawn through a long stove-pipe": Olmsted, "A Tour in the Southwest," *New-York Daily Times*, Mar. 15, 1854.

210 "This is only the branch of a Dogwood tree": an image of the postcard can be seen at https://www.pinterest.com/pin/535576580673266369.

210–1 "the Redlands of Eastern . . . floundered helplessly on": Olmsted, *Journey through Texas*, 67–68.

211 "We had entered our promised . . . were nowhere visible": Olmsted, *Journey through Texas*, 68.

211 "San Augustine made . . . mud": Olmsted, *Journey through Texas*, 68.

212 "there was but one man in . . . the merry party": Olmsted, *Journey through Texas*, 68–69.

214 "You got your West . . . fried mud cat": *Bernie*, directed by Richard Linklater (2012; Castle Rock Entertainment).

214 "the debasing doctrine of the equality of all men . . . in all future time": "Declaration of Causes: February 2, 1861: A Declaration of the Causes which Impel the State of Texas to Secede from the Federal Union," Texas State Library and Archives Commission, https://www.tsl.texas.gov/ref/abouttx/secession/2feb1861.html.

215 "a considerable . . . in grand decay.": Olmsted, *Journey through Texas*, 78.

215 **Republic of Fredonia:** For an overview and maps of the *empresario* era, including the Republic of Fredonia, see Stephens and Zuber-Mallison, *Texas: A Historical Atlas*, 70–79.

215 "Independence, Liberty, Justice": Stephens and Zuber-Mallison, *Texas: A Historical Atlas*, 79.

216 "put to the uses of the invading race": Olmsted, *Journey through Texas*, 79.

216 **"The jackass is the finest flower of Tex-ass":** There are many versions of the Marx Brothers' visit to Nacogdoches, including Arthur Marx, *My Life with Groucho* (New Jersey: Barricade Books, 1998), 24–26. For a more skeptical take, see Robert S. Bader, *Four of the Three Musketeers* (Evanston, IL: Northwestern University Press, 2016), 85–88.

CHAPTER 13

222 "The passion . . . extremes in Texas": Bainbridge, *The Super-Americans*, 18.

222 "which extends to the town": Olmsted, *Journey through Texas*, 361.

222 "There is no place in Texas more healthy": The speculators were the Allen brothers, from New York, and the quote is taken from an exhibit at the Heritage Society museum in Houston.

222 "Houston . . . subsistence": Olmsted, *Journey through Texas*, 361–2.

222 "completely terra incognito": Olmsted, *Journey through Texas*, 364.

223 **"The principal thoroughfare . . . not be easily overridden"**: Olmsted, *Journey through Texas*, 361, 366.

224 **"well-marked . . . battle-field"**: Olmsted, *Journey through Texas*, 366–7. For history of the San Jacinto battle, see Hardin, *Texian Iliad*, 207–17. For more on the monument and park, see pamphlet "Monumental Myths: A Talk Given by Paul Gervais Bell Jr., Dallas, March 5, 1999," at San Jacinto Battleground State Historic Park.

227 **"I fancied that you were in my arms, and we were felicitating ourselves"**: James L. Haley, *Sam Houston*, 231.

227 **"Big Drunk"**: James L. Haley, *Sam Houston*, 74.

227 **"Sam Houston and his . . . laughter at his expense"**: Olmsted, *Journey through Texas*, 104.

227 **"sea of blood and smoking . . . avalanche"**: James L. Haley, *Sam Houston*, 328, 397.

228 **"Suh, you prate about . . . and moral leprosy"**: Fogarty has slightly altered the historical quote, which can be found in James L. Haley, *Sam Houston*, 225. For more on this remarkable Texan, the Sam Houston Memorial Museum in Huntsville has an excellent and entertaining collection.

228 **"lowness, flatness, and . . . marshy pools"**: Olmsted, *Journey through Texas*, 364.

228 **"odd natural phenomenon . . . inflammable gas"**: Olmsted, *Journey through Texas*, 375–6.

228 **"permanently . . . syphilis"**: Block, *Sour Lake*, 36.

228 **"rude bathing-houses . . . Italian naphthas"**: Olmsted, *Journey through Texas*, 376.

228 **"a stunted hamlet"**: Olmsted, *Journey through Texas*, 374.

229 **"the largest producing field in the world"**: Block, *Sour Lake*, 153.

230 **"like a battalion of puddle ducks"**: Bertha Cornwell Museum at the Alma M. Carpenter Public Library, Sour Lake, TX.

231 **"sucking mire . . . village hotel"**: Olmsted, *Journey through Texas*, 377–9.

232 **"Lucas Gusher"**: Linsley, Rienstra, and Stiles, *Giant Under the Hill*, 2–3. For pictures of the gusher, see pages 108, 115, 124. Reenactments of the gusher (using water) are held at the Spindletop Gladys City Boomtown Museum in Beaumont, TX.

233 **"No, you dare not make war on . . . Cotton *is* king."**: Speech of Hon. J. H. Hammond, Senate, Mar. 4, 1858, *Congressional Globe*, Appendix for the First Session, Thirty-Fifth United States Congress, 68–71, https://memory.loc.gov/cgi-bin/ampage?collId=llcg&fileName=048/llcg048.db&recNum=83.

CHAPTER 14

234 **"You may all go to hell and I will go to Texas"**: Davy Crockett, 1835, quoted in James Atkins Shackford, *David Crockett: The Man and the Legend* (Lincoln: University of Nebraska Press, 1994), 212. This utterance was preceded by the words, "Since you have chosen to elect a man with a timber toe to succeed me . . . ," a reference to Crockett's wooden-legged opponent. There are many versions of the "go to hell" quote. See William C. Davis, *Three Roads to the Alamo*, 692, 74n.

234 **"Our journey through Eastern Texas was . . . bad weather"**: Frederick Law Olmsted to Anne Charlotte Lynch, Mar. 12, 1854, in Olmsted, *Papers of Frederick Law Olmsted*, 2:271.

234 **"an old original Texas settler, ranger, and . . . seen better days"**: Olmsted, *Journey through Texas*, 70, 73.

234–5 **"for provision as well as . . . reliable in every sense, would give brute courage to even a dyspeptic tailor"**: Olmsted, *Journey through Texas*, 73–5.

235 **"determined to begin at once . . . Borden's meat biscuit"**: Olmsted, *Journey through Texas*, 80–81.

235   **"portable meat glue"**: *Scientific American*, "New Article of Food—Meat Biscuit," Mar. 23, 1850, http://todayinsci.com/B/Borden_Gail/MeatBiscuit-SciAm.htm.

235   **"After preparing a substantial . . . recourse to it"**: Olmsted, *Journey through Texas*, 81.

235–236   **"frantic and . . . the blows"**: Olmsted, *Journey through Texas*, 86.

236   **"making, sailor-like, repairs to such articles as . . . Sunday and New Year's day"**: Olmsted, *Journey through Texas*, 86, 88.

236   **"the largest emigrant train we have . . . puddle by the roadside"**: Olmsted, "A Tour in the Southwest," *New-York Daily Times*, Mar. 21, 1854.

236   **"Oh my God! How tired . . . much longer"**: Olmsted, *Journey through Texas*, 88.

238   **what Olmsted called "the drift of things" in America**: Frederick Law Olmsted, "The Prospect for Civilization in America," postscript c. 1868, in Olmsted, *Papers of Frederick Law Olmsted*, 5:762.

239   **"reluctance of a southern-born man to be taxed, for a mutual . . . checks and deprived of exciting possibilities"**: Olmsted, *Journey through Texas*, 332–3.

242   **"a Soviet-style über-government"**: John Savage, "Bad Bill: Forever Agenda 21," *Texas Observer*, Apr. 2, 2015, https://www.texasobserver.org/bills-would-curb-agenda-21-influence-on-texas-2/.

249   **"Very melancholy . . . cursedly little people"**: Frederick Law Olmsted to Charles Loring Brace, Dec. 1, 1853, Olmsted Papers, Library of Congress, box 5, reel 4.

CHAPTER 15

250   **"We came to-day upon the first prairie of any . . . open country and a distant view"**: Olmsted, *Journey through Texas*, 89.

250   **"like the swell of the . . . islands in the large prairies"**: Olmsted, *Journey through Texas*, 89.

250–1   **"rather dolefully . . . a candle and a book or pencil"**: Olmsted, *Journey through Texas*, 96.

251   **"dirty persecutors, the hogs"**: Olmsted, *Journey through Texas*, 91.

251   **"behind a pair of frightful . . . a hungry lion, and route a whole herd"**: Olmsted, *Journey through Texas*, 93.

251   **"Supper was, however, eaten . . . on the table"**: Olmsted, *Journey through Texas*, 103.

251   **"We heard him whipping his puppy . . . dealing with his slaves"**: Olmsted, *Journey through Texas*, 117.

252   **"vastness and simplicity"**: Olmsted, *Journey through Texas*, 98.

253   **"it would still have struck us as the pleasantest place we had seen in Texas"**: Olmsted, *Journey through Texas*, 110.

253   **"fine situation . . . wood over prairie slopes"**: Olmsted, *Journey through Texas*, 110–1.

253   **"seat of empire"**: Siegel, *Poet President of Texas*, 97. The words are attributed to Mirabeau Lamar, an eccentric literati who succeeded Sam Houston as president of the Republic of Texas.

253   **"a really imposing . . . German turret"**: Olmsted, *Journey through Texas*, 110.

253–4   **"very remarkable number . . . and he was quietly persuaded to retire"**: Olmsted, *Journey through Texas*, 111–4.

255   **"De Saligny . . . Pig War"**: James L. Haley, *Sam Houston*, 241. For more on De Saligny and pigs, see Siegel, *Poet President*, 85–86, and Haley, *Sam Houston*, 216–7.

255   **"violating the sanctity"**: James L. Haley, *Sam Houston*, 123.

255   **"potterized"**: See Fischer and Walter, *Robert Potter*, 22–25.

255   **"infamy was wider than the world and deeper than perdition"**: Fischer and Walter, *Robert Potter*, 110.

256 **His lurid demise . . . named after him:** See Shuey, "Murder at Caddo Lake," 54–59.

256 **"A more reckless . . . even what it is":** Olmsted, *Journey through Texas*, 123–4.

258 **"Washington,** *en petit***":** Olmsted, *Journey through Texas*, 110.

260 **A leading talk radio . . . "of Local Militants":** The source of this conspiracy theory was Alex Jones. See Manny Fernandez, "As Jade Helm 15 Military Exercise Begins, Texans Keep Watch 'Just in Case,'" *New York Times*, July 15, 2015, https://www.nytimes.com /2015/07/16/us/in-texas-a-military-exercise-is-met-by-some-with-suspicion.html.

261 **"shaggy live oaks . . . always at right angles":** Olmsted, *Journey through Texas*, 231.

263 **"Texas is a mirror in which . . . bigger than life":** Bainbridge, *The Super-Americans*, 6.

264 **Then, under orders from . . . three weeks earlier:** *The Handbook of Texas Online*, s.v. "Goliad Massacre," by Harbert Davenport and Craig H. Roell, Texas State Historical Association, June 15, 2010, https://tshaonline.org/handbook/online/articles/qeg02.

264 **The Americans destroyed it as much as they . . . "dim damp vault-like" chapel:** Olmsted, *Journey through Texas*, 263–5.

265 **"but rather as vermin, to be exterminated":** Olmsted, *Journey through Texas*, 245.

CHAPTER 16

269 **"One sometimes wonders . . . stand on it":** McMurtry, *In a Narrow Grave*, 100.

269 **"a museum of living trees":** Frederick Law Olmsted to George Washington Vanderbilt, Dec. 30, 1893, in Olmsted, *Papers of Frederick Law Olmsted*, 9:726.

269 **"Years ago I rode alone for a full month through the North Carolina forests" . . . untamed forest that moved:** Frederick Law Olmsted to George Washington Vanderbilt, July 12, 1889, in Olmsted, *Papers of Frederick Law Olmsted*, 8:687.

270 **"a measured account":** Olmsted, "Preliminary Report upon the Yosemite and Big Tree Grove," Aug. 1865, in Olmsted, *Papers of Frederick Law Olmsted*, 5:500.

270 **"lacking the rich vigor and full foliage . . . the pains":** Olmsted, *Journey through Texas*, 129–30.

270 **"The groundswells . . . and gazed long on the sunny scene":** Olmsted, *Journey through Texas*, 148.

271 **"outposted":** Olmsted, *Journey through Texas*, 151.

271 **"three shabby homes":** Olmsted, *Journey through Texas*, 137.

272 **"the drift of things":** Frederick Law Olmsted, "The Prospect for Civilization in America," postscript c. 1868, in *Papers of Frederick Law* Olmsted, 5:762.

272 **"Today, just like the brave heroes . . . 'Enough is enough!'":** David Weigel, "In Texas Homecoming, Ted Cruz Remembers the Alamo," *Washington Post*, Feb. 24, 2016. For an enlightening and entertaining survey of Texas's influence on the nation, see Collins, *As Texas Goes*.

272 **"preeminence of positions . . . wanton mismanagement can forfeit":** Olmsted, *Journey through Texas*, 411.

273 **"and so the city bristles . . . with river-grass":** Olmsted, *Journey through Texas*, 148–9.

273 **The Alamo . . . "as an arsenal by the U.S. quartermaster":** Olmsted, *Journey through Texas*, 145.

273 **"a sacred memorial . . . hallowed ground":** Quote taken from exhibit at Long Barracks Museum at the Alamo. For an excellent overview of the desecration, preservation, and memory of the Alamo, see Turner, Cantrell, and Brundage, *Lone Star Pasts*, 57–67.

275 **"Old Betsy":** On the facts and legends surrounding Crockett's death, see Thompson, *Born on a Mountaintop*, 258–63, 283–90.

276 **"Much blood has been shed . . . a small affair"**: Santa Anna quoted in Hardin, *Texas Iliad*, 155. Richard Bruce Winders's *Sacrificed at the Alamo* sets the fight in the broader context of conflict with Mexico. For aspiring Alamaniacs, Bill Groneman's *Eyewitness to the Alamo* is compulsive reading from both sides of the battle.

276 **"heroic defense"**: Olmsted, *Journey through Texas*, 155.

277 **"God and Texas! Victory or Death!!"**: Travis's letters from the Alamo were widely published, with slight variations. I have quoted from his letter of Mar. 3, 1836, to the Texas Constitutional Convention. For this and other Travis letters, see Groneman, *Eyewitness*, 3–15.

279 **"We have no city, except . . . sallow Yankees"**: Olmsted, *Journey through Texas*, 149–50.

279 **"There is a permanent company of . . . ruddily picturesque"**: Olmsted, *Journey through Texas*, 159.

279 **"We were invariably received with . . . affectionate"**: Olmsted, *Journey through Texas*, 161.

279 **"blushing olive"**: Olmsted, *Journey through Texas*, 161.

279 **"animation of tongue and glance"**: Olmsted, *Journey through Texas*, 151–2.

279 **"deep, dark, liquid, and well-set"**: Olmsted, *Journey through Texas*, 161.

279 what he delicately called their **"soft embonpoint"**: Olmsted, *Journey through Texas*, 152.

279 **"The common dress was loose . . . petticoat"**: Olmsted, *Journey through Texas*, 162.

279 **"seemed lazily reluctant"** to cover the women's charms: Olmsted, *Journey through Texas*, 152.

280 He described . . . **"on imperturbable"**: Olmsted, *Journey through Texas*, 162–3.

280 **"of a rich blue and pure as crystal . . . bridge-rail"**: Olmsted, *Journey through Texas*, 149.

281 **"rattling life . . . clunking for vespers"**: Olmsted, *Journey through Texas*, 151.

281 As Olmsted observed . . . a near-forgotten heritage: Olmsted, *Journey through Texas*, 150–1.

281 **"All are real ruins . . . of the silent past"**: Olmsted, *Journey through Texas*, 155.

281–2 **"the strangely patient courage . . . ponderous but rudely splendid edifices"**: Olmsted, *Journey through Texas*, 154.

282 **"Imperfect Conversion"**: Quote taken from exhibit at Mission Concepción, San Antonio.

287 **"chief interest . . . jumble"**: Olmsted, *Journey through Texas*, 150–2.

CHAPTER 17

290 **"a sort of religious colony of Silesian Poles"**: Olmsted, *Journey through Texas*, 270.

290 **"approaching hardships of married life"**: Institute of Texan Cultures, San Antonio, TX.

290 **"bringing new crowns to old glory"**: *The Handbook of Texas Online*, s.v. "Soms-Braunfels, Prince Carl of," by Glen E. Lich and Günter Moltmann, Texas Historical Society, https://tshaonline.org/handbook/online/articles/fso03. See also Fehrenbach, *Lone Star*, 292–5, and Murphy and Johnson, *Cultural Encounters with the Environment*, 40–56.

291 **"The first German settlers . . . judiciously cultivated" fields**: Olmsted, "A Tour in the Southwest," *New-York Daily Times*, Apr. 4, 1854.

291 **"It caused us . . . COTTON—FREE-LABOR COTTON"**: Olmsted, *Journey through Texas*, 141.

291 **"the WEST . . . *beyond* Slavery"**: Olmsted, "A Tour in the Southwest," *New-York Daily Times*, Mar. 31, 1854.

291 *"seven wagon manufactories . . .* **in Germany"**: Olmsted, "A Tour in the Southwest," *New-York Daily Times*, Apr. 4, 1854.

292 **"all educated, cultivated . . . pleasant as that in Texas before; hardly in the South"**: Olmsted, "A Tour in the Southwest," *New-York Daily Times*, Apr. 4, 1854.

292 **"Patient, industrious and persevering . . . Southerners"**: Olmsted, "A Tour in the Southwest," *New-York Daily Times*, June 3, 1854.

292 **"In these associations you . . . degrades labor"**: Olmsted, "A Tour in the Southwest," *New-York Daily Times*, Apr. 14, 1854.

293 **"knew at once"**: Olmsted, "A Tour in the Southwest," *New-York Daily Times*, Apr. 4, 1854.

293 **"Texas Deutsch"**: For discussion of German as spoken in Texas, see the Texas German Dialect Archive, at http://sites.la.utexas.edu/hcb/files/2011/02/Boas_Weilbacher_TexasGermanDialectArchive_final.pdf. Also, Katy Vine, "Auf Wiedersehen to a Dialect," *Texas Monthly*, July 2013, https://www.texasmonthly.com/the-culture/auf-wiedersehen-to-a-dialect/.

295–6 **"Our local German . . . German alumni of 1848"**: *Neu Braunfelser Zeitung*, Mar. 20, 1857, Sophienburg Museum and Archives, New Braunfels, TX.

296 **"universal repugnance" to slavery**: Olmsted, "Appeal for Funds for the San Antonio Zeitung," Oct. 1854, in Olmsted, *Papers of Frederick Law Olmsted*, 2:315.

296 **"the manners and ideals of the Texans and of the Germans are hopelessly divergent"**: Olmsted, *Journey through Texas*, 431.

298 **"We should wear out about one horse a week, and would be robbed each day"**: Olmsted, *Journey through Texas*, 183.

298 **"first business . . . blocked our wheels"**: Olmsted, *Journey through Texas*, 165–6.

298 **they "gladly accepted an invitation . . . into the mountains to the northward"**: Olmsted, *Journey through Texas*, 187.

298 **"A Pause"**: Olmsted, *Journey through Texas*, 165.

298 **"infidel"**: Olmsted, *Papers of Frederick Law Olmsted*, 2:58. For more on Douai, see unpublished "Autobiography of Dr. Adolf Douai," translated from the German by Richard H. Douai Boerker, Olmsted Documentary Editing Project, University Archives and Special Collections, American University Library, Washington, DC. Also, Randers-Pehrson, *Adolf Douai, 1819–1888*.

298–9 **"There are certain persons . . . over the arid rocky elevations"**: Olmsted, *Journey through Texas*, 187–8.

299 **"A wide and magnificent . . . earning a tough livelihood chiefly by splitting shingles"**: Olmsted, *Journey through Texas*, 191, and Olmsted, "A Tour in the Southwest," *New-York Daily Times*, Apr. 24, 1854. The editors of Olmsted's papers identify the baron as "von Westphal" (or Westphalen), who is believed to have fled to Texas in 1848.

299 **After leaving the baron's "castle" . . . "the talk was worthy of golden goblets"**: Olmsted, *Journey through Texas*, 192–3.

299 **Their host, a formerly . . . "ingenuous, gentle and manly"**: Olmsted, *Journey through Texas*, 196.

300 **After supper . . . condemned to death or life imprisonment**: Olmsted, "A Tour in the Southwest," *New-York Daily Times*, Apr. 24, 1854, and Olmsted, *Journey through Texas*, 198.

300 **"It is a strange thing . . . their daily bread by splitting shingles"**: Olmsted, "A Tour in the Southwest," *New-York Daily Times*, Apr. 24, 1854.

300 **"unsurpassed"**: Olmsted, *Journey through Texas*, 426.

300 **"mental & moral capital of gentlemen"**: Frederick Law Olmsted to Charles Loring Brace, Dec. 1, 1853, in Olmsted, *Papers of Frederick Law Olmsted*, 2:232.

300 **"We have fallen among a German . . . may determine to become a settler"**: Frederick

Law Olmsted to Anne Charlotte Lynch, Mar. 12, 1854, in Olmsted, *Papers of Frederick Law Olmsted*, 2:273. John Olmsted later wrote that he'd been set upon settling, and that his wife liked the plan, but he became concerned about the schooling of their children and the effect of Texas's long hot summers on his fragile health.

302 **"for our own benefit . . . a future home":** Olmsted, *Journey through Texas*, 202.

CHAPTER 18

303 **"Sonoran":** Olmsted, *Journey through Texas*, 188.

303–4 **"The whole upper valley now . . . in the dale":** Olmsted, *Journey through Texas*, 213.

304 **"varied and stormy life":** Olmsted, *Journey through Texas*, 188.

305 **"insane mutual jealousy . . . effective cooperation":** Olmsted, *Journey through Texas*, 430.

306 **"greatly pleased":** Frederick Law Olmsted to Anne Charlotte Lynch, Mar. 12, 1854, in Olmsted, *Papers of Frederick Law Olmsted*, 2:271.

306 **In coming to America, German Forty-Eighters looked to the new world:** For more on Forty-Eighters, see the fine study of Honeck, *We Are the Revolutionists*, which includes a chapter on Texas and an overview of German activism in the US.

306 **Douai's mountain "excursion" and for his "invitation":** Olmsted, *Journey through Texas*, 187.

306 **"welcome acquaintances":** "Autobiography of Dr. Adolf Douai," translated from the German by Richard H. Douai Boerker, Olmsted Documentary Editing Project, University Archives and Special Collections, American University Library, Washington, DC, 114.

306 **The gathering of . . . political meeting, too:** Olmsted, *Journey through Texas*, 198.

306 **"visiting and visited by":** Olmsted, *Journey through Texas*, 222.

306 **"tour of observation":** Olmsted, "A Tour in the Southwest," *New-York Daily Times*, May 12, 1854.

306 **"put up a tent on the banks of Sister Creek":** Siemering, Burrier, Dietert, and Pue, *The Germans in Texas*, 3.

307 **"Slavery is an evil, the abolition of which is . . . the assistance of the general government":** Biesele, "Texas State Convention of Germans," 247–61, http://www.jstor.org .ezp-prod1.hul.harvard.edu/stable/30235334.

307 **"Western Texas":** Olmsted, "A Tour in the Southwest," *New-York Daily Times*, June 3, 1854.

307 **"A majority of the citizens of the whole . . . I hope to live to see here. YEOMAN":** Olmsted, "A Tour in the Southwest," *New-York Daily Times*, June 3, 1854.

308 **"The result of what . . . manifestly civilizing effect":** Frederick Law Olmsted to Elizabeth Baldwin Whitney, Dec. 16, 1890, in Olmsted, *Papers of Frederick Law Olmsted*, 9:246.

308 **"I have all my life been . . . of the future":** Frederick Law Olmsted to Frederick Law Olmsted Jr., Sept. 5, 1890, in Olmsted, *Papers of Frederick Law Olmsted*, 9:204.

308 **"immigration of one or two thousand staunch . . . pour in":** Adolf Douai to Frederick Law and John Hull Olmsted, Nov. 24, 1854, Letter File, box 2, Olmsted Documentary Editing Project. In his autobiography Douai also wrote of the Olmsteds: "They promised me active support when it came time to actively agitate for a free state of West Texas." "Autobiography of Dr. Adolf Douai," translated from the German by Richard H. Douai Boerker, University Archives and Special Collections, American University Library, Washington, DC, 114. For more on the plotting of Douai and the Olmsteds, see Roper, "Frederick Law Olmsted and Western Texas Free-Soil Movement," 58–64, and Sibley, *Lone Stars and State Gazettes*, 231–7.

308 **"I have a private . . . Freedom on this continent"**: Frederick Law Olmsted to Samuel Cabot, Jan. 22, 1857, Letter File, box 2, Olmsted Documentary Editing Project.

312 **Anti-immigrant fervor . . . Know-Nothings**: Lepore, *These Truths*, 263.

312 **"designing men"**: Biesele, "Texas State Convention of Germans," 259.

312 **"the press and many Americans spoke aloud of lynching"**: Adolf Douai to John Hull Olmsted, Sept. 4, 1854, Letter File, box 2, Olmsted Documentary Editing Project.

312 **"for freedoms sake in Western Texas . . . to save our paper"**: Adolf Douai to John Hull Olmsted, Sept. 4, 1854, Letter File, box 2, Olmsted Documentary Editing Project.

312 **"silently at work . . . *free labor* & real republicanism"**: Olmsted, "A Few Dollars Wanted to Help the Cause of Future Freedom in Texas," Oct. 1854, in Olmsted, *Papers of Frederick Law Olmsted*, 2:319.

312 **"I never before witnessed in friends of so short an acquaintance such a readiness to help"**: Adolf Douai to Frederick Law Olmsted, Dec. 9, 1854, Letter File, box 2, Olmsted Documentary Editing Project.

313 **"We see one and the same . . . of American life"**: Charles Riotte to Frederick Law Olmsted, Feb. 25, 1856, Letter File, box 2, Olmsted Documentary Editing Project.

313 **"vomit fire and poison against . . . revolutionary pressure"**: Charles Riotte to Frederick Law Olmsted, Feb. 25, 1856, Letter File, box 2, Olmsted Documentary Editing Project.

314 **"a sort of communism . . . what was lacked"**: Dielmann, "Emma Altgelt's Sketches," 377, http://www.jstor.org/stable/30240880. Altgelt also described jolly picnics in Sisterdale, where "wine was never wanting, although the pocketbooks of these learned men, who were impractical and not used to hard work, were often empty." Dielmann, "Emma Altgelt's Sketches," 376.

314 **Presbyterian missionary . . . "no church building or religious services"**: Rev. W. H. Buchanan, in *The Church at Home and Abroad* (Philadelphia: Presbyterian Board of Publication and Sabbath School Work, 1916), 485.

315 **"Our honest peasants understood farming better than we did"**: Julius Dresel, quoted in "Diary by Julius Dresel" (unpublished manuscript), trans. Johanna Dresel (1943), San Antonio Public Library. Pages provided to me by Bryden Moon. Dresel went on to become a prominent, early winegrower in California.

316 **"unusually large education . . . fine pictures of youthful yeomen as can be imagined"**: Olmsted, *Journey through Texas*, 196.

316 **Soldiers were . . . refused were summarily hanged**: Samuel Boyer Davis, "General Orders, No. 45: Headquarters Department of Texas; Houston, May 30, 1862," in *The War of the Rebellion: A Compilation of the Official Records of the Union and Confederate Armies*, series 1, vol. 9 (Washington, DC: Government Printing Office, 1883), 71–6.
     For more on German resistance to the Confederacy, see Walter D. Kamphoefner, "Texas Germans and the Confederacy," 440–55, http://www.jstor.org/stable/30242540.

316 **"Civil war is on the eve of breaking . . . no more coffee in the house"**: Barr, "Records of the Confederate Military Commission," 247–78, http://www.jstor.org.ezp-prod1.hul.harvard.edu/stable/30240967.

316 **"They offered the most . . . no prisoners to report"**: "Report of Lieut. C. D. McRae, Second Regiment Texas Mounted Rifles Division," Aug. 18, 1862, in *War of the Rebellion*, 614–6. There is considerable debate about the casualties at the Nueces, and other events related to the battle. For more, see Burrier, *Nueces Battle and Massacre*, and McGowen, "Battle or Massacre?," 64–86, http://www.jstor.org/stable/30241669.

317 **"used as shooting targets."**: Burrier, *Nueces Battle and Massacre*, 125.

317 **"If the south is victorious, it . . . emigrate again"**: Barr, "Records of the Confederate Military Commission," 251.

317 **"a dangerous and . . . to the Confederate States"**: Barr, "Records of the Confederate Military Commission," 248–9.

318 **"The sacrifice that we . . . expect to reap"**: "German Unionists in Texas," *Harper's Weekly*, Jan. 20, 1866, 39. The weekly also carried an engraving of the ceremony on the front page of that issue. For more on Comfort and its monument, see Ransleben, *A Hundred Years of Comfort;* and Ruth Kiel and Frank Kiel, *Comfort* (Charleston, SC: Arcadia Publishing, 2011).

319 **"in exile, but free"**: Olmsted, *Journey through Texas*, 198.

319 **"How times have changed since 1854 . . . free society"**: Siemering, *Germans in Texas*, 12.

319 **"Mr. Degener's salon"**: Siemering, *Germans in Texas*, 8.

319 **"There is hardly . . . their old song"**: *New Yorker Belletristishes Journal*, Nov. 29, 1882, 10, courtesy of Bryden Moon.

CHAPTER 19

320 **"Always in the evening we search out . . . travelling about, without definite aim, in an original but on the whole, very pleasant fashion"**: Frederick Law Olmsted to Anne Charlotte Lynch, in Olmsted, *Papers of Frederick Law Olmsted*, 2:273–4.

320–1 **"What is the beautiful? . . . element of human nature"**: "Address to the Prospect Park Scientific Association," in Olmsted, *Papers of Frederick Law Olmsted, Supplementary Series*, 1:151–4.

321 **"his most complete . . . wanted in parks"**: Olmsted, *Papers of Frederick Law Olmsted, Supplementary Series*, 1:14.

321 **"Pick up all the . . . useful to me"**: Frederick Law Olmsted to Frederick Law Olmsted Jr., Aug. 1, 1894, in Olmsted, *Papers of Frederick Law Olmsted*, 9:804–5. The influence of Olmsted's time in Texas was also evident in a letter to a biographer. "My best book was the Journey in Texas," Olmsted wrote, and "best also, for your purpose," because it showed an "important part of my education" as a landscape architect. Olmsted to Mariana Griswold Van Rensselaer, June 17, 1893, in Olmsted, *Papers of Frederick Law Olmsted*, 9:650.

322 **"quality of ease"**: "Address to the Prospect Park Scientific Association," Olmsted, *Papers of Frederick Law Olmsted, Supplementary Series*, 1:151–4.

323 **"Mr. Brown . . . two thousand rough miles"**: Olmsted, *Journey through Texas*, 45.

324 **J. D. B. DeBow . . . "be readily localized"**: Olmsted's exchange with DeBow appears in Olmsted, *Journey in the Back Country*, 398–400.

325–6 **"Mules, with very few exceptions . . . keep it in spite of all you can do"**: Riley, *The Mule: A Treatise*, 8, 36, 37, 42.

330 **"He was endowed with the hereditary bigotry of his race"**: Olmsted, *Journey through Texas*, 45.

330 **On another occasion . . . "some pumpkins"**: Olmsted, *Journey through Texas*, 227–8.

330 **"amenable to reason"**: Olmsted, *Journey through Texas*, 45.

330 **"symptom of insurrection"**: Olmsted, *Journey through Texas*, 228.

331 **"Our road took us over a rugged ridge"**: Olmsted, *Journey through Texas*, 191.

331 **"wide and magnificent"**: Olmsted, *Journey through Texas*, 191.

331 **"civilized life"**: "The Barbarizing Experience of Pioneers on the Frontier," in Olmsted, *Papers of Frederick Law Olmsted*, 5:684.

334–5 **"The whole prairies . . . seemed to swell with life"**: Olmsted, *Journey through Texas*, 233.

335 **"new-clothed in its most . . . and even verdure"**: Olmsted, "A Tour in the Southwest," *New-York Daily Times*, May 12, 1854.

335 **"perfume" of a shrub known in Texas as frijolito**: Frederick Law Olmsted to Anne Charlotte Lynch, in Olmsted, *Papers of Frederick Law Olmsted*, 2:274 and 275, 5n.

335 **"quick and perfectly transparent"**: Olmsted, *Journey through Texas*, 193.

336 **"I also shared Olmsted's writing . . . finding us exactly such a spot"**: "Address to the Prospect Park Scientific Association," in Olmsted, *Papers of Frederick Law Olmsted, Supplementary Series*, 1:152.

337–8 **Olmsted, for all his skill . . . "with streaks and spots, and clouds of soot and coal"**: This scene was described in Olmsted, "A Tour in the Southwest," *New-York Daily Times*, May 31, 1854, and in very similar form in *Journey through Texas*, 215–21.

338 **"blazed away without . . . for which they have an irresistible hankering."**: Olmsted, *Journey through Texas*, 214.

340 **"I have rarely seen any resort of wood-nymphs . . . would be loath to desecrate its deep beauty"**: Olmsted, *Journey through Texas*, 193.

340 **"Over we rolled . . . of Mr. Brown"**: Olmsted, *Journey through Texas*, 211.

340–1 **Elsewhere . . . "then broke into an uncontrollable fit of laughter"**: Olmsted, *Journey through Texas*, 251–2.

341 **"His house stands upon a prominence, which commands the beautiful valley in both directions"**: Olmsted, *Journey through Texas*, 196.

341–2 **"A man of marked attainments . . . rocky bluff of the Guadalupe"**: Olmsted, *Journey through Texas*, 192.

342 **"The delicious brook water has . . . thrown open to patients"**: Olmsted, *Journey through Texas*, 195.

342 **"To any friend of mine who has . . . to pass his exile than this"**: Olmsted, *Journey through Texas*, 194.

343 **"The water of both streams . . . like ornamental columns"**: Olmsted, *Journey through Texas*, 193–4.

CHAPTER 20

354 **"vagabond . . . off wool-gathering"**: Frederick Law Olmsted to Elizabeth Baldwin Whitney, Dec. 16, 1890, in Olmsted, *Papers of Frederick Law Olmsted*, 9:246.

354 **"We expect to go on to California"**: Frederick Law Olmsted to Anne Charlotte Lynch, Mar. 12, 1854, in Olmsted, *Papers of Frederick Law Olmsted*, 2:273.

354 **"California plan."**: John Hull Olmsted to Isaac Clinton Collins, Oct. 4, 1854, Letter File, box 2, Olmsted Documentary Editing Project.

354–5 **"company for any long route in Mexico . . . for the pleasure of the thing"**: Olmsted, *Journey through Texas*, 273.

355 **early April weather "Italian" and the prairie "a rolling sheet of the finest grass, sprinkled thick with bright, many-hued flowers"**: Olmsted, *Journey through Texas*, 275.

355 **"We saw that we were approaching the great chaparral desert of the Rio Grande valley"**: Olmsted, *Journey through Texas*, 284.

355 **"soldiers periodically gave . . . would be no greater nonsense"**: Olmsted, *Journey through Texas*, 298.

355 **"to procure at Fort Inge" . . . state his business, rather than spouting nonsense as if to babies:** Olmsted, *Journey through Texas*, 303–4. For more on John Woodland, see his entry in *The Handbook of Texas Online*, https://tshaonline.org/handbook/online/articles/fwo49.

356 **"I slept little . . . of an August grasshopper, and cannot be mistaken"**: Olmsted, *Journey through Texas*, 307–9.

356–7 **He also deflated fearful tales about . . . "for a more dreary country, of equal extent, I never saw"**: Olmsted, *Journey through Texas*, 312–4.

357 **"The cottages are scattered . . . from Texas as possible"**: Olmsted, *Journey through Texas*, 276. For more on the Alsatian settlements, see Weaver, *Castro's Colony*.

357 **Quihi, which Olmsted . . . "improvements":** Olmsted, *Journey through Texas*, 279.

358 **"stunted and rare":** Olmsted, *Journey through Texas*, 280.

358 **"a singular spectacle . . . of European peasant hamlets":** Olmsted, *Journey through Texas*, 280.

358 **"very coarse and masculine":** Olmsted, *Journey through Texas*, 281.

359 **"go back whar I belong":** Olmsted, *Journey through Texas*, 284.

359 **"adjacent to a singular conical rocky hill":** Olmsted, *Journey through Texas*, 279–85.

360 **"In riding sixty miles" . . . the slave catchers rode off:** Olmsted, *Journey through Texas*, 313–4.

360 **"dwarf forest of prickly shrubs":** Olmsted, *Journey through Texas*, 313.

360 **"a sudden flash of . . . hilly desert":** Olmsted, *Journey through Texas*, 314–5.

360–1 **On the Texas side . . . Cora Montgomery:** Olmsted, *Journey through Texas*, 315.

361 **"true miniature of Americanism":** Cora Montgomery, *Eagle Pass*, 1.

361 **"Perhaps, if we had known this, we should have been a little less disappointed":** Olmsted, *Journey through Texas*, 315.

361 **The riders came to . . . it was flea-ridden:** Olmsted, *Journey through Texas*, 315–8.

361 **That night . . . "in the establishment":** Olmsted, *Journey through Texas*, 337.

361 **"spoony fancies":** Frederick Law Olmsted to Frederick Kingsbury, Oct. 17, 1852, in Olmsted, *Papers of Frederick Law Olmsted*, 2:84. For more on Cazneau's ideology and her differences with Olmsted, see William T. Kerrigan, "Race, Expansion, and Slavery," 275–301, http://www.jstor.org.ezp-prod1.hul.harvard.edu/stable/30242080. Cazneau may also have authored the essay that popularized the phrase "manifest destiny." See Greenberg, *Manifest Destiny*, 97.

362 **"Every tub must stand on its own bottom":** "Notes on the Pioneer Condition," in Olmsted, *Papers of Frederick Law Olmsted*, 5:587.

362 **"barbarism":** "Notes on the Pioneer Condition," in Olmsted, *Papers of Frederick Law Olmsted*, 5:591.

362 **"Incompleteness . . . wilderness":** "Notes on the Pioneer Condition," in Olmsted, *Papers of Frederick Law Olmsted*, 5:596.

364 ***"standing guard* over the landing":** Olmsted, *Journey through Texas*, 319.

364 **"informal" passports:** Olmsted, *Journey through Texas*, 322.

364 **"not yet wakened from . . . from whom he had run away four or five years ago":** Olmsted, *Journey through Texas*, 319–23.

364 **"runaways were *constantly* arriving here":** Olmsted, *Journey through Texas*, 324. The estimate of escaped slaves is cited in Kelley, "'Mexico in His Head,'" 709–23. See also Jacoby, *Strange Career of William Ellis*, 10–12.

365 **"When they first got here . . . brought very soon":** Olmsted, *Journey through Texas*, 324.

365 **"In fact, a colored man . . . too rough to suit them":** Olmsted, *Journey through Texas*, 325.

365 **This time, the . . . all his earnings:** Olmsted, *Journey through Texas*, 338–9.

365 **"Where is the man who does not sometimes make a bad use of freedom?":** Olmsted, *Journey through Texas*, 339.

365–6 **"the great dry . . . is driven to assert his claim to manhood?":** Olmsted, *Journey through Texas*, 327.

368 **"tamed sort of Indians . . . I used to think.":** Olmsted, *Journey through Texas*, 288.

368 **Jack Woodland, called them "greasers":** Olmsted, *Journey through Texas*, 335.

369 **"a pleasant sketch of the natural socialism of the uncontaminated man":** Olmsted, *Journey through Texas*, 288.

369 **"noble savages of . . . of degrading nonsense to secure it"**: Olmsted, *Journey through Texas*, 289–90.

369 **The Olmsteds . . . "scalps we wore"**: Olmsted, *Journey through Texas*, 290–1.

369 **"Assuming as much native dignity as I could command . . . to translate"**: Olmsted, *Journey through Texas*, 291.

369 **"Sí, . . . corn, horses, and Germans"**: Olmsted, *Journey through Texas*, 292.

369 **"The trail, when found, . . . to be shot down at will"**: Olmsted, *Journey through Texas*, 294–5.

369–70 **"If my wife were in a frontier . . . vermin, to be exterminated"**: Olmsted, *Journey through Texas*, 297.

370 **"Nothing can be more . . . and angry depredations"**: Olmsted, *Journey through Texas*, 296.

370 **"the power of even a little . . . extermination will then, at least, be open"**: Olmsted, *Journey through Texas*, 297–8.

370 **"nominal"**: Olmsted, *Journey through Texas*, 285.

370 **"badly placed, in a military view"**: Olmsted, *Journey through Texas*, 314.

370 **four hundred troops . . . "from under their guns"**: Olmsted, "A Tour in the Southwest," *New-York Daily Times*, May 27, 1854.

370 **"afford but a feeble guard against marauders"**: Pryor, *Reading the Man*, 241.

370–1 **"desert of dullness . . . you in this paradise of the Texans"**: Pryor, *Reading the Man*, 249, 252.

371 **As illustration, he showed . . . fined one hundred dollars**: From displays at Eagle Pass Fort Duncan Museum, Eagle Pass, TX.

371 **"he who moves here and there"**: History of the Mexican Kickapoo, Milwaukee Public Museum, Milwaukee, WI, https://www.mpm.edu/research-collections/anthropology/online-collections-research/mexican-kickapoo/history.

371 **"Parolee-Kickapoo Indians pending clarification of status by Congress"**: "'Lost' Indian Tribe Seeks Recognition and a Home," *New York Times*, Dec. 26, 1981.

373 **"curt refusal and extreme suspicion"**: Ritzenthaler and Peterson, *The Mexican Kickapoo Indians*, 9.

375 **"mat-covered Woodland wigwams"**: Ritzenthaler and Peterson, *The Mexican Kickapoo Indians*, 11.

375 **"should not be too heavy for a horse"**: Ritzenthaler and Peterson, *The Mexican Kickapoo Indians*, 62.

375 **"almost fanatical will and effort to keep out foreign influences"**: Ritzenthaler and Peterson, *The Mexican Kickapoo Indians*, 11.

375 **"when the tribe becomes extinct, God will destroy the whole world by fire"**: Ritzenthaler and Peterson, *The Mexican Kickapoo Indians*, 46.

CHAPTER 21

377 **"trackless, bleak, rugged . . . moderately smooth"**: Olmsted, *Journey through Texas*, 339–40.

377 **"dreary, desolate . . . that I have ever seen"**: Olmsted, *Journey through Texas*, 341.

377 **"a dark mass of lofty trees"**: Olmsted, *Journey through Texas*, 343.

377–8 **"The place had a comfortable look . . . contented peasantry"**: Olmsted, *Journey through Texas*, 350.

378 **curiosity about "los Americanos"**: Olmsted, *Journey through Texas*, 344.

378 **Olmsted, in turn, made a "pretty study" . . . before resuming her labor**: Olmsted, *Journey through Texas*, 349.

378 **The brothers weren't sure, at first, how ... "were masters of the town":** Olmsted, *Journey through Texas*, 350.

378 **"I spurred my horse, and ... yelling and gesticulating violently":** Olmsted, *Journey through Texas*, 346.

378 **"squeezed his eye ... Colt and knife under each pillow":** Olmsted, *Journey through Texas*, 348, 352.

378 **"They seemed to regard us with a skulking malice, ... possible":** Olmsted, *Journey through Texas*, 353.

378 **"After one lonely, ... a friend":** Olmsted, *Journey through Texas*, 355. On Woodland's demise, see Townsend, "The Mays Massacre," 29–43.

381 **"Sahara":** Olmsted, *Journey through Texas*, 341.

382 **"comfortable" settlements Olmsted described:** Olmsted, *Journey through Texas*, 350.

385 **"prepared for more rapid travel," shedding "useless weight" for their journey out of Texas:** Olmsted, *Journey through Texas*, 356.

385 **"the hot, soggy breath of the approaching summer was extremely depressing":** Olmsted, *Journey through Texas*, 380.

386 **"the hope of invigorating weakened lungs":** Olmsted, *Journey through Texas*, xii.

386 **"abominable diet ... and unable to speak":** Olmsted, *Journey through Texas*, 380.

386 **"fresh, lusty, good-natured American stallion":** Olmsted, *Journey through Texas*, 379.

386 **"the alligator-bayous":** Olmsted, *Journey through Texas*, 406.

386 **"so prostrated by the heat ... useless expense & suffering":** John Hull Olmsted to Sophia Hitchcock, Aug. 13, 1854, Letter File, box 2, Olmsted Documentary Editing Project.

386 **"the wet country ... of steady travel":** Olmsted, *Journey through Texas*, 379–80.

386 **"From Richmond I went with my horse and dog direct to New York by the steamer":** Olmsted, *Journey in the Back Country*, 283.

386 **"Her tired bones have now found a last rest upon Staten Island":** Olmsted, *Journey through Texas*, 94.

386 **"Fred took many notes ... work with energy":** John Hull Olmsted to Isaac Clinton Collins, Oct. 4, 1854, Letter File, box 2, Olmsted Documentary Editing Project.

386 **"The great key ... *what to expect next*":** Frederick Law Olmsted to Bertha Olmsted and Sophia Stevens Hitchcock, early 1855, in Olmsted, *Papers of Frederick Law Olmsted*, 2:340.

387 **"useless weight":** Olmsted, *Journey through Texas*, 356.

387 **"much jaded":** Olmsted, *Journey through Texas*, 379.

CHAPTER 22

390 **"I am one of those men who work best with a strong head of steam on":** Frederick Law Olmsted to Henry Whitney Bellows, Oct. 3, 1861, in Olmsted, *Papers of Frederick Law Olmsted*, 4:211.

390 **"neither right nor best":** Olmsted, *Papers of Frederick Law Olmsted*, 9:249, 1n.

390 **"how such a loitering ... been ever since?":** Frederick Law Olmsted to Elizabeth Baldwin Whitney, Dec. 16, 1890, in Olmsted, *Papers of Frederick Law Olmsted*, 9:248.

390 **He also recalled ... "I have been selling being for doing," he wrote:** Frederick Law Olmsted to Elizabeth Baldwin Whitney, Dec. 16, 1890, in Olmsted, *Papers of Frederick Law Olmsted*, 9:246–8. On the sermon, see 251, 12n.

391 **"recognized litterateur":** Frederick Law Olmsted to John Olmsted, Nov. 8, 1855, in Olmsted, *Papers of Frederick Law Olmsted*, 2:376. Karl Marx referred to Olmsted in two letters, describing him as "genial." Marx to Engels, Sept. 22, 1856, and Oct. 30, 1856,

Biographical File, box 4, folder on Karl Marx, University Archives and Special Collections, American University Library, Washington, DC.

391 **But Fred chafed from . . . parental loan:** Frederick Law Olmsted to John Olmsted, Nov. 24, 1855, Letter File, box 2, Olmsted Documentary Editing Project.

391 **"feasible opportunity to forestall further aggressive movements of the slave powers":** Frederick Law Olmsted to George Perkins Marsh, Jan. 12, 1857, Letter File, box 2, Olmsted Documentary Editing Project.

391 **"the opposing forces face each other on line A.B.":** Frederick Law Olmsted to Samuel Cabot, Jan. 22, 1857, Letter File, box 2, Olmsted Documentary Editing Project.

391 **"In four years' time a line from Iowa continuously to the Gulf may be occupied with free labor farms," he wrote:** Frederick Law Olmsted to George Perkins Marsh, Jan. 12, 1857, Letter File, box 2, Olmsted Documentary Editing Project.

391 **"completely *turn* the flank of the South":** Frederick Law Olmsted to Samuel Cabot, Jan. 22, 1857, Letter File, box 2, Olmsted Documentary Editing Project.

391 **and "Slavery will retreat upon itself":** Frederick Law Olmsted to Edward Everett Hall, Jan. 10, 1857, in Olmsted, *Papers of Frederick Law Olmsted*, 2:398.

391 **"grand" scheme to win the "war between the power of Slavery and of Freedom":** Frederick Law Olmsted to Samuel Cabot, Jan. 22, 1857, Letter File, box 2, Olmsted Documentary Editing Project.

392 **"hopelessly in debt":** White and Kramer, *Olmsted South*, 131.

392 **"I have not determined . . . a permanently lucrative disposition of myself":** Frederick Law Olmsted to Samuel Cabot, Aug. 18, 1857, in Olmsted, *Papers of Frederick Law Olmsted*, 2:449.

392 **"I have to-day received . . . very closely for some time to come":** Frederick Law Olmsted to Samuel Cabot, Sept. 14, 1857, in Olmsted, *Papers of Frederick Law Olmsted*, 2:450.

392 **"nuisance" industries like boiling bones to make grease and glue:** See Ronald Korcak, "Bone Char Made in Central Park, New York," *Biochar Journal*, Nov. 2015, https://www.biochar-journal.org/en/ct/70. Olmsted referred to these "nuisances" in a letter to the board of commissioners of Central Park (Olmsted, *Papers of Frederick Law Olmsted*, 3:203–4) and wrote of touring low grounds steeped in the "overflow and mush of pig sties, slaughter houses and bone boiling works, and the stench was sickening." Olmsted, *Papers of Frederick Law Olmsted*, 3:90.

392 **"I'll take the boat . . . to me before morning, I'll do it":** Olmsted, "Autobiographical Fragment A: Passages in the Life of an Unpractical Man," in *Papers of Frederick Law Olmsted*, 3:86.

392 **"frontier" state of society:** Olmsted, *Journey through Texas*, 518.

392 **"elevate" the North:** Frederick Law Olmsted to Charles Loring Brace, Dec. 1, 1853, in Olmsted, *Papers of Frederick Law Olmsted*, 2:234.

393 **"The *New York Herald* . . . lowest denizens of the city":** "The Central Park and Other City Improvements," *New York Herald*, Sept. 6, 1857, 4, https://chroniclingamerica.loc.gov/lccn/sn83030313/1857-09-06/ed-1/seq-4.pdf.

393 **"The first real park made in this country . . . this country is dependent":** Frederick Law Olmsted to Parke Godwin, Aug. 1, 1858, in Olmsted, *Papers of Frederick Law Olmsted*, 3:201. Olmsted's belief in the democratizing power of parks, and other aspects of his landscape philosophy, reflected the influence of Andrew Jackson Downing, a leading horticulturalist and tastemaker. Downing was also an early advocate for a park in New York and recruited Calvert Vaux to work with him on landscape designs. Had Downing not died in a steamboat accident in 1852, at the age of thirty-six, he might well have become the principal architect of Central Park.

393 **"The strongest objection to me . . . practical" man:** Frederick Law Olmsted to John Hull Olmsted, Sept. 11, 1857, in Olmsted, *Papers of Frederick Law Olmsted*, 3:80.

393 **"You will, of course, be cautious not to give offence in your new position and particularly careful in your accounts"**: John Olmsted to Frederick Law Olmsted, Sept. 27, 1857, Olmsted Papers, Library of Congress, box 6, reel 5.

393 **he was glad . . . "turned out next election":** John Hull Olmsted to John Olmsted, Oct. 3, 1857, Olmsted Papers, Library of Congress, box 6, reel 5.

393 **"Dear dear Fred . . . we have held out such tenderness":** John Hull Olmsted to Frederick Law Olmsted, Nov. 13, 1857, Olmsted Papers, Library of Congress, box 6, reel 5.

394 **John went . . . "to the end his quiet ways":** Quoted in Kalfus, *Frederick Law Olmsted*, 374, 47n.

394 **"In his death I have lost not only a son but a very dear friend. You almost your only friend":** John Olmsted to Frederick Law Olmsted, Nov. 28, 1857, Olmsted Papers, Library of Congress, box 6, reel 5.

394 **"Glory! Hallelujah . . . what I was and felt":** Frederick Law Olmsted to Frederick Knapp, Apr. 9, 1865, in Olmsted, *Papers of Frederick Law Olmsted*, 5:349.

394 **Their plan was titled Greensward:** The plan can be found in Olmsted, *Papers of Frederick Law Olmsted*, 3:119–74.

394 **romantic "infinity":** John Hull Olmsted to Frederick John Kingsbury, Dec. 17, 1849, Letter File, box 1, Olmsted Documentary Editing Project.

394 **"Don't let Mary suffer while you are alive":** John Hull Olmsted to Frederick Law Olmsted, Nov. 13, 1857, Olmsted Papers, Library of Congress, box 6, reel 5.

394–5 **"comfortably pretty . . . but to talk with":** Olmsted, *Papers of Frederick Law Olmsted*, 3:59–60.

395 **"The steel of the larger, as pure as thy mind/Can be—just as cutting—can not be as kind":** Olmsted, *Papers of Frederick Law Olmsted*, 3:59–60.

395 **"I am capable of stronger . . . itself to that passion":** Frederick Law Olmsted to Calvert Vaux, Nov. 26, 1863, in Olmsted, *Papers of Frederick Law Olmsted*, 5:148.

395 **"used up, fatigued beyond recovery, an older man . . . blue" pills:** Frederick Law Olmsted to John Olmsted, Sept. 23, 1859, in Olmsted, *Papers of Frederick Law Olmsted*, 3:230.

395 **"close on the edge of a brain-fever":** Frederick Law Olmsted, quoted in Kalfus, *Frederick Law Olmsted*, 57.

395 **"litter chair":** Frederick Law Olmsted to John Olmsted, Oct. 21, 1860, in Olmsted, *Papers of Frederick Law Olmsted*, 3:274.

395 **"Park" entered an American encyclopedia for the first time, the entry written by Olmsted:** "Park," from the *New American Cyclopaedia*, 1861, in Olmsted, *Papers of Frederick Law Olmsted*, 3:346.

395–6 **"Both in conception and execution . . . have frowned on the theory of self-government":** *Atlantic Monthly*, Apr. 1861, quoted in Olmsted, *Papers of Frederick Law Olmsted*, 3:273, 330.

396 **"We are full of fight . . . everything before it":** Frederick Law Olmsted to John Olmsted, Apr. 17, 1861, in Olmsted, *Papers of Frederick Law Olmsted*, 3:342.

396 **"ultraists":** Olmsted, "A Tour in the Southwest," *New-York Daily Times*, May 13, 1854.

396 **"Black Republican":** For example and discussion of this term, see Bachmann, "The 1860 Campaign and the 'Black Republican President,'" *The Shelf* (blog), Oct. 6, 2012, http://blogs-test.harvard.edu/preserving/2012/10/06/the-1860-campaign-and-the-black-republican-president/.

396 **"Slave Power":** For a discussion of this phrase, see Foner, *Free Soil*, 96–98.

396 **"My thoughts are murder to the state":** Henry David Thoreau, "Slavery in Massachusetts," 1854, http://xroads.virginia.edu/~hyper2/thoreau/slavery.html. This was delivered as a talk during a July Fourth protest at which Garrison burned the Constitution (see next note).

396 **William Lloyd Garrison . . . "with tyranny!":** See Donald Yacovone, "A Covenant with Death and an Agreement with Hell," *Object of the Month* (blog), Massachusetts Historical Society, July 2005, https://www.masshist.org/object-of-the-month/objects /a-covenant-with-death-and-an-agreement-with-hell-2005-07-01. Also Mayer, *All on Fire*, 445.

397 **Lincoln spoke eloquently . . . real existence?":** Abraham Lincoln, "First Inaugural Address, of Abraham Lincoln," Mar. 4, 1861, Avalon Project: Documents in Law, History and Diplomacy, Yale Law School, http://avalon.law.yale.edu/19th_century /lincoln1.asp.

398 **"bonds of affection" were badly strained . . . "chorus of the Union," touched "by "the better angels of our nature":** Lincoln, "First Inaugural Address," Avalon Project.

399 **"pining" . . . "superintendent" of slaves flocking to Union lines:** Frederick Law Olmsted to Henry Whitney Bowles, June 1, 1861, in Olmsted, *Papers of Frederick Law Olmsted*, 4:118.

399 **"Talent and energy most . . . brought into close relations":** From Strong's diary, quoted in Olmsted, *Papers of Frederick Law Olmsted*, 4:110.

399 **"fanatical about his duty":** Henry Whitney Bellows, quoted in Olmsted, *Papers of Frederick Law Olmsted*, 1:378. Bellows also described Olmsted as an "unconscious tyrant" with "an indomitable pride of opinion," adding, "if a monarch he would rule with a rod of iron." Olmsted, *Papers of Frederick Law Olmsted*, 4:87.

399 **"Most insanitary habits of life . . . breakfasts on *strong coffee and pickles*!!!":** Strong diary quoted in Olmsted, *Papers of Frederick Law Olmsted*, 4:108.

399 **"all about the temporal wants of your wife and her babies":** Mary Olmsted to Frederick Law Olmsted, Aug. 4, 1861, Olmsted Papers, Library of Congress, box 7, reel 6. Fred had written her six days earlier about the Union defeat at Bull Run and declared: "Make the best of our affairs. I could not shrink from this war if it starved us all." Frederick Law Olmsted to Mary Olmsted, July 29, 1861, Olmsted Papers, Library of Congress, box 7, reel 6.

399 **"I want to exterminate the Slaveholders—or rather slaveholding and the state of society founded on it":** Frederick Law Olmsted to Henry Whitney Bellows, Oct. 3, 1862, in Olmsted, *Papers of Frederick Law Olmsted*, 4:440.

399 **"I would rather . . . them, damn them!":** Frederick Law Olmsted to Henry Whitney Bellows, July 4, 1863, in Olmsted, *Papers of Frederick Law Olmsted*, 4:642.

400 **"I believe many of them are capable of making military heroes":** Testimony before the American Freedmen's Special Inquiry Commission, Apr. 22, 1863, in Olmsted, *Papers of Frederick Law Olmsted*, 4:610.

400 **"soldier of the republic":** Frederick Law Olmsted to Henry Whitney Bellows, Oct. 3, 1862, in Olmsted, *Papers of Frederick Law Olmsted*, 4:440.

400 **"righteous hatred . . . stronger than my love of life":** Frederick Law Olmsted to Henry Whitney Bellows, July 4, 1863, in Olmsted, *Papers of Frederick Law Olmsted*, 4:642.

400 **Olmsted wrote that . . . "free use of the whole body of the people forever":** Olmsted, "Preliminary Report upon the Yosemite and Big Tree Grove," Aug. 1865, in Olmsted, *Papers of Frederick Law Olmsted*, 5:505–7.

400 **"The art is not" . . . public spaces, and other features:** Frederick Law Olmsted to Calvert Vaux, Aug. 1, 1865, in Olmsted, *Papers of Frederick Law Olmsted*, 5:422.

400–1 **"Of all American artists . . . and miscellaneous democracy":** Norton, quoted in Olmsted, *Papers of Frederick Law Olmsted*, 9:30.

401 **"blues":** Olmsted, *Papers of Frederick Law Olmsted*, 4:203.

401 **"the dumps":** Olmsted, *Papers of Frederick Law Olmsted*, 9:843.

401 **"faculties and . . . it's the worst feature in my life":** Frederick Law Olmsted to Frederick Knapp, Apr. 9, 1865, in Olmsted, *Papers of Frederick Law Olmsted*, 5:349–50.

401 **"park-making"**: Olmsted, *Papers of Frederick Law Olmsted*, 9:633.

401 or **"scenery-making"**: Olmsted, *Papers of Frederick Law Olmsted*, 9:624.

401 **"the severe and excessive exercise of the mind which leads to the greatest fatigue"**: Olmsted, "Preliminary Report upon the Yosemite and Big Tree Grove," Aug. 1865, in Olmsted, *Papers of Frederick Law Olmsted*, 5:503.

401 **"resist" and "recover" from the stresses of their hectic lives. "It is thus, in medical phrase, a prophylactic and therapeutic agent of vital value."**: Frederick Law Olmsted, "Mount Royal," quoted in Olmsted, *Papers of Frederick Law Olmsted*, 9:1011, 2n.

401 **"Upon my word Olmsted . . . bloodless figure as you insist upon doing"**: Calvert Vaux to Frederick Law Olmsted, Oct. 1859, quoted in Olmsted, *Papers of Frederick Law Olmsted*, 3:66.

401 **"*undemocratic* . . . I never for a moment sympathized"**: Calvert Vaux to Frederick Law Olmsted, July 31, 1865, in Olmsted, *Papers of Frederick Law Olmsted*, 5:419.

401–2 **"the big art work of the Republic"**: Calvert Vaux to Frederick Law Olmsted, June 3, 1865, in Olmsted, *Papers of Frederick Law Olmsted*, 5:385.

402 **"There is no other place in the world," he wrote, "that is as much home to me"**: Frederick Law Olmsted to Calvert Vaux, June 8, 1865, in Olmsted, *Papers of Frederick Law Olmsted*, 5:390.

402 **"artificial things"**: Beveridge and Rocheleau, *Designing the American Landscape*, 30.

402 **"poetic"**: Frederick Law Olmsted, "Address to the Prospect Park Scientific Association," in Olmsted, *Papers of Frederick Law Olmsted, Supplementary Series*, 1:151.

402 **"compel us" to "walk circumspectly," . . . drawing from them"**: Bender, *Toward an Urban Vision*, 176.

403 **"mystery and infinity"**: Frederick Law Olmsted, "Lecture to Architecture Students," in Olmsted, *Papers of Frederick Law Olmsted*, 9:1006.

403 **the first Otis passenger elevator was installed in a New York building**: See John C. Abell, "March 23, 1857: Mr. Otis Gives You a Lift," *Wired*, Mar. 23, 2010, https://www .wired.com/2010/03/0323otis-elevator-first/.

403 **"loch"**: Cook, *New York Central Park*, 171, https://archive.org/details/descriptionofnew 00cookiala/page/n7.

404 **"hundreds of thousands . . . easier circumstances"**: Frederick Law Olmsted to the Board of Commissioners of the Central Park, May 31, 1858, in Olmsted, *Papers of Frederick Law Olmsted*, 3:196.

404 **"The time will come . . . and piles of erect angular buildings"**: Frederick Law Olmsted to the Board of Commissioners of the Central Park, May 31, 1858, in Olmsted, *Papers of Frederick Law Olmsted*, 3:196.

404 **"these particularly individual and characteristic sources of landscape effects"**: Frederick Law Olmsted to the Board of Commissioners of the Central Park, May 31, 1858, in Olmsted, *Papers of Frederick Law Olmsted*, 3:196.

404 **"More mowing or dug ground I object to . . . Less wildness and disorder I object to"**: Frederick Law Olmsted to John Charles Olmsted, Sept. 12, 1884, in Olmsted, *Papers of Frederick Law Olmsted*, 8:212.

404 **"How will it be . . . new silk hat?"**: Frederick Law Olmsted, "The Spoils of the Park," 1882, in Olmsted, *Papers of Frederick Law Olmsted*, 7:635.

404 **fashion . . . "rocky, wild, sea-beaten"**: Frederick Law Olmsted to Mariana Van Rensselaer, June 29, 1888, in Olmsted, *Papers of Frederick Law Olmsted*, 8:528–9.

404 **"improvement . . . Nothing better can be done than to let it alone"**: Olmsted, "Improvement of Easton's Beach," Mar. 13, 1883, in Olmsted, *Papers of Frederick Law Olmsted*, 8:153.

405 **"elevate" and assimilate the masses "and force into contact" the rich and the poor, the**

highbrow and low: Frederick Law Olmsted to Charles Loring Brace, Dec. 1, 1853, in Olmsted, *Papers of Frederick Law Olmsted*, 2:232.

405 **"gregarious" aspect of parks . . . "presence to the pleasure of all others":** Frederick Law Olmsted, "Public Parks and the Enlargement of Towns," 1870, in *Civilizing American Cities*, 74–5. Also see Beveridge and Rocheleau, *Designing the American Landscape*, 47.

405 **"heart-hardening":** Beveridge and Rocheleau, *Designing the American Landscape*, 46.

407 **"excuse to a pair of . . . canopy of vine":** Cook, *New York Central Park*, 125–6.

407 **"picturesque, sylvan and rural":** Frederick Law Olmsted to Francis Newlands, Nov. 16, 1891, in Olmsted, *Papers of Frederick Law Olmsted*, 9:421.

408 **"Racial divisions . . . are not yet ready to mingle":** Rothstein, *Color of Law*, 51.

408 **"villages":** Frederick Law Olmsted to Mariana Griswold Van Rensselaer, June 11, 1893, in Olmsted, *Papers of Frederick Law Olmsted*, 9:644.

408 **"series of neighborhoods of a peculiar character":** Preliminary Report upon the Proposed Suburban Village at Riverside, Near Chicago, by Olmsted, Vaux, & Co., Landscape Architects. Sept. 1, 1868, https://www.fandm.edu/david-schuyler/urban/preliminary-report.

408 **"It is far & away the most . . . forming in this *period*":** Frederick Law Olmsted to John Charles Olmsted and Charles Eliot Norton, Oct. 2, 1893, in Olmsted, *Papers of Frederick Law Olmsted*, 9:701.

408 **"a very rich man who for his own . . . rarely good way":** Frederick Law Olmsted to Frederick Law Olmsted Jr., Dec. 5, 1895, in Olmsted, *Papers of Frederick Law Olmsted*, 9:956.

408–9 **"The public is more and more . . . to the future of our profession":** Frederick Law Olmsted to John Charles Olmsted and Charles Eliot Norton, June 3, 1894, in Olmsted, *Papers of Frederick Law Olmsted*, 9:789.

409 **"The Negroes have been . . . to have the more intelligent people of the South":** Frederick Law Olmsted to Thomas Clark, Aug. 5, 1889, in Olmsted, *Papers of Frederick Law Olmsted*, 8:708–9.

409 **"the best books ever written":** Olmsted, *Papers of Frederick Law Olmsted*, 9:352, 1n.

409 **"I have seen a tendency in recent . . . has been a tremendous one and I am well satisfied with the present results":** Frederick Law Olmsted to John Murray Forbes, July 2, 1891, in Olmsted, *Papers of Frederick Law Olmsted*, 9:352.

410 **"My memory as to . . . cannot be depended on to properly represent the firm":** Frederick Law Olmsted to John Charles Olmsted, May 10, 1895, in Olmsted, *Papers of Frederick Law Olmsted*, 9:920.

410 **"over-strung and nervous":** Olmsted, *Papers of Frederick Law Olmsted*, 9:951.

410 **"way to a realization of the truth":** Frederick Law Olmsted to Charles Eliot Norton, Sept. 26, 1895, in Olmsted, *Papers of Frederick Law Olmsted*, 9:950.

410 **"The firm! No. The Art!" "*Exit*, bowing, not ungratefully," "F.L.O.":** Frederick Law Olmsted to John Charles Olmsted and Charles Eliot Norton, Sept. 19, 1895, in Olmsted, *Papers of Frederick Law Olmsted*, 9:949.

410 **"gradual decay" of his "faculties":** Frederick Law Olmsted to John Charles Olmsted and Charles Eliot Norton, Sept. 19, 1895, in Olmsted, *Papers of Frederick Law Olmsted*, 9:950.

410 **"My father was a director of an Insane . . . is intense":** Frederick Law Olmsted to Charles Eliot Norton, Sept. 26, 1895, in Olmsted, *Papers of Frederick Law Olmsted*, 1:950.

410 **"slight hemorrhages on the brain":** Stevenson, *Park Maker*, 425.

411 **"I will never forget how shocked I . . . made such an impact":** X and Haley, *Autobiography of Malcolm X*, 179.

411 **"I represent pretty . . . on our side":** Olmsted, "The South," *New-York Daily Times*, Feb. 13, 1854.

411 **"I see what ought to be done but I can't get other men to see it"**: Frederick Law Olmsted to Henry Whitney Bellows, Aug. 16, 1863, in Olmsted, *Papers of Frederick Law Olmsted*, 4:697.

411 **"snubbed & set down and made of no account"**: Frederick Law Olmsted to Henry Whitney Bellows, Aug. 16, 1863, in Olmsted, *Papers of Frederick Law Olmsted*, 4:696.

411 **"First: I should not be under . . . in my practical sagacity"**: Frederick Law Olmsted to Henry Whitney Bellows, Aug. 16, 1863, in Olmsted, *Papers of Frederick Law Olmsted*, 4:698.

412 **"Seek the best society . . . fortunate sort of people"**: Frederick Law Olmsted to Frederick Law Olmsted Jr., Sept. 5, 1890, in Olmsted, *Papers of Frederick Law Olmsted*, 9:204.

412 **"loitering, self-indulgent, dilettante"**: Frederick Law Olmsted to Elizabeth Baldwin Whitney, Dec. 16, 1890, in Olmsted, *Papers of Frederick Law Olmsted*, 9:248.

413 **"from the cramped, confined, and controlling circumstances" of urban life:** Olmsted and Vaux (Firm), *Preliminary Report to the Commissioners for Laying Out a Park in Brooklyn, New York: Being a Consideration of Circumstances of Site and Other Conditions Affecting the Design of Public Pleasure Grounds*, 5, https://archive.org/details/preliminaryrepor1866olms /page/n1.

413 **"*a sense of enlarged freedom* is to all, at all times, the most certain and the most valuable gratification afforded by a park":** Olmsted and Vaux (Firm), *Preliminary Report*, 5. See also Menard, "Enlarged Freedom," 508–38.

BIBLIOGRAPHY

Books

Arreola, Daniel D. *Tejano South Texas: A Mexican American Cultural Province*. Austin: University of Texas Press, 2002.

Bainbridge, John. *The Super-Americans: A Picture of Life in the United States, as Brought into Focus, Bigger Than Life, in the Land of the Millionaires—Texas*. New York: Holt, Rinehart and Winston, 1972.

Baptist, Edward E. *The Half Has Never Been Told: Slavery and the Making of American Capitalism*. New York: Basic Books, 2014.

Barry, John M. *Rising Tide: The Great Mississippi Flood of 1927 and How It Changed America*. New York: Touchstone, 1998.

Beckert, Sven. *Empire of Cotton: A Global History*. New York: Vintage Books, 2014.

Bender, Thomas. *Toward an Urban Vision: Ideas and Institutions in Nineteenth Century America*. Baltimore: Johns Hopkins University Press, 1987.

Benfey, Christopher. *Degas in New Orleans: Encounters in the Creole World of Kate Chopin and George Washington Cable*. Berkeley: University of California Press, 1999.

Beveridge, Charles E., and Paul Rocheleau. *Frederick Law Olmsted: Designing the American Landscape*. Rev. ed. New York: Universe, 2000.

Blight, David W. *Race and Reunion: The Civil War in American Memory*. Cambridge, MA: Belknap Press, 2001.

Block, W. T. *Sour Lake, Texas: From Mud Baths to Millionaires, 1835–1909*. Liberty, TX: Atascosito Historical Society, 1995.

Blumenthal, Sidney. *The Political Life of Abraham Lincoln*. Vol. 2, *Wrestling with His Angel: 1849–1856*. New York: Simon & Schuster, 2017.

Bowman, John. *Wheeling: The Birthplace of the American Steamboat*. Wheeling, WV: J. Bowman, 2008.

Brands, H. W. *Andrew Jackson: His Life and Times*. New York: Doubleday, 2005.

Broyard, Bliss. *One Drop: My Father's Hidden Life—A Story of Race and Family Secrets*. New York: Back Bay Books/Little, Brown, 2008.

Burnette, Eric. *Parks for the People!: Profit, Power, and Frederick Law Olmsted in Louisville*. Louisville, KY: Holland Brown Books, 2017.

Burrier, William Paul, Sr. *Nueces Battle and Massacre: Myths and Facts*. San Antonio, TX: Watercress Press, 2015.

Campbell, Randolph B. *An Empire for Slavery: The Peculiar Institution in Texas, 1821–1865*. Baton Rouge: Louisiana State University Press, 1989.

———. *Gone to Texas: A History of the Lone Star State*. 2nd ed. New York: Oxford University Press, 2012.

Chernow, Ron. *Grant*. New York: Penguin Press, 2017.

Clark, Emily. *The Strange History of the American Quadroon: Free Women of Color in the Revolutionary Atlantic World*. Chapel Hill: University of North Carolina Press, 2013.

Clay, Cassius Marcellus. *The Life of Cassius Marcellus Clay: Memoirs, Writings, and Speeches, Showing His Conduct in the Overthrow of American Slavery, the Salvation of the Union, and the Restoration of the Autonomy of the States. In Two Volumes, Written and Compiled by Himself, and Illustrated with Engravings on Steel*. Cincinnati: J. F. Brennan, 1886.

Collins, Gail. *As Texas Goes: How the Lone Star State Hijacked the American Agenda*. New York: Liveright, 2012.

Cook, Clarence. *A Description of the New York Central Park*. New York: F. J. Huntington, 1869.

Davis, William C. *Three Roads to the Alamo: The Lives and Fortunes of David Crockett, James Bowie, and William Barret Travis*. New York: HarperCollins, 1998.

Dean, P. A. "Pap," Jr. *Colfax: Its Place in Louisiana*. Colfax, LA: Dean Art Features, 2003.

Desmond, Adrian J., and James R. Moore. *Darwin's Sacred Cause: How a Hatred of Slavery Shaped Darwin's Views on Human Evolution*. Boston: Houghton Mifflin Harcourt, 2009.

Eskew, Garnett Laidlaw. *The Pageant of the Packets: A Book of American Steamboating*. New York: Henry Holt and Company, 1929.

Faust, Drew Gilpin. *James Henry Hammond and the Old South: A Design for Mastery*. Baton Rouge: Louisiana State University Press, 1982.

Fehrenbach, T. R. *Lone Star: A History of Texas and the Texans from Prehistory to the Present; The People, Politics, and Events That Have Shaped Texas*. Updated edition. New York: Da Capo Press, 2000.

Fetherling, George, Jeanne Finstein, and Brent Carney. *Wheeling: A Brief History*. Wheeling, WV: Polyhedron Learning Media, 2008.

Fischer, Ernest G. *Robert Potter: Founder of the Texas Navy*. With foreword by Stephen L. Walter. Gretna, LA: Pelican, 2006.

Fisher, Lewis F. *The Spanish Missions of San Antonio*. San Antonio, TX: Maverick, 1998.

Foner, Eric. *Free Soil, Free Labor, Free Men: The Ideology of the Republican Party before the Civil War*. New York: Oxford University Press, 1970.

———. *Reconstruction: America's Unfinished Revolution, 1863–1877*. Updated edition. New York: HarperCollins, 2014.

Fuller, Randall. *The Book That Changed America: How Darwin's Theory of Evolution Ignited a Nation*. New York: Viking, 2017.

Greenberg, Amy S. *Manifest Destiny and American Territorial Expansion: A Brief History with Documents*. Bedford Series in History and Culture. Boston: Bedford / St. Martin's, 2012.

Groneman, Bill. *Eyewitness to the Alamo*. Dallas: Republic of Texas Press, 2001.

Haley, James L. *Sam Houston*. Norman: University of Oklahoma Press, 2002.

Ham, Ken. *The Lie: Evolution*. Green Forest, AR: Master Books, 2005.

Hamilton, Jeff, and Lenoir Hunt. *My Master: The Inside Story of Sam Houston and His Times by His Former Slave Jeff Hamilton as Told to Lenoir Hunt*. Austin: State House Press, 1992.

Hardin, Stephen L. *Texian Iliad: A Military History of the Texas Revolution, 1835–1836*. Austin: University of Texas Press, 1994.

Harrigan, Stephen. *The Eye of the Mammoth: Selected Essays*. Austin: University of Texas Press, 2013.

Hay, Jerry M. *Mississippi River: Historic Sites and Interesting Places; From Lake Itasca to the Gulf of Mexico*. Floyds Knobs, IN: Inland Waterways, 2014.

Hirsch, Arnold R., and Joseph Logsdon, eds. *Creole New Orleans: Race and Americanization*. Baton Rouge: Louisiana State University Press, 1992.

Hodge, Roger D. *Texas Blood: Seven Generations Among the Outlaws, Ranchers, Indians, Missionaries, Soldiers, and Smugglers of the Borderlands*. New York: Knopf Doubleday, 2017.

Honeck, Mischa. *We Are the Revolutionists: German-Speaking Immigrants and American Abolitionists after 1848*. Athens: University of Georgia Press, 2011.

Howe, Daniel Walker. *What Hath God Wrought: The Transformation of America, 1815–1848*. Oxford: Oxford University Press, 2007.

Hunter, Tera W. *Bound in Wedlock: Slave and Free Black Marriage in the Nineteenth Century*. Cambridge, MA: Belknap Press, 2017.

Jacoby, Karl. *The Strange Career of William Ellis: The Texas Slave Who Became a Mexican Millionaire*. New York: W. W. Norton, 2016.

Johnson, Walter. *River of Dark Dreams: Slavery and Empire in the Cotton Kingdom*. Cambridge, MA: Belknap Press, 2013.

———. *Soul by Soul: Life Inside the Antebellum Slave Market*. Cambridge, MA: Harvard University Press, 1999.

Jordan, Terry G. *German Seed in Texas Soil: Immigrant Farmers in Nineteenth-Century Texas*. Austin: University of Texas Press, 2004.

Kalfus, Melvin. *Frederick Law Olmsted: The Passion of a Public Artist*. New York: New York University Press, 1990.

Keith, LeeAnna. *The Colfax Massacre: The Untold Story of Black Power, White Terror, and the Death of Reconstruction*. New York: Oxford University Press, 2008.

Lane, Charles. *The Day Freedom Died: The Colfax Massacre, the Supreme Court, and the Betrayal of Reconstruction*. New York: Henry Holt, 2008.

Larson, Erik, *Devil in the White City: Murder, Magic, and Madness at the Fair That Changed America*. New York: Vintage Books, 2004.

Lemann, Nicholas. *Redemption: The Last Battle of the Civil War*. New York: Farrar, Straus and Giroux, 2006.

Lepore, Jill. *These Truths: A History of the United States*. New York: W. W. Norton, 2018.

Lincoln, Abraham. *The Portable Abraham Lincoln*. Bicentennial ed. Andrew Delbanco, ed. New York: Penguin Books, 2009.

Linsley, Judith Walker, Ellen Walker Rienstra, and Jo Ann Stiles. *Giant Under the Hill: A History of the Spindletop Oil Discovery at Beaumont, Texas, in 1901*. Austin: Texas State Historical Association, 2008.

Madsen, William. *Mexican-Americans of South Texas*. Case Studies in Cultural Anthropology. 2nd ed. New York: Holt, Rinehart and Winston, 1973.

Martin, Justin. *Genius of Place: The Life of Frederick Law Olmsted*. Cambridge, MA: Da Capo Press, 2011.

Mayer, Henry. *All on Fire: William Lloyd Garrison and the Abolition of Slavery*. New York: St. Martin's Press, 1998.

Meacham, Jon. *American Lion: Andrew Jackson in the White House*. New York: Random House, 2008.

McInnis, Maurie D. *Slaves Waiting for Sale: Abolitionist Art and the American Slave Trade*. Chicago: University of Chicago Press, 2011.

McMurtry, Larry. *In a Narrow Grave: Essays on Texas*. New York: Simon & Schuster Paperbacks, 2006.

Medley, Keith Weldon. *Black Life in Old New Orleans*. Gretna, LA: Pelican, 2014.

———. *We As Freemen: Plessy v. Ferguson*. Gretna, LA: Pelican, 2003.

Mellon, James, ed. *Bullwhip Days: The Slaves Remember: An Oral History*. New York: Grove Press, 1988.

Mitchell, Broadus. *Frederick Law Olmsted: A Critic of the Old South*. Baltimore: Johns Hopkins Press, 1924.

Montejano, David. *Anglos and Mexicans in the Making of Texas, 1836–1986*. Austin: University of Texas Press, 2003.

Montgomery, Cora. *Eagle Pass, Or, Life on the Border*. New York: George P. Putnam, 1852.

Mullins, Lashé D., and Charles K. Mullins. *A History of White Hall: House of Clay*. Charleston, SC: History Press, 2012.

Murphy, Alexander Bailey, and Douglas L. Johnson, eds. *Cultural Encounters with the Environment: Enduring and Evolving Geographic Themes.* With the assistance of Viola Haarmann. Lanham, MD: Rowman and Littlefield, 2000.

Olmsted, Frederick Law. *Civilizing American Cities: Writings on City Landscapes.* Edited by S. B. Sutton. New York: Da Capo Press, 1997.

———. *The Cotton Kingdom: A Traveller's Observations on Cotton and Slavery in the American Slave States Based upon Three Former Volumes of Journeys and Investigations by the Same Author.* Edited by Arthur M. Schlesinger. New York: A. A. Knopf, 1953.

———. *A Journey in the Back Country.* New York: Schocken Books, 1970.

———. *A Journey in the Seaboard Slave States: In the Years 1853–1854, with Remarks on Their Economy.* Vol. 1. New York: Knickerbocker Press, 1904.

———. *A Journey in the Seaboard Slave States: In the Years 1853–1854, with Remarks on Their Economy.* Vol. 2. Reprint ed. New York: Knickerbocker Press, 1904.

———. *A Journey through Texas: Or a Saddle-Trip on the Southwestern Frontier.* Lincoln: University of Nebraska Press, 2004.

———. *The Papers of Frederick Law Olmsted.* Vol. 1, *The Formative Years; 1822–1852.* Charles Capen McLaughlin and Charles E. Beveridge, eds. Baltimore: Johns Hopkins University Press, 1977.

———. *The Papers of Frederick Law Olmsted.* Vol. 2, *Slavery and the South: 1852–1857.* Charles E. Beveridge and Charles Capen McLaughlin, eds. Baltimore: Johns Hopkins University Press, 1981

———. *The Papers of Frederick Law Olmsted.* Vol. 3, *Creating Central Park, 1857–1861.* Charles E. Beveridge, Charles Capen McLaughlin, and David Schuyler, eds. Baltimore: Johns Hopkins University Press, 1983.

———. *The Papers of Frederick Law Olmsted.* Vol. 4, *Defending the Union: The Civil War and the U.S. Sanitary Commission; 1861–1863.* Jane Turner Censer, ed. Baltimore: Johns Hopkins University Press, 1986.

———. *The Papers of Frederick Law Olmsted.* Vol. 5, *The California Frontier, 1863–1865.* Victoria Post Ranney, ed.; Gerard J. Rauluk, assoc. ed.; Carolyn F. Hoffman, asst. ed. Baltimore: Johns Hopkins University Press, 1990.

———. *The Papers of Frederick Law Olmsted.* Vol. 6, *The Years of Olmsted, Vaux & Company, 1865–1874.* David Schuyler, Jane Turner Censer, Carolyn F. Hoffman, Kenneth Hawkins, and Charles Capen McLaughlin, eds. Baltimore: Johns Hopkins University Press, 1992.

———. *The Papers of Frederick Law Olmsted.* Vol. 7, *Parks, Politics, and Patronage: 1874–1882.* Charles E. Beveridge, Carolyn F. Hoffman, and Kenneth Hawkins, eds. Baltimore: Johns Hopkins University Press, 2007.

———. *The Papers of Frederick Law Olmsted.* Vol. 8, *The Early Boston Years: 1882–1890.* Ethan Carr, Amanda Gagel, and Michael Shapiro, eds. Baltimore: Johns Hopkins University Press, 2013.

———. *The Papers of Frederick Law Olmsted.* Vol. 9, *The Last Great Projects: 1890–1895.* David Schuyler and Gregory Kaliss, eds. Baltimore: Johns Hopkins University Press, 2015.

———. *Papers of Frederick Law Olmsted: Supplementary Series.* Vol. 1. Charles E. Beveridge and Carolyn F. Hoffman, eds. Baltimore: Johns Hopkins University Press, 1997.

———. *Walks and Talks of an American Farmer in England in the Years 1850–51,* Vol. 1. Whitefish, MT: Kessinger, 2000.

———. *Walks and Talks of an American Farmer in England,* Vol. 2. New York: G. P. Putnam, 1852.

Olmsted, Frederick Law, and Theodora Kimball Hubbard. *Frederick Law Olmsted, Landscape Architect, 1822–1903.* Vol. 2. Charleston, SC: Nabu Press, 2010.

Parker, Richard. *Lone Star Nation: How Texas Will Transform America.* New York: Pegasus Books, 2014.

Perry, Lewis. *Boats against the Current: American Culture between Revolution and Modernity, 1820–1860*. Lanham, MD: Rowman and Littlefield, 2002.

Potter, David M., and Don E. Fehrenbacher. *The Impending Crisis: 1848–1861*. New York: Harper & Row, 1976.

Powers, Ron. *Mark Twain: A Life*. New York: Free Press, 2005.

Pryor, Elizabeth Brown. *Reading the Man: A Portrait of Robert E. Lee through His Private Letters*. New York: Viking, 2007.

Randers-Pehrson, Justine Davis. *Adolf Douai, 1819–1888*. New York: Peter Lang, 2000.

Ransleben, Guido. *A Hundred Years of Comfort in Texas*. San Antonio, TX: Naylor Company, 1954.

Remnick, David. *King of the World: Muhammad Ali and the Rise of an American Hero*. New York: Random House, 1998.

Richard, Zachary. *The History of the Acadians of Louisiana*. Lafayette: University of Louisiana at Lafayette Press, 2013.

Richardson, Harold Edward. *Cassius Marcellus Clay: Firebrand of Freedom*. Lexington: University Press of Kentucky, 1996.

Riley, Harvey. *The Mule: A Treatise on the Breeding, Training, and Uses, to which He May Be Put*. Philadelphia: Clanton, Remsen and Haffelfinger, 1869.

Ritzenthaler, Robert E., and Frederick A. Peterson. *The Mexican Kickapoo Indians*. Milwaukee Public Museum Publications in Anthropology, no. 2. Whitefish, MT: Literary Licensing, 2015.

Rogers, Elizabeth Barlow. *Saving Central Park: A History and a Memoir*. New York: Alfred A. Knopf, 2018.

Roper, Laura Wood. *FLO, a Biography of Frederick Law Olmsted*. Baltimore: Johns Hopkins University Press, 1983.

Rothstein, Richard. *The Color of Law: A Forgotten History of How Our Government Segregated America*. New York: Liveright, 2017.

Rybczynski, Witold. *A Clearing in the Distance: Frederick Law Olmsted and America in the 19th Century*. New York: Scribner, 1999.

Sansing, David G., Sim C. Callon, and Carolyn Vance Smith. *Natchez: An Illustrated History*. Natchez, MS: Plantation, 2007.

Sibley, Marilyn McAdams. *Lone Stars and State Gazettes*. College Station: Texas A&M University Press, 1983.

———. *Travelers in Texas, 1761–1860*. Austin: University of Texas Press, 2012.

Sides, Hampton. *Blood and Thunder: The Epic Story of Kit Carson and the Conquest of the American West*. New York: Anchor Books, 2007.

Siegel, Stanley. *The Poet President of Texas: The Life of Mirabeau B. Lamar, President of the Republic of Texas*. Austin: Jenkins, 1977.

Siemering, A., William Paul Burrier, Helen Dietert, and Ronnie Pue. *August Siemering's Die Deutschen in Texas waehrend des Buergerkrieges: The Germans in Texas During the Civil War*. Tamarac, FL: Llumina Press, 2013.

Smiley, David L. *Lion of White Hall: The Life of Cassius M. Clay*. Gloucester, MA: Peter Smith, 1969.

Stephens, A. Ray, and Carol Zuber-Mallison. *Texas: A Historical Atlas*. Norman: University of Oklahoma Press, 2012.

Stevenson, Elizabeth. *Park Maker: A Life of Frederick Law Olmsted*. New Brunswick, NJ: Transaction Publishers, 2000.

Stowe, Harriet Beecher. *Uncle Tom's Cabin or, Life Among the Lowly*. With introduction by Darryl Pinckney. New York: Signet Classics, 1998.

Tanner, Lynette Ater, ed. *Chained to the Land: Voices from Cotton & Cane Plantations; From Interviews of Former Slaves*. Winston-Salem, NC: John F. Blair, 2014.

Thompson, Bob. *Born on a Mountaintop: On the Road with Davy Crockett and the Ghosts of the Wild Frontier*. New York: Crown Trade Group, 2012.

Trollope, Frances Milton. *Domestic Manners of the Americans*. Edited, with a history of Mrs. Trollope's adventures in America, by Donald Arthur Smalley. New York: Vintage Books, 1949.

Turner, Elizabeth Hayes, and Gregg Cantrell, eds. *Lone Star Pasts: Memory and History in Texas*. With foreword by W. Fitzhugh Brundage. College Station: Texas A&M University Press, 2006.

Twain, Mark. *Life on the Mississippi*. New York: Signet Classic, 2001.

Waters, Andrew, ed. *I Was Born in Slavery: Personal Accounts of Slavery in Texas*. Winston-Salem, NC: John F. Blair, 2003.

Weaver, Bobby D. *Castro's Colony: Empresario Development in Texas, 1842–1865*. College Station: Texas A&M University Press, 1985.

Weber, David J. *The Spanish Frontier in North America*. New Haven: Yale University Press, 1992.

White, Dana F., and Victor A. Kramer, eds. *Olmsted South: Old South Critic / New South Planner*. Westport, CT: Greenwood Press, 1979.

White, Richard D., Jr. *Kingfish: The Reign of Huey P. Long*. New York: Random House, 2006.

Williams, John Alexander. *West Virginia: A History*. 2nd ed. Morgantown: West Virginia University Press, 2001.

Winders, Richard Bruce. *Sacrificed at the Alamo: Tragedy and Triumph in the Texas Revolution*. Abilene, TX: State House Press, McMurry University, 2004.

Wright, Lawrence. *God Save Texas: A Journey into the Soul of the Lone Star State*. New York: Alfred A. Knopf, 2018.

Wyatt-Brown, Bertram. *Honor and Violence in the Old South*. New York: Oxford University Press, 1986.

X, Malcolm, and Alex Haley. *The Autobiography of Malcolm X*. New York: Ballantine, 1987.

Collections/Manuscripts

Frederick Law Olmsted Documentary Editing Project, University Archives and Special Collections, American University Library, Washington, DC.

Frederick Law Olmsted Papers, Manuscript Division, Library of Congress, Washington, DC. http://hdl.loc.gov/loc.mss/collmss.ms000067.

Journal Articles

Avillo, Philip J., Jr. "Phantom Radicals: Texas Republicans in Congress, 1870–1873." *Southwestern Historical Quarterly* 77, no. 4 (Apr. 1974): 431–44.

Barr, Alwyn. "Records of the Confederate Military Commission in San Antonio, July 2–October 10, 1862." *Southwestern Historical Quarterly* 71, no. 2 (1967): 247–78.

———. "Records of the Confederate Military Commission in San Antonio, July 2–October 10, 1862." *Southwestern Historical Quarterly* 73, no. 2 (1969): 243–74.

Bidwell, Percy W. "The New England Emigrant Aid Company and English Cotton Supply Associations: Letters of Frederick L. Olmsted, 1857." *American Historical Review* 23, no. 1 (Oct. 1917): 114–18.

Biesele, R. L. "The Texas State Convention of Germans in 1854." *Southwestern Historical Quarterly* 33, no. 4 (Apr. 1930): 247–61.

Chipman, Donald E. "Alonso De Leon: Pathfinder in East Texas, 1686–1690." *East Texas Historical Journal* 33, no. 1 (1995): 3–17.

Davis, Edwin Adams. "Bennet H. Barrow, Ante-Bellum Planter of the Felicianas." *Journal of Southern History* 5, no. 4 (Nov. 1939): 431–46.

Dielmann, Henry B. "Emma Altgelt's Sketches of Life in Texas." *Southwestern Historical Quarterly* 63, no. 3 (Jan. 1960): 363–84.

Hatcher, Mattie Austin. "Description of the Tejas or Asinai Indians, 1691–1722." *Southwestern Historical Quarterly* 31, no. 1 (July 1927): 50–62.

Hilt, Eric. "Economic History, Historical Analysis, and the 'New History of Capitalism.'" *Journal of Economic History* 77, no. 2 (June 2017): 511–36.

Johnson, Walter. "The Slave Trader, the White Slave, and the Politics of Racial Determination in the 1850s." *Journal of American History* 87, no. 1 (June 2000): 13–38.

Jones, Joseph. "Hail, Fredonia!" *American Speech* 9, no. 1 (Feb. 1934): 12–17.

Kamphoefner, Walter D. "New Perspectives on Texas Germans and the Confederacy." *Southwestern Historical Quarterly* 102, no. 4 (Apr. 1999): 440–55.

Kelley, Sean. "'Mexico in His Head': Slavery and the Texas-Mexico Border, 1810–1860." *Journal of Social History* 37, no. 3 (2004): 709–723.

Kerrigan, William T. "Race, Expansion, and Slavery in Eagle Pass, Texas, 1852." *Southwestern Historical Quarterly* 101, no. 3 (Jan. 1998): 275–301.

Kiel, Frank Wilson. "Treue Der Union: Myths, Misrepresentations, and Misinterpretations." *Southwestern Historical Quarterly* 115, no. 3 (Jan. 2012): 282–92.

Lack, Paul D. "Slavery and the Texas Revolution." *Southwestern Historical Quarterly* 89, no. 2 (Oct. 1985): 181–202.

McGowen, Stanley S. "Battle or Massacre?: The Incident on the Nueces, August 10, 1862." *Southwestern Historical Quarterly* 104, no. 1 (July 2000): 64–86.

Menard, Andrew. "The Enlarged Freedom of Frederick Law Olmsted." *New England Quarterly* 83, no. 3 (Sept. 2010): 508–38.

"New Article of Food—Meat Biscuit." *Scientific American* 5, no. 27 (1850): 213.

Nicholson, Carol J. "Elegance and Grass Roots: The Neglected Philosophy of Frederick Law Olmsted." *Transactions of the Charles S. Peirce Society* 40, no. 2 (Spring 2004): 335–48.

O'Neal, William B. "The Stagecoach Comes to Northern Kentucky." Apr. 22, 1952. Christopher Gist Historical Society Collection, Special Collections and Archives Department, Northern Kentucky University Library.

Olmstead, Alan L., and Paul W. Rhode. "Cotton, Slavery, and the New History of Capitalism." *Explorations in Economic History* 67 (Jan. 2018): 1–17.

Roper, Laura Wood. "Frederick Law Olmsted and the Western Texas Free-Soil Movement." *The American Historical Review* 56, no. 1 (Oct. 1950): 58–64.

Scheper, George L. "The Reformist Vision of Frederick Law Olmsted and the Poetics of Park Design." *New England Quarterly* 62, no. 3 (Sept. 1989): 369–402.

Shuey, Mary Willis. "Murder at Caddo Lake." *Southwest Review* 37, no. 1 (Winter 1952): 54–59.

Siegel, Stanley E. Review of *Robert Potter: Founder of the Texas Navy* by Ernest G. Fischer. *Southwestern Historical Quarterly* 80, no. 2 (Oct. 1976): 245–46.

Swanton, John R. "Source Material on the History and Ethnology of the Caddo Indians." *Bureau of American Ethnology Bulletin* 132 (1942): 1–332.

Townsend, E. E. "The Mays Massacre," West Texas Historical and Scientific Society Publications, no. 5 (1933): 29–43.

Ware, Leland. "'Color Struck': Intragroup and Cross-racial Color Discrimination." *Connecticut Public Interest Law Journal* 13, no. 1 (Fall–Winter 2013): 75–110.

Williamson, Samuel, Jr. "Slavery and the Founding of the University of the South." *Sewanee Theological Review* 52, no. 2 (Easter 2010): 136–38.

Newspaper Articles

Olmsted, Frederick Law. "The South," *New-York Daily Times*, Feb. 16, 1853, to Feb. 13, 1854.
———. "A Tour in the Southwest." *New-York Daily Times,* Mar. 6, 1854, to June 7, 1854.

Dissertations/Theses

Abrams, Nels. "The Making of Audubon Park: Competing Ideologies for Public Space." Master's thesis, University of New Orleans, 2010. https://scholarworks.uno.edu/td/1241.

Beveridge, Charles E. "Frederick Law Olmsted: The Formative Years 1822–1865." PhD diss., University of Wisconsin–Madison, 1966.

Cox, John David. "Traveling Texts: Southern Travel Narratives and the Construction of American National Identity." PhD diss., University of Mississippi, 2000.

Follett, Richard J., "The Sugar Masters: Slavery, Economic Development, and Modernization on Louisiana Sugar Plantations, 1820–1860." PhD diss., Louisiana State University, 1997.

Lewis, David Roberts. "Dissent to Duelling: Arguments against the Code Duello in America." Master's thesis, Vanderbilt University, 1984.

Sikes, William Henry, "The Malcontents of the Old World: German Revolutionaries in Early Texas (1842–1865)." Honors thesis, Wesleyan University, 2015. https://wesscholar.wesleyan.edu/etd_hon_theses/1408.

Internet Resources

"About *The Caucasian*. (Alexandria, La.) 1874–1875." Chronicling America: Historic American Newspapers. Library of Congress. http://chroniclingamerica.loc.gov/lccn/sn86053765/.

Beveridge, Charles E. "Olmsted—His Essential Theory." National Association for Olmsted Parks. http://www.olmsted.org/the-olmsted-legacy/olmsted-theory-and-design-principles/olmsted-his-essential-theory.

Darwin Correspondence Project. http://www.darwinproject.ac.uk/.

"The 1860 Campaign and the 'Black Republican President.'" *The Shelf.* Oct. 6, 2012. http://blogs-test.harvard.edu/preserving/2012/10/06/the-1860-campaign-and-the-black-republican-president/.

The Handbook of Texas Online. Texas State Historical Association. https://tshaonline.org/handbook/online/.

"History of the Mexican Kickapoo." Milwaukee Public Museum. https://www.mpm.edu/research-collections/anthropology/online-collections-research/mexican-kickapoo/history.

"1927 Bartholomew Study on African American Recreation in New Orleans." NOLA Parks History. May 23, 2014. https://web.archive.org/web/20160810114735/http://www.nolaparkshistory.org/category/segregation-of-new-orleans-parks/.

"Segregation in Audubon Park." NOLA Parks History. May 18, 2014. https://web.archive.org/web/20160810114735/http://www.nolaparkshistory.org/category/segregation-of-new-orleans-parks/.

Smith, Edward D. *Historic Resource Study: Cumberland, Maryland; Historical Data Chesapeake and Ohio Canal National Historical Park, MD–D.C.–W.Va.* http://www.npshistory.com/publications/choh/cumberland-hrs.pdf.

Texas German Dialect Archive. http://sites.la.utexas.edu/hcb/files/2011/02/Boas_Weilbacher_TexasGermanDialectArchive_final.pdf.

INDEX

Mudfest, 188–99, 205
mud-sill theory, 85–86
mules, 179, 188, 212, 216–17
    author's journey with, 323–53, 357
    Olmsted and, 202, 320, 323, 329–30,
        340–41, 354, 386
Mullins, Lashé, 79–81
Murdoch, Rupert, 154
Musée de f.p.c., 141
Museum of Death, 155
Muslims, 245–49, 397
Mussolini, Benito, 130

Nacimiento, 374
Nacogdoches, Tex., 215–17
NAFTA, 367, 382
Napoleon I, Emperor, 225, 286
Nashville, Tenn., 83–85, 87–93,
        96–97, 101
    integrity in, 93
    Olmsted in, 84, 87, 88, 91, 93, 97, 249
    Tennessee State Capitol, 88–91
    Tennessee State Museum, 90–92
Natchez, Miss., 110–20, 123, 134
    cotton trade in, 111
    Forks of the Road at, 114–15, 125
    Historic Natchez Tableaux, 113–15
    Longwood, 115–17
    Magnolia Hall, 112–16
    Olmsted in, 112, 114
    slave trade in, 111, 114–15, 125
    Spring Pilgrimage, 113
    Under-the-Hill, 110, 111, 122
Natchez Trace, 111
Natchitoches, La., 201–3, 205–6, 208, 215
National Park Service, 400
National Road, 23–27
Native Americans, see Indians
Navy SEALs, 260
Nebraska, 83, 98, 130
Neches River, 231
Nelken, Benjy, 105–7
Nelson, Willie, 262
Netanyahu, Benjamin "Bibi," 75
New Braunfels (Neu Braunfels), Tex., 291–97,
        300–301, 303, 305
New Braunfels Herald-Zeitung, 293, 295–96,
        312–13
New Deal, 237
New England, 12, 158
New England Emigrant Aid Company,
        391, 392
New Haven, 15
New Martinsville, W.Va., 52, 53
New Mexico, 370

New Orleans, La., 83, 101, 104, 111, 114, 137,
        138–53, 155–56, 178, 205, 279
    black-white relations in, 144–45
    Franklin Avenue Baptist Church, 146–50
    free blacks in, 141–42
    French Quarter, 141, 153, 155
    "grades of colored people" in, 138–39
    Hurricane Katrina and, 145, 146, 147, 150
    Olmsted in, 138–41, 145–46
    plaçage in, 139–41
    quadroon balls in, 140, 141
    slave market in, 139
    Treme, 141, 143, 145, 146
New Orleans *Times-Picayune*, 143
Newport, R.I., 404
New York, 368
New York, N.Y., 16, 83, 138, 402
    Central Park in, 4, 5, 124, 174, 392–96,
        399–407, 410–14
New-York Daily Times (*New York Times*),
        19, 143
    name change of, 19
    Olmsted as correspondent for, 3–7, 19–20,
        39, 51, 83–84, 91, 97–99, 171, 201–2,
        204, 291, 300, 301, 307, 390–91
    see also Olmsted, Frederick Law,
        Southern tour of
New York Harbor, 14
New York Herald, 393
New-York Tribune, 23
Nichols, Robert, 241–42
9/11 attacks, 237, 397
Nixon, Richard, 92
Noah's Ark, 64, 67, 71
Nome, Tex., 228
the North, 5, 7, 20, 98–99, 150–51, 292,
        392–93
    blacks in, 98
    financial panic in, 392
    Mason-Dixon Line, 29
    slavery and, 98–99
    visitors to South from, 4
North Carolina, 269, 409
    Biltmore Estate in, 4, 269, 408–12
Northup, Solomon, 117
Norton, Charles Eliot, 400–401
Nottoway, 134–36
Nueces River massacre, 316–18, 325, 341
Nutt, Haller, 116

oak trees:
    live, 124, 261, 270, 322
    post, 250, 252–53, 269–70, 322
Obama, Barack, 34, 74, 75, 91, 109, 144–45,
        238, 262, 397

.